T0224544

POWER SYSTEMS
DYNAMICS

Volume 1

F.P de Mello

authorHOUSE®

AuthorHouse™
1663 Liberty Drive
Bloomington, IN 47403
www.authorhouse.com
Phone: 1 (800) 839-8640

Published by AuthorHouse   01/28/2016

ISBN: 978-1-5049-6504-0 (sc)
ISBN: 978-1-5049-6503-3 (e)

Library of Congress Control Number: 2016901428

Print information available on the last page.

This book is printed on acid-free paper.

Volume I - Contents

FOREWORD

The PTI Power System Dynamics Course is designed to impart an understanding of the practical and theoretical aspects of power system dynamics and of the latest methodology of engineering analysis and simulation tools.

The material in this collection has been assembled under appropriate subject headings form PTI course notes, technical papers and internal technical memoranda.

Course content is assembled in three volumes. Volume I contains tutorial material largely extracted from PTI course notes. Volume III is a collection of problems and solutions.

Volume II is a compendium of reference papers and technical memoranda illustrating various aspects of Power System Dynamics.

A reader's guide to this material is included below in the form of a brief outline on the content of the major chapters of Volume I followed by an index relating particular subjects to the articles in Volume II.

VOLUME I

I. INTRODUCTION

"Dynamic Analysis and Control System Engineering in Utility Systems" - A keynote address to the IEEE Control Conference held in Albany in September 1995. It gives an overview of dynamic effects in Power Systems ranging from the slow dynamics of energy supply systems (power plant thermo-mechanical process) to the relatively fast electrical machine-network dynamics characteristic of stability problems.

The paper also addresses the evolution of computation techniques applied to the analysis of dynamic and control problems in the Electric Power Industry.

"Power System Dynamics – Overview" - A paper covering modeling requirements of various types of problems involved with electrical machine/network dynamics.

II. PRIME MOVER SYSTEM DYNAMICS

PTI Course Notes, "Generation Dynamics & Control", cover prime movers, governing and automatic generation control. The material is useful in developing an understanding of prime mover system response characteristics as well as of simplified analysis methods for phenomena where the prime mover dynamics predominate and the network voltage effects are neglected.

The simplifications of the Power System Process justified by the scope of the dynamic effects under consideration form an ideal example for the introduction of dynamics in the context of power systems. Included are references on prime mover models and Automatic Generation Controls.

III. LOAD FLOW FUNDAMENTALS

"Digital Computer Methods" - Chapter 10 of PTI course notes "Power Circuit Analysis II". Load flow phenomena are the most important aspect of power system behavior.

A discussion of numerical methods of load flow solution is covered in this material.

IV. SYNCHRONOUS MACHINES

Performance characteristics of synchronous machines are fundamental to many aspects of power system dynamics. PTI course notes, "Electrical Machine Dynamics I", cover the fundamentals of synchronous machine theory. The material on machine models (Section 4.7) is of particular importance to the understanding of machine behavior as a contributing factor in dynamics of power systems.

It is particularly important to understand the d-q transformation (starting in Section 4.3.4), the machine equivalent circuits and the per unit system (Section 4.4).

Class problems are helpful in exercising concepts. (Volume III).

V. POWER SYSTEM STABILITY - LOAD REJECTION - SUBSYNCHRONOUS OSCILLATIONS

PTI course notes "Electrical Machine dynamics II" cover the fundamentals of steady state, transient and dynamics stability.

Electrical self-excitation and subsynchronous oscillation phenomena are also discussed.

Class problems illustrate various principles involved with these phenomena.

VI. DYNAMIC ANALYSIS TOOLS

Appendices A through F of PTI course notes on Generation Dynamics and Control illustrate methods of solution of dynamic problems by the "Analog Computer Technique" and by equivalent digital techniques using numerical integration methods. This material is of fundamental importance to understanding of modeling of dynamic systems. Brief notes on frequency response techniques are also included.

VOLUME II

Reference material in Volume II falls under the following topics:

Methodology of Transmission Planning and Design Studies

Item 1   "Transmission System Design Studies:" Part II - Steady State and Dynamics Performance", PTI Newsletter, Issue #6, pp. 2&3

Item 2   "Some Aspects of Transmission Planning in Large Developing Countries"

Load Flow and VAR Support Problems

Item 3   "Voltage Collapse and Maximum Power Transfer Analyzed Using Current vs. Voltage Plots"

Item 4   "Considerations on Voltage Support Requirements in Receiving Systems Supplied Through Long Distance Transmission", PTI Memorandum

Item 29   "Voltage Control and Reactive Supply Problems"

Item 30   "Reactive Compensation in Power Systems"

Item 33   "Load Flow Techniques in System Dynamic Performance Assessments", PTI Memorandum

Item 38   "Voltage Collapse" and "Applications of the Optimal Power Flow to Analysis of Voltage Collapse Limited Power Transfer" and "Voltage Collapse Investigations with Time-Domain Simulation" and "Performance of Methods for Ranking and Evaluation of Voltage Collapse Contingencies Applied to a Large-Scale Network"

Transient and Dynamic Stability

Item 6   "Modern Concepts of Power System Dynamics - The Effect of Control"

Item 7   "Concepts of Synchronous Machine Stability as Affected by Excitation Control"

Item 8   "Dynamic Stability of Systems with Remote Generation"

Item 9   "Coordinated Application of Stabilizers in Multi-Machine Power Systems"

Equipment and Load Modeling

Load Rejection

Subsynchronous Oscillations

The presentation of a balanced treatment on the subject of power system dynamics presents a major challenge not only in terms of where to start, the chicken or the egg, but also in terms of relative emphasis on various aspects of the problem.

Our experience in dealing with and teaching about power system dynamics indicates that the development and understanding of the subject should proceed in the following order:

1.   Understanding of dynamic systems, their characterization by differential equations and the methods of solution of time dependent effects.

2. Understanding of dynamic effects of machines and controls and their characterization by mathematical models (block diagrams).

3. Understanding of the linear laws of Ohm and Kirchoff and the resulting nonlinear effects relating power flows, voltages and currents in a.c. networks.

4. Understanding of new phenomena which are of relevance to present and future applications including novel methods for their study and analysis (D.C. transmission, subsynchronous oscillations, shaft torques, supplementary stabilizing, etc.).

READING REFERENCES

Overview of Power System Dynamics

Vol. I   Section I - Introduction

"Process Dynamics in Electric Utility Systems"

"Power System Dynamics - Overview"

Dynamic Analysis Tools

"Dynamic Systems, Differential Equations - Transient and Steady State Solutions - Operation Impedance"

Vol. I   Section VI - Appendix A

"Laplace Transforms"

Vol. I   Section VI - Appendix B

Vol. III   Generation Dynamics and Control

Class Problems I, II

Homework Problem I

"Transfer Functions - Block Diagrams"

Vol. I   Section VI - Appendix C

Vol. III   Generation Dynamics and Control

Class Problem III

"Analog Computers - State Space - Numerical Methods of Differential Equation Solution"

Vol. I   Section VI - Appendix D

Vol. I   Section II - "Prime Mover System Dynamics"

Vol. I   Section VI - "FACE a Digital Dynamic Analysis Program"

Vol. III   Generation Dynamics and Control

Class Problems VII, XI

Homework Problem II

"Frequency Response Techniques"

Vol. I   Section VI - Appendix E

Vol. III   Generation Dynamics and Control

              Class Problems X, XII

"Process Control - Controller Tuning"

Vol. I   Section VI - Appendix F

Vol. III   Generation Dynamics and Control

              Class Problem XII

Power System Models for Generation Control

Vol. I   Section II -"Prime Mover System Dynamics" and references on Automatic Generation Control, Hydro Turbines and Fossil Fueled Steam Units

Vol. III   Generation Dynamics and Control

              Class Problems, Homework Problems

Power System Stability Concepts

Vol. I   Section V - "Power System Stability - Load Rejection - Subsynchronous Oscillations", pp. 1-32

Vol. III   Electrical Machine Dynamics II

              Class Problems I, II, III, IV, V, VI, VII

              Homework Problems I, II, III, IV

System Design for Stability

Vol. II   Item 2   "Some Aspects of Transmission Planning in Large Developing Countries"

             Item 6   "Modern Concepts of Power System Dynamics"

             Item 28   "Dynamic Aspects of Excitation Systems and Power System Stabilizers" and "Stabilizing Signals - Practical Considerations" and "Alternatives in Deriving Stabilizing Intelligence from Measurement of Electrical Power"

Load Rejection and Self Excitation

Load Flow Criteria - Reactive Support

Static Compensators - Voltage Collapse

Load Flow Criteria - Reactive Support

Static Compensators - Voltage Collapse (Continued)

Item 38   "Voltage Collapse" and "Applications of the Optimal Power Flow to Analysis of Voltage Collapse Limited Power Transfer" and "Voltage Collapse Investigations with Time-Domain Simulation" and "Performance of Methods for Ranking and Evaluation of Voltage Collapse Contingencies Applied to a Large-Scale Network" and "Power System Long Term Dynamics"

Induction Machines - Load Characteristics

Vol. I   Section V - "Power System Stability - Load Rejection – Subsynchronous Oscillations", pp. 72-79

Vol. II   Item 19   "Large Scale Induction Generators for Power Systems"

          Item 20   "Application of Induction Generators in Power Systems"

          Item 21   "Reclosing Transients in Induction Motors with Terminal Capacitors"

Vol. III Electrical Machine Dynamics - I

          Class Problems X, XI, XVII

          Electrical Machine Dynamics - II

          Class Problem VI

Series Capacitors - Subsynchronous Oscillations - Impact Torques

Vol. I   Section V - "Power System Stability - Load Rejection – Subsynchronous Oscillations", pp. 95-104

Vol. II   Item 26   "Subsynchronous Oscillations"

          Item 27   "Turbine Generator Impact Torques in Routine and Fault Operations"

          Item 31   "Subsynchronous Oscillation Stability Analysis" and "Shaft Torsional Oscillation Interactions Between Turbo- Generators in Parallel in Series Compensated Transmission Systems"

AC/DC Conversion

Variable Series Compensation

ACKNOWLEDGEMENTS

This edition of course notes on synchronous machines has involved a complete retyping of the notes last done in 1978, with considerable editing and upgrading of figures. This has involved a great deal of effort on the part of the following individuals whose dedication and skill is acknowledged with many thanks:

Mrs. Barbara Mountford who did an outstanding job on typing the notes and the numerous equations with difficult mathematical symbols.

Leonardo Lima and Arthur Pinheiro who edited, proof read the text and every equation, and upgraded the figures.

DYNAMIC ANALYSIS AND CONTROL SYSTEM ENGINEERING IN UTILITY SYSTEMS

FP de Mello
Consulting Engineer

INTRODUCTION

DYNAMIC PROCESSES

POWER SYSTEM PROCESS DYNAMICS
Electrical Machine and System Dynamics
System Governing and Generation Controls
Prime-Mover Energy Supply System
Other Areas involving Dynamics

HISTORICAL DEVELOPMENT OF DYNAMIC ANALYSIS TECHNIQUES
The AC and DC Network Analyzer
The Mechanical Differential Analyzer
The Analog Computer
The Digital Computer

IMPACT OF COMPUTERS ON POWER SYSTEM ENGINEERING
Batch versus Interactive Mode

CONTROL ANALYSIS AND DESIGN
The Oscillatory Stability Problem
Direct Digital Control

DYNAMIC ANALYSIS OF FOSSIL AND NUCLEAR PLANTS
Design of Plant Controls

MANAGEMENT AND HUMAN FACTORS

CONCLUDING REMARKS

REFERENCES

Key Note Address

Dynamic analysis and Control System Engineering

in Utility Systems.....F Paul de Mello

4th IEEE conference on Control Applications

Albany NY September 28-29, 1995

0-7803-2550-8/95$4.00©1995 IEEE

DYNAMIC ANALYSIS AND CONTROL SYSTEM ENGINEERING IN UTILITY SYSTEMS

FP de Mello
Consulting Engineer

INTRODUCTION

I am indeed flattered and pleased to address this conference on Control Applications. Having spent my entire career in the power industry, in the discipline of Power System Engineering, it is appropriate that I share with you my experience and views on control applications and dynamic analysis in this industry.

I will attempt to convey in a limited way an introspective appreciation of developments in analysis and control in Power Systems. Unlike many technologies which sprouted only within the last few decades, and which would not have come to being without the computer, the core and structure of the Power System is still composed of equipments which, except for size and sophistication, resemble other vintages dating back a whole century. Looking back, it is amazing that complex power systems were successfully designed, built and operated based on rule of thumb and slide rule calculations.

Dynamic analysis is not an end in itself but only one of the vital disciplines in the planning, design and operation of reliable electrical systems. It is interesting to contrast the practical from the impractical and try to understand the reasons why impractical analysis approaches have sometimes been advocated and supported much beyond what could be justified from common sense or economic viewpoints.

In the background, we should recognize the major events that have impacted the technology of control, namely: World War II and the Cold War, with Sputnik as a dramatic milestone. These events have been tremendous propellers of advancements in the technology of dynamic analysis. There were important differences however. The urgency for results in the race against Hitler within available time and resources focused World War II efforts on very practical approaches.

Sputnik intensified efforts in Space technology with its tremendous fallout in the technology of electronics, communication and computing hardware. It also gave rise to unprecedented federal research funding into analysis methods. Without the pressure of an ongoing war, and fostered by a backlash of feeling that sophisticated mathematics and analytical techniques had propelled the USSR ahead of the U.S., the discipline of control analysis often wandered into impractical approaches with no tangible applications in the real world.

An interesting cross-development was the advent of the

digital computer which has had far more impact on the technical and economic affairs of mankind than any single invention in the last 100 years. It is ironic that while the digital computer liberated analysts from the need for closed form solution of complex mathematical expressions, allowing more practical numerical solution approaches, so much effort has been and is being spent on analytical approaches, often bending the problem to fit the theory.

The changing structure of digital computing which no longer presents the serious human interface problems in terms of response time between the problem solver's question and the computer's answer, is having a profound effect on approaches to problem solution and control system design.

To this audience it is "coals to Newcastle" to elaborate on the meaning of the term "Dynamic Process". However, to ensure that the link is firmly established between physical systems and their mathematical models, the meaning of "order of the process", "linear and nonlinear", we will start with a couple of simple examples of dynamic processes.

A description of the power system dynamic process is next addressed as well comments on the historical development of simulation techniques. Finally, observations are offered on control analysis as applied to power plants and systems.

DYNAMIC PROCESSES

The behavior of variables in Dynamic processes is defined by differential and algebraic relations which describe the governing laws of physics. A simple example is the relationship between level in a tank, fluid flowing in and fluid being drawn out (Fig. 1).

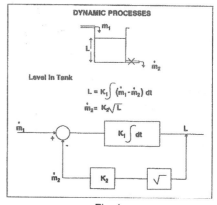

Fig. 1.

The level is proportional to the integrated difference between flow rate in and out, and the equation is a first order differential equation.

$$L = k_1 \int (\dot{m}_i - \dot{m}_2)\, dt \qquad 1$$

The flow rate out, $\dot{m}_2$ is an algebraic function of the level, in this case proportional to the square root of level.

$$\dot{m}_2 = k_2 \sqrt{L} \qquad 2$$

This set of equations is symbolically described by the block diagram in Fig. 1.

In state space format the equations are

$$\dot{X} = -K_1 K_2 \sqrt{X} + K_1 U \quad 3$$

where $X = L$ and $U = \dot{m}_1$

The next example shown in Fig. 2 is the case of a shaft linking two rotating masses of inertia J_1 and J_2.

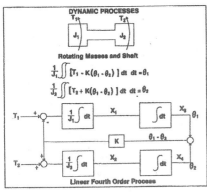

Fig. 2.

Newton's law of motion is used to define this dynamic system. If external Torques T_1 and T_2 are imparted to masses 1 and 2 and the shaft stiffness is K then the equations of motion, with damping neglected are:

$$\int\int [T_1 - K (\theta_1 - \theta_2)]dt\, dt = \theta_1 \quad 4$$

$$\int\int [T_2 + K (\theta_1 - \theta_2)]dt\, dt = \theta_2$$

This system of equations is described by the block diagram in Fig. 2.

Again, in state space format, it is described by

$$\dot{X} = |A|\,|X| + |B|\,|U| \qquad \text{where } X = \begin{vmatrix} X_1 \\ X_2 \\ X_3 \\ X_4 \end{vmatrix} \quad U = \begin{vmatrix} T_1 \\ T_2 \\ 0 \\ 0 \end{vmatrix}$$

$X_1 = d\theta_1 / dt$

$X_2 = d\theta_2 / dt$

$X_3 = \theta_1$

$X_4 = \theta_2$

$$A = \begin{vmatrix} 0, 0, -K, +K \\ 0, 0, +K, -K \\ 1, 0, 0, 0 \\ 0, 1, 0, 0 \end{vmatrix} \quad B = \begin{vmatrix} 1, 0, 0, 0 \\ 0, 1, 0, 0 \\ 0, 0, 0, 0 \\ 0, 0, 0, 0 \end{vmatrix}$$

The first example deals with a first order differential equation system. The system is nonlinear because of the square root relationship between flow and level. The second example is a fourth order linear system which will exhibit a pair of complex roots characterizing the torsional oscillatory mode between the two masses and a multiple pair of roots at the origin (S = 0).

The formulation of the relationships that describe the process physics has been known for scores of years, except where models for new processes had to be developed. In the days of the slide rule, the big difficulty was the solution of the equations to yield the response characteristics of the process, especially where the relations involved a high order set of nonlinear differential and algebraic equations. Today the digital computer has trivialized the solution process.

POWER SYSTEM PROCESS DYNAMICS

To the control systems engineer, the power system process can be described as in Fig. 3, identifying its many systems and subsystems in the

5

familiar pattern of several closed loops nested within one another.

The dimensions and complexity of power system dynamics can well be appreciated when one realizes that there are thousands of interacting elements such as generators with their prime movers, energy supply systems and controls, and that the mathematical representation of each element generally involves many interdependent variables, their interdependence being described by sets of high order, nonlinear differential and algebraic equations. In its simplest form, the power system comprising a single prime-mover, generator and load is a complex process. Adding to this the effects of large numbers of units within systems, and of interconnecting entire power systems from coast to coast, one can appreciate the dimensionality of the overall process.

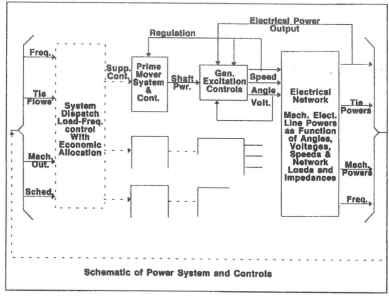

Fig. 3.

This high dimensionality of the problem made it important to use skill in the choice of simplifying assumptions aimed at cutting down size and complexity to suit the needs of the particular situation. An intimate knowledge of the process physics and the orders of magnitude of basic effects is fundamental to the tasks of cutting down the problem to a workable size.

Reduction of the dimensions is accomplished by equivalencing or aggregation, where several equipments, due to their similar characteristics and location, could be represented as one composite. The other opportunity for reducing the dimensionality of the mathematics is to recognize the bandwidth of interest, eliminating dynamic effects which are too fast or too slow to affect the results of the problem at hand.

With reference to Fig. 3, power system dynamic effects of prime interest can be categorized as belonging predominantly in one of the following areas:

1. Electrical machine and system dynamics

2. System governing and generation controls

3. Prime-mover-energy-supply system dynamics

Electrical Machine and System Dynamics

In the area of electrical machine dynamics, a prime concern is the ability of the power system to operate with synchronism and acceptable voltage conditions through severe credible disturbances. The emphasis of representation is on the network power flow and machine inertial relations. As excitation and prime-mover energy controls play more active roles, the need for more detail in their representation increases.

The elastic nature of the power system exhibiting poorly damped swings in power flow and related variables in the bandwidth of approximately 0.5 to 2 Hz, can be visualized in terms of the mechanical analog or masses, springs and dashpots of Fig. 4. The masses are analogous to the rotors of turbo-generators and the springs analogous to transmission links between generators. The nonlinear nature of the process is represented in the mechanical analog where the various levers, balljointed at a pivot, represent the angular positions of the turbo-generator rotors relative to a synchronous reference. The power flow between generators is analogous to the torques developed from forces in the springs, analogous to transmission links. Shown also are loads as force vectors acting on the spring network.

Fig. 5a shows transients in a generator's power and exciter voltage during and following a severe short circuit fault on the transmission cleared within a few cycles. The effects are generally over in a few seconds, in this case a successful recovery. In the industry this would be labeled as a stable case. The phenomena involve large disturbances and the prediction of performance necessitates the solution of a nonlinear set of state space and algebraic equations. Dimensions of the state vector can easily exceed 20000 in typical large interconnected systems.

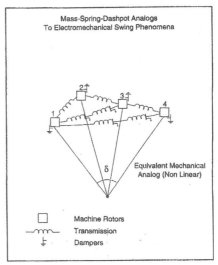

Fig. 4.

System Governing and Generation Controls

Problems that fall under the category of system governing are concerned with the frequency behavior of overall systems and power flow between systems for normal load changes i.e. small perturbations. Considerable lumping or equivalencing is justified in the representation of networks and electrical machines, while more detail is preserved in individual prime movers including energy supply system effects (boiler pressures, hydraulic heads), their governor systems and supplementary controls. Fig. 5b shows typical performance following small load changes.

Prime-Mover Energy Supply System

The third category, that of prime-mover energy supply systems, is concerned with such details as combustion, feedwater and temperature controls in the case of fossil steam prime-mover complex or a number of flow, pressure and rod controls in the case of nuclear plants. In this category, the turbine can be represented as a variable orifice and its dynamics are practically instantaneous relative to the many other pressure, flow and temperature effects of the plant multi-variable process (Fig. 5c).

Other Areas involving Dynamics

As shown in Fig. 5 and 6, the principal phenomena under the various categories fall in different spectra of duration of main effects. Also indicated in Fig. 6 are the important areas at the extremes of the duration spectrum which will not be addressed, but which deserve mention since they represent important areas of activity that may also be classified under the subject of dynamics.

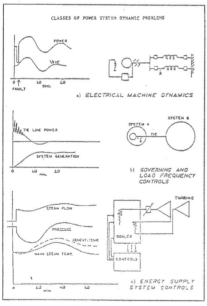

Fig. 5a...b...c

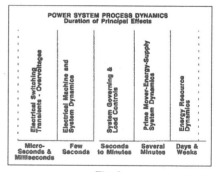

Fig. 6.

One of these is the important and distinct area of electrical system transients concerned with overvoltage studies. Prediction of the overvoltage levels resulting from switching transients and lightning surges is vital in insulation coordination design and proper application of overvoltage protection measures to ensure reliable power systems. The nature of the process dynamics in this area spans durations of microseconds and milliseconds. The need for a high degree of refinement and fidelity of representation of very high frequency phenomena made, for many years, the most practical method of study that of direct measurement on electrical scaled models of the system. Specialized laboratories (transient analyzers) with models of transmission lines, transformers, reactors, lightning arresters and switches are devoted to study of transient overvoltage performance of systems. Today many of these studies are being performed digitally with programs such as EMTP.

The other extreme in the duration spectrum involving hours, days and weeks concerns problems of management of energy resources, typically water, nuclear fuel and coal fuels. The nature of storage in these processes classifies them as dynamic and the techniques of simulation and prediction involve dynamic equations. The time duration in these processes is such that automatic control is usually not involved but rather the formulation of operating decisions and schedules implemented manually in response to results of sophisticated nonlinear programming techniques.

Fig. 7. The AC Network Analyzer

(Credit the Hall of History Foundation Schenectady, New York)

HISTORICAL DEVELOPMENT OF DYNAMIC ANALYSIS TECHNIQUES

To appreciate the progress through the last few decades in the area of large scale dynamic analysis, it is appropriate to recall the historical development of this technology from the 1930's to date. The power system process has presented computational challenges in many areas, but for the purposes of this discussion we will exclude the area of switching surge and traveling wave phenomena and the large area of dynamic and linear programming techniques used for operations scheduling and expansion planning studies. In the area of electrical system dynamics the basic computation problem falls into two main categories:

The power flow aspect which involves solution of a large set of coupled nonlinear algebraic equations.

The dynamic aspect which requires the solution of a large number of differential equations.

The AC and DC Network Analyzer

The AC network analyzer was used for over 30 years to solve the power flow problem. A simpler DC version was used for short circuit calculations. The AC simulation tool was a single phase scaled model of the network with resistances, inductances and capacitances assembled to represent power system elements, such as transmission lines, transformers and loads. Generators were represented by alternating voltage sources. Aside from its use in steady state power flow problems, the traditional transient stability problem was calculated through step by step hand calculations and repetitive load flow measurements, to yield the trajectories of machine speeds and angles following contingencies.

Fig. 7 shows typical AC network analyzer facilities with the capacity of representing about 30 generators and few dozen lines, transformers and loads used in the 40's, 50's and early 60's.

Although extremely modest in terms of dimensions and degree of representation, and extremely slow in terms of yielding documented results, the network analyzer had a unique advantage. It provided interactive features whereby the engineer felt immediate responses to his questions and acquired a feel for the problem as the instruments registered reactions to his inputs. This type of response so vital in exploratory studies, became unavailable when every question or trial was answered with the delay of hours or days as became the norm with the advent of the mainframe digital computer introduced to the industry in the 60's and 70's.

So here we are in the 1940's and early 50's. Solution capabilities for power, flow of 100 buses, 36 generators solved by the network analyzer. Dynamics of machine speeds and angles by hand calculations. Rudimentary representation of machines as sources behind reactance. Loads represented by constant impedances.

The Mechanical Differential Analyzer

The more general dynamic problem requiring the integration of coupled state space equations was unfeasible through manual calculation. The earliest machine solution of differential equations was done with the mechanical differential analyzer which consisted of a system of shafts, gears, and rotary to linear motion transducers. Variables were characterized by displacements which were plotted on X-Y plotters (Fig. 8).

Fig. 8. Mechanical Differential Analyzer

A mechanical differential analyzer capable of solving a 12th order differential equation occupied a space of 20 meters x 10 meters!

The Analog Computer

There is no single development that can match the contribution to the technology of dynamic simulation made by the introduction of the electronic operational amplifier and its use in solution of dynamic problems known as analog computation. Introduced following World War II, with the use of vacuum tube technology, operational amplifiers were used as the basic elements of analog computers composed of summers, integrators, inverters, scaling potentiometers, etc. Some of these devices, in the days of vacuum tube electronics, would weigh up to 30 lbs. and cost $1,000 or more. A 36 amplifier analog computer would cost over $100,000 equivalent to about a million of today's dollars. Although functionally equivalent to the mechanical differential analyzer, the electronic analog computer brought an order of magnitude improvement in problem solution capability (Fig. 9).

The unique advantage of the analog computer was the mode of operation, giving an almost instantaneous response to the investigators' questions. This response was always in the form of conveniently displayed recordings of the variables of interest.

Analog computers benefited from the exponential progress in solid state electronics, integrated circuits and chips. The cost of computational components came down by a factor of thousands to one. Analog computers had been the playground of control engineers and were used extensively in defense and industrial manufacturer's engineering facilities, as well as universities.

Fig. 9. Analog Computer

(Credit the Hall of History Foundation Schenectady, New York)

Although the advent and growth of the digital computer should have turned the analog computer practically obsolete by the late 70's, other factors such as interactive capability, computer system administration procedures, cost plus funding, and inertia to change favored their continuing use in many situations.

The Digital Computer

In the 1950's, when mainframe computers were seeing their first real boom, the extremely high cost of hardware and the awesome complexity of the computer-user interface led to almost total centralization of computer functions and bred a whole generation of professional "interpreters", "computer centers", programming departments, etc. Since the mid 50's, the pace of computer evolution has been staggering, with changes in capacity, speed and efficiency of orders of magnitude every few months. The development of high-level software permitting direct engineer-computer communication has also been extremely significant. The initial growth was entirely in the direction of size and speed, but, in the late 1960's, a few manufacturers began to "think small". The result was the first minicomputers.

The last two decades have seen many fold increases in the power of mini and micro computers, in their speed of execution, memory capacity (virtual memory these days) and both system and application software. The hand held calculator has become as common as a wrist watch and the microprocessor based home computer with capabilities greater than mainframes of a few years back as common as the TV set.

Digital Computer	
Early Large Centralized Main Frames	1955
Assembly Languare	
Rudimentary Software	
Computer Organizations	
Batch Processing	
Time Share	1968
Dedicated Single User Minicomputers	1970
Minicomputers in Local Time Share Configuration	1974
Minicomputers with Virtual Memory	1978
Distributed Processing	1980
Personal Computers and Workstations	1981

Fig. 10.

Fig. 10 and Fig. 11 highlight the salient milestones statistics of the digital computer evolution.

	Approximate number of instructions per second (IPS)	Price	Cost per IPS
	Computer Power and Cost		
	In the evolution of computer-ship technology, as information-processing speed has increased, the prices of computing devices have plummeted.		
1975 IBM Mainframe	10,000,000	$10,000,000	$1.0
1976 Cray 1	160,000,000	20,000,000	0.125
1979 Digital Vax	1,000,000	200,000	0.20
1981 IBM PC	250,000	3,000	0.012
1984 Sun Microsystems 2	1,000,000	10,000	0.010
1994 Pentium-chip PC	66,000,000	3,000	4.5×10^{-5}
1995 Sony PCX video game	500,000,000	500	1×10^{-6}
1995 Microunity set-top of box	1,000,000,000	500	0.5×10^{-6}

Fig. 11.

IMPACT OF COMPUTERS ON POWER SYSTEM ENGINEERING

From the point of view of large scale problem solution, the digital computer has offered ever increasing capabilities in size of problem, detail of representation, speed of solution, interactive operation and automated documentation. Compared with the network analyzer and the analog computer, the digital approach provides orders of magnitude improvements in all aspects. For a couple of decades, however, the power of the computer for engineering computation was muzzled by cost considerations and structure of organizations that considered computation as a function in itself.

From the beginning, due to the very high cost of hardware and lack of high level software, the computer resource required machine language specialists called programmers and keypunchers. The computing facility was operated as a common resource available to many departments in the corporation among which, of course, the accounting department became dominant. This gave rise to an accepted institutional structure which considered computers the domain of the data processing department controlling use of the machines. Several aspects of such administration of computer resources became very undesirable from the point of view of the engineering function. It has taken a long time to shed the CPU-sec culture whereby computer resources had to be utilized 24 hours a day. Today such resources spread through offices and homes are so powerful and so inexpensive that nobody worries about having them idle or shut off.

Batch versus Interactive Mode

In the bad old days, the engineer had to submit his job to be keypunched and lost control of the process until hours or days later when he was handed a mass of paper with computer printout, often containing incorrect results due to inadvertent input errors (Fig. 12).

This time lag between question and answer and the loss of control of the computation process during execution led to the practice of submitting many more cases than necessary and obtaining tons of computer output.

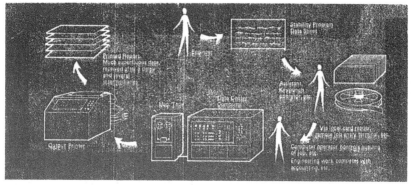

The Batch Syndrome

Interactive Facilities with Dedicated Computer

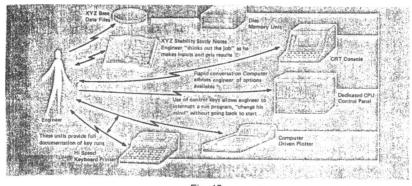

Fig. 12

In the field of control theory, we have noted a similar tendency of trying to delegate the job of optimization to the computer. For the past 30 years there has been an explosion of papers on optimal control theory. This approach in essence formulates a performance index and lets the computer execute the task of tuning (Fig. 13). Unfortunately in most of the cases it has not been practical to use such techniques either because the formulation of the problem for it to be susceptible to the mathematical methodology, forces an unrealistic model to be used, or because it is more productive to use the insights and inventiveness of the human brain functioning in an interactive environment where rapid results keep pace with the thinking process. The amount of effort in research on optimal control has far exceeded potential benefits from past, present and future applications.

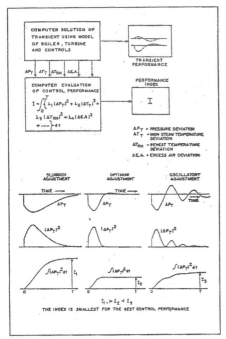

Fig. 13

Following a period of a couple of years with telephone connected time share computer services through teletype terminals, the real breakaway from the batch mode to the interactive mode occurred in the early 70's with the advent of the dedicated single user minicomputer. The analog computer concept of large scale dynamic simulation was now available for power system analysis. Specialized interactive software for power system simulation was developed at the 500 bus, 100 machine level on a minicomputer. Incredible as it may now seem this was done on a machine such as the Hewlett Packard-2100, with 64K of RAM.

From the days of the network analyzer when practical limits for load flow solutions were about 50 to 100 buses and 30 odd generators, and dynamic solutions were limited to step by step integrations of swing equations of two states per generator, i.e. a 60th order system handled by a mixture of hand calculations for the integrations and analyzer derived load flow solutions, present day computation capability is typically:

Power flow: 50000 buses, 100000 branches, 3000 generators, 50000 loads

Dynamic solution: 100,000 plus order differential equation solution of equipment models such as generators, excitation, prime-mover models, D.C. links, loads, special controls, etc.

The interactive approach first involved use of single user dedicated minicomputers. Soon the advent of virtual memory and large minicomputers such as Prime, Vax, Sun and IBM machines led to the multi-user installations with multi-monitor interfaces, workstations and local area networks.

The size, speed and modeling capability have continually increased to enable the simulation of the entire world if it were interconnected, including the kinds of detailed models of old and new equipment such as D.C. links, Static Var Compensators, FACTS devices and controls. Today this Power System Simulation capability is available on personal computers. As noted in Fig. 11, the hardware cost is no longer a factor.

A few years back there was novelty in the concept of interaction, graphic interface through a TV monitor. Today, the ubiquitous mouse, the medium of windows, the spreadsheet and computer graphics are second nature to the new generation of our children and grandchildren.

CONTROL ANALYSIS AND DESIGN

Control applications being the main theme of this conference, it is appropriate to present thoughts on approaches we have found most effective and useful in this area.

Prediction is the fundamental concept of control. Mathematical simulation is the tool used in prediction and understanding of the process behavior with or without controls. While linear analysis techniques, notably frequency response and process control principles, are essential to guide synthesis of appropriate control structures and their adjustments, there is no substitute to the use of time domain simulation, to as accurate a degree as possible.

In today's industrial competitive environment, experienced system engineers will usually bypass elaborate linear system analysis and rather concentrate resources on full scale simulation of the process and controls since this step is the final requirement for confirmation of a satisfactory system design.

In the majority of cases, control design is dictated by performance requirements under larger perturbations. Non linear phenomena such as rate limits, ceilings, saturation, control windup can be extremely important in determining control logic. A quantitative understanding of the physical process is the key to selection of the right control approach. An example or two is helpful to illustrate these principles.

The Oscillatory Stability Problem

Few problems of the industry have received more analytical effort than the problem of poor or negative damping of electromechanical oscillations between rotating machines or groups of machines in Power Systems. Reference was previously made to these phenomena with the mechanical analogs of Fig. 4. For about 3 decades this damping problem has been cured with the use of supplementary control of excitation, labeled Power System Stabilizers (PSS).

Recently the industry's enthusiasm has turned to the application of power electronics in the control of network reactive elements the so-called use of FACTS (Flexible AC Transmission). Among the applications considered for such devices is their use in damping of electromechanical power swings, the oscillatory stability problem mentioned above.

Referring to Fig. 14, it is apparent, from the physics of the mechanical mass-spring-dashpot analog, that excitation system stabilization, which acts like a dashpot on the masses, is ideally located relative to the storage elements participating in the oscillations, the turbine-generator rotors. This is much like the location of shock absorbers in a car, right next to the wheels.

Beside the matter of right location there is also the factor of amplification whereby, with a few watts or milli-watts in the control signal, KW of excitation power are directed to convert MW of power from the mechanical rotating mass to provide damping energy. The PSS concept does not require installation of massive power equipment. It merely directs transient action in already existing power equipments.

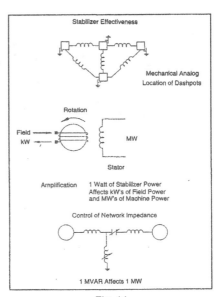

Fig. 14

In contrast, the control of power at the network level, through variable reactive elements, requires installation of equipment with MVA ratings comparable to the MW of power to be controlled i.e. in the vicinity of 1 MV Ar per MW. Evidently FACTS devices cannot compete with PSS in damping of oscillations and would only be used for such a purpose if their installation were justified for other reasons.

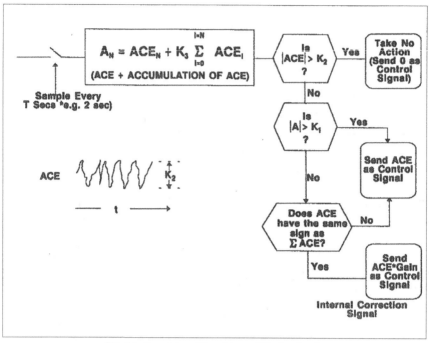

Fig. 15. Example of Non-Linear Filtering Logic

Direct Digital Control

The digital computer has made possible time domain simulation of high order nonlinear, continuous, or combination of continuous and discrete systems. Increasingly its logic and computational power is being applied in control equipments which traditionally had been of analog design. In new technologies such as power electronics (HVDC, Static Var Compensators, FACTS devices) control functions are now exclusively microprocessor based.

The control design methodology is no longer constrained by the differential equation behavior of analog hardware but free to use common sense with no constraints as to computation or logic and little need for analytically based control theory. Guided by sound control principles and armed with unlimited logic capability, the design process is non-analytical, rather one of intelligent trial and error. Where justified, adaptive functions can be easily incorporated and system requirements often dictate nonlinear control.

In the early days of digital control, elaborate sampled data control theories were developed motivated by the high cost of rapid sampling and unavailability of solid state switching. Sampling rates were a problem variable affecting feasibility and cost of the digital control. Digital simulation was also very expensive and ineffective in the batch environment. Analytical transform approaches to digital control design were thus developed and used in the 50's. Today sampling rates much beyond problem requirements are readily available at low cost and so is digital dynamic simulation capability down to the P.C. level.

The result is that there is little need for sampled data theory. Bandwidth considerations determine reasonable choices of sampling rates and full scale simulation which must be undertaken for the design process, discloses if there is deterioration due to too slow a sampling rate.

As an illustration of special control logic dictated by large disturbance performance, take the case of a Static Var Compensator whose function is to control voltage at some location in the network. The process is extremely simple with the dynamics of voltage change to change in compensator admittance being practically instantaneous while the dynamics of the compensator itself involve small time constants and perhaps a deadtime due to the firing controls. The voltage controller tuning is easy to do and the small perturbation control performance is rapid and well damped.

Simulation results show however that under the condition of a fault and subsequent clearing a few cycles later the normal control action cannot avoid a post fault severe overvoltage. The remedy, of course, is to limit the voltage error acting on the controls, a trivial code modification in the microprocessor control program.

As another example of a non-analytically based nonlinear control

take the case of automatic generation control (AGC), with the objectives of control of interchange power and frequency in interconnected systems. Fig. 15 shows the nature of control error with large noise components in a bandwidth of frequencies beyond the capability of control to follow. Even before the advent of direct digital control, AGC had a discrete component in the sense that control action was imparted through pulsing action applied to turbine governor load reference motors.

Examination of the control error statistical characteristics indicates a band of deviations which it is not possible to reduce by control because 'the frequencies of the deviations are too high in relation to the control response. The obvious conclusion is that, to avoid constant pulsing up and down of governor motors, a deadband should be provided so that as long as the control error is within the band, no action is taken. One other objective is to maintain the integrated power interchange (MWHRS) at the contractual value. That is the average or integral of the error should be maintained close to zero. Fig. 15 shows the nonlinear filtering logic which accomplishes both objectives. At sampling instants the error is measured and an accumulation of the error is calculated. Next, the magnitude of the error is compared with the deadband threshold level. If the error is below the threshold there is no need to promote pulsing action. However, in order to look at the second objective which is to maintain the integral of error close to zero the value of the accumulated error is compared with another threshold.

If the accumulated error exceeds this threshold the indication is that there is need to correct this integral. The next logic block checks if the sign of the error is the same as the sign of the integral. If this is the case control action would be indicated to correct the integral. If the sign is opposite then just allowing the error to persist i.e. taking no control action would work towards reduction of the integral.

The important point of this very effective and simple control logic is that in all cases control action is proportional to error. Correction of the integral is done by allowing or disallowing proportional control and not by imparting integral control which would introduce oscillatory tendencies.

The other point to be made with this example is that this control logic is based on common sense and not based on any formula or analytical procedure.

DYNAMIC ANALYSIS OF FOSSIL AND NUCLEAR PLANTS

Although we have dwelled on the dynamic problem of the electrical network, equally challenging is the use of dynamic simulation for the power plant process.

The solutions of equations describing the dynamics of thermomechanical process would be unthinkable without the power of the digital computer.

Fig. 16 shows some of the equations which describe the extremely nonlinear process and which can now be easily solved, in real time or faster. There would be hundreds of such equations along with other relations defining logic, control and auxiliary equipment.

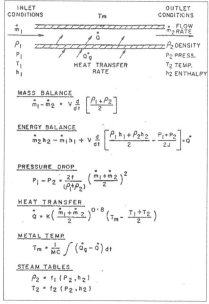

Fig. 16. Process Equations - Flow and Heat Transfer

Fig. 17. Nuclear Plant Training Simulator

Although the capability of modelling of plant dynamics has been available since the mid 60's, and should have been applied to the engineering of plant controls much more than it has, notable examples of the use of this technology are in the design of nuclear plant controls and of simulators for operator training of nuclear and fossil plants.

Fig. 17 shows one of the earliest simulators of this type built in the mid 60's. Basically it is a duplicate of the nuclear plant control room with practically every switch, indicating light, instrument and control device represented. In lieu of the plant however, a computer is programmed to simulate the process in real time. This must be accomplished by mathematical modeling of the physics for the right degree of fidelity and accuracy.

Progress in computer capability has permitted ever increased sophistication in simulators. However the most difficult task of all in a simulator project is the development of the software and the orderly management of the collective efforts of dozens of engineers and programmers.

Especially high level executive and data management software has been developed to improve the efficiency of software development. Experience from simulator projects has disclosed that one major value is derived from discovery of flaws in the plant design during the development stage. With the simulator project usually ahead of plant commissioning, such flaws can be corrected in time to avoid major hazards and costs.

Design of Plant Controls

Plant dynamics are fundamental to design of controls.

The synthesis of a control configuration for a complex process such as just described presents a real challenge to the control engineer. Attempts to automate the design process by optimization theories of modern control methodology have not been practical because the process is highly nonlinear, the control logic must recognize constraints such as valves at limits, etc., and the information available from the process generally involves much fewer states than the order of the system. The most practical approach will continue to be the use of simulation in an interactive manner whereby the engineer develops a design by an orderly process of trial and evaluation.

The options of accomplishing a given control function are many and the mix of feedforward, feedback, cross-coupling for interaction, and adaptive features that are used requires a strong element of creativity and judgment. Such difficult questions as sensitivity of the configuration to variations in process characteristics, reliability versus complexity, etc., must be carefully weighed.

Typical boiler-turbine control systems used to be configured as large operational amplifier analog type systems with hundreds of elements such as described in Fig. 18. Also

shown in this figure is the present evolutionary step in configuring the control system with digital computers rather than analog operational amplifier type systems. This step today with use of distributed processing promises major benefits to the plant control function. Digital control permits use of practically unlimited control logic, including such functions as nonlinear and adaptive control. Sophistication is often discouraged in the case of analog controls since it invariably involves more components, and complexity must be weighed against its effect on reliability. In the digital machine complexity, when needed, is easily implemented in software and has no significant effect on reliability.

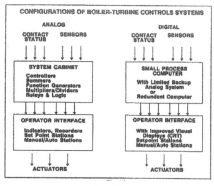

Fig. 18

The transition to Direct Digital Control, DDC, has, for the most part, replaced the old analog controls with a digital implementation of the same limited function.

Although the logic capability available in today's digital systems is literally infinite relative to what is used, extending the control function to handle the wide range of contingencies, without abdication to manual control, requires engineering effort through use of nonlinear multi-variable control design. This involves use of simulation which is again very feasible today with the use of digital computers to an extent never possible in the past with analog computers.

To illustrate, take the schematic of Fig. 19 showing the feedwater flow subloop for a once-through steam generator. The flow demand signal generated by another cascade control is shown to be limited so it cannot drop below, say 30%. A controller responds to the error between demand and flow feedback developing a signal to control the speed of the boiler feedpump through a function generator designed to linearize the speed/flow characteristic of the turbine driven pump. Fig. 19 shows the typical nonlinear flow/speed characteristic of a pump supplying the steam generator. There is no flow until the pump speed develops a discharge pressure equal to the steam generator pressure. From that point on, because of the squared law of pressure drop with flow, a very small change in speed produces a very large change in flow and this gain between flow and speed then decreases with increasing flow. A function generator to linearize this characteristic would only be correct at one value of steam generator pressure and supply pressure to the feed pump turbine which can vary appreciably depending on the steam source (extraction from main turbine or an auxiliary steam generator). Evidently it is a simple matter with

digital logic to adjust the compensation as a function of these additional variables (steam pressure to feed pump turbine) whereas this would have been discouragingly complicated to attempt with analog implementations.

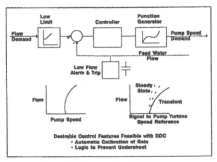

Fig. 19. Example of Subloop Control Problem

Another problem in this flow loop is the requirement to prevent flow from dropping below the minimum flow demand level. An alarm and time delay trip is provided to protect the unit from operation at flow rates below minimum. In the configuration of Fig. 19, there is no intelligence to the controls to indicate the rate at which the demand signal is approaching the minimum and the particular amount by which the flow is away from minimum. With digital logic it is fairly simple to use the combination of these two items of information to slow down control action in anticipation of the demand signal reaching the low limit, thereby preventing an undershoot in flow.

MANAGEMENT AND HUMAN FACTORS

In any project requiring use of large scale dynamic analysis and highly skilled engineering talent, a key ingredient to success is the proper use of the human resource and the proper matching of facilities and organization structure to the demands of the job.

We have seen too many undertakings requiring high levels of software effort which although deemed technically feasible, turned out failures due to human factors. Some of these are:

1. Experience and Continuity.

   It is vital that he leading human resources be applied so that the same individuals will be involved in the conceptual, developmental and final checkout phases of the project. In complex projects it is impossible to provide sufficient documentation to allow substitution of talent midstream. The longevity of engineers in a given function is a very important factor in determining success or failure of a given project.

2. Organization Structure.

   Inflexibility and rigidity in bureaucratic organizations have sometimes limited or frustrated the creative individual and leading to illogical approaches to problems. An example will illustrate.

During the conceptual stages of one of the first large scale nuclear plant operator training simulator, in the late 60's, it was felt that the advanced engineering resources of a manufacturer's department dealing with space programs, would bring to the project the latest in simulation technology.

To the surprise of some that were involved, these space technology engineers advocated a simulator built with analog operational amplifiers, thousands of them, ignoring the obvious advantage of the digital computer. The reason for such an approach became apparent. The organization of their department, following contemporary industry practice, set out computation as a separate section data processing function, manned by a hierarchy in charge of the of programmers, analysts and managers. An engineer's access to computers was only permitted through a process of defining his needs, to the computer section's analyst. This one in turn would execute the job and the final product formally delivered to the engineer.

This cumbersome obstruction had the obvious effect. Engineers preferred the analog route and built up monstrous hardware setups in a cost plus environment. There was no unnecessary human interface with the analog approach and, with no penalties placed on cost, this was the preferred way to get the job done. Naturally, even in those days of primitive computers, the simulator ended up being built with digital equipment.

CONCLUDING REMARKS

An overview of computation techniques for large scale system dynamic analysis is a task that would require volumes to do it justice.

We have attempted to cover the subject specific to the electric power industry of necessity in a superficial manner. Tracing back the state-of-the-art through a few decades one cannot fail to be amazed at the progress that has occurred, with the single most important element being the evolution of the digital computer and microelectronics. The availability of literally infinite computer calculating power at insignificant cost is causing great changes in the approach to control analysis and application of digital technology in control equipments.

By far the most important use of such resources is developing accurate process models. With these available for rapid experimentation by simulation, the control methodology that has existed for many years seems to be more than adequate to meet the usual objectives of control.

The potential for efficient use of these tools in analysis, design and operation of power systems is much larger than has been achieved to date. The bottleneck appears to be in the management and availability of properly trained human resources.

REFERENCES

1. F.P. de Mello, "Process Dynamics in Electric Utility Systems," ISA Paper 505-70, International Conference and Exhibit of ISA, October 26-29, 1970, Philadelphia, PA.

2. F.P. de Mello, "Modern Concepts of Power System Dynamics - The Effects of Control," IEEE Summer Power Meeting, 1970 Tutorial Paper.

3. C. Concordia, F.P. de Mello, "Concepts of Synchronous Machine Stability as Affected by Excitation Control," IEEE Transactions on Power Apparatus and Systems, Vol. 88, April 1969.

4. F.P. de Mello, D.N. Ewart, "FACE - A Digital Dynamic Analysis Program," 1967 PICA Conference Record, Power Industry Computer Applications Conference, pp. 83-94.

5. F.P. de Mello, "Plant Dynamics and Control Analysis," IEEE Transactions on Power Apparatus and Systems, Paper 63-1401, 1963, Vol. S82, pp. 664-678.

6. W.F. B'Rells, F.P. de Mello, R.J. Mills, "Automatic Generation Control: Part I - Process Modeling," IEEE Transactions on Power Apparatus and Systems,

Vol. PAS- 92, No. 2, March/April 1973, pp. 710-715.

7. W.F. B'Rells, F.P. de Mello, R.J. Mills, "Automatic Generation Control: Part II - Digital Control Techniques," IEEE Transactions on Power Apparatus and Systems, Vol. PAS-92, No. 2, March/April 1973, pp. 716-724.

8. F.P. de Mello, T.E. Kostyniak, R.J. Mills, J.M. Undrill, "Interactive Computation in Power System Analysis," IEEE Proceedings, (special issue on Computers in the Power Industry), 1974.

9. F.P. de Mello, "Power System Dynamics - Overview," Symposium on Adequacy and Philosophy of Modeling: Dynamic System Performance, IEEE Paper #75 CHO 970-4 PWR.

10. J.M. Undrill, F.P. de Mello, "Automatic Generation Control," tutorial paper, presented at 1978 IEEE Winter Power Meeting, New York, NY, Jan. 29-Feb. 3, 1978, New York, NY.

11. H.K. Clark, F.P. de Mello, L.N. Hannett, "Dynamic Aspects of Excitation Systems and Power System Stabilizers," First Symposium of Specialists in Electrical Operational Planning, Rio de Janeiro, Aug. 17-21, 1987.

12. F.P. de Mello, "Boiler Models for System Dynamic Performance Studies," IEEE Transactions Paper 90 SM 305-3 PWRS, Summer Meeting, July 1990.

13. F.P. de Mello, "Exploratory Concepts on Control of Variable Series Compensation in Transmission Systems to Improve Damping of Intermachine/System Oscillations," IEEE Transactions of Power Systems, Vol. 9, No. 1, February 1994, p. 102.

14. F.P. de Mello, J.C. Westcott, "Steam Plant Startup and Control in System Restoration," IEEE Transactions on Power Systems, Vol. 9, No. 1, February 1994, p. 93.

POWER SYSTEM DYNAMICS - OVERVIEW

F. P. de Mello
Power Technologies, Inc.
Schenectady, New York

INTRODUCTION

Dynamics of power systems cover a wide spectrum of phenomena, electrical, electromechanical and thermomechanical in nature. The power system process can encompass entire nations and continents and, therefore, involve a very high dimension of interacting systems with an immense array of variables.

An overview of the power system process was presented in Reference 1 where dynamic problems were classified under the major categories of (1) electrical machine and system dynamics, (2) system governing and generation control, and (3) prime-mover energy supply system dynamics and controls. Figure 1 illustrates the nature of problems in these categories.

A convenient visualization of the process showing coupling between major. variables is developed in the block diagram of Figure 2. In this diagram, one of the interfaces between mechanical and electrical systems is recognized in the shaft powers to generating units.

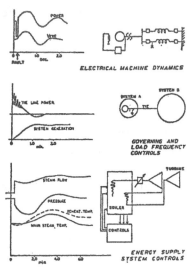

Figure 1. Classes of Power System Dynamic Problems

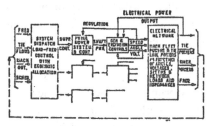

Figure 2. Schematic of Power System and Controls

There are many categories of problems which require emphasis on one or the other side of this interface. For instance, in electrical machine and network transients lasting a few seconds, the detail of the network, loads and machines is paramount, while variations in shaft power play a minor part. Simplifications in representation of the mechanical system are justified in such cases. On the other hand, where effects of significance are system frequency and interchange control lasting more than a minute, the amount of detail of the network can be reduced while the representation of the prime-mover/energy supply systems becomes paramount.

Obviously, the degree of detail of representation and the simplifying assumptions that can be made are a function of the particular problem. This fact places a great deal of importance on a grasp of the over-all process physics and a thorough understanding of the fundamentals.

Sometimes the interface between the areas which can be grossly simplified and others which must be detailed can shift considerably. Examples involve problems of subsynchronous resonance interactions with mechanical shaft natural frequencies; fast valving for transient stability; load rejection transients where prime mover overfrequency is an important effect; disturbances resulting in severe generation/load imbalances where the effects of significance may develop over many seconds.

Although the term "Power System Dynamics" can encompass a tremendous range of problems and effects, there has been a tendency to associate these problems with the phenomena of "Power System Stability," usually related to the question of whether or not a system remains in synchronism after a credible disturbance. The answer to such a question has usually involved simulations of one or two seconds in the normal system. The more difficult situations, however, involve stability problems that are less conventional and are characterized by phenomena that develop over several seconds. In these cases, load characteristics, excitation controls and prime mover characteristics are particularly significant. Often, even if instability does develop the question does not end there but rather one must ascertain system behavior following the loss of synchronism of one of its parts in order to properly design protective schemes which will ensure the survival of the majority of the system as well as minimize hazards to equipment. The point must, therefore, be made that "Power System Dynamics" is not merely "transient stability." Some of the major engineering aspects involving power system dynamics can require highly complex. analysis of system behavior. In these cases it is very important to (1) use relevant process models, (2) use computational tools tailored to the task, and (3) properly interpret the results.

MODELING DETAIL

The variations in process modeling that can be used depending on the phenomena of dominant importance are many.[1,2] We shall make our point by showing variations on modeling detail on the part dealing merely with generators and networks, recognizing that a wide range of modeling alternatives can also apply to phenomena involving other elements of the power system; namely, loads, excitation systems and prime mover systems.

Figures 3 to 10 summarize aspects of modeling detail involving machine and network. Figure 3 starts with the simple problem of a single phase alternating ideal voltage source connected to a linear network made up of resistance, inductance and capacitance elements. Figure 4 extends this problem to the 3-phase situation, still preserving the network as describable by linear differential equations and the source as ideal voltage sources.

Figure 5 evolves from the case of Figure 4 to include nonlinearities such as caused by saturation of magnetic elements. Here the solution techniques which use components are no longer applicable since superposition is not valid in nonlinear systems.

Figure 6 expands the detail with the representation of the generator by differential equations in the d and q axes accounting for the transients in rotor and armature currents and their effect on voltage product fluxes. Figure 6 represents the maximum of detail in both machine and network. Such effects as subsynchronous resonance, harmonics generated by saturation can be studied with this representation.

Figure 7 shows the next step wherein the network equations are reduced to solution of the fundamental frequency effects. This represents reduction of the network differential equations to algebraic equations solving for the fundamental frequency voltages and currents while preserving the time varying (differential equation) nature of fluxes and rotor speed giving rise to varying magnitude and frequency of generated voltages. Frequency effects on network impedances are included.

Figure 8 follows from the model of Fig. 7 by neglecting the effect of frequency variations in the generated voltages and in the network parameters. This is the degree of detail generally used in stability studies where machine rotor flux behavior must be accounted for both for their effect on synchronizing and damping torques.

Figures 9 and 10 show successive simplifications of the machine model with removal of the rotor flux differential equations and representation of source voltages as constant values behind constant reactances. Figure 10 uses the classical representation of constant voltage behind a transient reactance symmetrical in both axes.

These are merely examples of the wide range of modeling detail that can enter into a particular problem solution. The choice of the adequate model for the problem in question requires intimate knowledge of fundamentals and orders of magnitude of effects.

Source	Network	Nature of Results	Applications & Limitations	Solution Methods and Tools
Ideal sinusoidal source behind constant inductance with constant or varying frequency, single phase.	R, L, C linear elements - treated by differential equations.	Instantaneous time solution of voltages and currents.	Switching surges, recovery voltages. Applicable to <u>linear</u> single phase systems or to symmetrical 30 systems where transients do not involve imbalances.	TNA, analog computer. Digital computer (with traveling wave or lumped parameter solution methods). Digital differential analyzer.

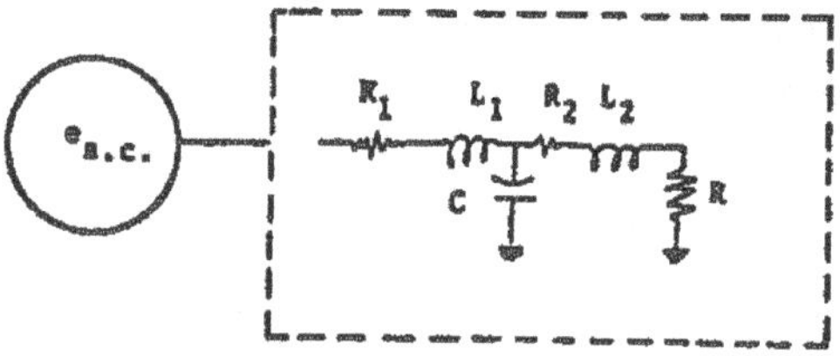

Figure 3

Source	Network	Nature of Results	Applications & Limitations	Solution Methods and Tools
Ideal sinusoidal balanced 30 sources behind constant inductances in each phase with constant or varying frequency (source inductance usually represented by X_d'').	R, L, C linear elements - treated by differential equations of 3 phases or differential equations of α, β and 0 networks.	Instantaneous time solution of phase voltages and currents and/ or α, β 0 components.	Switching surges, recovery voltages, short circuits. Applicable to linear 30 systems with or without imbalances. Duration of transients short relative to flux decay time constants of generators.	TNA, analog computer. Digital computer (with traveling wave or lumped parameter solution methods). Digital Differential Analyzer.

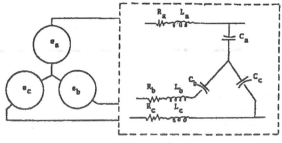

Figure 4

Source	Network	Nature of Results	Applications & Limitations	Solution Methods and Tools
Ideal sinusoidal balanced 3Ø sources behind constant inductances in each phase with constant or varying frequency (source inductance usually represented by X_d'').	R, L, C elements with nonlinear characteristics (magnetic saturation, thyrite resistors, etc.) differential equations of 3 phases.	Instantaneous time solution of phase voltages and currents.	Switching surges, recovery voltages, energization transients, short circuits. Applicable to nonlinear 3Ø systems with or without imbalances. Duration of transients short relative to flux decay time constants of generators.	TNA, analog computer. Digital computer (with traveling wave or lumped parameter solution methods). Digital differential analyzer.

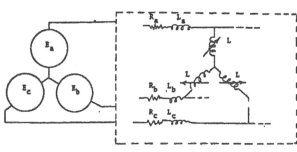

Figure 5

Source	Network	Nature of Results	Applications & Limitations	Solution Methods and Tools
Source represented by equations of flux behavior in d and q axes. Instantaneous terminal phase voltages derived from d, q, o transformation.	R, L, C elements with nonlinear characteristics (magnetic saturation, thyrite resistors, etc.) described by differential equations.	Instantaneous time solution of phase voltages, currents, powers, etc.	Switching surges, recovery voltages, energization transients, subsynchronous resonances, short circuits, load rejection transients. Applicable to nonlinear 30 systems with or without imbalances. Solution takes into account generator flux effects and is valid for short or long durations.	Analog computer (limited scope problem). Digital computer, scaled model of machines and network.

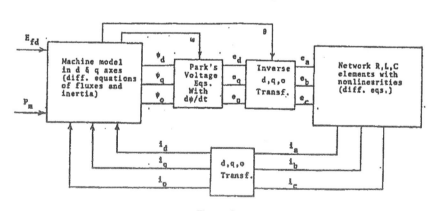

Figure 6

Source	Network	Nature of Results	Applications & Limitations	Solution Methods and Tools
Source represented by equations of flux behavior in d and q axes. Terminal voltage obtained as fundamental frequency positive sequence phasor by multiplying flux with speed. Armature and network transients neglected.	Z (jw), Y (jw) elements with nonlinear characteristics and frequency dependence. Network equations described by complex algebraic equations.	Fundamental frequency solutions of phase voltages and currents expressed as phasors, Machine angles, powers, etc.	Fundamental frequency transients following load rejections or other balanced network disturbances where frequency effects are significant. Applicable to balanced 30 systems for fundamental frequency effects over several seconds.	Analog computer (small size problem). Digital computer. Scaled models of machines and network.

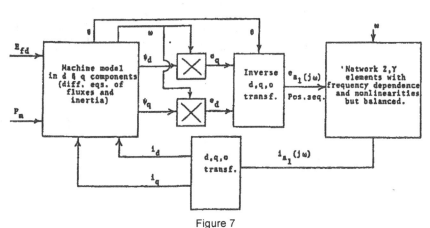

Figure 7

Source	Network	Nature of Results	Applications & Limitations	Solution Methods and Tools
Source representation same as in Fig. 7 except voltage taken equal to flux (speed assumed rated).	Z (jw), Y (jw) elements with or without nonlinear elements. Network equations described by complex algebraic equations. Negative and zero sequence network includes machine.	Fundamental frequency solutions of positive sequence voltages and currents as phasors. Machine angles, speeds, powers (average). (Negative and 0 sequence quantities can also be obtained).	Fundamental frequency transients following faults or other disturbances. Machine rotor angles, powers. Applicable to 30 systems for fundamental frequency effects over several seconds. Stability phenomena.	Analog computer (small size problem). Digital computer. Scaled models of machines and network. Hybrid computers.

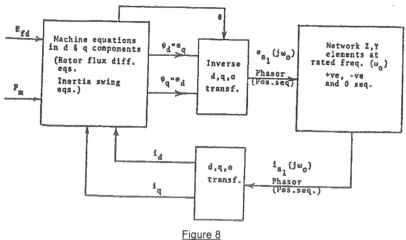

Figure 8

Source	Network	Nature of Results	Applications & Limitations	Solution Methods and Tools
Source represented as constant voltages behind appropriate reactances in d and q axes. "can be subtransient," transient, ` or steady-state (synchronous) depending on problem. Machine saliency included	$Z(jw_o)$, $Y(jw_o)$ elements with or without nonlinear elements. Network equations described by complex algebraic equations. Negative and zero sequence network includes machine.	Fundamental frequency solutions of sequence currents and voltages. If machine swing equations are included, rotor angle transients are obtained (stability)	Fundamental frequency network conditions. Symmetrical short circuit currents (balanced and unbalanced). With proper choice of machine reactances, may be used for stability calculations. Applicable to 30 systems for fundamental frequency effects. Used generally for conditions at some instant in time depending on value of source reactance and voltage used. If swing equations are solved (stability) transient reactance values are used and solution approximates conditions in first half second.	Digital computer.

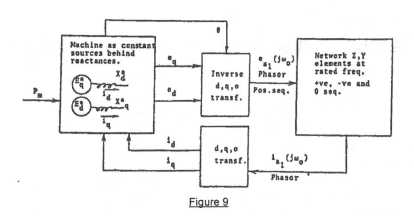

Figure 9

35

Source	Network	Nature of Results	Applications & Limitations	Solution Methods and Tools
Source represented as constant voltage behind an equivalent reactance. Machine saliency neglected.	$Z(jw_o)$, $Y(jw_o)$ elements with or without nonlinear elements. Network equations described by complex algebraic equation. Negative and zero sequence network includes machine.	Fundamental frequency solutions of sequence currents and voltages. If machine swing equations are included, rotor angle transients are obtained (stability-classical solution).	Applicable for short circuit studies (balanced and unbalanced) and first swing stability studies.	A-C network analyzer. Digital computer.

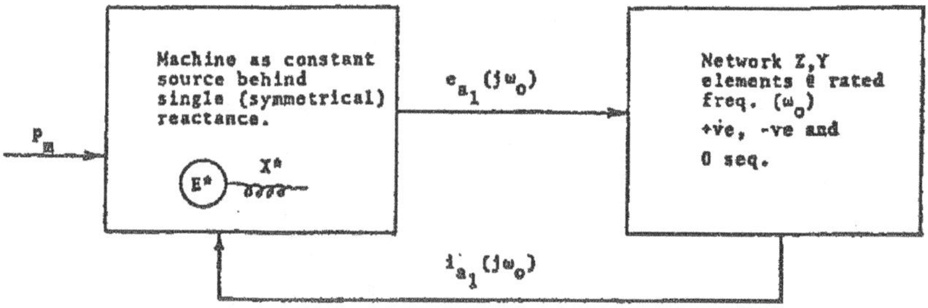

Figure 10

LOAD CHARACTERISTICS[3,6]

The sensitivity of results to load characteristics increases markedly in cases where the design of the power system is dictated by stability considerations. In many situations stability may not be governing. Location of loads and generation often results in extremely stiff systems where stability could only present a problem for rather severe disturbance criteria such as a 30 fault for 10 cycles. In such systems which essentially exhibit minor variations in voltage during realistic disturbances, accuracy of load representation may be relatively unimportant.

On the other hand, in systems where transmission design is pushed to limits dictated by stability, the dynamic behavior of loads becomes as significant as the disturbance criteria (severity and duration of fault).

Figure 11 illustrates the sensitivity of certain results to assumptions on load characteristics. The curves show the frequency behavior of a load area supplied by a significant amount of remote generation following the loss of this remote regeneration. Figure 11 shows how assumptions of load characteristics can alter the results of frequency behavior for this occurrence. With more than 75% of the real part of the load assumed to vary directly with voltage, the net result is a collapse in system voltage and a drastic reduction in connected load resulting in an eventual rise in system frequency rather than an expected drop in frequency.

When realistic load characteristics are modeled, with a certain percentage made up of induction motor loads, even more surprising results can develop. The induction motor load can exhibit an effective admittance about 4 to 5 times normal depending on the extent and duration of a voltage dip which could cause motors to stall. This is another stability type phenomenon where results are radically different depending on whether or not the disturbance was severe enough to cause motor stalling. Conceptually, one could think of the case as involving a single event, as the initial disturbance or a sequence of events where the initial disturbance is rapidly followed

by another involving a drastic increase in load admittance. The point is that the transition from one case to the other is so abrupt and leads to so widely differing results that system designers experiencing conditions on the optimistic side of the chasm may be lulled into a sense of security which could be drastically altered by a minor change in load assumptions.

Modeling of load characteristics remains one of the most important aspects of power system dynamics, deserving a great deal more attention and research than has been devoted by the industry to date.

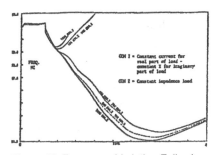

Figure 11. Frequency Variation Following Loss of Remote Generation

INTERPRETATION OF RESULTS

The interpretation of stability performance from simulation results of machine angle swing curves is at times difficult, especially in cases where the problem of instability develops beyond the first swing.

A discussion of some typical effects as revealed in stability swing curves follows:

1. First Swing Stability

The most clear-cut manifestation of instability is the pulling out of step in the first swing (Fig. 12).

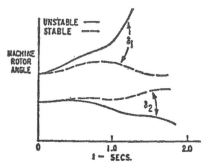

Figure 12. Machine Rotor Angle Transients Following Electrical Fault

2. Instability Following the First Swing

Several phenomena which might cause instability or what appears to be instability on subsequent swings are:

(a) Lack of damping of machine oscillations caused primarily by weak transmission and aggravated by voltage regulator action. Certain system conditions can exist which produce negative damping in machines even without action from voltage regulators.[5] This happens particularly in situations where a large load is served mainly by remote generation, with the local generation being a relatively small portion compared with the remote generation. The damping of the local generation can be negative in such cases. Figure 13 shows the case of undamped oscillations typical of such dynamic instability cases. It must be emphasized that the condition is a function of the state of the system following the disturbance rather than the transient shock of the disturbance itself. In other words, if the end state is obtained with the switching of a line, the instability characterized with build-up of oscillations will occur regardless of whether the switching of the line was preceded by a line fault. The shock of the fault would merely cause the oscillations to grow from larger initial amplitudes.

Dynamic instability can result in oscillations growing to a magnitude where eventual pull-out results. Sometimes the oscillations will grow to a certain magnitude and then sustain themselves at that magnitude. This can occur where the lack of damping is produced by voltage regulator action. As oscillations increase, the regulators and exciters begin to hit limits and ceilings and the effective gain of these devices is decreased. These situations result in so-called, limit cycles. Although in these cases pull-out and loss of synchronism may not occur, the performance of the power system is intolerable.

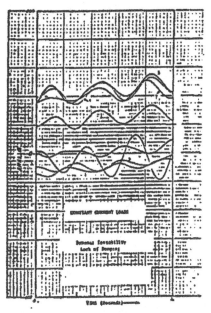

Figure 13

(b) In some instances, several modes of oscillation are excited by the disturbance such that, at some point beyond the first swing, a superposition of modes results in larger angle deviations and eventual pull-out of one or more plants. The loss of synchronizing power leading to pull-out is due to an excessive angle excursion reached some time after the first swing through an amplification effect due to superposition of modes. Figure 14 shows an example of this phenomenon. In this case, the disturbance was a 3Ø fault followed by the switching of a line section. Figure 15 shows that a less severe fault (2Ø ground fault), followed by the same switching operation results in stable conditions as the amplitude of subsequent angle swings did not reach the point where loss of synchronizing power occurs. This is in contrast to the phenomenon of lack of damping explained in (a) above where the phenomenon is a sustained growth in amplitude of individual modes of oscillations leading to eventual loss of synchronism or to a sustained state of oscillations, the magnitude of the disturbance affecting only the length of time before the oscillations reach a certain level or before pull-out occurs. In comparing Figure 15 with Figure 14, it should be noted that the time scales are different on the two sets of figures.

The phenomenon of amplification of angle excursions beyond the first swing through superposition of different modes is obviously aggravated by poor damping of these modes, since if good damping exists, the amplitude of the individual modes would be well reduced beyond the first swing.

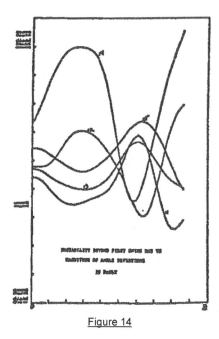

Figure 14

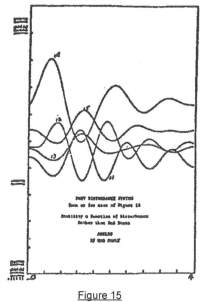

Figure 15

(c) The superposition of modes discussed in (b) above can also give rise to what appears to be dynamic instability discussed

in (a). Here, although the amplitude of the oscillations are initially not large enough to exhibit the nonlinear characteristics associated with the phenomenon of loss of synchronism, they appear to grow in amplitude. If the simulation run is terminated too soon, the real nature of the phenomena may not be revealed. Figure 16 shows this type of effect which is a "beat" phenomenon.

Evidently, where these cases occur, the system has marginal damping since for beats to be evident the modes of oscillation must last a long time.

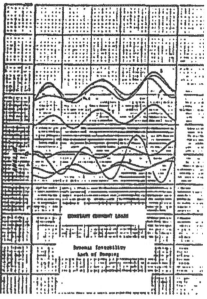

Figure 16

3. Sensitivity of Results

Whenever marginal stability cases are noted, exhibiting any of the phenomena discussed above, it is appropriate to establish the sensitivity of the results to various factors and assumptions. A marginally stable situation, especially where the instability phenomena are caused by poor or negative damping, is one that must be avoided by measures which establish a very decided degree of stability.

Figure 17 can be compared with Figure 13 to show the effects of the assumption on load characteristics (constant current for the real part for Figure 13 versus constant impedance for Figure 17) for a particular situation.

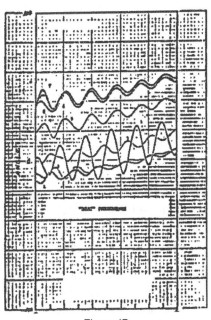

Figure 17

A poorly damped system although theoretically stable by mathematical definition, may be unacceptable from a system performance point of view. Random disturbances can keep the system in constant oscillations which at the frequency of about 1 Hz are intolerable to industrial and residential customers.

The top curves of Figure 18 show the swing performance of a large interconnected system following a severe disturbance. The bottom set of curves corresponds to the identical disturbance except that here the generators were simulated with modern static excitation systems and stabilizers. This is an empathetic demonstration of the potential benefits that can be derived from excitation systems designed to provide damping.

Evaluation of damping effects imposes increased demands on detail of modeling of synchronous machines, excitation systems and prime mover systems.

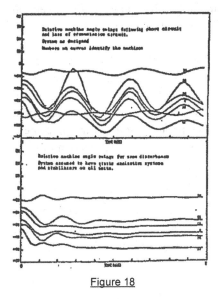

Figure 18

NEW TRENDS IN SOLUTION METHODS

Exploration of power system dynamic effects is critically a function of the ability of engineers to predict by simulation the behavior of systems. The less this ability the more conservative must be the design criteria and the greater must be the margins imbedded into designs. Most of the discussions on effects to be considered in power system dynamics become academic unless engineering solution methods are available to yield results within the constraints of time, cost and human endurance which are part of every real-life situation. The subject of new techniques in solution of power system problems, therefore, assumes major importance.[8]

The digital computer has probably had far more impact on the technical and economic affairs of mankind than any single invention in the last 100 years. But, like most inventions, it has gone through a very rapid evolution as have our concepts of its logical applications. The rate of evolution has increased manyfold in the last few years, and the management of computer resources has become a major factor in the realization of large engineering projects.

In order to appreciate the factors involved, let us review briefly the evolution of computation and the recent new directions that it is taking.

In the 1950's, for example, when large-scale computers were seeing their first real boom, the extremely high cost of hardware and the awesome complexity of the computer/ engineer interface led to almost total centralization of computer functions and bred a whole new generation of professional "interpreters," computer centers, programming departments, etc. Since the early 1950's, the pace of computer evolution has been staggering, and those working close to this field have grown used to seeing changes in size, speed, efficiency, etc. of orders of magnitude in just a few years. The development of high-level software permitting direct engineer/ computer communication has also been extremely significant. The initial growth was entirely in the direction of size and speed, but in the late 1960's several manufacturers began to "think small." The result was the first mini-computers and an even more accelerated progress in performance.

By almost any standard of measurement, computational costs have come down by a factor of 10 in just the last four years, and the trend is still downward. But, in addition to this, economies of scale in computers have disappeared for many applications.

With hardware costs becoming less significant, over-all costs are influenced by those features that permit increase in human efficiency. It matters little how fast and cheaply a load flow is performed if access to results is obtained with a day's time lapse instead of minutes.

With this in mind, it is apparent that computers should be as closely coupled to the person or function they serve as possible. Time-sharing was a significant step in this direction. The applications of autonomous dedicated computers is another.

A mini-computer today has the speed of the most advanced modern large computers and a memory size comparable to large machines of only a few years back.

Concurrently, a revolution has taken place in computer software. Whereas communication with computers used to require special machine language and the employment of specialized staff in such languages, today computer languages are easy to use and known by every new graduate engineer. Direct communication between engineer and computer is a mode of operation which is becoming increasingly popular.

This factor of eliminating a now superfluous human link between the engineer and the computer is probably as significant as the elimination of turn-around time through the use of dedicated interactive facilities.

Figure 19 shows the composition of a dedicated computer facility especially fitted with a complete set of interactive power system analysis programs. Interactive programs are designed so that engineers can examine results as the run progresses, make changes and adjustments, and essentially treat the problems as one would on an AC network analyzer or analog computer where there is a direct coupling without appreciable delay between the engineer's question and the analyzer or computer's answer. By having the ability to converse through a keyboard CRT and to examine the results on the screen, rapid experimentation can be made and the results outputted on hard copy only when a valid solution needs to be documented. In addition to printed output, an X-Y plotter provides means of presenting plotted results, such as are frequently needed in load flow studies and for the interpretation of dynamic simulation results.

The capacity of the interactive power system analysis programs handled by the minicomputer facility is quite large. Five hundred bus load flow problems, dynamic simulations of power systems with 50 generators and 250 buses including excitation and governor control effects are currently being executed with such speed that the bottleneck is now the ability of the engineer to digest the results. The dedicated facility is also used in the same role as a general-purpose analog computer for the solution of dynamic problems, such as analysis of excitation and governor controls, plant hydraulic hydraulic transients, etc.

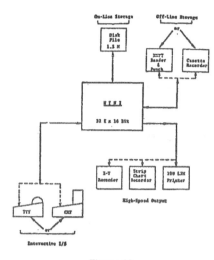

Figure 19

Dedicated Interactive Computer
System for Power System Analysis

CONCLUSIONS

The technological challenges of supplying the demands for electric energy in the present and foreseeable future require planning and design effort of scope and complexity unmatched in other industries.

Much of the complexity arises from the fact that in widespread interconnected systems analysis of any segment of the system additions must consider effects throughout the whole interconnected system. This is particularly the case where the size of each system addition is a significant fraction of the over-all system as is happening in developing nations.

The schedules inherent in much of this engineering work, often aggravated by surprise in equipment availability, load growth, and other unforeseen factors, has placed a very high premium on the speed and accuracy of solutions.

In presenting an overview of the subject of power system dynamics, we have had the opportunity of accentuating aspects which we believe are of major importance.

These aspects involve:

(1) Thorough understanding of the fundamentals, which is essential for the choice of the right model for the problem at hand, and for the interpretation of results.

(2) Accuracy of load modeling, especially in system configurations where stability is a governing criterion.

(3) The key requirement of providing computational tools designed for the task of dynamic analysis where interactive computation and rapid access to results is essential.

REFERENCES

1. F. P. de Mello, "Process Dynamics in Electric Utility Systems," ISA Paper 505-70, International Conference Exhibit of ISA, October 26-29, 1970, Philadelphia, Pa.

2. F. P. de Mello, "Modern Concepts of Power System Dynamics - The Effects of Control," IEEE Tutorial Publication 70M62-PWR, May, 1970, pp. 25-40.

3. F. G. McCrackin and W. R. Schmus, "Modern Concepts of Power System Dynamics - The Representation of System Load in Stability Studies," IEEE Tutorial Publication 70M62 - PWR, May 1970, pp. 41-46.

4. F. P. de Mello and C. Concordia, "Concepts of Synchronous Machine Stability as Affected by Excitation Control," IEEE Transactions on Power Apparatus & Systems, PAS-88, pp. 316-329, April, 1969.

5. F. P. de Mello and T. F. Laskowski, "Concepts of Power System Dynamic Stability," IEEE paper to be presented at the Joint Power Generation Conference, Miami, September, 1974.

6. W. Mauricio and S. Semlyen, "Effect of Load Characteristics on the Dynamic Stability of Power Systems," IEEE Transactions on PA&S, 1972, pp. 2295-2304

7. "System Load Dynamics Simulation Effects and Determination of Load Constants," prepared by Computer Analysis of Power Systems Working Group of the Analytical Methods Subcommittee, PA&S March/April, 1973, Vol. PAS-92.

8. J. M. Undrill, F. P. de Mello, T. E. Kostyniak and R. J. Mills, "Interactive Computation in Power System Analysis," Proceedings of IEEE, Special issue on Computation in the Power Industry, July, 1974.

Chapter 2

Power System Dynamics and Control

Contents

List of Figures

Generation Dynamics and Control

2.1 Introduction

The subject of Power System Dynamics is one of considerable complexity and very large dimensions.

Figure 1 is helpful in describing the chain of causes and effects and in identifying the many systems and subsystems which contribute to the magnitude of the problem of analysis and prediction of dynamic effects in power systems. These dynamic effects usually can be categorized under one of the following areas:

1) Prime-mover system Dynamics

2) Electrical machine Dynamics and excitation controls

3) Generation dynamics, i.e.; (System Governing and load frequency controls)

Under prime mover system dynamics one is concerned with the control and response of prime mover variables such as turbine shaft power, boiler pressures, temperatures and flows. Depending on the purpose the representations can range from very detailed ones taking into account many thermomechanical effects, such as are required for boiler control studies1, to fairly simple representations such as those concerned only with the effects of turbine shaft power over small excursions.

The area of electrical machine dynamics and excitation controls involves the study of network conditions and the behavior of electrical power flow, voltages, currents, etc. as affected by electromechanical transients that are set up between machines due to temporary unbalances between electrical and mechanical powers. These unbalances cause accelerations or decelerations of machine rotors giving rise to power-angle swings. These phenomena are normally studied under the subject of Power System Stability[5].

The third area of generation dynamics (system governing and load frequency controls) concerns the performance of overall power systems in relation to frequency and tie line powers. [2,3,4]

Examination of Figure 2.1 shows that problems in all of these categories must involve representations of all systems because of the coupling and closed loop feedback nature of the Power System.

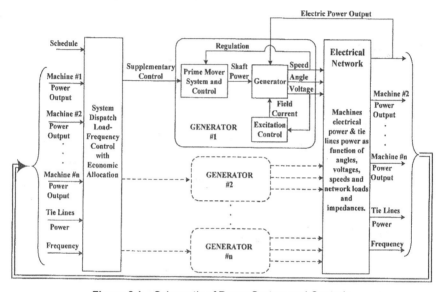

Figure 2.1 – Schematic of Power System and Controls

Fortunately, however, it is very seldom that all areas need be considered simultaneously in equal detail, and, depending on the particular phenomenon of concern, various simplifications can be made to represent the less important and less relevant effects. This leads to the need for special representations of Power Systems tailored to the specific problem rather than all-encompassing representations which consider all effects, both the relevant and the irrelevant. The need for these special representations is not only due to incentives of reducing computer costs, but mainly one related to limitations of data-gathering capability. Although computing capability has expanded by many billion times in the last 15 years, one is still faced with limitations in the capability of the human brain to absorb results and to feed in the correct input data. Hence, no matter how powerful the computing capability, it is important to solve the problem with the right degree of detail in the representation of relevant effects and a justifiable amount of simplification in the less important effects.

Opportunities for simplifications arise on several accounts:

a) Duration of effects and the resolution in time over which the effects are of significance. For instance, where transient stability phenomena over a second or two are the primary effects under investigation, it is not necessary to represent boiler transients which develop over several minutes. Again for this same problem, the other end of the spectrum of extremely fast transients such as switching transients of high frequencies need not be represented, allowing corresponding simplifications in the basic equations. Figure 2.2 classifies typical Power System Problems in the duration spectrum.

b) The range of variables may allow simplifications. For instance, in normal power system transients where frequency excursions are small, the simplifying assumption of constant speed in the generated voltage equations and constant frequency for the impedance parameters is perfectly justified. However, for load rejection conditions where the generator might undergo a significant speed transient, this assumption is no longer valid and for these problems one needs to represent speed as a variable. Additional peculiarities of the rejection case involve the need to represent saturation effects because of the possible range of voltage excursions.

c) Another opportunity for simplification involves the number of elements of a kind that needs to be represented. It is surprising how many problems can be solved and how many concepts can be developed with the study of the case of the single machine against infinite bus. Usually the greater the detail of a given effect that is to be studied, the more advisable it is to reduce the dimension of the system by considering a limited number of like elements. There are few fundamental effects that cannot be studied better on a 10-machine system representation than on a 100-machine representation. This is particularly true in the study of detailed control effects.

The art of reducing the number of elements is the art of "equivalencing". For instance, maintaining the identity of every unit of several in one plant is unnecessary for problems involving system disturbances which are felt equally by all such units. In such cases, lumping the many units into one equivalent unit gives a sufficient solution with greatly reduced computational burdens.

		PROBLEM AREA		
		Electrical Machine Dynamics and Excitation Controls	Governing and Load Frequency Controls	Prime-Mover and Energy Supply System Controls
DURATION OF PHENOMENA	Few Seconds	X		
	Several Seconds to Several Minutes		X	X

Figure 2.2 – Partitioning of Dynamic Problems by Duration of Effects

One important aspect of Power System Dynamics that is the subject of these notes, concerns the study of dynamics and control of generation known as governing and load frequency control. The development of an understanding of this area involves first, the description of the basic elements of the power system in terms of simplified mathematical models which adequately describe their behavior for purposes of power generation control analysis.

An understanding of the assumptions and limitations inherent in these models is essential to ensure that their application is limited to the solution of the appropriate class of problems.

The subject fits well into that of a feedback control problem. Figure 2.3 outlines the basic elements of the problem.

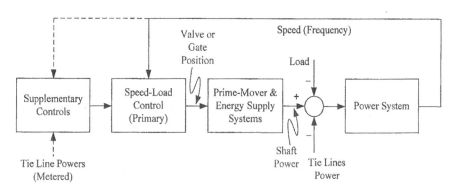

Figure 2.3 – Schematic Representation of Generation Control

Following logically the procedure of the control engineer in the understanding and tackling of control problems, we will first develop an understanding of the process and then proceed to close the primary and secondary control loops in that order.

Thus we will describe the blocks in Figure 2.3 in the following order:

1) The Power System

2) The Prime Mover-Energy Supply System

3) Primary Speed-Load Controls (Governing)

4) Supplementary Controls

The variables that link the various elements are labeled on Figure 2.3 For instance, in dealing with item (1), The Power System, we will concern ourselves with independent variables of shaft power and connected load and develop the model that describes the reaction of system frequency and tie line powers to changes in these independent variables. Likewise for the Prime Mover system the independent variable is valve or gate position and the model solves for shaft power and so on.

Supplementary material on methods of control analysis which will be helpful to the understanding of Power Generation Dynamics and Control are contained in Appendices A through F.

2.2 The Power System

For purposes of control analysis, elements such as generating units, prime movers, etc. are conveniently represented by linear differential equations which describe their performance for the small perturbation mode of operation.

Generating units are approximated by constant alternating voltage sources. The speeds or frequencies of these sources are determined by the momentum equations relating mechanical (accelerating) torques to the inertial torques developed by the machine rotors and the decelerating torques produced by electrical load.

2.2.1 Isolated Generator and Load

It is helpful to first examine the case of a single generator supplying an electrical load P_0 as in Figure 2.4.

$$T_m = \text{Mechanical Torque}$$
$$T_e = \text{Electrical Torque}$$

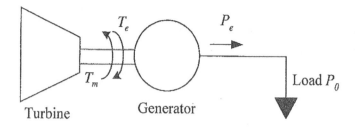

Turbine   Generator

Figure 2.4 – Isolated Generator Supplying Local Load

Under steady state conditions the generator of Figure 2.4 supplies load P_0 at constant frequency ω_0, and by definition of "steady state" the mechanical driving torque is equal to the electrical braking torque. Let us now examine the relations for small changes about the steady state. Subscript *"0"* is generally used to denote the quiescent or steady state value.

Figure 2.5 is a block diagram transfer function description of a generator's speed as function of torques. It defines relations between changes in speed ($p\delta$) and changes in torques (ΔT_m, ΔT_e).

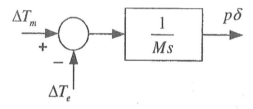

Figure 2.5 – Block Diagram for Generator

The relations of Figure 2.5 are described in operational form by

$$p\delta(s) = \frac{1}{Ms}\left[\Delta T_m(s) - \Delta T_e(s)\right] \qquad (II.1)$$

where M = Effective rotor inertia of the machine
        ΔT_m = Change in prime-mover torque
        ΔT_e = Change in electrical torque
        $p\delta$ = Deviation from normal frequency or speed (ω_0)
        $(\omega = \omega_0 + p\delta)$ = Actual frequency or speed of rotor inertia

Equation (II.1) can also be expressed in the time domain as

$$p\delta(t) = \frac{1}{M} \int \left[\Delta T_m - \Delta T_e \right] dt \qquad \text{(II.2)}$$

2.2.2 Derivation of M6

The equation of motion of a rotating body is

$$\frac{WR^2}{32.2} \alpha = T \text{ pound} - \text{feet} \qquad \text{(II.3)}$$

where WR^2 = moment of inertia in pound-feet^2

α = mechanical angular acceleration in radians/seconds^2
T   = accelerating torque in pound-feet

The mechanical angular acceleration α is equal to the electrical angular acceleration $d^2\delta/dt^2$ divided by the number of pairs of poles, P/2.

$$\therefore \alpha = \frac{2}{P} \frac{d^2\delta}{dt^2} \qquad \text{(II.4)}$$

where

$$P = \frac{2 \times 60 f}{rpm} = \text{no. of poles}$$

$$f = \text{frequency} \qquad \text{(II.5)}$$

$$\alpha \text{ is then equal to } \frac{rpm}{60f} \frac{d^2\delta}{dt^2}$$

Substituting Equation (II.5) in Equation (II.3)

$$T(\text{pound} - \text{feet}) = \frac{WR^2}{32.2} \frac{rpm}{60f} \frac{d^2\delta}{dt^2} \qquad \text{(II.6)}$$

Base torque may be defined as the torque required to produce base kW or kVA at rated speed or

$$T_{base} = \frac{(kW \text{ or } kVA)_{base}}{1.42 \times rpm \times 10^{-4}}$$

Expressing Equation (II.6) in per unit by dividing by T_{base}

$$\overline{T} = \frac{0.231 \times WR^a \times \overline{rpm}^2 \times 10^-}{\pi f \times kVA_{base}} \frac{d}{dt^2} \frac{\delta}{}$$ (II.7)

where $\overline{T}$ = torque in per unit.

The quantity

$$\frac{0.231 \times WR^2 \times \overline{rpm}^2 \times 10^{-6}}{kVA_{base}}$$

is known as H and has the dimensions of $\dfrac{kW \cdot s}{kVA}$ or seconds.

Equation (II.7) can then be written as

$$\overline{T}(p.u.) = \left(\frac{H}{\pi f}\right) \frac{d^2\delta}{dt^2}$$ (II.8)

where H is in seconds, f is in Hertz, δ is in radians and t is in seconds.

With the use of a new unit of time τ (radians) such that $\tau = \omega t = 2\pi f t$, Equation (II.8) becomes

$$\overline{T}(p.u.) = \frac{H(2\pi f)^2}{\pi f} \frac{d^2\delta}{dt^2}$$

$$= 4H\pi f \frac{d^2\delta}{dt^2}$$

M in radians $= (4H\pi f)$

$$= \frac{0.924 \times WR^2 \times (rpm)^2 \times \pi f \times 10^{-6}}{kVA_{base}}$$

Expressing torque in per unit, $p\delta$ in p.u. and t in seconds, we have

$$T = \frac{H}{\pi f} \frac{d}{dt} (p\delta \text{ in rd/s})$$

$$= \frac{H}{\pi f} \frac{d}{dt} (p\delta \text{ in p.u} \times 2\pi f)$$

$$= 2H \frac{d}{dt} (p\delta \text{ in p.u}) \qquad \text{(II.9)}$$

The significance of H expressed in seconds on machine base can be thought as the amount of time it takes the unit to change speed by 0.5 p.u. under a constant accelerating or decelerating torque of 1 p.u. Hence, in equations (II.1) or (II.2), $M = 2H$ s when T is in p.u. and $p\delta$ is in p.u.

The representation of Figure 2.5 can be used to simulate one machine or a group of closely coupled machines in a power system. When representing a group of machines, the inertia constant M is the composite sum of the inertias of all machines, the variable ΔT_m denotes the total change in system prime mover torque and ΔT_e denotes the total change in system electrical torque.

2.2.3 System Damping

The relationship in Figure 2.5 is between torque and speed. It is more meaningful to derive a relationship involving the basic variables of mechanical and electrical power. The relationship between power P and torque is given by

$$P = \omega T \qquad \text{(II.10)}$$

Expanding equation (II.10) in small oscillation form and neglecting second order terms

$$\Delta P = \omega_0 \Delta T + T_0 p\delta \qquad \text{(II.11)}$$

where $P = P_0 + \Delta P$

$T = T_0 + \Delta T$

$\omega = \omega_0 + p\delta$

From Equation (II.11)

$$\Delta T = \frac{\Delta P}{\omega_0} - \frac{T_0 \, p\delta}{\omega_0} \qquad \text{(II.12)}$$

Using relation (II.12) in Figure 2.5 and remembering that $\omega_0 = 1\ p.u.$ we develop the block diagrams of Figure 2.6 expressing deviation in per unit speed $p\delta$ as function of deviations in mechanical and electrical powers.

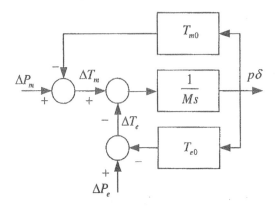

Figure 2.6 – Block Diagram for Generator Including Damping

Let us now examine the effects of speed deviations on mechanical and electrical power. Within the range of speed variations with which we are concerned the turbine mechanical shaft power is essentially a function of valve position and independent of frequency (in some types of hydro-turbines this is not always the case as speed deviations can affect the power developed in spite of constant gate position).

Depending on the particular load characteristics, electrical power can be affected by frequency and can be expressed as

$$P_e = P_L\,(1 + D'p\delta) \qquad\qquad (II.13)$$

where P_L is the connected load at normal frequency, and D' is the load frequency characteristic. In the special case of a purely resistive load with voltage maintained constant, electrical power would be independent of frequency, i.e.; D' would be zero in Equation (II.13).

In general, Power System loads are a composite of motor loads with various torque speed characteristics, lighting and heating loads. Changes in frequency cause changes in load due to changes in motor speeds as well as due to changes in voltage at the utilization points caused by changes in frequency. Representative values of system damping are $D' = 1\ or\ 2\ per\ unit$. A value of $D' = 2$ means that a 1% change in frequency would cause a 2% change in load based on connected load.

Developing equation (II.13) in small perturbation form, and neglecting second order terms

$$\Delta P_e = \Delta P_L (1 + D'P_{Lo} p\delta) \qquad (\text{II}.14)$$

Figure 2.7 shows the block diagram of the power system comprising one equivalent single machine and connected load P_{Lo} with a damping characteristic D'. The damping term $D'P_{Lo} = D$ is proportional to the connected load P_{Lo} and to the load's frequency sensitive characteristic D'. Thus D would be close to zero for a very lightly loaded system.

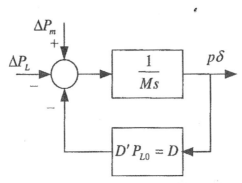

Figure 2.7 – Block Diagram for Generator Including Load Damping

2.2.4 Units

The per unit system is widely used in Power Systems analysis. It is convenient to select a base for powers ΔP_M, ΔP_L etc. This can be an arbitrary base although it is often selected as a base which is close to the rating of the system being represented. The value of kVA base chosen should be used in determining the value of M as in Equation (II.9).

The parameter D would likewise be expressed on this base. The variable $p\delta$ is usually expressed in per unit on rated frequency base.

As an example take the case of an isolated power system comprising two 500 MVA units supplying a connected load of 750 MW. The inertia constant H of each unit is 3.5 seconds on machine base. The load varies 1% per 1% change in frequency. Express the constants M and D of the block diagram of Figure 2.7 on a base of 1000 MVA.

Solution: - Combined system inertia H for the two units

   $= 2 \times 3.5$ on 500 MVA base

   or $2 \times 3.5 \times 500/1000 = 3.5$ on 1000 MVA base

$$\therefore M = 2H = 2 \times 3.5 = 7 \text{ on } 1000 \text{ MVA base}$$

System damping = 1 per unit change in load per 1 per unit change in frequency (load base = 750 MW).

Expressing D on 1000 MW base, $D = \dfrac{750}{1000} = 0.75$ p.u..

Figure 2.8 is the block diagram of this system on 1000 MVA base.

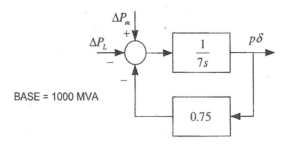

Figure 2.8 – Block Diagram for Generator – Numerical Example

The same system expressed on 500 MVA base would yield the constants

$$M = 7 \times \frac{1000}{500} = 14 \text{ and } D = 1 \times \frac{750}{500} = 1.5$$

The response of system frequency to a step change in load ΔP_L would be:

$$p\delta(s) = -\frac{\Delta P_L}{s} \frac{\dfrac{1}{Ms}}{1 + \dfrac{D}{Ms}} = -\frac{\Delta P_L}{sD\left(1 + s\dfrac{M}{D}\right)} \tag{II.15}$$

Figure 2.9 shows a time plot of the frequency change.

The initial rate of change at time t = 0⁺ is $\Delta P_L / M$ p.u./s. The final value is $- \Delta P_L / D$ and the time constant (time to 63% of change) is M/D seconds.

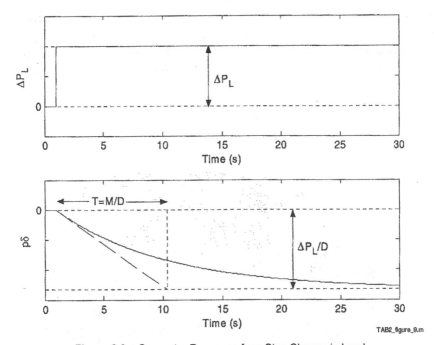

Figure 2.9 – Generator Response for a Step Change in Load

2.2.5 Electrical Coupling Between Machines

Evolving from the case of the isolated machine to that of machines operating in parallel or power systems operating interconnected, it is helpful to examine the case of two synchronous machines operating in parallel connected across a reactance X_{12} as in Figure 2.10.

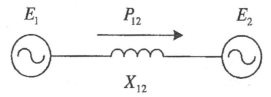

Figure 2.10 – Two Machines System

The power exchange between the two machines of Figure 2.10 is given by the familiar power-angle expression.[6] P_{12} is the power from voltage source E_1 to voltage source E_2.

$$P_{12} = \frac{E_1 E_2}{X_{12}} \sin \delta_{12} \qquad (\text{II.16})$$

The solution of the power angle equation in its nonlinear form is treated in analyses of transient stability where the effects of large upsets and large angular excursions are considered. For purposes of control analysis, we are interested in small changes about an operating point, and Equation (II.16) can be expressed in small oscillation form by the linear relation

$$\Delta P_{12} = \frac{E \cdot E_1}{X_{12}} \cos\left(\delta_{12_0}\right) \Delta \delta_{12}$$

The coefficient $(E_1 E_2/X_{12})$ $\cos\left(\delta_{12_0}\right)$ which can be seen on Figure 2.11 to be the slope $\Delta P_{12}/\Delta \delta_{12}$ of the power angle curve about the operating point is labeled T, the synchronizing power coefficient.[*]

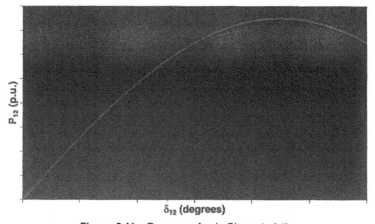

Figure 2.11 – Power vs. Angle Characteristic

The change in angle $\Delta \delta_{12}$ is obtained by integrating the change in frequency between machine 1 and 2, $p\delta_1 - p\delta_2$. It must be noted that this change in angle is with reference to a vector rotating at frequency $\omega_2 = \omega_0 + p\delta_2$.

In our previous block diagram presentations, we had expressed the variable $p\delta$ as per unit of rated frequency. To convert it to radians/sec. which, when integrated, will yield δ_{12} in radians for use in equation 16, it must be multiplied by ω_0 or 377 rd/s in a 60 Hz system.

The block diagram describing two coupled machines or groups of machines is shown on Figure 2.12. The synchronizing power coefficient T in the block diagram of Figure 2.12 is

---

[*] The symbol T for synchronizing torque coefficient should not be confused with the same symbol previously used for Torque.

$$\left[\frac{E_1 E_2}{x_{12}} \cos \delta_{12} \times \omega_0 \right]$$

Note that the power exchange between machines $\Delta P_{TL12} = \frac{T}{s}\left(p\delta_1 - p\delta_2\right)$ acts as a load to machine group 1 and as generation to machine group 2. This fact is indicated by appropriate signs into the summing junctions of the block diagram of Figure 2.12.

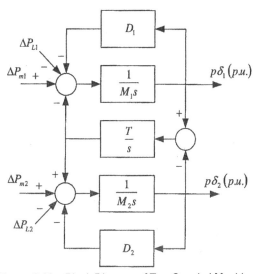

Figure 2.12 – Block Diagram of Two Coupled Machines

We have now derived a model of a two machine system, or of two power systems interconnected through a tie line - representing only the part of the system which forms system frequency and tie line interchange from prime mover and load power. Summarizing, the basic variables and constants that enter this model are:

ΔP_m = Change in prime mover power, p.u.

ΔP_L = Change in electrical load at nominal frequency, p.u.

$p\delta$ = Change in frequency from synchronous in p.u. of base frequency. (1 p.u. = 377 rd/s for 60 Hz systems)

ΔP_{TL} = Change in electrical power between machines in p.u.

M = Inertia constant = 2H secs on same base as prime mover or load power

D = System damping (p.u. power/p.u. $p\delta$)

T = Synchronizing power coeff. = 377 x p.u. power/radian.

Let us now examine the nature of this power system model. Using the formula $\frac{G}{1+GH}$ for block diagram reduction, (Appendix C), we will determine the one overall transfer function relating $p\delta_1$ to ΔP_{L1}. That is, we will keep all other inputs, ΔP_{m1}, ΔP_{m2} and $\Delta P_{L2} = 0$ and determine $p\delta_1$, for a step in ΔP_{L1}.

Starting from the block diagram of Figure 2.12; Figure 2.13 shows a series of reductions which will be self-evident.

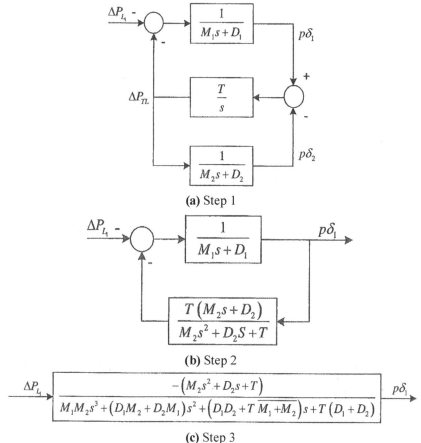

(a) Step 1

(b) Step 2

(c) Step 3

Figure 2.13 – Block Diagram Simplification

The final transfer function expression may be simplified further if we assume equal units, or areas with $M_1 = M_2$ and $D_1 = D_2$, whereupon

$$\frac{\Delta p\delta_1}{\Delta P_{L1}} = \frac{-\left(Ms^2 + Ds + T\right)}{(Ms + D)\left(Ms^2 + Ds + 2T\right)} \qquad (\text{II.17})$$

For this case the final value theorem shows that $\Delta p\delta_1$, $(t \to \infty)$ for a unit step change in ΔP_{L1} is $\dfrac{-T}{2TD} = \dfrac{-1}{2D}$.

The time response $\Delta p\delta_1$ to a unit step in ΔP_L is given by taking the inverse Laplace transform of

$$\Delta p\delta_1(s) = \frac{-\left(Ms^2 + Ds + T\right)}{sM^2\left(s + \dfrac{D}{M}\right)\left(s^2 + \dfrac{D}{M}s + \dfrac{2T}{M}\right)} \tag{II.18}$$

When $\left(\dfrac{D}{M}\right)^2$ is small relative to $\dfrac{2T}{M}$, this expression is approximately equal to

$$\frac{-\left(Ms^2 + Ds + T\right)}{sM^2\left(s + \dfrac{D}{M}\right)\left[\left(s + \dfrac{D}{2M}\right)^2 + \dfrac{2T}{M}\right]}$$

and the inverse is

$$K_1 + K_2 e^{\frac{D}{M}t} + K_3 e^{-\frac{D}{2M}t}\sin\left(\sqrt{\frac{2T}{M}}t + \psi\right) \tag{II.19}$$

K_1, K_2 and K_3 can be obtained by the rules of partial fractions and Laplace transformation. (Appendix B).

Figure 2.14 shows the behavior of the two equal interconnected systems to a sudden load change ΔP_{L1} in area 1, assuming there are no changes in prime mover powers.

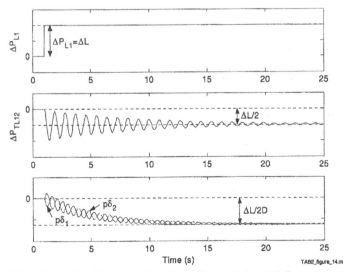

Figure 2.14 – Generators Response for a Step Change in Load (2 Generators System)

Note the final steady-state deviation of frequency in both areas which settle out to a value of $-\dfrac{\Delta L}{2D}$. Also, note the oscillations of $p\delta$ and P_{TL} with a frequency equal to $\dfrac{\sqrt{2T}}{M}$ which typically lies between 0.2 Hz and 2 Hz depending on the strength of T and the magnitude of M. The higher the strength of T, i.e.; the lower the reactance between machines or between systems, the higher is the oscillation frequency. The rate of decay of these oscillations is contributed by system damping D discussed before. Machine amortisseurs and field losses are also a source of damping especially at the higher frequencies.

Note that we have examined the behavior of the power system exclusive of the governor and prime-mover effects. This would be equivalent to operation under blocked governor.

Situations often arise where one must consider a finite system interconnected to a large system which, for practical purposes, may be taken as infinite ($p\delta_2 = 0$). For this case, the system block diagram is shown in Figure 2.15.

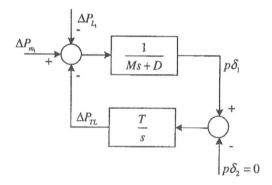

Figure 2.15 – Block Diagram of Machine Connected to Infinite System

The transfer function between $p\delta_1$ and ΔP_L shows that the steady-state frequency deviation is zero as one would expect since the system is tied to an infinite system whose frequency cannot change.

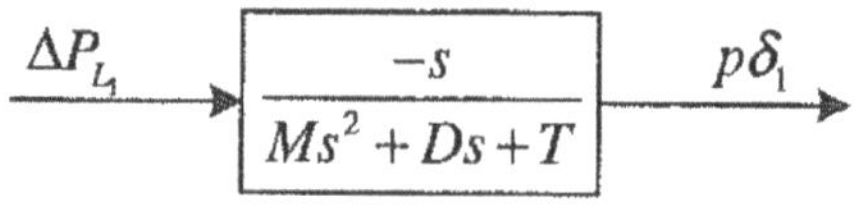

$$\Delta P_{L_1} \rightarrow \boxed{\dfrac{-s}{Ms^2 + Ds + T}} \rightarrow p\delta_1$$

Figure 2.16 – Transfer Function $\dfrac{p\delta_1}{\Delta P_{L1}}$ for Machine Connected to Infinite System

The transfer function between ΔP_{TL} and ΔP_L is:

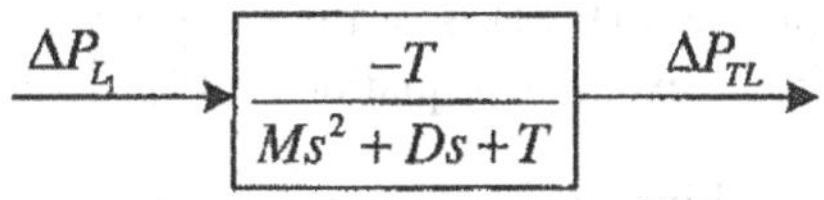

$$\Delta P_{L_1} \rightarrow \boxed{\dfrac{-T}{Ms^2 + Ds + T}} \rightarrow \Delta P_{TL}$$

Figure 2.17 – Transfer Function $\dfrac{\Delta P_{TL}}{\Delta P_{L1}}$ for Machine Connected to Infinite System

with a steady-state gain of -1, i.e.; all the load change in area 1 is supplied through the tie line from the neighboring infinite area.

Note that the oscillation frequency is $\sqrt{T/M}$ in rd/s where M is the inertia of the finite area and T the synchronizing power coefficient between areas.

2.2.6 Equivalencing

Some insight can be derived from the expressions of Figure 2.13 in order to arrive at logical ways by which multimachine systems may be approximated by reduced numbers of machines. One factor which justifies lumping of machines is when the disturbances of concern impinge with symmetry on several machines thereby not giving rise to intermachine oscillations. In the example of Figure 2.14, if the load change impinged with equal weight on both areas i.e.; if we had $\Delta P_{L1} = \Delta P_{L2} = \Delta P_{LI}$, then the mode of oscillations between machines would not be excited, there would be no change in tie flow and both frequencies would track the monotonic decay of Figure 2.14 without oscillations.

Obviously for such a case the behavior of the machines could be represented by that of one equivalent machine.

Another factor that justifies lumping of machines is when they are very tightly coupled, i.e.: when the value of the synchronizing power coefficient is large.

Take the expression at the bottom of Figure 2.13 relating frequency deviation $p\delta_1$ to load change in system 1, ΔP_{LI}

$$\frac{p\delta_1(s)}{P_{L1}(s)} = \frac{-\left(M_2 s^2 + D_2 s + T\right)}{M_1 M_2 s^3 + \left(D_1 M_2 + D_2 M_1\right)s^2 + \left(D_1 D_2 + T M_1 + M_2\right)s + T\left(D_1 + D_2\right)} \tag{II.20}$$

Taking the limit of this expression as $T \rightarrow \infty$ we have

$$\frac{p\delta_1}{P_{L1}} = \frac{-1}{\left(M_1 + M_2\right)s + \left(D_1 + D_2\right)} \tag{II.21}$$

One can note that expression (II.21) is of the same form as that for the single isolated area derived in the example, Equation (II.15).

The equivalent single machine has inertia equal to the sum of the inertias and the equivalent system damping is likewise equal to the sum of the individual system's damping terms.

2.2.7 Machine Electrical Power

In analyses of load-frequency controls, one must sometimes represent the metered electrical power from a machine or groups of machines. A simple way of deriving this power from the block diagrams developed so far will be shown here.

Going back to the block diagram of Figure 2.7 and adding the tie line power P_{TL} we have the representation of Figure 2.18 where we have preserved the identity of ΔP_e which is the actual electrical power of the unit, or equivalent unit.

In Figure 2.18 we have identified as X the output of the summing operation

$$\Delta P_m - \Delta P_e = X \tag{II.22}$$

hence, $\Delta P_e = \Delta P_m - X$

where X is the accelerating power.

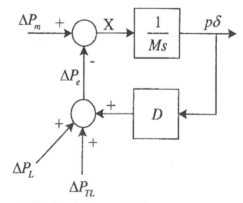

Figure 2.18 – Block Diagram for Generator Preserving ΔP_e

In the more common block diagram where the identity of ΔP_e is not preserved, we may derive the value ΔP_e from Equation (II.22), as is shown in the block diagram of Figure 2.19.

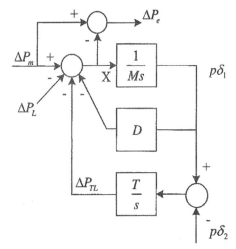

Figure 2.19 – Block Diagram for Two Machine System with Calculation of ΔP_e

In many studies, it may be necessary to preserve the identity of the prime movers, whereas the electrical behavior of the units can be adequately simulated by considering the units as one equivalent generator. For such a case, the representation would be as shown in Figure 2.20.

Note the formation of electrical powers as the mechanical powers less the corresponding accelerating powers. M_A is the sum of inertias in one area $= M_1 + M_2 + \dots$ where M_1, M_2, etc., are the individual units' inertias.

The models developed under this section entitled "The Power System" give some insight as to the dynamic behavior of generating units or whole power systems. We should stress that these models although adequate for study of governing and load frequency controls, are quite approximate. In particular the subject of damping involves effects which have been neglected namely; the damping torques developed in fields and amortisseurs of generating units. These are functions of the slips or relative speeds between units and for a multi-machine system would require the representation of generators and excitation systems in great detail. These damping torques are sometimes referred to as induction torques as contrasted with synchronous torques. Reference 7, in its Chapter 6, discusses the magnitude of these torques. Since they are affected materially by external impedance, these damping torques are not significant for the case of representing generation in one area as an equivalent single machine interconnected to another machine through, usually, a fairly high per unit impedance on the equivalent machine base. Another important source of positive or negative damping is the action of automatic voltage regulators. This subject is covered in the course notes dealing with oscillatory stability.

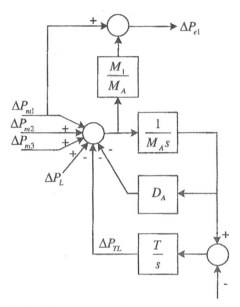

Figure 2.20 – Block Diagram for Two Area Equivalent System with Calculation of ΔP_e for Individual Generators

2.3　The Prime Mover and Energy Supply Systems

In the previous section we examined the behavior of the power system as described by deviations in frequency and tie line power in response to changes in prime mover power and in connected electrical load. We shall now describe another element of the loop, namely; the response of prime mover power to changes in valve or gate position.

2.3.1　Steam Turbines [2,3]

The power developed in a turbine is proportional to steam flow ($\dot{m}_s$): $P_m \propto \dot{m}_s\,(h_i - h_0)$ where P_m is the prime mover power, h_i and h_0 are inlet and exhaust steam enthalpies. Since h_i and h_0 are generally nearly constant the response of Pm follows that of the steam flow. In non-reheat turbines, the response of steam flow to a change in turbine throttle valves is almost instantaneous, i.e.; it exhibits a time constant of 0.2 to 0.3 seconds due to the small charging time of the turbine bowl volume. Assuming that the pressure of the steam supply holds essentially constant, then the response of turbine power to a change in valve position can be described by the transfer function of Figure 2.21 for a non-reheat turbine. The flow/pressure phenomena giving rise to this time constant are similar to those developed for the reheater in the following discussion.

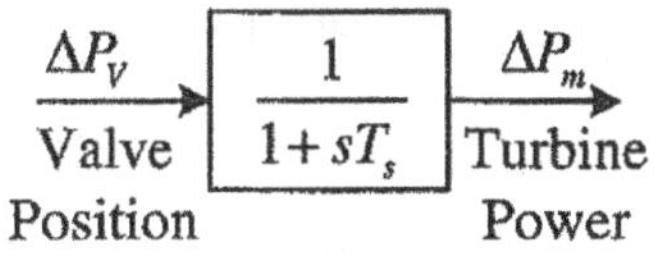

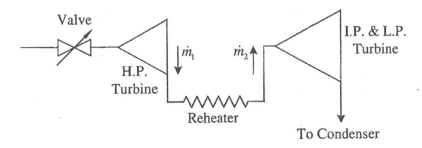

$$T_s = 0.2 \rightarrow 0.3 \text{ Sec. (Steam Bowl Time Constant)}$$

Figure 2.21 – Block Diagram for Non-Reheat Turbine Considering Constant Pressure

Figure 2.22 shows a schematic of reheat turbines.

Figure 2.22 – Schematic Diagram of Reheat Turbine

Although the change in flow in the high pressure turbine gets established with a very short time constant, as in Figure 2.21, the flow in the low pressure turbine can only change with the build-up of pressure in the reheater volume. The following equations describe approximately the phenomena of transient steam flow into the reheater and into the turbine stages downstream of the reheater[8].

$\dot{m}_1$ = steam mass flow rate into reheater (lbs/sec)

$\dot{m}_2$ = steam mass flow rate out of reheater into low pressure turbine (lbs/sec)

P = reheater pressure (psi)

ρ = average density of steam in reheater, (lbs/ft³)

V = volume of reheater and steam leads (ft³)

Continuity equation

$$V \frac{d\rho}{dt} = \dot{m}_1 - \dot{m}_2 \qquad (\text{II.23})$$

Flow equation

$$\dot{m}_2 = \left(\frac{\dot{m}_0}{P_{R0}} \right) P \qquad (\text{II.24})$$

where $\dot{m}_0$ is rated flow, P_{R0} is rated reheater pressure.

Now

$$\frac{d\rho}{dt} = \frac{dP}{dt}\frac{\partial\rho}{\partial P}\Big|_T \qquad\qquad\text{(II.25)}$$

where

$\dfrac{\partial\rho}{\partial P}\Big|_T$ (change in density of steam with respect to pressure) is determined from

steam tables.

Substituting Equation (II.25) and Equation (II.24) in Equation (II.23) and taking the Laplace transform of the resultant equation (neglecting initial conditions)

$$sV\frac{\partial\rho}{\partial P}\Big|_T \frac{P_{Ro}}{\dot{m}_0}\dot{m}_2(s) = \dot{m}_1(s) - \dot{m}_2(s)$$

$$\dot{m}_2(s) = \frac{\dot{m}_1(s)}{\left(1 + V\dfrac{\partial\rho}{\partial P}\Big|_T \dfrac{P_{R0}}{\dot{m}_0}s\right)} = \frac{\dot{m}_1(s)}{(1 + T_R s)} \qquad\qquad\text{(II.26)}$$

where T_R is the reheater time constant $= V\dfrac{\partial\rho}{\partial P}\Big|_T \dfrac{P_{R0}}{\dot{m}_0}$

A typical 300 MW unit with $P_{R0} = 600$ psi, $\dfrac{\partial\rho}{\partial P}\Big|_T = 0.0015$, $\dot{m}_0 = 500\dfrac{lbs}{s}$ and

$V = 3,000\,ft^3$ yields

$T_R = 5.4\ s.$

The overall transfer function of the prime mover power for a reheat turbine is obtained by summing the powers developed by the turbine stages upstream and downstream of the reheater. If C is the proportion of power developed in the high pressure turbine (about 0.3 near full load point), then the transfer function for the total power is

$$\frac{C}{1+T_s s} + \frac{(1-C)}{(1+T_s s)(1+T_R s)} = \frac{1+CT_R s}{(1+T_R s)(1+T_s s)}$$

Figure 2.23 shows the response of a reheat turbine power to a step change in throttle valve position.

Typical values of T_R are between 5 and 7 sec.

It should be noted that in the analysis above, a number of second order effects have been neglected. For instance, the assumption that high pressure turbine flow is directly proportional to admission pressure and turbine valve opening is valid for the critical flow regime where the ratio of downstream to upstream pressure is less than 0.5. Under this regime there are essentially no feedback effects of reheat pressure on flow through the high pressure turbine.

Near full load the regime is not quite critical, and a slight effect is actually felt between reheat pressure and main steam flow. Another second order effect is the transient charging of feedwater heaters affecting extraction flows from the turbine with corresponding effects on turbine power.

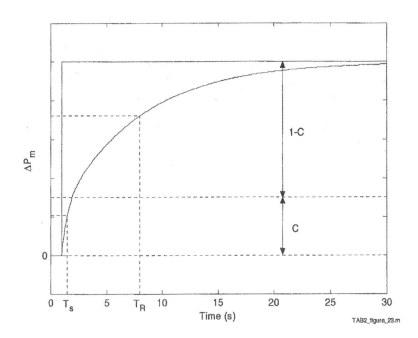

Figure 2.23 – Reheat Turbine Response for a Step Change in Throttle Valve Position

Although such effects are considered in detailed dynamic analyses of turbines as may be necessary in turbine speed control design studies, they can be neglected as being second order for the general system performance studies concerned with small perturbations around an operating point.

A more important effect on turbine response is the behavior of boiler pressure under changing demands of steam flow and under the effects of boiler controls.[9]

2.3.2 Boiler Effects

Since the steam supply system is not an infinite source, boiler pressure does vary transiently with changes in steam demand. Boiler dynamics is a very involved subject requiring the consideration of many simultaneous thermodynamic effects (Ref. 1, 10, 11, 12). However, for purposes of this discussion one can look at the boiler process in a very simplified fashion as shown on Figures 2.24a and b.[12]

Pressure in the boiler is affected by changes in steam mass within the boiler storage volume. These changes in stored mass result from transient imbalances between steam flow into the turbine and steam generation in the boiler. The throttle pressure differs from drum pressure by the amount of pressure drop across the superheaters. This pressure drop is approximately proportional to the square of the steam flow rate.

An equivalent electrical circuit which performs in analogous fashion to the boiler pressure phenomena for small changes in load is shown in Figure 2.24b where I_1 is analogous to steam generation, I_2 to steam flow to the turbine, R to the friction resistance presented by the superheaters and R_T to the resistance offered by the turbine at a given valve opening.

The voltage across the capacitor is analogous to drum pressure and the voltage across R_T is analogous to the throttle pressure P_T. In the above equivalent circuit representation, the change in turbine valve is represented by a change in R_T.

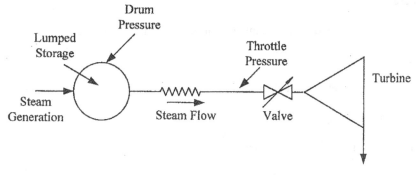

(a) Schematic Representation

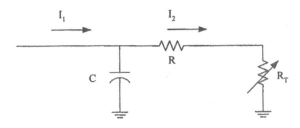

(b) Electrical Analog

Figure 2.24 – Boiler-Turbine System

For the first few seconds following a change in R_T or turbine valve, the voltage across the capacitor (drum pressure) does not change. However, the throttle pressure will suffer a deviation due to the change in friction drop ($R\Delta I_2$) in the superheaters and piping.

Since pressure drop is proportional to the square of flow, whereas voltage drop is linearly related to current, the above analogy is approximate and holds for small changes about an operating point. The value of resistance R varies with operating load level as can be seen from the following:

$$P_{DT} = \text{Pressure drop from drum to throttle} = K\dot{m}_s^2$$

where

$$K = \text{friction drop coefficient}$$

$$\dot{m}_s = \text{steam flow rate}$$

For small perturbations

$$\Delta P_{DT} = \text{change in pressure drop} = 2K\dot{m}_{so}\Delta\dot{m}_s \text{ from drum to throttle} \qquad (II.27)$$

where

$\dot{m}_{so}$ = steady state steam flow at the particular operating point

and

$\Delta \dot{m}_s$ = change in steam flow

In the analog of Figure 2.24b, $R = 2K\dot{m}_{so}$.

The effect of turbine valve changes can be represented in linearized small perturbation form as follows:

$$\dot{m}_s = K_v P_T \qquad (II.28)$$

where

P_T = Throttle Pressure

K_v = coefficient proportional to valve opening

For small perturbations, neglecting second order terms

$$\Delta \dot{m}_s = K_{vo}\Delta P_T + \frac{\Delta K_v}{K_{vo}}\dot{m}_{so} \qquad (II.29)$$

Steam generation (I_l) is proportional to heat release in the furnace, and follows this heat release with a small time constant (5 to 7 seconds) due to the waterwall metal and film coefficient. The process can therefore be represented by the block diagram of Figure 2.25, where subscript 0 denotes steady state value and prefix Δ denotes change from steady state value:

$\dot{m}_w$ = steam generation
P_D = drum pressure
P_T = throttle pressure
$\dot{m}_s$ = steam flow
K_v = coefficient proportional to valve opening
T_w = waterwall time constant
C_b = boiler storage constant

In the linear, small oscillation model shown in Figure 2.25, the parameters that change with load level are R and K_{vo}. All other parameters are essentially invariant.

Using the per unit system based on rated values, i.e.; base steam flow = full load steam flow, base pressure = rated pressure, etc., typical values of parameters in the block diagram of Figure 2.25 are:

Kv = coefficient proportional to load, 1.0 p.u. at full load

R = friction drop coefficient

   = 2 x (p.u. load level) x (p.u. pressure drop from drum to turbine throttle at full load)

The value of pressure drop at full load is about 10% or 0.1 p.u. so that at the full load operating point a typical value of R is 0.20 p.u.

The boiler storage constant C_b is related to the stored mass of saturated liquid and vapor as well as the mass of superheated steam in the superheaters and steam leads. Typically C_b represents the number of full load flow seconds for a one per unit change in pressure assuming a linear relationship between stored mass and pressure. This storage constant varies between 120 to 300 seconds in drum type boilers and 90 to 200 seconds in once-through units.[13]

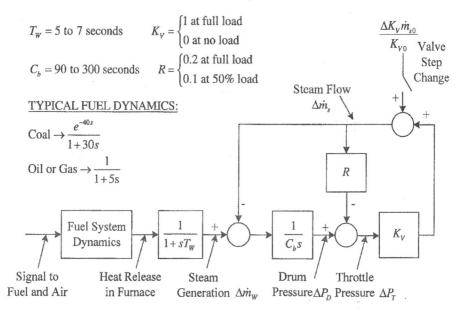

Figure 2.25 – Simplified Block Diagram of Boiler Process

Typical boiler pressure responses for step changes in turbine valve of 0.1 p.u. are shown on Figure 2.26.

Figure 2.26 shows the case of change in turbine valve where the boiler is left uncontrolled with a steady input of fuel and air. The action of boiler controls is to restore pressure back to set point and the promptness with which this can be done as well as the pressure deviation which would occur are a function of the dynamics of the fuel system.

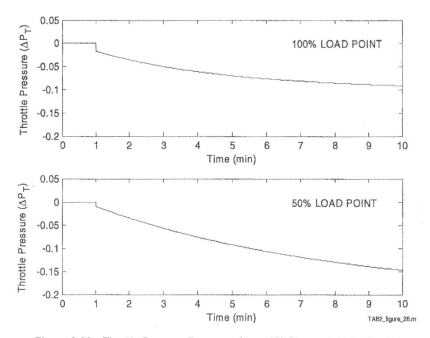

Figure 2.26 – Throttle Pressure Response for a 10% Change in Valve Position

Figure 2.27 shows representative pressure responses for coal fired and gas or oil fired boilers. The deviations in pressure in per unit multiplied by the per unit load at the particular operating point represent the per unit deviation in power due to pressure effects.

A simplified model of the prime mover system including pressure effects is shown on Figure 2.28.

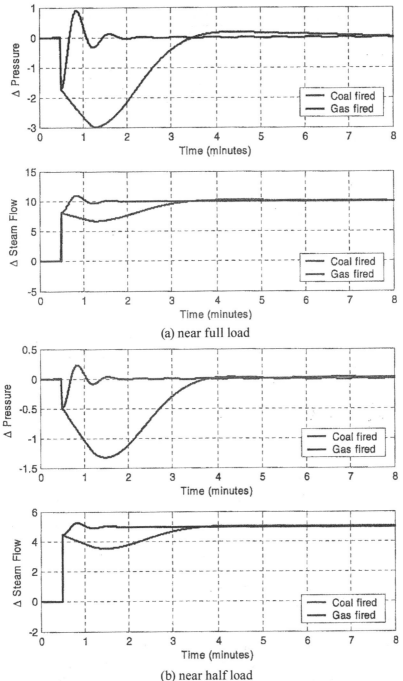

(a) near full load

(b) near half load

Figure 2.27 – Boiler Response for a Step Change in the Valve Position

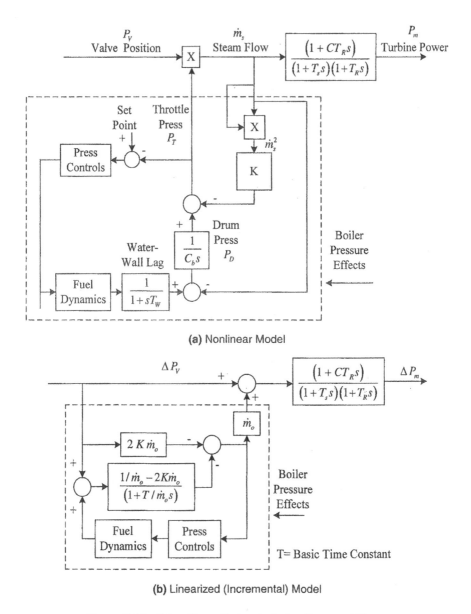

(a) Nonlinear Model

(b) Linearized (Incremental) Model

Figure 2.28 – Prime Mover System Including Pressure Effects

Hydro Turbines [3, 14]

The inertia of water flowing through penstocks gives rise to a curious phenomenon in hydraulic turbines. Upon opening of the gates, the initial effect is a drop in head at the turbine and a negative change in turbine power while the change in head is being used to accelerate the water column. As a result the initial change in turbine power is opposite in direction to the final change, and twice as large.

The transfer function can be approximated by:

$$\frac{\Delta P_m}{\Delta P_v} = \frac{(1 - T_w s)}{\left(1 + \frac{T_w s}{2}\right)} \tag{II.30}$$

where:

$$
\begin{array}{lll}
P_m & = & \text{Turbine mechanical power} \\
P_v & = & \text{Turbine gate position and} \\
T_w & = & \text{is the water starting time (varies with load point)}
\end{array}
$$

The derivations below assume an inelastic penstock and incompressible fluid. These assumptions can be justified in the majority of cases except for very long penstocks. They are included here to explain the physics which give rise to the transfer function in Equation (II.30). Appendix G contains more details on modeling of hydraulic turbines.

Figure 2.29 shows a penstock and turbine defining pertinent variables.

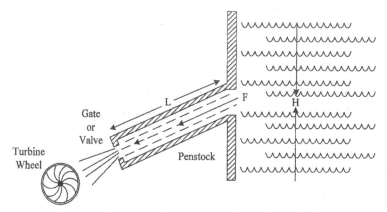

Figure 2.29 – Schematic Representation of Hydro Turbines

The flow rate of water in turbine and penstock is given by

$$q = G\sqrt{H} \tag{II.31}$$

where

$$H \quad = \quad \text{hydraulic head at the gate in ft.}$$
$$G \quad = \quad \text{factor proportional to gate position}$$
$$q \quad = \quad \text{water flow rate in cu. ft./sec.}$$
$$u \quad = \quad \text{velocity of water in penstock} = q/A \text{ ft./sec.}$$

For small perturbations about an operating point, Equation (II.31) can be written in linearized and normalized form as

$$\frac{\Delta q}{q_0} = \frac{1}{2}\frac{\Delta H}{H_0} + \frac{\Delta G}{G_0} \tag{II.32}$$

where subscript "0" denotes steady-state value and prefix "Δ" indicates small change from steady-state value.

Now by Newton's law we may write the acceleration equation for the water column as

$$L\rho \, \frac{d(\Delta q)}{dt} = -A\rho \, g\Delta H \tag{II.33}$$

where

$$\rho \qquad = \qquad \text{mass density}$$
$$A \qquad = \qquad \text{pipe area}$$
$$g \qquad = \qquad \text{acceleration of gravity}$$
$$L \qquad = \qquad \text{length of penstock}$$
$$\rho LA \qquad = \qquad \text{mass of water in conduit}$$
$$\rho g\Delta H \quad = \quad \text{incremental change of hydraulic head at turbine gate}$$

Equation (II.33) can be normalized by dividing both sides by $\rho g\Delta H_0 q_0$ and Laplace transformed.

$$A\frac{Lq_0}{gH_0}s\left(\frac{\Delta q}{q_0}\right) = -\left(\frac{\Delta H}{H_0}\right)$$

or

$$T_w s\left(\frac{\Delta q}{q_0}\right) = -\left(\frac{\Delta H}{H_0}\right) \tag{II.34}$$

where T_w is the nominal starting time $= Lq_0 / gH_0 A = Lu_0 / gH_0$

T_w can also be defined as the time required to accelerate the water in the penstock to the velocity u_0 under the action of a head H_0.

Substituting Equation (II.34) in Equation (II.32), we may express the change in flow rate as function of change in gate position

$$\frac{\Delta q}{q_0} = \frac{1}{1+\dfrac{T_w s}{2}} \frac{\Delta G}{G_0}$$

(II.35)

Now the turbine power is proportional to the product of pressure and flow rate, i.e.;

$$P_m \propto H_q$$

Expanding in linearized form and normalizing

$$\frac{\Delta P_m}{P_{m0}} = \frac{\Delta H}{H_0} + \frac{\Delta q}{q_0}$$

(II.36)

Substituting Equations (II.34) and (II.35) into Equation (II.36), we have

$$\frac{\Delta P_m}{P_{m0}} = \frac{1-T_w s}{1+\dfrac{T_w s}{2}} \frac{\Delta G}{G_0}$$

(II.37)

Figure 2.30 shows the response of a typical hydro turbine to a change in gate position.

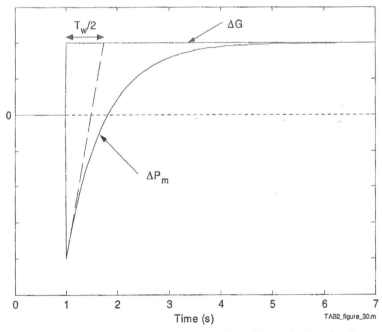

Figure 2.30 – Hydro Turbine Response to a Step Change in Gate Position

From the derivations above, it is apparent that the linearized value of T_w in the transfer function Equation (II.37) is proportional to the load point. That is, T_w at the 50% load point is approximately one half the value at around 100% load.

There are other dynamic phenomena that occur in hydro turbines. One of these is due to the compressibility of water and the elastic expansion of the penstock which give rise to traveling waves known as water hammer, usually of frequency high enough not to be of concern. [14]

Another phenomenon arises in cases where there is a surge tank at some intermediate point along the penstock giving rise to poorly damped oscillations between surge tank and reservoir. These oscillations are generally quite slow in the order of a few minutes per cycle and can generally be neglected in studies of governing and load frequency controls.

Figure 2.31 shows the block diagram of the non-linear relations for a hydro-turbine without surge tank, and Figure 2.32 shows the block diagram for the case where the surge tank is included.[5]

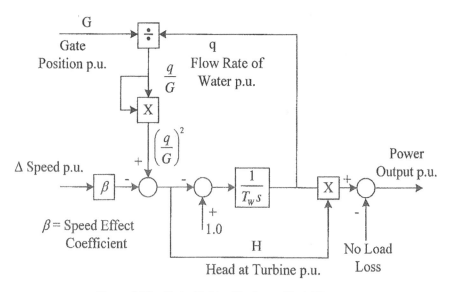

Figure 2.31 – Hydro Turbine Nonlinear Block Diagram

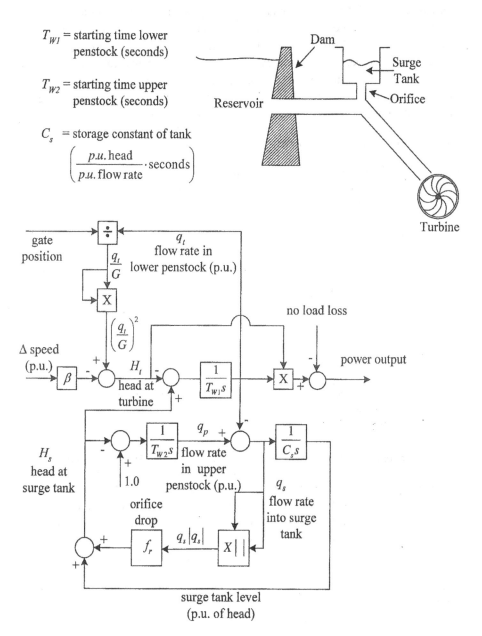

Figure 2.32 – Hydro Turbine Model Including Surge Tank

2.4 Primary Speed/Load Controls

Having described the dynamic characteristics of some prime mover and energy supply systems, we now proceed to describe the next link in the chain; namely, the primary speed/load controls. Historically these have been labeled speed governors; however, the term "governor" implies a mechanical speed sensor linked mechanically to control changes in input power, and since today a great many speed/load controls are electro-hydraulic, the term governor no longer universally describes this primary speed/load control function.[15]

2.4.1 Isochronous Governor

A simple governing mechanism is described in Figure 2.33.

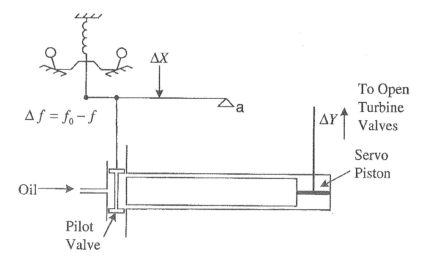

Figure 2.33 – Schematic Representation of Isochronous Speed Governor

Deviations in speed sensed by the flyballs cause displacement ΔX of the pilot valve which causes oil to flow through the main servo piston. This piston, in turn, closes or opens the turbine valve or gates depending on the direction of ΔX. It is important to note that a displacement ΔX of the pilot valve causes a rate of change of piston displacement, or a rate of change of valve position.

Steady-state is reached when the pilot valve holds equal oil pressure on both sides of the servo piston. Referring to Figure 2.33, we may write

$$\Delta X = k_1 \Delta f \tag{II.38}$$

where

Δf = freq. deviation $(f_0 - f)$

k_1 = proportionality constant

$$\frac{d}{dt}(\Delta Y) = k_2 \Delta X \qquad\qquad (II.39)$$

where k_2 is another proportionality constant.

$$\therefore \frac{d}{dt}(\Delta Y) = k_1 k_2 \Delta f$$

$$\Delta Y = \int k_1 k_2 \Delta f\, dt \qquad\qquad (II.40)$$

These relations are described in the block diagram of Figure 2.34.

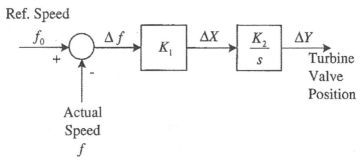

Figure 2.34 – Block Diagram of Isochronous Speed Governor

Because of the integrating action in the main servo piston, it is evident that ΔY will reach a new steady-state only when Δf goes to zero.

The governor with the configuration of Figure 2.33 will, therefore, reduce the frequency error to zero in the steady-state and move the valve position to whatever position is required to do so. It is known as an isochronous governor. Note that a frequency deviation can be caused by either a change in actual frequency or by change in the reference value f_0 which is accomplished by means of a change of pivot point (a) usually through a worm screw mechanism driven by a motor called "synchronizing motor" or speed level changer motor.

Isochronous governors are not used on multimachine systems because of the need for proper load sharing between machines. Load sharing is assured by providing regulation or speed droop in the governing or speed control action.

2.4.2 Governor with Speed Droop

Figure 2.35 shows the schematic of a governor with droop or steady state regulation. The droop characteristic is due to the linkage connecting the pilot valve to the main servo piston.

Referring to the block diagram of the isochronous governor in Figure 2.34, the effect of the feedback linkage in Figure 2.35 is represented by a feedback gain K_3 as in Figure 2.36.

Figure 2.37 shows the time response of the governor controlled valves to a step change in frequency deviation. T_G is known as the governor time constant usually in the order of a fraction of a second.

From the transfer function shown in Figure 2.37a

$$\frac{\Delta \text{ valve (p.u.)}}{\Delta \text{ frequency (p.u.)}} = \frac{1}{R(1+T_G s)} \tag{II.41}$$

one notes that the steady state value of frequency deviation Δf required to produce a one per unit change of turbine valve Δf is R. This parameter is known as speed regulation and can also be expressed in percent as $(N_0 - N)/N_R \times 100$ where N_0 is the steady state speed no load (valves closed) and N is the steady state speed at full load (valves wide open). N_R is rated speed. A 5% regulation means that a frequency deviation of 5% causes 100% change in valve position or output. In process control terminology the governor would be characterized as a proportional controller with a proportional gain of $1/R$ or a proportional band of $R \times 100\%$. (Appendix F).

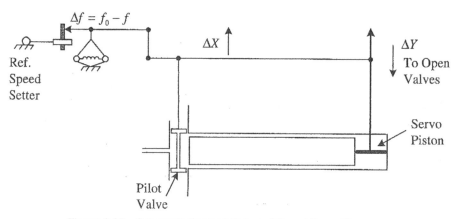

Figure 2.35 – Schematic Representation of Speed Droop Governor

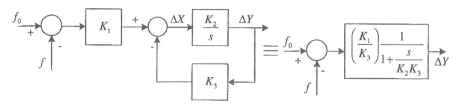

Figure 2.36 – Block Diagram of Speed Droop Governor

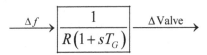

(a) Transfer Function

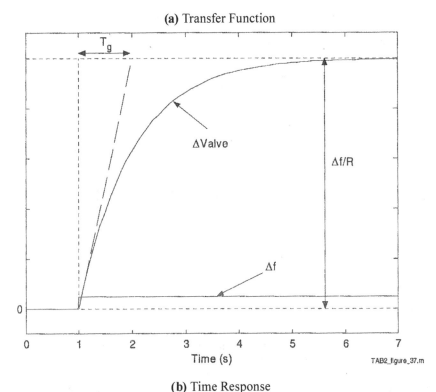

(b) Time Response

Figure 2.37 – Speed Droop Governor Response for a Step Change in Frequency

2.4.3 Governors with Transient Droop Compensation [16, 17, 18]

Hydro turbines, because of their peculiar response characteristics, require governors with special transient droop characteristics for stable speed control performance. The term transient droop implies that for fast deviations in frequency the governor exhibits a high regulation (low gain), while for slow changes and in the steady state the governor has a lower regulation R (high gain).

The schematic of Figure 2.38 shows the addition of a transient feedback through an oil chamber with an orifice.

The transfer function of the additional transient feedback ΔZ from valve position ΔY can be derived as follows. The transmission of motion, through the incompressible fluid in chamber C is

$$-\Delta Z = k_4 \Delta Y - \int \frac{\dot{Q}}{A}\, dt \qquad\text{(II.42)}$$

where $\dot{Q}$ = rate of volume flow of fluid out of enclosure C

A = area of piston

k_4 = constant due to linkage ratios

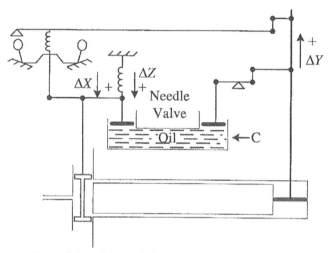

Figure 2.38 – Schematic Representation of Speed Droop
Governor with Transient Compensation

Also pressure of the fluid is proportional to displacement ΔZ due to spring compression and flow $\dot{Q}$ is proportional to pressure, hence we may write

$$\frac{\dot{Q}}{A} = -k_5 \Delta Z \qquad\text{(II.43)}$$

Substituting equation (II.43) in equation (II.42)

$$-\Delta Z = k_4 \Delta Y + \int K_s \Delta Z\, dt \qquad\text{(II.44)}$$

or in operational form

$$-\Delta Z(s)\left(1 + \frac{k_5}{s}\right) = k_4 \Delta Y(s)$$

i.e.:
$$\frac{\Delta Z(s)}{\Delta Y(s)} = \frac{k_4}{\left(1 + \frac{k_5}{s}\right)} = \frac{k_4 s}{k_5\left(1 + \frac{s}{k_5}\right)} \tag{II.45}$$

Hence the block diagram of the simple governor with droop of Figure 2.36 is modified by the additional feedback as shown on Figure 2.39.

The transient feedback function reduces the gain for fast changes but since in the steady state its output is zero the steady state gain is the same as for the case of Figure 2.37.

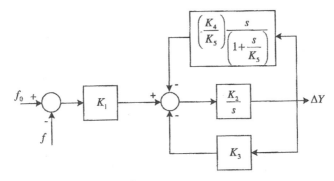

Figure 2.39 – Block Diagram of Speed Droop Governor with Transient Compensation

The overall transfer function of Figure 2.39 can be factored to yield the function

$$\frac{\Delta \text{ Valve}}{\Delta f} = \frac{\left(1 + sT_r\right)}{R\left(1 + s\frac{r}{R}T_r\right)\left(1 + sT_G\right)} \tag{II.46}$$

where R =   steady state regulation

   r =   transient regulation

   $\dfrac{rT_r}{R}$ =   washout time

   T_G =   governor time constant

Figure 2.40 describes the characteristics of the three types of governors or speed control devices discussed above.

Figure 2.41 presents the block diagram of a single area represented by a single combined inertia being powered by three different types of prime mover systems with their respective speed controls.

The performance of the system under these primary speed/load controls, also known as governing, is the subject of the next section.

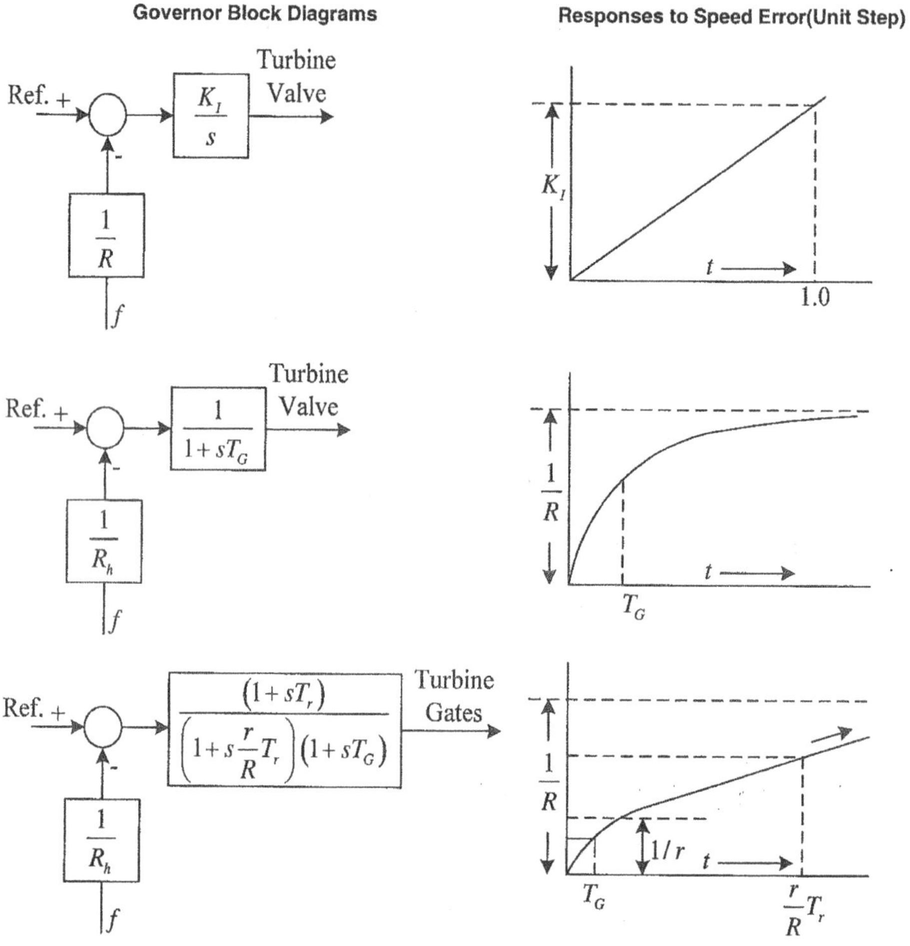

Governor Block Diagrams

Responses to Speed Error(Unit Step)

Figure 2.40 – Types of Speed Governor and Characteristic
Response for Step Change in Speed

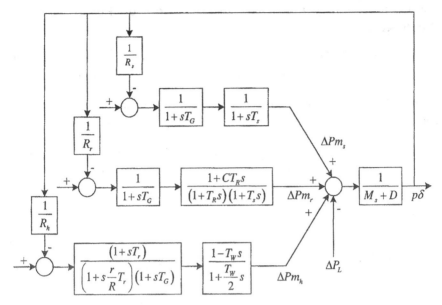

Figure 2.41 – Block Diagram of System with Different
Prime Movers and one Equivalent Generator

Where M = $\sum M_s + M_r + M_H$

D = Electrical load damping characteristic $\partial P_L / \partial \omega$

R_s = Nonreheat steam regulation

R_r = Reheat steam regulation

R_h = Hydro steady state regulation

r_h = Hydro transient regulation

T_R = Reheater time constant

T_w = Water inertia starting time

T_s = Turbine bowl charging time

T_G = Governor time constant

T_r = Hydro governor washout time

2.4.4 Governing or Primary Speed Control Performance - Single Area [2, 9, 15]

Let us now examine the transient behavior of a single isolated power system subjected to a load change, taking governing or speed control into account.

Figure 2.42 shows block diagrams for systems which are being represented by one equivalent machine (nonreheat steam, reheat steam and hydro).

Figure 2.43 shows block diagram simplifications for the purpose of arriving at an expression or transfer function between frequency and load change, taking into account the power system and Prime-mover system governing characteristics.

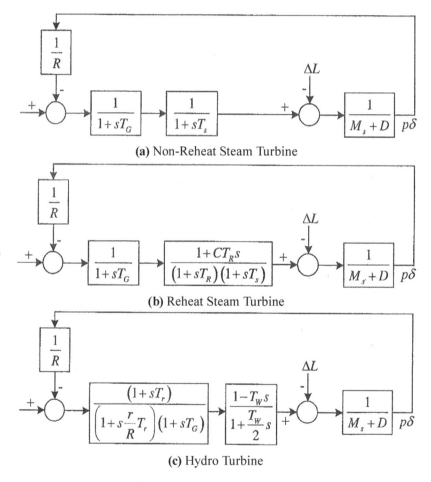

(a) Non-Reheat Steam Turbine

(b) Reheat Steam Turbine

(c) Hydro Turbine

Figure 2.42 – Closed Loop Diagram of Speed Governor Action

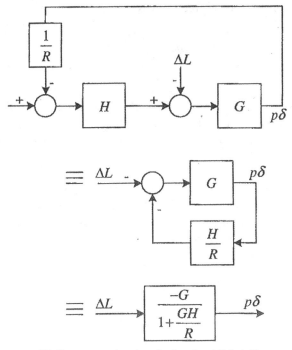

G is the power system transfer function $1/(Ms + D)$
H is the governor and prime-mover transfer function
Figure 2.43 – Block Diagram Reduction

The time response of frequency deviation following a step load change ΔL for these systems can be worked out by taking the inverse transform of the function

$$\frac{\Delta L}{s}\left(\frac{-G}{1+\dfrac{GH}{R}}\right)$$

or by solving the system of differential equations on an analog or digital computer. (Appendix D)

From the final value theorem (Appendix B), the final steady-state frequency deviation can be obtained by taking the steady-state value of the transfer function multiplied by ΔL (i.e.; the value of the function with $s = 0$).

$$p\delta \text{ steady state} = \Delta L \frac{-G}{1+\dfrac{GH}{R}}\Bigg|_{s=0}$$

This steady-state deviation in frequency is

$$p\delta = \frac{-\Delta L}{\dfrac{1}{R} + D} \tag{II.47}$$

for all three systems of Figure 2.42. Although, for the same value of R and D, the final deviation is the same for the three types of prime-mover systems, there are marked differences in the transient performance (peak deviations and recovery times) for these systems.

Figure 2.44 shows the nature of these responses. In order to illustrate the effect of governing, we have also included the response of frequency to a load change on a system where the prime-mover power is invariant (blocked governors). This was the case discussed in Figure 2.9.

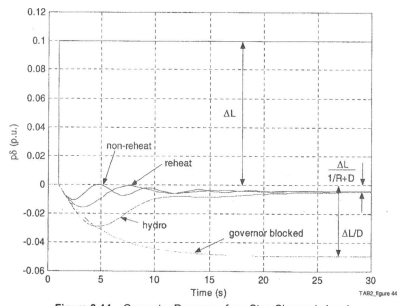

Figure 2.44 – Generator Response for a Step Change in Load

Inspection of Figure 2.41 and the derivation in Figure 2.43 shows that for a system composed of several prime movers with individual governors, the final frequency deviation following a load change ΔL is.given by

$$p\delta = \frac{-\Delta L}{1 / R_1 + 1 / R_2 + \ldots + D}$$

or

$$p\delta = \frac{-\Delta L}{1/R_{eq} + D} \tag{II.48}$$

where R_{eq} is the area's equivalent governor regulation

$$R_{eq} = \frac{1}{1/R_1 + 1/R_2 + \ldots} \tag{II.49}$$

The quantity $\left(\dfrac{1}{R_{eq}} + D\right)^{-1}$ is termed the area's composite regulating characteristic

which includes both prime-mover steady-state regulation and load damping. A representative value of this composite regulating characteristic for steam systems with a mixture of units in regulating range and others with governors blocked or valves wide open is between 15 and 20% on system base.

The steady state speed/load characteristic of a typical unit is shown on Figure 2.45. When the unit is not synchronized the adjustment of the speed/load changer merely changes the unit speed.

Once synchronized to the power system, adjustments of the speed/load reference produce changes in load and only minor effects on system frequency in proportion to the size of the unit relative to the power system.

In the general case of interconnected systems, the power system looks like an infinite system relative to the individual unit so that, once synchronized the effect of speed/load reference adjustments is primarily one of changing load on that unit

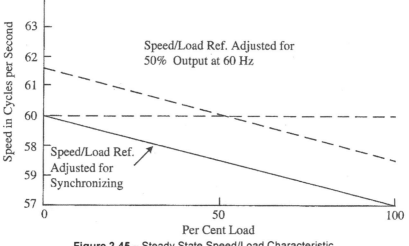

Figure 2.45 – Steady State Speed/Load Characteristic

Although the speed/load characteristic is shown on Figure 2.45 as a straight line with uniform slope, in actuality the characteristic is rather uneven averaging the straight line but exhibiting incremental slopes ranging from 2 to 12% depending on the position of the particular control valve in control range. Near the end of travel of a particular valve the incremental regulation is high while in the beginning or valve cracking point, the incremental regulation is low. Modern electro-hydraulic speed/load control systems attempt to minimize these variations in incremental regulation by characterization of valves with electronic function generators, or by the use of turbine first stage pressure feedback. [15]

2.4.5 Governing Performance - Interconnected Areas

The case of interconnected areas is no different from that of a single area as far as governing effects are concerned.

Building on the block diagram of Figure 2.12, Figure 2.45 shows two areas with a prime-mover in each area (in the general case several prime movers would be contributing in parallel in each area as shown on Figure 2.41).

The representation of Figure 2.46 considers elasticity between areas (i.e.; their individual frequencies can differ transiently although they will have to average the same value if the systems remain in synchronism).

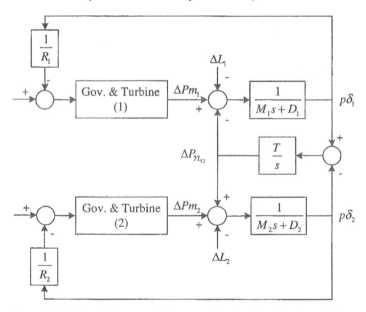

Figure 2.46 – Block Diagram of Frequency Control of a Two-Area System

The steady-state frequency deviation will be the same regardless of the area in which the load change occurs and will be given by

$$p\delta = \frac{-\Delta L}{\dfrac{1}{R_1} + \dfrac{1}{R_2} + D_1 + D_2} \tag{II.50}$$

This result can be derived from a reduction of the block diagram of Figure 2.46 or from the steady-state relations below which can be extracted from the same block diagram.

Examine the steady-state relations following a load change ΔL_1 in area 1:

$$p\delta_1 = p\delta_2 = p\delta \tag{II.51}$$

$$\Delta P_{m1} - \Delta P_{TL12} - \Delta L_1 = p\delta_1 D_1 = p\delta \, D_1 \tag{II.52}$$

$$\Delta P_{m2} + \Delta P_{TL12} = p\delta_2 D_2 = p\delta \, D_2 \tag{II.53}$$

$$\Delta P_{m1} = -p\delta / R_1 \tag{II.54}$$

$$\Delta P_{m2} = -p\delta / R_2 \tag{II.55}$$

Substituting Equations (II.54) and (II.55) in Equations (II.52) and (II.53)

$$-\Delta P_{TL12} - \Delta L_1 = p\delta \, (1/R_1 + D_1) \tag{II.56}$$

$$+\Delta P_{TL12} = p\delta \, (1/R_2 + D_2) \tag{II.57}$$

Solution of these equations yields

$$p\delta = \frac{-\Delta L_1}{\left(\dfrac{1}{R_1} + D_1\right) + \left(\dfrac{1}{R_2} + D_2\right)} \tag{II.58}$$

$$\Delta P_{TL12} = \frac{-\Delta L_1 \left(\dfrac{1}{R_2} + D_2\right)}{\left(\dfrac{1}{R_1} + D_1\right) + \left(\dfrac{1}{R_2} + D_2\right)} \tag{II.59}$$

$$\therefore \Delta P_{TL12} = \frac{+\Delta L_1 \left(\dfrac{1}{R_2} + D_2\right)}{\left(\dfrac{1}{R_1} + D_1\right) + \left(\dfrac{1}{R_2} + D_2\right)} \tag{II.60}$$

Inspection of the above equations shows that the steady-state frequency deviation is the same for a similar load change in area 2.

The tie line deviation reflects the governing and load regulation contribution from one area to the other.

These relationships, listed in Table I below, form the basis for the operation and philosophy of load frequency controls of interconnected systems.

Note in particular the sign of tie line deviation relative to frequency deviation as intelligence from which the location of the load change (whether in area 1 or area 2) can be derived.

A convenient way of describing governing and load damping effects is shown in Figures 47 for the case of a single area. Here we see that a load change ΔL is supplied through the effects of a frequency change acting on the governors of the connected units and acting on the frequency characteristic of the load.

Table I – Steady State Frequency and Tie Line Power Deviations

	Frequency deviation in both areas	Tie Line Deviation	
		Area 1	Area 2
Load change ΔL occurring in Area 1	$\dfrac{-\Delta L}{\left(\frac{1}{R_1}+D_1\right)+\left(\frac{1}{R_2}+D_2\right)}$	$\dfrac{-\Delta L\left(\frac{1}{R_2}+D_2\right)}{\left(\frac{1}{R_1}+D_1\right)+\left(\frac{1}{R_2}+D_2\right)}$	$\dfrac{+\Delta L\left(\frac{1}{R_2}+D_2\right)}{\left(\frac{1}{R_1}+D_1\right)+\left(\frac{1}{R_2}+D_2\right)}$
Load change ΔL occurring in Area 2	$\dfrac{-\Delta L}{\left(\frac{1}{R_1}+D_1\right)+\left(\frac{1}{R_2}+D_2\right)}$	$\dfrac{+\Delta L\left(\frac{1}{R_1}+D_1\right)}{\left(\frac{1}{R_1}+D_1\right)+\left(\frac{1}{R_2}+D_2\right)}$	$\dfrac{-\Delta L\left(\frac{1}{R_1}+D_1\right)}{\left(\frac{1}{R_1}+D_1\right)+\left(\frac{1}{R_2}+D_2\right)}$

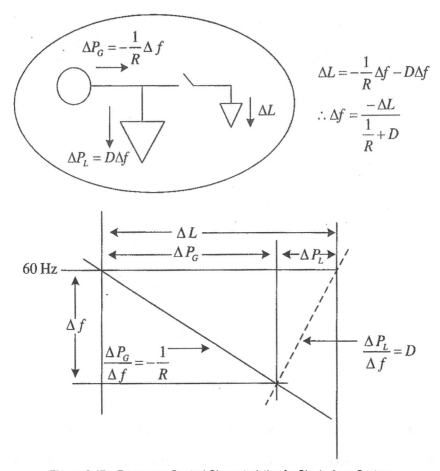

Figure 2.47 – Frequency Control Characteristic of a Single Area System

Similarly for the case of two interconnected systems, Figure 2.48 shows the changes in powers that arise upon the application of a load-change in area 1. The relations of Equations (II.58), (II.59) and (II.60) can be derived from inspection of the contributions of power changes from loads and generators as indicated in Figure 2.48.

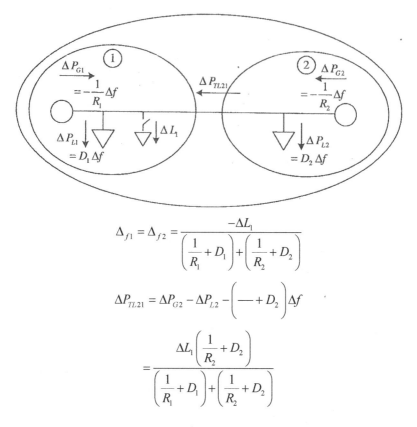

$$\Delta_{f1} = \Delta_{f2} = \frac{-\Delta L_1}{\left(\dfrac{1}{R_1} + D_1\right) + \left(\dfrac{1}{R_2} + D_2\right)}$$

$$\Delta P_{TL21} = \Delta P_{G2} - \Delta P_{L2} - \left(\frac{}{} + D_2\right)\Delta f$$

$$= \frac{\Delta L_1\left(\dfrac{1}{R_2} + D_2\right)}{\left(\dfrac{1}{R_1} + D_1\right) + \left(\dfrac{1}{R_2} + D_2\right)}$$

Figure 2.48 – Frequency Control Characteristic of Two Interconnected Systems

2.5 Supplementary Control or Automatic Generation Control

Study of the block diagrams and relationships, both dynamic and steady-state, developed so far reveals that there are two control means for changing prime-mover power. One of these is by virtue of the change in prime-mover speed through governing or primary speed control action. The other is by means of changes in the load reference or speed setter (speed changer motor) of the speed control, or governing mechanism.

In normal operation frequency deviations are very small, and the basic mechanism of controlling prime-mover power to match load in a given area is by manipulation of the load reference device, this action being labeled supplementary control.

From the standpoint of a given individual unit synchronized to a power system large in relation to the size of the unit, changes in load reference have little effect on system frequency but result in changes in mechanical and therefore electrical power out of the unit. These changes in electrical power, in turn, reflect into changes in the load flow through the transmission system.

If the mechanism of changing generation to match loads is left to the primary speed control action, then according to the characteristic shown on Figure 2.45, the only way a change in generation can occur is for a frequency deviation to exist. Restoration of frequency to rated value requires manipulation of the speed/load reference, known as generation control or supplementary control.

Generation control in a given area has the following objectives:

1) Matching area generation changes to area load changes.

2) Distributing these changes among generators so as to minimize operating costs.

Meeting the first of these objectives is known as supplementary control. Addition of the second objective is labeled supplementary control with economic allocation.

2.5.1 Supplementary Control - Isolated Power Systems

In an isolated power system, a mismatch between prime-mover power and connected load results in a frequency deviation of sufficient magnitude as required to bring a balance between mechanical and electrical powers. Frequency deviation is therefore a direct indicator of this mismatch between generation and connected load. Restoration of frequency deviation to zero through supplementary control does accomplish the objective of matching generation to load.

Figure 2.49 illustrates the block diagram of an isolated power system with supplementary control action. For illustration purposes, a system made up of reheat steam generation is shown. Reset action (Appendix F) or integral action in the supplementary control ensures zero frequency error in the steady state.

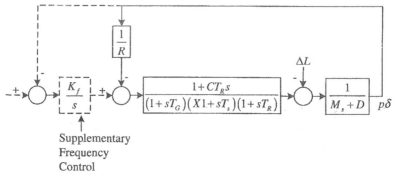

Supplementary
Frequency
Control

Figure 2.49 – Block Diagram of Isolated System with Supplementary Control

The gain of the integral action in the supplementary control is limited by control stability considerations. Sometimes proportional action is added to improve the stability of the supplementary control, or to permit faster action through supplementary control.

Figure 2.50 illustrates typical isolated area frequency performance with and without supplementary control following a step load change.

Evidently, the slower the overall system response of frequency to a change in load reference, the slower must be the supplementary control action for it to be stable. There are significant differences in control response between hydro and steam systems as illustrated in Figure 2.44 and Reference 9.

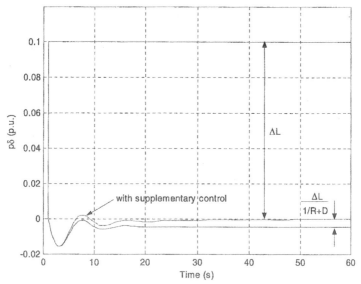

Figure 2.50 – Frequency Control in Isolated System
with and without Supplementary Control

2.5.2 Supplementary Control - Interconnected Power System

As discussed in previous sections, a mismatch between load and generation in interconnected systems results in deviations of tie flows and frequency. In the usual case of areas interconnected to others which are part of a very large power pool, frequency deviations are very small, and the basic effect of a load change in an area is felt as a deviation in the tie flow between the area and neighboring systems.

Keeping in mind the basic objective of supplementary control as being the restoration of balance between area load changes and area generation changes, this basic objective is met when control action restores frequency deviation to zero and tie line deviation to zero.

Inspection of Table I and some heuristic reasoning aimed at achieving non-interaction between control efforts in interconnected areas leads to the concept of the area control error (ACE) made up from tie line deviation added to frequency deviation weighted by a bias factor.

This concept also known as "tie-line bias load frequency control" is based on the following objectives.

Supplementary control in a given area should correct for load changes in that area but should not be acting to supply load changes in the other area beyond the contribution made by virtue of frequency deviation through its area regulating characteristic.

In effect, it is desired that if the load change is in area 1, there should be no supplementary control action in area 2, but only action in area 1.

From the values listed in Table I, it is noted that a load change in area 1 results in tie-line deviation from the point of view of area 1 of

$$\Delta P_{TL12} = -\frac{\Delta L_1 \left(\dfrac{1}{R_2} + D_2 \right)}{\left(\dfrac{1}{R_1} + D_1 \right) + \left(\dfrac{1}{R_2} + D_2 \right)} \qquad (II.61)$$

and a frequency deviation of

$$-\frac{\Delta L}{\left(\dfrac{1}{R_1} + D_1 \right) + \left(\dfrac{1}{R_2} + D_2 \right)} \qquad (II.62)$$

From the point of view of area 2, this load change in area 1 results in a tie-line deviation equal but opposite in sense to the tie-line deviation seen by area 1. That is,

$$\Delta P_{TL21} = + \frac{\Delta L_1 \left(\dfrac{1}{R_2} + D_2 \right)}{\left(\dfrac{1}{R_1} + D_1 \right) + \left(\dfrac{1}{R_2} + D_2 \right)} \qquad (\text{II.63})$$

Area 2 also feels the same frequency deviation.

$$p\delta = - \frac{\Delta L}{\left(\dfrac{1}{R_1} + D_1 \right) + \left(\dfrac{1}{R_2} + D_2 \right)} \quad \text{as felt by area 1.}$$

From these relations, it can be seen that using a weighting factor of $(1/R_2 + D_2)$ on frequency deviation for area 2 (known as bias factor), a supplementary control signal known as area control error (ACE) can be formed by adding tie-line deviations to this bias factor times the frequency deviation.

Thus, for area 2, this ACE would be $\Delta P_{TL21} + B_2 p\delta$, which, with $B_2 = (1/R_2 + D_2)$ would yield ACE = 0 for the case in question of load change in area 1.

For area 1, however, the ACE would be $\Delta P_{TL12} + B_1 p\delta$ which, with $B_1 + (1/R_1 + D_1)$ would yield ACE = ΔL.

We see, therefore, that the composite error signal made up of tie-line deviation plus a bias factor equal to the area's regulating characteristic $(1/R + D)$ has the right intelligence as to which area should exert supplementary control effort.

Although this concept is based on steady-state relations of system performance under governing duty, a number of dynamic studies (References 2,3,6) have confirmed that the use of a bias factor close to the area's steady-state regulating characteristic gives close to optimal control from the standpoint of dynamic non-interaction between areas.

Figure 2.51 shows the block diagram of two areas with supplementary control.

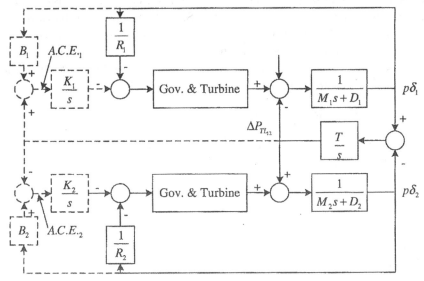

Figure 2.51 – Block Diagram of Two Areas System with Supplementary Control

It should be noted that steady-state considerations show that it is not critical to have the bias factors set exactly equal to regulating characteristic. As a matter of fact, in order to reach the final result of $\Delta P_{TL} = 0$ and $p\delta = 0$, almost any combination of area control errors which contain components of frequency and tie-line deviation will ensure the ultimate restoration of tie-line deviation and frequency deviation to zero. This is apparent from the fact that integral action ensures the reduction of area control error to zero in the steady state.

$$ACE_1 = k_1 \Delta P_{TL12} + B_1 p\delta = 0 \tag{II.64}$$

$$ACE_2 = k_2 \Delta P_{TL21} + B_2 p\delta = 0 \tag{II.65}$$

Thus, for non-zero values of k_1, k_2, B_1 and B_2 Equations (II.64) and (II.65) will yield $\Delta P_{TL} = 0$, $p\delta = 0$ independent of the values of k_1, k_2, B_1 and B_2.

A mode of control which will also satisfy the objectives of $\Delta P_{TL} = 0$, $p\delta = 0$, is to assign one area to control tie-line deviations (called flat tie-line control) and the other area to control frequency (called flat frequency control). In general this mode of control results in poorer dynamic performance than the mixed mode with tieline bias.

2.6 Load-Frequency Control with Economic Allocation

In addition to the task of controlling frequency and holding net interchange schedules, a very important secondary function is the distribution of the desired generation among the many sources so as to minimize operating costs. The theory of allocating generation to minimize production costs including the effect of losses is treated in another unit of the Power Technology Course. Since the essential principles involved in loading generators in accordance with theories of equal incremental costs are fairly straightforward, it appears worthwhile to give a brief explanation of these theories before we take up the discussion of methods of implementing automatic load frequency control with economic allocation of generation.

2.6.1 Coordination of Incremental Costs

From the input fuel cost versus output generation, by differentiation one can derive incremental cost curves as in Figure 2.52.

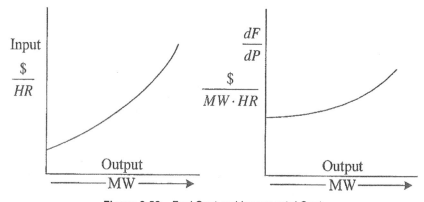

Figure 2.52 – Fuel Cost and Incremental Cost

Without resorting to methods of variational Calculus and LaGrange multipliers the principle of equal incremental loading for minimizing costs can be derived heuristically by the following reasoning.

Let the total load to be supplied by a couple of generators be P. Then if the individual generator loads are P_1 and P_2.

$$P_1 + P_2 = P \tag{II.66}$$

Let the total cost of production F be expressed by functions of the individual unit loadings

$$F = F_1(P_1) + F_2(P_2) \tag{II.67}$$

For a fixed total load P, equation 66 determines that any variation in loading on generator 1 must be equal and opposite to the variation in loading of generator 2 (neglecting the effect of losses)

i.e.;
$$\Delta P_1 = -\Delta P2 \tag{II.68}$$

The condition for minimum production costs can be obtained by differentiating equation 67 with respect to P_I and setting the expression equal to zero

i.e.,
$$\frac{dF}{dP_1} = -\frac{dF_1(P_1)}{dP_1} + \frac{dF_2(P_2)}{dP_1} = 0$$

i.e.;
$$\frac{dF_1(P_1)}{dP_1} = -\frac{dF_2(P_2)}{dP_1} = \frac{dF_2(P_2)}{dP_2} \qquad (II.69)$$

since $dP_1 = dP_2$ by Equation (II.68).

The Equations (II.69), $dF_1/dP_1 = dF_2/dP_2 = \lambda$ specify a criterion for loading generators so as to minimize production costs. They are called "coordination-equations."

The solution of the coordination equations to yield the desired total generation with proper loading distribution between units is indicated by the control scheme of Figure 2.53.

A controller moves the system production cost λ to the value which produces a total power, through summation of the individual unit powers, equal to the total desired power. The individual unit powers are related to λ by their individual incremental cost characteristics.

The control scheme of Figure 2.53 can also be visualized as an iterative solution of the coordination equations wherein the integrator K/s is replaced by some iterative logic which, in the simplest form, is no more than an accumulator with the proper gain or accelerating factor.

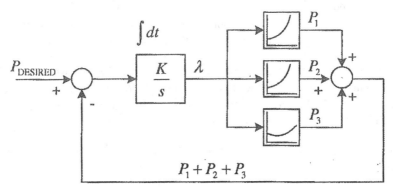

Figure 2.53 – Control Scheme for Solution of Coordination Equations

The solution scheme of Figure 2.53 whether implemented in its analog computer form or its equivalent numerical iteration form is helpful to the understanding of various schemes of automatic control implementation discussed in the following sections.

2.6.2 Implementation Schemes

Load Frequency Control

The simplest load frequency control system is that shown in Figure 2.54.

A signal proportional to area control error (ACE) is transmitted to the various units' speed changers, or load reference motors. The speed changer positions or load reference values change at rates proportional to the transmitted signal which is generally in the form of pulses.

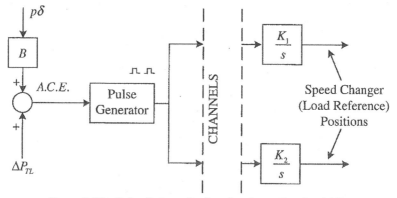

Figure 2.54 – Pulse Rate and/or Duration Proportional to ACE
Integral Action Provided by Speed Changer Motors

The actual speed changer positions or load references are therefore proportional to the integral of the ACE. The proportionality factors are obviously a function of the response settings of each unit labeled K_1, K_2 --- etc. in Figure 2.54.

The change in loading of each unit in response to control action would be rather indeterminate depending on the effective gains K_1, ... K_2 etc., and with this control scheme it is difficult to control the distribution of the change in generation which is a function of the effective responses of the various units.

The drawbacks of the scheme of Figure 2.54 are corrected by the system of Figure 2.55.

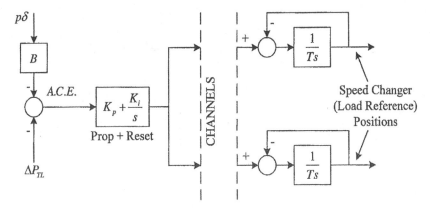

Figure 2.55 – Load Frequency Controls with Proportional + Integral action at Central Location. Unit Speed Changers Follow Common Signal through Position Feedback

Here we have added a load reference positioning system at the individual units. Integration is performed at one point, the master controller which develops a common load reference demand signal transmitted to the various units. By adjustment of the proportion of this common signal among units they can be made to share in the control action in any desired manner.

2.6.3   Addition of Economic Loading Equipment

The next evolutionary step in automatic load frequency control is shown on Figure 2.56.

The main control function is still like that of Figure 2.55 shown in the solid lines. The dashed lines show economic loading equipment which, through reset action, restores the proper distribution of generation among units; i.e., the loading distribution which maintains equal incremental costs. The way this scheme works can be readily understood from the basic scheme shown on Figure 2.53.

Proportional and integral action on ACE develops a demand for load reference positions which act through the primary regulating path to move generation and restore ACE to zero. This demand is also interpreted as λ since it is a common signal fed to the various unit incremental cost function generators. As indicated in Figure 2.56 these function generators develop the desired MW loadings. The error signals between desired and actual MW act in slow reset fashion to restore the distribution of generation in accordance with economics.

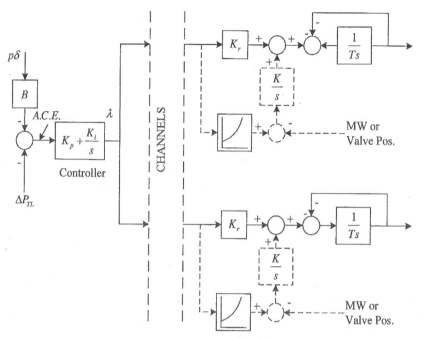

Figure 2.56 – Load Frequency Controls Including Incremental Costs Effects

Figure 2.57 shows typical control action for the case where there is no conflict between regulating duty and economics (i.e., machines with identical incremental cost characteristics) as well as for the case where the incremental characteristics are such as to call for most of the load change to be taken by one unit.

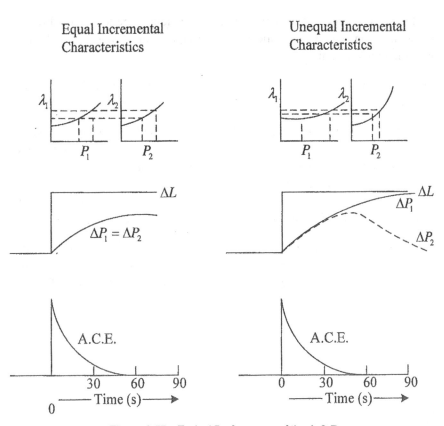

Figure 2.57 – Typical Performance of the A.C.E.

The scheme of Figure 2.56 was popular due to the fact that only one channel (λ) was necessary per plant. The incremental loading equipment was provided at the station. Some disadvantages were concerned with the problem of "bumpless" transfer, or necessary safeguards in case of loss of signal.

Also since the slope of the incremental characteristic can vary appreciably, this could at times impose problems related to rather large variations in reset gain in the economic loop.

2.6.4 Modern Implementation Schemes

The advent of the modern digital process control computer and recent great improvements in data transmission and communication equipment have led to the almost universal practice of developing the control logic including the process of economic allocation at the central location called the dispatch center.

In addition to the area control error, unit MW loadings are telemetered to the central location where economic allocation equipment develops the desired generation for each unit.

Figure 2.58 shows a method of economic allocation implemented with analog equipment.

The high gain integrator drives the total unit requirement to equal the area control error on a continuous and almost instantaneous basis, and in so doing generates the correct desired generation in accordance with the equations shown on Figure 2.58. The economic allocator assures that the total desired generation is distributed on a continuous and instantaneous basis among the various units in accordance with economics as determined by participation and base point settings.

The information for base points and participation settings is generated elsewhere through the solution of the coordination equations as in Figure 2.53, including the effect of losses where appropriate. This solution is expressed in the form of curves relating the loading of individual units to the total load.

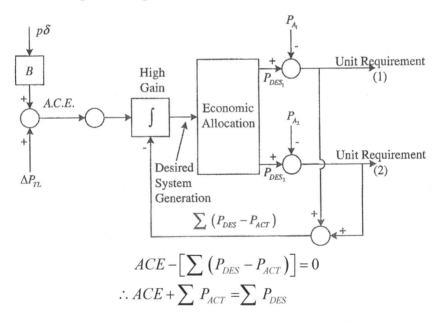

$$ACE - \left[\sum \left(P_{DES} - P_{ACT} \right) \right] = 0$$

$$\therefore ACE + \sum P_{ACT} = \sum P_{DES}$$

Figure 2.58 – Analog Implementation of Economic Allocation

Figure 2.59 illustrates the meaning of base point and participation setting.

Figure 2.60 shows details of the box labeled "Economic allocation" in Figure 2.58.

The values of base points and participation factors can be updated as needed by auxiliary equipment such as by a digital computer in digital directed analog controls.

A much more popular scheme these days is to perform the entire computation implied by Figure 2.60, digitally. This is done frequently enough that the effects of sampling are not felt, usually in the order of once every two to four seconds.

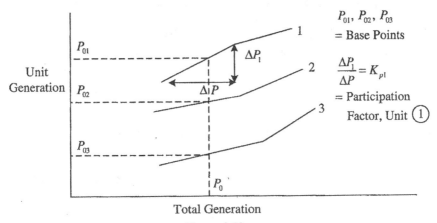

P_{01}, P_{02}, P_{03}
= Base Points

$\dfrac{\Delta P_1}{\Delta P} = K_{p1}$

= Participation
Factor, Unit ①

Figure 2.59 –

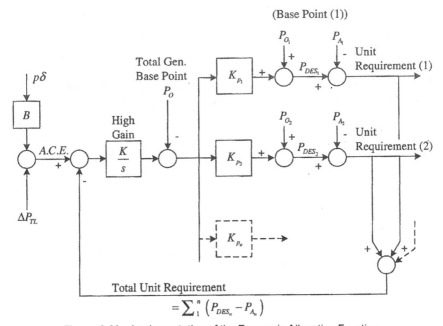

Figure 2.60 – Implementation of the Economic Allocation Function

Figure 2.61 outlines the basic computation of unit control error performed every T seconds by the load frequency control program. Note that the updating of economic loading parameters (bass points and participation settings) is performed much less frequently by an auxiliary program called the Economic Dispatch Program.

With the use of digital computers there are any number of sophisticated control logic schemes that may be executed. Nevertheless as a carryover from analog systems, two basic types have been used as indicated by Figure 2.62.

The scheme at the left shapes impulses to the various units as function of their individual errors, while the system at the right bases control action to all units on the Area Control Error, the Unit Control Errors being merely used to permit or block control action to the individual unit depending on whether or not the unit control error has the same polarity as Area Control Error.

Some differences in performance obtainable from these schemes are illustrated in Figure 2.63.

Basically, with the control action shaped to individual unit errors, better control is possible since each unit will home in to its desired generation with no overshoot. As shown on Figure 2.63 the scheme which shapes control pulses merely from ACE is likely to cause units to overshoot or undershoot their targets since the rate at which they are pulsed is not proportional to their individual errors.

Of course this disadvantage may be somewhat offset by basing the blocking or permitting of control action on unit control error plus rate of change of error.

Another point concerns the use of regulating forcing action, sometimes labeled "assist action." The idea here is that, depending on the size of the area control error, it may be desirable to move all units irrespective of the dictates of economic loading. Figure 2.64 shows that the first scheme permits this action by merely adding a "regulating" component from ACE with or without deadband to the unit control errors. When ACE is reduced to zero, the various units would automatically be reset to their economic loading points.

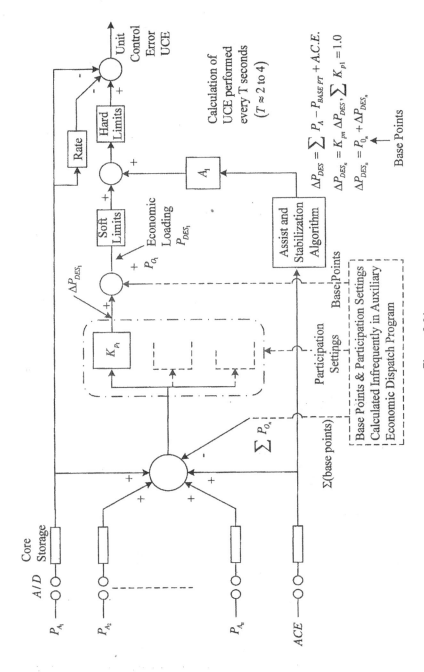

Figure 2.61

123

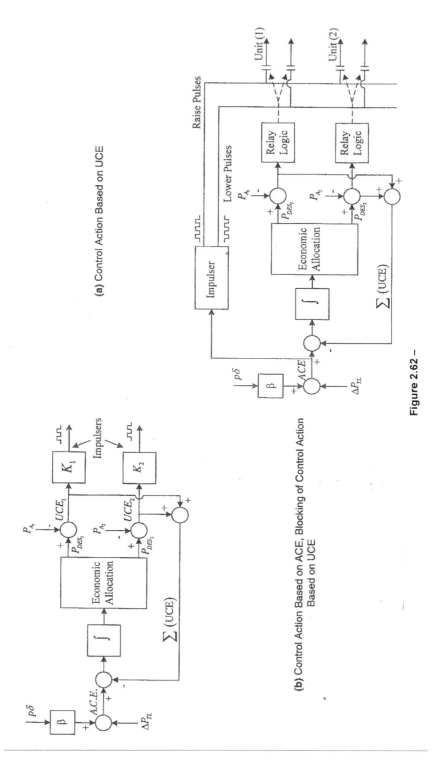

(a) Control Action Based on UCE

(b) Control Action Based on ACE, Blocking of Control Action Based on UCE

Figure 2.62 –

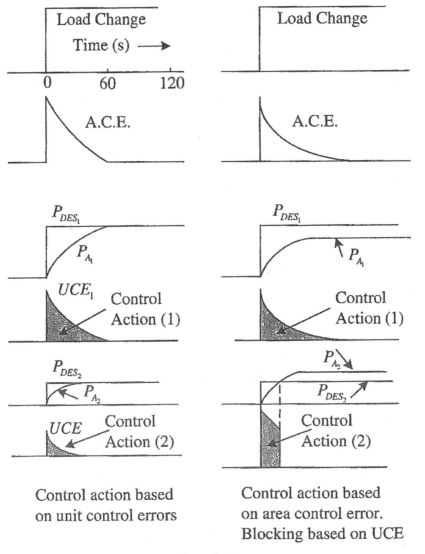

Figure 2.63

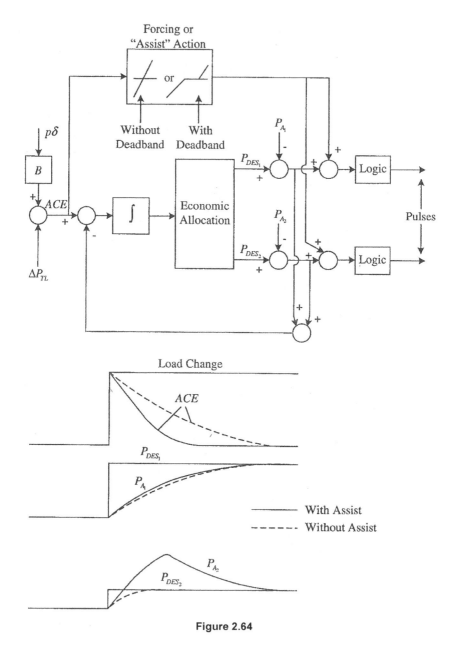

Figure 2.64

The implementation of forcing or "assist" action in the second scheme would call for bypassing of the blocking action of the economic logic, and units would respond to new levels to satisfy the load demand irrespective of economics. The subsequent restoration of loading to economic levels would have to rely on reversals of ACE within the "deadband" for which the "assist" action is inhibited.

It should be noted that a deadband on assist action is required with this scheme to permit selective rectification of ACE noise as the mechanism for restoration of economic loading.

The main feature of this second scheme is that it will never allow units to be moved in a direction opposite to ACE. Obviously this constraint, if deemed desirable, can also be achieved with a modification of the first scheme where control action is in response to unit control errors. Such modifications are especially easy to implement in modern digital implementations where it is a trivial matter to add the logic to block control action in a direction opposite to that called by the system requirement anytime the ACE exceeds a certain value.

There are many situations where the simultaneous shifting of generation is desired; i.e., with one generator picking up and others dropping load. If the rates at which the generation swap is accomplished are equal, there would be no effect on area control error.

One frequent occurrence is the commitment of a new unit or the disconnection of a unit. Upon synchronizing, a unit is loaded almost immediately to 10 or 15% of its rating. This act often creates a transient ACE considerably greater than might be caused by gradual and simultaneous controlled shifts in generation to achieve a new economic load distribution. Following the commitment of disconnection of units, there usually occurs a discontinuity in the economic loading of the now set of units requiring shifts in generation. These shifts can be accomplished in a controlled and deterministic manner in the scheme where there is an active subloop control for each unit. With the method in the second scheme the rate at which generation can be redistributed is rather undetermined and at the mercy of existence of plus or minus noise on ACE. As a practical consequence such reallocations are often done manually.

The ability to reallocate generation on command, independent of the existence of ACE, can be of particular value in the automatic implementation of system security measures.[16, 19] For instance, when a transmission system constraint suddenly requires reallocation of generation to avoid thermal overloading of transmission equipment, this can be accomplished safely and expediently by a new "security" dispatch which sets new base points and participation factors based on security constraints rather than economic criteria.

Another advantage of the first scheme is that it permits with relative ease the implementation of logic to effect random noise rejection on ACE (to reduce unnecessary and ineffective control action) without inhibiting the ability of units to maintain economic loading.[17] The use of such control concepts is much less straightforward in schemes which depend on the rectification of raise/lower noise in the ACE as the primary mechanism for bringing units to their economic loading targets. Removal of the "noise" through nonlinear adaptive filtering would destroy the means whereby units seek their economic targets in the second scheme.

Digital control permits implementation of a wide range of logic.[17, 38] An interesting application is in the provision of nonlinear filtering logic to minimize unnecessary and ineffective control action.[18, 38] It is characteristic of load frequency control systems that the control error contains random components with frequencies considerably higher than the closed loop response bandwidth of generation control.

Control action in response to these random components does not reduce ACE but merely imposes an unnecessary wear and tear on governor motors, turbine valves and other plant equipment.

The conventional approach with linear filtering accomplishes noise reduction at the expense of speed of response. Nonlinear digital logic can be designed to preserve the response capabilities for large and sustained error signals while rejecting control action for the small and high frequency (non-sustained) components of error.

One technique of distinguishing between random loads and sustained load requirements is to use a filtering technique similar to that described in Ref. 18. Basically, a decision is made on whether or not the error is in the direction to correct inadvertent interchange[38]. It may be noted that a crude nonlinear filter is just plain "deadband."

2.6.5 Pulsing Logic

Pulsing logic interprets the unit control error information into raise and lower pulses to the individual units. One scheme is to achieve proportionality between error and control effort by means of the repetition rate with which pulses are sent.[37]

An additional factor on control effort can be related to magnitude of ACE which can govern pulse duration. For instance, two levels of pulse duration could be used, a pulse duration for normal control and double this value in case of excessive ACE.

Pulsing logic may have the capability of vetoing pulses when these are called for in a direction opposite to the system load requirements anytime these requirements exceed a given level (ACE in excess of a certain value). Rate limiting can also be accomplished by a similar vetoing technique based on a comparison of the measured actual unit power relative to permissible unit power as limited by rate of change considerations.

Since an individual pulse of minimum duration still represents a finite amount of generation change, quantization logic is usually provided to establish a minimum error, or integral of error before pulsing action is taken. This can be done by accumulating unit control errors and comparing the accumulated value with a set threshold. When the threshold is exceeded, pulses are routed to the unit in question and the accumulator reset. It should be noted that this type of pulsing logic in a sense provides a certain amount of nonlinear random noise rejection.

2.7 Conclusions

In these notes we have attempted to cover the subject of Generation Dynamics and Control from the point of view of control action that can normally be imparted to the prime mover.

Of fundamental importance is the development of an understanding of the "process." Knowledge of the process has been developed with the help of mathematical models which describe the relationships between various pertinent variables. Almost any mathematical description of a process implies some degree of approximation or some qualifying assumptions. Knowledge of these assumptions and the range of conditions over which the models are valid are equally important.

A vital aspect of this subject is knowledge of control principles and associated techniques. We have included supplementary material on methods of dynamic analysis, simulation methods by analog computer and by digital techniques, and some background material on basic concepts of feedback control. We have attempted to present all this material in the context generation control. While much of the subject matter is technical, i.e., more closely associated with what may be termed a science - there are aspects of control philosophy which fall in the category of an art. Some thoughts on control philosophy seem appropriate.

The primary objective of generation control is very simply stated as the matching of generation against the demands of area loads and interchange schedules. An important secondary objective is the allocation of generation demands among various committed units so as to minimize operating costs. The first of these objectives is known as load frequency control and involves control of generation to reduce the area control error to zero in the steady state. The second objective is known as the economic dispatch control function and has generally been accomplished by distributing the loading among units so as to maintain equal incremental costs of generation on all units within control range, with proper account for penalties imposed by transmission losses.

Within these general objectives there is a wide range of possibilities of implementing dynamic control action following different philosophies.

In the past, the amount and type of control logic that could be provided, and indeed the motivation for a particular control philosophy, was to some extent influenced by the practical constraints of analog hardware implementation. With the use of digital computers this is no longer the case since it is a simple matter to accommodate with control software almost any degree of logic that may be desirable. This new freedom from hardware constraints in the implementation of control logic makes it a simple matter to implement a wide range of strategies as may be desired by the user.

Some general guidelines on control philosophy which should be kept in mind are:

Flexibility and Ease of Adjustment

Control performance criteria must include not only the easily identified objectives such as the minimization of area control error or inadvertent interchange, but also the important objective of minimizing unnecessary control action. The control logic should be designed to accommodate through simple adjustment the relative weight given to these often conflicting objectives.

Simplicity

The relative case of implementing almost any conceivable control logic by software should not lead to the adoption of unnecessarily complex structures. An important factor should be the ease with which a given control strategy can be understood and the ease with which its performance can be adjusted by choice of the proper "tuning" parameters. Simplicity will always remain a virtue.

F. P. deMello

Power Technologies, Inc.

References

1) Plant Dynamics and Control Analysis IEEE Transactions, Paper 63-1401, Power Apparatus and Systems, 1963, Vol. S82, pp. 664-78.

2) Economic Control of Interconnected Power Systems - Vol. II, L.K. Kirchmayer, John Wiley and Sons, 1959.

3) Tie-Line Power and Frequency Control of Electric Power Systems C. Concordia, L.K. Kirchmayer AZEE Transactions, Power Apparatus and Systems, Part III, Vol. 72. p. 562 and Part III, Vol. 73, Part III-A, 1959, p. 33.

4) Effect of Speed-Governor Dead Band on Tie-Line Power Frequency Contral Performance C. Concordia, L.K. Kirchmayer, E.A. Szymanski AIEE Transactions, Power Apparatus and Systems, 1957.

5) FACE Multimachine Power System Simulator Program D.N. Ewart, R.P. Schulz PICA, 1969.

6) Power System Stability - Vol. I S.B. Crary, John Wiley & Sons.

7) Power System Stability - Vol. II, S.B. Crary, John Wiley & Sons.

8) Effect of Steam Turbine Reheat on Speed-Governor Performance, C. Condordia, ASME Paper 58-A-36.

9) Effect of Prime-Mover Response and Governing Characteristics on System Dynamic Performance, C. Concordia. F.P. deMello. L.K. Kirchmayer, R.P. Schulz, American Power Conference, April, 1966.

10) Simulation as a Design Tool for Plant Jack McDonough Boiler Controls, W.M. Stephens and D.N. Ewart (Co-authors), ISA, 7th National Power Instrumentation Symposium Proceedings, 1964, pp. 35-46.

11) Analysis and Design of Controls for a Once-Through Boiler Through Digital Simulation, D.J. Ahner, C.E. Dyer, and V.C. Summer (Co-authors), ISA, 9th National Power Instrumentation Symposium Proceedings, 1966, pp. 11-30.

12) Boiler Pressure Control Configurations, F.P. Imad (Co-author), Conference Paper 31-PP-67-12, IEEE Winter Power Meeting, January, 1967.

13) A Review of the Effect of Heat Storage upon the Performance of Modern Steam Generators, W.G. Schuctzenduebel, Combustion, February, 1965, p. 26.

14) Dynamic Response of Hydro Plant, R. Oldenburger, J. Donelson, AIEE Transactions, Part III (PAS), Vol. 81, p. 403.

15) Introduction to the Basic Elements of Control Systems for Large Steam Turbine Generators, M.A. Eggenberger, GET-3096A.

16) Logic-Adaptive Process for Control and Security in Interconnected Power Systems, M. Couvreur, IEEE Transactions, Power Apparatus and Systems, December 1968, Vol. 87, p. 1979.

17) A Comprehensive Direct Digital Load Frequency Controller, C.W. Ross, Conference Paper, IEEE, PICA Conference 1967.

18) Error Adaptive Control Computer for Interconnected Power Systems, C.W. Ross, IEEE Transactions, Power Apparatus and Systems, July 1966.

19) Adaptive Control of Electric Power Systems, R. Renchan and M. Convreur, CIGRE Paper 319, June 1966.

20) Performance of Interconnected Systems Following Disturbances, C. Concordia, IEEE Spectrum Vol. I, June, 1965, pp. 68070, 77-80.

21) Some Aspects of Tie-Line Bias Control on Interconnected Power Systems, N. Cohn, AIEE Transactions, 75, Part III, February 1957.

22) Power Response of Modern Reheat Turbine Generators to Load Dispatching Signals, M.A. Eggenberger, ASME Transaction 65 WA/PWR - IEEE Working Group on Power Plant Response to Load Changes.

23) Power Plant Response, J. Baker, W.D. Marsh, P.H. Light. J. Dobelson and F.P. deMello, Report by IEEE Working Group, IEEE Transactions, Power Apparatus and Systems, March 1967, p. 384.

24) Must Define Requirements to Get Proper Reserve, J.B. Tice, Electrical World, November 20, 1967.

25) Servomechanisms and Regulating System Design, H. Chestnut and R.W. Mayer, John Wiley & Sons, Inc. Vol. I (1951).

26) Transients in Linear Systems - Vol. I, Gardner and Barnes, John Wiley & Sons, Inc. (1942).

27) Modern Operational Mathematics in Engineering, Churchill and Ruc, McGraw-Hill Book Co. (1944).

28) Mathematical and Physical Principles of Engineering Analysis, Johnson & Walter, McGraw-Hill Book Co. (1944).

29) Linear Systems, Schwarz and Friedland, McGraw-Hill Book Co. (1965).

30) Servomechanism Analysis, Thaler and Brown, McGraw-Hill Book Co. (1953).

31) Differential Equations - A Modern Approach, Hochstadt, Holt, Rinehart & Winston, San Francisco, California (1964).

32) On the Automatic Control of Generalized Passive Systems, Chien, Hrones & Reswick, ASME Transactions, Vol. 74, No. 2, Feb. 1952, p. 175.

33) Techniques of Process Control, Buckley, John Wiley & Sons, Inc. (1964).

34) Optimum Settings for Automatic Controllers, J.G. Ziegler and M.B. Nichols, ASME Transactions, Vol. 64, pp. 769-775, 1942.

35) A More Precise Method for Tuning Controllers, C. Smith and P.W. Murrill, ISA Journal, May 1966, pp. 50-58.

36) Face - A Digital Dynamic Analysis Program, D.N. Ewart and F.P. deMello, Power Industry Computer Applications Conference, May 15-17, 1967.

37) Automatic Generation Control - Part I Process Modelling - F.P. deMello, R.J. Mills and W.F. B'Rells, IEEE Transactions, PAS, March/April 73, p. 710.

38) Automatic Generation Control - Part II Digital Control Techniques - F.P. deMello, R.J. Mills and W.F. B'Rells, IEEE Transactions PAS, March/April 73, p. 716.

39) Automatic Generation Control - F.P. deMello, J.M. Undrill, presented at the IEEE Energy Control Center Design Tutorial in Mexico City, July, 1977.

40) MW Response of Fossil Fueled Steam Units - IEEE Working Group on Power Plant Response to Load Changes, F.P. deMello and D.N. Ewart, presented at the Joint Power Generation Conference, Sept. 1972.

PRIME MOVER MODELS AND AUTOMATIC GENERATION CONTROL

- "Effect of Prime-Mover Response and Governing Characteristics on System Dynamic Performance"
- "Automatic Generation Control"
- "MW Response of Fossil Fueled Steam Units"
- "Automatic Generation Control: Part I - Process Modeling"
- "Automatic Generation Control: Part II - Digital Control Techniques"
- "Dynamic Models for Fossil Fueled Steam Units in Power System Studies"
- "Boiler Models for System Dynamic Performance Studies"
- "Hydraulic Turbine and Turbine Control Models for System Dynamic Studies"
- "Hydraulic Turbine Units and Hydro Governing"
- "BWR Capabilities for Utility Load Following and Regulation Requirements"
- "Dynamic Models for Combined Cycle Plants in Power System Studies"
- "A Governor/Turbine Model for a Twin-Shaft Combustion Turbine"
- "Steam Generators and Boiler-Turbine Controls"

Effect of Prime-Mover Response and Governing Characteristics on System Dynamic Performance

C. Concordia
F.P. de Mello
L.K. Kirchmayer
R.P. Schulz

EFFECT OF PRIME-MOVER RESPONSE AND GOVERNING CHARACTERISTICS ON SYSTEM DYNAMIC PERFORMANCE

C. CONCORDIA
Consulting Engineer

F. P. deMELLO
Senior Application Engineer
System Planning and Control

L. K. KIRCHMAYER
Manager, System Planning
and Control

and

R. P. SCHULZ
Application Engineer
System Planning and Control
Electric Utility Engineering Operation
General Electric Company
Schenectady, New York

INTRODUCTION

Prime-mover response and governing characteristics are of fundamental importance to power system load and frequency control. These response characteristics also play a major role during emergencies if portions of power systems are left with large unbalances between generation and load.

The adequacy of generation-transmission system design traditionally has been tested by its ability to withstand the first few seconds of generator power angle oscillations following faults or switching operations in the electrical network. For this type of momentary disturbance, barring the use of fast valve action for energy control,[1] the normal response of prime-mover mechanical powers has usually been too slow to materially affect the critical phenomena of transient stability in networks, justifying the assumption of constant prime-mover mechanical power which is often made in the course of studying these phenomena. However, as a next step in reliability, it is becoming common practice nowadays, with large interconnected systems, to study the behavior of interconnecting tie-lines on the assumption that a generator has already become unstable and has been lost. Such studies must extend over longer time periods and include the effects of prime-mover governor control.[2]

As a further step beyond these types of disturbances, which involve only momentary severe unbalances between electrical load and mechanical power among one or more sources, there are the admittedly more rare and much more difficult to analyze cases of upsets which result in large sustained unbalances between generation and load. In these cases the performance of the power system, the changes in load flow distribution across transmission

139

ties, and sometimes the ability of the power system to ride through the upset, are largely dependent on the response and governing characteristics of various prime-mover systems. Close examination of this problem is indicated, particularly in cases where prime-mover responses may be significantly dissimilar in different portions of interconnected systems.

Performance of the system is affected by the manner in which the spinning reserve is allocated, and we see digital dispatching computers as an important means of providing reserve surveillance and

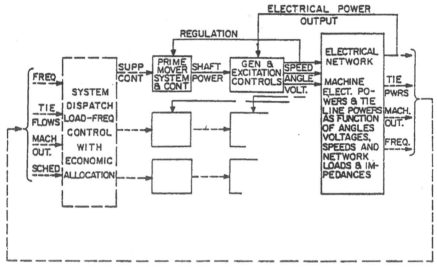

Fig. 1--Schematic of power system and controls.

corrective strategy for best overall distribution of reserve.[3]

It is the purpose of this paper to describe the pertinent phenomena and discuss the implications of prime-mover response in the light of normal and emergency load change duty.

BASIC CONCEPTS

The mechanism of maintaining equilibrium between prime-mover power and electrical load demands can be described briefly with reference to the schematic of Fig. 1.

Load changes originate in the network either due to normal switching or changing of loads or, in the case of upsets, due to abrupt loss of major generation, transmission equipment, or of major load-carrying ties. These changes in electrical connected load reflect themselves instantaneously as changes in electrical power among the various generating units, with an initial distribution governed by the network load flow laws applied to existing machine rotor angles.[4]

The resulting unbalance between prime-mover power and

generator electrical power will cause accelerations or decelerations of the various machine rotors which, with the passing of time, develop into changes in speeds and machine rotor angles.

Restoring forces, namely, changes in machine electrical powers, develop in response to angular changes between generator rotors, and oscillations in angle and electrical powers are set up such that the average electrical power on each unit equals its mechanical power less an amount proportional to the unit's average acceleration. These oscillations have periods of from less than a second to a few seconds, depending on the stiffness of electrical tie between machines relative to the inertia of these machines. It is characteristic of machines which are closely tied electrically to act like an equivalent large machine; and the oscillations of significance become those between groups of machines or between major power systems across limited capacity ties, with typical periods of up to ten seconds.

The final change in speed of all units will be arrested when balance is again restored between total mechanical power and electrical load demanded by the network.

For the case of constant prime-mover (blocked governors), this balance is obtained by virtue of the change in connected load with frequency. Typically, this load damping characteristic amounts to between 1 and 2 percent change in connected load for a 1 percent change in frequency. For this limiting situation, where prime-mover power is assumed unchanging, the frequency transient phenomena are described entirely by the machine inertias, system load damping characteristics and electrical tie strengths between machines, and the frequency deviation will be established within ten seconds or so, although oscillations between machines will persist for several additional seconds.

For the more realistic case of active governors, the frequency deviation produces changes in prime-mover power, and the final frequency change is primarily a function of the equivalent governor regulation, which is usually considerably more effective than the load characteristic in limiting the extent of the frequency dip. It should be noted, however, that changes in prime-mover power occur with varying delays, depending on the response characteristics of the prime-mover system.

Final control action on the prime movers is through the supplementary load frequency control action, which returns frequency and tie-line power interchange to schedule within a minute or more. This control action is also affected by the dynamic response characteristics of prime-mover systems, which will be reviewed briefly before leading on to a discussion on their effect on system dynamic performance.

RESPONSE CHARACTERISTICS OF PRIME MOVERS

By prime-mover response, we mean the time response of prime mover shaft power to control signals calling for changes in output. These response characteristics are influenced by the dynamics of turbines and associated energy sources, such as boilers, hydraulic systems, as well as by associated control devices, i.e., governors, boiler-turbine controls, etc. A brief review of these characteristics for some common types of prime-mover systems follows:

Conventional Steam Single Reheat and Double Reheat

Generation is changed on conventional steam turbine units by moving the governor-controlled valves. In normal system operation the motion of these valves is directed by:

1. Flyball action or other speed-sensor action in response to changes in unit and, therefore, system frequency.

2. Changes in speed changer motor position (governor synchronizing motor).

Control valve position responds very fast (in less than a second) to flyball action or to changes in speed changer motor position.[5]

Assuming constant boiler pressure, turbine mechanical power, in turn, responds to valve position changes as follows: About 30 percent of the final change, which is due to the turbine upstream of the reheater, comes about within a fraction of a second, and the remaining 70 percent will follow with a time constant of about 5 to 8 seconds, due to the charging time of the reheater volume.[6]

Figure 2 shows a response of turbine mechanical power following a step change in turbine valve for this ideal case of constant boiler pressure. Since the steam source is not infinite, boiler pressure does suffer deviations which affect the response of steam flow and mechanical power. Figure 2 also shows a typical response trace for a drum-type unit, including the effects of boiler pressure deviations and subsequent

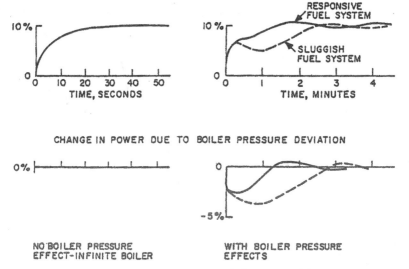

CHANGE IN POWER DUE TO BOILER PRESSURE DEVIATION

NO BOILER PRESSURE
EFFECT-INFINITE BOILER

WITH BOILER PRESSURE
EFFECTS

Fig. 2—Step change in speed changer position.

pressure restoration by combustion controls. The fast pressure control performance shown corresponds to about the best that can be obtained in coal-fired units with no dead time in fuel systems. It is more representative of oil-and gas-fired units, as many coal-fired units have considerably slower pressure controls. The slow pressure control performance is typical of certain coal-fired units with significant lags in the fuel system.[7]

The effect of double reheat is to add a second lag of from 5 to 8 seconds to the portion of mechanical power developed in the turbine downstream of the second reheater.

In most conventional steam units, changes in generation are initiated by turbine control valves, and the boiler controls respond with necessary immediate control action upon sensing changes in steam flow and deviations in pressure. Energy is transiently drawn from or put into boiler storage, since the inputs to the boiler are relatively slow in relation to the speed with which a turbine valve can move.

Once-Through Units

The basic difference between the response of once-through units and that of conventional drum-type units lies in the method of coordinating the control of the boiler-turbine unit. The somewhat lower stored energy in the once-through boiler and requirement of closer coupling between firing rate and feedwater flow has led to greater caution in control of these units, with the evolution of varying degrees of coordination between the turbine load demand and the inputs to the boiler.[8, 9]

The evolution of more sophisticated boiler controls will probably permit obtaining response characteristics from once-through units comparable to, if not better

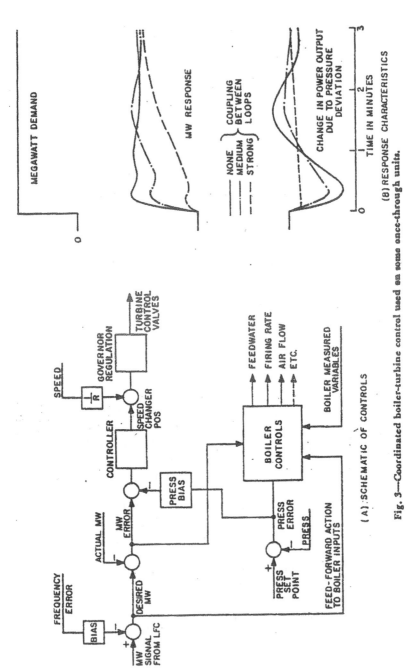

Fig. 3—Coordinated boiler-turbine control used on some once-through units.

Fig. 3—Coordinated boiler-turbine control used on some once-through units.

than, those of conventional units. However, to date, the coordination between turbine and boiler has involved use of the turbine valve in varying degrees as a boiler pressure regulator. Turbine valve motion is inhibited in deference to boiler pressure deviations, thereby affecting in varying degrees the response of turbine power.[10]

A common type of coordinated once-through boiler-turbine controls is shown functionally in Fig. 3A. To achieve the coordination between boiler variables and turbine demand, it is necessary to make the speed changer motor respond to intelligence other than, and in addition to, load control signals. This is done by integrating the load frequency control pulses to develop a signal indicative of demand for Mw which can be altered by other inputs. This signal is modified by a frequency deviation bias matching the unit's governor droop characteristic to develop the desired Mw. Without this bias the Mw feedback loop would undo whatever motion of turbine valves might have occurred from governor action. Comparison with the unit's actual output develops the Mw error, which is sent with the desired Mw signal to the boiler controls. Turbine speed changer position is directed to reduce a combination of Mw error and pressure error to zero, while the boiler controls likewise are directed to reduce the pressure error biased by the Mw error to zero. The sense of the cross-coupled Mw error and pressure error biases is in the direction such that a positive Mw error (Mw lower than

demand) would cause the turbine valve to open and the boiler controls to call for more feedwater, fuel, and air, whereas a positive pressure error (pressure lower than set point) would call for closing of the turbine valve while simultaneously increasing the feedwater.

Figure 3B shows response characteristics for varying degrees of coupling between Mw and pressure error, including the case where the loops are not coupled.

Hydraulic Turbine Units

Hydraulic turbine power plants have an inherent characteristic (inertia of the water column) which causes them to have shaft power responses that are considerably slower than those in a steam turbine.

Because a change in the position of the gate at the foot of the penstock produces an initial short-term turbine power change which is opposite in sense to that sought, hydraulic turbine governors are designed to have relatively large transient droops, with long resetting times, in order to obtain stable frequency regulation under isolated operating conditions. Consequently, the response of a moderate head hydraulic turbine plant to speed changes or to changes in speed-changer setting is relatively slow, as shown in Fig. 4.

Response Limitations

In large interconnected systems, the normal instantaneous

changes in connected load are a very small percentage of the total capacity; hence, frequency changes are small, and the flyball action (governor action) is normally an imperceptible ripple. Generation is usually changed manually or through supplementary control, and, normally, the rate of change, whether done manually or by automatic supplementary control, does not exceed 3 to 5 percent of machine capacity per minute, and on the large new steam units is often limited to less than 2 percent per minute.[11]

During system upsets, such as system separation or loss of generation where portions of systems may be left isolated with large unbalances of generation and load, governor action may be called upon to make large changes within a few seconds. Now, even though the turbine valve may be capable of responding 100 percent within this period of time, there are other factors which do not allow such unrestricted motion, and these pertain to boiler and turbine

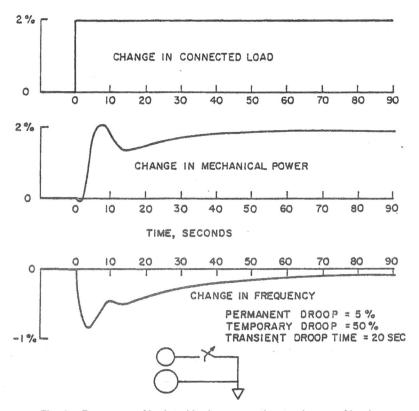

Fig. 4—Response of isolated hydro generation to change of load.

safety. On the way up, that is, valve opening action, the valve motion may be limited by the turbine load limit, which can be set to ride a certain value above operating point to prevent turbine loading above the capacity of mills, pumps or other auxiliaries on line. In the event of very large changes, if not limited by the load limit, unit loading may be arrested by the turbine initial pressure regulator which can be set to prevent boiler pressure from dropping below about 90 percent of rated value. This is done to prevent carryover of water from the boiler.

Other factors that sometimes limit the magnitude of generation change that can be taken in this almost instantaneous fashion involve combustion controls which may not stand the large upset, due to possible large transient mismatches in fuel and air and attendant danger of explosions, or in the feedwater controls which may not be able to hold drum level within safe limits.[12]

These factors, therefore, make it generally impractical to take instantaneous load changes greater than 20 percent on large conventional steam units, and there are

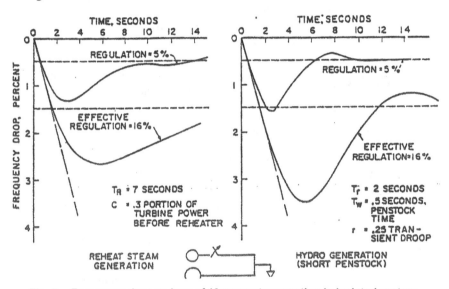

Fig. 5—Frequency drop on loss of 10 percent generation in isolated system.

some units that cannot stand instantaneous changes over 10 percent.

In the case of once-through units using the coordinated control philosophy, it is usual to limit the maximum rate at which load demand can change, and this can be done upstream of the point where the frequency bias signal is injected, or downstream of this point. In the first case, the unit response to governor action following frequency upsets would be faster than for the case where the rate limit is on the Mw demand signal downstream of the point where the frequency bias is injected.

Hydro units usually have no intentional response limitations, as the plant equipment is often protected by the inherent limits of speed changer maximum rate and governor transient droop.

It should be noted that large changes on a given unit imply that reserve has been concentrated in a few units. These large changes in power, if brought about by governor action, would require too large a frequency deviation. Alternately, if not produced by governor regulation, these changes would require special control action.

PERFORMANCE UNDER SYSTEM GOVERNING AND LOAD CONTROL

The significance of prime-mover response on power system dynamic performance is illustrated by examining transient performance following abrupt load changes in certain limiting situations. One of these situations is the case of an equivalent single unit supplying an isolated load. This case approximates conditions where the bulk of power generation in an isolated area is of the same type. Another case of interest concerns the isolated system with prime-movers of dissimilar characteristics. Additional cases explore effects of prime-mover characteristics in a system tied to a very large interconnected pool.

Single Equivalent Unit in Isolated Area

The case of a single equivalent unit in an isolated area is often studied to determine

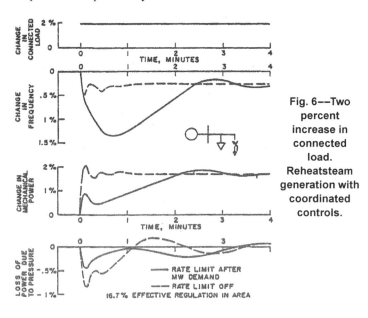

Fig. 6—Two percent increase in connected load. Reheatsteam generation with coordinated controls.

the responsiveness of power generation in limiting frequency excursions following a large upset, which results in the area under study to be separated from the multistate power grid.

Figure 5 shows the frequency deviations for the case of a load increase in an isolated power system with different types of generation and varying amounts of effective regulation. Only governor action is being considered, as the slower resetting of frequency deviation to normal through supplementary control is of secondary significance in terms of affecting peak deviations.

The peak deviation in frequency can be greater than the final value. This is shown on Fig. 5, depicting frequency transients, following a loss of generation for a typical reheat steam system and a typical hydro system. Figure 5 shows that the ratio of peak deviation relative to the final deviation of frequency is related to the value of steady-state regulation and is amplified by lags in the response of the prime-mover system.

The frequency transient initially follows the response determined by system inertia, as can be seen by noting that all curves near time zero approach asymptotically the curve of deviation that would occur with blocked governors.

The effective regulation is inversely proportional to the number of units in governing range. The results show the advantages of distributing regulation through many units by keeping their governors active.[13]

Figure 6 shows the performance that would result for the case of an isolated system composed of steam generation with coordinated boiler-turbine controls such as those advocated for once-through boilers[14] (Fig. 3A), with response characteristics as in Fig. 3B, middle curve.

The effects of introducing rate limiting of the Mw demand signal downstream of the point where the frequency bias signal is introduced is clearly shown on Fig. 6.

Dissimilar Units in Isolated Area

The effects of having generation with dissimilar response characteristics are illustrated on Fig. 7 which shows the case of an isolated system being supplied in part (50 percent) by conventional reheat steam, and the remainder by units with response characteristics shown on Fig. 3B, middle curve.

This case illustrates the fact that the transient load-flow conditions in networks following large upsets can be very sensitive to the response characteristics of generation in the various parts of the system. Entire interconnected systems can be reviewed as a huge single area, and the results of Fig. 7 have significance for this case, too. It is conceivable that, due to dissimilar response characteristics, a large load upset might result in overloading of ties in locations otherwise considered remote from the location of the upset.

Load Changes in Area Interconnected With Large Pool

Although the examples cited are pertinent for the case of a large upset relative to the total interconnected system capacity, a more common occurrence is that of an upset which is small relative to total interconnected system capacity, although not necessarily small relative to the utility in which it occurs. In these cases the frequency deviation is small with the bulk of the load change being supplied by the large interconnected capacity. Restoration of balance within the utility must rely on relatively slow supplementary control action (correction of load change within a minute or more).

Figure 8 puts into perspective the phenomena for this case, showing the load change being initially supplied by the interconnecting

ties, and then being corrected by supplementary control. Figure 8 shows the range of response to be expected as a function of the type of prime-mover system. In the case of the reheat steam generation with coordinated boiler turbine controls, the adjustments are as in Fig. 3B, using strong cross coupling with the pressure control loop.

CONCLUSIONS

The effect of prime-mover response on system dynamic performance has been illustrated in the light of several typical situations that can arise in power system operation. Recognition of these effects will become of increasing importance when

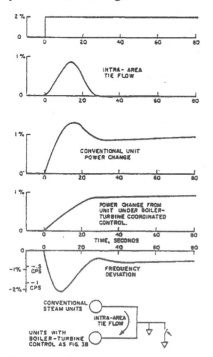

Fig. 7--Load change on isolated area.

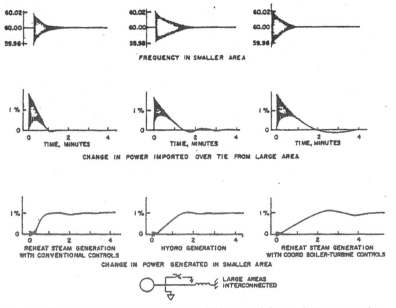

Fig. 8—Effect of load increase in area tied to much larger interconnection.

planning transmission capability between systems or parts of systems.

Closer attention to the response capabilities of various units and to the spreading of the governing duties as uniformly as possible among many units will be significant in reducing the severity of system upsets. In particular, boiler-turbine controls should be designed so as not to unnecessarily restrict the response of units beyond the inherent limits imposed by thermal stresses and safety of plant equipment.[15]

The role of digital dispatching systems will be expanded to recognize the phenomena of response capability in the scheduling of generation. At the power plants, we foresee extending the functions of plant automation computers to monitor the status of plant equipment including evaluation of stress conditions, to give on-line calculated indications of immediate response capability.

REFERENCES

1. DeMello, F. P., Ewart, D. N. and Temoshok, M., "Turbine Energy Controls Aid in Power System Performance," Paper presented at 1966 American Power Conference, Chicago, April 26-28, 1966. (See Authors' Index, this Volume).

2. Concordia, C., "Dynamic Concepts of Interconnected Systems," Paper presented at the 18th Annual Southwestern IEEE Conference, Dallas, Tex., April 20-22, 1966.

3. Fiedler, H. J. and Kirchmayer, L. K., "Developments in the Control of Interconnected Systems," Paper presented at 9th National Power Instrumentation Symposium, Detroit, Mich., May 16-18, 1966.

4. Concordia, C., "Effect of Prime Mover Speed Control Characteristics on Electric Power System Performance," *IEEE Conference Paper* 31CP65-778, presented at National Power Conference, Albany, N. Y., September 19-23, 1965.

5. Eggenberger, M. A., "Power Response of Modern Reheat Turbine Generators to Load Dispatching Signals," *ASME Paper* 65-WA/PWR-5.

6. Concordia, C., "Effect of Steam-Turbine Reheat on Speed-Governor Performance," *ASME Paper* 58-A-36; abstracted in *Mech. Eng.*, 81, 95 (1959) February.

7. Stephens, W. M., de Mello, F. P. and Ewart, D. N., "Simulation as a Design Tool for Plant Jack McDonough Boiler Controls," *Proc. National Power Instrumentation Symposium, 7,* 35-46 (1964).

8. Argersinger, J. I., Laubli, F., Voegli, E. F. and Scutt, E. D., "Development of an Advanced Control System for Supercritical Pressure Units," *IEEE Conf. Paper* CP63-1409, presented at National Power Conference, Cincinnati, Ohio, September 22-26, 1963.

9. Durrant, O. W. and Loeser, J. K., "Boiler-Turbine Control System for Application to Universal Pressure Boilers," *IEEE Conf. Paper* CP 63-1410 presented at National Power Conference, Cincinnati, Ohio, September 22-26, 1963.

10. Morgan, W. S. and Grimes, A. S., "Load-Frequency Control of Supercritical Units on the A.E.P. System," *IEEE Conf. Paper* 31CP66-59, presented at 1966 Winter Power Meeting, New York, January 31- February 4, 1966.

11. "Power Plant Response, IEEE Committee Report," *IEEE Transactions Paper* 31TP65-771, presented at National Power Conference, Albany, N. Y., September 19-23, 1965.

12. O'Brien, J. T., "Dynamic Testing of Power Plants," *Proc. National Power Instrumentation Symposium*, 6, 105-12 (1963).

13. Concordia, C., "Performance of Interconnected Systems Following Disturbances," *IEEE Spectrum*, 2, 68-72, 77-80 (1965) June.

14. Grant, I. E., Shuss, J. A., Hottenstine, R. H. and Daniels, J. H., "Automation of Bull Run Unit No. 1," Paper presented at

11th Annual Southwestern ISA Conference, Chattanooga, Tenn., April 27-29, 1965.

15. Summer, J. C., de Mello, F. P., Ahner, D. J. and Dyer, C. E., "Analysis and Design of Controls for a Once-Through Boiler, Through Digital Simulation,"

.

Paper presented at Ninth National Power Instrumentation Symposium, Detroit, Mich., May 16-18, 1966.

16. Kirchmayer, L. K., "Economic Control of Interconnected Systems," New York: Wiley, 1959.

Automatic Generation Control

F.P. de Mello
J.M. Undrill

AUTOMATIC GENERATION CONTROL

F. P. de Mello, Fellow, IEEE   J. M. Undrill, Senior Member, IEEE

Power Technologies, Inc.
Schenectady, New York

INTRODUCTION

Automatic Generation Control is the controlling link between the dispatch office and the generating plants that it supervises. The dispatcher, with the aid of the optimization and security analysis functions covered in companion papers, decides on the correct level of internal generation for his system and contracts to purchase or sell power in order to meet his company's load in the most economic manner. The automatic generation control[1] function (AGC) is assigned the responsibility of adjusting generator outputs to meet the overall system objectives of:

i)   Regulating frequency to the scheduled value.

ii) Maintaining net interchange of power across the company's boundaries at the value required by the several interchange contracts in force at each instant.

The AGC system is a compendium of equipment and computer programs implementing closed loop feedback control of frequency and net interchange. Generator outputs, tie-line flows, and frequency are measured, compared with setpoints, and adjusted to correct error in the controlled quantities. As with any feedback system, dynamic behavior is of prime importance. Correspondingly, the prime technical objective in the design of the AGC system is the correct accommodation of the dynamic characteristics of the power system to achieve prompt, smooth, and stable maneuvering of generation in response to system disturbances and changes of operating setpoints.

This paper reviews the AGC function as implemented by a modern dispatch office digital computer system.

THE TASK OF AGC

Process Response Characteristics

Load Sharing by Turbine Governors

The most direct control influence on power system frequency and generator load distribution is exerted by the turbine governors. Each turbine speed (frequency, f) and power, P_{gi}, are related by a "permanent droop," R_i, where

$$R_i = \frac{\delta f}{\delta P_{gi}} \qquad \text{Hz/MW} \qquad (2.1)$$

The sensitivity of system load to frequency is expressed by a damping factor, D_{eff}, where

$$D_{eff} = \frac{\delta P_{load}}{\delta f} \qquad \text{MW/Hz} \qquad (2.2)$$

It is permissible for governing analysis purposes to assume that all turbine/generators rotate at the same (synchronous) speed.[2] This being the case, system acceleration and frequency are determined by the collective action of all governors as shown by Figure 1a.

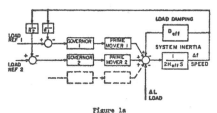

Figure 1a

Collective Action of All System Governors in Determining Variations of Average Frequency

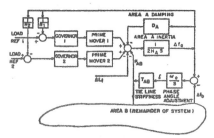

Role of Differences in Frequency of Adjacent Subsystems in Determining Net Power Interchange Between Them

It may readily be shown that a change in load will produce a steady-state change in frequency given by

$$\Delta f = a \frac{\Delta L}{\left(D_{eff} + \dfrac{1}{R_{eff}} \right)} \qquad \text{Hz} \qquad (2.3)$$

where

$$\frac{1}{R_{eff}} = \frac{1}{R_1} + \frac{1}{R_2} + ----+ \frac{1}{R_n} \qquad (2.4)$$

and

ΔL = load change expressed in terms of additional power at rated frequency, in MW.

Normal practice is to set the permanent droop, R, of every governor so that a load change from zero to rated output is associated with the same speed change. The value of this speed change is from 3 to 5 percent in most power systems. Figure 2 illustrates the steady-state relationship between load change, frequency change, and increase in power output provide by governor action.

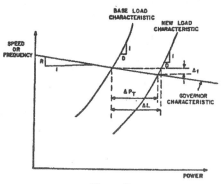

Figure 2

Relationship Between Nominal Load Change, ΔL, Total Turbine Power Change, ΔP_T, and Frequency Change, Δf, Under Governor Action

The power output increase of each individual unit under governor control is given by

$$\Delta P = \cfrac{\Delta L}{R_i \left(D_{eff} + \cfrac{1}{R_{eff}} \right)} \qquad (2.5)$$

Since the governor droops are set to an agreed per-unit value on the basis of rated turbine powers, a system frequency change would ideally change the outputs of all units in proportion to their ratings. This ideal is seldom attained because most load changes are so small in relation to the capacity of the system that some governors remain within their deadbands leaving a subset of the system's total capacity to accept the load. The key point, nevertheless, is that natural governor action causes changes in electrical load to be distributed essentially in proportion to unit ratings.

Figure 1a applies to a complete system without recognition of the effect of the load change on the constituent parts of its transmission network. Most large power systems are made up of a number of interconnected subsystems with power flow across their boundaries being the subject of commercial interest. The basic dynamic load balance of Figure 1a may be restated as in Figure 1b for the case of an individual subsystem within the overall interconnection. Here all units of the subsystem are viewed as rotating at identical speed at all times, but the elastic characteristic of the electrical ties between subsystems allows the speeds of different subsystems to differ during transients. This viewpoint is acceptable because only net power flows between subsystems are of concern to AGC. The steady-state frequency change caused by a load change within this subsystem continues to be given by the application of (2.3) with respect to the whole interconnected system. The change in the tie-line power flow follows from the natural loading distribution implied by (2.5). The dynamic response of frequency and tie-line flow are determined by:

i)   The transient load response of the turbine governors and prime movers.

ii) The elastic synchronizing effect of the tie lines.

The representative form of the response to a load change within the subsystem with control action being contributed by governors only is shown by the solid curves in Figure 3. The high-frequency oscillatory component is associated with tie-line elasticity and is of interest to AGC work only in that it represents a noise component in tie-line power flow measurements. The slower transient component represents the transient behavior of the prime movers, while the final offsets of net interchange and frequency are the result of the governor steady-state characteristics noted above.

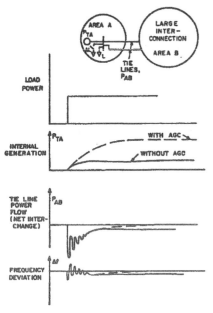

Figure 3
Variation of Internal Generation
and Net Interchange Following
Load Disturbance in Utility A

Generating Unit Load Response

The effect of key importance to AGC is the balance between total generator electrical power and total turbine power within a given subsystem of the complete power system. Total generator electrical power is determined by the subsystem's (e.g., company's) electrical load and the net power flow over the tie lines. Total turbine power, which the AGC system must match to the electrical load, is determined by the response of the individual prime movers to load control actions.

All adjustment of generator power output is effected by changing the turbine load setting. Depending upon unit type, the load reference may be implemented directly at the governor, or may have boiler controls interposed between it and the governor. A typical load control arrangement is shown in Figure 4.

The response of generator power to a change i governor reference is determined by the dynamic response characteristic of the turbine and energy supply.

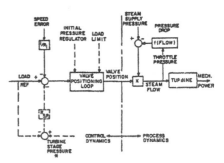

Figure 4
Functional Block Diagram of
Typical Turbine Controls

The modeling needed to characterize this may range from a single time constant, in the case of a simply configured gas turbine, to the level typified by Figure 5 which shows a model of a large drum-type boiler and reheat turbine.[3] Careful consideration is needed to determine, for each plant type, both:

i)   The natural response characteristic as determined by the form and time constant values of the principal transfer-function blocks.

ii) Limitations placed on plant load change rate by thermal stress considerations (steam turbines), hydraulic surge (hydro plants), nuclear reactor safety, and so on.

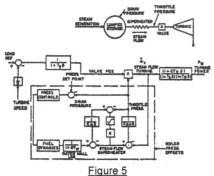

Figure 5
Dynamics of Turbine Power
Including Boiler Pressure Effects

While details need not be considered here, the breadth of unit response characteristics[3] that AGC must recognize can be indicated by the following summary of some principal unit characteristics:

a) The natural response of drum-type steam units with "turbine leading" control arrangements to small load change requests can be very rapid with the pertinent time constants being measured in seconds. Load changes exceeding a small band (say, 5 percent) about the initial operating point must, however, be executed at a rate far below that implied by the natural small disturbance response.

b) The natural response of units with "boiler leading" control arrangements,

where the boiler controls are interposed between the load reference and the governor, is generally determined by the steam generation process, with pertinent time constants being measured in minutes. Hence, such units do not have the initial quick response capability normally associated with conventionally controlled drum-type steam units.

c) The use of integrated boiler-turbine controls, depending upon specific design, results in plant response characteristics covering the whole spectrum between the forms a) and b) covered above.

d) The initial natural response of hydro units is intermediate between the two steam unit extremes covered above. The pertinent time constants are measured in seconds, but are longer than those pertaining to drum-type units. Most hydro units, however, can change load at their maximum natural rate without restriction over their entire operating range.

Figure 6 illustrates these general forms of prime mover loading response.

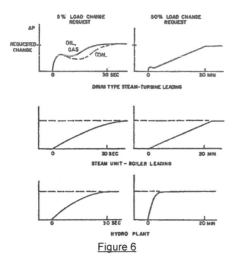

Figure 6
Variation of Unit Response Time
with Unit Type and Magnitude of
Requested Load Change

Basic AGC Actions

The control objective of AGC may be illustrated with reference to Figure 7. Subsystem S, a member of the interconnected system, is committed to maintain net interchanges of power, P_{Ad}, P_{Bd}, and P_{Cd} with its neighbors. Since the routing of power is not to be controlled, the subsystem can meet its commitments by maintaining a net outward interchange power flow of $(P_{Ad} + P_{Bd} + P_{Cd})$ while simultaneously holding its own frequency at the scheduled value. Each subsystem in the interconnection has a similar generation control requirement. The subsystem enclosed by a net interchange boundary is referred to as a control area.

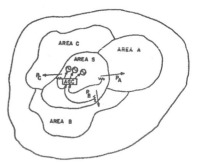

Figure 7
Interchanges Between a Utility,
S, and its Neighbors

Now, without AGC, any load change or other disturbance within the control area will result in the majority of the required power increment being supplied by the interconnection via the tie lines according to the natural governing characteristic, as illustrated by Figure 3. This will drive the net interchange away from its scheduled value.

The principal objective of an AGC system is to adjust the load reference settings of units within the control area to override the natural governing effect and hold net interchange and frequency at their scheduled values. The additional task of AGC is to ensure that each control area contributes its proper share to the system generation adjustments needed to hold system frequency at scheduled value.

AGC is, then, a reset control action superimposed over the natural governing action to cancel steady-state deviations of net interchange and frequency. The desired effect of AGC is shown by the dotted curves in Figure 3.

Since frequency is equal at all points of the interconnection in the steady state, this common control objective can be maintained by having each utility control its generation independently to achieve a zero steady-state value of a quantity termed Area Control Error, ACE.[4, 5] ACE is defined, for each control area by:

ACE = Net Interchange Error + B_f * frequency error (2.6)

For the case of Figure 7, ACE is given by:

$$ACE = (P_{Ad} + P_{Bd} + P_{Cd}) - (P_A + P_B + P_C) + B_f \Delta f \quad (2.7)$$

It should be noted that this control error requires each control area to measure quantities only at its boundaries and requires no intelligence on external conditions or on internal loads.

The parameter, B_f, is called frequency bias. As shown in Reference 4, a steady-state analysis may be made to find a value of B_f such that each AGC system produces steady-state generation changes only when they are needed to compensate for a change of load or interchange schedule within its own control area. It is emphasized, however, that the power system is seldom, if ever, in the steady state, and that the AGC system must be designed to respond correctly to dynamic variations in ACE. In view of this, dynamic rather than static analysis should be used as the basis for the overall design of the AGC system and B_f, like other parameters, should be viewed in terms of its effect on system dynamic behavior.[6]

The AGC system is working correctly when the inevitable and continual variations of net interchange error and frequency error are held within acceptable bounds by plant output adjustments that are within thermodynamic (or hydraulic) limitations and are acceptable to the plant operators.

The control of generation to meet AGC objectives involves action at three levels as follows:

First - the required individual generator outputs having been determined, their load reference setpoints must be manipulated to achieve these outputs.

Second- given a set of scheduling rules, the outputs requested of individual generators must be determined so as to meet the objective of zero ACE.

Third - the generator loading rules must be updated continually to recognize optimum dispatch principles, boiler-turbine load changing limitations, and transmission security.

Normal variations of system load and normal operating disturbances require the control actions in the first two levels to occur on a second-by-second basis, while the third level is required to revise the loading rules at intervals ranging from a few minutes (in most U.S. companies) to hours. Second-by-second actions at the first two levels are handled by the AGC system. The third level of action is discussed in companion papers.

STRUCTURE OF THE AGC SYSTEM

AGC Elements

The simplest AGC system would be that needed by a utility with one generator and one interconnection point. The principal elements of such an AGC system, as shown in Figure 8, are:

i) An inner loop using controller, L(s), which positions the governor reference to achieve a desired generator power output.

ii) An outer loop using controller, K(s), to alter the desired generator power output in response to changes in ACE.

The detailed design and construction of AGC equipment is influenced by the requirements of security and noise-free performance of the information paths between the widely-spaced measurement points, controllers, and generating unit. Nevertheless, the general procedures

for designing a control system of the form shown in Figure 8 are well recognized. Figure 8 may be reduced for analysis purposes to the block diagram shown in Figure 9.

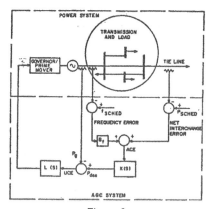

Figure 8
Basic Form of AGC for System With Single Generator and Interconnection

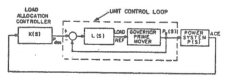

Figure 9
Two-Loop Structure of AGC

Good feedback system design practice recommends that:

a) The inner controller, L(s), be set up to achieve prompt, stable following of the intermediate signal, $P_{des}(s)$, by the output quantity, $P_g(s)$.

b) Given proper performance of the inner loop, the outer controller K(s) should exert control of the output, P_g, by adjustments of P_{des} that are within the bandwidth that the inner control loop is able to follow.

In a real power system with many generators and interconnection points, the simple system of Figure 8 must be expanded to include several unit control loops operating in parallel as shown in Figure 10. It is vital to note, however, that the basic structure of inner and outer control loops remains unchanged; all that happens is that the single inner loop of Figure 8 is joined by several parallel inner loops, one for each generating unit, while the design principle stated above stands.

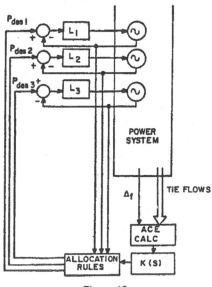

Figure 10
Multiple Unit Control Loops in
AGC of Multiunit Control Area

The inner control loop of Figures 8, 9, and 10 is called the Unit Control Loop while we shall refer to the outer path as the load allocation loop.

Early AGC systems, developed in the 1950's were based on the analog control equipment prevailing at the time. The disposition of equipment and the selection of signals to be sent between dispatch office and the generating units was determined in many instances by the availability and economics of analog tone telemetry channels. Analog AGC control schemes began to be superseded by all-digital systems in the mid-1960's and the use of digital telemetry, and digital computation is now the universal choice for new installations.

The flexibility and security of modern digital data transmission allows the location at which the control loops are implemented to be selected on the basis of logical convenience rather than equipment economics. Present practice favors placement of both unit control loop and load allocation loop logic in the centralized dispatch office computer, since all the required data is already available in this location for independent reasons. It would be entirely practical, however, to implement unit control loops in individual small computers located at the generating units without changing the fundamental organization of the AGC process.

Unit Control Loop

The unit control loop is a simple servo system whose task is to match generator output to a megawatt setpoint. While the equipment used to build the unit control loop varies between AGC system vendors, the transfer function achieved is generally equivalent to the basic reset arrangement shown in Figure 11a. A unit control error is computed and accumulated to give the load reference signal which continues to be adjusted until measured generator output matches the setpoint. One representative mechanization of this loop is shown schematically in Figure 11b. The operating sequence of this loop recurs at intervals of two to four seconds and is as follows:

i) The unit control program is started in the AGC computer. It picks up the generator power setpoint from the load allocation loop program and the actual generator power from telemetry tables. The unit control error is computed as

$$UCE = K_u(P_{des} - P_g) \qquad (3.1)$$

ii) The unit control program generates a request to drive the governor control motor in the raise or lower direction by a specified amount and sends this request in digitally encoded form to the telemetry system.

iii) The next telemetry outgoing transmission carries the request for movement to generating unit controller. The unit controller closes the power contactor of the governor reference motor for a preset time, usually a fraction of a second, to accumulate the requested raise/lower step onto the present reference position.

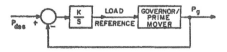

Figure 11a
Simple Reset Form of Unit Control Loop

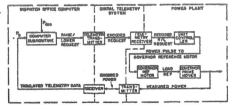

Figure 11b
Digital Computer/Telemetry
Implementation of Basic Unit Control Loop

The resolution and rate-of-change capability of this scheme are determined by the number of bits used to transmit the raise/lower signal. An "ideal" arrangement would be to transmit the computed UCE directly to the unit controller as the raise/lower signal, using the same number of bits as used to compute UCE. While this approach may be practical in a few specialized applications where the unit controller includes a small computing unit, it is not widely favored because:

a) It would require an elaborate and expensive decoding capability in the unit controller, and would not be compatible with many existing unit controller designs.

b) There is an incentive to minimize the number of

bits used for the AGC raise/ lower message so that a single digital data channel of limited baud rate can be shared with other telemetry functions, or be "party-lined" to several generating units.

c) The required resolution and response rate does not require a large number of bits for the raise/lower message.

The basic minimum message format uses two bits and is able to request a single quantum of raise or lower motion as shown in Figure 12. Such a simple scheme would impose a fixed relationship between control resolution, maximum rate-of-change and unit control loop repetition interval. If resolution of x percent is needed, the worth of one governor motor motion request must be x percent of unit output. Then if telemetry retransmits the message every T seconds, the maximum possible rate of change of generator output is

$$\frac{x}{T} \text{ percent per second.}$$

A 1/4 percent resolution and 4-second repetition interval then gives a maximum rate-of-change of

$$\frac{.25}{4} \times 60 = 3.75 \text{ percent per minute.}$$

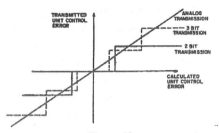

Figure 12
Approximation of Calculated
ACE by Digital Signal Composed
of Limited Number of Bits

This is a reasonable rate-of-change limit for sustained load ramping of thermal generating units, but is unrealistically restrictive for regulating purposes. Steam units can be maneuvered very rapidly over the limited range of 5 to 10 percent of their output, and most hydro units can move at a much higher rate over their entire no-load-to-full-load range. To take advantage of this the unit control loop should be able to move the governor reference signal at a rate of 10 to 15 percent per minute.

Such a rate of change capability may be achieved while retaining the previously mentioned resolution and repetition interval by adding one or more bits to the basic two-bit telemetry message format to allow specification of the amount of governor motor motion to be produced by each request.

The final format of the telemetry message and the logic by which the governor motor motion request is derived from the calculated unit control error is limited only by the ingenuity of the individual AGC vendors. The form of telemetry message and unit controller logic used to transmit AGC instructions and translate them into load reference changes must be expected to evolve continuously as manufacturers produce new telemetry equipment and as turbine governors make increasing use of digital control technology.

Regardless of its details, the important point is that each unit control loop is implemented as a self-contained entity and must operate satisfactorily as a prerequisite for the application of the AGC load allocation loop.

Load Allocation Loop

As indicated above and in Figure 10, the outer loop of the AGC must manipulate the unit control loop inputs in such a way that the present system generation is raised by an amount equal to ACE; ACE being a statement of the additional generation needed to return the net interchange and frequency to scheduled values.

A simple arrangement for determining unit control loop setpoints, P_{des}, at any instant is illustrated in Figure 13. In this arrangement, ACE is added to the present total system generation and the new total is allocated according to a set of "splitting factors" to the several generating units. While this load allocation scheme would give a workable AGC system, it would not satisfy several key requirements of AGC. Its principal drawbacks are:

a) It is poorly suited to the economic allocation of generation because economic loading rules are inevitably nonlinear and, hence, would require the splitting factors to be updated frequently as functions of total generation.

b) It forces the steady-state gain of the outer loop transfer function, K(s), to be unity, even though the optimum gain for effective regulation may be greater than unity.

c) It forces the allocation of ACE to be made in the same proportions as the allocation of base generation.

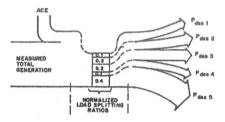

Figure 13
Simple Allocation of Total Load to Unit Control Loop Setpoints

The more widely used method of load allocation is a linearization of the exact economic loading rules to express each unit's output in terms of a "base point", P_{bi}, and a "participation factor", a_i, as shown in Figure 14. The participation factors are normalized so that $\Sigma a_i = 1$, and, hence, the allocation of the required total generation is given by

$$P_{desi} = P_{bi} + (\Sigma P_{gi} + ACE - \Sigma P_{bi})a_i \quad (3.2)$$

This method of load allocation allows the AGC and optimum dispatch functions to be linked by having the economic dispatch update the "P_b" and "a" values at intervals of about 5 minutes, or whenever the conditions of the old linearization become invalid.

Since the summation of a_i is unity, the allocation (3.2) still gives a net gain of unity in the outer loop of Figure 9. It is therefore common to provide one or more additional load allocation paths to increase the gain with which ACE is applied to the generator outputs, as illustrated in Figure 15. Such additional paths may use allocation factors, b_i, that are different from those determined by economic loading rules. The generator power allocation in this case becomes

$$P_{desi} = P_{bi} + (\Sigma P_{gi} + ACE - \Sigma P_{bi}) a_i + b_i ACE$$
$$= P_{bi} + (\Sigma P_{gi} - \Sigma P_{bi}) a_i + (a_i + b_i) \quad (3.3)$$

The value of the summation of the b_i factors depends on the gain desired in the outer loop transfer function, $K(s)$, of Figure 9.

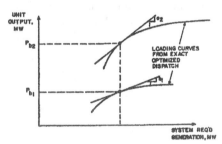

Figure 14
Allocation of Unit Outputs According to Base Points and Participation Factors Determined by Optimum Dispatch Calculation

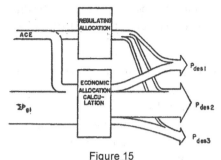

Figure 15
Use of Two Allocation Paths in Parallel to Allow ACE to be Allocated with Net Gain Other than Unity, and with Distribution Other than Economic Distribution

The most commonly cited reason for assigning different values to the a_i and b_i factors is that the regulating capabilities of generating units are not necessarily in proportion to their economic participation factors. In fact, low operating costs are usually associated with large steam or nuclear units which are much less tolerant of maneuvering than are smaller units having higher running costs. It is quite common, therefore, to find a unit being assigned a relatively large value of a_i and relatively small value of b_i, and vice versa.

Secondary allocation paths as characterized by the factors, b_i, may be used to obtain temporary strong corrective action by the AGC system in emergencies. This may be achieved, for example, by using two independent secondary paths, having sets of unit allocation factors by b_{1i} and b_{2i}, with the first path being active at all times and the second being active only when ACE exceeds a suitable threshold value. The terms "emergency action" and "assist action" have been used to describe this form of supplementary load allocation.

It will be noted that the scheme shown in Figure 15 allocates the system load entirely on the basis of optimum dispatch when ACE is zero. The occurrence of an upset, say a load increase, will create a nonzero ACE. This ACE will be allocated according to the sums $(a_i + b_i)$, hence increasing generation and canceling itself. When ACE returns to zero, the new total generation is again allocated on the basis of optimum dispatch only.

AGC Refinements

Relation to Basic Elements

The basic elements described above represent the core of the AGC system. The implementation of any AGC system within a digital supervisory control system requires that tie flows, frequency and generator powers be measured, telemetered at the required interval of two to four seconds, and fed to subroutines executing the unit control and load allocation loop calculations. It also requires that the outgoing raise/lower signals be telemetered out to the units on completion of each AGC subroutine execution.

Execution of the AGC subroutines, once telemetry requirements have been handled, consumes only a small fraction of the capacity of a typical dispatch office computer. Hence, once the basics have been provided, a broad range of refinements may be added to the AGC process by the simple addition

of code to the AGC subroutines of the central computer. The following paragraphs summarize some of the refinements found in up-to-date digital AGC systems.

ACE Filtering

The most important refinement of the basic process is the filtering of the ACE signal to avoid unneeded control action.[7,8] ACE contains a strong random component, corresponding to random variations of load and may also contain significant components at the natural frequencies of rotor angle oscillations. The frequency band of these variations in ACE extends right through the bandwidth of the AGC system, hence favoring a nonlinear filtration process which can reject variations of ACE on the basis of both magnitude and frequency.

Rejection of small high frequency variations may be handled by standard linear filtering. Additional logic is needed to recognize that small values of ACE do not require control action, even when they are within the AGC bandwidth and have been passed by high frequency cutoff filtration. One way of avoiding excessive control response to small values of ACE is illustrated by Figure 16. This form of filtration recognizes that a large value of ACE is a fair indication of a significant event and that control action should begin immediately, while small ACE values generally indicate that all is normal and that control action may reasonably be delayed. Filtering action of the general type illustrated by Figure 16 should be accompanied by logic to ensure that any persistent offset in a sequence of ACE values falling below the threshold of Figure 16 will be detected and passed through to the load allocation process.

References 7 and 8 give details of two ACE filtering schemes meeting these general objectives.

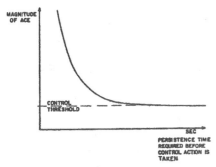

Figure 16
Nonlinear Characteristic Rejecting Control Action in Response to Small Values of ACE

Command and Permissive Control

The straightforward implementation of the two-loop control structure described in the preceding two sections allows the load of any unit to be changed in either direction at any time. This form of control action is termed[1] "command" control in the AGC context.

An alternative to command control is the "permissive" form of control[1] in which the raise/lower signaling logic can generate raise signals only when ACE is positive and vice versa. This method of control is claimed to reduce the control activity of the generating units since it can adjust their loads only in the direction required to reduce the value of ACE.

Pure permissive control has the disadvantage that it impairs the ability of the AGC to handle the valid and important situation where the load of an individual unit must be adjusted in opposition to the trend of system load and the load of other units. This need arises, for instance, when a large efficient unit is returned to service during a period of flat or declining system load and is to be brought up to full load to displace the output of other more expensive units.

The ease with which digital computers accommodate changes in control logic makes it quite practical to take advantage of the strong points of both command and permissive control methods. One approach, for example, operates on a command basis allowing both raise and lower requests, while ACE is small but switches to a permissive arrangement when ACE exceeds a suitable threshold.

Rate Limiting

Rate limiting in the unit control loops is highly desirable but is complicated by the nonlinear response characteristics of the majority of generating units. Rate limiting logic should recognize the following factors:

i) The quantity to be rate limited is actual generator output, not load reference.

ii) The relationship between load reference setting and unit output may be highly nonlinear, including both flat spots in the steady-state characteristic and varying transfer function lags.

iii) The permissible rate-of-change of actual unit output depends upon the immediate past history of load changes of that unit.

In view of these factors, the rate limiting of the unit control loops should be implemented by giving the loop the capability of moving the load reference at a rapid rate and by inhibiting this capability only when actual unit output is observed to exceed its permissible rate-of-change.

Non-Following Detection

Because rate limiting of the type described above can move the load reference quite rapidly, it is essential that the unit control loop be able to inhibit transmission of raise/lower signals promptly when:

i) The unit is taken off automatic control at the plant.

ii) The output of the unit fails to follow the load reference within a reasonable tolerance while in automatic control model.

The first condition may readily be accommodated by telemetering the status of the control-room control mode switch to the AGC computer. Failure to follow while in automatic mode may be detected by comparing a quantity such as integrated unit control error with a set of reasonable bounds. Detection of failure-to-follow should produce an operator alarm, deactivation of the unit control loop and reassignment of the economic dispatch parameters P_{bi} and a_i for the units remaining under automatic control.

Provisions for Telemetry Failure

While the non-following detection logic provides a degree of protection from incorrect operation in the event of telemetry failure, the AGC function should be advised of telemetry failures by the telemetry-driving software and should be able to adapt its operation automatically. The telemetry remote station or controller at each generating unit, as well as the central computer, should be able to detect loss of telemetry inputs, stuck contacts, and other likely causes of erroneous operation. While the details of telemetry failure detection depend on the specific structure of the equipment, the AGC logic should be able to respond to failures by:

• Suspending operation of an individual unit control loop.

• Suspending all AGC action.

• Continuing AGC action with certain telemetered data items

being replaced by manual data entries.

- Informing the operator whenever its mode of operation is altered or requires alteration.

Alternative Control Modes

The AGC system should recognize that system dispatch often requires generator loading to be controlled according to criteria other than economic operation and cancellation of ACE. The AGC should, correspondingly, be capable of controlling each unit to a power setpoint, P_{des}, determined according to a variety of special criteria. This can readily be accomplished in the schemes described above by accepting the input signal, P_{des}, of the unit control loop from an independent source rather than from the outer loop of the AGC. The independent source could be a manual separate entry by the operator or, as in the case of a preplanned load program, it could be an independent computer subroutine which calculates the desired unit power as a function of time of day. In either case it will be noted that the unit control loops, by themselves, constitute an effective control system for generation not falling within the realm of classical AGC requirements.

AGC TUNING AND PERFORMANCE

Operating Realities

The overriding concern in evaluating AGC performance is its influence on the power plants that it controls. The plant maneuvering that it produces must, above all else, be gentle and reasonable from the viewpoint of the plant operator. Any attempt by AGC to exert sudden control actions, or actions that appear to him to be arbitrary, creates immediate difficulties for the operator who must continually anticipate required changes in status of feedpumps, coal mills, oil guns, and so on to keep the plant operating safely. This implies that only simple control strategies will be accepted in AGC, and that smooth well-damped response is preferred over rapid neutralization of ACE.

Tuning

AGC is a well-understood control process applied to a system whose response is well understood in principle but widely variable in detail. Because it must accommodate wide variations in system response characteristics, must work with inputs containing significant noise components, and must give inherently smooth response, AGC systems should be tuned for slow reset action with an overall low-pass filter form of response.

Immunity from noise effects is best achieved by tuning the individual subloops for smooth, strongly damped response, hence assuring that each will function reliably by itself regardless of the validity of the action of the others. It is important that the AGC subroutines allow each individual unit control subloop to be tested and retuned individually at any time with the power system in normal operation. Tuning derived from optimal control theories and assuming that the entire AGC system is in service with valid telemetry data inputs is not acceptable; a practical AGC system is likely to be called on regularly to operate on a "partial control", basis while some of its subsections are out-of-service.

It is critical to note that practical AGC systems are strongly nonlinear for all magnitudes of disturbance and that their nonlinearities are essential to their proper operation. As a result, simulation of realistic disturbances, followed by test observations during field installation, have proved to be the only viable way of handling AGC optimization work, of proving new ideas, and of assuring safe performance. Simulation of the system environment that an AGC system will experience can be achieved with a high degree of realism, and it is usually practical to preset the majority of the parameters of a new AGC system on the basis of simulations, leaving only key parameters such as overall loop gains to be finalized during commissioning tests.

Currency of Telemetered Data

AGC is a feedback control system and, as with all feedback systems, its stability and ability to react to changing inputs are sharply influenced by phase lags in the receipt of its measured outputs or in the transmission of its control signals.

The optimum performance of the AGC system therefore depends very heavily on the correct timing of the telemetry scan and control output cycles.

Experience has shown that the complete AGC process, including load allocation and output of raise/ lower signals to the unit controllers, should be repeated every two to four seconds. The receipt of telemetered inputs, calculations, and transmission of control signals by the generating units would ideally be instantaneous. This is impractical because the economics of digital telemetry schemes make it necessary to scan the many measurement points used by AGC on a sequential basis. Experience, again, has shown the AGC process to be tolerant of the input data age variations that result from carefully coordinated and timed telemetry arrangements. It must be noted, however, that proper timing of the telemetry scan cycle and the execution of the AGC subroutines in the real-time operating system of the dispatch computer are essential to high-quality AGC performance.

REVIEW

The AGC system is a feedback control whose task is to hold a utility's net interchange and frequency at scheduled values. The operation, design and tuning of this control can readily be understood on the basis of straightforward feedback system theory, with proper recognition of power plant dynamic response being the key consideration.

AGC serves to link system optimum scheduling and security analysis functions with the power system by maneuvering generating units to their scheduled loadings. This linkage is achieved by having dispatch calculations hand over new unit base point and loading participation factors at intervals, ranging from minutes to hours, depending upon the utility's particular scheduling needs.

The overriding concern in the design and application of AGC is its effect on power plant operations, and up-to-date AGC systems include many special logic elements tailored to minimize unnecessary control action at the power plants. AGC is both an optimizing control during normal system operation and a first line of corrective action in emergencies. Improvements in the quality and flexibility of generation control are increasingly recognized as justification for the installation of digital computer-based supervisory control systems.

REFERENCES

[1] IEEE Standard 94, "Definitions for Terminology for Automatic Generation Control on Electric Power Systems," IEEE Transactions on Power Apparatus and Systems, Vol. PAS-89, pp. 1358-1364, 1970.

[2] "Process Dynamics in Electric Utility Systems, ISA Paper 505-70, International Conference and Exhibit of ISA, October 26-29, 1970, Philadelphia, Pennsylvania.

[3] "MW Response of Fossil Fueled Steam Units," IEEE Working Group on Power Plant Response to Load Changes, IEEE Transactions on Power Apparatus and Systems, Vol. PAS-92, pp. 455-463, 1973.

[4] L. K. Kirchmayer, Economic Control of Interconnected Systems, Wiley, New York, 1959.

[5] N. Cohn, Control of Generation and Power Flow on Interconnected Systems, Wiley, New York, 1966.

[6] D. N. Ewart, "Automatic Generation Control--Performance Under Normal Conditions," U.S. ERDA Publication CONF-750867, pp. 1-13, 1975.

[7] F. P. de Mello, R. J. Mills, W. F. B'Rells, "Automatic Generation Control - II: Digital Control Techniques," IEEE Transactions

on Power Apparatus and Systems, Vol. PAS-92, pp. 716-724, 1973.

[8] C. W. Ross, "Error Adaptive Control Computer for Interconnected Power Systems," IEEE Transactions on Power Apparatus and Systems, Vol. PAS-85, pp. 742-749, 1966.

MW Response of Fossil Fueled Steam Units

IEEE Working Group on
Power Plant Response to Load Changes

MW RESPONSE OF FOSSIL
FUELED STEAM UNITS

IEEE Working Group On
Power Plant Response To Load Changes*

INTRODUCTION

The IEEE Working Group on Power Plant Response has been in existence under the joint sponsorship of three IEEE Subcommittees. These subcommittees are the Power Plant Controls Protection and Automation Subcommittee of the Power Generation Committee, the System Controls Subcommittee and Systems Operations Subcommittee of the Systems Engineering Committee. The purpose of the Working Group is to study the subject of power plant MW response characteristics in the context of their role in meeting normal load changes.

The last significant achievement of the Working Group was the preparation of the IEEE Transactions paper in 1965 entitled "Power Plant Response",[1] reporting on the results of a questionnaire sent to the utility industry. Within the past year the Working Group set out as a task the preparation of a paper dealing with MW response of Fossil Fueled Steam Units.

Megawatt response (i.e. the ability of generating units to change Megawatt output in response to changes in power system Megawatt requirements) is an important aspect of power system planning and operation. A study of the possible and probable Megawatt response requirements of a power system and of the capabilities of the available units to singly and collectively respond to these changing system requirements requires an understanding of; 1) system response requirements, 2) the normal response capabilities of the various kinds of units and their associated auxiliaries, and 3) unit operating conditions which may vary or limit the normal unit response capabilities.

The factors which affect response capabilities of units may include:

1. Inherent turbine and turbine control characteristics.

2. Inherent boiler and boiler control characteristics.

3. Characteristics of major plant auxiliary systems.

4. Operating and maintenance practices.

This paper is one of several envisioned by the Working Group on Power Plant Response to clarify the various facets of Megawatt response and, hopefully, provide a uniform basis for future work on this aspect of power system planning and operation.

Some aspects of Megawatt Response are discussed as they pertain to Fossil-Fueled Steam Units. It is hoped that this paper may serve as an inspiration for additional papers for other kinds of units (i.e. hydro, nuclear, gas turbines and combined cycle units) and for additional fossil-fueled steam unit papers on such topics as variations in response with various fuels, operating experiences and test results.

RESPONSE DUTIES IMPOSED BY THE SYSTEM

A key criterion of performance of a generating unit is its ability to change output in response to system needs. These needs may be classified into four major categories as follows:[2]

1. Ability to follow normal daily load changes.

2. Ability to supply replacement power following the loss of generation within the system (tie-line thermal back-up).

3. Ability to participate in frequency regulation.

4. Special needs.

A measure of this ability is the response rate, often expressed in MW/min (megawatts per minute), or in percent of rated capability per minute. When meeting the more rapid system needs; i.e., tie-line thermal backup and frequency regulation, it is recognized that the unit may have the capability to respond quickly over a limited range.

A plot of response rate in percent MW/min versus the number of minutes for which this rate can be sustained, plotted on log-log scales, provides a valuable means of characterizing unit response capability over a broad spectrum.

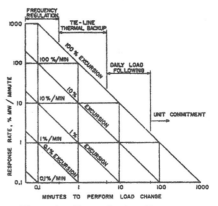

Figure 1. Power System Response Requirements Representation

Figure 1 illustrates these scales. The results of any single test or limitation would appear as a point on this plot. The composite characteristic of a boiler or turbine often can be expressed as a continuous curve on these axes.

Shown on Figure 1 are a set of straight lines which serve as guides to interpreting the unit data. The horizontal characteristic lines are identified as rate limits. Any unit limitation which can be expressed as a limit in rate of response would appear as a horizontal line on these scales. For example, if the MW demand on a unit is prevented from changing faster than 10% per minute, this limitation would appear as a horizontal line along the 10% per minute axis.

The parallel lines slanting downward from left to right are excursion limits. It is apparent that a unit which can change load at 10% per minute for 10 minutes would move through 100% of the capability of the unit; thus the intersection of 10% per minute and 10 minutes is a point on the 100% excursion line, as is 100% per minute for one minute. Similarly, 10% per minute for one minute falls on the 10% excursion line. Thus, any unit limitations which can be characterized as an excursion limit would appear as a line with a -45° slope on these axes. An example might be a restricted range of operation depending upon the number of coal mills operating or the number of burners in service.

The vertical lines may be thought of as separating the various system needs in the time spectrum. These are much more arbitrary than the horizontal and slanted lines, but they do serve to provide additional interpretation into unit characteristic curves which will be plotted on these scales.

Unit Commitment

Generation changes required for times greater than 60 minutes in the future have been arbitrarily designated as beyond the scope of simple regulation or load following and have been categorized as being in the domain of unit commitment. It is assumed that additional units can be brought on the line, or other measures taken, to meet system response needs more than one hour in the future.

Normal Daily Load Following

Times between five minutes and sixty minutes fall in the spectrum of normal daily load following where the basic need for response is to meet the daily load cycle with proper economic allocation between units. Normal maximum rates of change of loads seldom exceed 2%/min. of system peak load.[1] Other factors such as available reserve and economic allocation may require individual units to respond at rates up to 5%/min.

Tie Line Thermal Backup

Response within between about 15 seconds and 5 minutes can be important for tie-line thermal backup.[2,3] This is the time span over which automatic or manual generation control can be of critical importance to maintain tie lines within their thermal limits. Often the normal boiler and turbine lags and governor deadbands are such that it takes about 15 to 20 seconds to start to change generation significantly by means of automatic generation control in response to a major system upset.

Normal Frequency Regulation

The region of normal primary frequency regulation is between three seconds and twenty seconds.[4,5,6,7] It takes about three seconds for a typical governor to arrest a frequency drop caused by a sudden application of load to a system, and by 20 seconds the frequency is restored to the steady-state as indicated by the system frequency response characteristic.[8]

Special Needs

Times faster than 3 seconds fall into the area of phase angle readjustment and transient stability. Although normal speed control action in turbines is too small to affect the phenomena of electrical system transient stability, modern turbine speed control systems have the capability of fast valve shut-off (fractions of a second) provided for the control of turbine overspeed under load rejection.[9,10] If other plant conditions can be met, this capability can be used to advantage to provide a sharp temporary decrease in turbine power upon detection of an abrupt loss in electrical power output such as occurs during faults on the transmission system.[11,12]

A variation of this idea is to accomplish an almost instantaneous reduction of power with recovery to a reduced level compared to initial loading.

This type of action and other run-back actions that might occur due to loss or malfunction in some plants auxiliaries are not within the scope of this paper which deals primarily with the response capability of units to meet load changes, the critical direction being almost always in the increasing direction.

No attempt is made in this paper to quantify the system needs for response, but rather simply to identify the categories. However, in each category, minimum system needs do exist and units which do not meet these minimum needs must have their response deficiency made up by other units which carry their own share as well. System designers must recognize the possibility that the non-performing units may at some time become isolated from the remainder of the system.

To summarize, the set of axes on Figure 1 offers a means of characterizing response characteristics of particular units over a broad spectrum. In general, characteristic curves can be drawn against these axes which indicate limiting response capability under given conditions. Thus, response needs which approach these limiting curves will require the unit to operate in a non-linear mode, while response needs well below the limiting curves can be met with linear response from the unit. The limitations which delineate linear and non-linear response will be subsequently discussed.

GENERATION CONTROL

The means of changing turbine shaft power in conventional steam units in fossil-fired plants are shown in Figure 2.[9,10] The turbine speed control mechanism controls the effective valve area at the high pressure turbine admission in response to error signals between the speed/load reference and the load level corresponding to the incremental gain $(1/R_1)$ multiplied by speed deviation. The actual steam flow to the turbine is primarily a function of the effective valve area and the turbine throttle pressure. In

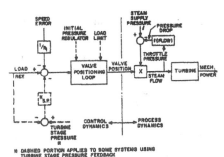

Figure 2. Functional Block Diagram of Turbine Controls

normal system operation, the motion of the valves is directed by:

1. Primary speed control or governing action in response to frequency deviations.

2. Supplementary governor control (or changes in speed/load reference) done manually or by means of automatic generation control.

Primary Speed Control Action

Figures 3A and 3B are helpful to the understanding of the primary speed control function.

Here the power system is represented by one composite inertia M of the interconnected power system, and the composite load frequency (damping) characteristic (change in

load with change in frequency) D.[4] The composite prime-mover incremental regulation is shown as R. Steady-state analysis of such a system shows that, in the linear range, the frequency deviation as a function of the load change and these parameters is

$$\Delta f = \frac{-\Delta L}{(1/R + D)} \qquad (1)$$

where $(1/R + D)$ is the system frequency response (regulation) characteristic. The steady-state contribution of generation change of an individual prime-mover would be

$$\Delta PG = \frac{\Delta L(1/R_1)}{(1/R + D)} \qquad (2)$$

where R_1 is that prime-mover's regulation expressed in the same units as that of the composite system.

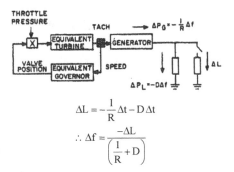

$$\Delta L = -\frac{1}{R}\Delta t - D\Delta t$$

$$\therefore \Delta f = \frac{-\Delta L}{\left(\frac{1}{R} + D\right)}$$

Figure 3a. Effect of Increased Load on Frequency

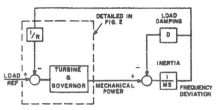

Figure 3b.   Primary Speed
Control or Governing Device

Expression (2) shows that under normal conditions, the magnitude of change due to primary speed control is related to the load disturbance and to the ratio of the unit's regulating characteristic to the interconnected system frequency-response (regulation) characteristic.

Barring major system upsets, the largest likely system load/generation unbalance that could come about in a step fashion would be that due to the loss of the largest unit. In the North American interconnection with 250,000 MW of connected capability, such an event (loss of a 1200 MW unit) would cause a change of generation on individual units of approximately

$$\frac{1200\left(\dfrac{1}{.05}\right)}{250000\left(\dfrac{1}{.05}+1\right)} = 0.4\%$$

if all units were in a linear regulating range, assuming 5% regulation and a load-frequency characteristic of 1. If only a third of the units were to have active primary speed controls, the change in generation on a given unit in regulating range would be

$$\frac{1200\left(\dfrac{1}{.05}\right)}{250000\left(\dfrac{1}{.05\times3}+1\right)} = 1.25\%$$

It is reasonable to expect this normal primary speed control action to be very small although essential for frequency stability of the power system.

During major system upsets, such as system separation, where portions of systems may be left isolated with large unbalances of generation and load, this primary speed control action may be called upon to make large changes within about 5 to 20 seconds. Under such conditions, the rate of opening of the turbine valves may be limited by the available hydraulic force in turbine mechanism. A typical value of this rate limit on opening control valves might be in the vicinity of 10% per second (600% per minute). This value is illustrated on Figure 4 as curve "A". The amount of opening action of turbine valves may be inhibited by the load limit setting, action of the initial pressure regulator, or other action relating to the boiler-turbine control system. Sometimes, the load limit may be set at a given percentage of unit capacity above the existing load level to offer a degree of protection to the boiler and turbine. Curve "B" in Figure 4 illustrates this limitation, assuming the load limit is set 10% above the existing generation level.

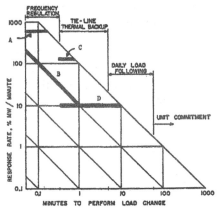

Curve A - 600%/min - Max Rate of Valve Motion
Curve B - 10% Excursion - Representing Load
          Limit
Curve C - 133%/min - Max Rate of Supplementary
          Control Down
Curve D - 10%/min - Max Rate of Supplementary
          Control Up

Figure 4. Limiting Conditions

Area Supplementary Control

The other means of changing generation is through the speed load reference (speed changer motor) done manually or by automatic generation control, also called supplementary control.[8]

In many units, the load reference and, hence, turbine valves, can be made to move through full travel in 45 seconds (133%/min) by manual means. In some modern electrohydraulic turbine control systems, the load reference action is rate limited to 10%/min for generation increases and up to 133%/min for generation decreases. These rates are identified on Figure 4 as curves C and D respectively. Although the capability of changing generation rapidly by manual means exists, it should be noted that when under manual control, it is unlikely that the unit would be subjected to changes in excess of what conditions in the boiler would permit since the operator making the change would be cognizant of the conditions in the plant.

In the automatic generation control mode, the supplementary governor controls are usually adjusted to have maximum rates of change less than ±9%/min.

Supplementary governor control attempts to match area generation to area loads usually considering production economics.[4,13] As previously mentioned, normal maximum rate of change of loads do not impose duties on individual units in excess of 5%/min. However, during contingencies such as the loss of a block of generation, generation in a given area may have to be shifted at maximum rates to relieve loading on tie lines.[6,7,3] The important consideration is not only the rate of change but the duration and therefore the total magnitude of the change. Under these situations response limitations are not only determined by process lags but primarily by permissible deviations and rate of change of process parameters such as temperatures, pressures, levels and corresponding stresses. The past loading history of the unit is also a factor since thermal stresses are a function of temperature variations with time.[14]

EQUIPMENT CHARACTERISTICS

Inherent Turbine and Turbine Control

On some units with electrohydraulic control systems the non-linear effects of valve lift-flow characteristics and boiler pressure effects are largely compensated by means of turbine stage pressure feedback (Figure 2), use of which provides a nearly linear relationship between control error and steam flow.[9,10]

Additional features in the control system are the load limit which is adjustable by the operator and which sets an upper limit to the valve opening, and the initial pressure regulator which superposes a closing action proportional to pressure deviation below a set value, usually 90% of rated pressure. The time lags associated with response of shaft power to changes in effective valve areas are indicated in the transfer function of the turbine (Figure 5). These lags are due to the highly predictable charging times of the volumes in the high-pressure turbine bowl and in the reheater and associated steam leads.

Assuming boiler pressure constant, turbine mechanical power responds to changes in valve position as follows: About 30% of the final change is contributed by the high-pressure turbine upstream of the reheater and is established almost instantaneously while the remaining 70% follows with the more gradual change in reheater

pressure due to the charging time of the reheater volume.[4,5]

Figure 5 shows a response trace of turbine mechanical power to change in valve position for this case of constant boiler pressure.

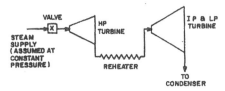

$$\frac{\Delta P_M}{\Delta V} = \frac{(1 + CT_R S)}{(1 + T_S S)(1 + T_R S)}$$

ΔP_M =	CHANGE IN TURBINE MECHANICAL POWER
ΔV =	CHANGE IN VALVE FLOW AREA
C =	FRACTION OF POWER IN HP SECTION (0.25 TO 0.35)
T_S =	BOWL TIME CONSTANT (0.3 TO 0.5 SEC)
T_R =	REHEATER TIME CONSTANT (5 TO 8 SEC)

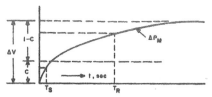

Figure 5. Response of Turbine Shaft Power

Inherent Boiler and Boiler Control Characteristics

Since the steam supply volume is not infinite, boiler pressure does suffer deviations which affect the response of steam flow and mechanical power.

Figure 6 contains an approximate model of a drum-type boiler and controls.[15,16] In general, the same form of a model relating overall pressure, flow and energy input effects can also apply to once-through units.

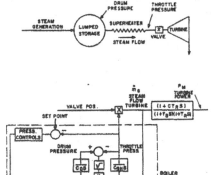

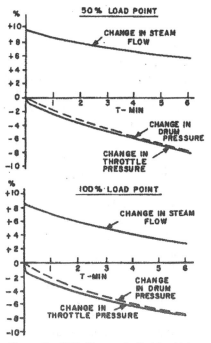

Figure 6. Dynamics of Turbine Power Including Boiler Pressure Effects

Figure 7 shows response traces of steam flow following step changes in turbine valve flow area, assuming no change in energy input to the boiler. In this case, the change in steam flow will be transient as energy is drawn from boiler storage. One can then visualize the contribution to change in steam flow as being from the two causes:

1. due to change in valve flow area

2. due to boiler pressure deviations

The effect of controls applied to the energy supply system (boiler controls) is to restore pressure within response capabilities of the fuel supply system.

Figure 8 shows typical pressure deviation performance representative of fast responding fuel systems (oil and gas) and the slower responding systems such as those in many coal-fired plants.

The prime-mover system and its control methods for changing generation as described previously, is representative of many drum-type steam units and a few once-through units operating in the turbine leading (boiler following) mode.[17,18,6] In this mode, changes in generation are initiated by turbine control valves and the boiler controls respond with appropriate action upon sensing changes in steam flow and pressure. The turbine has access to the boiler's stored energy and generation changes within reasonable magnitudes occur with a characteristic response as previously described. From a system governing point of view, this rapid response characteristic is beneficial, improving the quality of frequency control. Evidently, the rapid response can be at the expense of deviations in boiler variables, especially if the magnitude of the change is large.

Figure 7. 10% Change In Turbine Valve With No Change In Input To Boiler

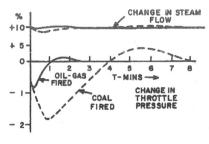

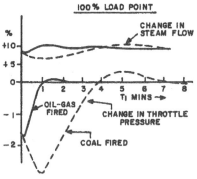

100% LOAD POINT

Figure 8. 10% Change In Turbine Valve Boiler Controls Active

Another mode of control is the boiler leading (turbine following) mode where turbine control valves are made to regulate boiler pressure and changes in generation are initiated by changing inputs to the boiler. The fast action of turbine control valves can accomplish almost perfect pressure control so that boiler pressure can be maintained essentially constant. Under this mode of control, no use is made of the stored energy in the boiler. The power output to the turbine will, therefore, closely follow changes in boiler steam generation as caused by changes in input to the boiler. Figure 9 shows the basic response characteristics of the turbine leading and boiler leading modes. In the former, a change in power generation is accomplished directly by action on the turbine valves. In the latter, a demand for change in power

generation acts on the boiler inputs and the turbine valves respond as the change in energy level is developed in the boiler. The power response is thereby delayed by the lags in the fuel system and boiler storage.

A compromise between the desire for fast generation response and the desire for boiler safety and limitation of deviations of boiler pressures and temperatures led to the adoption of control modes commonly known as coordinated, integrated or direct energy balance, offering an adjustable blend of the two previously described schemes. [6,17,18,19,20] This need for close coordination of the boiler and turbine has been more pressing in the case of once-through boilers where there are more strict requirements for balanced conditions between feedwater flow and firing rate and where there is closer coupling between feed pump and turbine valve than in the case of drum-type units.

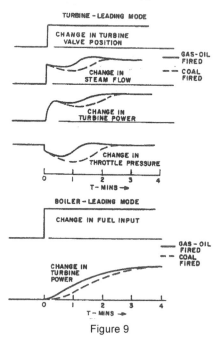

Figure 9

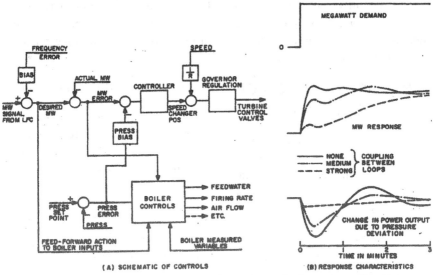

Figure 10. Coordinated Boiler-Turbine Control Used On Some Once Thru Units

The general philosophy of coordinated or integrated boiler turbine controls is described functionally in Figure 10A. A signal indicative of load demand is established by integrating automatic generation control signals. This signal is combined with other inputs to form the unit desired generation used to drive the turbine valves in a closed loop to match actual generation to the desired generation, and to provide feed forward signals to the boiler inputs. The modifications to the load demand signal are:

1. Frequency bias to match the units steady-state speed regulation (governor droop).

2. Pressure error acting to control valves for pressure regulation.

The relative strength of the pressure error introduced in such a scheme determines the response of the unit as shown in Figure 10B. A variation of coordinated controls where the turbine valve is primarily the pressure regulator and boiler inputs are actuated basically from load demand, is to introduce a transient offset in pressure set point from load demand and thereby speed up the response by forcing action.

A more recent evolution is the concept of non-interaction with pressure effects by controlling valve flow area to match demand rather than controlling MW to match demand, and to introduce action in response to pressure error only in the event that pressure error exceeds certain tolerances.[17,20] With such a scheme the unit exhibits response characteristics of the turbine leading mode for limited changes.

The mode of operation with sliding pressure, although not very common, can have a marked effect on the response of units.

CHARACTERIZATION OF RESPONSE

From the point of view of the basic turbine control elements of Figure 2 and their use in supplementary control, these different control methods can be classified as:

1. Systems which behave in a turbine leading manner for small changes, with some limiting action due to pressure error for larger changes.

2. Systems which introduce additional lags to the basic turbine response for small or large changes.

In defining response characteristics, it will be recognized that in addition to the basic process dynamic lags, there are response limitations imposed by operating practice or imposed automatically by rate limiting the demand signal.

Although all the above described factors complicate the definition of response capabilities of boiler turbine units, the characterization of response information may be attempted from the point of view of the two basic means of changing generator output; namely, (1) through primary speed control action, and (2) through supplementary control action.

In each case, identification of response characteristics in the linear range and in the non-linear, or limiting range is desirable.

Primary Speed Control Action

The response capabilities for primary speed control action or governing can best be obtained from test information with step changes in load reference or some equivalent means of obtaining a near step change of turbine valves of approximately 5% in less than 1 sec. The turbine shaft power response is predictable given the boiler pressure deviation under such step changes and given the storage volumes in reheater and high-pressure bowl. Since the intent of the test is to determine the throttle pressure response, the method of implementing the step change (whether via the load reference or the load limit) is not critical as long as the resulting change in valve position occurs in about a second or less. A record of the change can best be obtained from measurement of the change in first stage pressure.

In addition to the time response of this pressure deviation which can be characterized as in Figure 11, the other parameter of importance is the maximum magnitude of the change that the unit will permit without dangerous consequent occurrences (excessive deviations in drum level, temperature, O_2, etc.).[21,22,23,24] Sometimes this maximum excursion in load is limited to less than this critical value by means of the load limit setting.

These limitations should be identified as rate or excursion limits and plotted on the scales of Figure 4.

Referring to Figure 11, the governing response capabilities can be characterized by figures in the following table, covering a small excursion (5%) and the limiting excursion ΔL. For the sake of illustration representative figures are entered for a coal fired unit of moderate size (300-500 MW) at the 75% load level.

First Stage Pressure Response Characteristics		
Initial Load Level	Ramp Rate of About 2%/Min. for 5 Mins.	Maximum Ramp Rate
50% 75%	ΔL, T, ΔL_1, T_1, T_2, T_3	ΔL, T, ΔL_1, T_1, T_2, T_3

Initial Load Level	Pressure Deviation Characteristics for Approximate 5% Load Change				Pressure Deviation Characteristics- Max. Permissible Load Change			
	ΔL % of Rated	ΔP_1	ΔP_2	T_1 Secs.	T_2	ΔL % of Rated	ΔP_1	ΔP_2	T_1 Secs.	T_2
50% 75%	5%	1%	3%	50	180					

In the case of integrated or coordinated boiler-turbine control systems, it is presumed that any action through the turbine primary speed control is sustained through appropriate biasing of the load demand with frequency error, and that such biasing action is not subjected to rate limiting.[6] If this is not the case the resulting effect on response should be recognized and reported.

Supplementary Control Action

Supplementary control action is typically a pulsing type of action which, if sustained, develops into a ramp of the load demand or load reference. Referring to Figure 12, the response may again be characterized by figures in the following table:

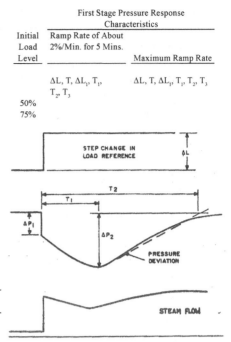

Figure 11. Suggested Measurements for Characterization of Response in Primary Speed Control

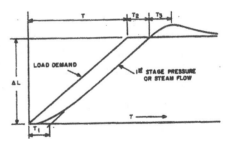

Figure 12. Suggested Measurements for Characterization of Response in Supplementary Control

As indicated in Figure 12, from a practical measurement point of view, the unit response characteristics may be derived from a record of steam flow or first stage pressure.

Several items which should be considered are:

1. For the maximum ramp rate which it is possible to implement by automatic supplementary controls, the duration of the ramp T and, hence, the excursion ΔL which is permissible.

2. Under these response duty conditions, the effective time lag, T_1, between initiation of the load reference ramp and start of the turbine response.

3. Time lag, T_2, between cessation of ramp and time the turbine output (steam flow) changes by ΔL.

4. Overshoot ΔL, if any.

5. Time for the peak of the overshoot, T_2, if applicable.

In addition to these characteristics, which may exhibit non-linear rate limiting effects, it would be valuable to have the response characteristics for a moderate ramp, say of 2%/min for 5 minutes.

The response capabilities of units so determined by tests would represent valuable data which are not presently readily available.[25] The manner in which the tests are conducted is very important. For the supplementary control tests, these should preferably be conducted from the dispatch office without particular warning so that the real operating conditions and constraints are observed.

For instance, as the supplementary controls are made to ramp a given unit, the plant operators should be allowed to react as necessary (place mills on, etc.). If the unit is tripped off control, this fact should be noted along with comments on the reasons and limiting factors.

Some excellent examples of unit response tests have been reported in the literature and can be used to illustrate the interpretation of results. Reference 19 contains results of tests on several coal, oil and gas-fired once-through supercritical units. Figures 13 and 14 are reproductions from that paper and show the response of a 550 MW gas-fired unit for a 65 MW load change at 50 MW per minute and a 165 MW load change at 10 MW per minute. Note that no apparent overshoot on MW response occurred for either test.

Since the boiler variables remained within limits, it is possible to plot these test results on the scales of Figure 1. One point can be plotted at 50/550 = 9.1% per minute for 65/60 = 1.3 minutes. This is point 1 on Figure 15. A second point, point 2 on Figure 15, occurs at 10/550 = 1.8% per minute for 165/10 = 16.5 minutes. If both of these points represent limiting, or nearly limiting conditions on the unit, a straight line connecting these points, as shown dashed on Figure 15, would represent a characteristic limiting curve for the particular unit. It would be helpful to obtain data at intermediate ramp rates as well.

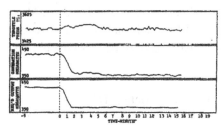

Figure 13. 65 MW Load Change at 50 MW Per Min, 550 MW Supercritical Unit-Gas Fired

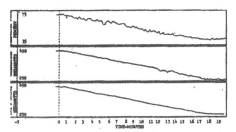

Figure 14. 165 MW Load Change at 10 MW Per Min, 550 550 MW Supercritical Unit-Gas Fired

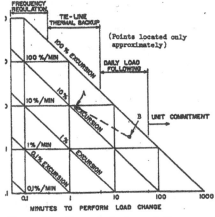

Figure 15. Characterization of Response of 550 MW Gas-Fired Boiler-Turbine

CONCLUSIONS

The IEEE Working Group on Power Plant Response has contributed this paper on the subject of Power Plant Response confined to fossil fired steam units with the following objectives:

1. Illustrate and discuss the many aspects of response, including typical duties imposed by the system and capabilities of units.

2. Suggest common methods of characterizing response which may serve a useful purpose to system planners and operators.

3. Encourage the submission of field test data which may be classified and compared within a common reference frame.

It is hoped that this paper will be followed by several others with theoretical and test data that will define within the framework herein established, the response capabilities of prime movers of all types.

REFERENCES

1. Power Plant Response, IEEE Working Group on Power Plant Response to Load Changes, IEEE Trans., PAS, March 1967, pp. 384.

2. J.B. Tice, "Must Define Requirements to Get Proper Reserve," Electrical World, November 20, 1967.

3. M. Couvreur, "Logic-Adaptive Process for Control and Security in Interconnected Power Systems,"

IEEE Trans., PAS, vol. 87, pp. 1979, December 1968.

4. L.K. Kirchmayer, "Economic Control of Interconnected Power Systems," vol. II, John Wiley & Sons, 1959.

5. C. Concordia, "Effect of Steam-Turbine Reheat on Speed Governor Performance," ASME paper 58-A-36.

6. C. Concordia, F.P. deMello, L.K. Kirchmayer, and R.P. Schulz, "Effect of Prime-Mover Response and Governing Characteristics on System Dynamic Performance," American Power Conference, April 1966.

7. C. Concordia, "Performance of Interconnected Systems Following Disturbances," IEEE Spectrum, vol. 1, pp. 68, 70, 77-80, June 1965.

8. "IEEE Standard Definitions of Terms for Automatic Generation Control on Electric Power Systems," IEEE Trans., PAS, pp. 1358-1364, July/August 1970.

9. M.A. Eggenberger, "Introduction to the Basic Elements of Control Systems For Large Steam Turbine Generators," G.E. Technical Manual, GET-3096A.

10. M. Birnvaun, E.G. Noyes, "Electro-Hydraulic Control for Improved Availability and Operation of Large Steam Turbines," ASME-IEEE, National Power Conference, Albany, New York, September 19-23, 1965.

11. F.P. deMello, D.N. Ewart, M. Temoshok, and M.A. Eggenberger, "Turbine Energy Controls Aid In Power System Performance," Proceedings of American Power Conference, 1966, vol. 28, pp. 438-445.

12. P.G. Brown, F.P. deMello, E.H. Leufest, and R.J. Mills, "Effects of Excitation, Turbine Energy Control and Transmission on Transient Stability," IEEE Trans., PAS, pp. 1247-1252, July/August 1970.

13. N. Cohn, "Control of Generation and Power Flow on Interconnected Systems," John Wiley & Sons, 1966.

14. D.P. Timo and G.W. Sarney, "The Operation of Large Steam Turbines to Limit Cyclic Thermal Cracking," ASME Publication 67-WA/PWR-4.

15. C.C. Young, "Equipment and System Modeling for Large Scale Stability Studies," PICA Conference Paper, Session V, pp. 163, 1971.

16. F. Laubli and F.H. Fenton, "The Flexibility of the Supercritical Boiler as a Partner in Power

System Design and Operation, Part I and II", IEEE Trans., PAS, pp. 1711 and 1719, July/August 1971.

17. D.J. Ahner, F.P. deMello, C.E. Dyer, and V.C. Summer, "Analysis and Design of Controls for a Once-Thru Boiler Through Digital Simulation," ISA Proceedings, 9th National Power Instrumentation Symposium, 1966, pp. 11.

18. T.W. Jenkins, Jr., and B. Littman, "Response Capability in the Control of Large Generating Units," IEEE Conference Paper 71 CP 73 PWR, January 1971.

19. F.H. Fenton, J.V. Pigford, "Rapid Response and Maneuverability are Obtainable from Supercritical Plants," ISA Instrumentation in the Power Industry, vol. 13, 1970, ISA Trans., Vol. 9, #4, 1970.

20. O.W. Durrant, H.D. Vollmer, "Need for a Strategy for Boiler-Turbine-Generator Operation and Control," IEEE Conference Paper 71 CP 244-PWR, January 1971.

21. E.H. MacDonald and J.T. O'Brien, "Unit Response Testing," IEEE Conference Paper 31 CP 65-772.

22. A. Klopfensteion, "Response of Steam and Hydro Generating Plants to Generation Control Tests," AIEE Trans., 1960.

23. D.G. Blodgett, "Performance of Spinning Reserves During System Frequency Transients," IEEE Conference Paper 63-225.

24. K.H. Workman and H.D. Volmer, Jr., "Frequency Response Tests on WH Sammis Plant No. 6 Unit," IEEE Trans., PAS, pp. 1734, July/August 1971.

25. M.A. Eggenberger, "Power Response of Modern Reheat Turbine Generators to Load Dispatching Signals," ASME Trans., 1960.

Automatic Generation Control
Part I - Process Modeling

F.P. de Mello
R.J. Mills
W.F. B'Rells

AUTOMATIC GENERATION CONTROL
PART I - PROCESS MODELING

F.P. deMello   R.J. Mills   W.F. B'Rells

Power Technologies, Inc.
Schenectady, New York

ABSTRACT

In the study and evaluation of Automatic Generation Control, time domain simulations of the power system process and control logic are the only practical method of attack. This paper outlines methods and philosophy of modeling the elements of power systems which have been found useful in simulation studies of Automatic Generation Control.

INTRODUCTION

Automatic Generation Control has evolved rapidly from the time when the function was performed manually, through the days of simple analog systems to the present application of sophisticated direct digital control schemes. Whereas in the past the extent and type of control logic that could be provided and indeed the motivations behind particular control philosophies were largely influenced by the practical constraints of analog hardware, the use of digital computers and high-speed data communication systems today allows a new degree of freedom permitting, through software, the implementation of a wide range of control strategies.

The key to development of improved control strategies lies in the ability to test them on mathematical models of the process and controls.

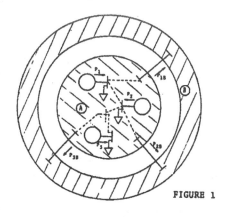

FIGURE 1

TRANSACTIONS PAPER

T 72 598-1. A paper recommended by the IEEE Power System Engineering Committee of the IEEE Power Engineering Society for presentation at the IEEE PES Summer Meeting, San Francisco, Cal., July 9-14, 1972. Manuscript submitted February 17, 1972; made available for printing May 22, 1972.

This paper, which is the first of a group of two papers, presents a description of process models which are representative of the dynamics encountered in Automatic Generation Control and which have been particularly useful in control design studies. The Part II paper will discuss various aspects in the development of digital control logic for Automatic Generation Control.

Modeling of the Power System Process

Models of the Power System Process are necessary for the design and development of control logic. The process of design, of necessity, must be by simulation with trials of different strategies tested on realistic models of the system.

Figure 1 is a schematic of a model system showing a control area 'A' whose generation is represented by three equivalent units.

Area 'A' is tied to a very large interconnected System 'B' through tie lines as indicated. Figures 2 and 3 contain the mathematical block diagram representations of this basic model. As can be seen, the emphasis of representation is on the prime mover systems.

The model is made up of the following parts.

(1) The Electro-Mechanical Subsystem

This is made up of machine inertia load damping the synchronizing coefficients. The model determines the conversion of mechanical power into electrical power and stored energy (frequency change). Inputs are machine mechanical power and connected load. Since the purpose is to study control strategies, an incremental model is adequate.

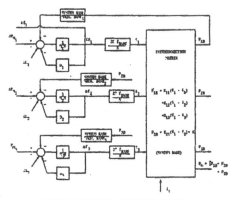

THE ELECTRO-MECHANICAL
SUBSYSTEM
FIGURE 2

The number of inertias representing machines, or groups of machines, the inertia, synchronizing coefficient and damping parameters are chosen to yield frequencies of oscillation in the range of 0.4 Hz to 2 Hz, which is typical of power systems. It is recognized that although these frequencies are beyond the bandwidth of supplementary control effectiveness, they must be considered in evaluation of sampling and filtering requirements.

The philosophy in modeling for this process is to have a prototype that is typical of the phenomena involved. There is no need to model a specific power system duplicating an existing situation since systems are constantly evolving and changing and control strategies should be designed to be insensitive to these changing characteristics. On the other hand, the model should be faithful to an extent that it exhibit typical oscillation effects.

The composition of prime movers should also be representative of different types with varying responsiveness of boiler controls.

(2) The Prime Mover/Energy Supply System

Figure 3 shows the model of the prime mover system including representation of boiler pressure effects. These effects include the long-term dynamics of fuel flow and steam flow on boiler drum pressure. Included also are representations for the combustion controls.

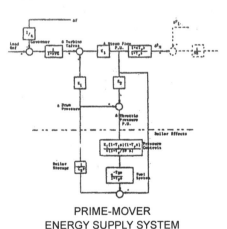

PRIME-MOVER
ENERGY SUPPLY SYSTEM
FIGURE 3

Although the model is basically that for a drum type boiler, similar responses have been observed for once - through boilers and pressurized water reactors. Three different responses were used for the study representing characteristics of coal fired units with poorly tuned (oscillatory) combustion controls, coal fired units with well tuned controls and well tuned gas or oil fired units.

Figure 4 shows the throttle pressure response for these three types for a step in turbine valve. Appendix A lists the constants used for the models. Examination of the constants in Figure 3 shows that the dynamics of the turbine itself, including the charging of the reheater, are fast relative to the boiler effects.

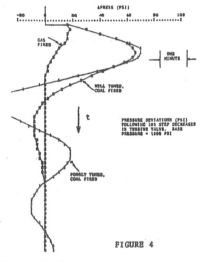

FIGURE 4

(3) Load Reference Actuator

Figure 5 is a block diagram of the load reference and its actuation by means of pulses. The input is a dimensionless pulse and the output has units of per unit load reference on machine base. The gain of the pulse integrator is, therefore, per unit load reference position per pulse. Typical values of this gain are from 0.0005 pu/pulse to 0.003 pu/pulse.

In real plants, the physical equipment represented by this model may vary considerably. In some, the raise-lower pulses are repeated by contact closures which ramp a load reference motor (or electronic integrator). In plants supplied with integrated or coordinated boiler - turbine control systems, the pulses ramp an electronic integrator which develops the demand for the unit. In still other plants, the impulses may be received directly by a turbine control computer (DEH) and the accumulation performed numerically. The essential point is that although the hardware configuration may vary, the functional performance of all these systems are analogous.

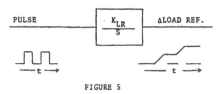

FIGURE 5

(4) Load Disturbance Models

In order to test various control schemes, realistic load disturbance characteristics must be simulated.

Power system load changes may be characterized as being composed of several components:

(a) Fairly slow (0.01 to 0.30 pu/ hour) ramp change in load lasting over many minutes.

(b) Rapidly varying components with no sustained change, but with a typical frequency spectrum. This will be called the "noise" component.

(c) An occasional step change due to disconnection of a unit, loss of a block of load or switching on of a major block of load.

A typical load pattern for an area is shown in Figure 6. Also shown on Figure 6 is the short - term ("noise") variation which is what remains after removal of the sustained change component. "Short - term" describes those components whose frequency spectrum exceeds the bandwidth of effective automatic generation control.

Typical loads for each area can, therefore, be synthesized by adding the actual load trend to the higher frequency components. Appendix B describes a manner of modeling the random component of load.

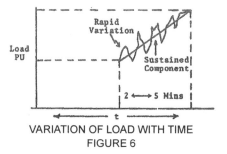

VARIATION OF LOAD WITH TIME
FIGURE 6

Model Responses

An insight into the dynamic behavior of the model can be obtained from a succession of step changes to test out particular subsystems.

The behavior of the electro - mechanical subsystem (machine

inertia and synchronizing coefficient effects) is described in Figure 7 which shows the responses of electrical powers, the tie line power and machine speeds following a step electrical load change applied to machine three with mechanical powers held constant. The simulation was done by numerical methods on a digital computer using a 0.2 second time step which is sufficiently small to approximate the continuous process.

The process of changes in electrical output through a series of oscillations starting from the initial upset to eventually match the mechanical power is apparent in Figure 7. Eventually, all the load change is carried through the ties by the outside world which was assumed infinite for this study.

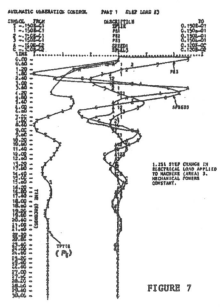

FIGURE 7

The effects of this disturbance, as seen by the boilers is small and of brief duration. Hence, no significant amount of long-term pressure excursions are excited and the system has essentially returned to a steady - state after 30 seconds.

Figures 8 and 9 show the responses, near-term and longer - term respectively, to a step change in the load reference of machine one, which may be considered as the response to a pulse transmitted to the machine with proper account for scaling of magnitudes. Inspection of Figure 8 shows several effects. First, as the load reference of machine one is increased, this results in a speed increase in that machine which integrates into an angle increase and corresponding electrical load increase. The load increase opposes the speed rise and the process is oscillatory with power swings between machines, with periods ranging from 1.5 to 2 seconds for this case. The power output of machine one at first takes a rapid increase (high pressure turbine contribution) and then oscillates about an increasing mean (effect of reheater time constant). The longer term effects in Figure 9 show that since the outside world is infinite, frequency is essentially back to normal and therefore the powers of machines two and three are back to normal to match their mechanical powers. Thus, all the change in power generated by machine one is being transmitted to the outside world (neglecting losses). The long - term behavior of P_{E1} and P_{TIE} reflect the transient behavior of the boiler pressures and combustion control effects which exhibit poor tuning conditions for this unit. Figure 10 shows the corresponding case for machine two with more optimally tuned combustion controls and Figure 11, the case of gas or oil fired unit which, due to much smaller lags in the fuel system, permits better control of pressure.

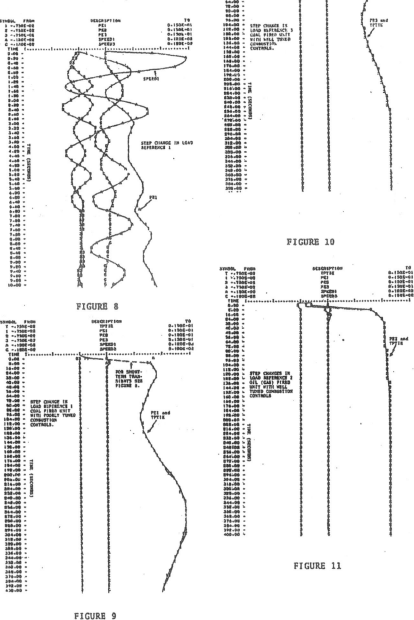

FIGURE 8

FIGURE 9

FIGURE 10

FIGURE 11

CONCLUSIONS

The synthesis of control strategies using the logic capability of digital computers requires evaluation of results by simulation using both deterministic as well as statistical load disturbances. This paper presents examples of models which have been used for the development of such strategies, as explained in Part II of this series. The variables shown are the true quantities rather than measured quantities. Transducer lags and filters should be included in any control design study.

APPENDIX A

Model Parameters

The electro - mechanical subsystem (swing equations) see Figure 2.

Interconnection matrix:

$$|P| = |K| \quad |\delta = \delta_o|$$

$$|K| = \begin{vmatrix} K_{11} & K_{12} & K_{13} \\ K_{21} & K_{22} & K_{23} \\ K_{31} & K_{32} & K_{33} \end{vmatrix}$$

$$= \begin{vmatrix} 6 & 3 & 6 \\ 3 & 3 & 3 \\ 6 & 3 & 9 \end{vmatrix}$$

$M_1 = M_2 = M_3 = 8$

$D_1 = D_2 = D_3 = 1$

System base/Mach$_1$ base = 8

System base/Mach$_2$ base = 4

System base/Mach$_3$ base = 1.6

The Prime - Mover/Energy Supply System (Fig. 3)

1/R	C	T_r	T_G	K_1	K_2	K_3	C_B
6.67	0.3	7	0.5	0.85	0.095	0.92	200

T_D	T_F	K_I	T_J	T_R	
60	25	0.019	90	69	Coal fired - well tuned
74	25	0.025	90	69	Coal fired - poorly tuned
0	10	0.030	26	69	Gas or oil fired

APPENDIX B

Loads for each area were synthesized by adding the actual load trend to a random high frequency component. This random high frequency component was derived as follows.

Obtain a series of normally distributed random numbers having a mean of zero and an appropriate standard deviation. Then process this series through a low pass filter (i.e., exponentially smooth the signal) as shown in Figure 12. Each value represents the signal at model calculation intervals (0.2 second).

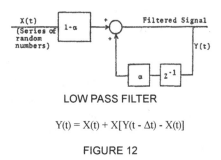

LOW PASS FILTER

Y(t) = X(t) + X[Y(t - Δt) - X(t)]

FIGURE 12

Using this randomly generated load with the filtering constant of α = 0.96, the resulting area control error which includes the dynamics of the electro - mechanical subsystem is shown in Figure 13.

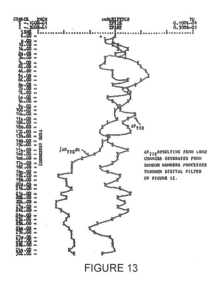

FIGURE 13

Unfortunately, the integral of the random ACE signal has the characteristics shown in Figure 13 where this integral shows that there are long periods of time during which the integral remains away from the zero line. This type of behavior is predicted by the first arc sine law, Reference 6, and is inconsistent with the assumed variation of load shown in Figure 6 where it is assumed that the integral of the high frequency component will oscillate around zero while the long-term variation in the integral of the load is taken into account by the load trend. In order to correct this problem, the signal obtained from the filtering in Figure 12 is corrected to force the integral to zero at frequent, though random, intervals. It consists of the following steps:

A. Choose a rectangularly distributed number, N, between 5 and 20. (N will be the number of signal samples between zero crossings of the integral and is chosen somewhat arbitrarily.)

B. Calculate the integral of the signal from t_o to $t_o + N\Delta t$.

C. If the integral obtained in (B) is not zero, modify the signal samples in this interval according to Y_i (modified) = Y_i (filtered) - (i-1)ε, where ε is chosen such that the integral of the filtered signal will be zero at t - NΔt.

D. Return to Step (A) to obtain another series of signals.

REFERENCES

(1) F.P. deMello, "Process Dynamics in Electric Utility Systems", ISA Paper 505 - 70 presented at the ISA International Conference and Exhibit, October 26-29, 1970.

(2) LK Kirchmayer, "Economic Control of Interconnected Systems", John Wiley & Sons, New York, 1959.

(3) C. Concordia, "Effect of Steam-Turbine Reheat on Speed-Governor Performance", ASME Paper 58-A-36; abstracted in Mechanical Engineering, 81, 95, February, 1959.

(4) C. Concordia, F.P. deMello, L.K. Kirchmayer and R. P. Schulz, "Effect of Prime-Mover Response

and Governing Characteristics on System Dynamic Performance", Proceedings of American Power Conference, 1966.

(5) M.A. Eggenberger, "Power Response of Modern Reheat Turbine Generators to Load Dispatching Signals", ASME Paper 65-WA/PWR-5 Annual Winter Meeting, Chicago, Illinois, November 7-11, 1965.

(6) Feller, "An Introduction to Probability Theory and Its Applications", John Wiley & Sons, Vol. 1, Page 80.

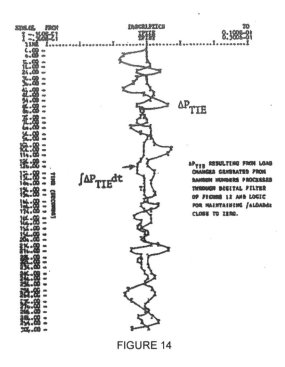

FIGURE 14

Automatic Generation Control
Part II - Digital Control Techniques

F.P. de Mello
R.J. Mills
W.F. B'Rells

AUTOMATIC GENERATION CONTROL
PART II - DIGITAL CONTROL TECHNIQUES

F.P. deMello   R.J. Mills   W.F. B'Rells

Power Technologies, Inc.
Schenectady, New York

ABSTRACT

Techniques are described for the application of automatic digital generation control and for the evaluation of performance from indices which measure the effectiveness of control relative to the control effort. The basic objectives of generation control are reviewed and non - conventional control logic is described with non - linear filtering features designed to be effective in following basic load trends and large deviations while reducing control action in response to the higher frequency random components. Examples of simulations are included.

INTRODUCTION

The application of digital computers in the control of the power generation process has opened a wide range of opportunities for improved control through strategies using the logical and computational capacity of computers.

The functions and objectives of automatic generation control are discussed. Quantitative evaluations of performance are established and tested on models of the power system process and associated controls.

Control logic design is unconventional and is based on educated trials and evaluations. Proper account is taken of the control duty requirements imposed by load changes which typically have random components in a frequency spectrum considerably higher than the bandwidth of supplementary control.

Examples of digital logic used in automatic generation control are given and demonstrated on simulations of the process modeled as explained in Reference 1.

Control Performance Criteria

Generation control in a given area has the following objectives:

(1) Matching area generation changes to area load changes. This is equivalent to control of tie - line interchange to match schedules and control of frequency.

(2) Distributing these changes among generators so as to minimize operating costs,

with due observance of additional constraints such as might be introduced by security considerations.

TRANSACTIONS PAPER

T 72 487-7. A paper recommended by the IEEE Power System Engineering Committee of the IEEE Power Engineering Society for presentation at the IEEE PES Summer Meeting, San Francisco, Cal., July 9-14, 1972. Manuscript submitted February 18, 1972; made available for printing May 22, 1972.

Meeting the first of these objectives is known as supplementary control in which the concept of tie - line bias[2,3,4,5] is almost universally used. In this concept, the Area Control Error (ΔP_{TL} + 10BΔf) provides each area with approximate intelligence as to the location of the load change and directs control action with a minimum of interaction. Addition of the second of these objectives is labeled supplementary control with economic allocation.

When trying to quantify the first of these objectives, that is, the minimization of area control error, one must develop certain performance indices which properly describe the effectiveness of control and the control effort involved. There is a point beyond which control effort is ineffective and even counter-productive, as it may well amplify the control error through action which is out of phase with the effects of the disturbance.

In this regard, speaking in terms of traditional linear control system design techniques, the tuning criteria for generation control must consider the effects of the bandwidth of the disturbances which invariably exceed the bandwidth of the closed loop control system. Evidently, this closed loop cannot be tuned to the criteria of 25% over-shoot and 1/4 decay ratio (Reference 6). It must be more than critically damped or else the control system will cause amplification of the error in the spectrum of the cross-over frequency.

A number of recent efforts to apply optimization theory to the load frequency control problem have been unrealistic, yielding control strategies in simulations fast enough to influence the power-angle swings following load steps. These have been direct results of great sophistication in the mathematics of control optimization but gross inaccuracies in process modeling such as unrealistically small time constants in responses of prime-movers (justified perhaps in the case of non-reheat units) and disregard of non-linearities such as dead-bands and velocity limits.

The statistical nature of the load disturbances which the generation control attempts to follow should be represented in order to evaluate control performance (Ref. 7). The control performance can be characterized by the following indices.

A. Standard deviation of Area Control Error

$$\sigma_{ACE} = \sqrt{\frac{1}{t} \int_0^t \left(ACE(t) \right)^2 dt}$$

or its equivalent in sampled (discrete) form where the sampling rate is high enough to avoid aliasing problems. Using the models in Reference 1, this sampling rate is 0.2 second.

$$\sigma ACE = \sqrt{\frac{\sum_{i=1}^N \left(ACE_i \right)^2}{N-1}}$$

This sampling rate which is dictated by the fidelity required to model digitally the continuous process is not to be confused with the calculating rate for digital control action to be described later.

B. Integral of Area Control Error or its equivalent in discrete form:

$$\int_0^t ACE \ dt \quad \underline{or} \quad \Delta t \sum_{i=0}^{i=N} ACE_i$$

C. Measure of control effort taken as the accumulation of control pulses without regard to sign (raise or lower).

Minimization of these three indices is one measure of control performance.

Digital Control Techniques

With the means for evaluating control performance by simulation, including the effects of random disturbances, the control task involves a number of trials of different strategies and evaluation of results.

Unlike the design of linear and continuous systems which are constrained within the framework of linear differential equations and for which one can apply a number of analytical techniques (frequency response, root locus, optimal control theory), the field of nonlinear digital or discontinuous control is unbounded. Synthesis often relies on inspired common sense and analysis must invariably resort to time domain simulations. At this point a word of caution: The relative ease of implementing almost any conceivable control logic by software should not lead one to the adoption of unnecessarily complex structures. An important consideration will always be the ease with which a given control strategy can be understood and with which its performance can be adjusted by choice of the proper "tuning" parameters. Simplicity will always remain a virtue.

A major benefit possible with digital control logic is through the provision of nonlinear filtering to minimize unnecessary and ineffective control action in response to the higher frequency components of control error. The conventional approach with linear filtering or over-damped tuning of the control loop accomplishes attenuation at the expense of speed response. Non - linear logic can be designed to preserve maximum response capabilities for large and sustained error signals while rejecting control action for the small and high frequency (non-sustained) components of error.

In Figure 1 is shown an approach to generation control taking these principles into consideration. A brief description of the control logic and typical results will illustrate some of the philosophy that is involved.

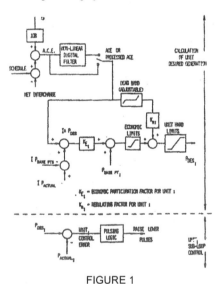

FIGURE 1

The control system can be viewed in two stages. One is the unit sub - loop control whereby an individual unit's generation is brought to match the desired generation for that unit. The other stage involves the determination of individual unit's desired generation based on regulating and economic requirements.

Unit Control Logic

Control action to each individual unit is primarily a function of the unit's control error defined as the difference between desired and actual generation. This permits tuning of control action to the individual unit's dynamic response characteristics and provides unit control without overshoot since control action is in proportion to the error of the quantity being controlled. It also allows a great deal of flexibility in reallocation of generation based on criteria which may require generation shifts other than those required to satisfy incremental demands determined by area control error. Safeguards are provided to assure that control action is not taken in a direction opposite to that called by the system to meet system loads anytime the area control error is in excess of a set amount. If this amount is set to zero, only units with control error of the same polarity as the area control error will receive control pulses. If this condition is met, however, the control pulses will still be proportional to the unit errors.

The ability to reallocate generation on command, independent of the existence of area control error, can be of particular value in automatic implementation of system security measures. For instance, when a transmission system constraint suddenly requires reallocation of generation to avoid thermal over loading of transmission equipment this could be accomplished safely and expediently by a new over-riding "security" dispatch which sets new desired generation values for each unit. Another advantage of individual unit control based on unit control error is that it permits the use of random noise rejection logic on area control error without inhibiting the ability of units to maintain themselves at the desired economic loading level. This noise rejection feature would be harder to implement in systems which rely on the rectification of raise/lower noise in the area control error as the primary mechanism for bringing units to their economic loading targets. An important feature of this system is also that it permits a predictable rate of redistribution of generation whenever an event such as the commitment of a new unit causes a discontinuity in the economic dispatch.

Figure 2 gives an example of unit pulsing logic. At each control actuation time, such as once every two seconds, a decision is made on whether to send no pulse, a short raise or lower pulse, or a long raise or lower pulse. The flow chart has been simplified to exclude logic for detection of "unit not tracking" and additional algorithms and logic to check that the unit does not exceed its permissible sustained rate of change limit.

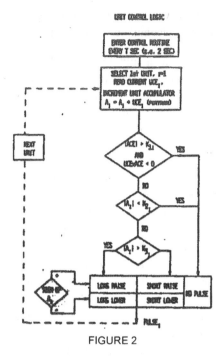

FIGURE 2

First a check is made on whether the area control error is greater than a tolerance K_1. If "no", the program continues with control calculations. If "yes", another check is made on whether the unit control error UE is of the same sign as the area control error ACE. If "yes", then the control calculations proceed. If "no", then control action is by-passed for that unit at that time.

The remaining calculations for unit control involve an accumulation of UCE, and a comparison of this accumulation A with two threshold values K_2 and K_3, with $K_3 > K_2$. If the accumulation A is greater than K_3, then a long pulse is routed through. If $K_2 < A < K_3$, a short pulse is routed. In both these cases, the accumulator is reset to zero. If $A < K_2$, then no pulse is given and the accumulator is not reset.

It should be noted that the technique of accumulating unit errors provides some degree of high frequency noise filtering and is very effective in avoiding unnecessary swinging of units.

Tuning of sub-loops is accomplished first by testing the response of individual unit controls to step changes in desired power. Figures 3 and 4 show typical responses on a greatly magnified scale for the case of the unit with poorly adjusted combustion controls, (Reference 1). The step was 0.025 pu. The threshold value K_2 for the accumulator was 0.01 pu of machine base. Inspection of the plot shows the effect of the accumulation of unit control error and the threshold value K_2. Note that as the unit error approaches zero the pulses are given less frequently although the pulse size remains the same. Note also, in the longer duration plot (Figure 4), the effect of boiler pressure and the control action which holds power close to the desired value in spite of boiler pressure effects.

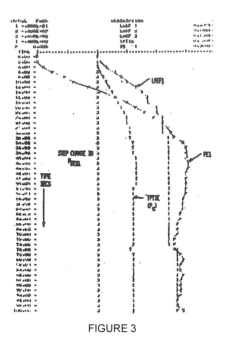

FIGURE 3

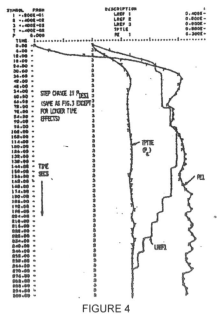

FIGURE 4

Figure 5 is a similar case of step change in desired power for a machine with responsive and well tuned combustion controls (gas or oil fired boiler). The results are essentially the same as in Figure 4 except for a lesser effect of boiler pressure excursions.

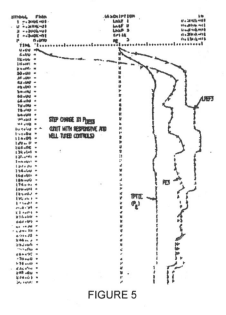

FIGURE 5

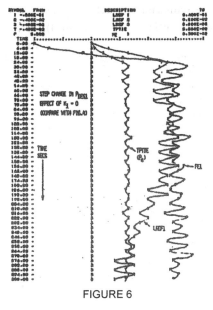

FIGURE 6

Other items of concern are the performance when a unit is taken to its high or low limit, the effect of the tolerance K_2 on pulsing, the effect of filters on the measured values of power, etc.

If there were no dead-band or accumulator on unit control error, there would be a pulse sent every two seconds (except for the rare case when the error is identically zero), see Figure 6. With K_2 a finite amount (about 0.01 pu), the pulsing action is reduced to a small fraction of the time while average power is still maintained at the desired value.

The effect of loop gain defined as the worth of a pulse in per unit of rating is illustrated in Figure 7, where this gain is four times the value used in the case of Figure 4. It is evident that this sub-loop can tolerate wide ranges of gain adjustment without adverse effects.

Figures 8 and 9 demonstrate the effects of selective blocking of control action when the area control error is above a certain value and control action in response to unit error is in a direction to increase the area control error. The need for redistribution of generation can often call for units to move in opposite directions. In Figure 8, due to the fact that the rates of motion of the two units are not the same, the net effect is an increase of area control error. With the selective blocking logic based on the magnitude and direction of area control error, Figure 9 shows the redistribution action without any adverse effects on area control error.

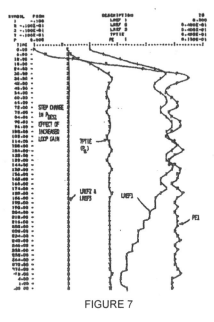

FIGURE 7

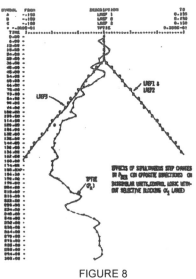

FIGURE 8

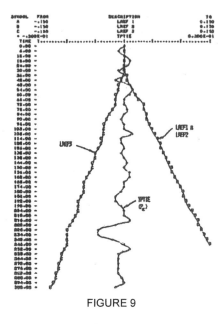

FIGURE 9

Unit Desired Generation

Figure 1 contained a typical calculation scheme to develop desired generation set points for various units under control. The economic participation factors and base points are developed in an auxiliary economic dispatch program run less frequently as loading conditions or the passage of time (e.g., once every five minutes) may dictate.

Disregarding limits, the change in desired generation is computed as the sum of an economic component and a regulating component. The economic component is derived by allocating the total change in desired generation

$$(\Sigma P_{ACTUAL} - \Sigma P_{BASE\ PTS} + ACE)$$

to the various units in accordance with the economic participation factors. The regulating component allocates a portion of the ACE in accordance with regulating factors. A dead-band may be used on this regulating action.

The economic limits are computed in the auxiliary economic dispatch program taking into account the constraints of permissible rate of change. The total unit desired generation is also subjected to the "Hard" limits set for the unit. In some systems, these limits are set at the plant by the plant operators and read into the computer either as telemetered data or manual input.

Random Noise Rejection

In addition to the noise filtering obtainable with the unit pulsing logic, there can be considerable merit in processing the basic input to the control system through filtering logic designed to eliminate unnecessary and ineffective control action thereby accomplishing additional objectives such as minimization of the integral of ACE which, in large measure, can accomplish the minimization of inadvertent interchange. Figure 10 illustrates a simple type of logic which does an effective job of non-linear filtering and reducing the integral of ACE without using integral control.

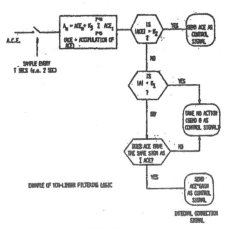

FIGURE 10

The ACE, sampled every two seconds, is sent as an input to the unit control error calculations if it exceeds a threshold value K_2. If not, the magnitude of an accumulator A containing the last sample of ACE added to a gained accumulation of ACE is compared with another threshold value K_1. If the value in this accumulator is smaller than K_1, then no action is taken since it is an indication first, that the ACE is small and second that the integral of ACE is also small requiring no action.

If the value of A is greater than K_1, then another test is made to check the sign of ACE relative to the sign of ΣACE. If their signs are opposite, advantage of this fact is taken to let conditions continue without control action since the existence of ACE will reduce the integral. If the signs are equal, then it is concluded that control action is needed to correct the integral and this is done by sending ACE times a gain factor as the control signal. It should be noted that control action, when sent, is always proportional to the latest sample of ACE rather than proportional to the accumulated ACE. This method of integral correction with proportional control action is inherently very stable and effective.

The performance of this logic is illustrated in a simulation on Figure 11 where, in addition to random noise in loads, a step load is subjected in an area followed by a step in the reverse direction. K_2 was chosen such that in the presence of noise only, the band of ACE would remain below K_2, 90% of the time. K_1 was chosen only slightly larger than K_2 so that the integral of ACE would be forced back close to zero. Magnitude scales have been left out of Figure 11, as they would convey little information without more detailed description of the case in question.

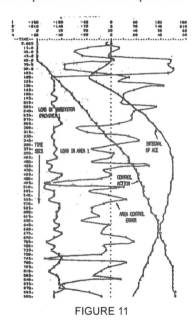

FIGURE 11

Filtering Considerations

A fundamental requirement in digital control is that the sampled signal not contain components of frequencies higher than the sampling frequency, to avoid aliasing problems (Figure 12).

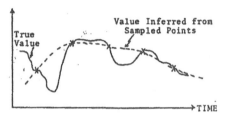

Illustration of Aliasing
FIGURE 12

Evaluation of the effects of filtering can be made using simulation methods as explained in Reference 1. Plots of the results are difficult to interpret and better calculations can be made in terms of performance indices.

These indices are:

(1) Control effort defined as the sum of the absolute values of all pulses given in the duration of a run.

(2) Standard deviation of the true continuous ACE and its integral (IACE).

(3) Standard deviations of the sampled values of $ACE_{SAMPLED}$ and of the accumulation of $ACE_{SAMPLED}$.

Some of these effects are illustrated in the table below.

Run 1 lists the performance of the system subjected to just pure load noise, with no sustained load changes and with all pulsing action blocked. The model was set up without analog filtering on the signals to be sampled. Note that the value of σACE derived from the two second samples is not significantly different from the true value of σACE derived from the nearly continuous measurement (0.2 second calculation interval). The value of σIACE inferred from accumulation of two second samples is 17 times larger than the true σIACE [12.46 versus 0.75]. This is a striking illustration of the effects of aliasing of sampled input signals. High frequency components are aliased into apparent low frequency components thus giving an indication of a false trend. Comparison of σIACE with σACE for the sampled case gives an indication of this effect since the low frequencies are amplified by the integral.

Run 1F was identical to Run 1 except that two second time constant analog filters were included in series with the ideal sensors for the measured quantities. As can be noted, this practically eliminates the aliasing problem.

STANDARD
DEVIATIONS

RUN	CONTROL EFFORT	$\sigma\left[\begin{smallmatrix}\text{SAMPLE}\\\text{ACE}\end{smallmatrix}\right]$	$\sigma\left[\begin{smallmatrix}\text{ACCUMULATION}\\\text{OF SAMPLED ACE}\end{smallmatrix}\right]$	$\sigma\left[\begin{smallmatrix}\text{SAMPLE}\\\text{ACE}\end{smallmatrix}\right]$	$\sigma\left[\begin{smallmatrix}\text{ACTUAL}\\\int\text{ACE dt}\end{smallmatrix}\right]$
1	0	0.99	12.46	1.2	0.75
1F	0	0.33	1.35	1.0	0.75

CONCLUSIONS

The generation control function provides ample opportunities for application of unconventional control techniques using the logic capabilities of digital computers. Examples of such techniques are documented in this paper. Of particular note are the following points:

(1) The power system process is one where the disturbances occur with bandwidths higher than the capabilities of the control system. Hence, it is important that control action not amplify the error components in the critical frequencies.

(2) The criteria for control performance are highly non-linear. The main objective of control is often the minimization of the integral of area control error. The minimization of instantaneous excursions of area control error is not of significance except for large excursions.

(3) Another important objective is the minimization of control effort.

(4) The control strategies that accomplish these objectives can be tested by simulation with the computation of appropriate performance indices that reflect some quantitative measure of the

control objectives. Such simulations should take proper account of the random nature of the load disturbances.

(5) In the use of digital techniques with sampled data, one should be especially careful that the sampled data is representative of the average value of the signal over the sampling period. Unless proper filtering is provided, the control action can easily be directed to correct an entirely false error signal full of aliasing components.

This paper illustrates some of the considerations which should figure in the generation control problem and gives examples of nonlinear control logic found to be effective in accomplishing the control objectives which, of necessity, must remain subjective.

REFERENCES

(1) FP deMello, RJ Mills and WF B'Rells, "Automatic Generation Control, Part I - Process Modeling", companion paper.

(2) N. Cohn, "Some Aspects of Tie - Line Bias Control on Interconnected Power Systems," Transactions AIEE, Vol. 75, Pt. III, pp. 1415-1428.

(3) N. Cohn, "Considerations in the Regulation of Interconnected Areas", IEEE Transactions Power Apparatus and Systems, PAS-86, No. 12, December, 1967.

(4) LK Kirchmayer, "Economic Control of Interconnected Power Systems, Vol. II, John Wiley & Sons, 1959.

(5) N. Cohn, "Control of Generation and Power Flow on Interconnected Systems", John Wiley & Sons, 1966

(6) JG Ziegler and NB Nichols, "Optimum Settings for Automatic Controllers", ASME Transactions, Vol. 64, pp. 769-775, 1942.

(7) CW Ross, "Error Adaptive Control Computer for Interconnected Power Systems", IEEE Transactions, Power Apparatus and Systems, July, 1966.

Dynamic Models for
Fossil Fueled Steam Units in Power System Studies

**Working Group on Prime Mover and Energy Supply
Models for System Dynamic Performance Studies**

DYNAMIC MODELS FOR FOSSIL FUELED STEAM UNITS IN POWER SYSTEM STUDIES

Working Group on Prime Mover and Energy Supply
Models for System Dynamic Performance Studies

SUMMARY

A working group on Prime Mover and Energy Supply Models for System Dynamic Performance studies under the IEEE System Dynamic Performance Subcommittee was established in 1987 to collect technical information on dynamic characteristics of prime mover and energy supply systems that can affect power system performance during and following disturbances such as faults, loss of generation or loads and system separation.

This paper presents an update of models on fossil fired steam turbines including boiler effects and special speed control logic.

It complements a previous IEEE Committee Report (Ref 1) on dynamic models for steam and hydro turbines, expanding the steam turbine models to include special turbine control and boiler effects.

Figure 1 shows the nature of the prime mover system model. The main variable of interest for power system dynamic performance studies is mechanical shaft power P_{mec} which is affected by turbine control valve and intercept valve flow areas and boiler main steam pressure P_T. Generic models are suggested for the subsystems described in the turbine including reheater effects block, and the boiler block.

Examples of speed/load control logic offered by some turbine manufacturers are given as well as descriptions of different types of integrated boiler turbine controls.

The structure of the models, with defined interfaces between subsystems, permits adaptation to specific equipments such as the particular offerings of control logic deferring the control and intercept valve action.

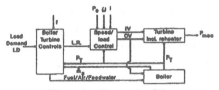

Figure 1. Elements of the
Prime Mover System

DYNAMIC MODELS FOR FOSSIL FUELED STEAM UNITS IN POWER SYSTEM STUDIES

Working Group on Prime Mover and Energy Supply
Models for System Dynamic Performance Studies

ABSTRACT

A working group on Prime Mover and Energy Supply Models for System Dynamic Performance studies under the IEEE System Dynamic Performance Subcommittee was established in 1987 to collect technical information on dynamic characteristics of prime mover and energy supply systems that can affect power system performance during and following disturbances such as faults, loss of generation or loads and system separation.

A principal objective of the working group is to develop prime mover/energy supply models for use in power system simulation programs. The last endeavor in this area was the IEEE Committee report (Ref. 1) in 1973 entitled "Dynamic Models for Steam and Hydro Turbines".

This paper presents an update of models on fossil fired steam turbines including boiler effects and special speed control logic. It does not replace the previous IEEE Committee Report containing much valuable data on turbine models and their parameters. It should be considered as complementary to that reference expanding the models to account for special turbine control and boiler effects.

KEY WORDS

Boiler-Turbine Dynamic Models, Boiler-Turbine Controls.

INTRODUCTION

The response of prime mover shaft power can at times be an important variable affecting the dynamic performance of electrical networks.

In many cases involving the behavior of systems during temporary disturbances such as electrical faults, prime mover power can be considered essentially constant over the few seconds of interest, since speed deviations are small and of high enough frequency (swing modes) not to cause appreciable changes in mechanical power through normal turbine primary speed control. In some cases, however, where provision is made for fast valving or discrete control in response to acceleration, prime mover effects can be significant even if the phenomena of interest span only a few seconds.

Prime mover response over a period of several seconds and few minutes can be significant to system behavior following disturbances resulting in significant imbalance between generation and load.

Paper was prepared by F. P. de Mello (Chairman) with contributions from P. Anderson, J. Doudna, J. H. Fish, III, P.A.L. Hamm, T. J. Hammons, J. D. Hurley, P. Kundur, R. Schulz, G. Tandy, C. W. Taylor and T. Younkins.

Figure 1 shows the functional relationship of the prime mover system in the context of the overall power system. It is the purpose of this paper to detail the model structures that apply to the speed-governing system and turbine and energy system including special control logic and boiler effects for fossil fueled turbines. These model structures should be capable of establishing the dynamic response of the prime mover system's mechanical power over the time span of fractions of a second to a few minutes as might be required to analyze effects of disturbances, especially those that involve significant prime mover control action. Control action can then transcend the normal near linear behavior of governing systems under small perturbations, since overrides such as power load unbalance relays, emergency speed controls, fast valving, initial pressure regulators come into play. An important factor is the steam supply system and its pressure controls. Various modes of coordinated boiler turbine control are in use as are also a

number of implementations of variable pressure operation.

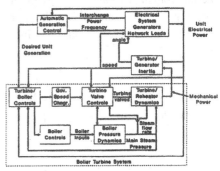

Figure 1. Functional block diagram showing relationship of prime mover system controls to complete system

In Figure 1 the basic process variables that play a role are indicated, as are the equipment modules which define these variables. The electric system performance, (voltages, powers, frequency, etc) is affected by the action of generators, condition of the network and behavior of loads. The prime mover system couples with the electrical system through mechanical power with its effect on generator rotor speed and angle.

The prime mover/energy supply system shown within the dashed line boundaries in Figure 1, responds to commands for generation changes from manual or automatic generation control (AGC) and from speed deviations. Internal plant variables that affect mechanical power, are shown as the turbine valves and boiler main steam pressure.

The turbine control logic operating on control and intercept

227

valves responds mainly to speed deviations. There may be override action from main steam pressure (initial pressure regulator) and electrical power (power load unbalance, fast valving, etc.)

Turbine/boiler controls can be of various kinds, from boiler follow, turbine follow to different types of coordinated boiler/turbine control. The automatic generation control determines the desired unit generation and imparts control action through the governor speed changer or through the turbine boiler coordinated controls.

Although Figure 1 shows the interaction of input and output variables for the case of a unit under full state-of-the-art automatic control there are many units where the control is greatly simplified including operation with many inputs on manual operator control.

A logical approach to the task of modelling such a complex system is to consider the various components as modules and to couple these through the variables that interact. Figure 2 shows the basic structure of the prime mover and energy supply system.

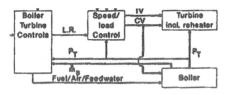

Figure 2. Elements of the Prime Mover Energy Supply System

The turbine/reheater block defines mechanical power as function of main steam pressure (P_T), control valve flow area (CV) and intercept valve flow area (IV). The "Boiler" block models boiler main steam pressure (P_T) and steam flow rate ($\dot{m}s$), as function of turbine control valve flow area (CV) and of fuel, air and feedwater which are essentially the energy inputs to the boiler. The pressure effects of the reheater are included in the turbine model.

The speed/load control block details the turbine control logic in response to changes in speed/load reference (L.R.), speed (ω), main steam pressure (P_T) through the initial pressure regulator, and possibly, in the case of fast valving applications, in response to changes in electrical power (P_e) and generator current (I).

The "boiler turbine controls" block develops the load reference L.R. input to the speed/load controls in response to the load demand (LD) set either manually or by AGC. Other inputs to the control logic, depending on the type of coordinated controls being used, are plant frequency (f) main steam pressure (P_T) and steam flow rate ($\dot{m}s$).

In its simplest form, the boiler and turbine controls are decoupled, with generation changes implemented directly through the load reference (LR) and the boiler controls responding to changes in steam flow ($\dot{m}s$) and pressure (P_T).

Modeling details of the various blocks of Figure 2 are developed in the following sections. As far as possible conventions for block diagram representation in reference 2 have been followed.

TURBINE MODELS

Reference 1 details the various types of turbine systems, ranging from nonreheat, tandem compound single and double reheat, to cross compound single and double reheat.

A general model that would accommodate all types is shown in Figure 3.

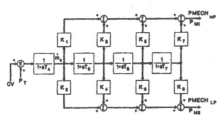

Figure 3. Generic Turbine Model

The coefficients K_1 to K_8 determine the contributions from various turbine sections. In the case of cross compound units the individual shaft mechanical power $PMECH_{HP}$ and $PMECH_{LP}$ must be modeled explicitly. The time constants represent the charging time of various volumes, the most significant of which is the reheater volume. In most cases, the turbine response is adequately modeled by three time constants, the high pressure turbine bowl, T_4, the reheater T_5 and the crossover T_6. The additional time constant T_7 is needed in the case of double reheat units.

The model in Figure 3 includes boiler pressure effects but does not allow for control of intercept valves. An enhancement to the model to accommodate intercept valve control action in the case of reheat turbines is shown on Figure 4 where the intercept valve flow area IV as well as the control valve flow area CV are specified by the speed load control block. Included is a limit on reheat pressure PR_{MAX} to account for safety valve action.

In the above representation, the input variables CV and IV are to be interpreted as flow areas of the control and intercept valves respectively. Any non-linearities between control signals and valve flow areas are assumed to be included in the turbine control logic module.

The parameters K_1 to K_8 representing the contributions to mechanical power of various turbine sections should, strictly speaking, not be constants but functions of stage efficiency and enthalpy drop across the stage. This enthalpy drop in turn is a function of the pressures across the stage.

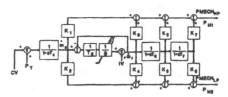

Figure 4. Generic Turbine Model Including IV Effects

For large excursions such as occur with fast valving, a more rigorous representation of the turbine may be necessary. (Ref. 11, 12)

A convenient per unit system that is widely used in power system dynamic performance studies considers base power as the rated MVA of the generator. The parameters K_1 to K_8 can therefore be expressed in terms of mechanical power in per unit of this base MVA. In some programs turbine rated MW is used as base.

TURBINE SPEED/LOAD CONTROLS

In the steam path to the turbine sections there are the main steam stop valves (SV) and the control valves (CV) in series at the admission to the turbine, and the intercept stop (ISV) and intercept control valves (IV) at the admission to the intermediate pressure turbine downstream of the reheater. For a normally functioning control system the stop valves provide merely a backup redundant means of stopping steam flow and therefore need not be modeled. The control logic that governs the positioning of CV's and IV's is very specific to the make and vintage of the particular turbine, although the basic requirements are quite generic.

These general requirements cover speed regulation under normal load change duty (primary speed control) as well as means of limiting overspeed for the more drastic events such as a partial or full load rejection. Whereas for the normal load change and primary speed control duty it is customary to use control valves with straightforward proportional control on speed error, the limitation of overspeed for the more severe disturbances involves both IV's and CV's often using very fast closure such as provided by spring loaded mechanisms. The controls thus have non linear and discrete characteristics based on the degree of measured acceleration or other signals indicative of acceleration.

The turbine speed/load control model can usually be generic when limited to normal primary speed control and normal supplementary load control (AGC). For problems involving large accelerations enlisting the discrete and nonlinear actions provided in the particular design, the speed/load control block should be defined by the manufacturer. The basic outputs to be defined are the CV and IV flow areas. The inputs to the particular logic could be speed, acceleration, electrical power, generator current, etc., depending on the particular design.

Reference (1) contains approximate mathematical representations for typical mechanical hydraulic (MHC) and electrohydraulic (EHC) speed governing systems. These continue to be useful for a large class of problems. In accordance with the conventions used in reference (13), the block diagrams should indicate the type of limiting action as windup or non windup.

Figure 5 is extracted from reference (1) with the proper annotation for non windup limiting action.

Recognizing that it is not possible to incorporate into one generic model the many variations of control logic in various makes and vintages of turbines, there is still value in describing some specific examples.

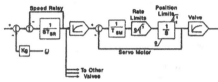

Figure 5. Approximate Representation of Mechanical-Hydraulic Speed Governing System

MHC Systems (GE)

The block diagram in Figure 6 shows typical control logic for General Electric's MHC systems. However as noted in Reference 2, from which the block diagram of Figure 6 is derived, there can be variations in overspeed control features for individual units.

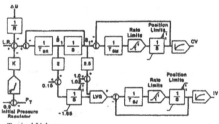

Typical Values
R = 0.06 p.u.
T_{SR} = 0.05 - 0.15 sec   Position Limits CV 1, 0
T_{SM} = 0.15 - 0.25 sec   Position Limits IV 1, 0
T_{SI} = 0.2 - 0.25 sec
Rate Limits CV = 0.2, -0.6
Rate Limits IV = 0.2, -0.5

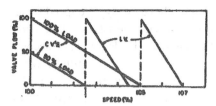

Figure 6. MHC System (GE)

An explanation of the block diagram of Figure 6 follows. A hydraulic servo, called the speed relay, develops an output proportional to the load reference signal LR less any contribution from speed deviation ($\Delta\omega$) through the primary speed control gain (1/R). The response time constant of the speed relay is labeled T_{SR} and the rate of change of the servo output S_1, is called S_1.

The control valves flow area, a function of valve position is shown to follow the speed relay output S_1 through a servo piston with a time constant T_{SM} subject to rate limits and position limits.

The intercept valves are controlled by a servo piston with time constant T_{SI} subject to rate and position limits, following the lower of two signals through a low value gate (LVG). As indicated in Figure 6, these signals are derived from S_1 (acceleration) and command to control valve S_1.

In the steady state S_1 is zero, hence the signal out of the integrator to the LVG should normally be at the upper limit of 1.02 p.u.

The signal to the LVG derived from S_1 is shown to be (1.0+ 2.5 S_1).

This implies a steady state speed versus flow area characteristic for the CV and IV as indicated in Figure 6. To account for the possibility of nonlinear valve/flow area characteristics, function generators are included in the block diagram of Figure 6.

If the rate of change of the speed relay signal is large enough in the negative direction, the IV could transiently respond in the closing direction to help limit the overspeed.

Typical values for the parameters of the block diagram are also listed in Figure 6.

EHC Systems (G.E.)

In addition to the speed control as provided in MHC systems and described in Figure 6, EHC systems have two features: the IV trigger and the power/load unbalance (PLU) relay.

The IV trigger will fast close the IV's whenever load is greater than 0.1 p.u. and the control error signal to the IV servovalve is greater than 0.1 p.u. in the closing direction. This translates into a speed deviation of $\Delta\omega$ > 0.05 (L.R.) + 0.002 p.u. Following the IV trip, the IV servovalve control will be blocked for one second, following which time the IV servovalves are free to respond to speed control.

The power/load unbalance relay is designed to fast close the control valves (CV) and (IV) upon detection of load rejections. Figure 7 shows the logic based on a mismatch between the average of the 3 generator phase currents and reheat pressure, which is indicative of the steady state generation level.

The PLU relay logic is shown schematically in Figure 7. This circuit trips during load rejections whenever generator three phase current, I_{30}, decreases faster than a preset rate, and turbine power exceeds I_{30} by preset amount (0.4 p.u.). Turbine power is indicated by cold reheat pressure ψ_R; and the rate of current decrease limit is established with a washout time constant, T_1, as shown in Figure 7. The circuit will reset only when $\psi_R - I_{30} <$ 0.4 p.u. The use of current rather than generator electrical power prevents the circuit from tripping during temporary power system faults, since under fault conditions the current will increase temporarily rather than decrease.

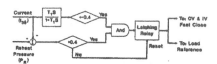

Figure 7. Rate Sensitive Power Load Unbalance Relay

When the PLU relay trips: all CV's and IV's will fast close completely by tripping; the load reference will be removed from the CV and IV control signals and the load reference will run back toward a minimum value at a rate of about 2.2%/sec. About one second after tripping, all CV's and the IV will respond to their respective control signals. However, the load reference portion of these signals will not be restored until the PLU relay resets, at which point the load reference runback stops and the load reference remains as its then present value.

Figure 8 shows the block diagram for the EHC (G.E.) system. The positioning command to the CV is developed by the LR less speed deviation times the gain 1/R. The initial pressure regulator can introduce action in the closing direction if main steam pressure falls below the initial pressure regulator set point (0.9). The IV's respond to overspeed in the same manner as in the MHC systems with the flow speed characteristic as in Figure

function is sometimes provided to improve transient stability on partial loss of load such as could occur following a close-in fault. This function has generally been referred as fast valving.

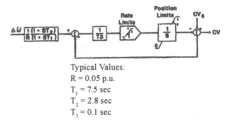

Typical Values:
R = 0.05 p.u.
T_1 = 7.5 sec
T_2 = 2.8 sec
T_3 = 0.1 sec

Rate Limits = -0.5 (closing), -0.4 (opening)

Note: The typical values for T_1 and T_2 assume that the turbine impulse stage pressure feedback is in service.

Figure 9. DEH Controls (Westinghouse)

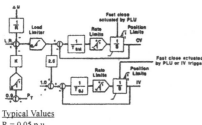

Typical Values
R = 0.05 p.u.
T_{SM} = 0.1 - 0.2 sec
T_{SI} = 0.1 - 0.2 sec
Time to fast close = 0.15 sec
Rate limits CV = -0.2, 0.1
Rate limits IV = -0.2, 0.1

Figure 8. EHC Control Logic (GE)

DEH Control System (Westinghouse)

Figure 9 shows the block diagram for the normal speed control function of the Digital Electro-Hydraulic controls of Westinghouse.

In addition to the normal speed control function, an overspeed protection controller is provided to prevent overspeed on complete loss of load. A "close intercept valves" (CIV)

The CIV function is based on a mismatch between turbine mechanical power and electrical load. The turbine reheat pressure located on HP exhaust on fossil units and LP inlet on nuclear units is compared to generated electrical power. If they differ by an adjustable setpoint, the CIV action is set.

CIV causes the intercept valves to close in approximately 0.15 seconds. If the generator breaker remains closed, this condition is detected as a partial load loss. The interceptor valves remain closed for a period of time (or usually from 0.3 to 1.0 seconds). After the time delay the intercept valves reopen. For the CIV action to occur again 10 seconds must elapse and turbine pressure and MW must be approximately equal. Closing the intercept valves provides a momentary reduction in a generator output and aids in maintaining power system stability.

On complete loss of load, the "load drop anticipator of overspeed" function causes rapid closure of control and intercept valves. This action is triggered when turbine power is greater than 30% and the generator breaker opens.

The overspeed action causes rapid control and intercept valve closures when turbine speed is equal to, or greater than, 103 percent of rated speed. The intercept valves are opened when the speed drops below 103 percent and an elapsed time of 5 seconds following breaker opening occurs. Since the breaker open condition causes the Reference to reset to rated speed, the speed error signal of the normal speed control loop holds the governor valves closed until the speed decreases to rated speed. At this time, the governor valves opens to maintain rated speed.

Turbine Controls (NEI Parsons, Ltd.)

In the UK, on the part of the two major manufacturers, the introduction of EHC systems was carried out in a manner which gave a fast opening as well as a fast closing capability of the steam valves. This enables "fast valving" actions to be implemented by injecting a relatively simple demand signal into the electronic systems, without necessitating special hardware such a dump valves in the valve control mechanisms. This has enabled models with relatively simple adaptations to serve in this area.

While it may be impractical to include models that represent variations on the same theme, one of the features stressed in UK controls is accounting for deadband, which could be present due to imperfections of mechanical equipment or which could also be deliberately introduced to avoid excessive movement of steam valves due to continuous system frequency deviations avoiding consequential perturbations to the boiler controls. Figure 10 shows two types of deadband, with and without hysteresis. The other feature is to account for transducer and filters in the speed measurement.

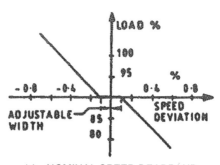

(a)   NOMINAL SPEED DEADBAND

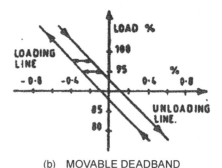

(b)   MOVABLE DEADBAND

Figure 10.   Types of Deadband

Figure 11 shows a turbine control model for typical its manufactured by C. A. Parsons including the effect of overspeed limiters which bypass the main droop setting and provide strong closing action to limit overspeed under load rejection conditions. Also shown is the speed versus CV flow area characteristic.

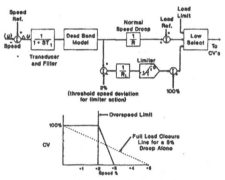

Figure 11. Examples of Parson's Controls

There are also a number of intercept valve sequencing systems sometimes including bypass valves. From a modeling point of view, any of these schemes can be easily programmed and it seems logical to break out the turbine control logic functions as separate modules whose inputs are speed, load reference, and other specific variables such as generator current, power, etc. as used in particular implementations.

BOILER MODELS

The process physics of a boiler can be visualized from the schematic in Figure 12 showing an equivalent lumped volume storing steam at an internal pressure labeled drum pressure in series with superheater and steam leads with their friction drop effects.

The energy input to the boiler, which is primarily the heat released in the furnace, generates steam in the waterwalls ($\dot{m}\omega$).

The distributed nature of the process is approximated by a couple of lumped storage volumes connected through an orifice representing the friction pressure drop effects through superheater and steam leads. By far the larger storage is in waterwalls and drum containing saturated steam and water. In once through units the bulk of the storage is in the transition region (high specific heat).

Also shown in Figure 12 is a low order nonlinear boiler model defining pressure and main steam flow effects as a function of turbine control valve area CV and energy input to the boiler.

As indicated, throttle pressure P_T in the storage volume defined by the constant C_{SH} is proportional to the integral of flow in ($\dot{m}$) minus flow out ($\dot{m}_s$) of the volume. Flow into the storage C_{SH} and out of the storage C_D, ($\dot{m}$) is obtained as proportional to the square root of pressure difference between the two volumes. Drum pressure P_D is developed as proportional to the integral of the difference between steam generation ($\dot{m}_w$) and steam flow out of the volume ($\dot{m}$).

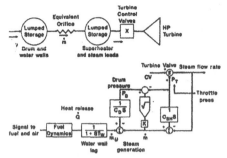

Typical Values

T_w = 5 to 7 sec	C_V = 1 at full load
C_D = 90 to 300 sec	O at no load
C_{SH} = 5 to 15 sec	K = 3.5

Typical Fuel Dynamics

$$\text{Coal} \rightarrow \frac{\xi^{-408}}{1+308} \quad \text{Oil and gas} \rightarrow \frac{1}{1+58}$$

Figure 12. Model of Boiler Pressure Effects

Steam generation $\dot{m}_w$ follows the heat release in the furnace with a time lag due to the heat capacitance of the water wall metal. Finally the response of heat release in the furnace to a command for a change in energy input to the boiler is very much a function of the fuel system dynamics. For oil or gas fired boilers, these dynamics are relatively fast, representative of fuel valve and air damper response times. For coal fired units it can be quite slow reflecting the lags in the coal feeder and pulverizer process.

The nonlinear nature of the boiler process is due principally to the square root relationship between pressure drop and flow and to the fact that steam flow is proportional to the product of control valve flow area CV and throttle pressure P_T.

In general, the same form of a boiler model relating pressure, flow and energy effects can also describe the response of once through units.

Figure 13 shows the inherent response of steam flow and boiler pressures to a change in turbine control valve flow area with no changes in energy input to the boiler. In this case, the change in steam flow will be transient as energy is drawn from boiler storage. One can then visualize the contribution to change in steam flow as being from the two causes:

1. Due to change in valve flow area.
2. Due to boiler pressure deviations.

Typical parameter values are listed on Figure 12. In general, due to the need for larger furnaces in coal fired units their storage time constants C_0 are larger than for oil or gas fired units. It is relatively easy to conduct tests such as those in Figure 13 and 14 to derive the model parameters for a specific unit.

In conventional boiler control systems changes in turbine control valve act as the disturbance to the process and the ensuing restoration of energy input to match the demand for steam is provided by control action based on pressure error and sometimes by a combination of pressure error and steam flow, or combination of pressure error and valve flow area.

Figure 14 shows typical pressure deviation performance representative of fast responding fuel systems (oil and gas) and the slower responding systems such as those in many coal-fired plants.

Boiler Turbine Controls

The prime-mover system and the control method for changing generation as described previously, is representative of many drum-type steam units and a few once-through units operating in the boiler following mode. In this mode, changes in generation are initiated by turbine control valves and the boiler controls respond with appropriate action upon sensing changes in steam flow and pressure. The turbine has access to the boiler's stored energy and generation changes within reasonable magnitudes occur with a characteristic response as previously described. From a system governing point of view this rapid response characteristic is beneficial, improving the quality of frequency control. Evidently, the rapid response can be at the expense of deviations in boiler variables, especially if the magnitude of the change is large.

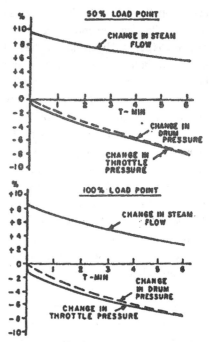

Figure 13. 10% Change in Turbine Valve - With No Change in Input to Boiler

Another mode of control is the boiler leading turbine mode where turbine control valves are made to regulate boiler pressure and changes in generation are initiated by changing inputs to the boiler. The fast action of turbine control valves can accomplish almost perfect pressure control so that boiler pressure can be maintained essentially constant.

Under this mode of control, no use is made of the stored energy in the boiler. The power output to the turbine will, therefore, closely follow changes in the boiler steam generation as caused by changes in input to the boiler. Figure 15 shows the basic response characteristics of the turbine leading and boiler leading modes. In the former, a change in power generation is accomplished directly by action on the turbine valves, whereas in the boiler leading mode the power response is delayed by the lags in the fuel system and boiler storage. A compromise between the desire for fast generation response and the desire for boiler safety and limitation of deviations of boiler pressures and temperatures led to the adoption of control modes commonly known as coordinated, integrated or direct energy balance, offering an adjustable blend of the two previously described schemes. This need for close coordination of the boiler and turbine has been more pressing in the case of once-through boilers where there are more strict requirements for balanced conditions between feedwater flow and firing rate and where there is closer coupling between feed pump and turbine valve than in the case of drum-type units.

The general philosophy of coordinated or integrated boiler turbine controls is described functionally in Figure 16A, (9). A signal indicative of load demand is established either manually or by integrating automatic generation control signals. This signal is combined with other inputs to form the unit desired generation used to drive the turbine valves in a closed loop to match actual generation to the desired generation, and to provide feed forward signals to the boiler inputs. The modifications to the load demand signal are:

1. Frequency bias to match the units' steady-state speed regulation (governor droop).

2. Pressure error acting to control valves for pressure regulation.

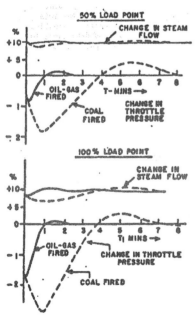

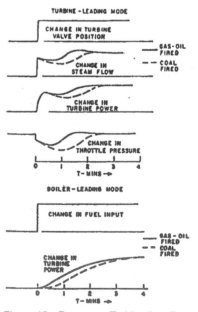

Figure 14. 10% Change in Turbine Valve Boiler Controls Active

Figure 15. Response Turbine Leading and Boiler Leading Modes

The relative strength of the pressure error introduced in such a scheme determines the response of the unit as shown on Figure 16B. A variation of coordinated controls where the turbine valve is primarily the pressure regulator and boiler inputs are actuated basically from load demand, is to introduce a transient offset in pressure set point from load demand and thereby speed up the response by forcing action.

A more recent evolution is the concept of noninteraction with pressure effects by controlling valve flow area to match demand rather than controlling MW to match demand, and to introduce valve control action in response to pressure error only in the event that pressure error exceeds certain tolerances. With such a scheme the unit exhibits response characteristics of the turbine leading mode for limited changes.

Figure 17 shows a generic Boiler-Turbine Control model structure that can accommodate practically any mode of coordinated control.

The MW demand signal, either developed manually or by AGC, is biased by frequency error to match the turbine governor droop characteristic forming the desired MW for the unit. This MW desired signal is biased by pressure error. The actual measured MW is subtracted from the pressure biased MW desired signal to form an error which integrates into a change in the Turbine Load reference L.R. The pressure error bias can be put through a dead band if desired. The bias coefficient K_D can also be made adaptive (proportional to load reference). Instead of control of MW, the MW desired signal may also be interpreted as a load reference demand in which case K_M would be set to zero and K_L set to unity. In this case, there would be no need for a frequency bias K_F.

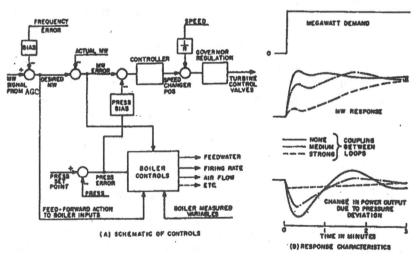

(A) SCHEMATIC OF CONTROLS

(B) RESPONSE CHARACTERISTICS

Figure 16. Coordinated Boiler-Turbine Control Used on Some Once Through Units and Drum Units

The boiler control portion can accommodate any degree of control action from complete boiler follow to complete turbine follow by appropriate setting of the parameters in the various blocks. The model would also be capable of representing variable pressure control modes.

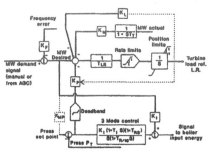

Figure 17. Generic Boiler Turbine Controls

CONCLUSION

The primary objective of this working group paper is to present prime mover/energy supply models limited to fossil fired steam units for use in power system dynamic performance studies.

While ideally it would be desirable to present models of all types and vintages of boiler-turbine systems and their controls, practical considerations dictate against trying to achieve this goal in one paper.

The prime mover systems and controls have been presented within a structure that can accommodate a variety of types and philosophies of controls. This structure is shown in Figure 2 as consisting of subsystems, some of which can be described by generic models and others that may

have to be tailored to the specific application.

A subsystem under the generic category is the turbine model including reheater developing mechanical power from three input variables, control valve flow area, CV, intercept valve flow area, IV and boiler main steam pressure P_T.

Another component susceptible to treatment by a generic model is the boiler with inputs from fuel/air/feedwater, and control valve flow area (CV) and outputs as main steam pressure (P_T) and steam flow (ṁs). These two subsystems can thus be integrated into one boiler turbine generic model.

Less susceptible to generic treatment, is the subsystem labeled speed/load control. Typical turbine control logic offered by some manufacturers has been described at a level that supports model definition. The basic outputs of this subsystem are the IV and CV flow areas. Inputs to the model are the speed/load reference (LR) speed, boiler pressure and other special inputs such as generator current, electrical power.

A logical remaining subsystem is that labeled Boiler Turbine Controls whose outputs are commands to the turbine load reference and to the energy inputs to the boiler. Inputs to this model are load demand, (LD) main steam pressure (P_T), steam flow (ṁs) and plant frequency. Models defining commonly used boiler turbine controls have been presented with provision, depending on the setting of constants, for a wide range of control modes and response adjustments.

The effects of abnormal voltage and frequency on auxiliary equipment and hence on boiler/turbine response are not included in these models. Some guidance is provided in reference 15.

REFERENCES

1. "Dynamic Models for Steam and Hydro Turbines in Power System Studies," IEEE Committee Report. Transactions In Power Apparatus & Systems, Vol. 92, No. 6, Nov./ Dec. 1973, pp. 1904-1915.

2. Task Force on Stability Terms and Definitions, "Conventions for Block Diagram Representation", IEEE Trans. on Power Apparatus and Systems, Vol. PWRS-1, No. 3, August 1986.

3. L.H. Johnson and T.D. Younkins, "Steam Turbine Overspeed Control and Behavior During System Disturbances," Transactions In Power Apparatus & Systems, Vol. 100, No. 5, May 1981, pp 2504-2511.

4. F. P. de Mello and D. N. Ewart, "MW Response of Fossil-Fueled Steam Units", IEEE Working Group on Power Plant Response to Load Changes," IEEE Transactions on Power Apparatus and Systems, Vol. PAS-92, No. 2, March/April 1973, pp. 455-463,

5. Hughes, F. M., "Improvement of Turbogenerator Transient Performance by Control Means," Proc. IEE, Vol. 120, No. 2, Feb. 1973, pp. 233-240.

6. Dent, F. G., "Microgovernor - A Replacement of Existing Large Steam Turbine Governing Controls," IEE Conference on Refurbishment of Power Station Electrical Plant, Nov. 1988, Conference Publication No. 295, pp. 128-132.

7. Ham, P. A. L., "The Application of Digital Control to Turbine-Generators," ibid, pp. 138-142.

8. Ham, P. A. L. and Green, N. J., "Developments and Experience in Digital Turbine Control," IEEE Transactions on Energy Conversion, Sept. 1988, Vol. 3, No. 3, pp. 568-574.

9. Concordia C. de Mello, F, Kirchmayer, L. and Schultz, R, "Effect of Prime-Mover Response and Governing Characteristics on System Dynamic Performance," American Power Conference, 1966, Vol. 28, pp 1074-85.

10. Hammons, T. J., Fleming, R. J. and Ewer, M. H., "Bibliography of Literature on Steam Turbine-Generator Control Systems,"

IEEE Committee Report, IEEE Trans. on Power Apparatus and Systems, 1983, Vol. PAS-109, (9), pp. 2959-2970.

11. Hammons, T. J., Fleming, R. J. and Ewer, M. H., "Update of Bibliography of Literature on Steam Turbine-Generator Control Systems," IEEE Committee Report, IEEE Trans. on Energy Conversion, 1988, Vol. EC-3, (3), pp. 560-567.

12. Kundur, P, Beaulieu R.E., Munro, C. Starbuck, P.A., "Steam Turbine Fast Valving: Benefits and Technical Considerations." Canadian Electrical Association - Position paper ST 267, March 24-26, 1986.

13. Younkins, T.D., Kure-Jensen, J. et al, "Fast Valving With Reheat and Straight Condensing Steam Turbines," IEEE Transactions Power Apparatus and Systems", Vol. PWR S-2, No. 2, May, 1987.

14. IEEE Committee Report, "Excitation System Models for Power System Stability Studies", IEEE Transactions on Power Apparatus and Systems, Vol. 2, February 1981.

15. Schulz, R.P., Turner, A.E., and Ewart, D.N., "Long Term Power System Dynamics", Report to EPRI for RP90-7, Vol. I, June 1974, Vol. II, October 1974.

Boiler Models for System Dynamic Performance Studies

F.P. de Mello

BOILER MODELS FOR SYSTEM DYNAMIC PERFORMANCE STUDIES

F. P. de Mello, Fellow

Power Technologies, Inc.
P.O. Box 1058
1482 Erie Boulevard
Schenectady, New York 12301-1058

ABSTRACT

The dynamic response of boiler pressure is a mass-volume-energy balance relationship which can be derived from changes in turbine valve position and boiler energy input. The response characteristics so derived are compared with more simplified models which preserve the essential nonlinear characteristics of the process. It is shown that the dominant influence on the pressure response comes from the pressure controls tuning.

Errors in modeling the steady state response of the boiler itself are neutralized by the controls.

The use of simplified boiler models in power system dynamic performance studies is justified.

KEYWORDS

Boiler-turbine response, boiler-pressure control, boiler-models.

INTRODUCTION

The dynamic response of boilers can be of importance in predicting the behavior of power systems through upsets involving significant imbalances between generation and loads beyond the 3-5 second time period considered in typical transient stability simulations. Simplified models of the steam generating process have been suggested to account for pressure effects on the response of steam turbines[1].

A boiler model based on first principles of mass, energy and volume balance is derived to lend insight on the parameters that figure in the model. The relations apply to a drum-type boiler. Typical parameter values used are for a 270 MW, 2400 psi coal-fired unit[2].

The model is limited to pressure/flow effects. The saturation characteristics of water/steam are the dominant energy storage contributors. Storage in superheaters is considered from the mass, volume, and pressure effects of superheated steam assuming constant temperature.

The validity of the simplified models is established with comparisons of their response characteristics against those obtained with the more rigorous solution of the physics from first principles. Methods of deriving the parameters of the simplified models are given.

The Boiler Process

Figure 1 is a schematic of the boiler process.[3] Steam generated in the waterwalls is separated in the drum from where it flows through the primary and secondary superheaters on to the high pressure (HP) turbine. It then re-enters the boiler to the reheater where its energy level is increased. It flows through the intermediate and low pressure turbine to the condenser.

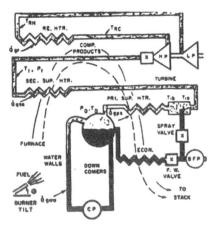

Figure 1.   Boiler Process

The combustion products path is also shown. The waterwalls absorb radiant heat in the furnace. The hot gases leaving the furnace transfer heat by radiation and convection to the secondary superheater, reheater primary superheater and economizer in succession.

Constant volume circulating pumps maintain an essentially constant rate of circulation through the downcomers and waterwalls.

Desuperheating spray water is introduced between the primary and secondary superheater sections for control of main steam temperature.

In this design burner tilts are used to control reheat temperature and the firing rate is used to control pressure while feedwater flow is controlled to maintain drum level. The modeling considers pressure/flow effects only.

Referring to Figure 2, the relations defining the process dynamics for this subsystem are based on the following assumption:

(1) Feedwater at enthalpy h_{fw} and flow rate $\dot{m}_w$ mixes with saturated water from drum and the mixture flows down the downcomer at a constant recirculation rate $\dot{m}_r$. In natural circulation boilers the buoyancy head versus head loss due to friction drop characteristics also tend to maintain a constant recirculation.

(2) Heat absorbed by fluid in waterwalls is uniformly distributed i.e. proportional to length or volume.

(3) Velocities of steam and water are assumed equal.

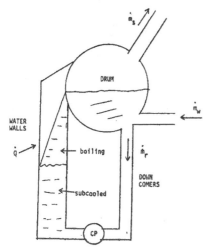

Figure 2. System Defining Steam Generation and Pressure

For the system with boundaries shown on Figure 3, the following equations apply:

Mass Balance

$$d/dt\,[M_f + M_{SC} + M_g] = \dot{m}_w - \dot{m}_s \qquad (1)$$

where

M_f = Mass of saturated liquid in waterwalls and drum

M_{SC} = Mass of subcooled liquid in waterwalls

M_g = Mass of saturated vapor in waterwalls and drum

$\dot{m}_w$ = feedwater flow rate

$\dot{m}_r$ = recirculation flow rate

$\dot{m}_s$ = steam flow rate out of drum

Volume Balance

$$(M_f + M_{SC})\,v_f + M_g v_g = V \qquad (2)$$

where

vf = specific volume of saturated water

vg = specific volume of saturated steam

V = volume of waterwalls and drum

Energy Balance

$$\frac{d}{dt}\left[M_f h_f + M_{sc}\frac{(h_f + h_r')}{2} + M_g h_g - \frac{144V}{J}P_D\right]$$

$$= \dot{Q}_w + \dot{m}_r h_r'$$

$$- (\dot{m}_r - \dot{m}_w)\,h_f$$

$$-\dot{m}_s h_g \qquad (3)$$

where

h_f = enthalpy of saturated water

h_r' = enthalpy of water entering waterwalls

h_g = enthalpy of saturated steam

P_D = drum pressure

$\dot{Q}_w$ = heat transferred from tubes to fluid in waterwalls

Variables to be solved are: M_f, M_g, M_{SC}, P_D, h_r and h_r' given as inputs $\dot{m}_w$, $\dot{m}_s$, $\dot{m}_r$, $\dot{Q}_w$.

M_{SC} is calculated as proportional to the volume required to heat the incoming fluid from h_r' to h_f. Since $\dot{m}_r$ is constant, this translates into being proportional to $(h_f - h_r')/\dot{Q}_w$. A small time constant is used to represent residence time effects. The block diagram defining the calculation of M_{SC} is shown in Figure 4 where the subscript "o" denotes the variables' quiescent values. T_{SC} is the residence time of the subcooled fluid, approximately equal to $M_{SC}/\dot{m}_r$.

Calculation of hr and hr1

The enthalpy of water entering the downcomers is obtained from the mixing equation:

$$h_r = \frac{(\dot{m}_r - \dot{m}_w)h_f + \dot{m}_w h_{fw}}{\dot{m}_r} \qquad (4)$$

where h_{fw} is the enthalpy of feedwater. The enthalpy of the water entering the waterwalls h_r^1 is the same as h_r delayed by the transport time in the downcomers which is approximated as a time constant (Figure 5).

Equations (1) and (2) can be expressed as

$$M_f + M_g = \int (\dot{m}_w - \dot{m}_s)\,d_t - M_{SC} = A \qquad (5)$$

and

$$M_f v_f + M_g v_g = V - M_{SC} v_f = B \qquad (6)$$

from which $M_f = (Av_g - B)/(v_g - v_f)$ (7)

and $M_g = (B - Av_f)/(v_g - v_f)$ (8)

Equation (3) can be expressed as

$$M_f h_f + M_g h_g - \frac{144V}{J}P_D = \int(\dot{Q}_w + \dot{m}_r h_r^1$$

$$- (\dot{m}_r - \dot{m}_w)\,h_f$$

$$- \dot{m}_s h_g)dt$$

$$- M_{SC}\left(\frac{(h_f + h_r^1)}{2}\right)$$

$$= C \qquad (9)$$

or $P_D = \dfrac{J}{144V}\left[-C + M_f h_f + M_g h_g\right]$ (10)

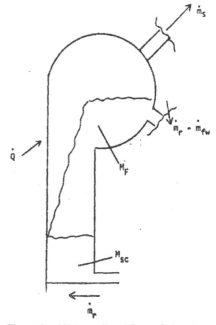

Figure 3. Waterwall and Drum Subsystem

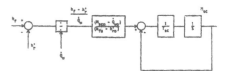

Figure 4. Computation of Subcooled Resident Mass

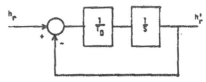

Figure 5. Computation of Enthalpy at Waterwall Inlet

Saturated steam properties, v_f, v_g, h_f, h_g, are all functions of P_D. For the range of 2300 to 2800 psi, approximate expressions are:

$vf = 0.02934 - 0.0078 \, (P_D/1000) + 0.003 \, (P_D/1000)^2$

$vg = 0.52968 - 0.22085 \, (P_D/1000) + 0.0245 \, (P_D/1000)^2$

$hf = 684.2 - 93.5 \, (P_D/1000) + 45 \, (P_D/1000)^2$

$hg = 1083.3 + 116.5 \, (P_D/1000) - 45 \, (P_D/1000)^2$ (11)

Calculation of Heat Flux From Tubes to Fluid in Waterwalls

The heat flux from tubes to fluid $\dot{Q}_w$ is assumed to be proportional to the temperature difference between metal and fluid. Temperature of the fluid is basically a function of drum pressure. Figure 6 shows the relations in block diagram form.

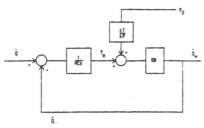

Figure 6. Computation of Heat Flux from Tube Metal to Fluid

where

MC = heat capacitance of waterwalls
KW = heat transfer coefficient between tubes and inner fluid
$\dot{Q}$ = heat flux from furnace to waterwalls

Storage in Superheaters

The effect of superheater volume is considered assuming temperature is constant. The distributed nature of the process is approximated as in Figure 7 with three lumped volumes linked by orifices to represent pressure to flow squared, the pressure flow effects are modeled by the following set of algebraic and differential equations:

$P_D = P_1 + (\dot{m}_3)^2 K_1 \quad P_1 = P_2 + (\dot{m}_{12})^2 K_2$

$P_2 = P_3 + (\dot{m}_{23})^2 K_3$ (13)

$\dot{m}_T = K_v P_3$ (14)

where K_1, K_2, K_3 are coefficients relating pressure drop to flow rate square, K_v is proportional to turbine valve flow area, and the symbol P denotes pressure at the volume denoted by the suffix.

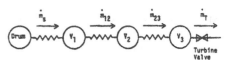

Figure 7. Lumped Representation of Superheaters

Flow rates between volumes are calculated from the continuity equations

$$\dot{m}_{23} = \dot{m}_T + V_3 \frac{\partial \rho_3}{\partial p_3} \frac{dP_3}{dt} \quad \dot{m}_{12} = \dot{m}_{23} + V_2 \frac{\partial \rho_2}{\partial p_2} \frac{dP_2}{dt}$$

$$\dot{m}_s = \dot{m}_{12} + V_1 \frac{\partial \rho_1}{\partial p_1} \frac{dP_1}{dt}$$ (15)

where

V_1, V_2 and V_3 are the volumes of the lumped superheater sections and ρ_1, ρ_2, ρ_3 are the densities of steam in these volumes.

Calculation of Drum Level

Defining

$$M_{fd} = \text{mass of liquid in drum}$$

$$V_D = \text{volume of drum}$$

Volume of waterwalls occupied by the steaming mixture =

$$(V - V_D) - M_{SC}*V_f \quad (16)$$

The proportion of this volume occupied by liquid is

$$1 - \frac{\dot{m}_{ws}V_g}{2\left((\dot{m}_r - \dot{m}_{ws})(v_f + m_{ws}v_g)\right)} \quad (17)$$

where

$$\dot{m}_{ws} = \text{steam generation}$$

$$= \dot{m}_s + \frac{dM_q}{dt} \quad (18)$$

Mass of saturated liquid in waterwalls

$$M_{fww} = \frac{1}{v_f}(V - V_D - M_{SC}V_f)\frac{\dot{m}_r v_f + \dot{m}_{ws}(v_g/2 - v_f)}{\dot{m}_r v_f + \dot{m}_{ws}(v_g - v_f)} \quad (19)$$

Mass of fluid in drum $M_{fd} = M_f - M_{fww}$ (20)

Change in drum level

$$DL = \frac{(M_{fd} - M_{fdo}) \times v_f}{DA} \quad (21)$$

where DA = drum cross section area

The Computation Scheme

The computation of the above set of nonlinear algebraic and differential equations is done by numerical integration and differentiation methods as well as iterative solution of simultaneous algebraic relations.

Figure 8 is a flow chart of the computation steps implemented on a PC. Not shown is the initialization of states which can be derived from the equations, setting derivatives of states equal to zero for the given operating condition defined by a given turbine valve opening and throttle pressure.

A, B and C are functions of states (outputs of integrators) as defined in relations 5, 6, and 9. In the flow chart, the numbers in brackets refer to the equations used to calculate the particular variables.

Results

The above equations were solved for a boiler with the following basic data defined for full load operating conditions of 480 lbs/sec steam output at 2400 psi, 1000°F.

$$V_{ww} = 2850 \text{ cu ft}$$

$$V_D = 950 \text{ cu ft}$$

$$V_1 \frac{\partial \rho_1}{\partial p_1} = 3.8, \ P_1 = 2550$$

$$DA = 270 \text{ sq. ft.}$$

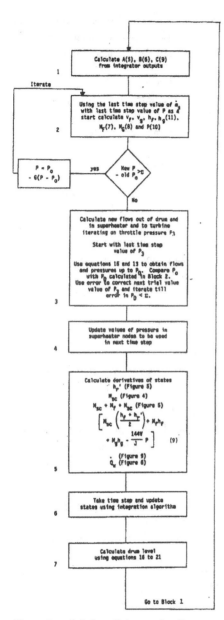

Figure 8. Solution Scheme for Process Equations

$$V_2 \frac{\partial \rho_2}{\partial p_2} = 2.5, P_2 = 2460$$

$$V_3 \frac{\partial \rho_3}{\partial p_3} = 1.0, P_3 = 2400$$

$$\dot{m}_r = 2000 \text{ lbs/sec, } P_D = 2640$$

The boiler response characteristics to step changes in turbine valve flow area and heat flux are illustrated in Figures 9 and 10 with feedwater flow put on control from drum level with a simple proportional and integral control.

$$K_p = 100 \text{ lbs/in}$$

$$-K_I = 0.1 \text{ lbs/in}$$

Figures 9 and 10 show the response of pressure, steam flow and drum level for step changes in turbine valve flow area and heat flux respectively around the full load and half load operating points.

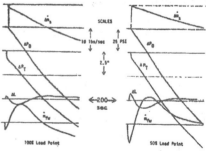

Figure 9. 2% Step Change in Valve Flow Area

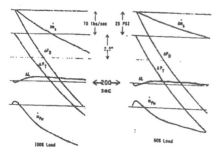

Figure 10. Step Change in Heat Flux

k_w	=	waterwall heat transfer coefficient BTU/sec°F
C_D	=	main component of boiler storage PSI/lb
C_{SH}	=	equivalent component of boiler storage lumped at turbine end. PSI/lb
K	=	friction drop coefficient lb/sec x /PSI 1/2
CV	=	turbine control valve flow area lb/sec x PSI
CM	=	metal capacitance BTU/°F
K_M	=	steam generation per BTU lb/BTU
K_T	=	$\partial T_{sat}/\partial P_{sat}$ °F/PSI
KH	=	$\partial [h_g - h_{fw}]/\partial P$ BTU/PSI

Examination of the pressure response in Figure 9 reveals an interesting effect of pressure on steam generation. Basically this is a positive feedback effect, as less BTU are needed to generate steam with increases in pressure level.

Inspection of the boiler response characteristics in Figures 9 and 10 suggests a simple model shown on Figure 11 which is essentially similar to that presented in Figure 6 of reference 1 except that the positive feedback effect from pressure on steam generation has been included.

The process of heat transfer from metal to inner fluid in the waterwalls is through temperature difference between metal and inner fluid. Metal temperature is obtained from integration of heat flux into and out of the tube walls divided by the tube heat capacitance.

The steam generated from a given amount of heat flux is influenced by the drum pressure through a multiplying effect as noted in Figure 11.

The parameters of this model are defined as follows:

The storage constant ($C_D + C_{SH}$) can be defined as the change in mass of steam stored in waterwalls, drum, and superheaters and steam leads per change in drum pressure. The contribution to this storage constant from superheaters is approximated as

$$\sum V_1 \left.\frac{\partial \rho_1}{\partial p_1}\right| T$$

where V_1 is the superheater section volume and

$$\sum V \left.\frac{\partial \rho_1}{\partial p_1}\right| T$$ is the partial density with respect to pressure at an average constant temperature in the section.

The contribution from the waterwalls and drum (C_D) containing saturated fluid is more complicated and can be derived from considering the system as in Figure 12 where M_f and M_g are the resident masses of saturated water and steam respectively.

The small perturbation form of the mass balance, volume balance and energy balance equations for this subsystem are:

$$\frac{dM_f}{dt} = \Delta \dot{m}_s - \frac{dM_g}{dt} \qquad (22)$$

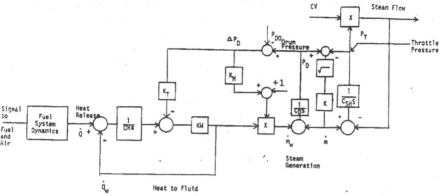

Figure 11. Simplified boiler model with pressure effect on steam generation

$$V_{go} \frac{dM_g}{dt} + M_{go} \frac{\partial v_g}{\partial p} \frac{dP}{dt} + v_{fo} \frac{dM_f}{dt} + M_{fo} \frac{\partial v_f}{\partial p} \frac{dP}{dt} = 0 \quad (23)$$

and

$$\Delta \dot{Q} - \Delta \dot{m}_s h_{go} - \dot{m}_{so} \frac{\partial h_g}{\partial p} \Delta P$$

$$= M_{go} \frac{\partial h_g}{\partial p} \frac{dP}{dt} + h_{go} \frac{dM_g}{dt} + M_{fo} \frac{\partial h_f}{\partial p} \frac{dP}{dt}$$

$$+ h_{fo} \frac{dM_f}{dt} \quad (24)$$

Solution of these equations for $\Delta \dot{m}_s \backslash dP/dt$ yields the storage factor

$$\frac{\Delta \dot{m}_s}{\frac{dP}{dt}} = C = \frac{\left[M_{go} \frac{dP_g}{dP} + M_{fo} \frac{dP_f}{dP} - \frac{(h_{go} - h_{fo})}{(V_{go} - V_{fo})} \left(M_{go} \frac{dV_g}{dP} + \frac{dV_f}{dP} \right) \right]}{\left[h_{go} + \frac{h_{fo} V_{go} - h_{go} V_{fo}}{V_{go} - V_{fo}} \right]} \quad (25)$$

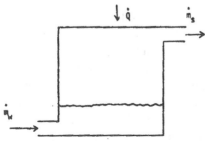

Figure 12. Saturated Water and Steam System

The most significant term in the numerator of the expression is

$$M_{fo} \frac{\partial h_f}{\partial p}$$

hence the larger the resident mass of saturated water the greater is the storage factor.

The validity of expression (25) was checked through a number of simulation runs using the full solution of the equations outlined in Figure 8. The storage constant C was determined through solving for the rate of change of pressure for a given change in flow out of the boiler.

An additional 30% to 35% of storage can be attributed to the superheaters. Thus the storage constant for a typical 2400 psi coal-fired boiler in the range of 300 MW would be in the order of 180 sec.

For an oil or gas-fired unit the storage time constant would be in the order of $120 \approx 150$ sec because of the smaller furnace and waterwall volume used in designs for those types of firing.

Use of the Simplified Model

One of the problems with use of models is obtaining the proper model parameters.

Referring to the simplified model of Figure 11, there are nine basic boiler parameters to be derived. Expressing these in per unit, the constants C_D and C_{SH} will be in units of seconds. Although $(C_D + C_{SH})$ can be derived from the physical dimensions and characteristics of the boiler and use of first principles of mass balance, energy balance etc. as illustrated in this paper, a more practical approach is to derive the parameters from simple tests and from knowledge of the boiler steady state performance characteristics.

$(C_D$ and $C_{SH})$ can be derived from the initial rate of change of drum pressure following a change in steam flow out of the boiler. For instance if for a 2400 psi boiler, a step change in turbine valve position results in a 2% change in steam flow, and the initial rate of change of drum pressure is recorded as 16 psi/min, the constant

$$(C_D + C_{SH}) = \left(\frac{16}{2400 \times 60 \times .02} \right)^{-1}$$

$$= 180 \text{ seconds}$$

with the variables, pressure and steam flow, expressed in per unit of rated. Experience has shown that splitting the total storage constant $(C_D$

$+ C_{SH})$ as 10% for C_{SH} and 90% for CD yields a good approximation to the boiler pressure response.

The parameter K is obtained from a knowledge of the pressure drop between drum and admission to the turbine. For instance if at full load ($\dot{m}_s$ = 1 pu) the drum and throttle pressures are 2640 and 2400 psi respectively, then

$$k \sqrt{\frac{2640 - 2400}{2400}} = 1.0 \quad \text{or} \quad K = 3.16$$

The parameter K_T relates the change in saturation temperature with pressure. Keeping the temperature as degrees F and pressure in per unit

$$K_T = \frac{\partial T}{\partial p} \times 2400$$

K_T typically for a 2400 psi unit (drum pressure around 2640 psi) = 0.057 x 2400 = 137.

Typically K_W can be estimated from the assumption of 25°F drop for full load steam generation. Hence

$$K_W = \frac{1}{25} = 0.04$$

The value of heat capacitance CM can be obtained from the mass of water wall tubes multiplied by specific heat of metal. From experience with modeling of boilers it is found that the effective time constant of heat transfer from waterwalls to inner fluid is in the order of 7 seconds. Hence CM/KW = 7 or CM = 0.7.

$$K_H = \partial[hg - h_{fw}]/\partial P$$

For a 2400 psi unit with enthalpy at the economizer outlet of 560 BTU/lb $K_H = -0.12$, BTU/lb psi.

In per unit

$$K_H = \frac{-0.12}{520} \times 2400 = -0.55$$

where $520 = h_{go} - h_{fwo}$.

Using these parameters in the model of Figure 14 yields the responses to turbine valve step and heat release step changes as in Figures 13 and 14 which correspond very closely to those in Figures 9 and 10 obtained from the more elaborate modeling of the process physics.

Response With Pressure Control

Assuming that the fuel system dynamics are characterized by a dead time of 20 secs in series with a time constant of 30 secs

$$\frac{\Delta Q}{\Delta s} = \frac{\varepsilon^{-20s}}{1 + 30s}$$

a three mode control (proportional, integral and rate) operating on pressure error, properly tuned for the process lags, yields the responses to step changes in turbine valve in Figure 15 using the detailed model and in Figure 16 using the simplified model.

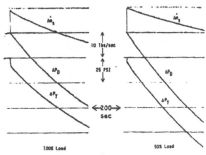

Figure 13. Step Change in Valve Flow Area for Model of Figure 11

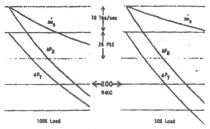

Figure 14. 2% Step Change in Heat Flux for Model of Figure 11

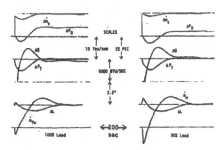

Figure 15. Detailed Model with Pressure Control 2% Step Increase in Valve Flow Area

The controller function is

$$\frac{K_I(1 + T_I s)(1 + T_R s)}{s\left(1 + \dfrac{T_R}{10\ s}\right)}$$

with $K_I = 0.04$, $T_I = 100$ sec, $T_R = 30$ sec.

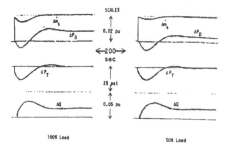

Figure 16. Simplified Model With Pressure Control 2% Step Increase in Valve Flow Area

One notes that the simplified model's response is almost identical to that of the more detailed model.

A Simpler Model

The pressure-temperature effect on steaming rate (K_T) in the block diagram of Figure 11 is a transient effect and not very significant. The pressure-enthalpy effect on steaming rate (K_H) affects the steady state gains between valve flow area and pressure and between heat flux and pressure.

Since control effects with integral action can neutralize variations in steady state process gain, the control performance of boiler pressure under changes in turbine valve flow area is basically the same where the effects of K_T and K_H are ignored in the block diagram of Figure 11. The model is then identical to that of Figure 6, reference (1) and is shown in Figure 17.

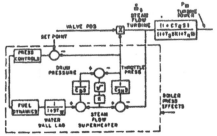

Figure 17. Dynamics of Turbine Power Including Boiler Pressure Effects

Figure 18 shows the response of this model to a step change in valve flow area with no change in energy input. The parameters in this model were the same as those used in the model of Figure 11 except for the elimination of the constants K_T, K_H, M_C and K_W and the introduction of T_W = 7 sec as the water wall time constant.

One notes that the differences between the response of this model and those of the previous two models lie in the steady state gain.

The responses with pressure controls with same settings used with the previous two models are shown in Figure 19. By comparing these with those in Figures 15 and 16 one concludes that the simpler model of Figure 19 is quite valid when used together with pressure controls.

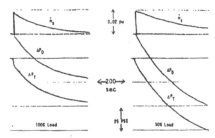

Figure 18. Model as in Figure 17 Without Pressure Controls

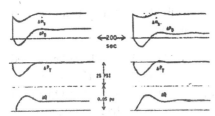

Figure 19. Model of Figure 19 With Pressure Controls 2% Step Change in Valve Flow Area

CONCLUSIONS

In certain studies of power system dynamic performance, steam turbine mechanical power response including boiler pressure effects may be significant, requiring the modeling of the steam supply system. This paper has demonstrated the validity of simplified boiler models that have previously been used to represent these effects.

Boiler response characteristics derived from modeling of the basic energy balance, mass balance and volume balance relations using physical boiler parameters were compared with those obtained from two other simplified models, one which matched both the steady state and transient open loop boiler response characteristics and a simpler model which matches the initial open loop response. It is shown that both simplified models yield acceptable results when used to yield the boiler response including pressure controls.

Suggestions are made on how to derive parameters to be used with these models.

A partial list of references in boiler modeling and control is also cited (4-10).

REFERENCES

1. F. P. de Mello and D. N. Ewart, "MW Response of Fossil Fueled Steam Units, IEEE Working Group on Power Plant Response to Load Changes", IEEE Transactions on Power Apparatus and Systems, Vol. PAS-92, No. 2, March/April 1973, pp. 455-463.

2. F. P. de Mello, D. N. Ewart and W. M. Stephens, "Simulation as a Design Tool for Plant Jack McDonough Boiler Controls", ISA 7th National Power Instrumentation Symposium Proceedings, 1964, pp. 35-46.

3. F. P. de Mello, "Plant Dynamics and Control Analysis", IEEE Transactions on Power Apparatus and Systems, Paper 63-1401, 1963, Vol. S82, pp. 664-678.

4. Durrant, O. W. and Loeser, J. K., "Boiler-Turbine Control System for Application to Universal Pressure Boilers", IEEE Conference Paper CP63-1410, ASME-IEEE National Power Conference, Cincinnati, Ohio, September 22-25, 1963.

5. Profos, P., "Dynamics of Pressure and Combustion Control in Steam Generators", Sulzer Technical Review, V37, No. 4, 1955, pp. 1-15.

6. Chien, K. L., Ergin, E. I., Ling C., and Lee, A., "Dynamic Analysis of a Boiler", ASME V 80, December 1958, pp. 1809-1819.

7. McDonald, J. P. and Kwatny, H. G., "A Mathematical Model for Reheat Boiler-Turbine-Generator Systems", IEEE Paper 70 CP221-PWR, PES Winter Power Meeting, New York, New York, January 25-30, 1970.

8. Ahner, D. J., de Mello, F. P., Dyer, C. E and Summer, V. C., "Analysis and Design of Controls for a Once-Through Boiler Through Digital Simulation", Proc. 9th National Power Instrumentation Symposium, Detroit, May 16-18, 1966.

9. de Mello, F. P. and Imad, F. P., "Boiler Pressure Control Configurations", IEEE Paper CP31, IEEE Winter Power Meeting, New York, New York, January 29-February 3, 1967.

10. Anderson, P. M., "Modeling Thermal Power Plants for Dynamic Stability Studies":, Book Cyclone Copy Center, Ames, Iowa 1974.

F. P. de Mello graduated with a B.Sc and M.Sc degrees in Electrical Engineering from MIT in 1948.

In 1948 he joined Rio Light and Power and Sao Paulo Companies in Brazil and for the next seven years held positions of increasing technical responsibility in system planning and design studies.

From 1955 to 1969, he worked in the General Electric Company Electric Utility Engineering Operation where he specialized in studies of dynamics and electrical machines, excitation control, prime-mover systems, overall power systems and boiler dynamics.

Mr. de Mello joined Power Technologies, Inc. at the time of its formation in August of 1969 as a Principal Engineer, Dynamics and Control. He was appointed Vice President in 1973.

He is presently a Principal Consultant for Power Technologies, Inc.

Hydraulic Turbine and Turbine Control Models for System Dynamic Studies

Working Group on Prime Mover and Energy Supply Models for System Dynamic Performance Studies

HYDRAULIC TURBINE AND TURBINE CONTROL MODELS FOR SYSTEM DYNAMIC STUDIES

Working Group on Prime Mover and Energy Supply
Models for System Dynamic Performance Studies

ABSTRACT

A working group on Prime Mover and Energy Supply Models for System Dynamic Performance Studies under the IEEE System Dynamic Performance Subcommittee was established in 1987 to collect technical information on dynamic characteristics of prime mover and energy supply systems that can affect power system performance during and following disturbances such as faults, loss of generation or loads and system separation.

A principal objective of the working group is to develop prime mover/energy supply models for use in power system simulation programs. The last endeavor in this area was the IEEE Committee Report (Ref. 1) In 1973 entitled "Dynamic Models for Steam and Hydro Turbines".

KEY WORDS

Hydraulic Turbine Dynamic Models, Hydro-Turbine Controls, Power System Dynamic Performance.

1.0 INTRODUCTION

The 1973 IEEE Committee report "Dynamic Models for Steam and Hydro Turbines in Power System Studies" (1) has been used widely. Even in 1973, however, it was realized that more work needed to be done. Since then, modeling requirements have increased greatly and more detailed models have been implemented in the advanced simulation programs.

The older models were considered adequate for typical first swing stability simulations common in the early 70s. Nowadays, models for the following types of studies are also needed:

Longer transient stability program simulation -up to and beyond ten seconds are now routine. In this longer time frame, prime mover and prime mover action can affect results.

Low frequency oscillations.

Islanding and isolated system operation.

System restoration following a break-up.

Load rejection.

Load acceptance.

Water-hammer dynamics.

Pump storage generation with complex hydraulic structures.

Paper preparation was coordinated by F. P. de Mello (Chairman) and R. J. Koessler with contributions from J. Agee, P. M. Anderson, J. H. Doudna, J. H. Fish III, P. A. L. Hamm, P. Kundur, D. C. Kee, C. J. Rogers and C. Taylor.

91 SM 462-2 PWRS   A paper recommended and approved by the IEEE Power System Engineering Committee of the IEEE Power Engineering Society for presentation at the IEEE/PES 1991 Summer Meeting, San Diego, California, July 28 - August 1, 1991. Manuscript submitted February 1, 1991; made available for printing June 19, 1991.

Other developments requiring new models include the widespread use of electric-hydraulic speed control both in new construction and in modernization of older power plants. It is better to use models describing the actual equipment rather than make approximations to fit existing mechanical governor models. The tremendous increase in computer power eliminates the need for less detailed models.

This report recommends hydraulic models suitable for a relatively wide range of studies. The two main sections of the report provide models for 1) prime movers including water supply conduit and 2) prime mover speed controls. The section on prime mover models includes both linear and nonlinear controls. Non-linear models are required where speed and power changes are large, such as in islanding, load rejection, and system restoration studies.

The block diagram of Figure 1 shows the basic elements of a hydro turbine within the power system environment. Excluded from the scope of this report are models for generation load control and electrical load dynamics.

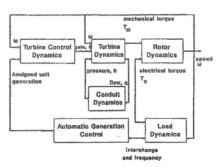

Figure 1.   Functional Block Diagram Showing Relationship of Hydro Prime Mover System and Controls to Complete System

2.0 MODELING OF TURBINE CONDUIT DYNAMICS

2.1   Non-linear Model Assuming a Non-Elastic Water Column

The block diagram in Figure 2 represents the dynamic characteristics of a simple hydraulic turbine, with a penstock, unrestricted head and tail race, and with either a very large or no surge tank.

The penstock is modeled assuming an incompressible fluid and a rigid conduit of length L and cross-section A. Penstock head losses h_1 are proportional to flow squared and f_p is the head loss coefficient, usually ignored.

From the laws of momentum, the rate of change of flow in the conduit is

$$\frac{d\overline{q}}{dt} = \left(\overline{h_o} - \overline{h} - \overline{h_1}\right) g\,A\,/\,L \tag{1}$$

where:

$\overline{q}$ = turbine flow rate, m3$_{/sec}$
A = Penstock area, m^2
L = Penstock length, m
I = is the acceleration due to gravity, m/sec^2
$\overline{h_o}$ = is the static head of water column, m
$\overline{h}$ = is the head at the turbine admission, m
$\overline{h_1}$ = is the head loss due to friction in the conduit, m

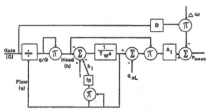

Figure 2. Non-Linear Model of Turbine - Non-Elastic Water Column Expressed in per unit this relation becomes

$$\frac{dq}{dt} = \frac{\left[1 - h - h_I\right]}{T_w} \tag{2}$$

where h and h_1 are the head at the turbine, and head loss respectively in per unit, with h_{base} defined as the static head of the water column above the turbine.

T_w, called water time constant or water starting time, is defined as:

$$T_w = \left(\frac{L}{A}\right)\frac{q_{base}}{h_{base}\,g} \text{ secs} \tag{3}$$

q_{base} is chosen as the turbine flow rate with gates fully open (Gate position G = 1) and head at the turbine equal to h_{base}. It should be noted that the choice of base quantities is arbitrary.

The system of base quantities defined above has the following advantages:

- Base head (h_{base}) is easily identified as the total available static head (i.e. lake head minus tailrace head)..
- Base gate is easily understood as the maximum gate opening.

Having established base head and base gate position, the turbine characteristics define base flow through the relationship:

$$q = f\,(gate,\,head)$$

The per unit flow rate through the turbine is given by:

$$q = G\sqrt{h} \qquad (4)$$

In an ideal turbine, mechanical power is equal to flow times head with appropriate conversion factors.

The fact that the turbine is not 100% efficient is taken into account by subtracting the no load flow from the actual flow giving the difference as the effective flow which, multiplied by head, produces mechanical power. There is also a speed deviation damping effect which is a function of gate opening (6).

Per unit turbine power, P_m, on generator MVA base is thus expressed as:

$$P_m = A_t h (q - q_{nl}) - DG\Delta\omega \qquad (5)$$

where q_{nl} is the per unit no-load flow, accounting for turbine fixed power losses. A_t is a proportionality factor and is assumed constant. It is calculated using turbine MW rating and generator MVA base.

$$A_t = \frac{\text{Turbine MW rating}}{(\text{Generator MVA rating})h_r \left(q_r - q_{nL}\right)} \qquad (6)$$

where h_r is the per unit head at the turbine at rated flow and q_r is the per unit flow at rated load.

It should be noted that the per unit gate would generally be less than unity at rated load.

The parameter A_t defined by Equation 6 converts the gate opening to per unit turbine power on the volt-ampere base of the generator and takes into account the turbine gain. It should be noted, however, that in some stability programs, A_t is used to convert the actual gate position to the effective gate position, i. e. $A_t = 1/(G_{FL} - G_{NL})$ as described in (6). A separate factor is then used to convert the power from the turbine rated power base to that of the generator volt-ampere base.

2.2 Linear Models

Neglecting friction losses in the penstock, a small perturbation analysis of the relationships in Figure 2 yields the block diagram of Figure 3.

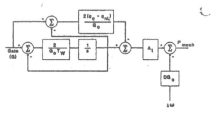

Figure 3.   Linearized Model of Turbine - Non-Elastic Water Column

From this figure, the change in mechanical power output can be expressed as:

$$\Delta P_m = \frac{A_1 \left(1 - T_1 s\right)\Delta G}{\left(1 + T_2 s\right)} - DG_o\Delta\omega \qquad (7)$$

where

G_o = per unit gate opening at operating point

T_1 = $(q_o - q_{nl})T_W$

T_2 = $G_o T_W / 2$

q_o = per unit steady state flow rate at operating point

Note that G_o = q_o

264

With the damping term neglected, equation 7 is similar to the commonly used classical penstock/turbine linear transfer function

$$\frac{\Delta P_m}{\Delta G} = \frac{1 - G_o T_w s}{1 + \frac{G_o T_w s}{2}} \times A_t \qquad (8)$$

where $G_o T_w$ is an approximation to the effective water starting time for small perturbations around the operating point.

Other, more elaborate linear models have been proposed (2,3,4,5). They require more detailed turbine data.

Linear models are useful for studies of control system tuning using linear analysis tools (frequency response, eigenvalue etc.). Their use in time domain simulations should be discouraged since in addition to being limited to small perturbations, they do not offer any computational simplicity relative to the non-linear model.

2.3 Traveling Wave Models

While the modeling of the hydraulic effects using the assumption of inelastic water columns is adequate for short to medium length penstocks, there is sometimes need to consider the effects which cause traveling waves of pressure and flow due to the elasticity of the steel in the penstock and the compressibility of water. For long penstocks the travel time of the pressure and flow waves can be significant.

An analysis of the partial differential equations in time and space defining pressure and flow rate at each point in the conduit gives rise to the classical traveling wave solution which, with the boundary conditions of zero change in head at the penstock inlet and the flow/gate/head relationship at the turbine, yields the block diagram of Figure 4.

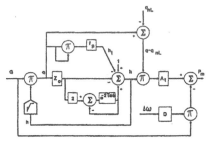

Figure 4.   Non-Linear Model of Turbine Including Water Column Traveling Wave Effects

This block diagram incorporates the traveling wave transfer function between head and flow rate:

$$\frac{h(s)}{q(s)} = \frac{-Z_o \left(1 - e^{-2T_e s}\right)}{\left(1 + e^{-2T_e s}\right)} \qquad (9a)$$

also written as

$$-Z_o \tan h (T_e s) \qquad (9b)$$

Z_o is the surge impedance of the penstock in per unit expressed as:

$$Z_o = \frac{q_{base}}{h_{base}} \frac{1}{\sqrt{g\alpha}} \qquad (10)$$

and T_e, the wave travel time is

$$T_e = L/a \qquad (11)$$

where:

α = pg (1/K + D/fE)

ρ = density of water

K = bulk modulus of water

D = internal penstock diameter

f = wall thickness of penstock

E = Young's modulus of pipe wall material

q_{base} = base flow

h_{base} = base head

g = acceleration due to gravity

L = length of penstock

a = wave velocity = $\sqrt{\dfrac{g}{\alpha}}$

Noting that the water time constant in the penstock

$$T_W = \frac{q_{base}L}{Ah_{base}g} \qquad (12)$$

and expression 11 for T_e, it follows that

$$T_W = Z_o T_e \qquad (13)$$

Typical values for wave velocity are in the range of 1000 to 1200 m/sec.

In the block diagram of Figure 4 the effect of friction head loss in the penstock is shown proportional to flow squared.

An alternative numerical method of time simulation of traveling wave effects is the method of characteristics solution, detailed in reference 9. An example of this solution technique is given in Section 4.4.

The dynamics of turbine power are an almost instantaneous function of head across the turbine and gate or nozzle opening including deflector effects where applicable. The head across the turbine is a function of the hydraulic characteristics upstream of the turbine and also downstream in cases where the flow in the draft tube and/or tailrace is constrained as in the case of Francis or Kaplan Turbines. In the case of Pelton (impulse) turbines, the downstream pressure is atmospheric hence the hydraulic effects are only from the conduits between the reservoir and turbine.

This modular separation of effects is shown in Figure 1 with the distinct blocks labeled "Turbine Dynamics" and "Conduit Dynamics". The model of the combined system, turbine and conduit, is shown in Figures 2 and 3 for the simple penstock/turbine system without elasticity effects and in Figure 4 considering elasticity effects. Particular hydraulic conduit arrangements may require special modeling in cases such as constrained or vented tunnels, individual penstocks fanning out from a common pressure shaft etc. The basic models for conduits can be put together to describe the specific arrangement, much as the basic models of electric components are used to describe specific networks.

Examples of models for more complex hydraulic systems are given in Sections 2.4 to 2.6.

2.4 Non-Linear Model Including Surge Tank Effects.

Non-Elastic Water Columns.

In hydro plants with long supply conduits, it is common practice to use a surge tank. The purpose of the surge tank is to provide some hydraulic isolation of the turbine from the head deviations generated by transients in the conduit. Many surge tanks also include an orifice which dissipates the energy of hydraulic oscillations and produces looping. The hydraulic model shown in Figure 5 includes presentation of:

- penstock dynamics
- surge chamber dynamics
- tunnel dynamics
- penstock, tunnel and surge chamber orifice losses

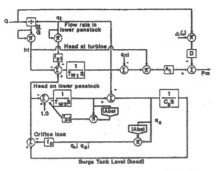

Figure 5. Non-Linear Model of Turbine Including Surge Tank Effects - Non-Elastic Water Column

Flow base, head base and water time constants are determined as in 2.1. C_s, storage constant of surge tank, is defined as:

$$C_s = \frac{A_s * h_{base}}{q_{base}} \, secs \qquad (14)$$

where

A_s = surge tank cross section area, m^2

Upper and lower penstock head losses are proportional to flow rate squared through loss coefficients f_{p1} and f_{p2}.

Head losses in the orifice to the surge tank are proportional to the coefficient f_o times flow rate times absolute value of flow rate to maintain direction of head loss. The same applies to head loss in the upper penstock where flow can reverse.

The head across the lower penstock is defined by the level of the surge tank, which can undergo low frequency oscillations (in the order of .01 Hz) between surge tank and reservoir.

The inclusion of surge tank effects is warranted in cases where dynamic performance is being simulated over many seconds to minutes.

2.5 Non-Linear Model Including Surge Tank Effects.

Elastic Water Column In Penstock

In cases where traveling wave effects in the penstock are important the model of Figure 5 is modified to that of Figure 6. Here the upper penstock or tunnel is considered inelastic because the dynamic effects contributed by that system and surge chamber involve low frequency effects, while the high frequency response components are contributed by the lower penstock which is subject to abrupt gate or flow area changes. The difference between the model in Figure 6 and that in Figure 4 is that the head acting on the lower penstock is the surge tank level rather than the constant reservoir elevation taken as 1 pu.

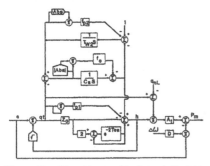

Figure 6. Non-Linear Model of Turbine With Surge Tank Effects and Traveling Wave Effects in Penstock

2.6 Non-Linear Model of Multiple Penstocks and Turbines Supplied from Common Tunnel, Inelastic Water Columns

Figure 7 shows a configuration where a pressure shaft or tunnel brings water to a manifold from which penstocks fan out to several turbines. The coupling effect of head variations at the manifold is illustrated in the model of Figure 8 for the case of three turbines and their penstocks with water starting times of T_{w1}, T_{w2} and T_{w3} respectively and a tunnel water starting time of T_w.

The model of Figure 8 is derived from the basic momentum equations for each conduit and eliminating the variable head at the manifold through use of the continuity equation forcing the flow in the upper tunnel to be equal to the sum of the flows in the penstocks.

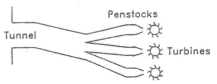

Figure 7. Penstock Arrangement Fanning Out From Manifold From Sinale Tunnel

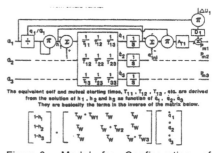

Figure 8. Model for Configuration of Figure 7 - Non-Elastic Water Column

2.7 Non-Linear Model of Multiple Penstocks and Turbines Supplied From Common Tunnel, Elastic Water Columns in Penstocks and Tunnel

Figure 9 shows the model accounting for traveling wave effects in the penstocks and tunnel.

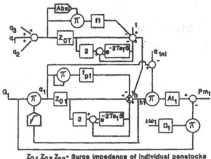

Figure 9. Model for Configuration of Figure 7 - Including Traveling Wave Effects in Penstocks and Tunnel

This model incorporates the single penstock model of Figure 4 and introduces the effect of the tunnel by using the same form of transfer function between downstream head and flow, which, for the tunnel is the sum of flows in the penstocks.

Whereas the algebraic loop between flow and head of the simple penstock can be solved in closed form, these loops in Figure 9 are best solved by iteration.

3.0 HYDRO TURBINE CONTROLS

Hydro turbines, because of their initial inverse response characteristics of power to gate changes, require provision of transient droop features in the speed controls for stable control performance. The term "transient droop" implies that, for fast deviations in frequency, the governor exhibits high regulation (low gain) while for slow changes and in the steady state the governor exhibits the normal low regulation, (high gain).

From a linear control analysis point of view, the case of a hydro turbine generator supplying an isolated load can be represented by the block diagram of Figure 10.

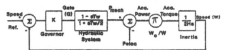

Figure 10. Linear Model of Hydro Turbine and Speed Controls Supplying Isolated Load

Conventional frequency response and Bode plot analysis of this control system shows that a pure proportional controller would have to be tuned with a very low gain for acceptable stability yielding a very poor (high) regulation. This is evident from Figure 11 showing the open loop asymptotic gain and phase angle plots and in Figure 12 showing the response to a step change in electrical load for different values of proportional gain K. This example using a water starting time T_w of 2 sec and inertia constant H of 4 sec, shows that a proportional control gain would be limited to about 3 per unit for acceptable stability which would imply an unacceptably high regulation of 33%.

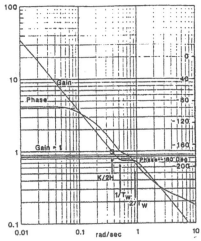

Figure 11. Bode Plot of Open Loop Function in Figure 10 with Proportional Governor

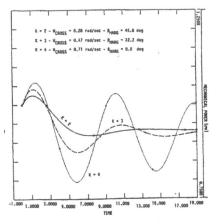

Figure 12. Response of Mechanical Power for a Step Change in Electrical Power in System of Figure 10 with Proportional Governor

Transient gain reduction is thus necessary to provide acceptable steady state regulation with adequate stability.

3.1 Governors - Proportional Control with Transient Droop

Figure 13 shows the model block diagram of a typical governor in which the turbine gate is controlled by a two stage hydraulic position servo. The physical meaning of the parameters used in the model is as follows:

T_p - Pilot valve and servo motor time constant

Q - Servo gain

T_g - Main servo time constant

R_p - Perm anent droop

R_t - Transient droop

T_R - Reset time or dashpot time constant

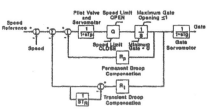

Figure 13. Model of Typical Hydro-Turbine Governor

The permanent droop determines the speed regulation under steady state conditions. It is defined as the speed drop in percent or per unit required to drive the gate from minimum to maximum opening without change in speed reference. As noted in Section 3.0. due to the peculiar dynamic characteristics of the hydraulic turbine, it is necessary to increase the regulation under fast transient conditions in order to achieve stable speed control. This is achieved by the parallel transient droop branch with washout time constant T_R.

Because of the choice of the per unit system, with maximum gate opening defined as unity, the speed limits must be defined, for consistency, as fractions of the maximum gate opening per second.

The Bode diagram in Figure 14 gives an asymptotic plot of the inverse of the feedback path $1/h_1$ i.e.

$$\frac{1}{h_1} = \frac{1 + sT_R}{sT_R R_t} \tag{15}$$

and the forward function g

$$g_1 = \frac{1}{R_p \left(1 + \dfrac{s}{QR_p}\right)} \tag{16}$$

(For the purpose of clarity, the effects of servomotor time constants have been neglected in this figure. Their effect is significant only if their poles occur before or near crossover frequency).

The closed loop response (C.L.R.) of such a g_1/h_1 control loop is

$$C.L.R. = \frac{g_1}{\left(1 + g_1 h_1\right)} \tag{17}$$

If $g_1 \ll 1/h_1$, then: $gh_1 \ll 1$ and C.L.R. is approximately $= g_1$.

If $1/h_1 \ll g$, then: $g_1 h_1 \gg 1$ and C.L.R. is approximately $= 1/h_1$.

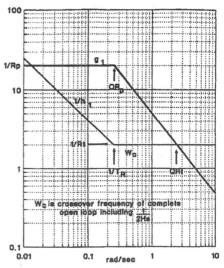

Figure 14. Bode Diagram of Governor in Figure 13, Forward and Inverse Feedback Function

Hence, the closed loop response may be approximated by plotting both g_1 and $1/h_1$ and choosing the lowest of both gain responses at any frequency as an approximation to the closed loop response at that frequency. Referring to Figure 14, the speed-regulating control loop will "see" the governor as having a gain of $1/Rp$ in the steady state, and a "transient" gain of $1/Rt$ for phenomena above the $1/T_R$ frequency range. An equivalent time constant of $1/(QRt)$sec will result from the second intersection of the g_1 and $1/h_1$ traces.

The speed regulating loop will have acceptable stability if:

- a) The transient gain, $(1/Rt)$ does not exceed

$$\frac{1}{R_t} \leq 1.5 \frac{H}{T_w} \qquad (18)$$

- b) Crossover frequency, W_c, approximately equal to $1/(2HRt)$, occurs somewhere in the region between $1/T_R$ and QRt. This reduces phase lag contributions from the governor.

Several authors have proposed relations for temporary droop, Rt, and dashpot time constant, T_R:

For temporary droop Ref 11 and 12 propose values of T_w/H, while Ref. 7 proposes the following formula

$$R_t = T_w/H*[1.15 - (T_w - 1)*0.075]$$

All three will result in crossover frequencies that are close to $1/2T_w$, and, therefore, satisfy condition (a).

Regarding the dashpot time constant, Ref 11 suggests a value of 4 times T_w, Ref 12 proposed a T_R equal to five times T_w and Ref 7 proposes

$$T_R = T_w*[5 - (T_w - 1)*0.5] \qquad (20)$$

For crossover frequencies in the order of $1/2T_w$, $1/T_R$ values in the order of $1/5T_w$ will minimize "low frequency" phase lag contributions from the governor.

Reference 7 suggests large values of Q, the servosystem gain, to attain improved performance characteristics. The typical maximum values of 5 to 10 reported in that

same paper, will minimize the "high frequency" phase lag contributions from the governor.

3.2 Other Types of Governors

There are cases where specific governors require more complex representation than in Figure 13. The differences may be due to added time constants in hardware and also where derivative action is included.

Figure 15 shows an example of more complex representations.

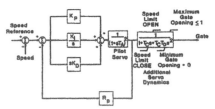

Figure 15. PID Governor Including Pilot and Servo Dynamics

3.2.1 PI Governor (KD = 0)

Neglecting the pilot servo and additional servo dynamics in Figure 15, shown in the Bode diagram of Figure 16 are the inverse of the internal loop feedback path $1/h_1$. i.e. $1/Rp$, and the forward gain g, i.e. KP + KI/s. When comparing the resulting frequency response characteristics with those of Figure 14 it is apparent that both governors achieve the same objective, i.e. transient droop increase.

Tuning objectives are identical: Transient droop Rt is given by 1/KP, KP/KI is equivalent to the dashpot time constant T_R, and care must be taken that crossover does not occur at frequencies that are close to the inverse of the smaller servomotor time constants.

3.2.2 PID Governor

The purpose of the derivative is to extend the crossover frequency beyond the constraints imposed on PI governors. Figure 17 shows the governor loop frequency response when the PID governor is tuned according to the authors of Reference 10.

$$Rt = 1/KP = 0.625T_w/H$$
$$T_R = KP/KI = 3.33\ T_w \qquad (21)$$
$$KP/KD > 3/T_w$$

Transient gain (1/Rt) has been increased by 60% over normal PI values. This results in roughly the same increase in crossover frequency, and thereby, in governor response speed. The detrimental effects on stability are averted by the phase lead effects resulting from derivative action. There is a risk, however, that the rise in magnitude due to the derivative action, compounded with that resulting from the hydraulic system, may result in a second crossover at higher frequencies. Due to the high phase lags at these frequencies, a second crossover will certainly result in governor loop instability. This is the reason for the minimum limit imposed on the value of KP/KD.

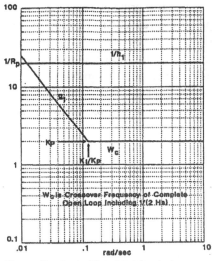

Figure 16. Bode Plot of P-I Control

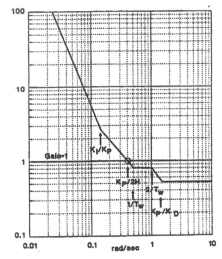

Figure 17. Bode Plot of PID Control

3.3 Enhanced Governor Model

The governor model described in Figure 18 has modeling capabilities not frequently found in typical hydro plant models. Its features may be critical for the correct simulation of partial or total load rejections:

Buffering of gate closure may produce a reduction in overpressures under load rejection. It also reduces impact loadings on the gate linkage and limits the magnitude of the pressure pulsations while the gates are fully closed during the decay of load collection overspeed.

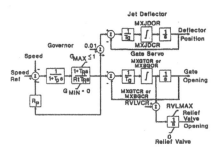

Rp	Permanent Droop
Rt	Temporary Droop
TR	Dashpot Time Constant
Tp	Pilot Valve Time Constant
Tg	Gate Servo Time Constant
MXGTOR	Maximum Gate Opening Rate
MXGTCR	Maximum Gate Closing Rate
MXBGOR	Maximum Buffered Gate Opening Rate
MXBGCR	Maximum Buffered Gate Closing Rate
GMAX	Maximum Gate Limit
GMIN	Minimum Gate Limit
RVLVCR	Relief Valve Closing Rate
RVLMAX	Maximum Relief Valve Limit
MXJDOR	Maximum Jet Deflector Opening Rate
MXJDCR	Maximum Jet Deflector Closing Rate

Figure 18. Enhanced Governor Model Used In Load Rejection Studies

In some installations a relief valve is attached to the turbine casing providing a bypass for the flow. It is operated directly from the governor or the gate mechanism of the turbine. The amount of water bypassed is sufficient to keep the total discharge through the penstock fairly constant, hence controlling pressure rise.

Turbine flow, as used for turbine power calculations, is determined in this case as:

$$\text{Turbine Flow} = \frac{\text{Openstock} \times \text{GateOpening}}{\text{Gate.Opn.} + \text{Rel.Vlv.Opn.}} \qquad (22)$$

In long-penstock impulse turbines, rapid reductions in water velocity are not allowed to avoid the pressure rise which would occur. To minimize the speed rise following a sudden load rejection, a governor-controlled jet deflector is sometimes placed between the needle nozzle and the runner. The governor moves this deflector rapidly into the jet, removing part or all of the power input to the turbine.

Turbine flow in this case is calculated as:

Turbine Flow = Openstock x Min(1.,DefPos./ Gate Opn.)   (23)

In Figure 18, position limits are shown on the controller. Limits could also be included on the jet and gate servos.

4.0 EXAMPLES OF ANALYSIS AND SIMULATION

A sample system with all hydraulic and control parameters defined in the Appendix serves to illustrate various aspects of dynamic performance and simulation approaches.

4.1 Governor Loop Stability

Traveling wave effects may become a significant factor when analyzing governor loop stability. Figure 19 shows magnitude and phase lags for the classical linear hydro turbine model (Eq. 8, $G_o = 1$, $T_w = 2$ sec) and for the same ideal model when traveling wave effects are considered ($T_e = 1$ sec) (14). The larger magnitudes in the traveling wave model will result in higher crossover frequencies. Higher crossover frequencies, compounded with larger phase lags, result in smaller phase margins, and therefore less stable performance than when assuming a lumped-parameter model.

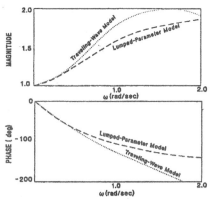

Figure 19. Magnitude and Phase Lag Versus Frequency of $\Delta P_m/\Delta G$ Function - Lumped Parameter and Traveling Wave Models

These effects have usually a negligible impact on PI controller stability. They should not be neglected, however, when analyzing PID controller. This is illustrated in the example in Table 1, where traveling-wave modeling is shown to have a significant impact on PID controller stability.

It can be shown that the per unit error in the head/flow transfer function due to ignoring traveling wave effects is approximately equal to

$$error = \frac{-T_e^2 s^2}{3} \qquad (24)$$

Their significance is therefore larger for long penstocks. Long penstocks result in larger water time constants and therefore lower governor response speed. The larger bandwidth in PID controllers is most attractive in such conditions. Traveling wave analysis thus becomes critical.

4.2 Linear vs. Non-Linear Hydraulic Model (Inelastic Flow)

The advantages of nonlinear versus linear models become apparent when both models are subjected to large excursions in turbine loading. Figure 20 shows the models' responses to a relatively small (0.01 pu) step in gate position. Figure 21 shows simulation results for a larger (0.2 pu) step. For comparison purposes, the governor representation was deactivated in both models and both no-load flow and speed deviations were set to zero in the nonlinear model.

Table 1. Governor Loop Stability for Typical Controller Tuning and Alternative Hydraulic Models

Controller	Hydraulic Model	Cross Frequency	Phase Margin
PI	Lumped Parameter	0.30 rad/sec	19.5 deg
PID	Lumped Parameter	0.51 rad/sec	20.0 deg
PI	Traveling Wave	0.30 rad/sec	18.1 deg
PID	Traveling Wave	0.54 rad/sec	13.8 deg

$H = 4$ sec, $T_w = 2$ sec, $T_e = 1$ sec
PI Controller: $KP = 2$, $KI = 0.25$
PID Controller: $KP = 3.2$,
$KI = 0.48$, $KD = 2.13$

The hydraulic system parameters were:

$$T_w = 1.83 \text{ sec}$$
$$A_t = 1.004$$
$$G_0 = 0.762 \ pu$$

The linear model falls to represent the increases in effective water time with changes in penstock flow.

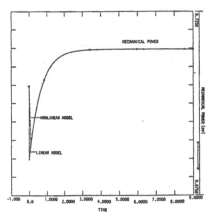

Figure 20. Mechanical Power Response to 0.01 pu Step in Gate Position. Linear vs. Non-Linear Model

4.3 Effect of Surge Tank

Surge tank effects should be included in dynamic analyses of hydro plants when the time range of interest is comparable to the surge tank natural period. For shorter time periods, the simpler short-term model can be used.

$$\text{Surge Tank Natural Period} = 2\pi \sqrt{\frac{A_s \times L_t}{A_t \times g}} \text{ secs} \qquad (25)$$

where

A_s = surge tank cross section area

A_t = Tunnel cross section area
L_t = Length of tunnel
g = gravity constant

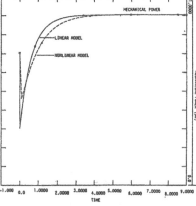

Figure 21. Mechanical Power Response to .2 pu Step in Gate Position. Linear vs. Nonlinear Model

Figure 22 shows the result of simulating a 0.1 pu step load increase on an isolated hydro plant with and without surge tank effects. The surge tank natural period is 3 minutes. For the normal 3 to 5 sec transient stability range simulation results are almost identical. For longer simulation intervals, surge tank level starts falling, and mechanical power recovery lags behind that of the short-term model, which assumes an infinite surge tank.

Simulation of surge tank dynamics is necessary when the tank is small enough to be emptied by a large load increase (8). Long-term simulations are valuable in establishing acceptable operating procedures that avoid such catastrophic consequences.

For plants with more complex layouts, "high frequency" oscillations resulting from pendulum action between surge chambers and other hydraulic resonant modes may interfere with the governor's speed-regulating loop. Dynamic simulations and frequency response analyses representing these "long-term" effects are required tools in such types of analyses (8).

4.4 Traveling-Wave Hydraulic Simulation

The results shown in Figure 22 were for the case of inelastic conduits and incompressible fluid. Taking into account the effect of elasticity and compressibility leads to a traveling wave solution method described in Figure 23. This method of calculation of traveling wave effects is an alternative to implementation of the Figure 6 model with time delay of transport time simulation of the wave.

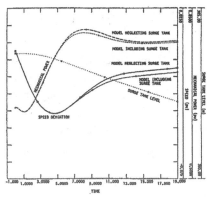

Figure 22. Response of Mechanical Power and Speed to a 0.1 pu Load Increase - With and Without Surge Tank Effects

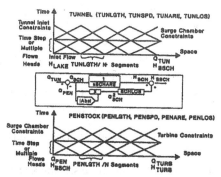

Figure 23. Solution of Traveling Wave Effects by Method of Characteristics

Flows and heads along the penstock and tunnel are analyzed in terms of a continuity equation

$$\frac{a^2 \partial Q}{gA \partial x} + \frac{Q \partial H}{A \partial x} + \frac{\partial H}{\partial t} + \frac{Q}{A} \sin \theta = 0 \qquad (26)$$

where:

a - conduit wave velocity

g - gravitational acceleration

A - cross-sectional area

Θ - conduit slope

and an equation of motion:

$$g\frac{\partial H}{\partial x} + \frac{Q\partial Q}{A^2\partial x} + \frac{\partial Q}{A\partial t} + g\frac{dfloss}{dx}Q|Q| = 0 \quad (27)$$

Time-space lattices such as those shown in Figure 23 are defined for each of the conduits, and both equations are simultaneously solved using the method of characteristics (9).

The accuracy of the results is proportional to the number of segments into which the conduit is divided. Practical application of these models seems to suggest that a minimum of ten segments is required.

Time and space increments are related by conduit wave velocity. Time increments must be equal to or multiples of the simulation time step. The minimum size requirements on simulation time step may create additional computational burdens for large system simulations.

Simultaneous consideration of two or more conduits, while using a unique simulation time step makes it impossible to "fit" an exact lattice on each conduit. Recognizing the problem uncertainties, particularly on conduit wave velocity, conduit lengths are adjusted to the nearest increment.

The sine term in (26) recognizes pressure rises, and therefore, specific volume and flow reductions, resulting from reductions in elevation. This complicates the initialization process (flows along the same conduit are not equal in the steady-state), but has negligible effects in simulation results. Horizontal conduits may be assumed.

The additional computational burden of programming and running a traveling-wave model has to be weighed against the error caused by the use of an inelastic model. As previously mentioned, the per-unit errors are proportional to the square of conduit travel time times the square of the main frequency of the dynamic phenomena. As shown in Section 4.1 this per-unit difference will usually be negligible unless very long penstocks are studied or unless governor bandwidth has been expanded by derivative action. A critical case run under both assumptions assesses the difference.

This is shown in Figure 24, where the hydro plant described in the Appendix ($T_w = 1.83$ s, Te = 0.42 s) is subjected to a 0.2 pu increase in load under isolated conditions. Except for some transient high frequency effects, the difference between the elastic and inelastic solutions is negligible.

There are times, however, when traveling wave analysis is essential. The analysis of overpressures and pressure pulsations due to total load rejection is generally carried out with this type of tool. A closed or almost closed gate gives rise to poorly attenuated traveling waves of pressure.

Figure 25 shows a total gate closure simulation for the system described in the Appendix. For gate positions at or near total closure, the inelastic simulations of scroll case head and penstock flows are no longer applicable, and are replaced by an algebraic, steady-state solution of the penstock. Surge chamber levels and tunnel flows are not affected by these high-frequency effects. Frequency control is not affected either since turbine power is practically zero at these small gate openings.

The effect of buffering the gate closure is shown in Figure 26 for the same total load rejection simulation as in Figure 25, but with a maximum buffered closing rate of -0.05 pu/sec, applied after gate opening is less than 0.15 pu. Overpressures and pressure pulsations are significantly reduced, at the expense of a larger overspeed.

Figure 27 shows the same total load rejection as in Figure 25, but including simulation of a relief valve with a -0.01 closing rate. Both overpressures and overspeed are significantly improved by relief valve operation.

Figure 28 simulates total load rejection including jet deflector action with a -0.5 closing rate. While gate closing rate has been reduced to a tenth of its value in Figure 25, reducing overpressures, the jet deflector manages to control speed.

5.0 CONCLUSIONS AND RECOMMENDATIONS

This paper has presented a number of different models for hydraulic turbines and for their speed controllers. The models vary in complexity, and are meant to be used for the study of power system problems of different types. General recommendations for their use are given below.

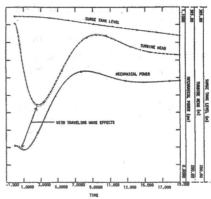

Figure 24. Mechanical Power. Head and Surge Tank Level Response to a 0.2 pu Load Increase With and Without Traveling Wave Effects

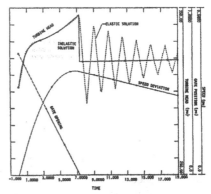

Figure 25. Speed and Head Response to a Full Load Rejection With and Without Traveling Wave Effects

It is recognized that specific applications may require the development of special models including effects such as deadbands, hysteresis, etc. One of the objectives of the paper is to present the basic physics of hydraulic turbines and their controls recognizing that, in the state of the art, the development of code for a particular model is routine once the physics are well defined.

5.1 Transient Stability Studies

The slow response of the turbine controls and hydraulic system makes their effect on first swing stability negligible. In interconnected systems which have low frequency inter-area modes below about 0.5 Hz, the governor and turbine action may influence the damping of these modes. Depending on the governor control parameters, the turbine may either add or subtract from the natural damping of the mode.

In studies of small isolated power systems, the governor and turbine characteristics play an important part in the response of the system frequency to disturbances. Here the action of the governor speed regulation and the response of the turbine must be included in the model. The effects of gate position and speed limits can be significant in such cases, and should thus correspond to those in service in the modeled plants.

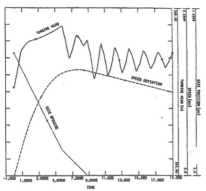

Figure 26. Speed and Head Response to a Full Load Rejection With Gate Buffering

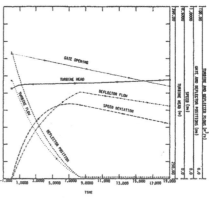

Figure 28. Speed, Head and Flow Response to a Full Load Rejection with Jet Deflector Operation

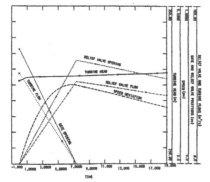

Figure 27. Speed, Head and Flow Response to a Full Load Rejection With Relief Valve Operation

The turbine model of Section 2.1 coupled with a governor model chosen from that of Section 3.1 or Section 3.2 as appropriate is recommended for use in transient stability programs. A simple linear turbine model is not recommended since its parameters would have to be adjusted as a function of operating conditions and the accuracy of representation would be affected by the magnitude of the perturbations.

5.2 Small Signal Stability

In small signal stability studies, it is the effect of the governors and turbines on the damping of low frequency inter-area modes which is of concern. These effects can be modeled adequately by linearizing the non-linear turbine and governor models about the appropriate operating point. Fixed time constant linearized models of the turbine without adjustment for operating point are not recommended.

Linear models are also used for guidance in speed control tuning using linear control analysis techniques. The most critical condition for such studies of governor adjustments would be with the unit supplying an isolated load at maximum output.

5.3 Special Applications

In special circumstances, additional complexity must be included in the turbine and governor models to study the detailed response of the plant to disturbances, or to study the effect of the units on long-term dynamics. Other instances requiring additional complexity are studies of interactions between turbine hydraulic dynamics including draft tube pulsations and electromechanical power oscillations. In such cases, the model must correspond as closer as possible to the actual turbine and controls that exist at the ???etailed modeling of special controls, such as those discussed in Section 3.3, and the penstock, including traveling wave effects and surge tank

dynamics, as in Sections 2.3 and 2.4, may be required.

APPENDIX

Sample System (Figures 5, 6 and 18)

Rated Generator MVA:	100. MVA
Rated Turbine Power:	90.94 MW
Rated Turbine Flow:	71.43 m³/s
Rated Turbine Head:	138.9 m
Gate Position at Rated Cond:	0.90 pu.
No-Load Flow, qN_L:	4.3 m³/s
Permanent Droop, R_p:	0.05 pu.
Temporary Droop, R_t:	0.45 pu.
Dashpot Time Constant, T_R:	8. s
Pilot Time Constant, T_p:	0.02 s
Servo Time Constant, T_g:	0.5 s
Maximum Gate Opening Rate, MXGTOR:	0.1 pu./s
Maximum Gate Closing Rate, MXGTCR:	-0.1 pu./s
Maximum Gate Limit, GMAX:	1. pu.
Minimum Gate Limit, GMIN:	0. pu.
Lake Head:	307.0 m
Tail Head:	166.4 m
Penstock Length	465 m
Penstock Cross Section	15.2 m²
Penstock Wave Velocity:	1100 m/s
Penstock Head Loss Coeff., fpl:	0.0003042 m/(m³/s)²
Tunnel Length:	3850 m
Tunnel Cross Section:	38.5 m²
Tunnel Wave Velocity:	1200 m/s
Tunnel Head Loss Coeff., fp2:	0.0010112 m/(m³/s)2
Surge Chamber C. Section:	78.5 m²
S.Ch. Orifice Head Loss C., fo:	0.0040751 m/(m³/s)²
Turbine Damping:	0.5 pu/pu

REFERENCES

1. IEEE Committee Report, "Dynamic Models for Steam and Hydro Turbines in Power System Studies", IEEE Trans. Vol. PAS-92, pp. 1904-1915.

2. J.L Woodward, "Hydraulic-Turbine Transfer Function for Use

in Governing Studies", Proc. IEE, Vol. 115, pp. 424-426, March 1968.

3. J.R. Smith et al., "Assessment of Hydroturbine Models for Power System Studies", Proc. IEE, Vol. 130, Pt. C. No. 1, January 1983.

4. P.W. Agnew, "The Governing of Francis Turbines", Water Power, pp. 119-127, April 1974.

5. R. Oldenburger, J. Donelson, "Dynamic Response of a Hydroelectric Plant", Trans. AIEE, Vol. 81, Pt. III, pp. 403-418, 1962.

6. J.M. Undrill and J.L. Woodward, "Non-Linear Hydro Governing Model and Improved Calculation for Determining Temporary Droop", IEEE Trans. Vol. PAS-86, No. 4, pp. 443-453, April 1967.

7. P.L. Dandeno, P. Kundur and J.P. Bayne, "Hydraulic Unit Dynamic Performance Under Normal and Islanding Conditions - Analysis and Validation", IEEE Trans., Vol. PAS-97, No. 6, pp. 2134-2143, November/December 1978.

8. J.M. Undrill and W. Strauss, "Influence of hydro plant design on regulating and reserve response capacity", IEEE Trans., Vol. PAS 74, pp. 1192-1200, July/August 1974.

9. V.L. Streeter and E.B. Wylle, "Fluid Mechanics" (McGraw-Hill, New York, 1975).

10. S. Hagihara, H. Yokota, K. Goda, K. Isaobe, "Stability of a Hydraulic Turbine Generating Unit Controlled by PID Governor", IEEE Trans., Vol. PAS 98 No 6, pp. 2294-2298, Nov/Dec 1979.

11. L. M. Hovey, "Optimum Adjustment of Hydro Governors on Manitoba Hydro System", AIEE Trans., Vol. 81, Part III, pp. 581-587, Dec 1962.

12. F. R. Schleif and A. B. Wilbor, "The Coordination of Hydraulic Turbine Governors for Power System Operation", IEEE Trans. Vol. PAS 85, pp. 750-758, July 1966.

13. L. K. Kirchmayer, "Economic Control of Interconnected Systems, Vol. II, Chapter I", John Wiley and Sons Inc. 1959.

14. C. K. Sanathanan, "Accurate Low Order Model for Hydraulic Turbine-Penstock", IEEE Trans., Vol. EC-2, No. 2, pp. 196-200, June 1987.

Hydraulic Turbine Units and Hydro Governing

Extracted from PTI course notes:
"Power Technology Course"

F. P. de Mello
J.M. Undrill

Power Technologies, Inc.

APPENDIX

HYDRAULIC PENSTOCK TRANSFER FUNCTION

The performance of hydro electric turbines is dominated by the effects of water inertia, water compressibility and pipe wall elasticity in the penstock or pressure tunnel feeding the turbine.

The effect of water inertia is to cause changes in turbine flow to lag behind changes in turbine gate opening. This introduces phase lag into the speed governing loop and hence has a destabilizing effect on the generating unit.

The effect of elasticity is to cause traveling waves of pressure and flow in the pipe. These wave effects are of little consequence when the pipe line is short in relation to the wave velocity; but they can build up to destructive levels in cases where resonance between the penstock and the governing system causes standing waves and local magnification of pressure oscillations.

Elastic Analysis

Consider a short slice of an elastic penstock, as shown in Figure G-1.

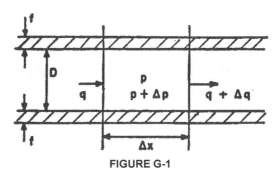

FIGURE G-1

Let the pressure in this slice increase by Δp. The corresponding change in volume due to stretching of the pipe walls is

$$\Delta V = \frac{\pi D^3 \Delta x}{4 Ef} \Delta p \qquad \text{(G-1)}$$

(E=Young's Modulus of pipe wall material)

The increase in mass of water in the pipe section is given by

$$\Delta m = \rho (\Delta V + \Delta V') \qquad \text{(G-2)}$$

where $\Delta V'$ is due to the compressibility of the water in the section and ρ is the density of water.

$$\Delta V' = \frac{\pi D^2 \, \Delta x}{4K} \Delta p \qquad \text{(G-3)}$$

(K=bulk modulus of water)

Combining 1,2, and 3 gives:

$$\Delta m = \frac{\rho \pi D^2}{4} \Delta x \left(\frac{1}{K} + \frac{D}{fE} \right) \Delta p \qquad \text{(G-4)}$$

The change in mass of water within the pipe section during the period, ΔT, is given by the difference in inflow and outflow

$$\Delta m = \rho q \Delta t - \rho (q + \Delta q) \Delta t = -\rho \Delta q \Delta t \qquad \text{(G-5)}$$

Combining 4 and 5 gives:

$$\frac{\Delta q}{\Delta x} = -A \left(\frac{1}{K} + \frac{D}{fE} \right) \frac{\Delta p}{\Delta t} \qquad \text{(G-6)}$$

where A = pipe internal cross section area.

Next, noting that $\Delta p = \rho g \Delta h$ and taking infinitesimally small values for Δx and Δt gives:

$$\frac{\partial q}{\partial x} = -\alpha A \frac{\partial h}{\partial t} \qquad \text{(G-7)}$$

where

$$\alpha = \rho g \left(\frac{1}{K} + \frac{D}{fE} \right) \qquad \text{(G-8)}$$

Next, writing the equation of motion of the fluid in the pipe section gives:

$$A \Delta x \rho \frac{\partial u}{\partial t} = A \Delta p$$

where u is the velocity of water

Whence, since q=Au, and $\Delta p = \rho g \Delta h$

$$\frac{\partial q}{\partial t} = -Ag\frac{\partial h}{\partial x} \qquad \text{(G-9)}$$

We now wish to obtain a transfer function relating head and flow at the turbine gate, when the pipe length, L, is given.

Assume that the turbine gate is located at x=0 and the open intake of the pipe is at x = -L. Taking the LaPlace transforms of 7 and 9 with no disturbance for $t \leq 0$ gives:

$$\begin{bmatrix} \dfrac{dq(s)}{dx} \\ \\ \dfrac{dh(s)}{dx} \end{bmatrix} = \begin{bmatrix} 0 & -\alpha As \\ \\ -\dfrac{s}{gA} & 0 \end{bmatrix} \cdot \begin{bmatrix} q(x,s) \\ h(x,s) \end{bmatrix} \qquad \text{(G-10)}$$

The Solution of this equation is:

$$q(x,s) = c_1 e^{\sqrt{\frac{\alpha}{g}}s} + c_2 e^{\sqrt{\frac{\alpha}{g}}s} \qquad \text{(G-11)}$$

$$h(x,s) = -Z_o\left(c_1 e^{\sqrt{\frac{\alpha}{g}}s} - c_2 e^{\sqrt{\frac{\alpha}{g}}s} \right) \qquad \text{(G-12)}$$

where $Z_o = \dfrac{1}{A\sqrt{\alpha g}}$ is the <u>surge impedance</u> of the pipe line.

The required transfer function relates q(o,s) and h(o,s).

We consider the case where the intake end of the pipe is fed by a large reservoir, so that h(-L,s) = 0.

Putting h(-L,s) = 0 in (12) gives:

$$\frac{c_1}{c_2} = e^{2\sqrt{\frac{\alpha}{g}}Ls} \qquad \text{(G-13)}$$

Substituting this into 11 and 12 for x = 0 then gives:

$q(o,s) = c_1 + c_2$

$$= c_1\left(1 + e^{-2\sqrt{\frac{\alpha}{g}}\,La}\right)$$

$$h(o,s) = Z_o\,(c_1 - c_2)$$

$$= -Z_o c_1\left(1 - e^{-2\sqrt{\frac{\alpha}{g}}\,La}\right)$$

Hence, the required transfer function is:

$$\frac{h(s)}{q(s)} = \frac{-Z_o\left(1 - e^{-2T_e s}\right)}{\left(1 + e^{-2T_e s}\right)} \tag{G-14}$$

where

$$T_e = \sqrt{\frac{\alpha}{g}}\,L \;=\; \text{wave travel time} \tag{G-15}$$

Transfer function 14 refers to absolute (foot pound second or MKS) units.

To convert to the per unit form the numerator and denominator of 14, are divided by q_o and h_o respectively, to give:

$$\frac{\dfrac{h(s)}{h_o}}{\dfrac{q(s)}{q_o}} = \frac{\dfrac{-Z_o q_o}{h_o}\left(1 - e^{-2T_e s}\right)}{\left(1 + e^{-2T_e s}\right)}$$

Hence, by redefining Z_0 as per unit value, we obtain the per unit form transfer function

$$\frac{h(s)}{q(s)} = \frac{-Z_0\left(1 - e^{-2T_e s}\right)}{\left(1 + e^{-2T_e s}\right)} \tag{G-16}$$

where

$$Z_0 = \frac{q_o}{Ah_o\sqrt{\alpha g}} \tag{G-17}$$

Figure G-2 shows the block diagram defining the solution of flow rate q, head h and mechanical power P_m for the case considering elasticity of the water column. The head loss due to friction losses fr q × |q| is included as are also the no-load losses q_{nl}. The parameter At is needed to convert the product of $(q-q_{nl})$h to per unit mechanical power. The parameter D accounts for the effect of turbine speed variations ΔW on turbine efficiency.

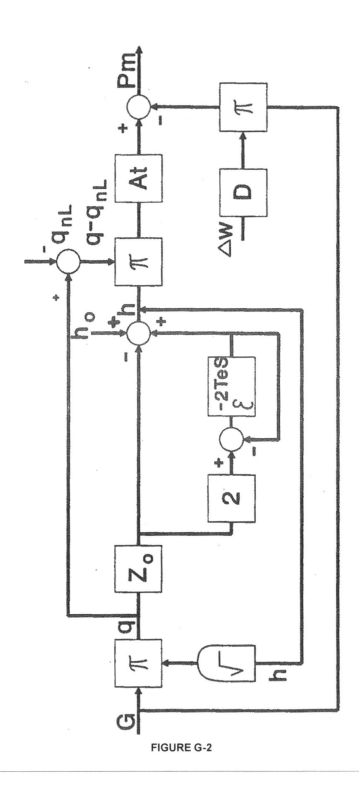

FIGURE G-2

Inelastic Analysis

In the case where the penstock is short and wave effects are unimportant, it is sufficient to analyze the penstock water column on the basis of water inertia alone. Here, considering Fig. G-3, the mass of water on the penstock is

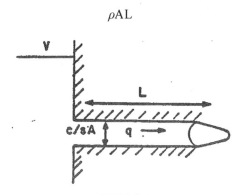

FIGURE G-3

and the equation of motion is

$$\rho AL \frac{du}{dt} = -A\Delta p$$

whence

$$\frac{dq}{dt} = \frac{A}{\rho L}\Delta p$$

or

$$\frac{L}{Ag}\frac{dq}{dt} = -\Delta h$$

Converting to per unit form by dividing by q_o and h_o gives

$$\frac{Lq_o}{Ag}\frac{d\left(\dfrac{q}{q_o}\right)}{dt} = -h_o\left(\frac{\Delta h}{h_o}\right)$$

or writing in terms of per unit variables

$$T_w \frac{dq}{dt} = -h \qquad \text{(G-18)}$$

where

$$T_w = \frac{Lq_o}{gAh_o} = \frac{Lu_o}{gh_o} \qquad \text{(G-19)}$$

Notice that $T_w = Z_o T_e$ in per unit form. T_w is the <u>water inertia time constant</u> of the penstock.

Summary of Per Unit Form

<u>Elastic</u>

$$\frac{h(s)}{q(s)} = -Z_s \frac{\left(1 - e^{-2T_e s}\right)}{1 + e^{-2T_e s}}$$

$$\alpha = \rho g \left(\frac{1}{K} + \frac{D}{fE}\right)$$

$$Z_o = \frac{q_o}{Ah_o} \frac{1}{\sqrt{\mu g}}$$

$$T_e = \sqrt{\frac{\alpha}{g}} L$$

$$\text{wave velocity} = \sqrt{\frac{g}{\alpha}}$$

K = Bulk Modulus of Water
E = Young's Modulus of Pipe Wall
D = Pipe Inside Diameter
f = Pipe Wall Thickness
L = Pipe Length

<u>Inelastic</u>

$$T_w \frac{dq}{dt} = -h \qquad \frac{h}{q} = -T_w s$$

$$T_w = \frac{Lu_o}{gh_o} = \frac{Lu_o}{gAh_o}$$

$$T_w = Z_o T_e$$

EFFECT OF PENSTOCK ON TURBINE RESPONSE

Let the penstock transfer function be

$$\frac{h(s)}{q(s)} = T(s) = -T_w s \tag{G-20}$$

The turbine power P_m in per unit, assuming 100% efficiency is

$$Pm = qh$$

$$\text{Also } q = G\sqrt{h}$$

These can be linearized and normalized about the operating point and LaPlace transformed to yield

$$\overline{q}(s) = \overline{G}(s) + \frac{1}{2}\overline{h}(s) \tag{G-21}$$

$$P_m(s) - \overline{q}(s) + \overline{h}(s) \tag{G-22}$$

where $\overline{G}$ is the change in gate opening in per unit of operating point, $\overline{q}$ is the change in flow per unit of operating point flow, $\overline{h}$ is the change in head in per unit of normal and $\overline{p}$ is the change in power in per unit of operating point power.

Combining 20, 21, and 22 gives:

$$\overline{q}(s) = \frac{1}{1 - .5T(s)}\overline{G}(s)$$

$$\frac{\overline{P}(s)}{G(s)} = \frac{1 + T(s)}{1 - .5T(s)} \tag{G-23}$$

In the inelastic case $T(s) = T_w s$ and this simplifies to:

$$\frac{P_m(s)}{G(s)} = \frac{1 - T_w s}{1 - .5T_w s} \tag{G-24}$$

The transfer function $\frac{P_m(s)}{G(s)}$ is plotted for some typical penstock parameters in Figures G-4 and G-5, both in the elastic case and in the inelastic case.

The parameter values used are:

> Tw = 1 Second
> q_o = 1 pu (full load)
> T_e = 0.5 sec. (elastic case)

A T_e value of 0.5 second corresponds to a steel penstock whose length would typically be of the order of 1000 feet (300 meters).

In both the inelastic and the elastic case the phase of the turbine power lags behind the gate signal, with the lag being limited to 180° in the inelastic case but being unlimited in the elastic case.

That the phase lag introduced by the penstock is detrimental to system governing stability is illustrated in Fig. G-6 which shows the governing loop of a hydro plant feeding an isolated or inertialess load.

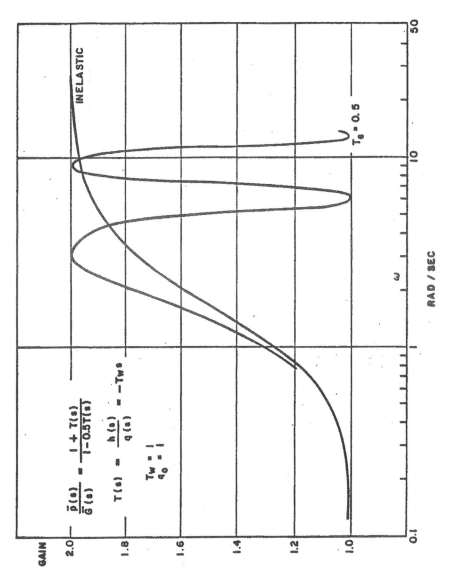

FIGURE G-4

295

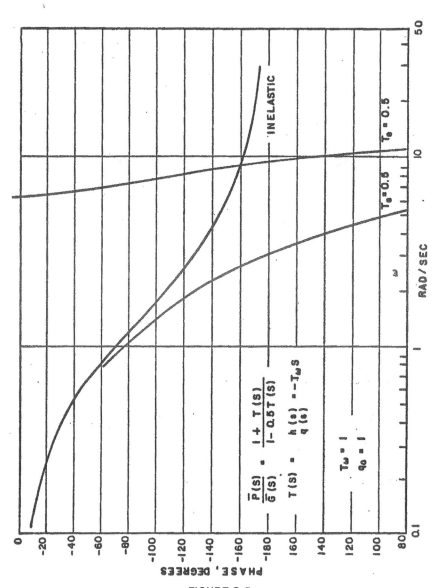

FIGURE G-5

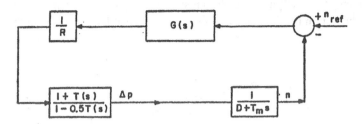

Hydro plant governing loop - isolated load

Tm = generator + load inertia

$$D = \frac{\delta \, load}{\delta \, speed} + \frac{\delta \, turbine \, output}{\delta \, speed}$$

G(s) = governor compensation function

FIGURE G-6

Since R is $\simeq$ 0.03 the governor loop gain (1/R) is approximately 30. Further, the phase shift of the generator inertia, $(1/(D + T_m s))$ adds an additional lag to that produced by the penstock characteristic. It is necessary, therefore, for the governor transfer function G(s) to either reduce the loop gain at frequencies in the region of 180° lag, produce a substantial phase lead, or both.

GOVERNOR TRANSFER FUNCTIONS

A widely used governor transfer function which satisfies these requirements is the following:

$$G(s) = \frac{1 + T_r s}{1 + \frac{r}{R} T_r s} \tag{G-25}$$

where:

        R = steady state regulation, or permanent droop
        r = temporary droop
        T_r = relaxation time constant for temporary droop action

The general characteristic of this transfer function is shown in Fig. G.7.

It will be seen that this governor transfer function produces a reduction in transient (high frequency) gain while leaving the steady state gain unchanged.

The values of r and T_r must be chosen so as to produce an acceptable amount of gain reduction in the frequency band where the open loop phase is in the region of 180°.

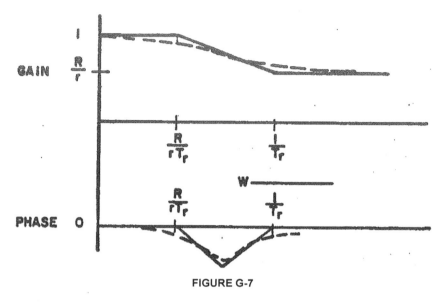

FIGURE G-7

A great deal of research has been expended on the question of optimum values for r and T_r. Well accepted criteria for hydro plants where <u>elasticity effects are not of large magnitude</u> are

$$r \ 2T_w/T_m \ \text{to} \ 2.5T_w/T_m$$
$$T_r \ 4T_w \ \text{to} \ 5T_w$$

SURGE TANKS

In hydro plant layouts where a long supply conduit is required it is fairly common practice to use a surge tank. The purpose of the surge tank is to provide a degree of hydraulic isolation of the turbine from the head deviations generated by transients in the longest portion of the conduit. Many surge tanks also include an orifice whose head loss serves to dissipate the energy of hydraulic oscillations and to produce a damping effect.

A representative hydraulic system incorporation a surge tank is shown in Fig. G-8.

The effect of the surge tank is best illustrated by an example. Consider the case where the tunnel is relatively long but where wave effects are not of major significance, so that the tunnel may be characterized by its inertia constant.

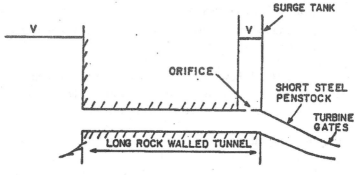

Plant configuration Using Surge Tank
FIGURE G-8

The system differential equations are:

<u>Tunnel Inertia</u> $\quad T_{wt} \dfrac{dq_t}{dt} = h_u - h_s$ $\qquad$ (G-26)

<u>Penstock Inertia</u> $\quad T_{wp} \dfrac{dq_p}{dt} = h_s - h_g$ $\qquad$ (G-27)

<u>Surge Tank Inflow</u> $\quad A_t \dfrac{dq_\ell}{dt} = q_t - q_p$ $\qquad$ (G-28)

The system algebraic equations are:

<u>Orifice Head Drop</u> $h_s = h_l + k_o (q_t - q_p) \,|\, (q_t - q_p)|$ $\qquad$ (G-29)

<u>Turbine Gate Flow</u> $q_p = k_t G h_g^{\frac{1}{2}}$ $\qquad$ (G-30)

where

h_u	=	reservoir head (constant)
h_s	=	head at penstock entrance
h_g	=	head at turbine gate
qt	=	tunnel flow
qp	=	penstock flow
$h\ell$	=	head in surge tank
k_o	=	orifice head loss constant
k_t	=	turbine gate head characteristic
G	=	turbine gate opening
T_{wt}	=	tunnel inertia constant

T_{wp} = penstock inertia constant

A_t = surge tank area in terms of seconds at rated flow to produce 1 p.u. head rise.

Figures G-9, G-10 and G-11 show the behavior of this hydraulic system for a severe transient, the rejection of nearly all load from the turbine. The turbine gates are closed linearly from 1 p.u. opening to 0.2 p.u. opening in 4 seconds.

These figures show that the surge tank allows the tunnel flow to decelerate slowly while the penstock flow is decelerated rapidly by the gate closure. The unbalance between tunnel and penstock flow is taken up by an increase in surge tank level, as shown in Fig. G-11. Figures G-9 and G-10 show transients for a range of surge tank orifice constants. With k_o = 1000 the surge tank is hardly effective and the head rise is essentially that produced if there had been no surge tank. With k_o = 0.001 the surge tank is extremely effective in limiting head rise at the turbine gate, but the rise in surge tank level could be excessive and the oscillation of the hydraulic system would have inadequate damping.

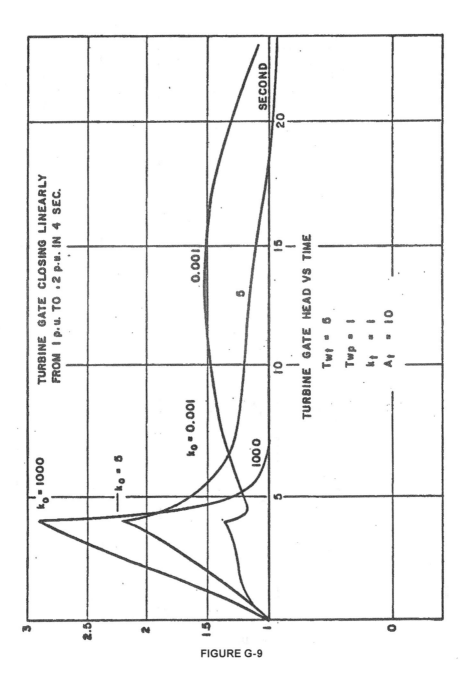

FIGURE G-9

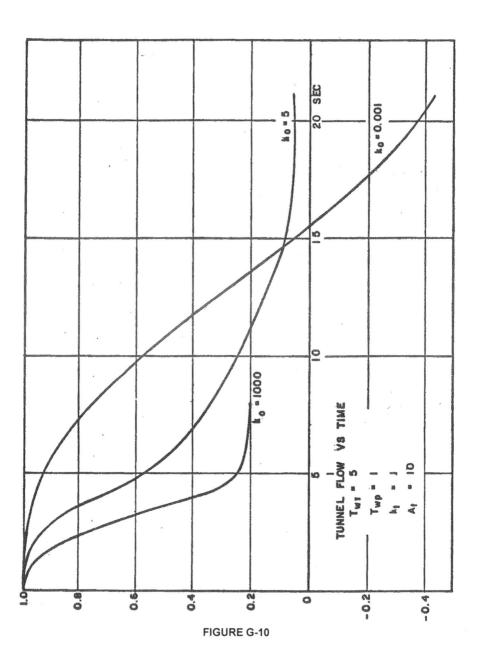

FIGURE G-10

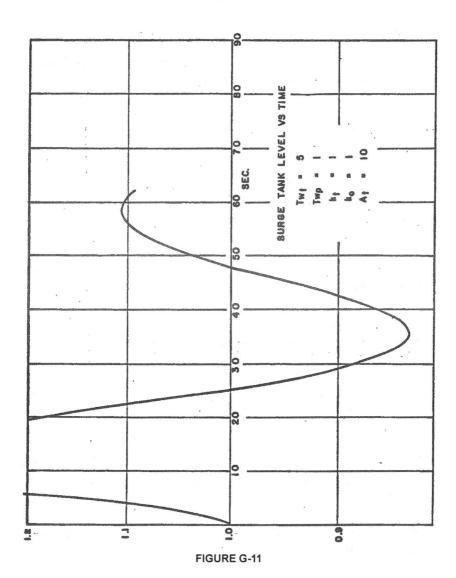

FIGURE G-11

303

HYDRO BIBLIOGRAPHY

1. Hovey, L.M., "Optimum Adjustment of Hydro Governors on Manitoba Hydro System," AIEE Trans, Pt 111 (Power Apparatus and Systems), Vol. 81, 1962, pp. 581-587.

2. Undrill, J.M. and Woodward, J.L., "Nonlinear Hydro Governing Model and Improved Calculation for Determining Temporary Droop," IEEE Trans. on Power Apparatus and Systems, Vol. PAS-86, No. 4, April, 1967.

3. Young, C.C. and Webler, R.M., "A New Digital Computer Program for Predicting Dynamic Performance of Electric Power Systems," 1967 PICA Conference Record, pp. 21-30.

4. Concordia, C. and Kirchmeyer, L.K., "Tie-Line Power and Frequency Control of Electric Power Systems - Part II," AIEE Trans. Pt. III A (Power Apparatus and Systems), Vol. 73, 1954, pp. 131-146.

5. Concordia, C. and Kirchmayer, L.K., "Tie-Line Power and Frequency Control of Electric Power Systems," AIEE Trans. Pt. III A (Power Apparatus and Systems), Vol. 72, 1953, pp. 562-572.

6. Hovey, L.M. and Bateman, L.A., "Speed Regulation on a Hydro Station Supplying an Isolated Load," AIEE Trans. Pt. III (Power Apparatus and Systems), Vol. 81, 1962, pp. 364-371.

7. Schleif, F.R. and Johnstone, L.M., "Experiences with Hydraulic Prime Mover Controls," ASME Trans., Journal of Engineering for Power, April, 1961, pp. 189-193.

8. Oldenburger, R. and Donelson, J., Jr., "Dynamic Response of a Hydroelectric Plant" AIEE Trans. Pt. III A (Power Apparatus and Systems), Vol. 81, No. 10, Oct. 1962, pp. 403-419.

9. Oldenburger, R. and Goodson, R.E., "Hydraulic Line Dynamics," Proceedings of the 2nd IFAC Conference, 1963, Paper 439-4.

10. Leum, M., "The Development and Field Experience of a Transistor Electric Governor for Hydro Turbines," IEEE Transactions on Power Apparatus and Systems, Vol. PAS-85, April, 1966, pp. 393-402.

11. Ramey, D.G. and Skooglund, J.W., "Detailed Hydro Governor Representation for System Stability Studies," Sixth PICA Conference Proceedings, May, 1969, pp. 490-501; IEEE Transactions on Power Apparatus and Systems, Vol. PAS-89, January, 1970, pp. 106-112.

12. Schleif, F.R. and Wilbor, A.B., "The Coordination of Hydraulic Turbine Governors for Power System Operation," IEEE Transactions on Power Apparatus and Systems, Vol. PAS-85, July, 1966, pp. 750-756.

13. Avery, C.L., "Field Adjustment of Hydraulic Turbine Governors," ASME Trans. Journal of Engineering for Power, Jan. 1961, pp. 61-68.

14. Stone, H.M., "Field Testing and Adjusting of Hydraulic Turbine - Generator to Improve System Regulation," ASME Trans. Journal of Engineering for Power. Jan. 1961, pp. 53-60.

15. IEEE Committee, "Power Plant Response," IEEE Trans. on Power Apparatus and Systems, Vol. PAS-86, No. 3, March, 1967, pp. 391-394.

16. Joint AIEE and ASME Committee, "Recommended Specification for Speed - Governing of Hydraulic Turbines Intended to Drive Electric Generators," AIEE Report, No. 605, September, 1960.

17. Concordia, C. et al, "Effect of Prime Mover Response and Governing Characteristics on System Dynamic Performance," Proceedings of the American Power Conference, Vol. 28, 1966.

18. Almeras, P., "Influence of Water Inertia on the Stability of Operation of a Hydro-electric System," Engineers' Digest, Vol. 4, 1947, pp. 9-12, 55-61.

19. Gibson, W.L. and Shelson, W., "An Experimental and Analytical Investigation of a Differential Surge-Tank Installation," ASME Trans., 1956, pp. 925-940.

20. McCaig, I.W., "Application of Computer and Model Studies to Problems Involving Hydraulic Transients," ASME Trans., Journal of Basic Engineering, Dec. 1959, pp. 433-445.

21. Oja, V., "Frequency Response Methods Applied to the Study of Turbine Regulation in the Swedish Power System," Asme Trans., Nov. 1954, pp. 1325-1333.

22. Long, L.O., "Outlook on the Relationship between Load-Frequency Control and Turbine Governors on Interconnected Power Systems", Engineering Journal, Dec. 1961, pp. 42-54.

23. Concordia, C., Crary, S.B. and Parker, E.E., "Effect of Prime - Mover Speed Governor Characteristics on Power-Swings," AIEE Trans., Vol. 60, 1941, pp. 559-567.

24. Schleif, F.R. and Wilbor, A.B., "The Coordination of Hydraulic Turbine Governors for Power System Operation," IEEE Trans. on Power Apparatus and Systems, Vol. PAS-85, No. 7, July, 1966, pp. 750-757.

BWR Capabilities for Utility Load Following and Regulation Requirements

F.P. de Mello
J.J. Hogle

BWR CAPABILITIES FOR UTILITY LOAD FOLLOWING AND REGULATION REQUIREMENTS

F. P. deMello   J. J. Hogle

Electric Utility system needs for response and controllability of given generating units vary considerably depending on the particular unit's expected mode of operation which may range from base load to peaking duty. However, since technological improvements in efficiency characteristics of future units may cause changes in the operating pattern of presently base loaded units, it is well to view the response requirements conservatively by assuming unit loading patterns more severe than those of the over-all power system load. On this basis the requirements imposed by needs of typical power systems are reviewed as are also the capabilities of the BWR to meet these needs.[1,2]

SYSTEM NEEDS

1. Daily Load Following

   From the point-of-view of realistic system demands, the unit must have the ability to change load daily over a wide range, at rates up to approximately 5%/min. which is the normal maximum rate for supplementary controls or automatic dispatch system (ADS) controls. To give it wide operating flexibility, the range should be typically from 100% to 35%.

2. Tie-Line Thermal Backup

   With such a load following capability, the unit would also be available for more abnormal power reallocations as might be called upon during system upsets to alleviate thermal overloading of tie lines. When a large generation deficiency occurs in an area of a large interconnected system, the transmission ties initially will make up the deficiency. However, if this results in over-loading the lines, only a matter of minutes may be available before limiting temperatures on the conductors are reached. The 5%/minute ADS rate has been adequate to take care of such requirements.

3. Isolation System Frequency Recovery

Another consideration is the ability of the unit to respond to unusually large frequency deviations under speed control action at a rapid rate, i.e., within about ten seconds. Such duty might be imposed very infrequency during abnormal disturbances such as might result in system isolation coupled with a new area generation deficiency.

Should extreme losses in generation result in system separation, the quick response of spinning reserve will minimize the amount of load shedding that will be necessary in those areas with generation deficiencies. Thus, the capability to increase generation by 10% in 10 seconds plus sustained changes of 20% or more in 30 seconds would aid in minimizing the initial disturbance and speeding the restoration of load that had to be shed initially. However, it is probable that the only time that nuclear generation will be under 80% load is when there will also be a large amount of fossil capacity on line running at its minimum of 20 to 30%. Hence, unless the system separation also isolates the nuclear generation from the fossil reserve, it might be argued that the wide range quick-response capability of nuclear generation will seldom be exercised.

4. Normal System Frequency Regulation

Under normal steady-state operation, it is desirable that the inherent droop, time constants, and transient compensation of the prime mover speed control and associated control systems be coordinated to yield characteristics similar to and compatible with those of existing generation. The duty imposed by normal frequency regulation through speed control, as distinct from supplementary control, is seldom exercised over more than 1 to 2% of load range.

It should be noted that in the past, the governing response characteristics for this small excursion mode have seldom been considered as a system design factor. For instance, such considerations have not inhibited the use of hydro generation for which the small oscillation response characteristics are often several times slower than those of fossil steam generation. Likewise, the more limited speed control response of reheat vs. nonreheat units has not been a factor in barring the use of the reheat and double reheat cycle, except in a few cases of isolated power systems where the short term response for large upsets is a major system design need. In the future more attention will be devoted to these aspects of system performance due to the better understanding of their effects on dynamic stability of interconnected operation.

Load Rejection Capability

There is a great variation in the need to maintain generating units on the line in spite of severe load reduction due to the system splitting into unbalanced segments of load and generation. Hence, the ability for a plant to ride through and continue to operate following essentially 100% load rejection should be an available design option, though not necessarily a standard product feature. It should be noted that similar capability on large fossil units has seldom been provided.

On the other hand, some amount of load rejection or reduction capability is necessary in all plants. The capability of reducing load by about 35% at speed control actuation rates would probably satisfy a large majority of system situations.

In addition to satisfying normal speed control needs and system isolation requirements, there occasionally may be instances where it would be desirable to employ an early valving option[4] (rapid closure of control or intercept valves and subsequent reopening within few seconds) to enhance plant stability. To date, such fast valving schemes have been mainly in investigation phases and the first few fast valving applications on fossil generating units have yet to go into operation.

BWR CAPABILITY

Response Characteristics

The single cycle Boiling Water Reactor (BWR) plant, with recirculation flow control is capable of meeting or exceeding the requirements listed above, in view of the following performance characteristics.

1. Within the recirculation flow control range, the BWR can change power at an average rate of about 30% per minute over the range from 65% to 100% power (Curve A on Fig. 1) automatically by ADS or supplementary control, or under operator control. To cover the minimum 35% power level of a daily load swing, the operator would move control rods to shift the flow control line (or band) down to perhaps Curve C on Fig. 1. Operation on this lower curve would permit an average rate of about 15% per minute over a range 33 to 50% power level.

Fig. 2 shows a typical daily load curve which spans a range of 40% to 100%. Twice in each 24 hours the operator would move control rods to shift the flow control band as needed to maintain automatic load following. The "60%" and "100" rod patterns refer to control rod patterns which, at rated recirculation flow, result in 60% and 100% power levels, respectively. For example, Curve A on Fig. 1 is a 100% rod pattern and Curve C is a 50% rod pattern. Depending on reactor size, an operator can change power by control rods at rates from 2% to 4% per minute.

The BWR will not be limited by Xenon poisoning, even at end of core life, when following the power cycle shown in Fig. 2. The excess reactivity built into the core plus the long Xenon time constant relative to the load cycle combine to keep the reactor from being limited.

2.   The BWR has excellent rapid response capability, as shown in Fig. 3, which shows steam flow responses to step demands. Although the fastest demands through speed control action originating from a system disturbance will be spread over a period of several seconds (since speed cannot change instantly), the step demand curves of Fig. 3 are useful in assessing the capability of the unit to respond under large system disturbances which might result in isolation of the power system with a simultaneous unbalance between load and generation.

In the direction of load rejection (negative steps), the fast steam bypass system will respond almost instantaneously. A 25% bypass system will permit handling up to 35% negative step demand from rated power without scram. A few utilities may require the capability of 100% load rejection without scram. For such a requirement, the bypass capacity can be increased to 105%.

Performance under System Speed and Load Control

Predictions of BWR plant performance under typical electrical system load upset situations are shown on Figs. 4 and 5.

The case illustrated in Fig. 4 is that of a hypothetical power system supplied entirely by BWR generation, connected through tie lines to a large interconnected system. An abrupt generation deficiency of 10% develops in the area as might be caused by the tripout of one or more units. The deficiency is almost instantaneously made up by a change of power over the ties. The tie-line power deviation is then restored in about a minute through load control action. This type of performance is comparable to what can be achieved with supplementary controls on conventional boiler following fossil generation if these controls are set up to respond at the rate of 10%/min. It should be noted that in many instances the supplementary controls on fossil generation are limited to maximum rates considerably lower than 10%/min. In such cases the restoration of tie-line power to schedule would take considerably longer than the one minute shown on Fig. 4. Another factor that affects generation response is the capacity available to respond. In the example of Fig. 4, it was assumed that the spinning reserve capacity was available uniformly distributed among all units. Any reduction in this reserve capacity will correspondingly reduce the rate at which such large generation deficiencies can be made up.[5]

The case illustrated in Fig. 5 describes control performance for an upset situation which resulted in system isolation and a net 10% deficiency in generation. With steady-state speed regulation of 5% distributed over all units, the frequency recovery is not appreciably different than would be the case for the same hypothetical situation with fossil generation. The peak frequency excursion lasting only a few seconds is about the same as would be obtained with fossil-fired boiler-following generation with an effective regulation of 10%.

The BWR plant is also capable of frequency regulation duty, as indicated by Fig. 6, which shows ample response to ±1.0% steps in demand with different periodicity, or Fig. 7 where the demand signal is random. This type of response is comparable to that of conventional fossil generation.

For line fault disturbances, preliminary analyses indicate that early valve operation (fast closure and reopening of turbine intercept valves) to improve transient stability can be utilized on a BWR plant without scramming the reactor.

"Blackout" Start

The BWR can start up and generate a significant amount of power without running the recirculation pumps, reactor core flow being supplied by natural circulation. Without the large amount of power required by the recirculation pumps, the auxiliary power requirements are within the capacity of the standby AC power (diesel generators); hence, the plant can start up without external power. Once a few percent power is being generated, the main generator can then supply all the auxiliaries including the recirculation pumps and thus "bootstrap" up to higher power levels.

REFERENCES

1. J. B. Tice, "Must Define Requirements to Get Proper Reserve," Electrical World, November 20, 1967.

2. C. Concordia, F. P. deMello, L. K. Kirchmayer, R. P. Schulz, "Prime-Mover Response and System Dynamic Performance," IEEE Spectrum, October, 1966.

3. O. W. Durrant, R. P. Siegfried, <u>Electric World</u>, August 12, 1968, "Pulling Boiler through System Upset Calls for Ready Plan," p. 31-34.

4. F. P. deMello, M. A. Eggenberger, D. N. Ewart, M. Temoshok, "Turbine Energy Controls Aid in Power System Performance," American Power Conference, Chicago, April 26-28, 1966.

5. C. Concordia, "Performance of Interconnected Systems Following Disturbances," <u>Spectrum</u>, June, 1965.

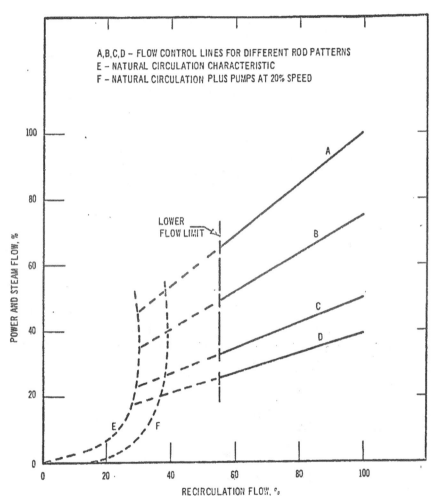

TYPICAL BWR POWER - FLOW CHARACTERISTICS
FIGURE 1

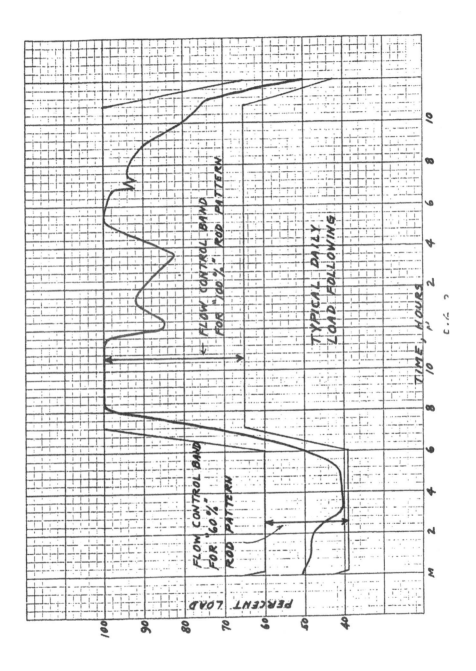

TYPICAL DAILY
LOAD FOLLOWING

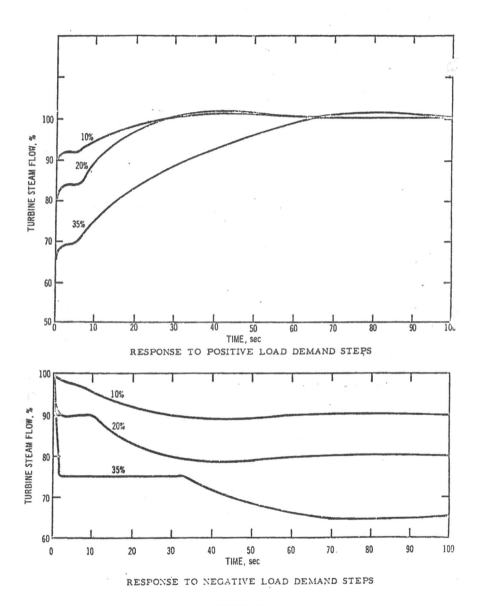

RESPONSE TO POSITIVE LOAD DEMAND STEPS

RESPONSE TO NEGATIVE LOAD DEMAND STEPS

FIGURE 3

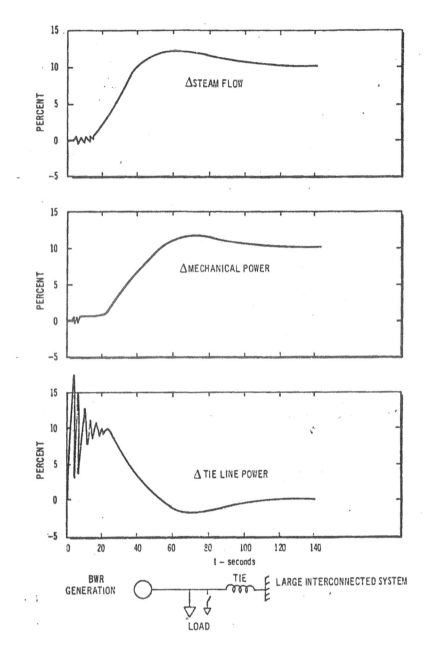

10 PERCENT STEP LOAD INCREASE IN AREA TIED TO LARGE
INTERCONNECTION BWR GENERATION WITH SUPPLEMENTARY
CONTROL

FIG. 4

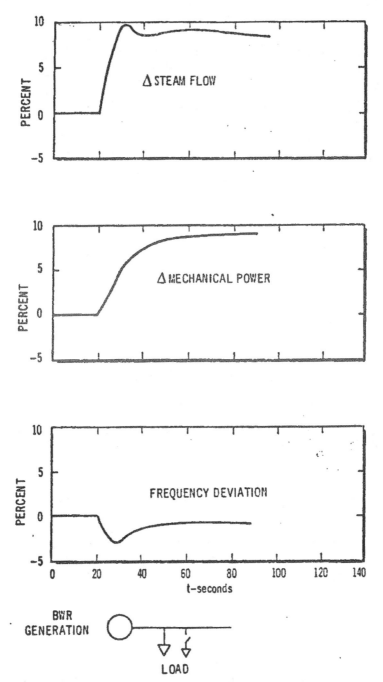

10 PERCENT STEP LOSS IN GENERATION. ISOLATED NETWORK
SUPPLIED WITH BWR GENERATION GOV REGULATION = 5 PERCENT

FIG. 5

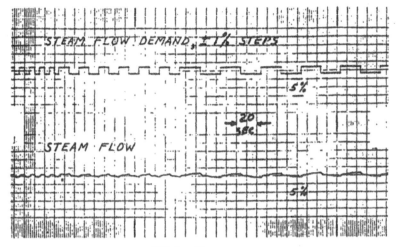

FIG. 6

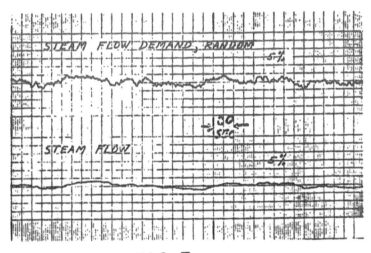

FIG. 7

BWR SMALL SIGNAL RESPONSE

Dynamic Models for Combined Cycle Plants in Power System Studies

Working Group on Prime Mover and Energy Supply Models for System Dynamic Performance Studies

DYNAMIC MODELS FOR COMBINED CYCLE PLANTS IN POWER SYSTEM STUDIES

Working Group on Prime Mover and Energy Supply Models for System Dynamic Performance Studies

Abstrat - This paper is the third of a series of papers prepared by the Working Group on Prime Mover and Energy Supply Models for System Dynamic Performance Studies.

It describes various aspects of combined cycles made up of gas turbine, waste heat recovery boiler and steam turbine and develops models designed to simulate the response of the combined cycle plant for use in system dynamic performance studies.

KEY WORDS

Combined cycle plants, combustion turbines, heat recovery steam generators, prime mover dynamic models

INTRODUCTION

The Working Group on Prime Mover and Energy Supply Models for System Dynamic Performance Studies, under the IEEE System Dynamic Performance Subcommittee has as its principal objective the development of prime mover/energy supply models for use in power system simulation programs. Two previous working group papers have dealt with fossil fueled steam units [1] and hydro turbines [2].

This paper contains modeling information on gas turbine - steam turbine combined cycles which are becoming increasing contributors to the world's power generation. The

Paper was prepared by F. P. de Mello (Chairman) and D. J. Ahner with contributions from P. M. Anderson, J. H. Doudna, P. Kundur, L. M. Richardson, G. Tandy, C. W. Taylor and F. Van de Meulebroeke.

94 WM 185-9 PWRS A paper recommended and approved by the IEEE Power System Engineering Committee of the IEEE Power Engineering Society for presentation at the IEEE/PES 1994 Winter Meeting, New York, New York, January 30 - February 3, 1994. Manuscript submitted August 2, 1993; made available for printing November 29, 1993.

response characteristics of this generation configuration differ substantially from those of conventional steam cycles and must be understood and modeled correctly to determine the dynamic interaction of the prime movers with the grid transmission characteristics.

There are several different combined cycle configurations and control variations available from various manufacturers. These configurations may incorporate steam injection from the heat recovery system to control NO_x emissions, Heat Recovery Steam

Generator (HRSG) supplementary firing, multiple steam generation pressure levels, reheat or nonreheat steam cycles and integral HRSG deaerators. In addition gas turbines may modulate gas flows to different degrees and control turbine firing or exhaust temperatures over given ranges of operation. Each of these options has a unique power response characteristic.

This paper discusses and illustrates a typical steam configuration and gas turbine control system characteristics and response. To clarify the illustration, a nonreheat, dry NO_x configuration has been selected with limited turbine air flow modulation to maintain gas turbine firing temperature. A single shaft, constant speed gas turbine configuration has been used with variable inlet guide vanes.

There is no intent of establishing a recommended model structure for combined cycle plants in this paper. It is recognized that there are many variations in the composition of cycle components and the particular logic of controls. The purpose of the paper is to serve as an illustration of modeling requirements for this type of plant and to motivate contributions based on existing or future installations.

TYPICAL COMBINED CYCLE CONFIGURATION

A typical combined cycle plant configuration is shown in Fig. 1. This arrangement consists of an unfired three pressure level with a single shaft gas turbine, HRSG and single steam turbine (HRSG) operating at steam conditions of 1250 psi/950°F and 450 psi/475°F. The low pressure drum provides steam for feedwater deaeration. The steam turbine has no uncontrolled extraction and all feedwater deaeration is accomplished with low temperature gas turbine

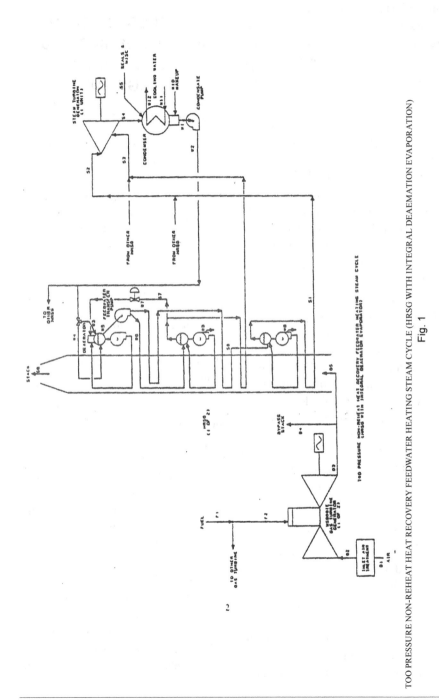

TOO PRESSURE NON-REHEAT HEAT RECOVERY FEEDWATER HEATING STEAM CYCLE (HRSG WITH INTEGRAL DEAEMATION EVAPORATION)

Fig. 1

exhaust heat in an integral HRSG deaerator. 1250 psi high pressure throttle steam and the 450 psi admission steam expand to a condenser pressure of 2" Hg. The steam turbine operates under sliding pressure with initial pressure regulation at low load conditions.

In multiple gas turbine unit combined cycle configurations, the steam flows are generally combined as shown in Fig. 1 for admission to a single steam turbine. The gas turbine units modulate in parallel to provide good partial load performance which also results in uniform steam mixing conditions. The gas turbines are provided with variable compressor inlet guide vanes to maintain good steam conditions over partial load ranges. These guide vanes reduce gas turbine compressor air flow thus decreasing stack loss and maintaining high gas turbine exhaust temperature at reduced gas turbine loads. The range of guide vane operation and control strategy may vary somewhat among turbine manufacturers, however, the basic objective is to maintain high steam temperature operation at lower loads.

Fig. 2 shows the chain of submodels of the combined cycle described above, identifying the input and output variables of each submodel and the coupling between the blocks. From left to right these blocks are: the speed/load control, the fuel and air flow controls, the gas turbine and the heat recovery boiler with steam turbine.

The detail of each of these submodels is developed in the next section.

PROCESS PHYSICAL RELATIONSHIPS AND MODEL BLOCK DIAGRAMS

Speed/Load Control

Fig. 3 shows the speed governor using the same symbols as in references 3 and 4. The inputs to the speed governor are the load demand V_L and the speed deviation ΔN. The output is a fuel demand signal, F_D.

Fuel and Air Controls

The control scheme for fuel and air flow rates is shown in Fig. 4. Where applicable the symbols for control parameters have been maintained the same as in references 3 and 4.

Inlet guide vanes are modulated to vary air flow over a limited range. This allows maintaining high turbine exhaust temperatures and thus, steam cycle efficiency at reduced loads. Over this load range, the fuel and guide vanes are controlled to maintain constant gas turbine inlet temperature. This is functionally accomplished by scheduling air flow with load demand F_D and setting the turbine exhaust temperature reference, T_R, to that value which is calculated to result in the desired load with the scheduled air flow at constant turbine inlet temperature. This exhaust temperature reference may be calculated from the basic gas turbine thermodynamic relations:

$$T_R = T_f \left[1 - \left(1 - \frac{1}{x}\right) n_T \right] \qquad (1)$$

where T_R = reference exhaust temperature in per unit of the absolute firing temperature at rated conditions

$x = [PR]^{\frac{\gamma-1}{\gamma}}$ cycle isentropic pressure ratio parameter

or

$$x = \left[PR_o \cdot W \right]^{\frac{\gamma-1}{(\gamma_2)}}$$

where

PR$_o$ = design cycle pressure ratio (turbine inlet pressure divided by ambient pressure)

γ = ratio of specific heats, c_p/c_V

W = air flow in pu of design air flow (W_o)

n_T = turbine efficiency

Tf = turbine inlet temperature in pu of design absolute firing temperature

The per unit air flow required to produce a specified power generation at the given gas turbine inlet temperature T_f, is given by the turbine power balance:

$$W = \frac{P_G \cdot K_o}{T_f \left(1 - \frac{1}{x}\right) n_T - T_1 \dfrac{(x-1)}{n_c}} \qquad (3)$$

where P_G = power output in pu of rated

$$K_o = \frac{kW_o \cdot 3413}{W_o \cdot T_{fo} \cdot C_p} \qquad (4)$$

kW$_o$, W$_o$, T$_{fo}$, C$_p$ = base net output (kW), air flow (lbs/sec), turbine inlet temperature (^{O}R), average specific heat (BTU/lb x ^{O}F)

T$_i$ = compressor inlet temperature in pu of design absolute firing temperature

n_c = compressor efficiency

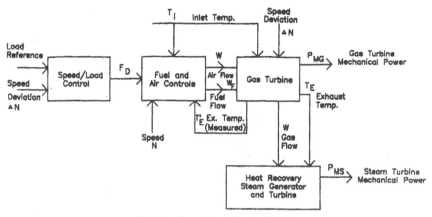

Fig. 2. Combined Cycle Model

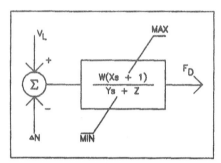

Fig. 3. Speed Load Controls

Combustor pressure drop, specific heat changes and detailed treatment of cooling flows has been deleted for purposes of illustration of the general unit behavior. These performance effects have been incorporated into equivalent compressor and turbine efficiency values.

Also for practical purposes the steady state gas flow through the turbine is considered the same as air flow through the compressor (W).

Equations 2) and 3) determine the air flow W and pressure ratio parameter, x for a given power generation, P_G, at a specified per unit ambient temperature,

T_i. The reference exhaust temperature, T_R is then given by equation 1), with $T_f = 1.0$. The air flow must of course be subject to the control range limits.

Block A in Fig. 4 contains the calculation of desired air flow W_D and desired exhaust temperature reference T_R, over the design range of air flow variation through vane control. These desired values of W_D and T_R are functions of F_D (desired turbine output from speed/load controls) and ambient temperature T_i and are determined by the solution of equations 2 and 3 with appropriate limits on W_D and T_R. The response of the vane control is modeled with a time constant T_V with non windup limits corresponding to the vane control range. The actual air flow W is shown as product of vane opening and shaft speed. The exhaust temperature reference T_R is fed through a time lag and appropriate limits to the exhaust temperature controls.

The measured exhaust temperature T_E' is compared with the limit value T_R and the error acts on the temperature controller, again represented with the same symbols as in references [3,4]. Normally T_E' is less than T_R causing the temperature controller to be at the MAX limit (about 1.1 pu). Should T_E' exceed T_R, the controller will come off limit and integrate down to the point where its output takes over as the demand signal for fuel, V_{ce}, through the "low select" block. The fuel valve positioner and fuel flow control is represented as in reference 1 yielding the fuel flow signal W_F as another input to the gas turbine model.

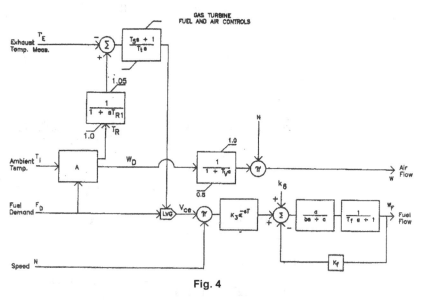

Fig. 4

Gas Turbine

Fig. 5 shows the relationships used to develop gas turbine mechanical power P_{MG} and exhaust temperature T_E.

The gas turbine net output (turbine power less compressor power) is determined from equation 3) where T_f is the calculated turbine inlet temperature, and the air flow W is specified by the inlet guide vane schedule and compressor speed. The turbine inlet temperature T_f is determined from the combustor heat balance.

$$T_f = T_D + \frac{W_f K_2}{W} = T_i \left[1 + \frac{(x-1)}{\eta_c} \right] + \frac{W_f}{W} \cdot K_2 \quad (5)$$

where

$K_2 = \dfrac{\Delta T_o}{T_{fo}} =$ design combustor temperature rise in pu of absolute firing temp (6)

T_D = compressor discharge temperature in per unit of design absolute firing temperature

W_f = fuel flow in per unit of design air flow (W_o)

W_{fo} = design fuel flow in per unit of design air flow

The gas turbine exhaust temperature T_E is now given by equations 1) and 2) using the turbine inlet temperature, equation 5).

Mechanical power P_{MG} is shown to be a function of T_f and flow rate of combustion products (W). Since in many applications speed deviations can be significant, the speed effects are also included.

The blocks involving dynamics follow the definitions in reference 3. They include the combustor time delay E_{CR}, the compressor discharge volume time constant T_{CD} and the turbine and exhaust system transport delay E_{TD}. The location of the time constants and time delays in the block diagram of Fig. 5 does not necessarily follow their relation

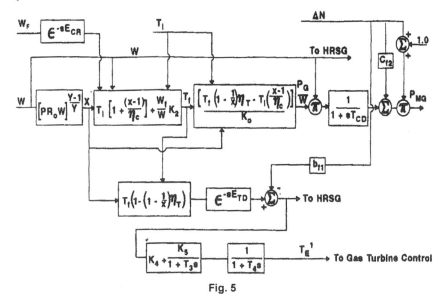

Fig. 5

to the process physics. For instance the compressor volume time constant T_{CD} is located downstream of the turbine power block $\frac{P_G}{W}$. This does not alter the effect of this time constant on the variable of interest which is P_{MG}.

It should be noted that the effect of this time constant on the output of the HRSG is negligible compared to the storage lags in the steam generator.

The radiation shield and thermocouple lags as defined in reference 3 are used to develop the measured exhaust temperature T_E' from the actual exhaust temperature T_E.

Steam Power Determination

The HRSG steam system reacts to the changes in gas turbine exhaust flow W, and exhaust temperature, T_E. The transient gas heat flux to the high and low pressure steam generation sections may be closely approximated by using the relations for constant gas side effectiveness. The exhaust gas and steam absorption temperatures through the HRSG shown in Fig. 1, are indicated in Fig. 6. [1]

$$\eta_{g1} = \frac{T_{ex} - T'}{T_{ex} - Tml} \qquad (7)$$

$$\eta_{g2} = \frac{T' - T''}{T' - Tm_2} \qquad (8)$$

where T' and T'' are the gas pinch point temperatures shown in Fig. 6 and, Tm1, Tm2 are the average metal temperatures in the HP and LP evaporation sections, respectively.

The gas heat absorption by the respective HRSG section is then given by:

$$\dot{Q}_{g1} = W\eta_{g1} \left(T_{ex} - T_{ml}\right) + \left(\dot{Q}_{ec1} + \dot{Q}'_{ec1}\right) \quad (9)$$

$$\dot{Q}_{g2} = W\eta_{g2} \left(T' - T_{m2}\right) + \left(\dot{Q}_{ec2} - \dot{Q}'_{ec1}\right) \quad (10)$$

where $\dot{Q}_{ec\ 1,2}$ 1,2 $and\ \dot{Q}_{ec\ 1}$ are the HP and IP economizer heat fluxes.

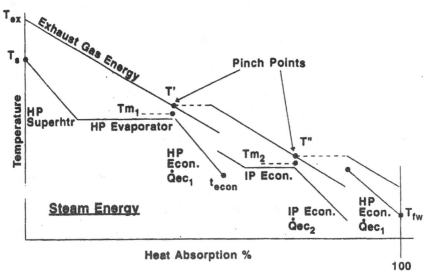

Fig. 6

The respective economizer heat absorption is approximated by using the generic constant effectiveness expression.

$$\dot{Q}_{ec} = n_{ec} \left(Tg - Ti\right)\dot{m}$$

where

$\dot{Q}_{ec}$ = the heat flux absorbed by the heating section

T_g = hot side gas temperature
T_i = the cold side water temperature
$\dot{m}$ = flow rate of water

The relations above are listed to illustrate the physics of the process involved in the block "Gas Path Relations" of Fig. 7. As noted in the next section, this level of modeling detail is not justified except where studies of plant controls are the principal objective.

Fig. 7 develops a lumped parameter simplified structure of the HRSG and steam turbine model following the approach described in reference 6.

Given the heat fluxes absorbed by the high pressure and intermediate pressure steam generators, $\dot{Q}_{G1}$ and $\dot{Q}_{G2}$, steam pressure in each drum P_{DH} and P_{DI} is developed by integrating the difference between steam generation and steam flow out of each section. Steam generation follows heat flux (Q_{g1}, Q_{g2}) with a short lag due to metal heat capacitance (MC_1, MC_2) and heat transfer film coefficient (HW_1, HW_2).

The heat fluxes $\dot{Q}_1$ and $\dot{Q}_2$ from metal to the steaming mixture are proportional to the temperature differences between metal and steaming mixture (T_{M1} - T_{S1}) for the high pressure boiler and (T_{M2} - T_{S2}) for the intermediate pressure boiler. The saturation temperature TS_1 and TS_2 are functions of drum pressures P_{DH} and P_{DI} for the high pressure and intermediate pressure boilers respectively. Steam generations are proportional to the beat fluxes $\dot{Q}_1$ and $\dot{Q}_2$ through the constant R_1 and R_2. The boiler and steam leads inner volume is split in two lumped volumes whose storage constants are shown as C_{B1} and C_{T1} for the high pressure boiler and C_{B2} and C_{T2} for the low pressure boiler.

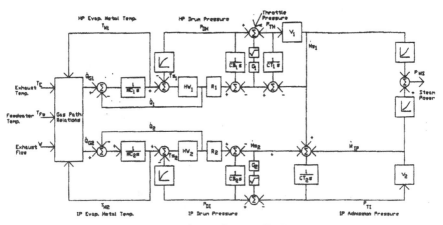

Fig. 7. Steam System Model

The changes in gas heat flux are established by the gas temperature profile which tends to peg about the pinch points as shown by the dotted gas characteristics shown in Fig. 6. This is the point of closest approach of the gas to the evaporator metal temperature.

The IP sections therefore experience higher temperature difference as exhaust temperature decreases. The deaerator is assumed pegged at a constant pressure.

The steam flow rates between the two volumes in each boiler is determined from the pressure drop relationship with flow rate being proportional to square root of pressure drop (proportionality constants G_1 and G_2). The flow rate to the high pressure turbine is proportional to the valve coefficient V_1 and throttle pressure. The turbine pressure at the point of the low pressure steam admission is shown to be proportional to turbine flow coefficient V_2 and total steam flow $\dot{m}_{S1} = \dot{m}_{S2}$, with a small time constant C_{T2} to account for steam volume effects. The steam turbine mechanical power is a function of the steam flow rates $\dot{m}_{S1}$ and $\dot{m}_{ip}$.

Practical Expedient in Modeling of HRSG and Steam Turbines

Inspection of the process physics described in Fig. 7 reveals that the steam turbine mechanical power response follows changes in gas turbine exhaust energy with basically two time lags for the high pressure contribution and two lags for the low pressure contribution. These lags correspond to the tube metal heat capacitance time constants in the order of 5 seconds and the boiler storage time constants in the order of 50 to 100 seconds.

It is very likely that the total contribution to mechanical power from the two pressure boilers can be approximated with a two time constant model. The gain between gas turbine exhaust energy and steam turbine output will in general be a nonlinear function which can be derived from steady state measurements through the load range, or from design heat balance calculations for rated and partial load conditions.

The resulting simplified model would thus have the form in Fig. 8.

SAMPLE RESULTS

For a combined cycle plant modeled as in Figs. 3, 4, 5 and 8 with parameters listed in Appendix I, Figs. 9 to 11 show some response results for a step change in KW demand (a step in F_D of Fig. 2).

Fig. 9 shows the response of several variables to a 10% step increase in F_D from an initial operating point of 0.95 pu.

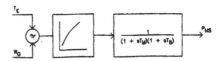

Fig. 8. Simplified Steam Turbine Power Response Model

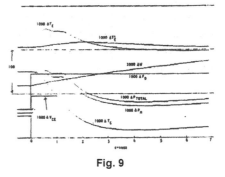

Fig. 9

The step change in F_D reflects into a similar change in fuel demand signal V_{CE}. The increase in firing causes an increase in the exhaust temperature beyond the exhaust temperature limit reference causing the temperature controller output T_C to come off its limit and override the F_D demand signal. This can be seen from the V_{CE} trace following the T_C signal around one second after the step change.

The total power (gas turbine plus steam turbine) as well as the gas turbine power are plotted with a slight offset. One can see that in the time frame of a few seconds there is no appreciable contribution from the steam turbine. The responses of the actual exhaust temperature T_E and of the measured temperature T'_E are also shown as is also the change in air flow. In this operating region close to full load, increases in load demand are quickly offset by the temperature controller.

Fig. 10 shows the response to a negative 10% step change from the same operating point (0.95 pu). There is no interference from the temperature controller and the power output responds both transiently and in steady state to the power demand signal. In the time scale of Fig. 10, 0 to 7 secs, the contribution of the steam turbine is hardly noticeable. Fig. 11 is a repeat of the Fig. 10 with time scale of 0 to 25 secs.

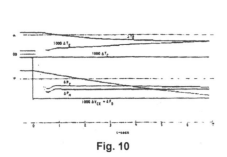

Fig. 10

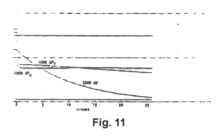

Fig. 11

The results shown on Fig. 9 are for the case where the output of the override temperature control is initially at a limit which is higher than the KW demand signal F_D. One thus sees a temporary increase in gas turbine output later overridden by the temperature control.

In schemes concerned with optimizing efficiency in the range of variable guide vane control, the prime concern is to observe rigid control of firing temperature as inferred by measurement of air flow and exhaust temperature. In such cases, increases in load demand in the range of variable guide vane control, would result in the slower response characteristic following air flow. This aspect could be of importance in isolated power system applications where spinning reserve and frequency control is shared by combined cycle units.

One other effect that may need consideration in isolated power system applications (system restoration scenarios are some of them) is the effective negative speed droop characteristics in the region where the fuel controls are following temperature limit rather than speed. In this mode of operation where fuel is dictated by temperature control, a decrease in speed, due to its effect on air flow, would cause a decrease in fuel and therefore a decrease in power.

CONCLUSIONS

The increasing use of combined cycle plants as part of power systems' generation mix brings an industry need for modeling these types of plants in assessments of system dynamic performance. This need is more acute in some developing countries where combined cycle plants form a significant proportion of the systems generating capacity.

This working group paper presents the modeling requirements for a particular type of combined cycle plant as an example of the subsystems, including controls, that play a role in the dynamic performance of this type of plant.

It is hoped that the paper will serve as a pattern for future contributions on modeling of existing or future installations.

APPENDIX

MODEL PARAMETERS AND TYPICAL DATA

The bases for the variables and the values of parameters used in illustrating the characteristics of the combined cycle plant are listed below.

Parameter Values

Fuel and Air Controls   Figure 4

K_3 = 0.7
K_6 = 0.3
a   = 10
b   = 1
c   = 0
K_f = 1
T_f = 0.01
T_5 = 3.3
T_t = 0.45
T_V = 10

Gas Turbine   Figure 5

E_{CR} = 0.1
E_{TD} = 0.04
T_3 = 15
T_4 = 3
K_4 = 0.8
K_5 = 0.2
T_{CD} = 0.1

Steam Turbine   Figure 8

T_M = 5
T_B = 20

COMBINED CYCLE PLANT RATED CONDITIONS

Power		
	Gas Turbine	82 MW
	Steam Turbine	45 MW
	Total Net Power	127 MW
Heat Consumption		930 x 10⁶ Btu/hr
Heat Recovery Steam Generator		
	High pressure	1250 psia
	High pressure flow	251,000 #/hr
	High pressure temperature	950°F
	Intermediate Pressure	
	Intermediate Pressure flow	420 psia
	Intermediate Pressure temperature	82,000 #/hr
		500°F

Fuel and Air Controls, Combustor and Gas Turbine and HRSG, Figs. 4, 5, & 7

VARIABLE	BASE
T_R, Exhaust temperature reference	Design exhaust absolute temperature at rated load, 40°F ambient temperature
T_E, Actual exhaust temperature	Design exhaust absolute temperature at rated load, 40°F ambient temperature
T'_E, Measured exhaust temperature	Design exhaust absolute temperature at rated load, 40°F ambient temperature
W_D, Desired air flow	Design air flow at rated load
W, Actual air flow	Design air flow at rated load
N, Speed	Rated speed
W_F, Fuel flow	Design air flow at rated load
T_F, Firing temperature	Design firing absolute temperature at rated load
P_{MG}, Gas turbine mechanical power	Rated generator MVA
T_{M1}, T_{M2}, High and intermediate pressure steaming sections metal temp	°F
T_{S1}, T_{S2}, High and low pressure saturation temperature	°F
P_{DH}, High pressure boiler drum pressure	Boiler throttle pressure at rated load
P_{DI}, Low pressure boiler drum pressure	Intermediate pressure turbine admission pressure at rated load
M_1, M_{S1}, High pressure boiler section steam flow	High pressure turbine steam flow at rated load
M_2, M_{S2}, Low pressure boiler section steam flows	Intermediate pressure turbine steam flow at rated load
P_{MS}, Steam turbine mechanical power	Rated generator MVA

REFERENCES

1. Working Group on Prime Mover and Energy Supply Models for System Dynamic Performance Studies, "Dynamic Models for Fossil Fueled Steam Units in Power System Studies", IEEE Trans.-PWRS May 91 pp. 753-761, 90SM 327-7.

2. Working Group on Prime Mover and Energy Supply Models for System Dynamic Performance Studies, "Hydraulic Turbine and Turbine Control Models for System Dynamic Studies", IEEE Trans. PWRS, Vol. 7, No. 1, February 1992, 91SM 462-2.

3. W. I. Rowen, "Simplified Mathematical Representations of Heavy-Duty Gas Turbines", ASME, Vol 105(1) 1983 (Journal of Engineering for Power, Series A, October 1983), pp 865-869.

4. LN Hannett and Afzal Khan, "Combustion Turbine Dynamic

Model Validation from Tests",
IEEE Trans. February 1993, Vol.
8, pp 152-158.

5. WI   Rowen,   "Simplified
    Mathematical   Representations
    of Single Shaft Gas Turbines on
    Mechanical Drive Service". Trans.
    ASME Paper 92-GT-22.

6. FP de Mello, "Boiler Models for
    System Dynamic Performance
    Studies", IEEE Trans. PWRS,
    February 91, pp 66-74.

A Governor/Turbine Model for a Twin-Shaft Combustion Turbine

L.N. Hannett

G. Jee

B. Fardanesh

A GOVERNOR/TURBINE MODEL FOR A TWIN-SHAFT COMBUSTION TURBINE

Louis N. Hannett,
Senior Member
Power Technologies, Inc.
Schenectady, NY

George Jee, Senior Member
Consolidated Edison
Company
New York, NY

B. Fardanesh, Member
New York Power Authority
New York, NY

ABSTRACT

A twin shaft gas turbine unit was tested for the governor response to disturbances. A computer simulation model is presented as well as the test data which was used to derive values for the model parameters.

KEY WORDS

Keywords: Gas turbine, simulation model, testing method.

INTRODUCTION

The Consolidated Edison Company of New York, Inc. is among several New York utilities participating in a statewide research project funded by New York Power Authority and the Empire State Electric Research Corporation to field test a number of hydro and thermal units. The objective of this project is to validate and update the models for generators, excitation systems, and governors used in the computer simulation studies. In parallel with identifying values for model parameters, the existing model structures are also examined, and, whenever needed, refinements are made to achieve better matches of simulation results with field recordings of staged tests.

94 WM 188-3 PWRS A paper recommended and approved by the IEEE Power System Engineering Committee of the IEEE Power Engineering Society for presentation at the IEEE/PES 1994 Winter Meeting, New York, New York, January 30 - February 3, 1994. Manuscript submitted July 26, 1993; made available for printing December 6, 1993.

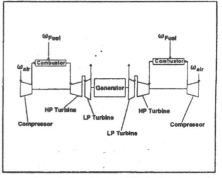

Fig. 1. Gas Path of Twin-Shaft Combustion Turbine

In the Fall of 1992, a 46.5 MVA (0.9 pf) combustion turbine unit in Con Edison's Astoria Plant complex was tested. This unit is part of a block of combustion turbines in the complex which are utilized for peak load shaving, spinning reserve, system restoration and voltage control. The combustion turbine was manufactured by Pratt & Whitney with controls manufactured by Hamilton Standard. This paper presents the model that was developed for this combustion turbine and its controls and identification of values for model parameters from tests.

MODEL STRUCTURE

The arrangement of turbine components is shown in Fig. 1. As shown in that figure, the generator is located in the center with a twin-shaft combustion turbine on each side.

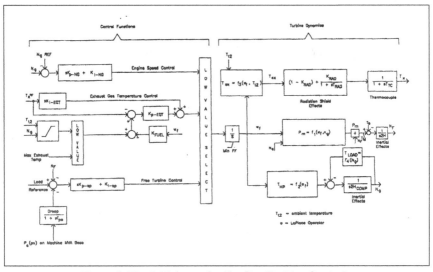

Figure 2. Block Diagram for the Gas Turbine Controls

Twin shafts connect the compressors and the HP turbines and another shaft connects the generator to the LP turbines. Air is supplied to two combustors by twin compressors driven by two high pressure turbines. Part of the energy of the high pressure temperature gas from the combustors is extracted in the HP turbines to drive the compressors. During startup, the diesel engines drive the compressors until sufficient pressure is obtained before entering the combustors. Then fuel is burned and the combustion turbine becomes self-sustaining.

When the turbine generator is on-line, the shaft connecting the generator and LP turbine will be rotating close to synchronous speed (called free turbine speed), and variation of fuel flow will result in variation of power output of the generator. Since the compressor and HP turbine form a separate system, variation of fuel flow will affect the rotational speed (called the engine speed) of these two components as determined by the load on the compressors (i.e. the air flow/ pressure characteristics) and power of the HP turbines. Thus, the engine speed varies for different loads affecting the air flow and gas temperatures.

The design of the controls considers the effect that changes in fuel flow has on engine speed and air flow. The block diagrams for the controls are shown in Fig. 2, where the input signals are:

1. N_g, the engine speed in per unit
2. N_f, the free turbine speed in per unit
3. T_x, exhaust temperature in °F
4. T_{t2}, ambient temperature or inlet air temperature in °F
5. P_e, generator electrical power (pu on machine MVA base)

The fuel flow is regulated by a servo, which is represented in Fig. 2 by a reset controller 1/s. The input to the fuel servo is one of three signals which enter a low value select. These signals are:

1. Free Turbine Control
2. Exhaust Gas Temperature Control
3. Engine Speed Control

FREE TURBINE CONTROL

This control provides the normal governing control for the unit. The input signals are the free turbine speed and electrical power. The control function produces from the error signal a proportional-derivative action to the servo considering the reset response of the servo, the total response when this control is in command is that of proportional-integral control. If free turbine speed is the only signal being measured, then the device will operate

as an isochronous governor. For parallel operation with other units, droop is introduced by including in the error signal electrical power scaled by a gain (droop). Thus, if the unit is operating at full load, i.e. $P_e = 1$ p.u., on machine base and the unit trips, the final speed deviation will equal the speed droop setting.

ENGINE SPEED CONTROL

The structure for this control is similar to that for free turbine control. The value for N_{gREF} is actually the maximum value that is allowed for engine speed as a function of the inlet air temperature. This controller when in command is an isochronous control on engine speed, and it serves to limit fuel flow so that engine speed will not exceed a certain value. Maximum values are selected for base load, peak load, and emergency peak load.

EXHAUST GAS TEMPERATURE CONTROL

The input signals for the exhaust gas temperature controls are inlet air temperature, engine speed and turbine exhaust temperature. This control is in command whenever the exhaust temperature exceeds the exhaust temperature reference, or when the unit is picking up load faster than the turbine dynamics can handle. The latter condition is due to the fact that the exhaust temperature responds faster due to increases in fuel flow before the moderating action of air flow with increase in engine speed.

Thus, the second condition serves as a rate limiter for load pickup.

TURBINE DYNAMICS

The turbine dynamics are represented by a set of functions which can be determined by steady-state measurements. These functions are:

1. $P_m = f_1 (w_f, N_g)$
   $T_m = P_m/N_f$

where P_m = mechanical power in the LP turbine

w_f = fuel flow

N_g = engine speed

N_f = free turbine speed

2. $T_{HP} = f_2 (w_f)$

where T_{HP} = torque developed by the HP turbine

3. $T_{ex} = f_3 (w_f, T_{t2})$

where T_{ex} = turbine exhaust temperature

T_{t2} = inlet air temperature

4. $T_{LOAD} = f_4 (N_g)$

where T_{LOAD} = load torque on the compressor assuming a torque-speed characteristic

Additional dynamics are included for inertial effects and lags from radiation effects and thermocouple measurements similar to those cited in [1].

SUGGESTED TEST PLAN

The following test plan is suggested based on the experience with the tests that were conducted. This test plan includes additions to that which was used during the tests conducted in the fall of 1992.

Signals which should be measured for the dynamic response are:

1. Engine Speed, N_g
2. Free Turbine Speed, N_f
3. Electrical Power, P_e
4. Exhaust Temperature, T_x
5. Engine Speed Control Output
6. Exhaust Gas Temperature Control Output
7. Free Turbine Speed Control Output

The tests consist of collecting steady-state measurements and performing dynamic load change tests. The steady-state measurements were collected with the unit on-line at different load levels. In addition to the above signals, the following quantities were recorded:

1. Fuel Flow
2. Inlet Air Temperature or the Ambient Temperature, T_{t2}

If possible, air flow and compressor outlet pressure should also be recorded.

The dynamic response characteristics were obtained from load rejection tests and fast load pickup.

TESTS CONDUCTED IN FALL OF 1992

The following signals were measured for the dynamic response by using a PC based digital recorder:

1. Two Phase-to-Phase Voltages on the Generator Side of the Main Breaker
2. Two Generator AC Line Currents
3. Free Turbine Speed
4. Exhaust Temperature
5. Engine Speed Control Output
6. Exhaust Gas Temperature Control Output
7. Free Turbine Speed Control Output

The digitized values of phase voltages and generator AC line currents can be post-processed to obtain electrical power. A sudden change in electrical power serves to identify the instant that switching took place.

Steady-state measurements were made at different loads with increments of 10% of the unit's MVA rating. Two dynamic tests were load rejections with the unit initially carrying 4.5 MW and 12.1 MW. A third dynamic test was a rapid pick-up from no load to full load.

MODEL DERIVATION

The steady-state data was used to identify the turbine functions as shown in Figs. 3 and 4. The gains in the control functions were determined from the dynamic response.

The analysis of the steady-state data usually involved preparing graphs such as the one shown in Fig. 3. In this figure, the quantity electrical power is plotted as a function of fuel flow. The functions, f_1, f_2, f_3, and f_4 were represented by look up tables in the simulation model.

The digitized data from the load rejection were used to estimate the control gains. A PC digital signal processing program was used to combine individual signals to form the error signal, e.g., load reference $- N_f - \frac{Droop}{1+STpc} P_e(s)$. The error signal was differentiated and the quantities $error(t)$ and $\frac{derror(t)}{dt}$ are compared with the control signal to obtain the values for the proportional gain and integral gain.

The final check was to run digital simulations of the tests and compare the model output variables with the recorded signals. When necessary, adjustments were made to fine tune the model response until a match was made with the recorded measurements. The values for the derived model parameters are listed in Table 1. Look up tables used in the

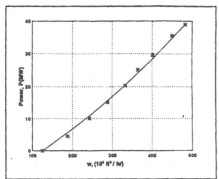

Fig. 3. Electrical Power vs. Fuel Flow

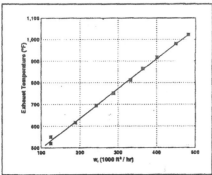

Fig. 4. Exhaust Temperature vs. Fuel Flow

model for power and fuel flow are also listed in Table 1 in per unit with base values being 46.5 MW and 482,000 ft³/hr.

A sample of the comparison plots are shown in Figs. 5-8. The plots from the simulation of the 6 MW load rejection are shown in Figs. 5 and 6 for the free turbine speed and free turbine speed control output. Plots from the load pickup tests are shown in Figs. 7 and 8.

CONCLUSIONS

The process of model derivation by tests has been illustrated for a twin shaft combustion turbine. This process involves first a thorough analysis of the physics of the

TABLE 1						
Values for Gas Turbine Parameters						
H_{gen}	Droop	K_{p-sp}	K_{1-sp}	T_{pe}	K_{p-EGT}	K_{1-EGT}
2.51	.05	8.0	40	.6 sec	.00557	.00125
Maximum Exhaust Temp		N_{G-REF}	K_{p-NG}	K_{1-NG}	T_{INLET}	$T_{INLET\ REF}$
1190 °F		1.0	2.0	8.0	50°F	50°F
Minimum Fuel Flow		H_{COMP}	T_{RAD}	K_{RAD}	T_{TC}	K_{FUEL}
.19		.5	6 sec	.6	.5 sec	100

Exhaust Temperature Reference Table				
N_g (pu)	0	0.698	.989	1.00
T_{XREF}	671°F	671°F	1358°F	1358°F

Fuel Flow Versus Power Table - $F_1\ (w_f, n_g)$				
w_f (pu)	.259	.390	.502	1.0
Power	0	.097	.216	.838

Fuel Flow Versus Engine Speed Table - $F_2\ (w_f)$							
w_f (pu)	.259	.310	.390	.60	.77	.875	1.0
N_g	.780	.830	.879	.940	.975	.97	1.0

Fuel Flow Versus Exhaust Temperature - $F_3\ (w_f)$		
w_f (pu)	.259	1.0
T_x	525°F	1050°F

Engine Speed Versus Load Torque - $F_4\ (N_g)$		
N_g	0	1.0
T_{LOAD}	0	1.0

N_g base $=$ 5190.5 rpm

w_f base $=$ 482,000 ft³/hr

P_e base $=$ 46.5 MW

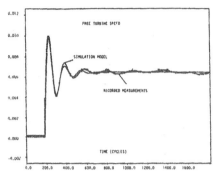

Fig. 5. Comparison of Simulation Results and Recorded Measurements: Free Turbine Speed Following 6.05 MW Load Rejection

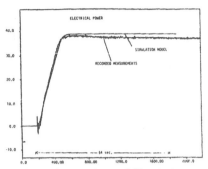

Fig. 7. Comparison of Simulation Results and Recorded Measurements: Electrical Power During Load Acceptance Tests

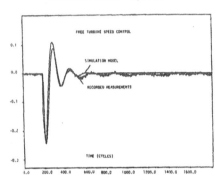

Fig. 6. Comparison of Simulation Results and Recorded Measurements: Free Turbine Speed Control Output Following 6.05 MW Load Rejection

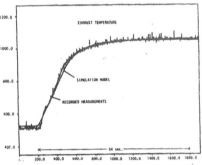

Fig. 8. Comparison of Simulation Results and Recorded Measurements: Exhaust Temp. Using K_{rad} = 0.6, T_{rad} = 6 sec During Load Acceptance Test

process and controls which determine the model structure including pertinent variables and parameters.

The recommended test procedure includes careful documentation of steady-state characteristics and capture of dynamic responses of important process variables during feasible tests consisting of rapid load changes and load rejections. An intelligent trial and error process is then used to adjust model parameters until reasonable matches are obtained between tests and digital simulations. As can be noted, the process and its controls are extremely non-linear and there is no other practical procedure of model derivation than the one described, even when the turbine dynamics were represented by hydraulic and thermodynamic equations. If this approach is taken, then performance data would be required for each component, i.e. the compressor, combustor, and turbines.

It is hoped that the model of the twin shaft combustion turbine presented will be useful for studies of system dynamic performance.

A field testing program was conducted to obtain data for use in the computer simulation model development. The steps for the testing procedure and model derivation are presented.

ACKNOWLEDGEMENTS

This work was sponsored by the Consolidated Edison Company of New York, ESEERCO, and the New York State Power Authority. The authors would like to acknowledge the contributions of Reza Ghafurian, Steve Tourian, Anna Yee and Firooz Mirbaha of Con Edison.

REFERENCES

1. W.I. Rowen, "Simplified Mathematical Representations of Heavy Duty Gas Turbines", Transactions of ASME, Vol. 105(1), 1983, pp. 865-869.

2. IEEE Committee Report, "Dynamic Models for Steam and Hydro Turbines in Power System Studies", IEEE Transactions on Power Apparatus and Systems, Vol. 92, No. 6, November/ December 1973, pp. 1904-1915.

3. ASME Performance Code Committee No. 20.1, "Speed and Load Governing Systems for Steam Turbine-Generator Units", ANSI/ASME-PTC20.1-1977.

4. St. Pierre, C.R., "Impact Loading of Isolated Generators", IEEE Transactions on Industry Applications, Vol. 1A-17, No. 6, November/December 1981, pp. 557-566.

Louis N. Hannett graduated from Clarkson University in 1971 receiving a B.S. in Electrical Engineering with honors. Upon graduation, he joined Power Technologies, Inc. as an analytical engineer and was promoted to senior engineer in 1982. He has contributed to the area of dynamic stability and model of electrical machines. Mr. Hannett is a senior member of the IEEE and is a registered professional engineer with the State of New York.

George Jee received the B.S. degree in engineering from Newark College of Engineering of Newark, New Jersey in 1974 and the M.S. in engineering from New Jersey Institute of Technology in 1978. He also completed the General Electric Power System Engineering course in 1979. He joined Consolidated Edison Company of New York, Inc. in 1975 and in 1984 was promoted to Subsection Manager, System Performance. He had also served as an Industry Advisor to EPRI on two optimal power flow development projects. Since March 1993, Mr. Jee has held the position of Section Manager, Energy Strategy Department.

Behruz (Bruce) Fardanesh (M'83) received his B.S. in Electrical Engineering from Sharif Technical University in Tehran, Iran. He also received his M.S. and Doctor of Engineering degrees both in Electrical Engineering from the University of Missouri-Rolla and Cleveland State University in 1981 and 1985, respectively. Since 1985 he has been teaching at Manhattan College where he holds the rank of Associate Professor of Electrical Engineering. Currently, he is working as a senior R&D Engineer at the New York Power Authority. His areas of interest are power systems operations, dynamics, and control.

Steam Generators and Boiler-Turbine Controls

Extracted from PTI course notes:
"Steam Generation Control"

STEAM GENERATOR TYPES

Drum Type and Once-Through

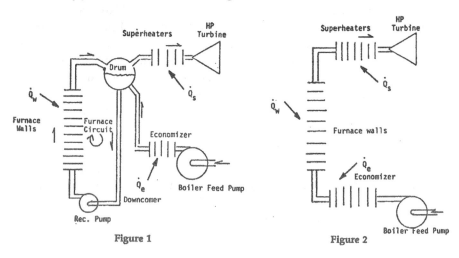

Figure 1   Figure 2

Figs. 1 and 2 are schematics of the two basic types of steam generators in use today. Fig. 1 indicates the fluid circuitry associated with the so-called conventional or drum-type unit. In this system the pressure level is always below the critical point of steam, 3206.2 psi (i.e., steam has latent heat).

Feedwater is preheated in the economizing section and flows into the drum, downcomer, water wall or furnace circuit. Since steam generation occurs in the water wall sections, and the recirculation flow rate around the furnace circuit is five to ten times that of the generated steam flow, depending on the load the unit is carrying, the water wall exit flow is a low quality mixture of steam and liquid, and the furnace circuit remains essentially in a saturated condition at the existing drum pressure. Mechanical separators in the drum insure that negligible moisture is carried over into the superheating sections. The steam is superheated to rated steam temperature conditions in the superheating sections and passes on into the high pressure turbine. Recirculation can be either natural, due to density effects, or forced by recirculation pumps.

At this point, some comments on the response characteristics and dominant effects which occur transiently in this type of unit are appropriate. consider the response for a change in the turbine throttle valve position or equivalently, load. The increase in steam taken from the boiler results in a decreasing boiler pressure. This decreasing pressure is arrested by increasing the steam generation in the furnace walls through increased fuel input. The large change in the specific volume of the fluid in flashing from liquid to steam is the physical mechanism by which pressure drop is arrested. Note that changing feedwater flow results in essentially just a change in drum level. Thus, in conventional units, combustion is used for pressure control, and feedwater basically follows the steam flow to insure that an adequate supply of liquid is in the boiler at all times.

Another important aspect of this type unit, particularly from an analytical modeling standpoint, is the fact that the fluid properties and conditions in each section of the boiler under normal operating conditions are well defined; that is, liquid in the economizer, saturation conditions in the furnace circuit and superheated steam in the superheaters. This permits the equations describing the fluid properties for a particular condition to be used throughout a given section (i.e., furnace circuit, superheater, etc.), without the complex problem of trying to describe the properties of the fluid if it were to undergo drastic changes in properties in a particular subsection.

Consider Fig. 2 which shows the fluid circuitry of the once-through boiler. These units may operate under subcritical and supercritical conditions (i.e., above 3606.2 psi). Note that the flow of fluid through the boiler is continuous, and that as heat is added along the fluid path, the fluid properties change in a continuous manner.

The pressure level in this type unit is basically specified by the flow being forced through the entire boiler circuit by the feed pump. Changes in fuel input will have essentially a transient effect due to the expansion or condensation of the fluid within the boiler until the new operating conditions are achieved. Since these units operate in the higher pressure ranges, the changes in the fluid specific volume are relatively smaller than conventional units, thus diminishing the effect of heat addition on pressure. In this type unit then, feedwater has a dominant effect on pressure.

Another important difference in characteristics and, hence, control requirements of once-through versus drum-type boilers relates to the fact that the steady state flow rate of fluid in the furnace tubes for once-through boilers is proportional to load in the normal operating range of 30 to 100%, whereas it is almost independent of load or of feedwater flow in the case of drum-type boilers. In drum boilers, changes in feedwater flow or steam flow do not materially affect the fluid flow rate in water wall tubes and, hence, there is no concern of major imbalance between heat flux to the tubes and heat absorption to the inner fluid. For once-through boilers, however, it is important to keep a close match between the once-through flow rate i.e., feedwater flow and fuel flow, since only a few seconds of a major imbalance can result in rapid rise of tube temperatures and burn out. Fuel and feedwater flow must, therefore, be moved in unison and corrections in the ratio of fuel to feedwater should be made within well-defined limits in a slow reset recalibration mode to correct for temperature deviations.

Balanced Draft or Pressurized Furnaces

Another feature of steam generators is whether their furnaces operate pressurized or under negative pressure (balanced draft). In the former case, only forced draft fans are needed, whereas, in the latter, a set of induced draft fans is placed at the exit of the gas path just before the stack.

The trend is to go to balanced draft units due to the need to add scrubbers and limit pollution of the atmosphere.

Fuel and Air Control Characteristics

Oil and Gas Fired Boilers - Control of fuel in oil and gas-fired boilers is relatively easy, as it involves modulation of a fuel valve. The response of fuel flow to valve change is almost instantaneous, hence the fuel flow subloop is handled very simply with a proportional and reset controller.

Airflow is usually changed by modulation of fan damper position (FD and/ or ID) hence the airflow subloop can likewise be handled with simple reset controllers. In the case of balanced draft boilers, the control action to the fans must be properly coordinated to hold furnace draft and satisfy airflow demand.

Fig. 3 shows a commonly used control scheme for coordination of fuel and air controls in oil or gas-fired boilers. Fuel demand is derived from a LO-SELECT station which compares the basic fuel and air demand signal with measured and characterized air flow. In this way one ensures that fuel cannot run ahead of air. Should for any reason air flow lag or

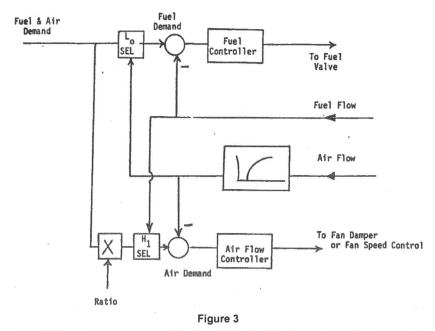

Figure 3

not respond to a demand signal, the LO-SELECT station would hold fuel in balance with the available air flow.

The air flow demand signal in similar fashion is the output of a HI-SELECT station which compares demand derived from the basic fuel and air demand with actual fuel flow.

The basic demand signal is modified by a ratio calibration which is either manually set or is directed by a slow auxiliary loop controlling excess air to the desired value by sensing percent 0_2.

The airflow measurement is processed through a function generator to impart the desired non-linear characteristic between fuel demand and air demand (minimum airflow is usually 30% or higher even when fuel flow is zero).

<u>Pulverized Coal-Fired Boilers</u> - Pulverized coal-fired boilers provide fuel to the furnace as a mixture of finely ground coal dust and air (Fig. 4). Coal is introduced to a coal mill through a coal feeder which drops coal from a hopper to the mill. Rollers in the mill grind the coal to a fine dust which is transported through coal pipes to the burners by primary air. Each mill usually supplies coal to four corner mounted burners at a given elevation. Four or five mills feed the burners at a like number of different elevations.

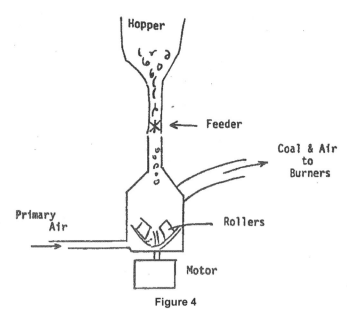

Figure 4

Firing rate is changed basically by changing the feeder speed, that is, the rate of flow of coal into the mill. Evidently there is a lag between the time feeder speed is changed and actual change of pulverized coal in the furnace. This lag is sometimes quite variable and the dynamics of coal mills are indeed a mystery. Primary air flow is kept constant in many cases. In others, primary air is made to vary in proportion to feeder speed.

The response of fuel in the furnace to changes in feeder speed exhibits considerable lags. These lags can also be variable as a function of the condition of the mill (amount of wear and/or the actual coal inventory of fines in the mill).

Conceptually one may think of the pulverizer process in terms of the block diagram of Fig. 5 where the fuel flow to the furnace is shown as being proportional to some function of level of fines in the mill.

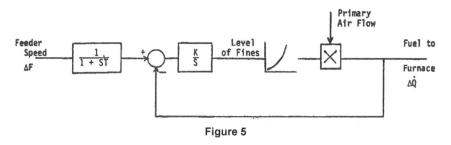

Figure 5

The net result is that the response of the mill is usually characterized by a dead time in series with a time lag.

$$\frac{\Delta \dot{Q}}{\Delta F} = \frac{e^{-ST_1}}{\left(1+ST_2\right)}$$

where T_1 = 30 to 60 sec.

T_2 = 15 to 30 sec.

In schemes where some change in primary air flow is effected simultaneous with a change in feeder speed, a small, almost instantaneous change, in fuel flow results, provided the coal mill inventory is not depleted.

The important point is that the response of fuel in the furnace to a change in feeder speed is usually not measurable. An inferential measure of fuel is usually taken as feeder speed. This fact makes the control of fuel and air in coal-fired boilers radically different than for oil and gas-fired boilers.

Fig. 6 shows the functional diagram of a fuel control system designed for coal firing. Pressure error works through the pressure controls (proportional and reset with additional stabilization for process lags) to set a fuel demand to a cascaded controller which almost instantly satisfies this demand by sending the proper signal to the various feeders. The purpose of the cascaded fuel controller is to assure the same gain between the pressure controls and the actual fuel in the boiler, irrespective of number of mills in operation.

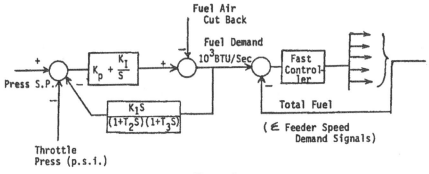

Figure 6

Air Flow Controls in Coal-Fired Boilers - The problem of matching air to the fuel in coal-fired plants arises due to the fact that there is no direct measure of the fuel being burned--only inferential measures such as coal-feeder speeds which are only approximately indicative of the BTU being burned (within 10% or so in the steady state). During transients the relationship between coal feeder speed and BTU in the furnace is further complicated by fuel system (pulverizer) lags which can be long and variable.

Because of the relative inaccuracies between feeder speed and actual fuel BTU, it has been the practice in coal-fired plants to set the air flow from measured steam flow which, in the steady state, is a more reliable indication of fuel burned.

The idea of supplementing this relationship between air flow and steam flow in the steady state with transient action from the signal to the fuel system is not recommended because of the possibility of a runaway positive feedback situation. It would be possible to have the signal calling for increases in fuel to momentarily fail to increase the heat release in the furnace (due to fuel system upsets, insufficient number of mills or unpredictably large pulverizer dead time) while it succeeded in increasing air flow. Now, since increased air flow causes a drop in pressure, this would cause the pressure controls to further call for more fuel and air. The air would respond ahead of the fuel decreasing the pressure still further and a runaway positive feedback situation could result. Evidently, where the fuel system characteristics are not completely predictable and repeatable, it is impractical to use the signal to the fuel system to call for transient changes in air flow.

The transient shaping of the air flow can be provided directly from steam flow. This avoids the positive feedback aspects of the previous alternative, but in order to provide good transient matching of air to fuel, it relies on repeatable and predictable fuel system characteristics.

A more positive, as opposed to inferential, measure of actual fuel in the furnace can be synthesized from steam flow added to term proportional to rate of change of drum pressure.

Boiler Pressure Effects

Since the steam supply system is not an infinite source, boiler pressure does vary transiently with changes in steam demand. Boiler dynamics is a very involved subject requiring the consideration of many simultaneous thermodynamic effects. However, for purposes of this discussion one can look at the boiler process in a very simplified fashion as shown on Figs. 7 and 8.

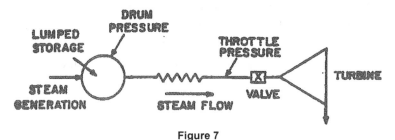

Figure 7

Schematic of Boiler Turbine System

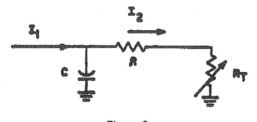

Figure 8

Electrical Analog of Boiler Pressure Flow Phenomena

Pressure in the boiler is affected by changes in steam mass within the boiler storage volume. These changes in stored mass result from transient imbalances between steam flow into the turbine and steam generation in the boiler. The throttle pressure differs from drum pressure by the amount of pressure drop across the superheaters. This pressure drop is approximately proportional to the square of the steam flow rate.

An equivalent electrical circuit which performs in analogous fashion to the boiler pressure phenomena for small changes in load is shown in Fig. 15 where I_1 is analogous to steam generation, I_2 to steam flow to the turbine, R to the friction resistance presented by the superheaters and R_T to the resistance offered by the turbine at a given valve opening.

The voltage across the capacitor is analogous to drum pressure, and the voltage across R_T is analogous to the throttle pressure P_T. In the above equivalent circuit representation, the change in turbine valve is represented by a change in R_T.

For the first few seconds following a change in R_T or turbine valve, the voltage across the capacitor (drum pressure) does not change. However, the throttle pressure will suffer a deviation due to the change in friction drop ($\Delta I_2 R$) in the superheaters and piping.

Since pressure drop is proportional to the square of flow, whereas voltage drop is linearly related to current, the above analogy is approximate and holds for small changes about an operating point. The valve of resistance R varies with operating load level as can be seen from the following:

P_{DT} =   Pressure drop from - $K\dot{m}_s^2$ drum to throttle

where

K   =   friction drop coefficient

$\dot{m}_s$ =   steam flow rate

For small perturbations

ΔP_{DT} =   change in pressure drop = $2K\dot{m}_{so}\Delta m_s$ from drum to throttle

where

$\dot{m}_{so}$ =   steady state steam flow at the particular operating point

and

$\Delta \dot{m}_s$ =   change in steam flow

In the analog of Fig. 8, $R = 2 K\dot{m}_{so}$.

The effect of turbine valve changes can be represented in linearized small perturbation form as follows:

$$\dot{m}_s = K_v P_T \tag{5}$$

where

$$K_v \quad = \quad \text{coefficient proportional to valve opening}$$

For small perturbations, neglecting second order terms

$$\Delta \dot{m}_s = K_{vo}\Delta P_T + \frac{\Delta K_v}{K_{vo}}\dot{m}_{so} \tag{6}$$

Steam generation (I_1) is proportional to heat release in the furnace, and follows this heat release with a small time constant (5 to 7 seconds) due to the waterwall metal and film coefficient. The process can therefore be represented by the block diagram of Fig. 9.

Where

subscript o denotes steady state value

prefix Δ denotes change from steady state value

$\dot{m}_w$ = steam generation

P_D = drum pressure

P_T = throttle pressure

$\dot{m}_s$ = steam flow

K_v = coefficient proportional to valve opening

T_w = waterwall time constant

C_b = boiler storage constant

In the above linear, small oscillation model, the parameters that change with load level are R and K_{vo}. All other parameters are essentially invariant.

Using the per unit system based on rated values, i.e.; base steam flow = full load steam flow, base pressure = rated pressure, etc., typical values of parameters in the block diagram of Fig. 16 are:

K_v = coefficient proportional to load, 1.0 p.u. at full load

R = friction drop coefficient

= 2 x (p.u. load level) × (p.u. pressure drop from drum to turbine throttle at full load)

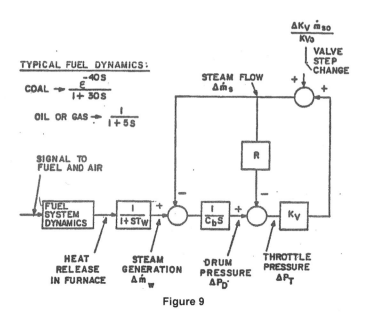

Figure 9

Simplified Block Diagram of Boiler Process

The value of pressure drop at full load is about 10% or 0.1 p.u. so that at the full load operating point a typical value of R is 0.20 p.u.

The boiler storage constant C_b is related to the stored mass of saturated liquid and vapor as well as the mass of superheated steam in the superheaters and steam leads. Typically C_b represents the number of full load flow seconds for a one per unit change in pressure assuming a linear relationship between stored mass and pressure. This storage constant varies between 120 to 300 secs. in drum type boilers and 90 to 200 secs. in once-through units.

Typical boiler pressure responses for step changes in turbine valve are shown on Fig. 10.

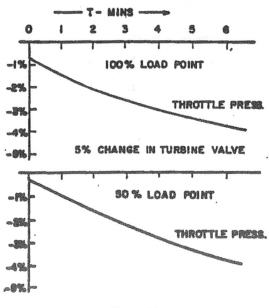

Figure 10

Figure 10 shows the case of change in turbine valve where the boiler is left uncontrolled with a steady input of fuel and air. The action of boiler controls is to restore pressure deviation which would occur are a function of the dynamics of the fuel system. Figure 11 shows representative pressure responses for coal fired and gas or oil fired boilers. The deviations in pressure in per unit multiplied by the per unit load at the particular operating point represent the per unit deviation in power due to pressure effects.

A simplified model of the prime mover system including pressure effects is shown on Fig. 12.

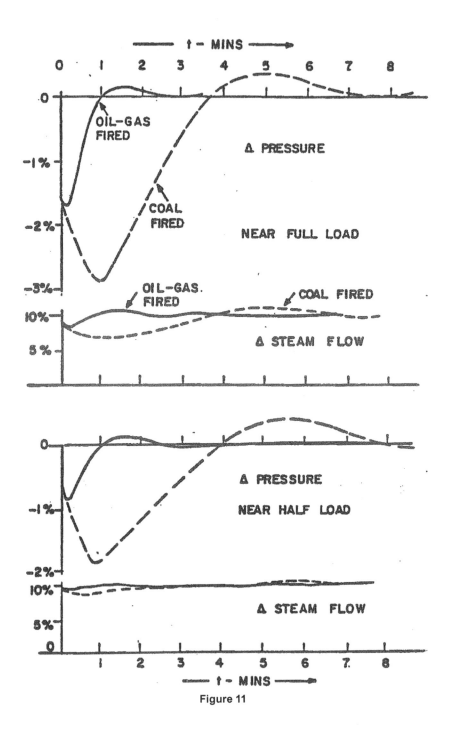

Figure 11

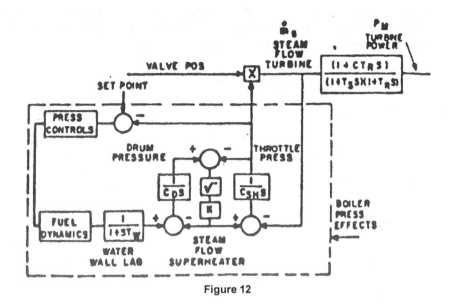

Figure 12

Dynamics of Turbine Power Including Boiler Pressure Effects

Steam flow to the high pressure turbine is proportional to the control valve flow area multiplied by throttle pressure which is obtained from the boiler model. The pressure drop between drum and throttle is proportional to the steam flow rate squared. Both drum pressure and throttle pressure are represented as states (outputs of integrators or storage volumes).

The boiler storage is represented primarily by the coefficient C_D with the coefficient C_{SH} representing a small storage effect in the steam leads. It is computationally convenient to represent this small storage effect so that the steam flow computation is straight forward, without need for iterations.

Steam generation follows the heat release in the furnace with a small (7-10 sec.) water wall lag. Steam generation minus steam flow into the superheaters integrates into a change in drum pressure through the storage constant C_D. Steam flow into the superheaters minus steam flow into the turbine integrates into a change of throttle pressure through the storage constant C_{SH}.

The pressure control adjustment is very much a function of the fuel and air system response which was discussed in the section "Fuel & Air Control Characteristics".

The response characteristics of once-through steam generators is similar to that of drum-type units and hence the same model of Fig. 9 is applicable. The main difference is that in the case of once-through units, the energy inputs are closely coordinated, fuel, air and feedwater. Whereas in the case of drum-type units, feedwater control is primarily devoted to holding drum level and is, therefore, not closely coupled to the fuel and air controls.

BOILER-TURBINE CONTROLS

The main objectives of boiler-turbine controls are:

1. To attend to the turbine demands for energy as expediently as possible within the storage and auxiliary system capabilities of the plant.

2. To maintain process conditions, pressure temperatures and flow rates (feedwater, fuel and air) at optimum and safe values under load demand disturbances as well as other upsets such as fuel disturbances, losses of auxiliaries, etc.

The demands on control performance are obviously related to the severity of load change response solicited from a given steam generating unit. Several philosophies of control have evolved in attempts to accommodate the need or capability for rapid load changes versus the need to control critical plant variables (temperatures and pressures). A review of these philosophies is appropriate as an introduction to principles of control of once-through boiler and in particular the coordination of boiler-turbine controls.

Conventional Practice

Most conventional drum-type steam units are operated in the boiler following mode wherein changes in generation are initiated by turbine control valves, and the boiler controls respond with necessary control action upon sensing the changes in steam flow and deviations in pressure. In this mode, the turbine has access to the stored energy in the boiler and load changes within reasonable magnitudes occur with fairly rapid response, as shown on Fig. 13. This characteristic is beneficial from a governing standpoint improving the quality of frequency control, and it is characteristic of conventional steam systems to maintain a fairly narrow band of frequency due to this fast governor action. It is also beneficial in arresting frequency sags following large upsets. The boiler controls must be responsive and stable to withstand this mode of operation.

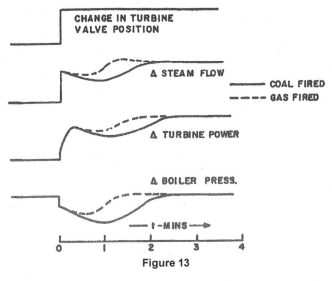

Figure 13

Boiler-Follow Mode

Turbine-Following Mode

The turbine-follow mode, on the other hand, involves use of the turbine control valves to regulate boiler pressure. This can be done with practically no time delay so that under this mode, boiler pressure suffers virtually no transient deviations, and no use is made of stored energy in the boiler. Steam flow through the turbine and, therefore, turbine power follows closely the amount of steam generation, i.e., the input to the boiler. Control of boiler variables is easy under this mode of operation, although the response of turbine power is considerably slower. The units' power output does, however, reflect both the intentional and unintentional variations in fuel input which in the case of coal-fired units can be a problem. The turbine following mode is lacking in the main functional requirement of a power plant which is to meet electrical load demands as expediently as possible. Governing action would be quickly washed out by the action of the pressure controls.

Fig. 14 shows response characteristics of a turbine following plant where the change in load demand actuates a corresponding change in fuel and feedwater input, and the turbine valve maintains constant boiler pressure. The output power is delayed by the lags in fuel system and storage time constants of the boiler. The dimension of the control task is reduced appreciably as boiler input becomes an independently specified variable rather than a process dependent quantity including feedback.

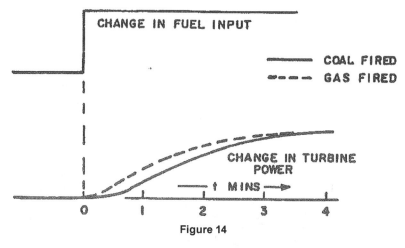

Figure 14

Turbine-Follow Mode

Coordinated Boiler-Turbine Controls

Recognizing the advantages and disadvantages of both previously discussed modes of operation and control and the need for varying degrees of compromise between the desire for fast response to load changes and the desire for boiler safety and good quality of control of steam conditions, a logical control mode is one that offers an adjustable blend of the two previously described schemes. This need for coordination of the boiler turbine is more pressing in the case of once-through boilers where the process interactions between feed pump, firing, and turbine valve are closer coupled than was the case with drum-type boilers with their large saturated liquid storage and insulating effect of having saturation pegged at the drum.

A type of coordinated controls that has been described in the literature is shown functionally in the schematic of Fig. 15. To achieve this coordination, it is necessary to make

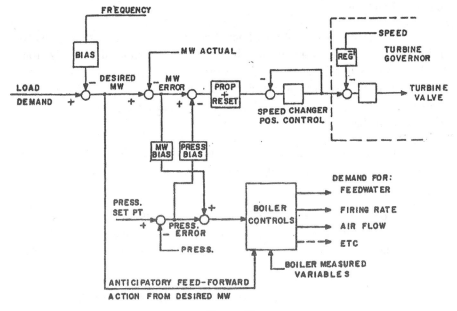

Figure 15

Coupling of Turbine Load Controls with Boiler Controls

the speed changer motor respond to intelligence other than and in addition to load control signals. This is done by integrating the load control pulses to develop a signal indicative of demand for MW which can be altered by other inputs. This signal is modified by a frequency deviation bias matching the unit's governor droop characteristic to develop the desired MW. Comparison with the unit's actual output develops the MW error. The desired MW signal as well as the MW error signal are sent to the boiler controls. Turbine speed changer position is directed to reduce a combination of MW error and pressure error to zero while the boiler controls likewise are directed to reduce the pressure error biased by the MW error to zero. The sense of the cross-coupled MW error and pressure error biases is in the direction such that a positive MW error (MW lower than demand) would cause the turbine valve to open and the boiler controls to call for more feedwater fuel and air, whereas a positive pressure error (pressure lower than set point) would call for closing of the turbine valve while simultaneously increasing the feedwater, fuel and air.

Analysis shows that the control systems come to rest when both the MW error and pressure errors are restored to zero and transiently the cross coupling is in the direction to attenuate interacting effects of the MW feedback and pressure feedback loops. Depending on the cross coupling strength between pressure and

MW loops, the load response can be adjusted to any degree between that shown on Fig. 13 and Fig. 14.

Another variation of coordinated controls where the turbine valve is primarily the pressure regulator and boiler inputs are actuated basically from load demand is to introduce a transient offset in the pressure set point from load demand. With such an arrangement, on a step increase in load demand, the pressure set point moves down with a timed washout causing the turbine valve to open immediately.

One important aspect of these methods is the role of the turbine valve as the basic boiler pressure regulator. Relying on turbine valve for this role has drawbacks as follows:

1. Constant motion of speed changer motor due to the normal process noise, fuel disturbances, etc., which can be significant in the case of coal-fired plants. Pressure deviations would be eliminated at the expense of MW deviations.

2. Reliance on turbine valves for pressure control removes the incentive to do a good control job on the boiler input variables. If responsibility for good and stable pressure control is not assigned to the boiler input variables, this can become a problem under the condition of valves wide open, at which point the turbine valves are beyond control range.

3. In those cases where a transient offset in pressure set point activated from load demand is not provided, the use of turbine valves for pressure control does materially reduce the load response capability of the unit.

Improved Method of Boiler-Turbine Control Coordination

Keeping in mind the disadvantages of continuous pressure control by means of turbine valves and the overall objectives of quick load response within reasonable limits of boiler storage capability, the scheme of Fig. 16 meets these objectives.

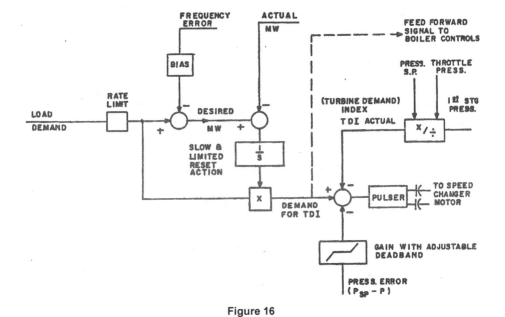

Figure 16

Control System Coordinating Turbine Load Demands with Boiler Plant Capabilities

The features of the configuration of Fig. 16 may be understood in the light of the following considerations applying to the basic scheme of Fig. 15.

The MW feedback loop without adequate cross coupling from pressure error presents stability and potential runaway problems if for some reason the boiler fails to keep in step with the demand. That is, without biasing action from pressure error, the MW loop will cause valve overtravel in attempting to satisfy MW demand, irrespective of boiler pressure. An analogous situation occurs with the use of first stage pressure feedback, whereas this condition would be avoided if a suitable indication of valve position (if linear with flow) were used.

Examine now the significance of combining pressure error to the MW demand. To prevent interaction of the pressure and MW loops, the gain of the pressure bias cross coupling term would be adjusted such that the turbine valve would not attempt to correct the component of MW error due to the pressure not being at set point, but would allow the pressure loop to accomplish this component correction. This means that the cross coupling gain would be $\dfrac{MW}{P} = K_v$ or the equivalent turbine valve opening. Since MW in the steady state are proportional to valve position times pressure, the combination of MW added to the negative pressure error gained by the noninteracting value K_v (Fig. 16), which is proportional to load level, can be interpreted as turbine valve opening, i.e.,

$$MW = K_v P = K_v(P_o + P_e)$$

or

$$(MW - K_v P_e) = K_v P_o$$

where K_v is proportional to valve opening, P_o = pressure set point and P_e = pressure error.

To the extent that the pressure error cross coupling term is gained by K_v, the combination of MW and this pressure error term can be replaced by the equivalent turbine valve opening. Any added strength of this pressure error beyond K_v inhibits turbine response and provides some degree of pressure regulation by means of the turbine valves.

In view of the above considerations and in keeping with basic philosophy of taking advantage of stored energy in the boiler within safe limits, the scheme of Fig. 16 accomplishes the required degree of noninteraction between the MW loop without inhibiting turbine valve motion as long as pressure error is within a safe band. The response of this system to load demand pulses as well as to governing signals through the turbine is compatible with that of conventional units - exhibiting fast response for limited changes. This type of response is also compatible with dynamics of load-frequency controls.

As shown on Fig. 16, the load demand, which can be derived either from the load control signal or set manually, establishes the desired turbine demand index (TDI) which is equivalent to turbine valve position.

This index is derived from first stage pressure by multiplying it by the ratio of pressure set point to actual pressure. It is, therefore, the first stage pressure that would result for the given valve position at the pressure corresponding to pressure set point. Aside from convenience of measurement, this index avoids the nonlinear relationship between valve position and flow, and thus forms an ideal feedback signal instead of actual valve position, which was mentioned previously as being desirable. Essentially, TDI is a direct measured indication of the turbine flow demand compensated for throttle pressure deviations from set point.

The difference between demand and actual TDI acts on the speed changer controller to move the turbine valves. The demand signal for TDI is slowly calibrated by integrated MW error from demand. This has no significant dynamic effect and is a convenient feature especially under base load operation where a MW demand level can be set and the proper TDI will be called for regardless of condenser, heater and other conditions which may affect the steadystate relationship between TDI and MW.

Variable Pressure Controls

Considerations of improved turbine efficiency at part load and reduced temperature gradients within the turbine led to the adoption, in some cases, of variable pressure mode of operation.

In this mode the turbine valves are left wide open and turbine load follows boiler pressure. The response to changes in load demand, therefore, follows the boiler pressure response to pressure set point changes.

THE PSS/E TGOV5 MODEL

TGOV5 is a model of a steam turbine and boiler which represents governor action, main, reheat and low pressure effects, including boiler effects. The boiler controls will handle practically any mode of control including coordinated, base, variable pressure and conventional. The control mode is selected by the proper choice of constants. A functional block diagram of TGOV5 is shown in Fig. 17 and a detailed diagram in Fig. 18.

'TGOV5' Functional Block Diagram

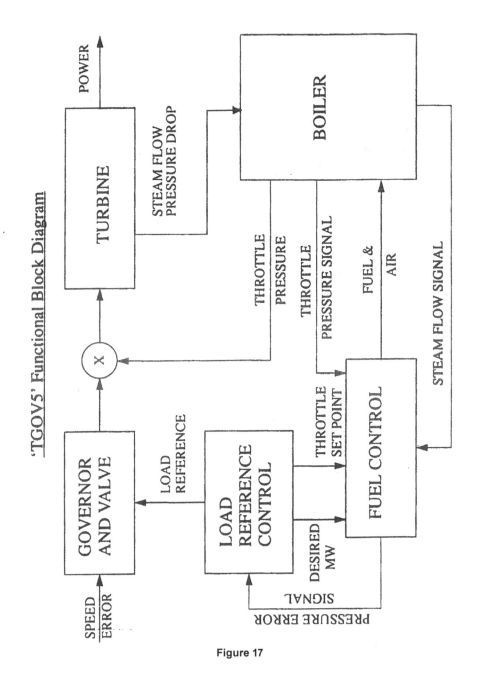

Figure 17

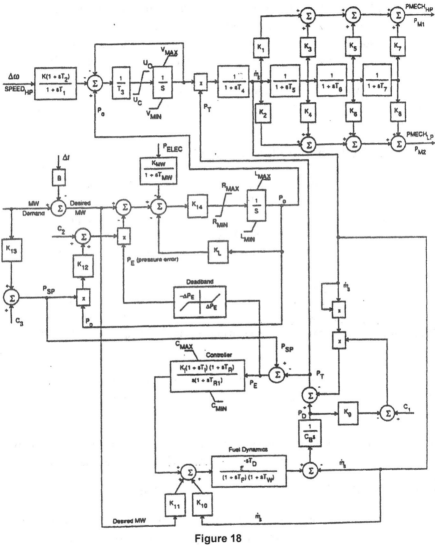

Figure 18

Governor Turbine Model

The governor turbine model is similar to the IEEEG1 model. It can be used for tandem and cross-compound units.

P_o is the load reference. The valve has rate limits and minimum and maximum limits. Steam flow is proportional to the product of throttle pressure and valve area rather than just proportional to valve position as in the standard governor models. Proper selection of the time constants and gains allows the modeling of the reheater and intermediate and low pressure turbine effects.

The variables of the governor that interface with the other portions of the model are P_o (load reference of the governor), P_T (throttle pressure) and $\dot{m}_s$ (steam flow).

Models of Boiler and Boiler-Turbine Controls

Drum pressure, P_D, is proportional to the integral of steam generation less steam flow out of the boiler. Throttle pressure, P_T, is equal to drum pressure less a pressure drop across superheaters and steam leads. This pressure drop varies as square of steam flow and also with density of steam. The pressure drop coefficient is shown to be a function of boiler pressure to accommodate the case of variable pressure operation.

Steam generation is controlled by the inputs to the boiler (fuel and air for drum units and fuel, air and feedwater for once-through units) which are driven by a three mode controller. Provision is made to introduce anticipation from steam flow or MW demand signal.

The three mode controller has non-windup limits. K_I can be set to zero to model the fuel and air control on manual. To model two mode control, set T_R and T_{RI} to zero.

The time delay is modeled by a fourth order approximation. This allows the modeling of long time delays without an inordinately long delay table.

Pressure Set Point And Load Reference Control

A MW demand is modified by the frequency bias and pressure error in the coordinated control front end. This bias demand signal is matched by the load reference motor position with appropriate rate limits. There is the possibility of the load demand signal to act on the pressure set point for the case of variable pressure operation. The gain of pressure error modifying the MW demand signal can be set as a constant or proportional to the product of pressure set point P_{sp} and load reference P_o.

The MW demand signal is stored in VAR(L+2). External logic to change the MW demand (such as due to AGC pulsing) could be added to the CONEC subroutine.

The initialization of the model is dependent upon the gains K_{13} and K_{14} and may require that the CON C_3 be changed from its original value. VAR(L+6) is used to store the changed value of C_3. If K_{13} is zero, then C_3 is set equal to P_{sp} and the MW demand signal is set equal to either

- electrical power in per unit on machine base (K_{MW} = 1.0)
- P_o (K_L = 1.0)
- zero (K_{MW} and K_L = 0.0)

Setting K_{14} to zero locks the load reference at its original value. If K_{13} and K_{14} are both zero, the MW demand signal is used only if K_{11} is non-zero. If K_{13} and K_{14} are both non-zero, the MW demand is set as above and C_3 is calculated to get the proper relationship between the pressure set point and MW demand.

On certain control strategies, C_2 may also need to be calculated. In mode 1, VAR(L+5) is set either to the value of CON(J+31) or a calculated value depending on the sign of the CON's value. If C_2 is negative, VAR(L+5) is set to electrical power in per unit on machine base. This allows the pressure error bias signal to be proportional to machine initial loading.

Model Constants

The following is an explanation of the model constants:

K	is the inverse of the governor speed droop
T_1 and T_2	are the governor controller lag and lead time constants (seconds)
T_3	is the valve servomotor time constant for the control valves (seconds)
U_o	is the control valve open rate limit (p.u./second)
U_c	is the control valve close rate limit (p.u./second)
V_{max}	is the maximum valve area (p.u.)
V_{min}	is the minimum valve area (p.u.)
T_4	is the steam flow time constant (seconds)
T_5, T_6 and T_7	are the first reheater time constant, second reheater time constant and crossover time constant. They may be set to zero if all steps are not necessary, for example, if there is not a second reheat stage.
K_1, K_3, K_5 and K_7	are the fractions of the HP unit's mechanical power developed by the various turbine stages. The sum of these constants should be one for a non-cross-compound unit.

K_2, K_4, K_6 and K_8	are similar fractions of the LP unit's mechanical power. These should be zero for a non-cross-compound unit. For a cross-compound unit, the sum of K_1 through K_8 should equal one.
K_9	is the adjustment to the pressure drop coefficient as a function of drum pressure.
K_{10}	gain of anticipation signal from main stream flow
K_{11}	gain of anticipation signal from load demand
K_{12}	gain for pressure error bias
K_{13}	gain between MW demand and pressure set point
K_{14}	inverse of the load reference servomotor time constant (= 0.0 if the load reference does not change)
R_{MAX}	is the load reference positive rate of change limit (p.u./second)
R_{MIN}	is the load reference negative rate of change limit (p.u./second)
L_{MAX}	is the maximum load reference
L_{MIN}	is the minimum load reference
C_1	is the pressure drop coefficient
C_2	is the gain for the pressure error bias
C_3	is an adjustment to the pressure set point
B	is the frequency bias for load reference control
C_B	is the boiler storage time constant (seconds)
K_I	is the controller integral gain
T_I	is the controller proportional lead time constant (seconds)
T_R	is the controller rate lead time constant (seconds)
T_{RI}	is the inherent lag associated with lead T_R (usually about $T_R/10$) (seconds)
C_{MAX}	is the maximum controller output
C_{MIN}	is the minimum controller output
TD	is the time delay in the fuel supply system (seconds)
T_F	is the fuel and air system time constant (seconds)
T_W	is the water wall time constant (seconds)
P_{sp}	is the initial throttle pressure set point
T_{MW}	is the MW transducer time constant (seconds)
K_L	is the feedback gain from the load reference (0.0 or 1.0)
K_{MW}	is the gain of the MW transducer (0.0 or 1.0)
ΔP_e	is the deadband in the pressure error signal for load reference control (p.u. pressure)

Typical Data

There are four basic boiler/turbine control strategies:

- Conventional Control

Most conventional drum-type steam units are operated in the boiler follow mode wherein changes in generation are initiated by turbine control valves and the boiler controls respond with necessary control action upon sensing the changes in steam flow and deviations in pressure. In this mode the turbine has access to the stored energy in the boiler, and load changes within reasonable magnitudes occur with fairly rapid response.

- Turbine-Follow

The turbine-follow mode involves use of the turbine control valves to regulate boiler pressure. This can be done with practically no time delay so that under this mode boiler pressure suffers virtually no transient deviations, and no use is made of stored energy in the boiler. Steam flow through the turbine and, therefore, turbine power follows closely the amount of steam generation, i.e., the input to the boiler. The response of turbine power is considerably slower than conventional control.

- Coordinated Optimal

The coordinated optimal mode recognizes the advantages and disadvantages of the conventional and turbine follow modes and the need for varying degrees of compromise between the desire for fast response to load changes and the desire for boiler safety and good quality of control of steam conditions. A new demand signal is modified by a frequency deviation bias matching the unit's governor droop characteristic to develop the desired MW. Comparison with the unit's actual output develops the MW error. The desired MW signal as well as the MW error signal are sent to the boiler controls. Turbine speed changer position is directed to reduce a combination of MW error and pressure error to zero while the boiler controls likewise are directed to reduce the pressure error biased by the MW error to zero. Depending on the cross coupling strength between pressure and MW loops, the load response can be adjusted to any degree between that of the conventional and turbine follow modes. There is the possibility of disabling the pressure error effect within an adjustable deadband.

- Variable Pressure

  In the variable pressure control mode, the pressure set point is proportional to MW demand. The pressure error between set point and actual throttle pressure drives steam generation. There is no coupling of demand signal to turbine control valve position.

The TGOV5 model can simulate each of the control strategies by judicious setting of the model gains. Actual plant controls could be variants of the standard control philosophies or combinations of them.

To help the user in his understanding of these controls, typical data is given for each control mode for both coal and oil/gas fired units in Table 1 and Table 2 respectively. As with all typical data, the applicability of this data to any specific implementation of control strategy on a specific unit requires sound engineering analysis and judgement. Typical data for several governing systems is given in the IEEE Committee Report "Dynamic Models for Steam and Hydro Turbines in Power Systems", IEEE Transactions on Power Apparatus and Systems, Vol. PAS-92, pp. 1904-1915, 1973.

Additional details of turbine control logic are given in "Dynamic Models for System Dynamic Performance Studies", IEEE Transaction on Power Apparatus and Systems, Vol. 6, No. 2, May 1991, pp 753-761.

Table 1
TGOV5 Typical Data For Coal-Fired Units

(where data not shown, use the data shown in the conventional control column)

CON	Conventional	Coordinated Optimal	Turbine Follow	Variable Pressure
K	20			
T_1	0			
T_2	0			
T_3	.15			
U_o	.4			
U_o	-.4			
V_{MAX}	.9			
V_{MIN}	.2			
T_4	.4			
K_1	.3			
K_2	0			
T_5	9			
K_3	.4			
K_4	0			
T_6	.5			
K_5	.3			
K_6	0			
T_7	0			
K_7	0			
K_8	0			
K_9	0			.67
K_{10}	0			
K_{11}	0		1.0	
K_{12}	0			1.0
K_{13}	0			1.0

CON	Conventional	Coordinated Optimal	Turbine Follow	Variable Pressure
K_{14}	5	1.0		0
R_{MAX}	.0005			.1
R_{MIN}	-.0005			-.1
L_{MAX}	.9			
L_{MIN}	.2			
C_1	.2			.87
C_2^*	0	-1	15	
C_3	1			0
B	0	20	20	20
C_B	200			
K_I	.02		0	
T_I	90			
T_R	60			
T_{RI}	6			
C_{MAX}	1.1			1.1
C_{MIN}	0.5		0	.1
T_D	60			
T_F	25			
T_W	7			
P_{sp}	1.0			.9
T_{MW}	10^6	1.0		
K_L	0.0			
K_{MW}	1.0			
ΔPe	0.0			

* When C_2 is negative the C_2 VAR is set to P_{elec} in p.u. on MBASE.

Table 2

TGOV5 Typical Data Oil or Gas-Fired Units

(where data not shown, use the data shown in the conventional control column)

CON	Conventional	Coordinated Optimal	Turbine Follow	Variable Pressure	CON	Conventional	Coordinated Optimal	Turbine Follow	Variable Pressure
K	20				K_{14}	5	1.0		0
T_1	0				R_{MAX}	.0005			.1
T_2	0				R_{MIN}	-.0005			-.1
T_3	.15				L_{MAX}	.9			
U_o	0.4				L_{MIN}	.2			
U_o	-0.4				C_1	.2			.87
V_{MAX}	.9				$C_2{}^{2*}$	0	-1	15	
V_{MIN}	.2				C_3	1.0			0
T_4	.4				B	0	20	20	20
K_1	.3				C_B	150			
K_2	0				K_I	.04		0	
T_5	9				T_I	70			
K_3	.4				T_R	30			
K_4	0				T_{RI}	3			
T_6	0.5				C_{MAX}	1.1			1.1
K_5	.3				C_{MIN}	0.5		0	0.5
K_6	0				T_D	0			
T_7	0				T_F	5			
K_7	0				T_W	7			
K_8	0				P_{sp}	1.0			0.9
K_9	0			.67	T_{MW}	10^6	1.0		
K_{10}	0				K_L	0.0			
K_{11}	0		1.0		K_{MW}	1.0			
K_{12}	0			1.0	ΔP_e	0.0			
K_{13}	0			1.0					

* When C_2 is negative the C_2 VAR is set to P_{elect} in p.u. on MBASE.

Tests and Parameter Derivation

From the foregoing description of turbines, boilers and boiler/turbine controls, it should be evident that the response of turbine shaft power to changes in speed or in load demand is a function of some basic major equipment parameters, such as boiler storage constants, pressure drop coefficients, etc., as well as, and perhaps more importantly, on the particular control configuration and control adjustments.

Referring to the parameters in Fig. 12 and also in Fig. 18, the following tests are suggested:

Determination of C_D in Fig. 19 or C_B in Fig. 18. (boiler storage constant)

One fairly easy test is to obtain the boiler storage time constant is as follows:

With the unit operating at a substantial load (50 to 100%) place the fuel and air controls on manual and abruptly give a 2 or 3% change in turbine valve, either by changing the load reference or by releasing the load limit setting against the governor. The throttle pressure will register a deviation similar to that shown in Fig. 10. Following the initial abrupt drop in pressure, the initial rate of change of pressure divided by the measured initial per unit change in steam flow will give the reciprocal of the parameter C_D of Fig. 12 or C_B of Fig. 18.

Another test that would disclose not only this boiler storage constant but also additional lags in the fuel system is to again have the fuel, air and turbine valve on manual at a substantial loading condition and to impart a change in fuel and air, recording the change in throttle pressure.

The parameter K in Fig. 12 and C_1 in Fig. 18 can be derived from steady state measurement of drum pressure and throttle pressure at a particular load ($\dot{m}_{so}$). Let these pressures be P_{DO} and P_{TO}, all values in per unit.

Then

$$K = \frac{\dot{m}_{so}}{\sqrt{P_{DO} - P_{TO}}}$$

and

$$C_1 = \frac{P_{DO} - P_{TO}}{\dot{m}_{so}^2} - P_{DO} * K_9$$

The term $P_{DO} * K_9$ is used in the case of variable pressure operation to account for variations in steam density with pressure.

The other parameters are mainly control parameters. The most expedient way of determining these would be to conduct step changes in load demand with controls on automatic and registering the deviations in steam flow and pressure similar to those shown in Figs. 11 and 14.

Governors, Prime Movers and Boilers

1. L.N. Hannett, J.W. Feltes, B. Fardanesh, "Field Tests to Validate Hydro Turbine-Governor Model Structure and Parameters", presented at the 1994 IEEE Winter Power Meeting, New York.
2. F.P. de Mello, et al, "Dynamic Models for Combined Cycle Plants in Power system Studies", IEEE Working Group for Prime Mover and Energy Supply Models for System Dynamic Performance Studies.
3. R.T. Byerly, F.P. de Mello, et al, "Dynamic Models for Steam and Hydro Turbines in Power System Studies", IEEE Task Force on Overall Plant Response, IEEE Transactions on Power Apparatus and Systems, Nov./Dec. 1973.
4. F.P. de Mello, et al, "Hydraulic Turbine and Turbine Control Models for System Dynamic Studies", IEEE Working Group for Prime Move and Energy Supply Models for System Dynamic Performance Studies, paper 91 SM 462-2 PWRS, presented at the 1991 IEEE Summer Power Meeting.
5.(*) W.I. Rowen, "Simplified Mathematical Representations of Heavy Duty Gas Turbines", Journal of the American Society Mechanical Engineers, October 1983.
6. F.P. de Mello, et al, "Dynamic Models for Fossil Fueled Steam Units in Power System Studies", IEEE Transactions on Power systems, Vol. 6, No. 2, May 1991, pp. 753-761.
7.(*) R.M. Wright, "Understanding Modern Generator Control", IEEE Transactions on Energy Conversion, Vol. 4, No. 3, September 1989, pp. 453-457.
8. F.P. de Mello, "Boiler Models for System Dynamic Performance Studies", IEEE Transactions on Power Systems, Vol. 6, No. 1, February 1991, pp. 66-74.
9. L.N. Hannett, A. Khan, "Combustion Turbine Dynamic Model Validation from Tests", IEEE Transactions on Power Systems, Vol. 8, No. 1, February 1993, pp. 152-158.
10. F.P. de Mello, et al, "MW Response of Fossil Fired Steam Units", IEEE Transactions on Power Apparatus and Systems, Vol. PAS-92, No. 2, March/ April 1973, pp. 710-715.
11. L.N. Hannett, G. Jee, B. Fardanesh, "A Governor/Turbine Model for a Twin Shaft Combustion Turbine", IEEE paper 94 WM 188-3 PWRS, presented at the IEEE Power Engineering Society 1994 Winter Meeting, New York.

---

* Copy not included in notes due to copyright laws.

Chapter 3

Power System Dynamics

Contents

List of Figures

Load Flow Fundamentals

3.1 Introduction

The three problems encountered most frequently in power system analysis are load flow, short circuit and power system stability. This chapter is devoted almost entirely to the load flow computer program which is the basic engineering tool in planning, design and operation of a power system. A brief discussion of short circuit computer calculations as they differ from load flow computations is included at the end of the chapter. Computer solution of system stability problems requires an understanding of the dynamic behavior of electrical machinery and will be discussed in the "Electrical Machine Dynamics" courses.

In this chapter all quantities are in per unit and all AC voltages and currents are steady state quantities, represented by phasors. The bar representing per unit values and the (~) representing phasors are therefore deleted.

3.2 Load Flow Analysis

Load flow solutions provide bus voltages and power flow in the transmission system for specified generation and load conditions. This information is needed to test the system's ability to transfer energy from generation to load without overloading particular lines and test the adequacy of voltage regulation by shunt capacitors, shunt reactors, tap changing transformers and the var supplying capability of rotating machinery. Solution methods based on both the Y-bus and the Z-bus network representation are presented.

If the vector [**I**] containing the bus currents shown in Figure 3.1 are known the bus voltages [**E**] can be obtained by

$$[\mathbf{E}] = [\mathbf{Z}][\mathbf{I}] \tag{III.1}$$

where [**Z**] is the bus (nodal) impedance matrix. Conversely, if the bus voltages are known, the bus currents are obtained by:

$$[\mathbf{I}] = [\mathbf{Y}] [\mathbf{E}] \tag{III.2}$$

where [**Y**] is the bus (nodal) admittance matrix. Both the impedance and admittance bus matrices were described in some detail in Chapter 1. Both (III.1) and (III.2) are linear equations. If in equation (III.1) the currents are specified (known), the solution [**E**] is arrived at directly by matrix multiplication. If a mixture of currents and voltages were specified, the unknown currents and voltages could be evaluated by a variety of mathematical techniques for solving sets of simultaneous linear equations.

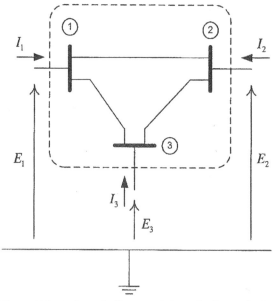

Figure 3.1 – Schematic Representation of a Power System

Partly because of tradition and partly because of the physical characteristics of generation and load, the electrical conditions at each bus are described in terms of active and reactive power rather than by bus current. In a load flow study, therefore, the electrical conditions at a bus are described by four quantities.

P - Active power into the transmission network
Q - Reactive power into the transmission network
$|E|$ - Magnitude of bus voltage (voltage to ground)
δ - Angle of bus voltage referred to as common reference

The bus current is related to these quantities as follows:

$$I = \frac{S^*}{E^*} = \frac{P - jQ}{|E|} e^{j\delta} \qquad (III.3)$$

In order to define the load flow problem to be solved, it is necessary to specify two of the four quantities at each bus. For generation it is reasonable to specify P and $|E|$ because these quantities are controllable through governor and excitation controls, respectively. For the loads, one generally specifies the real power demand P and the reactive power Q. Since there are losses in the transmission system and these losses are not known before the load flow solution is obtained, it is necessary to retain one bus where P is not specified. At this bus, called a swing bus (sometimes "slack bus"), $|E|$ as well as δ are specified. Since δ is specified (that is, held constant during the load flow solution), it is the reference angle for the system. The swing bus is therefore also called the reference bus. Table 3.1 summarizes the standard electrical specifications for the three bus types. The classifications "generator bus" and "load bus" should not be taken literally. There will, for example, be occasions where a pure load bus may be specified by P and $|E|$.

Table 3.1 – Standard Powerflow Bus Types

	SPECIFIED QUANTITIES			
Bus Type	P	Q	$|E|$	δ
"Generator" (*PE*-bus)	X		X	
"Load" (*PQ*-bus)	X	X		
Swing bus			X	X

Bus specification is the tool with which the engineer manipulates the load flow solution to obtain the desired information. Because of their importance, bus specifications will be discussed in more detail later using the more precise nomenclature indicated in parenthesis (e.g. "PE-bus").

The objective of the load flow solution is to determine the two quantities at each bus that are not specified. The specification of P and Q rather than the injected current / transfers a linear network problem to a non-linear problem that can not be readily solved by closed form matrix techniques. Rather, the load flow solution is obtained by an interaction procedure.

3.2.1 Solution Methods

Descriptions of load flow methods for A-C systems are often rather complex and not easily accessible. The apparent complexity, however, is more due to the nomenclature required for complex algebra than to the basic concepts of the solution method. In the following section, the basic techniques used in load flow programs are illustrated quite simply by considering the load flow solution to a D-C system. Applications to A-C problems are described in subsequent paragraphs.

3.3 Basic Load Flow Solution Concepts Illustrated on a D-C System Problem

In Figure 3.2, bus 3 is a load bus with specified per unit power. Bus 2 is a generator bus with power specified and bus 1 is the swing bus with voltage specified. The voltages E2 and E3 are sought.

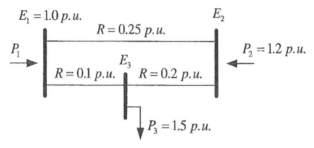

Figure 3.2 – D.C. Network for Power Flow Calculation

The system equations on an admittance basis are:[*]

$$\begin{bmatrix} I_1 \\ I_2 \\ I_3 \end{bmatrix} = \begin{bmatrix} 14 & -4 & -10 \\ -4 & 9 & -5 \\ -10 & -5 & 15 \end{bmatrix} \begin{bmatrix} E_1 \\ E_2 \\ E_3 \end{bmatrix} \qquad \text{(III.4)}$$

For bus no. 2

$$I_2 = Y_{21}E_1 + Y_{22}E_2 + Y_{23}E_3 \qquad \text{(III.5)}$$

or

$$E_2 = \frac{1}{Y_{22}}\left(I_2 - \left(Y_{21}E_1 + Y_{23}E_3\right)\right) \qquad \text{(III.6)}$$

Substituting

$$I_2 = \frac{P_2}{E_2} \qquad \text{(III.7)}$$

$$E_2 = \frac{1}{Y_{22}}\left(\frac{P_2}{E_2} - \left(Y_{21}E_1 + Y_{23}E_3\right)\right) \qquad \text{(III.8)}$$

---

[*] See Chapter 1 for formation of the Y=bus matrix.

This is a non-linear equation in E2. By substituting the admittance values, the specified voltage E1 and powers P2 and P3, the following system of simultaneous equations is obtained.

$$E_2 = \frac{1}{9}\left(\frac{1.2}{E_2} + 4 \times 1.0 + 5E_3 \right)$$

$$E_3 = \frac{1}{15}\left(\frac{-1.5}{E_3} + 10 \times 1.0 + 5E_2 \right)$$

(III.9)

There are several schemes for solving Equation (III.9).

3.3.1 Gauss-Seidel Iteration

This method is briefly as follows:

1. Assign an estimate of E2 and E3.

2. Compute a new value for E2 using the initial estimates for E2 and E3.

3. Compute a new value for E3 using the initial estimate for E3 and the just computed value for E2.

4. Repeat (2) and (3) using the latest computed voltages, E2 and E3 until the solution is reached. One complete computation of E2 and E3 is one iteration.

With numbers:

Initial estimate: $E_2 = E_3 = 1.0$

First Iteration: $E_2 = \frac{1}{9}\left(\frac{1.2}{1.0} + 4 \times 1.0 + 5 \times 1.0 \right) = \frac{1}{9}(1.2 + 9) = 1.133$

$E_3 = \frac{1}{15}\left(\frac{-1.5}{1.0} + 10 \times 1.0 + 5 \times 1.133 \right) = 0.944$

Second Iteration: $E_2 = \frac{1}{9}\left(\frac{1.2}{1.133} + 4 \times 1.0 + 5 \times 0.944 \right) = 1.087$

$E_3 = \frac{1}{15}\left(\frac{-1.5}{0.944} + 10 \times 1.0 + 5 \times 1.087 \right) = 0.923$

Third Iteration: $E_2 =$

(To be completed

by the student) $E_3 =$

In general, for the mth iteration:

$$E_2^m = \frac{1}{9}\left(\frac{1.2}{E_2^{m-1}} + 4 + 5 \times E_3^{m-1} \right)$$

$$E_3^m = \frac{1}{15}\left(\frac{-1.5}{E_3^{m-1}} + \ddot{u} + \times E_2^m \right)$$

(III.10)

Convergence Criteria

The computed voltages are said to converge when, for each iteration, they come closer and closer to the actual solution satisfying the network equations. Since the computer time increases linearly with the number of iterations, it is necessary to have the computer program make a check after each iteration and decide whether the last computed voltages are sufficiently close to the true solution or whether further computations are required. The criterion specifying the desired accuracy is called the convergence criterion.

A reliable convergence criterion is the so-called power mismatch check. Based on the last computed voltage solution, the power at each bus is computed and compared with the specified bus power. The difference - Power mismatch - is a measure of how close the computed voltages are to the true solution. If the maximum mismatch is obtained at bus "I", the convergence criterion is stated as follows:

$$\Delta P_{max} = \Delta P_i = \left| P_i' - E_i \left(\sum_{k=1}^{n} Y_{iK} E_K \right) \right| < \varepsilon_P$$

(III.11)

where the "prime" indicates specified bus quantity. The tolerance ε_p is generally specified in the range of 0.001 $p.u. \leq \varepsilon_p \leq 0.01$ $p.u.$

A different convergence check evaluates the maximum change in any bus voltage from one iteration to the next. A solution with desired accuracy is assumed when the change is less than a specified small value ε_E (e.g. $\varepsilon_E = 0.0001$ $p.u.$):

$$\Delta E_{max} = \Delta E_i = \left| E_i^{m-1} - E_i^m \right| < \varepsilon_E$$

(III.12)

A voltage check is dependent on the rate of convergence and is thus less reliable than the power check. However, the voltage check equation (III.12) is much faster than the power check equation (III.11) and since $\Delta P_{max} > \varepsilon_p$ until ΔE_{max} is quite small one may economically use a procedure where computation of ΔP_{max} is avoided until $\Delta E_{max} < \varepsilon_E$.

Table 3.2 shows the voltages and power at buses 2 and 3 after each iteration for the 3-bus system.

It is seen that the voltage solution is within 1% of its true value after only 2 iterations, but that 6 iterations would be required to meet a convergence criterion of $\Delta P_{max} < 0.001$. The convergence is asymptotic; i.e., a particular bus voltage approaches the final value in smaller and smaller increments and is always greater or always less than the desired solution.

Table 3.2 – **Gauss-Seidel Solution of Example System**

It. No.	E_2	E_3	P_2	P_3	ΔP_{max}
1	1.1333	0.9444	1.6748	-1.4166	0.4748
2	1.0867	0.9230	1.2670	-1.4660	0.0670
3	1.0799	0.9183	1.2680	-1.4923	0.0180
4	1.0781	0.9171	1.2043	-1.4981	0.0043
5	1.0776	0.9168	1.2010	-1.4995	0.0011
6	1.0775	0.9168	1.2003	-1.4999	0.0003
7	1.0775	0.9168	1.2001	-1.5000	0.0001

3.3.2   The Newton Raphson Method

Applied to A-C power systems, the Gauss Seidel iteration scheme converges rather slowly. In some cases it does not converge at all. A much faster convergence is obtained with the Newton Raphson Method which sometimes is referred to simply as the Newton Method. Typically, this method reaches (for all practical purposes) an exact solution after only 4 or 5 iterations. Before applying the method on the 3-bus D-C problem, the fundamentals of "linearizing" a non-linear equation are reviewed:

Consider a non-linear function $F(x)$ of a variable x as illustrated in Figure 3.3.

If the numerical value of $F(x)$ and its derivatives are known at x_0, the value of F at $x_0 + \Delta x$ is:

$$F\left(x_0 + \Delta x\right) = F\left(x_0\right) + \left.\frac{dF(x)}{dx}\right|_{x=x_0} \Delta x + \phi$$

where $\left.\dfrac{dF(x)}{dx}\right|_{x=x_0}$ is the first derivative of $F(x)$ at $x = x_0$ and ϕ is the contribution form second and higher order terms.

Neglecting ϕ yields the <u>linear</u> approximation

$$F(x_0 + \Delta x) \approx F(x_0) + \left.\frac{dF(x)}{dx}\right|_{x=x_0} \Delta x \qquad (III.13)$$

Figure 3.3 should provide the necessary mental calibration.

A function of two variables $F(x, y)$ is <u>linearized</u> in a similar manner:

$$F(x_0 + \Delta x, y_0 + \Delta y) \approx F(x_0, y_0) + \left.\frac{\partial F(x,y)}{\partial x}\right|_{\substack{x=x_0 \\ y=y_0}} \Delta x + \left.\frac{\partial F(x,y)}{\partial y}\right|_{\substack{x=x_0 \\ y=y_0}} \Delta y$$

and the <u>change</u> in F resulting from small changes in x and y:

$$\Delta F(x_0, y_0) = F(x_0 + \Delta x, y_0 + \Delta y) - F(x_0, y_0) \approx \left.\frac{\partial F(x,y)}{\partial}\right|_{\substack{x\ x \\ y\ y}} x \quad \left.\frac{\partial F(x,y)}{\partial}\right|_{\substack{x\ x \\ y\ y}} \Delta y \quad (III.14)$$

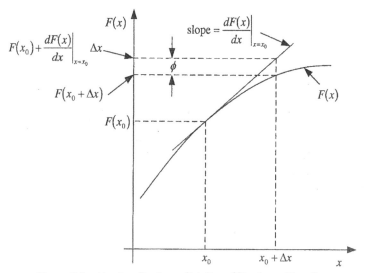

Figure 3.3 – Newton-Raphson Solution of Nonlinear Equation

In equation (III.14) $\left.\dfrac{\partial F(x,y)}{\partial x}\right|_{\substack{x=x_0 \\ y=y_0}}$ is the partial derivative of $F(x,y)$ with respect to x
at $x = x_0$ and $y = y_0$ (obtained by straight differentiation holding y constant $= y_0$).
Similarly $\left.\dfrac{\partial F(x,y)}{\partial y}\right|_{\substack{x=x_0 \\ y=y_0}}$ is the partial derivative of F with respect to y.

In the 3-bus D-C system, the bus powers can be expressed as non-linear functions
of the bus voltages.

$$P_1(E_1, E_2, E_3) = E_1(Y_{11}E_1 + Y_{12}E_2 + Y_{13}E_3)$$
$$P_2(E_1, E_2, E_3) = E_2(Y_{21}E_1 + Y_{22}E_2 + Y_{23}E_3) \qquad \text{(III.15)}$$
$$P_3(E_1, E_2, E_3) = E_3(Y_{31}E_1 + Y_{32}E_2 + Y_{33}E_3)$$

Small changes in bus voltages (ΔE) will cause corresponding small changes in bus powers (ΔP). Then from equation (III.14) a linearized approximation to the power change as a function of voltage changes can be obtained as:

$$\begin{bmatrix} \Delta P_1 \\ \Delta P_2 \\ \Delta P_3 \end{bmatrix} = \begin{bmatrix} \dfrac{\partial P_1}{\partial E_1} & \dfrac{\partial P_1}{\partial E_2} & \dfrac{\partial P_1}{\partial E_3} \\ \dfrac{\partial P_2}{\partial E_1} & \dfrac{\partial P_2}{\partial E_2} & \dfrac{\partial P_2}{\partial E_3} \\ \dfrac{\partial P_3}{\partial E_1} & \dfrac{\partial P_3}{\partial E_2} & \dfrac{\partial P_3}{\partial E_3} \end{bmatrix} \begin{bmatrix} \Delta E_1 \\ \Delta E_2 \\ \Delta E_3 \end{bmatrix} \qquad \text{(III.16)}$$

or symbolically:

$$[\Delta P] = [J] \times [\Delta E]$$

where $[J]$, the <u>Jacobian</u> matrix, contains the partial derivatives of power with respect to voltages for a <u>particular</u> set of voltages, E_1, E_2, and E_3. When one or more of the voltages changes substantially, a new Jacobian matrix must be computed.

In the load flow problem, E_1 is specified. That is, $\Delta E_1 = 0$. Also, since ΔP_1 does not enter the computations explicitly, equation (III.16) may be reduced to:

$$\begin{bmatrix} \Delta P_2 \\ \Delta P_3 \end{bmatrix} = \begin{bmatrix} \dfrac{\partial P_2}{\partial E_2} & \dfrac{\partial P_2}{\partial E_3} \\ \dfrac{\partial P_3}{\partial E_2} & \dfrac{\partial P_3}{\partial E_3} \end{bmatrix} \begin{bmatrix} \Delta E_2 \\ \Delta E_3 \end{bmatrix} \qquad \text{(III.17)}$$

Changes in E_2 and E_3 due to changes in P_2 and P_3 are obtained by inverting $[J]$ to obtain:

$$[\Delta E] = [J]^{-1}[\Delta P] \qquad \text{(III.18)}$$

The Newton-Raphson load flow solution method is then principally as follows:

1. Assign estimates of E_2 and E_3 (for example, $E_2 = E_3 = 1.0$).

2. Compute P_2 and P_3 from equation (III.15)

3. Compute the differences (ΔP) between computed and specified powers:

$$\Delta P_2 = P_2 - P_2'$$

$$\Delta P_3 = P_3 - P_3'$$

(III.19)

where the "prime" indicated specified value.

4. Since $\Delta P \neq 0$ is caused by errors in the voltages, it seems that the voltages should be incorrect by an amount that is closely approximated by ΔE as evaluated from equation (III.18). Therefore, the new estimate for the bus voltages is:

$$\begin{bmatrix} E_2 \\ E_3 \end{bmatrix}_{New} = \begin{bmatrix} E_2 \\ E_3 \end{bmatrix}_{Old} - [J]^{-1} \begin{bmatrix} \Delta P_2 \\ \Delta P_3 \end{bmatrix}$$

(III.20)

This is the basic equation in the Newton-Raphson method. The negative sign is due to the way ΔP was defined.

5. Recompute and invert the Jacobian matrix using the last computed voltages and compute the new estimate for the voltages using equations (III.19) and (III.20). Repeat procedure until ΔP_2 and ΔP_3 are less than a small value ε_1 (convergence criterion).

For the 3-bus D-C system, the elements of the Jacobian matrix are obtained by partial differentiation of equation (III.15):

$$\frac{\partial P_2}{\partial E_2} = Y_{21} E_1 + 2Y_{22} E_2 + Y_{23} E_3$$

$$\frac{\partial P_2}{\partial E_3} = E_2 Y_{23}$$

(III.21)

$$\frac{\partial P_3}{\partial E_2} = E_3 Y_{32}$$

$$\frac{\partial P_3}{\partial E_3} = Y_{31} E_1 + 2Y_{32} E_2 + 2Y_{33} E_3$$

3-Bus D-C System Example

With initial voltage estimates of $E_2 = E_3 = 1.0$, the elements of the initial Jacobian matrix are:

$$\frac{\partial P_2}{\partial E_2} = -4 + 2 \times 9 - 5 = 9$$

$$\frac{\partial P_2}{\partial E_3} = -5$$

$$\frac{\partial P_3}{\partial E_2} = -5$$

$$\frac{\partial P_3}{\partial E_3} = -10 - 5 + 2 \times 15 = 15$$

Therefore:

$$[J] = \begin{bmatrix} 9 & -5 \\ -5 & 15 \end{bmatrix}$$

and:

$$[J]^{-1} = \frac{1}{110} \begin{bmatrix} 15 & +5 \\ +5 & 9 \end{bmatrix}$$

From equation (III.15):

$$\Delta P_2 = 1.0(-4+9-5)-1.2 = -1.2$$

$$\Delta P_3 = 1.0(-10-5+15)+1.5 = +1.5$$

$$\begin{bmatrix} E_2 \\ E_3 \end{bmatrix} = \begin{bmatrix} 1.0 \\ 1.0 \end{bmatrix} - \begin{bmatrix} 0.136 & 0.0455 \\ 0.0455 & 0.082 \end{bmatrix} \begin{bmatrix} -1.2 \\ +1.5 \end{bmatrix}$$

$$\begin{bmatrix} E_2 \\ E_3 \end{bmatrix} = \begin{bmatrix} 1.0 \\ 1.0 \end{bmatrix} - \begin{bmatrix} -0.095 \\ 0.068 \end{bmatrix} = \begin{bmatrix} 1.095 \\ 0.932 \end{bmatrix}$$

Second Iteration:

$$[J] = \begin{bmatrix} 11.05 & -5.47 \\ -4.66 & 12.48 \end{bmatrix}$$

$$\Delta P_2 = 0.114$$

$$\Delta P_3 = 0.102$$

$$\begin{bmatrix} E_2 \\ E_3 \end{bmatrix} = \begin{bmatrix} 1.095 \\ 0.932 \end{bmatrix} - \begin{bmatrix} 11.05 & -5.47 \\ -4.66 & 12.48 \end{bmatrix}^{-1} \begin{bmatrix} 0.114 \\ 0.102 \end{bmatrix} = \begin{bmatrix} 1.079 \\ 0.916 \end{bmatrix}$$

Table 3.3 shows the voltages and the power deviation for each iteration. It is noted that $\Delta P_{max} < 0.001$ after the third iteration.

The convergence is not asymptotic as was the case with the Gauss-Seidel iteration scheme.

Digital computer programs solving large power system load flows do not explicitly compute the Jacobian inverse. Rather, the voltage correction ΔE is obtained by a numerical technique known as Gaussian Elimination. This technique is much faster and requires much less storage than matrix inversion.

Table 10.3 – Newton-Raphson Solution of Example System

ITERATION NO.	ΔP_2	ΔP_3	E_2	E_3
Initial			1.0	1.0
1	-1.2	1.5	1.09545	0.931818
2	0.115	0.102	1.07851	0.916183
3	0.01410	-0.0115	1.07741	0.916644
4	-0.00035	-0.00089	1.07749	0.916753
5	-0.000087	+0.000065	1.07749	0.916751
After 5ᵗʰ Iteration	0.000002	0.000006		

3.3.3 The "Ward and Hale" Method

In their pioneering work (published in 1956, ref. 1), J. B. Ward and H. W. Hale introduced a method that uses only the diagonal elements of the Jacobian matrix making the inversion of the matrix trivial. Equation (III.20) is then:

$$
\begin{bmatrix} E_2 \\ E_3 \end{bmatrix}_{New} = \begin{bmatrix} E_2 \\ E_3 \end{bmatrix}_{Old} = \begin{bmatrix} \dfrac{1}{\dfrac{\partial P_2}{\partial E_2}} & 0 \\ 0 & \dfrac{1}{\dfrac{\partial P_3}{\partial E_3}} \end{bmatrix} \begin{bmatrix} \Delta P_2 \\ \Delta P_3 \end{bmatrix}
$$

or:

$$
E_{2New} = E_{2Old} - \frac{1}{\dfrac{\partial P_2}{\partial E_2}} \Delta P_2
$$

$$
E_{3New} = E_{3Old} - \frac{1}{\dfrac{\partial P_3}{\partial E_3}} \Delta P_3
\qquad (III.22)
$$

Rather than first computing ΔP for all buses and then computing the new voltages as indicated by (III.22), Ward and Hale chose to postpone the computation of ΔP_3 and $\dfrac{\partial P_3}{\partial E_3}$ till after the new value of E_2 was established. The "Ward and Hale" method is thus a Gauss-Seidel iteration of equation (III.22).

For the three-bus D-C system, the procedure is as follows (note the similarity with the procedure described on page 3-3):

1. Assign an estimate of E_2 and E_3.

2. Compute a new value for E_2 using the initial estimates for E_2 and E_3:

a) $$\Delta P_2 = E_2 \left(E_1 Y_{21} + E_2 Y_{22} + E_3 Y_{23} \right) - P_2'$$

b) $$\frac{\partial P_2}{\partial E_2} = Y_{21} E_1 + 2 Y_{22} E_2 + Y_{23} E_3$$

c) $$E_{2New} = E_{2Old} - \frac{\Delta P_2}{\frac{\partial P_2}{\partial E_2}}$$

3. Similarly, compute a new value for E_3 using the initial estimate for E_3 and the just computed value for E_2.

4. Repeat (2) and (3) using the latest computed voltage E_2 and E_3 until the solution is reached. One complete computation of E_2 and E_3 is one iteration.

3-Bus D-C System Example

1. $E_2 = E_3 = 1.0$

   First Iteration

   a) $\Delta P_2 = -1.2$

2. b) $$\frac{\partial P_2}{\partial E_2} = 9$$

   c) $E_{2New} = 1.0 - \dfrac{1.2}{9} = 1.1333$

   a) $\Delta P_3 = E_3 \left(E_1 Y_{31} + E_2 Y_{32} + E_3 Y_{33} \right) - P_3'$

   $= 1.0(1.0(-10)+1.133\times(-5)+1.0\times15)+1.5$

   $= 0.833$

3. b) $\dfrac{\partial P_3}{\partial E_3} = Y_{31} E_1 + Y_{32} E_2 + Y_{33} E_3$

   $= -10+(-5)1.133+2\times15\times1.0 = 14.33$

c) $E_{3New} = 1.1333 - \dfrac{0.489}{11.5} = 1.091$

Second Iteration

a) $\Delta P_2 = 1.1333(1.0\times(-4)+1.1333\times9+0.9418\times(-5)) = 0.489$

2. b) $\dfrac{\partial P}{\partial E_2} = 1.0(-4)+2\times9\times1.133-5\times0.9418 = 11.5$

c) $E_{3New} = 1.1333 - \dfrac{0.489}{11.5} = 1.091$

$\Delta P_3 = 0.249$

3. $E_{3New} = 0.922$

The convergence characteristics of this procedure are shown in Table 3.4.

Table 3.4 – Ward-Hale Solution of Example System

ITERATION NO.	ΔP_2	ΔP_3	E_2	E_3
Initial			1.0	1.0
1	-1.200000	0.833333	1.1.33333	0.941860
2	0.489457	0.247869	1.091466	0.922493
3	0.121468	0.056403	1.080457	0.917898
4	0.025919	0.011272	1.078071	0.916970
5	0.005053	0.002154	1.077604	0.916792
6	0.000960	0.000407	1.077515	0.916758
7	0.000181	0.000077	1.077498	0.916752
8	0.000034	0.000014	1.077495	0.916751
9	0.000006	0.000003	1.077494	0.916750
10	0.000001	0.000001	1.077494	0.916750

This method also converges asymptotic and it appears that a more rapaid convergence would result by making the voltage correction a little larger than

that predicted by equation (III.22). Instead of $\Delta E_i = -\left(\dfrac{1}{\dfrac{\partial P_i}{\partial E_i}}\right)\Delta P_i$ one could use:

$$\Delta E_i = -\alpha \left(\frac{1}{\dfrac{\partial P_i}{\partial E_i}} \right) \Delta P_i \qquad (\text{III.23})$$

where α is a so-called <u>acceleration factor</u>. For A-C systems, $\alpha = 1.6$ is often used for both the real and the imaginary components of the voltage corrections. <u>Acceleration factors of this magnitude are also used in the Gauss-Seidel method described on page 3-4</u>.

3.4 The A-C Load Flow Program

The basic concepts of load flow solutions were described in the previous section using a d-c power system as a numerical example. This section presents the basic equations required for the a-c load flow solution based on the Ward and Hale method and also includes a brief discussion of load flow programs based on the impedance matrix network representation. Detailed equations for the various methods including the Newton-Raphson method are given in the literature (Reference 2).

As far as the user of the load flow program is concerned, the details of the method used is not significant as long as he knows the program's features and limitations. The last portion of this section describes common and not so common features of load flow programs and how such programs can be manipulated to provide the desired information for system planning and design.

3.4.1 Basic Equations for Load Flow Solution on an Admittance Basis

The system equations are:

$$[\mathbf{I}] = [\mathbf{Y}]\,[\mathbf{E}] \qquad (\text{III.24})$$

The current at bus i in terms of bus quantities:

$$I_i = \frac{P_i - jQ_i}{E_i^*} \qquad (\text{III.25})$$

From equation (III.24) (n-bus system)

$$I_i = \sum_{k=1}^{n} Y_{ik} E_k \qquad (\text{III.26})$$

Solving for E_i:

$$E_i = \frac{1}{Y_{ii}} \left(I_i - \sum_{\substack{k=1 \\ k \neq i}}^{n} Y_{ik} E_k \right) \qquad \text{(III.27)}$$

Substituting equation (III.25) in equation (III.27):

$$E_i = \frac{1}{Y_{ii}} \left(\frac{P_i - jQ_i}{E_i^*} - \sum_{\substack{k=1 \\ k \neq i}}^{n} Y_{ik} E_k \right) \qquad \text{(III.28)}$$

This is the A-C version of equation (III.9) used in the basic Gauss-Seidel iteration scheme. Equation (III.28) represents *(n-1)* non-linear equations. (The swing bus voltage is specified and need not be computed.)

The Ward and Hale approach utilizes the diagonal elements of the Jacobian matrix. Since the voltage and power quantities at each bus are complex numbers, the diagonal "elements" are actually 2 by 2 matrices. Having computed the prevailing deviations between specified and computed bus quantities (ΔP, ΔQ for load buses; ΔP, $\Delta/E/$ for generator buses) the corrections to the real and imaginary components of the bus voltage are obtained by inverting these 2 by 2 matrices. In the following discussion, *"e"* and *"f"* are the real and imaginary components of the bus voltages:

$$E_i = e_i + jf_i \qquad \text{(III.29)}$$

Load bus (*P* and *Q* specified):

$$\begin{bmatrix} \Delta P \\ \Delta Q \end{bmatrix} = \begin{bmatrix} \dfrac{\partial P}{\partial e} & \dfrac{\partial P}{\partial f} \\ \dfrac{\partial Q}{\partial e} & \dfrac{\partial Q}{\partial f} \end{bmatrix} \begin{bmatrix} \Delta e \\ \Delta f \end{bmatrix} \qquad \text{(III.30)}$$

Generator bus (*P* and *E* specified)

$$\begin{bmatrix} \Delta P \\ \Delta E \end{bmatrix} = \begin{bmatrix} \dfrac{\partial P}{\partial e} & \dfrac{\partial P}{\partial f} \\ \dfrac{\partial |E|}{\partial e} & \dfrac{\partial |E|}{\partial f} \end{bmatrix} \begin{bmatrix} \Delta e \\ \Delta f \end{bmatrix} \qquad \text{(III.31)}$$

The matrices may be inverted analytically. That is, the voltage corrections are computed directly from equations of form:

$$\Delta e = F_1 \,(\Delta P, \Delta Q)$$
$$\Delta f = F_2 \,(\Delta P, \Delta Q)$$
Load Bus

$$\Delta e = F_3 \,(\Delta P, \Delta |E|)$$
$$\Delta f = F_4 \,(\Delta P, \Delta |E|)$$
Generator Bus

(III.32)

The mechanics of the A-C load flow solution using the basic Gauss-Seidel iteration scheme or the Ward and Hale method is the same as illustrated on the D-C problem. The <u>convergence criteria</u> may include $\Delta P_{max} < \varepsilon_p$, $\Delta Q_{max} < \varepsilon_Q$ and $\Delta |E|_{max} < \varepsilon_{|E|}$. The last criterion (voltage check) is generally omitted. <u>Acceleration factors,</u> if used, will be applied to both Δe and Δf in equation (III.32).

The basic Gauss-Seidel iteration, the "Ward and Hale" method or combinations of the two are widely used in the industry. These methods are referred to by such partially descriptive names as" "The nodal iterative method", "The Gauss-Seidel method" and "The Y-bus method". The basic advantage of these methods over the Newton-Raphson method and impedance based load flow solutions is their relatively limited computer storage requirements.

3.4.2   Comment on the Newton-Raphson Method

The Jacobian matrix may be arranged as follows:

$$\begin{bmatrix} [\Delta P] \\ [\Delta Q] \\ [\Delta |E|] \end{bmatrix} = [J] \begin{bmatrix} [\Delta e] \\ [\Delta f] \end{bmatrix}$$

If N_G generator buses and N_L load buses are represented, the number of rows in $[J]$ will be:

for ΔP: $N_L + N_G$

for ΔQ: N_L

for $\Delta |E|$: N_G

TOTAL: $2(N_L + N_G) = 2(N - 1)$

The Jacobian matrix can be arranged in many different ways to fit the particular programming techniques selected. The voltage corrections can also be expressed in polar form $\Delta E = \Delta |E| \,|\underline{\Delta\delta}$. One successful program using this approach is described in Reference 3.

The Newton-Raphson approach may yield a nearly exact solution after as little as 4 iterations (4 computations of the Jacobian matrix and 4 solutions for the unknown voltages).

3.4.3 Impedance Matrix Method

In this case, the transmission network is represented by:

$$[E - E_R] = [Z] [I] \qquad \text{(III.33)}$$

where E_R is the specified voltage of the swing bus or reference bus.

Equation (III.33) yields the voltage difference between a bus i and the swing bus (R) as a function of the <u>bus currents</u> entering the transmission network at <u>all</u> the buses in the system. See Figure 3.4. Since the voltage element corresponding to the swing bus is zero, the elements of the row and column in the Z matrix that corresponds to the swing bus are all zero and are generally omitted from the matrix. The dimension of the matrix is thus $(n-1)$ by $(n-1)$. The Z-bus matrix as defined here does not include any shunt element to ground. The shunt elements at a bus i with total admittance y_i are included in the bus current.

$$I_i = \frac{P_i - jQ_i}{E_1 *} - y_i E_i \qquad \text{(III.34)}$$

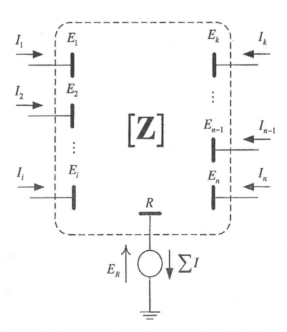

Figure 3.4 – Impedance Matrix Representation of the Network

411

Using a Gauss-Seidel iterative technique, the impedance method yields acceptable solutions after as little as 5 iterations, while the admittance methods (excluding Newton-Raphson) typically require 20 or more iterations.

The reason for the relatively slow convergence of the traditional admittance based load flow is the fact that when computing the current for bus i from the network equations, only the conditions at buses connected directly to bus i are considered. (In the Y-matrix, the mutual terms to all other buses are 0). The Z-matrix, on the other hand, is a "full" matrix (no zero elements.)[*] Therefore, the current at one bus influences the voltages at all the other buses when evaluating equation (III.33).

3.4.4 Comparison of Load Flow Solution Methods

<u>Computer Storage Considerations</u>

The complete complex Y-matrix or Z-matrix has about $2n^2$ elements. Even in a big computer, the available storage space for the network matrix may be limited to, say, 40,000 elements. If all elements were to be stored, a maximum of about 140 buses could be represented. Since the matrices are symmetric, only the upper triangle needs to be stored and it may be possible to represent about 250 buses. This would be the maximum size that could be represented by a basic impedance based load flow, since all the elements of the Z-matrix are generally non-zero. The Y-matrix, however, is a sparse matrix since each element Y_{ik} will be non-zero only if there is a direct connection (transmission line or transformer) between buses i and k. Since zero elements do not have to be stored, a 1000 or even a 2000 bus load flow can be run without difficulties on present computer installations.

In addition to the space requirements for the Y-matrix, the Newton-Raphson method needs storage space for the elements of the Jacobian matrix. For large power system problems, exploitation of this scarcity is required to reduce storage and computer time to reasonable levels. The Jacobian matrix has the same scarcity structure as the Y-matrix. For example, the element $\frac{\partial P_i}{\partial e_k}$ is non-zero only for $i = k$ and when bus i is directly connected to bus k

<u>Versatility</u>

Load flow programs on an admittance basis that do not use the complete Jacobian matrix may not yield a solution for unusual system conditions, such as when the circuit impedance between two buses is very small, zero or negative. (Negative impedances may result from three-winding transformer equivalents.) The Newton-Raphson method and the impedance method can handle such situations without difficulty.

---

[*] Zero elements may occur in some special cases.

Speed

The Newton-Raphson method seems to have an edge over other admittance methods as well as present impedance based methods. Figure 3.5 shows the convergence characteristics of the Newton-Raphson method, the impedance matrix method and an asymptotically converging admittance method. (The information is taken from H.W. Dommel's discussion of Reference 3.) The curves show how the real and imaginary component of a particular bus voltage converges from the initial estimate of $E = 1.0 + j0$ to the solution $E = 0.95 + j0.11$.

It should be noted that the time per iteration is much shorter for the admittance method than for either the Newton-Raphson or the impedance matrix method.

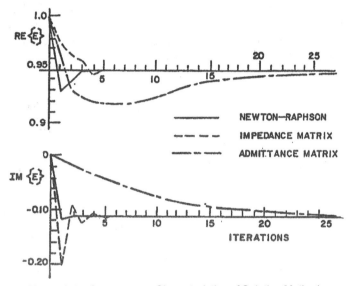

Figure 3.5 – Convergence Characteristics of Solution Methods

3.5   The A-C Load Flow Program as an Engineering Tool

Load flow programs can be used in several different ways, depending upon the nature of the problem being investigated. If one is interested in bus voltages and circuit power flow for a completely specified existing or planned system, one may wish to represent a large number of buses in complete detail. Load flow studies representing 1000 to 2000 buses are not unusual in the industry. The size of the system represented, however, is not necessarily a good measure of the usefulness of the output data. If the objective of the study is to evaluate the effect of future generation or transmission alternatives; it may prove more useful to limit detailed representation to the local system which is well known to the user and to represent remote areas by equivalents. These equivalents, then, can easily be varied to cover the possible range of operation of the remote areas without going into the operating details of these areas. Provided the engineer is experienced in network solution work and also has a good theoretical understanding of the subject, he will probably find frequent manipulation on a 100-200 bus load flow more rewarding than occasional runs with a 1000 bus system.

Frequently, the main objective of the study is to find out whether or not a specific system design alternative produces bus voltages within acceptable limits. If not, one may modify the system and try again until an acceptable solution is found. However, a more efficient procedure would be to artificially specify the acceptable limits for bus voltages and then read from the program output the reactive power supply required to maintain this voltage. Such studies, typical for early planning consideration, may conveniently be solved on 10-100 bus load flows which are easily accommodated on time-sharing systems. The following paragraphs are intended to illustrate the versatility of the A-C load flow program for network planning.

Example Network

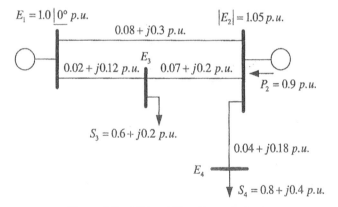

Figure 3.6 – AC Load Flow Example System

In the system in Figure 3.6, buses 1 and 2 are specified as generator buses while buses 3 and 4 are load buses. The line charging listed gives the admittance of one leg of the π equivalent for the transmission circuit. The solution to this load flow problem was obtained from a time-share load flow program using the Ward and Hale approach.

Figure 3.7 shows the load flow solution which includes computed bus voltages, the current flows, and the real and reactive power flows between the buses indicated. It is seen that the voltage at bus 4 (0.933) is about 12% below the voltage at bus 2 (1.05). One way of reducing this difference would be to add shunt capacitance at bus 4. Instead of using a trial and error procedure, one can specify bus 4 as a generator bus with voltage magnitude at the acceptable lower limit, say 0.95 per unit. Figure 3.8 shows the load flow solution for this specification.

NO. ITERATIONS= 13				CIRCUIT FLOW				BUS	POWERS
FROM BUS	MAG. V	ANG. V	TO BUS	MAG. I	ANG. I	P	Q	P	Q
1	1.000	0.	2	0.238	66.8	0.094	-0.219	0.548	-0.263
			3	0.457	5.5	0.454	-0.044		
2	1.050	-2.363	1	0.183	239.5	-0.090	0.169	0.900	0.898
			3	0.246	-55.5	0.155	0.206		
			4	0.939	-34.4	0.836	0.523		
3	0.996	-3.172	1	0.454	181.7	-0.450	0.039	-0.600	-0.200
			2	0.283	118.9	-0.150	-0.239		
4	(0.933)	-9.914	2	0.959	143.5	-0.800	-0.400	-0.800	-0.400

PROGRAM STOP AT 840

USED   .36 UNITS

Figure 3.7 – Time-Share Computer Output of Solution to Load Flow Problem Figure 3.6

NO. ITERATIONS= 13							
FROM BUS	MAG. V	ANG. V	TO BUS	MAG. I	ANG. I	P	Q
1	1.000	0.	2	0.237	67.2	0.092	-0.218
			3	0.455	5.4	0.453	-0.043
2	1.050	-2.328	1	0.181	240.0	-0.088	0.168
			3	0.246	-55.1	0.156	0.206
			4	0.890	-29.4	0.832	0.425
3	0.996	-3.159	1	0.452	181.7	-0.449	0.038
			2	0.283	119.3	-0.151	-0.238
4	(0.950)	-9.930	2	0.907	148.3	-0.800	(-0.319)

Figure 3.8 – Solution with Voltage Bus 4 Specified as 0.95 p.u.

The difference in total reactive power going into bus 4 in the second and first computer output is the reactive power compensation required to raise the voltage at bus 4 from 0.933 to 0.95 per unit.

$$\Delta Q = -0.319 - (-0.4) = 0.081 \text{ p.u.}$$

In the above example, a load bus was specified as a generator bus or more specific as a "PE-bus". There are a number of different bus specifications that can be used either to accurately represent the operation modes of the system or as artifices in arriving at specific design information as in the second load flow solution in the above example.

Bus Specifications

There are four types of bus specifications:

I.   Local - Unconditional

II. Local - Conditional

III. Remote - Conditional

IV. Remote - Unconditional

I. Local - Unconditional Bus Specifications

The specifications discussed previously (load bus, generator bus, and swing bus) are all of this type:

PQ- bus Specified: P, Q

This bus specification is normally used to represent load buses. The primary concern at this bus is whether or not the resulting voltage magnitude will be within acceptable limits.

PE-bus Specified: $P, |E|$

This bus type is normally used for generator buses with or without local loads. The specification assumes that an unlimited reactive power supply is available. The output may yield a reactive power output that is beyond the capability of the generator.

$E\delta$ bus Specified: $|E|, \delta$

This is the swing bus or the voltage reference bus. If the active and reactive powers at generator loads are not properly matched, the load flow solution may show unrealistic power input to the swing bus.

II. Local Conditional Bus Specifications

Buses of this type may change characteristics during the load flow computations.

PQ/PE bus   Specified: $P, |E|$ and $Q_{min} \leq \qquad \leq \qquad _{max}$

This bus is commonly used for specification of generator buses recognizing the inherent limit in the generator's capability of supplying reactive power. The bus voltage magnitude will be held constant at the specified value until the reactive power limits are violated. When this occurs, the bus is effectively a "PQ-bus" and the voltage magnitude will change to satisfy the system conditions.

III. Remote Unconditional Bus Specifications

PE-bus   Specified: P, $|E|$, and a remote bus that will adjust reactive power supply to keep $|E|$ constant.

This bus specification simulates a remote control scheme used in some systems. The specification can also be used as an artifice to obtain specific design information.

IV. Remote Conditional Bus Specifications

P_iE_i/P_iQ_k-bus   Specified: P and $|E|$ at bus i; $Q_{min} \leq Q \leq Q_{max}$ at bus k

This bus type will keep the voltage at bus "i" constant by adjusting the reactive power supply at bus "k" without violating the reactive power limits at this bus.

The above list is not exhaustive, but it is representative for the type of bus specifications allowed in the most versatile load flow programs existing today. In addition to bus specifications, there are three other useful system specifications in common use.

3.5.1 Automatic Tap Changing Transformers for Voltage Control

Autotransformers are often equipped with automatic tap changers for voltage regulations. Since the tap setting is a function of the voltage solution, it cannot be specified as input to the load flow program. Normally, the tap changing is controlled in such a manner that the voltage magnitude at the specified bus is kept constant. The specification is, however, a conditional one in that a maximum tap changing range also is specified. When the automatic tap changing feature is used in connection with representation of a manual tap changing transformer, the output of the load flow program will show the tap setting that produces the desired bus voltage.

3.5.2 Automatic Phase Shifting Transformers

Automatic phase shifting transformers can be used to control the power in a circuit that is connected in series with the transformer. If such controls do not exist in the system, the automatic phase shifting feature can be used to obtain the phase angle required for a specified power flow in the series circuit.

3.5.3 Area Power Interchange Control

Load flow studies for normal operating conditions often require a specified power export out of an area. Programs with area interchange control have provisions for holding the power out of the area constant by controlling the power at one generator.

3.6 Short Circuit Analysis

Short circuit solutions provide current flows and voltages in the transmission system during specified fault conditions. One of the principal purposes of short circuit studies is to determine the interrupting capability required for circuit breakers at each switching location. In this case one is generally interested in the maximum currents the breaker may be exposed to during symmetrical three phase faults on each side of the breaker. For protective relaying design it Is necessary to determine voltages and currents for asymmetric as well as symmetric faults at many locations in the system.

A short circuit solution could be obtained by the same techniques as used in load flow programs, but because of the frequent need to evaluate a large number of fault conditions, more efficient and less accurate) procedures are used. Short circuit programs are commonly based on the following assumptions.

1. All shunt elements including loads and line charging are neglected.

2. All tap changing transformers are assumed to be at their nominal tap setting.

3. Each generator is represented by constant voltage behind its subtransient reactance.

4. No current is flowing in any portion of the system prior to the fault. That is, all voltages behind the generator reactances are equal in magnitude and phase angle.

5. Balanced transmission line impedances are assumed allowing the use of symmetrical components for analysis of unsymmetrical faults. The negative and positive sequence system impedances are normally assumed equal and coupling between adjacent circuits is recognized in the zero sequence system only.

With these assumptions and representing the system by the Z-bus matrix, the short circuit solution for any specified fault type and fault location can be obtained by non-iterative techniques: Typically the procedure may be as follows:

1. Build the positive sequence Z-bus matrix with ground as reference, but with no shunt element included.

2. Build the corresponding zero sequence Z-bus matrix recognizing mutual coupling between adjacent circuits.

3. For specified fault types, compute voltage and current flow at the faulted bus and at any other desired location in the system. With the positive and zero sequence Z-bus matrix established such computations require only simple arithmetic operations. Often the current flow at the fault is described in terms of the "fault MVA" and the "contributions to the fault MVA" from the lines connected to the faulted bus.

Short circuit programs are often set up to evaluate a large number of fault cases without manual intervention. Some programs will, for example, systematically remove lines connected to the faulted bus one at a time. Such system changes require modification of the Impedance matrix elements associated with the buses where short circuit information is desired.

References

1. J. B. Ward, H. W. Hale, "Digital Computer Solution of Power Flow Problems", AIEE Transactions, PAS, June 1956.
2. "Computer Methods in Power Systems Analysis" - Stagg and El Abiad (McGraw Hill).
3. W. F. Tinney, C. E. Hart, "Power Flow Solutions by Newtons Method", IEEE Transactions, PAS, Nov. 1967, p. 1449.

Chapter 4

Synchronous Machines

Contents

List of Figures

Synchronous Machines

4.1 Introduction

The dynamic behavior of machines in Power Systems is of fundamental importance to the overall performance and integrity of power supply. In these notes, we attempt to develop an understanding of the performance of machines with derivations of models and modeling techniques based on the physical laws which describe the pertinent phenomena relating to fluxes, voltages, currents and rotational speeds. Emphasis is on developing an understanding of the dynamic performance characteristics of machines rather than on exploration of machine design methods.

A set of problems and their solutions in a separate volume complement these notes.

Traditionally, machine behavior has been examined under steady-state and under transient conditions. Sometimes the bridge between the two conditions has not been too clear. Various simplifications have been used in the past to approximate the effects under transient conditions. We shall attempt to present the subject as a unified treatment where the steady-state relations fall out naturally from the general solution.

In dealing with a.c. circuit theory we have become used to representing synchronous generators as ideal voltage sources behind some impedance.

This is a useful concept but may serve to unnecessarily restrict one's understanding of synchronous machine behavior. In order to explain machine performance with this simplified model, one needs to adopt some artificial concepts of changing source voltages and changing reactances. (Figure 4.1).

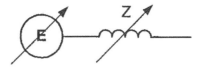

Figure 4.1 – Synchronous Machine as a Variable Voltage
Source behind Variable Impedance

From a conceptual point of view it is better to start from first principles and visualize the generated voltage as the product of flux with rotational speed. The e.m.f. thus obtained is the source voltage which is connected to the a.c. network through the stator leakage reactance and stator resistance.

The behavior of air gap flux as a function of machine loading, excitation etc., is governed by differential equations which define its response to these variables. The model of the generator is therefore described as in Figure 4.2.

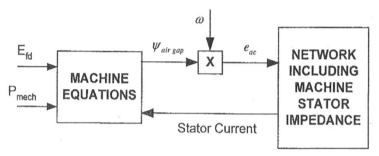

Figure 4.2 – Structure of the Synchronous Machine Model

Although these notes deal primarily with Synchronous Machines, there are analogous methods for induction machines which are also included.

With these introductory comments let us now develop the equations describing machine behavior from fundamental relationships of flux, m.m.f., voltage and current.

4.2 Description of a Synchronous Machine

Figure 4.3 is a schematic representation of a two-pole, synchronous machine. The windings on the stator are 3-phase windings, uniformly distributed with centers 120° apart.

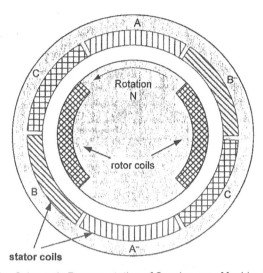

Figure 4.3 – Schematic Representation of Synchronous Machine Windings

The basic relationships are the same for machines with more than two pairs of poles since the armature will likewise be wound with corresponding multiple sets of coils. Hence, if we define relationships in terms of electrical degrees where 180 electrical degrees is the angle between adjacent north and south poles, the number of pairs of poles should make no difference in the way that a machine can be analyzed.

The relationship between mechanical and electrical degrees is:

$$p/2 \text{ (mechanical degrees)} = \text{electrical degrees}$$

where p/2 is the number of pairs of poles.

Examine first the magnetomotive force produced by balanced sinusoidal currents flowing in the stator. The distribution of windings around the stator is usually designed to yield a fairly sinusoidal wave shape, with little harmonic content. For illustration purposes, however, examine the case of Figure 4.4 which develops the winding of a 3-phase alternator with two slots per pole per phase and a 5/6-pitch winding. The slots are labeled by numbers and the letters A, B, C indicate the coil sides for phases a, b and c. Circles around the letters represent trailing coil sides.

The 5/6-pitch winding means that the coil sides marked A which lie in the top of slot 1 and in the bottom of slot 6 are in the same coil. The coil belts for the three phases are displaced by 120° electrical degrees from one another. The belts which contain leading coil sides are enclosed by dotted lines.

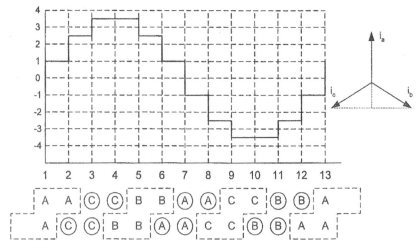

Figure 4.4 – Magnetomotive Force Produced by Balanced Stator Currents

Take conditions at the instant that phase "a" current is at the peak of the sinusoid; i.e., $I_a = I_m$. From the phase relations indicated on Figure 4.4, phase currents I_b and I_c will be $I_b = -I_m/2$ and $I_c = -I_m/2$ The magnetomotive force developed along the periphery of the stator is readily established by superposing the contributions from each coil carrying the appropriate value of current at the instant in question. This is seen to approximate a sinusoid with. Its peak centered about the center of phase "a". With a greater number of slots, the distribution of the windings can be made to yield an almost pure sinusoidal spacial distribution of MMF. This is desirable to minimize losses and telephone interference due to harmonics.

If we now take conditions at a later time, say 90 electrical degrees later, and repeat the procedure with the values of current for this instant; i.e.,

$$I_a = 0, I_b = +\sqrt{3/2}\, I_m, I_c = -\sqrt{3/2}\, I_m,$$

we would note that the MMF wave has now advanced 90° in its spatial distribution.

A graphical study of the MMF wave at successive instants of time gives a visual conception of the motion of rotating magnetic fields. These rotating fields occur only in polyphase machines, both synchronous and induction. The rotational speed of the MMF wave around the stator periphery is proportional to the frequency of the armature currents and, for rated steady-state conditions, is exactly equal to the rotational speed of the MMF wave due to the motion of the rotor field in synchronous machines.

The rotation effect of the MMF wave can be derived mathematically as follows:

Define α as the angle along the periphery of the stator referenced with respect to the center of phase "a". Then, assuming a uniform balanced sinusoidal spatial distribution of the phase coils along the stator slots, the MMF contribution from each phase at a particular time is proportional to:

$$MMF_a \propto i_a \cos \alpha$$

$$MMF_b \propto i_b \cos(\alpha - 2\pi/3) \qquad \text{(IV.1)}$$

$$MMF_c \propto i_c \cos(\alpha + 2\pi/3)$$

where i_a, i_b and i_c are the instantaneous values of the currents in the three phases.

For balanced sinusoidal currents with peak magnitude I_m and frequency ω, we may write

$$i_a \propto I_m \sin(\omega t)$$

$$i_b \propto I_m \sin(\omega t - 2\pi/3) \qquad \text{(IV.2)}$$

$$i_c \propto I_m \sin(\omega t + 2\pi/3)$$

where we have chosen arbitrarily the count of time "t" from the instant when i_a is going through zero and increasing.

From (IV.1) and (IV.2), the total MMF wave is proportional to:

$$MMF = MMF_a + MMF_b + MMF_c$$

$$\propto I_m \left[\sin(\omega t)\cos(\alpha) + \sin\left(\omega t - \frac{2\pi}{3}\right)\cos\left(\alpha - \frac{2\pi}{3}\right) + \sin\left(\omega t + \frac{2\pi}{3}\right)\cos\left(\alpha + \frac{2\pi}{3}\right) \right] \text{(IV.3)}$$

By means of trigonometric identities, (IV.3) is reduced to

$$MMF \propto \frac{3}{2} I_m \sin(\omega t - \alpha) \qquad \text{(IV.4)}$$

Expression (IV.4) shows that the MMF wave travels around the periphery with a velocity ω. Therefore, for conditions of synchronous speed operation and balanced currents in the stator, the MMF wave produced by these currents appears stationary as viewed from the rotor.

Figure 4.5 illustrates this fact by showing the rotor structure relative to the stator MMF.

In Figure 4.5 is also shown the MMF due to excitation in the rotor field. The net MMF which produces flux across the air gap is obtained by superposing these two components. The relative phase of the armature reaction MMF relative to the field excitation MMF is a function of the load, both in magnitude and power factor.

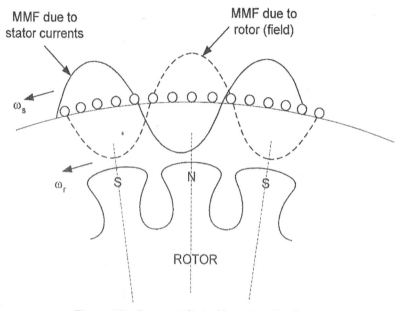

Figure 4.5 – Rotor and Stator Magnetomotive Forces

4.3   Development of Basic Relations

In this section we shall develop from first principles the fundamental equations describing a machine. The development includes the important d-q transformations leading to Park's equations which are universally used to describe machine behavior.

Although the development is quite straightforward, the danger is to get overwhelmed with terminology and symbols. For this reason an introductory description of the development is presented here and shown schematically in the flowchart below. Figure 4.6 presents the synchronous machine windings in terms of the d-q transformation.

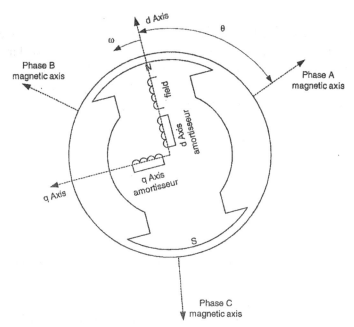

Figure 4.6 – Schematic Representation of Rotor Windings (*d-q* axes)

SYNCHRONOUS MACHINE ANALYSIS

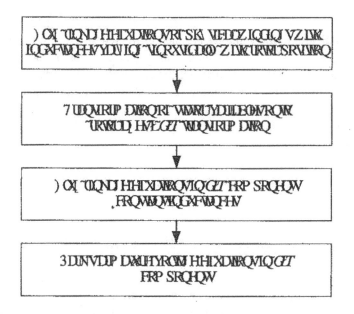

Step 1

The machine is composed of a number of windings in the stator and in the rotor. The electromagnetic characteristics of these windings and associated magnetic structure can be expressed with the help of fundamental circuit theory relating flux linkages to currents through self and mutual winding inductions. The basic winding inductances (self and mutual) are defined by lower case ℓ with appropriate subscripts, e.g.

$$\psi_a = -\ell_{aa}i_a + \ell_{ab}i_b + ...+ \ell_{afd}i_{fd}$$

Step 2

The basic stator physical winding inductances are described as functions of rotor position. They are seen to vary as trigonometric functions of the rotor angle with relation to the stator. The constant coefficients entering these trigonometric expressions for the inductances are labeled with upper case symbols, e.g.

$$\ell_{afd} = \ell_{afd}\cos\theta$$

where L_{afd} is a constant equal to the mutual inductance between field *(fd)* and phase "*a*" winding at the position of maximum coupling between these two windings ($\theta = 0°$).

Step 3

The flux linkages in the windings are then expressed in terms of the windings currents (i_a, i_b, i_c for the phase windings and i_{fd}, i_{kd}, i_{kq}, etc. for the rotor windings) and the inductances (self and mutual) which in turn are expressed as trigonometric functions of rotor angle. From these relationships the combinations of phase currents multiplied by trigonometric functions of rotor angle from the inductance expressions suggest the use of the *d-q* components and the transformation relationships

$$i_d = +\frac{2}{3}[i_a\cos\theta + i_b\cos(\theta - 2\pi/3) + i_c\cos(\theta + 2\pi/3)]$$

$$i_q = -\frac{2}{3}[i_a\sin\theta + i_b\sin(\theta - 2\pi/3) + i_c\sin(\theta + 2\pi/3)]$$

Step 4

The flux linkage equations for the rotor windings are next expressed as functions of rotor winding currents and the *d* & *q* components of armature currents. The equations thus expressed have *d* & *q* currents multiplied by constant inductance terms.

Step 5

The d-q transformations are also applied to armature flux linkages and voltages. Armature winding voltage equations

$$e_a = \frac{d\psi_a}{dt} - ri_a$$

are then expressed in terms of the transformation variables d & q leading to Park's equations

$$e_d = \frac{d\psi_d}{dt} - \omega\psi_q - ri_d$$

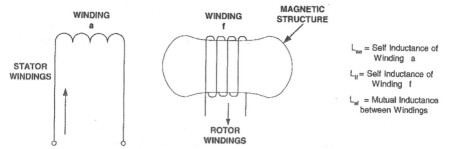

Figure 4.7 – Schematic Representation of Self and Mutual Inductances

4.3.1   Flux and Flux Linkages in Armature

The flux produced by a given MMF is a function of the reluctance of the magnetic circuit over which the MMF acts.

The reluctance of a material is defined as the ratio of the MMF acting on it and the resultant flux

$$R = \frac{F}{\psi} \qquad\qquad (IV.5)$$

where

R	= reluctance
ψ	= flux in webers
F	= magnetomotive force (amp turns)

The reluctance of the closed flux path through stator iron, across the air gap, through the rotor iron and back across the air gap is a composite reluctance made up contributions due to the air gap and iron parts.

$$R = R_a + R_i \qquad \text{(IV.6)}$$

The permeance is the reciprocal of the reluctance. Since the reluctance is inversely proportional to the permeability of the material, a major contribution to this reluctance is due to the air gap.

In viewing the magnetic circuit for MMF's in the stator, it is noted that the permeance of this circuit will change with the position of the rotor due to the variations in the air gap. This is particularly more pronounced in the case of salient pole machines.

In general, the variation will be periodic with a period equal to the space between poles. A good assumption is that this variation is sinusoidal. Hence, the permeance of the magnetic circuit as viewed from a fixed point in the stator could be expressed as a function of the angle between that point and the location of the center of a pole in the rotor; i.e.,

$$P = P_0 + P_2 \cos 2\theta \qquad \text{(IV.7)}$$

where θ is the angular distance between the point on the stator and the center of a pole. Permeance is a property which enters in the determination of inductance of windings. Actually, inductance of a coil is defined as the ratio of flux linkages in the coil to the current in the coil which produces these flux linkages. When permeance is independent of flux, inductance is a constant. From the theory of magnetic coupling of circuits, such as is used in analysis of transformers, for any given instant of time, we may define self and mutual inductances between armature circuits and rotor circuits and write the total flux linkages in the phase "a" armature circuits as

$$\psi_a = -\ell_{aa} i_a + \ell_{ab} i_b + \ell_{ac} i_c + \\ + \ell_{afd} i_{fd} + l_{akd} i_{kd} + l_{akq} i_{kq} \qquad \text{(IV.8)}$$

where

ℓ_{aa}	=	self inductance of stator winding "a"
ℓ_{ab}	=	mutual inductance between stator winding "a" and "b"
ℓ_{ac}	=	mutual inductance between stator winding "a" and "c"
$\ell_{afd}, \ell_{akd}, \ell_{akq}$	=	mutual inductances between stator winding "a" and rotor field winding (fd), d-axis amortisseur winding (kd) and q-axis amortisseur winding (kq), respectively

At this point we should clarify what is meant by the d and q axes, and field and amortisseur circuits.

Looking at the pole faces of the rotor, Figure 4.8 identifies the d and q axes as well as the rotor circuits made up of field circuits, d-axis amortisseur and q-axis amortisseur.

The d-axis is located at the peak of the MMF wave produced by the field while the q-axis is 90 electrical degrees leading. There are numerous closed paths for currents in the rotor. These may be lumped into equivalent circuits as follows:

1) The field circuit which carries the field direct current excitation.

2) An equivalent closed circuit which links the d-axis flux called the d-axis amortisseur winding. In salient pole machines, this is made up of conducting bars deliberately inserted in the pole face. In solid iron, round rotor machines, the conducting paths in the solid iron form an equivalent amortisseur effect.

3) One or more equivalent closed circuits concentric with the q-axis called the q-axis amortisseur.

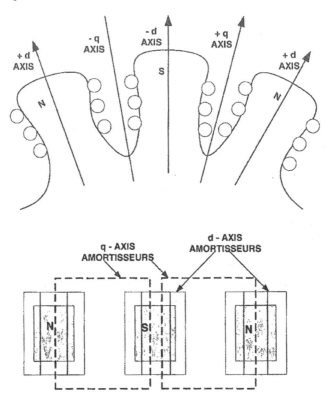

Figure 4.8 – Rotor Amortisseur Windings (d and q axes)

If the machine were a static device, the various inductances in (IV.8) would be constant such as in the case of a transformer, barring saturation effects. In the synchronous machine, however, because of the motion of the rotor, these armature winding inductances are a function of the rotor position. From the previous discussion of the variation of permeance as function of rotor position, as well as from consideration of the variable coupling between rotor circuits and armature circuits as function of rotor position, it follows that the mutual inductances between rotor and stator circuits are:

$$\ell_{afd} = L_{afd} \cos \theta \qquad \text{(IV.9)}$$
$$\ell_{akd} = L_{akd} \cos \theta \qquad \text{(IV.10)}$$
$$\ell_{akq} = -L_{akq} \sin \theta \qquad \text{(IV.11)}$$

where L_{afd}, L_{akd} and L_{akq} are constant, maximum values of these mutual inductances which occur when the corresponding rotor circuits are concentric with the phase "a" stator circuit.

The equations for the mutual inductances of the other phases "b" and "c" are similar to those for phase "a" except that the angle θ is replaced by $(\theta - 2\pi/3)$ and $(\theta + 2\pi/3)$ respectively.

The self inductance of phase "a", ℓ_{aa} has the form of the permeance given in equation (IV.7):

$$\ell_{aa} = L_{aa0} + L_{aa2} \cos 2\theta \qquad \text{(IV.12)}$$

From the geometry of the magnetic path, it is evident that the mutual inductance between stator phases is a minimum whenever the q-axis bisects the angle between the phases; i.e.,

$$\ell_{ab} = L_{ab0} + L_{ab2} \cos(2\theta + \pi/3) \qquad \text{(IV.13)}$$
$$\ell_{ac} = L_{ac0} + L_{ac2} \cos(2\theta - \pi/3) \qquad \text{(IV.14)}$$

Because of symmetry, the coefficients L_{abo}, L_{aco}, L_{bco} are all equal as are also the coefficients L_{ab2}, L_{ac2}, L_{bc2}, L_{aa2}, L_{bb2} and L_{cc2}.[2]

When expressions (IV.12), (IV.13) and (IV.14) as well as similar ones, with appropriate phase displacement, for phases "b" and "c" are substituted in (IV.8) or in analogous expressions for phases "b" and "c", it is noted that the flux linkage expression in terms of instantaneous phase currents turn out to be a function of rotor position.

---

[2] See Class Problem II.

One such expression is included to illustrate the form. Similar expressions with proper changes in subscripts apply to phases "b" and "c".

$$\psi_a = -i_a[L_{aa0} + L_{aa2}\cos2\theta]\, L_{ab0}[i_b + i_c] +$$

$$+ L_{aa2}i_b\cos\left(2\theta + \frac{\pi}{3}\right) + L_{aa2}i_c\cos\left(2\theta - \frac{\pi}{3}\right) \qquad \text{(IV.15)}$$

$$L_{afd}i_{fd}\cos\theta + L_{akd}i_{kd}\cos\theta - L_{akq}i_{kq}\sin\theta$$

4.3.2   Flux Linkages in the Rotor

Flux linkages with the rotor circuits can be written using relations (IV.9), (IV.10) and (IV.11) for the mutual inductances between stator circuits and rotor circuits. The self inductances of the rotor circuits are constants since the permeances of the magnetic circuits in the d and q axes are constants.

The rotor flux linkage equations are written as:

$$\psi_{fd} = L_{ffd}i_{fd} + L_{fkd}i_{kd} - L_{afd}\left[i_a\cos\theta + i_b\cos\left(\theta - \frac{2\pi}{3}\right) + i_c\cos\left(\theta + \frac{2\pi}{3}\right)\right] \qquad \text{(IV.16)}$$

$$\psi_{kd} = L_{fkd}i_{fd} + L_{kkd}i_{kd} - L_{akd}\left[i_a\cos\theta + i_b\cos\left(\theta - \frac{2\pi}{3}\right) + i_c\cos\left(\theta + \frac{2\pi}{3}\right)\right] \qquad \text{(IV.17)}$$

$$\psi_{kq} = L_{kkq}i_{kq} + L_{akq}\left[i_a\sin\theta + i_b\sin\left(\theta - \frac{2\pi}{3}\right) + i_c\sin\left(\theta + \frac{2\pi}{3}\right)\right] \qquad \text{(IV.18)}$$

Here L_{ffd}, L_{kkd}, and L_{kkq} are the self inductances of the field, direct-axis amortisseur and quadrature axis amortisseur circuits respectively. L_{fkd} is the mutual inductance between field and direct axis amortisseur. It should be noted that there is no magnetic coupling between the d and q axes since they are orthogonal; i.e., displaced by 90°.

4.3.3 Voltage Relations

The laws of electromagnetic induction applied to any continuous circuit or coil such as shown on Figure 4.9 can be expressed as:

$$e = \frac{d\psi}{dt} - ri \qquad (IV.19)$$

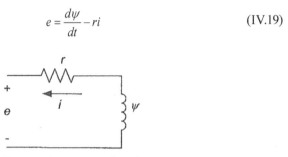

Figure 4.9 – Inductive Circuit

Where e is the voltage appearing across the terminals of the coil, ψ is the flux linkage in the coil, i is the current flowing through the coil and r is the resistance of the coil. Note the directions of voltage and current in Figure 4.9.

Relation (IV.19) applied to the case of a static circuit such as that in a transformer coil or transmission line can be expressed as

$$e = L\frac{di}{dt} - ri \qquad (IV.20)$$

where $L = \frac{\psi}{i}$ is the inductance of the circuit. It should be stressed that equation (IV.20) is a special case of the general equation (IV.19) where the circuit is static and linear. In the general case, the rate of change of flux linkages $\frac{d\psi}{dt}$ can be composed of terms due to changing currents (transformer action) as well as terms due to flux linkages being cut by rotation or motion, or terms due to changes in magnetic properties as occur with saturation of magnetic materials.

Equation (IV.19) applied to the armature circuits becomes:

$$e_a = \frac{d\psi_a}{dt} - ri_a$$

$$e_b = \frac{d\psi_b}{dt} - ri_b \qquad (IV.21)$$

$$e_c = \frac{d\psi_c}{dt} - ri_c$$

Applied to the field circuit, we have

$$e_{fd} = \frac{d\psi_{fd}}{dt} + ri_{fd} \qquad \text{(IV.22)}$$

Note that the choice of signs is due to the definition of the current direction relative to the voltage across the winding. In the case of the field, it is customary to look at the current as flowing into the field as a result of the applied voltage e_{fd}.

Similarly for the direct and quadrature axes amortisseur circuits, we have

$$0 = \frac{d\psi_{kd}}{dt} + ri_{kd} \qquad \text{(IV.23)}$$

$$0 = \frac{d\psi_{kq}}{dt} + ri_{kq} \qquad \text{(IV.24)}$$

The zeros on the left-hand side of (IV.23) and (IV.24) come from the closed nature of the circuits, with zero impressed or applied voltage.

Equations (IV.21) to (IV.24) could be solved in this form with the flux linkage relationships described in terms of actual phase and rotor currents, and inductances which are functions of rotor positions (see relations (IV.15), (IV.16), (IV.17) and (IV.18)).

The equations in terms of these variables are nonlinear and rather unwieldy. It turns out that a much simpler and more elegant mathematical treatment can be obtained by using new transformed variables for circuits, voltages and fluxes.

4.3.4   The dq0 Transformation

Study of expressions (IV.16), (IV.17) and (IV.18) shows that in the equations associated with the rotor flux linkages, the armature currents combine in a clear pattern involving rotor position as follows:

For the d axis

$$i_a \cos\theta + i_b \cos(\theta - 2\pi/3) + i_c \cos(\theta + 2\pi/3)$$

θ is the angle by which the direct axis leads the center of phase "a".

and for the q axis

$$i_a \sin\theta + i_b \sin(\theta - 2\pi/3) + i_c \sin(\theta + 2\pi/3)$$

This leads to the definition of new variables defined as i_d and i_q by:

$$i_d = K[i_a \cos\theta + i_b \cos(\theta - 2\pi/3) + i_c \cos(\theta + 2\pi/3)] \quad\quad \text{(IV.25)}$$
$$i_q = -K[i_a \sin\theta + i_b \sin(\theta - 2\pi/3) + i_c \sin(\theta + 2\pi/3)] \quad\quad \text{(IV.26)}$$

The value of the constant K is chosen so that, for balanced sinusoidal currents i_a, i_b, i_c with peak magnitude I_m

$$i_a = I_m \sin(\omega t)$$
$$i_b = I_m \sin(\omega t - 2\pi/3) \quad\quad\quad\quad \text{(IV.27)}$$
$$i_c + I_m \sin(\omega t + 2\pi/3)$$

the peak magnitudes of i_d and i_q are equal to I_m.

Substituting (IV.27) in (IV.25) and (IV.26)

$$i_d = K I_m \left[\sin(\omega t)\cos\theta + \sin\left(\omega t - \frac{2\pi}{3}\right)\cos\left(\theta - \frac{2\pi}{3}\right) + \sin\left(\omega t + \frac{2\pi}{3}\right)\cos\left(\theta + \frac{2\pi}{3}\right) \right] =$$
$$= K\frac{3}{2}I_m \sin(\omega t - \theta) \quad\quad\quad\quad \text{(IV.28)}$$

$$i_q = -K I_m \left[\sin(\omega t)\sin\theta + \sin\left(\omega t - \frac{2\pi}{3}\right)\sin\left(\theta - \frac{2\pi}{3}\right) + \sin\left(\omega t + \frac{2\pi}{3}\right)\sin\left(\theta + \frac{2\pi}{3}\right) \right] =$$
$$= -K\frac{3}{2}I_m \cos(\omega t - \theta) \quad\quad\quad\quad \text{(IV.29)}$$

By choosing $K = 2/3$, we have

$$i_d = +\frac{2}{3}\left[i_a \cos\theta + i_b \cos\left(\theta - \frac{2\pi}{3}\right) + i_c \cos\left(\theta + \frac{2\pi}{3}\right) \right] \quad\quad \text{(IV.30)}$$

$$i_q = -\frac{2}{3}\left[i_a \sin\theta + i_b \sin\left(\theta - \frac{2\pi}{3}\right) + i_c \sin\left(\theta + \frac{2\pi}{3}\right) \right] \quad\quad \text{(IV.31)}$$

which, for balanced currents as in (IV.27), result in

$$i_d = I_m \sin(\omega t - \theta)$$

$$i_q = -I_m \cos(\omega t - \theta)$$

Relations (IV.30) and (IV.31) are called the d and q transformations of the 3-phase currents. To be completely general; i.e., to give complete degree of freedom to values of the phase currents i_a, i_b and i_c, we need to express these by three new variables of which two have been selected as i_d and i_q. A convenient third variable is the zero-sequence current defined as

$$i_0 = \frac{1}{3}[i_a + i_b + i_c]$$ (IV.32)

Under balanced conditions or any conditions for which $i_a + i_b + i_c = 0 \Rightarrow i_0 = 0$

Relations (IV.30), (IV.31) and (IV.32) can be conveniently expressed in matrix notation as

$$\begin{bmatrix} i_d \\ i_q \\ i_0 \end{bmatrix} = \begin{bmatrix} 2/3\cos\theta & 2/3\cos(\theta - 2\pi/3) & 2/3\cos(\theta + 2\pi/3) \\ -2/3\sin\theta & -2/3\sin(\theta - 2\pi/3) & -2/3\sin(\theta + 2\pi/3) \\ 1/3 & 1/3 & 1/3 \end{bmatrix} \begin{bmatrix} i_a \\ i_b \\ i_c \end{bmatrix}$$ (IV.33)

The inverse transformation of (IV.33) is:

$$\begin{bmatrix} i_a \\ i_b \\ i_c \end{bmatrix} = \begin{bmatrix} \cos\theta & -\sin\theta & 1 \\ \cos(\theta - 2\pi/3) & -\sin(\theta - 2\pi/3) & 1 \\ \cos(\theta + 2\pi/3) & -\sin(\theta + 2\pi/3) & 1 \end{bmatrix} \begin{bmatrix} i_d \\ i_q \\ i_0 \end{bmatrix}$$ (IV.34)

Similar transformations apply to flux linkages and voltages; i.e., phase voltage e_a, e_b, e_c can similarly be transformed into e_d, eq and e_o components and vice versa.

The physical meaning of the components i_d and i_q is that they are proportional to the components of MMF in the direct and quadrature axes respectively produced by the resultant of all three armature currents i_a, i_b and i_c.

For the case of balanced currents of frequency ω and a rotor speed ω' expressions (IV.28) and (IV.29) become

$$i_d = I_m \sin(\omega t - \omega't + \phi)$$ (IV.35)
$$i_q = -I_m \cos(\omega t - \omega't + \phi)$$ (IV.36)

where $\theta = \omega't - \phi$, is the angle between the d-axis and the center of phase "a". If the frequency of the stator currents is synchronous with the rotor frequency, then $\omega = \omega'$ and (IV.35) and (IV.36) become

$$i_d = I_m \sin\phi$$ (IV.37)
$$i_q = -I_m \cos\phi$$ (IV.38)

Expressions (IV.37) and (IV.38) show that the components i_d and i_q are d.c. (constant) quantities for the case of balanced armature currents with frequency synchronous with the rotor speed. This fact ties in nicely with the concept of the rotating MMF wave set up by balanced armature currents described in Section

4.2. This MMF wave travels with the same velocity as the rotor, hence, relative to the rotor the wave appears stationary. The fact that in balanced steady state operation the currents i_d and i_q are d.c. quantities is important to remember, especially since, later on, in the construction of steady state vector diagrams, i_d and i_q are treated as phasors representing the spacial distribution of MMF's. These can be easily confused with phasors representing a.c. quantities.

In (IV.35) and (IV.36) when $\omega \neq \omega'$, i_d and i_q will be sinusoids with slip frequency of $(\omega - \omega')$. This occurs in the case of induction motors for which $\omega > \omega'$ and induction generators for which $\omega < \omega'$.

4.3.5 Rotor Flux Linkages in *dq0* Components

Expressing the rotor flux linkage equations (IV.16), (IV.17) and (IV.18) in terms of i_d and i_q yields:

$$\psi_{fd} = L_{ffd} i_{fd} + L_{fkd} i_{kd} - \frac{3}{2} L_{afd} i_d \tag{IV.39}$$

$$\psi_{kd} = L_{fkd} i_{fd} + L_{kkd} i_{kd} - \frac{3}{2} L_{akd} i_d \tag{IV.40}$$

$$\psi_{kq} = L_{kkq} i_{kq} - \frac{3}{2} L_{akq} i_q \tag{IV.41}$$

The fact that the current component "i_0" does not enter the rotor flux linkage equations is significant. It means that zero sequence components of the armature current produce no net MMF across the air gap. This fact is also evident from the basic expression for MMF due to armature currents as derived by:

$$MMF \propto i_a cos(\alpha) + i_b \cos\left(\alpha - \frac{2\pi}{3}\right) + i_c \cos\left(\alpha + \frac{2\pi}{3}\right) \tag{IV.42}$$

For any zero sequence component i_0, substitution of $i_a = i_b = i_c = i_0$ in (IV.42) shows that the MMF due to these components is zero.

All inductances in (IV.39) to (IV.41), barring saturation effects, are constants.

4.3.6 Armature Flux Linkages in *dq0* Components

Use of the same *d, q, 0* transformations (IV.33) for flux linkages and currents converts the armature phase flux linkage equations (IV.15) into armature *d, q* component flux linkage equations.

That is, the new variables are

$$\psi_d = +\frac{\ddot{u}}{\ddot{u}}\left[\psi_a\cos\theta + \psi_b\cos\left(\theta - \frac{\pi}{}\right) + \psi_c\cos\left(\theta + \frac{\pi}{}\right)\right]$$

$$\psi_q = -\frac{2}{3}\left[\psi_a\sin\theta + \psi_b\sin\left(\theta - \frac{2\pi}{3}\right) + \psi_c\sin\left(\theta + \frac{2\pi}{3}\right)\right] \tag{IV.43}$$

$$\psi_0 = \frac{1}{3}\left[\psi_a + \psi_b + \psi_c\right]$$

and i_d, i_q, i_0, similarly related to phase currents.

This process is an exercise in algebra and trigonometric identities which yield the following armature flux linkage equations:

$$\psi_d = -\left[L_{aa0} + L_{ab0} + \frac{3}{2}L_{aa2}\right]i_d + L_{afd}i_{fd} + L_{akd}i_{kd} \tag{IV.44}$$

$$\psi_q = -\left[L_{aa0} + L_{ab0} - \frac{3}{2}L_{aa2}\right]i_q + L_{akq}i_{kq} \tag{IV.45}$$

$$\psi_0 = -[L_{aa0} - 2L_{ab0}]i_0 \tag{IV.46}$$

Defining a new set of armature inductances as:

$$L_d = L_{aa0} + L_{ab0} + \frac{3}{2}L_{aa2} \tag{IV.47}$$

$$L_q = L_{aa0} + L_{ab0} - \frac{3}{2}L_{aa2} \tag{IV.48}$$

$$L_0 = L_{aa0} - 2L_{ab0} \tag{IV.49}$$

The armature flux linkage equations become:

$$\psi_d = -L_d\,i_d + L_{afd}i_{fd} + L_{akd}i_{kd} \tag{IV.50}$$

$$\psi_q = -L_q\,i_q + L_{akq}i_{kq} \tag{IV.51}$$

$$\psi_0 = -L_0\,i_0 \tag{IV.52}$$

Note that equations (IV.50), (IV.51) and (IV.52) in terms of the transformed variables contain all constant inductance terms. This is the basic reason for the use of d, q, 0 components in dealing with electric machinery problems.

Although the d, q variables have complete physical meaning when applied to conditions on the rotor, their meaning relative to stator quantities is somewhat more abstract, being a mathematical transformation much as is the case with symmetrical components.

4.3.7 Voltage Equations in *dq0* Components – Park's Equations

The basic voltage equations for the armature circuits are:

$$e_a = \frac{d\psi_a}{dt} - ri_a$$

$$e_b = \frac{d\psi_b}{dt} - ri_b \qquad \text{(IV.53)}$$

$$e_c = \frac{d\psi_c}{dt} - ri_c$$

Voltage transformation equations are:

$$e_d = +\frac{2}{3}\left[e_a \cos\theta + e_b \cos\left(\theta - \frac{2\pi}{3}\right) + e_c \cos\left(\theta + \frac{2\pi}{3}\right) \right]$$

$$e_q = -\frac{2}{3}\left[e_a \sin\theta + e_b \sin\left(\theta - \frac{2\pi}{3}\right) + e_c \sin\left(\theta + \frac{2\pi}{3}\right) \right] \qquad \text{(IV.54)}$$

$$e_0 = \frac{1}{3}\left[e_a + e_b + e_c \right]$$

Substitution of (IV.53) in (IV.54) and use the *d-q* transformation relations for currents yields:

$$
\begin{bmatrix} e_d \\ e_q \\ e_0 \end{bmatrix} = -\begin{bmatrix} r & & \\ & r & \\ & & r \end{bmatrix}\begin{bmatrix} i_d \\ i_q \\ i_0 \end{bmatrix} + \frac{2}{3}\begin{bmatrix} \cos\theta & \cos\left(\theta - \frac{2\pi}{3}\right) & \cos\left(\theta + \frac{2\pi}{3}\right) \\ -\sin\theta & -\sin\left(\theta - \frac{2\pi}{3}\right) & -\sin\left(\theta + \frac{2\pi}{3}\right) \\ \frac{1}{2} & \frac{1}{2} & \frac{1}{2} \end{bmatrix}\frac{d}{dt}\begin{bmatrix} \psi_a \\ \psi_b \\ \psi_c \end{bmatrix} \qquad \text{(IV.55)}
$$

Expressing ψ_a, ψ_b and ψ_c in terms of ψ_d, ψ_q and ψ_0 with the use of the inverse transformation (IV.34):

$$
\begin{bmatrix} \psi_a \\ \psi_b \\ \psi_c \end{bmatrix} = \begin{bmatrix} \cos\theta & -\sin\theta & 1 \\ \cos(\theta - 2\pi/3) & -\sin(\theta - 2\pi/3) & 1 \\ \cos(\theta + 2\pi/3) & -\sin(\theta + 2\pi/3) & 1 \end{bmatrix} \begin{bmatrix} \psi_d \\ \psi_q \\ \psi_0 \end{bmatrix}
\qquad \text{(IV.56)}
$$

Differentiating (IV.56) with respect to time

$$
\frac{d}{dt}\begin{bmatrix} \psi_a \\ \psi_b \\ \psi_c \end{bmatrix} = \begin{bmatrix} \cos\theta & -\sin\theta & 1 \\ \cos\left(\theta - \dfrac{2\pi}{3}\right) & -\sin\left(\theta - \dfrac{2\pi}{3}\right) & 1 \\ \cos\left(\theta + \dfrac{2\pi}{3}\right) & -\sin\left(\theta + \dfrac{2\pi}{3}\right) & 1 \end{bmatrix} \frac{d}{dt}\begin{bmatrix} \psi_d \\ \psi_q \\ \psi_0 \end{bmatrix} +
$$

$$
+ \frac{d\theta}{dt}\begin{bmatrix} -\sin\theta & -\cos\theta & 0 \\ -\sin\left(\theta - \dfrac{2\pi}{3}\right) & -\cos\left(\theta - \dfrac{2\pi}{3}\right) & 0 \\ -\sin\left(\theta + \dfrac{2\pi}{3}\right) & -\cos\left(\theta + \dfrac{2\pi}{3}\right) & 0 \end{bmatrix} \begin{bmatrix} \psi_d \\ \psi_q \\ \psi_0 \end{bmatrix}
\qquad \text{(IV.57)}
$$

Substituting equation (IV.57) in equation (IV.55):

$$
\begin{bmatrix} e_d \\ e_q \\ e_0 \end{bmatrix} = - \begin{bmatrix} r & & \\ & r & \\ & & r \end{bmatrix} \begin{bmatrix} i_d \\ i_q \\ i_0 \end{bmatrix} +
$$

$$
+ \frac{2}{3}\begin{bmatrix} \cos\theta & \cos\left(\theta - \dfrac{2\pi}{3}\right) & \cos\left(\theta + \dfrac{2\pi}{3}\right) \\ -\sin\theta & -\sin\left(\theta - \dfrac{2\pi}{3}\right) & -\sin\left(\theta + \dfrac{2\pi}{3}\right) \\ \dfrac{1}{2} & \dfrac{1}{2} & \dfrac{1}{2} \end{bmatrix} \begin{bmatrix} \cos\theta & -\sin\theta & 1 \\ \cos\left(\theta - \dfrac{2\pi}{3}\right) & -\sin\left(\theta - \dfrac{2\pi}{3}\right) & 1 \\ \cos\left(\theta + \dfrac{2\pi}{3}\right) & -\sin\left(\theta + \dfrac{2\pi}{3}\right) & 1 \end{bmatrix} \frac{d}{dt}\begin{bmatrix} \psi_d \\ \psi_q \\ \psi_0 \end{bmatrix} +
$$

$$
\frac{2}{3}\frac{d\theta}{dt}\begin{bmatrix} \cos\theta & \cos\left(\theta - \dfrac{2\pi}{3}\right) & \cos\left(\theta + \dfrac{2\pi}{3}\right) \\ -\sin\theta & -\sin\left(\theta - \dfrac{2\pi}{3}\right) & -\sin\left(\theta + \dfrac{2\pi}{3}\right) \\ \dfrac{1}{2} & \dfrac{1}{2} & \dfrac{1}{2} \end{bmatrix} \begin{bmatrix} -\sin\theta & -\cos\theta & 0 \\ -\sin\left(\theta - \dfrac{2\pi}{3}\right) & -\cos\left(\theta - \dfrac{2\pi}{3}\right) & 0 \\ -\sin\left(\theta + \dfrac{2\pi}{3}\right) & -\cos\left(\theta + \dfrac{2\pi}{3}\right) & 0 \end{bmatrix} \begin{bmatrix} \psi_d \\ \psi_q \\ \psi_0 \end{bmatrix}
\qquad \text{(IV.58)}
$$

It should be noted that the first matrix product results in the identity matrix (the two matrices are the inverse of each other). Therefore, equation (IV.58) can be simplified as:

$$
\begin{bmatrix} e_d \\ e_q \\ e_0 \end{bmatrix} = -\begin{bmatrix} r & & \\ & r & \\ & & r \end{bmatrix}\begin{bmatrix} i_d \\ i_q \\ i_0 \end{bmatrix} + \frac{d}{dt}\begin{bmatrix} \psi_d \\ \psi_q \\ \psi_0 \end{bmatrix} +
$$

$$
+ \frac{2}{3}\frac{d\theta}{dt}\begin{bmatrix} A & B & 0 \\ C & D & 0 \\ 0 & 0 & 0 \end{bmatrix}\begin{bmatrix} \psi_d \\ \psi_q \\ \psi_0 \end{bmatrix}
$$

(IV.59)

where

$$
A = -\sin\theta\cos\theta - \sin\left(\theta - \frac{2\pi}{3}\right)\cos\left(\theta - \frac{2\pi}{3}\right) - \sin\left(\theta + \frac{2\pi}{3}\right)\cos\left(\theta + \frac{2\pi}{3}\right) = 0
$$

$$
B = -\cos^2\theta - \cos^2\left(\theta - \frac{2\pi}{3}\right) - \cos^2\left(\theta + \frac{2\pi}{3}\right) = -\frac{3}{2}
$$

$$
C = +\sin^2\theta + \sin^2\left(\theta - \frac{2\pi}{3}\right) + \sin^2\left(\theta + \frac{2\pi}{3}\right) = +\frac{3}{2}
$$

$$
D = +\sin\theta\cos\theta + \sin\left(\theta - \frac{2\pi}{3}\right)\cos\left(\theta - \frac{2\pi}{3}\right) + \sin\left(\theta + \frac{2\pi}{3}\right)\cos\left(\theta + \frac{2\pi}{3}\right) = 0
$$

Applying these trigonometric simplifications, matrix equation (IV.59) reduces to

$$
e_d = \frac{d\psi_d}{dt} - \psi_q\frac{d\theta}{dt} - ri_d
$$

(IV.60)

$$
e_q = \frac{d\psi_q}{dt} + \psi_d\frac{d\theta}{dt} - ri_q
$$

(IV.61)

$$
e_0 = \frac{d\psi_0}{dt} - ri_0
$$

(IV.62)

Equations (IV.60), (IV.61), and (IV.62) are called Park's equations in honor of Mr. R. H. Park who developed their use.

These equations are in a form very similar to the equations of a static coil except for the rotational e.m.f. terms $-\psi_q\dfrac{d\theta}{dt}$ and $\psi_d\dfrac{d\theta}{dt}$ arising from rotor motion where $\dfrac{d\theta}{dt} = \omega$ = rotor angular speed in electrical radians/second.

These rotational e.m.f. terms are the dominant terms of equations (IV.60) and (IV.61). The terms $\frac{d\psi_d}{dt}$ and $\frac{d\psi_q}{dt}$ are sometimes referred to as the transformer action terms.

Note that under steady state conditions with balanced sinusoidal currents in the armature phases, the fluxes ψ_d and ψ_q like the voltages e_d, e_q and currents i_d, i_q are d.c. quantities (i.e. the terms $\frac{d\psi_d}{dt}$ and $\frac{d\psi_q}{dt}$ are zero). There are many conditions where these terms can be dropped from the equations without causing errors of any significance. In other situations such as we shall encounter in the determination of transient short circuit torques and d.c. offsets in short circuit currents, these terms play an important role and cannot be neglected.

In many texts dealing with synchronous machines the symbol for d/dt is labeled by the operator "p". In this form Park's equations are:

$$e_d = p\psi_d - \psi_q p\theta - r i_d \tag{IV.63}$$
$$e_q = p\psi_q + \psi_d p\theta - r i_q \tag{IV.64}$$
$$e_o = p\psi_o - r i_o \tag{IV.65}$$

4.3.8   Torque and Power

The instantaneous power measured at the machine terminals is given by:

$$P = e_a i_a + e_b i_b + e_c i_c$$

In terms of $d, q, 0$ components the expression for power is

$$P = \frac{3}{2}\left[e_d i_d + e_q i_q + e_0 i_0 \right] \tag{IV.66}$$

and under normal balanced operation with e_o and $i_o = 0$

$$-\left[e_d i_d \quad e_q i_q \right] \tag{IV.67}$$

If there were no losses in the machine or changes in magnetic stored energy, the torque would be equal to P/ω' where ω' is the rotor speed.

A more thorough analysis of the expression for power can be obtained by substituting (IV.60), (IV.61), and (IV.62) in (IV.66) giving:

$$P = \frac{3}{2}\left[\left(\frac{d\psi_d}{dt} - \psi_q \frac{d\theta}{dt} - r i_d \right) i_d + \left(\frac{d\psi_q}{dt} + \psi_d \frac{d\theta}{dt} - r i_q \right) i_q + \left(\frac{d\psi_0}{dt} - r i_0 \right) i_0 \right] \tag{IV.68}$$

The terms of (IV.68) can be rearranged as:

$$P = \frac{3}{2}\left(i_d \frac{d\psi_d}{dt} + i_q \frac{d\psi_q}{dt} + i_0 \frac{d\psi_0}{dt} \right) +$$
$$+ \frac{3}{2}\left(i_q \psi_d - i_d \psi_q \right) \frac{d\theta}{dt} -$$
$$- \frac{3}{2}\left(ri_d^2 + ri_q^2 + ri_0^2 \right)$$
(IV.69)

This equation can be interpreted as:

Power Output = (rate of decrease of armature magnetic energy)
+ (power transferred across air gap) – (armature resistance loss)

The air gap torque can be obtained from the second term of (IV.69) by dividing

the air gap power by the rotor speed $\dfrac{d\theta}{dt}$.

$$T = \frac{3}{2}\left(i_q \psi_d - i_d \psi_q \right)$$
(IV.70)

Equation (IV.70) could also have been derived from the basic consideration of forces acting on conductors as being the product of currents times the flux.

4.3.9   Summary of Basic Relations

Recapping briefly the development of these basic relations:

1) Flux linkages were derived for each physical winding in stator and rotor using actual phase currents and rotor currents, and actual self inductances of the windings and mutual inductances between windings, e.g.

$$\psi_a = -\ell_{aa} i_a + \ell_{ab} i_b + \ell_{ac} i_c + \ell_{afd} i_{fd} + \ell_{akd} i_{kd} + \ell_{akq} i_{kq}$$
(IV.8)

2) The values of inductances were established as function of the geometry of the magnetic circuit and rotor position. e.g.

$$\ell_{aa} = L_{aao} + L_{aa2} \cos 2\theta$$
(IV.12)

$$\ell_{afd} = L_{afd} \cos \theta$$
(IV.9)

$$\ell_{ab} = L_{abo} + L_{ab2} \cos (2\theta + \pi/3)$$
(IV.13)

3) Expressions for flux linkages in both stator and rotor circuits in terms of the fundamental winding inductances and basic currents were seen

to involve non-linear inductance terms varying sinusoidally with rotor position.

4) Basic voltage expressions of the form

$$e = \frac{d\psi}{dt} - ri \qquad \text{(IV.19)}$$

can be written for every circuit. However, using the flux linkage equations expressed in terms of phase currents and inductances, the resultant voltage equations are non-linear and unwieldy.

5) The d, q, 0 transformation was introduced by recognition of a logical grouping of currents multiplied by appropriate trigonometric functions of rotor angle relative to the center of phase "a". With these transformations of variables the form of the equations turns into a set of linear algebraic equations for flux linkages and linear differential equations for voltages. The d, q, 0 transformation for any variable y such as current, voltage or flux linkage is:

$$\begin{bmatrix} y_d \\ y_q \\ y_0 \end{bmatrix} = \begin{bmatrix} 2/3\cos\theta & 2/3\cos(\theta-2\pi/3) & 2/3\cos(\theta+2\pi/3) \\ -2/3\sin\theta & -2/3\sin(\theta-2\pi/3) & -2/3\sin(\theta+2\pi/3) \\ 1/3 & 1/3 & 1/3 \end{bmatrix} \begin{bmatrix} y_a \\ y_b \\ y_c \end{bmatrix}$$

and the inverse transformation is:

$$\begin{bmatrix} y_a \\ y_b \\ y_c \end{bmatrix} = \begin{bmatrix} \cos\theta & -\sin\theta & 1 \\ \cos(\theta-2\pi/3) & -\sin(\theta-2\pi/3) & 1 \\ \cos(\theta+2\pi/3) & -\sin(\theta+2\pi/3) & 1 \end{bmatrix} \begin{bmatrix} y_d \\ y_q \\ y_0 \end{bmatrix}$$

where the variable y would be ψ, e, or i.

6) In terms of the transformed variables, i_d, i_q and i_0, the rotor flux linkage equations become linear equations with constant inductance terms, e.g.,

$$\psi_{fd} = -L_{ffd}i_{fd} + L_{fkd}i_{kd} - 3/2\,L_{afd}i_d \qquad \text{(IV.39)}$$

$$\psi_{kd} = -L_{fkd}i_{fd} + L_{kkd}i_{kd} - 3/2\,L_{akd}i_d \qquad \text{(IV.40)}$$

$$\psi_{kq} = -L_{kkd}i_{kq} - 3/2\,L_{akq}i_q \qquad \text{(IV.41)}$$

7) Similarly, expressed in terms of the $d, q, 0$ variables, the armature flux linkage terms become linear equations with constant inductance terms as follows:

$$\psi_d = -L_d i_d + L_{afd} i_{fd} + L_{akd} i_{kd} \tag{IV.50}$$

$$\psi_q = -L_q iq + L_{akq} i_{kq} + L_{akq} i_{kq} \tag{IV.51}$$

$$\psi_0 = -L_0 i_0 \tag{IV.52}$$

8) The basic voltage equations when expressed in terms of $d, q, 0$ components develop into the well-known Park's equations relating voltages to fluxes, rates of change of fluxes, rotational speeds and currents; e.g.,

$$e_d = \frac{d\psi_d}{dt} - \psi_q \frac{d\theta}{dt} - r i_d \tag{IV.60}$$

$$e_q = \frac{d\psi_q}{dt} + \psi_d \frac{d\theta}{dt} - r i_q \tag{IV.61}$$

$$e_0 = \frac{d\psi_0}{dt} - r i_0 \tag{IV.62}$$

9) Voltage equations for the rotor coils are:

$$e_{fd} = \frac{d\psi_{fd}}{dt} + r_{fd} i_{fd} \tag{IV.22}$$

$$0 = \frac{d\psi_{kd}}{dt} + r_{kd} i_{kd} \tag{IV.23}$$

$$0 = \frac{d\psi_{kd}}{dt} + r_{kq} i_{kq} \tag{IV.24}$$

4.4   Per Unit Systems

The fundamental purpose of the per unit system developed for synchronous machines is to allow the form of the equations describing the machine to be expressed in terms of an electrical equivalent circuit.

The behavior of machine variables is thereby better visualized by the physical insight that is lent by the equivalent circuit and the familiar laws that govern circuit behavior.

The steps in the following development are:

1) Express machine equations (in d & q components) in per unit by dividing variables by appropriate base quantities.

2) The choice of rotor and stator kVA bases is guided by the convenience of having reciprocal mutuals between rotor and stator in the flux linkage equations.

3) The choice of rotor winding current bases is guided by the desire to have the same per unit mutual inductance between armature and rotor circuits much as is done by choice of appropriate current bases in transformers yielding equivalent circuits without need for ideal transformers between circuits.

4.4.1   General Relations

In the foregoing, the units for the various variables were:

I	=	Amperes (A)
ψ	=	Weber-turns (Wb-turn)
MMF	=	Amperes-turns (A-turn)
E	=	Volts (V)
R	=	Ohms (Ω)
L	=	Henries (H)
θ	=	radians (rd)
t	=	second (s)

There are many advantages to expressing equations in normalized or dimensionless form. This calls for a discussion of the per unit system undertaken in this Section.

Since, with the per unit system, equation terms become dimensionless through division of the variables and parameters by their "base" values, it is easy to lose track of dimensions which must necessarily remain implied. For instance, when base frequency is taken as rated frequency, per unit inductance becomes the same as per unit reactance. In some texts, reactance symbols (X) are used where truly these should be inductance symbols (L).

In all previous basic equations, currents and voltages have been expressed as instantaneous values. In the case of stator sinusoidal quantities, these have been expressed in terms of the peak values of the sine wave. It should be remembered that in the choice of base quantities, once voltage, current and frequency bases are picked, the bases for the remaining variables or circuit parameters such as flux linkages, resistance, inductance, etc., are automatically set by fundamental relations such as:

$$\psi_{base} = \frac{e_{base}}{\omega_{base}} \ [Wb] \quad R_{base} = \frac{e_{base}}{i_{base}} \ [\Omega] \quad L_{base} = \frac{\psi_{base}}{i_{base}} = \frac{e_{base}}{\omega_{base} i_{base}} \ [H]$$

One other point to remember is that in deriving per unit quantities, the variables should be divided by their appropriate bases. For instance, if the value of voltage is a peak value, in order to express it in per unit, it should be divided by the "peak voltage base."

4.4.2 Stator Base Values Definition

$e_{s_{base}}$ = peak value of rated line-to-neutral voltage (V)

$i_{s_{base}}$ = peak value of rated line current (A)

ω_{base} = synchronous (electrical) speed = $2\pi f_0$ (377 rd/s for 60 Hz machines)

$$Z_{s_{base}} = \frac{e_{s_{base}}}{i_{s_{base}}} \ [\Omega] \tag{IV.71}$$

$$L_{s_{base}} = \frac{Z_{s_{base}}}{\omega_{base}} \ [H] \tag{IV.72}$$

$$\psi_{s_{base}} = L_{s_{base}} i_{s_{base}} = \frac{e_{s_{base}}}{\omega_{base}} \ [Wb.turn] \tag{IV.73}$$

In defining a power or volt-ampere base, following the practices in transformer and three-phase power system circuit analysis, the 3-phase volt-amp base is defined as:

$$3\phi \ VA_{base} = 3E_{s_{base}} \times I_{s_{base}} \tag{IV.74}$$

Where $E_{s_{base}}$ is the line to neutral rms voltage

$$E_{s_{base}} = \frac{e_{s_{base}}}{\sqrt{2}} \ [V] \tag{IV.75}$$

and $I_{s_{base}}$ is the rms line current base

$$I_{s_{base}} = \frac{i_{s_{base}}}{\sqrt{2}}[A] \qquad \text{(IV.76)}$$

Hence,

$$3\phi\ VA_{base} = \frac{3}{2}e_{s_{base}} \times i_{s_{base}} \qquad \text{(IV.77)}$$

and

$$1\ \text{phase}\ VA_{base} = 1/2\left(e_{s\ base}\right)\left(i_{s\ base}\right) \qquad \text{(IV.78)}$$

Using the above definitions, let us convert the basic Park's Equations (IV.60) and (IV.61) into per unit form. In the following, quantities will be understood to be in per unit if labeled by a bar. Take Equation (IV.60):

$$e_d = \frac{d\psi_d}{dt} - \psi_q\frac{d\theta}{dt} - ri_d \qquad \text{(IV.60)}$$

$$\psi_{kq1} = L_{kkq1}i_{kq1} + L_{kq12}i_{kq2} + ... - \frac{3}{2}L_{akq1}i_q \qquad \text{(IV.41)}$$

$$\psi_{kq2} = L_{kq12}i_{kq1} + L_{kkq2}i_{kq2} + ... - \frac{3}{2}L_{akq2}i_q$$

where L_{ffd}, L_{kkd_1}, L_{kkd_2} ... are the self inductances of the direct axis field, amortisseur circuit 1 and amortisseur circuit 2 respectively, and terms like $L_{kd_{12}}$ denote the mutual inductance between amortisseur circuits 1 and 2.

4.4.4   Choice of Rotor kVA Base

In the following we shall limit illustration of the methods to developing the per unit form of equations (IV.39) and (IV.40). By analogy all necessary relations for the remaining equations will turn out to be obvious.

Dividing terms of (IV.39) and (IV.40) by the appropriate base quantities,

$$\frac{\psi_{fd}}{\psi_{fd_{base}}} = \frac{L_{ffd}}{L_{fd_{base}}} \frac{i_{fd}}{i_{fd_{base}}} + \frac{L_{fkd1}}{L_{fd_{base}}} \frac{i_{kd1}}{i_{kd1_{base}}} \frac{i_{kd1_{base}}}{i_{fd_{base}}} +$$

$$+ \frac{L_{fkd2}}{L_{fd_{base}}} \frac{i_{kd2}}{i_{kd2_{base}}} \frac{i_{kd2_{base}}}{i_{fd_{base}}} + \cdots - \frac{3}{2} \frac{L_{afd}}{L_{fd_{base}}} \frac{i_d}{i_{s_{base}}} \frac{i_{s_{base}}}{i_{fd_{base}}}$$

(IV.94)

where $\psi_{fd_{base}} = L_{fd_{base}} i_{fd_{base}}$ and

$$\frac{\psi_{kd1}}{\psi_{kd1_{base}}} = \frac{L_{fkd1}}{L_{kd1_{base}}} \frac{i_{fd}}{i_{fd_{base}}} \frac{i_{fd_{base}}}{i_{kd1_{base}}} + \frac{L_{kkd1}}{L_{kd1_{base}}} \frac{i_{kd1}}{i_{kd1_{base}}} +$$

$$+ \frac{L_{kd12}}{L_{kd1_{base}}} \frac{i_{kd2}}{i_{kd2_{base}}} \frac{i_{kd2_{base}}}{i_{kd1_{base}}} + \cdots - \frac{3}{2} \frac{L_{akd1}}{L_{kd1_{base}}} \frac{i_d}{i_{s_{base}}} \frac{i_{s_{base}}}{i_{kd1_{base}}}$$

(IV.95)

where $\psi_{kd1_{base}} = L_{kd_{base}} i_{kd1_{base}}$

From the terms in (IV.94) by defining per unit inductances as follows:

$$\overline{L}_{fda} = \frac{L_{afd}}{\dfrac{2}{3} L_{fd_{base}} \dfrac{i_{fd_{base}}}{i_{s_{base}}}}$$

(IV.96)

$$\overline{L}_{fkd1} = \frac{L_{fkd1}}{L_{fd_{base}} \dfrac{i_{fd_{base}}}{i_{kd1_{base}}}}$$

(IV.97)

$$\overline{L}_{fkd2} = \frac{L_{fkd2}}{L_{fd_{base}} \dfrac{i_{fd_{base}}}{i_{kd2_{base}}}}$$

(IV.98)

$$\overline{L}_{ffd} = \frac{L_{ffd}}{L_{fd_{base}}}$$

(IV.99)

Equation (IV.94) can now be written in per unit form as:

$$\overline{\psi}_{fd} = \overline{L}_{ffd}\overline{i}_{fd} + \overline{L}_{fkd1}\overline{i}_{kd1} + \overline{L}_{fkd2}\overline{i}_{kd2} + \ldots - \overline{L}_{fda}\overline{i}_d \qquad \text{(IV.100)}$$

Similarly (IV.95) can be written in per unit form as:

$$\overline{\psi}_{kd1} = \overline{L}_{kd1f}\overline{i}_{fd} + \overline{L}_{kkd1}\overline{i}_{kd1} + \overline{L}_{kd12}\overline{i}_{kd2} + \ldots - \overline{L}_{kd1a}\overline{i}_d \qquad \text{(IV.101)}$$

where

$$\overline{L}_{kd1a} = \frac{L_{akd1}}{\dfrac{2}{3}L_{kd1_{base}}\dfrac{i_{kd1_{base}}}{i_{s_{base}}}} \qquad \text{(IV.102)}$$

$$\overline{L}_{kd1f} = \frac{L_{fkd1}}{L_{kd1_{base}}\dfrac{i_{kd1_{base}}}{i_{fd_{base}}}} \qquad \text{(IV.103)}$$

$$\overline{L}_{kkd1} = \frac{L_{kkd1}}{L_{kkd1_{base}}} \qquad \text{(IV.104)}$$

$$\overline{L}_{kd12} = \frac{L_{kd12}}{L_{kd1_{base}}\dfrac{i_{kd1_{base}}}{i_{kd2_{base}}}} \qquad \text{(IV.105)}$$

Examine first the mutual terms in (IV.100) and (IV.101) $\overline{L}_{fkd_1}$ and $\overline{L}_{kd_{1}f}$. For these to be reciprocal we must equate expressions (IV.97) and (IV.103) from which is derived

$$L_{fd_{base}}\frac{i_{fd_{base}}}{i_{kd1_{base}}} = L_{kd1_{base}}\frac{i_{kd1_{base}}}{i_{fd_{base}}}$$

or

$$L_{fd_{base}}\left(i_{fd_{base}}\right)^2 = L_{kd1_{base}}\left(i_{kd1_{base}}\right)^2 \qquad \text{(IV.106)}$$

Expression (IV.106) merely confirms that in order to have reciprocal mutual per unit inductances between any two static circuits, the base volt-amps in both circuits must be the same. This is derived from (IV.106) by multiplying both sides by ω_{base} and using the identity

Note that we have not yet tied down the relationships between $i_{fd_{base}}$, $i_{kd1_{base}}$ and $i_{kd2_{base}}$ in (IV.85). Defining

$$\bar{L}_{afd} = \frac{L_{afd}}{L_{s_{base}} \dfrac{i_{s_{base}}}{i_{fd_{base}}}} \tag{IV.86}$$

$$\bar{L}_{akd1} = \frac{L_{akd1}}{L_{s_{base}} \dfrac{i_{s_{base}}}{i_{kd1_{base}}}} \tag{IV.87}$$

$$\bar{L}_{akd2} = \frac{L_{akd2}}{L_{s_{base}} \dfrac{i_{s_{base}}}{i_{kd2_{base}}}} \tag{IV.88}$$

we may rewrite (IV.85) as:

$$\bar{\psi}_d = -\bar{L}_d \bar{i}_d + \bar{L}_{afd} \bar{i}_{fd} + \bar{L}_{akd1} \bar{i}_{kd1} + \bar{L}_{akd2} \bar{i}_{kd2} + \dots \tag{IV.89}$$

By analogous developments we may perunitise (IV.51) and (IV.52) into the form shown in (IV.90) and (IV.91):

$$\bar{\psi}_q = -\bar{L}_q \bar{i}_q + \bar{L}_{akq1} \bar{i}_{kq1} + \bar{L}_{akq2} \bar{i}_{kq2} + \dots \tag{IV.90}$$

$$\bar{\psi}_0 = -\bar{L}_0 \bar{i}_0 \tag{IV.91}$$

where

$$\bar{L}_{akq1} = \frac{L_{akq1}}{L_{s_{base}} \dfrac{i_{s_{base}}}{i_{kq1_{base}}}} \tag{IV.92}$$

and

$$\overline{L}_{akq2} = \frac{L_{akq2}}{L_{s_{base}} \dfrac{i_{s_{base}}}{i_{kq2_{base}}}} \tag{IV.93}$$

Now take the rotor flux linkage equations (IV.39), (IV.40) and (IV.41) again generalized to include the possibility of more than one amortisseur circuit,

$$y_{fd} = L_{ffd}i_{fd} + L_{fkd1}i_{kd1} + L_{fkd2}i_{kd2} + \ldots - \frac{3}{2}L_{afd}i_d \tag{IV.39}$$

$$y_{kd1} = L_{fkd1}i_{fd} + L_{kkd1}i_{kd1} + L_{kd12}i_{kd2} + \ldots - \frac{3}{2}L_{akd1}i_d \tag{IV.40}$$

$$y_{kd2} = L_{fkd2}i_{fd} + L_{kd12}i_{kd1} + L_{kkd2}i_{kd2} + \ldots - \frac{3}{2}L_{akd2}i_d$$

$$y_{kq1} = L_{kkq1}i_{kq1} + L_{kq12}i_{kq2} + \ldots - \frac{3}{2}L_{akq1}i_q \tag{IV.41}$$

$$y_{kq2} = L_{kq12}i_{kq1} + L_{kkq2}i_{kq2} + \ldots - \frac{3}{2}L_{akq2}i_q$$

where L_{ffd}, L_{kkd_1}, L_{kkd_2} ... are the self inductances of the direct axis field,

amortisseur circuit 1 and amortisseur circuit 2 respectively, and terms like $L_{kd_{12}}$ denote the mutual inductance between amortisseur circuits 1 and 2.

4.4.4 Choice of Rotor kVA Base

In the following we shall limit illustration of the methods to developing the per unit form of equations (IV.39) and (IV.40). By analogy all necessary relations for the remaining equations will turn out to be obvious.

Dividing terms of (IV.39) and (IV.40) by the appropriate base quantities,

$$\frac{\psi_{fd}}{\psi_{fd_{base}}} = \frac{L_{ffd}}{L_{fd_{base}}}\frac{i_{fd}}{i_{fd_{base}}} + \frac{L_{fkd1}}{L_{fd_{base}}}\frac{i_{kd1}}{i_{kd1_{base}}}\frac{i_{kd1_{base}}}{i_{fd_{base}}} +$$

$$+ \frac{L_{fkd2}}{L_{fd_{base}}}\frac{i_{kd2}}{i_{kd2_{base}}}\frac{i_{kd2_{base}}}{i_{fd_{base}}} + \ldots - \frac{3}{2}\frac{L_{afd}}{L_{fd_{base}}}\frac{i_d}{i_{s_{base}}}\frac{i_{s_{base}}}{i_{fd_{base}}} \tag{IV.94}$$

where $\psi_{fd_{base}} = L_{fd_{base}}i_{fd_{base}}$ and

$$\frac{\psi_{kd1}}{\psi_{kd1_{base}}} = \frac{L_{fkd1}}{L_{kd1_{base}}} \frac{i_{fd}}{i_{fd_{base}}} \frac{i_{fd_{base}}}{i_{kd1_{base}}} + \frac{L_{kkd1}}{L_{kd1_{base}}} \frac{i_{kd1}}{i_{kd1_{base}}} +$$

$$+ \frac{L_{kd12}}{L_{kd1_{base}}} \frac{i_{kd2}}{i_{kd2_{base}}} \frac{i_{kd2_{base}}}{i_{kd1_{base}}} + \ldots - \frac{3}{2} \frac{L_{akd1}}{L_{kd1_{base}}} \frac{i_d}{i_{s_{base}}} \frac{i_{s_{base}}}{i_{kd1_{base}}} \qquad \text{(IV.95)}$$

where $\psi_{kd1_{base}} = L_{kd_{base}} i_{kd1_{base}}$

From the terms in (IV.94) by defining per unit inductances as follows:

$$\overline{L}_{fda} = \frac{L_{afd}}{\dfrac{2}{3} L_{fd_{base}} \dfrac{i_{fd_{base}}}{i_{s_{base}}}} \qquad \text{(IV.96)}$$

$$\overline{L}_{fkd1} = \frac{L_{fkd1}}{L_{fd_{base}} \dfrac{i_{fd_{base}}}{i_{kd1_{base}}}} \qquad \text{(IV.97)}$$

$$\overline{L}_{fkd2} = \frac{L_{fkd2}}{L_{fd_{base}} \dfrac{i_{fd_{base}}}{i_{kd2_{base}}}} \qquad \text{(IV.98)}$$

$$\overline{L}_{\ddot{u}} = \frac{L_{\ddot{u}}}{L_{fd_{base}}} \qquad \text{(IV.99)}$$

Equation (IV.94) can now be written in per unit form as:

$$\overline{\psi}_{fd} = \overline{L}_{ffd} \overline{i}_{fd} + \overline{L}_{fkd1} \overline{i}_{kd1} + \overline{L}_{fkd2} \overline{i}_{kd2} + \ldots - \overline{L}_{fda} \overline{i}_d \qquad \text{(IV.100)}$$

Similarly (IV.95) can be written in per unit form as:

$$\overline{\psi}_{kd1} = \overline{L}_{kd1f} \overline{i}_{fd} + \overline{L}_{kkd1} \overline{i}_{kd1} + \overline{L}_{kd12} \overline{i}_{kd2} + \ldots - \overline{L}_{kd1a} \overline{i}_d \qquad \text{(IV.101)}$$

where

$$\overline{L}_{kd1a} = \frac{L_{akd1}}{\dfrac{2}{3} L_{kd1_{base}} \dfrac{i_{kd1_{base}}}{i_{s_{base}}}} \quad\quad (IV.102)$$

$$\overline{L}_{kd1f} = \frac{L_{fkd1}}{L_{kd1_{base}} \dfrac{i_{kd1_{base}}}{i_{fd_{base}}}} \quad\quad (IV.103)$$

$$\overline{L}_{kkd1} = \frac{L_{kkd1}}{L_{kkd1_{base}}} \quad\quad (IV.104)$$

$$\overline{L}_{kd12} = \frac{L_{kd12}}{L_{kd1_{base}} \dfrac{i_{kd1_{base}}}{i'_{kd2_{base}}}} \quad\quad (IV.105)$$

Examine first the mutual terms in (IV.100) and (IV.101) $\overline{L}_{fkd_1}$ and $\overline{L}_{kd_1 f}$. For these to be reciprocal we must equate expressions (IV.97) and (IV.103) from which is derived

$$L_{fd_{base}} \frac{i_{fd_{base}}}{i_{kd1_{base}}} = L_{kd1_{base}} \frac{i_{kd1_{base}}}{i_{fd_{base}}}$$

or

$$L_{fd_{base}} \left(i_{fd_{base}} \right)^2 = L_{kd1_{base}} \left(i_{kd1_{base}} \right)^2 \quad\quad (IV.106)$$

Expression (IV.106) merely confirms that in order to have reciprocal mutual per unit inductances between any two static circuits, the base volt-amps in both circuits must be the same. This is derived from (IV.106) by multiplying both sides by ω_{base} and using the identity

$$\omega_{base} L_{base} i_{base} = e_{base}.$$

Next examine the mutual terms between rotor circuit and armature and vice-versa in expressions (IV.100) and (IV.89). For the mutual terms between armature and rotor circuits to be reciprocal

$$\overline{L}_{afd} = \overline{L}_{fda}$$

or from the definitions of $\overline{L}_{afd}$ and $\overline{L}_{fda}$ in (IV.86) and (IV.96)

$$\frac{L_{afd}}{L_{s_{base}} \dfrac{i_{s_{base}}}{i_{fd_{base}}}} = \frac{L_{afd}}{\dfrac{2}{3} L_{fd_{base}} \dfrac{i_{fd_{base}}}{i_{s_{base}}}}$$

i.e.

$$L_{s_{base}} \left(i_{s_{base}} \right)^2 = \frac{2}{3} L_{fd_{base}} \left(i_{fd_{base}} \right)^2 \qquad \text{(IV.107)}$$

By multiplying both sides of (IV.107) by ω_{base} and using the identity $\omega_{base} L_{base} i_{base} = e_{s_{base}}$ we have

$$\frac{3}{2} e_{s_{base}} i_{s_{base}} = e_{fd_{base}} i_{fd_{base}} \qquad \text{(IV.108)}$$

From (IV.77) we note that (IV.108) is equivalent to stating that to obtain reciprocal per unit mutual inductances between rotor circuits and armature, the base volt-amp base in the rotor circuits must be equal to the 3ϕ-volt amp RMS base chosen for the stator.

A similar derivation using expressions associated with q-axis circuits will yield the same conclusion in connection with the requirement for reciprocal per unit mutuals between any other rotor circuit and armature.

4.4.5 Choice of Rotor Current Bases

Having concluded that all rotor circuits should have their base volt-amp equal to the 3ϕ-volt amp base chosen for the stator, the next decision concerns the choice of a current or voltage base for the rotor circuits.

In this choice we are guided by the desire to develop an equivalent circuit as simple as possible much like is done in the case of transformers where, by choice of appropriate voltage bases for the windings, equivalent circuits can be derived without need for interposing ideal transformers.

Referring to (IV.50) and (IV.51) the self inductance of the armature d and q axis windings L_d and L_q can be broken into a leakage component corresponding to the leakage flux linkages which do not link the rotor and a component corresponding to the flux linkages which link the rotor:

$$L_d = L_{\ell d} + L_{ad} \tag{IV.109}$$

$$L_q = L_{\ell q} + L_{aq} \tag{IV.110}$$

It should be noted that L_{ad} is not a mutual inductance between the d-winding and the field but rather the portion of the d-winding self-inductance whose flux linkages are coupled to the rotor. The leakage inductances in the d and q axes are generally assumed equal and labeled L_ℓ. This approximation is generally justified especially in the case of round rotor machines.

In a way similar to development of equivalent circuits in transformers, the avoidance of interposing ideal transformers between windings in the equivalent circuit can be achieved by picking the bases such that all per unit mutual reactances between windings are equal.

Referring to (IV.89) and (IV.90) we will impose the requirement that

$$\overline{L}_{ad} = \overline{L}_{afd} = \overline{L}_{akd1} = \overline{L}_{akd2} \tag{IV.111}$$

and

$$\overline{L}_{aq} = \overline{L}_{akq1} = \overline{L}_{akq2} \tag{IV.112}$$

From (IV.111) and using the definitions given in (IV.86), (IV.87) and (IV.88)

$$\overline{L}_{ad} = \frac{L_{ad}}{L_{s_{base}}} = \overline{L}_{afd} = \frac{L_{afd}}{L_{s_{base}} \dfrac{i_{s_{base}}}{i_{fd_{base}}}}$$

$$= \overline{L}_{akd1} = \frac{L_{akd1}}{L_{s_{base}} \dfrac{i_{s_{base}}}{i_{kd1_{base}}}} \tag{IV.113}$$

$$= \overline{L}_{akd2} = \frac{L_{akd2}}{L_{s_{base}} \dfrac{i_{s_{base}}}{i_{kd2_{base}}}}$$

From equation (IV.113) we derive the relationship between current bases for the various circuits in the d-axis:

$$i_{fd_{base}} = \frac{L_{ad}}{L_{afd}} i_{s_{base}}$$

$$i_{kd2_{base}} = \frac{L_{ad}}{L_{akd}} i_{s_{base}} = \frac{L_{afd}}{L_{akd1}} i_{fd_{base}} \tag{IV.114}$$

$$i_{kd2_{base}} = \frac{L_{ad}}{L_{akd2}} i_{s_{base}} = \frac{L_{afd}}{L_{akd2}} i_{fd_{base}} = \frac{L_{akd1}}{L_{akd2}} i_{kd1_{base}}$$

Similarly for the q-axis

$$i_{kq1_{base}} = \frac{L_{aq}}{L_{akq1}} i_{s_{base}}$$

$$i_{kq2_{base}} = \frac{L_{aq}}{L_{akq2}} i_{s_{base}} = \frac{L_{akq1}}{L_{akq2}} i_{kq1_{base}} \tag{IV.115}$$

We have now completed the derivation of per unit constants for a synchronous machine representation system known as the reciprocal per unit L_{ad} system.

The various equations will be repeated here for ready reference:

4.4.6   Summary - Per Unit Equations

Stator flux linkages

$$\begin{aligned}
\overline{\psi}_d &= -\left(\overline{L}_\ell + \overline{L}_{ad}\right)\overline{i}_d + \overline{L}_{ad}\,\overline{i}_{fd} + \overline{L}_{ad}\,\overline{i}_{kd_1} + \overline{L}_{ad}\,\overline{i}_{kd_2} + \dots \\
\overline{\psi}_q &= -\left(\overline{L}_\ell + \overline{L}_{aq}\right)\overline{i}_q + \overline{L}_{aq}\,\overline{i}_{kq_1} + \overline{L}_{aq}\,\overline{i}_{kq_2} \\
\overline{\psi}_0 &= -\overline{L}_0\,\overline{i}_0
\end{aligned} \tag{IV.116}$$

Note that $\overline{L}_\ell + \overline{L}_{ad} = \overline{L}_d$ and $\overline{L}_\ell + \overline{L}_{aq} = \overline{L}_q$.

Rotor flux linkages

$$\begin{aligned}
\overline{\psi}_{fd} &= -\overline{L}_{ad}\,\overline{i}_d + \overline{L}_{ffd}\,\overline{i}_{fd} + \overline{L}_{fkd_1}\,\overline{i}_{kd_1} + \overline{L}_{fkd_2}\,\overline{i}_{kd_2} \\
\overline{\psi}_{kd_1} &= -\overline{L}_{ad}\,\overline{i}_d + \overline{L}_{fkd_1}\,\overline{i}_{fd} + \overline{L}_{kkd_1}\,\overline{i}_{kd_1} + \overline{L}_{kd_{12}}\,\overline{i}_{kd_2} \\
\overline{\psi}_{kd_2} &= -\overline{L}_{ad}\,\overline{i}_d + \overline{L}_{fkd_2}\,\overline{i}_{fd} + \overline{L}_{kd_{12}}\,\overline{i}_{kd_1} + \overline{L}_{kkd_{12}}\,\overline{i}_{kd_2} \\
\overline{\psi}_{kd_1} &= -\overline{L}_{aq}\,\overline{i}_q + \overline{L}_{kkq_1}\,\overline{i}_{kq_1} + \overline{L}_{aq_1}\,\overline{i}_{kq_2} \\
\overline{\psi}_{kq_2} &= -\overline{L}_{aq}\,\overline{i}_q + \overline{L}_{aq}\,\overline{i}_{kq_1} + \overline{L}_{kkq2}\,\overline{i}_{kq_2}
\end{aligned} \tag{IV.117}$$

Note that the various per unit self-inductances can be broken into a leakage component and a mutual component with the stator which, by choice of the per unit system is L_{ad} in the d-axis and L_{aq} in the q-axis:

$$\overline{L}_{ffd} = \overline{L}_{ad} + \overline{L}_{fd}$$

$$\overline{L}_{kkd_1} = \overline{L}_{ad} + \overline{L}_{kd_1}$$

$$\overline{L}_{kkd_2} = \overline{L}_{ad} + \overline{L}_{kd_2}$$

$$\overline{L}_{kkq_1} = \overline{L}_{aq} + \overline{L}_{kq_1}$$

$$\overline{L}_{kkq2} = \overline{L}_{aq} + \overline{L}_{kq_2}$$

It should be noted that the leakage components between rotor circuits would be as follows:

1) Leakage inductance between amortisseur kd_1 and field

$$= \overline{L}_{kkd_1} - \overline{L}_{fkd_1}$$

2) Leakage component between amortisseur kd_2 and amortisseur kd_1

$$= \overline{L}_{kkd_2} - \overline{L}_{kd_{12}}$$

Whereas to be perfectly general the per unit mutuals between rotor circuits can be different than the per unit mutual inductance between rotor circuits and armature $\left(\overline{L}_{ad} \right)$, the approximation is usually made that $\overline{L}_{fkd_1} = \overline{L}_{kd_{12}} = \overline{L}_{ad}$.

Stator Voltages

$$\overline{e}_d = \frac{d}{dt}\overline{\psi}_d - \overline{\omega}\overline{\psi}_q - \overline{r}\overline{i}_d$$

$$\overline{e}_q = \frac{d}{dt}\overline{\psi}_q + \overline{\omega}\overline{\psi}_d - \overline{r}\overline{i}_q \qquad \text{(IV.118)}$$

$$\overline{e}_0 = \frac{d}{dt}\overline{\psi}_0 - \overline{r}\overline{i}_0$$

Rotor Voltages

$$\overline{e}_{fd} = \frac{d}{dt}\overline{\psi}_{fd} + \overline{r}_{fd}\overline{I}_{fd}$$

$$0 = \frac{d}{dt}\overline{\psi}_{kd_1} + \overline{r}_{kkd_1}\,\overline{i}_{kd_1} + \overline{r}_{kd_{12}}\,\overline{i}_{kd_2}$$

$$0 = \frac{d}{dt}\overline{\psi}_{d_2} + \overline{r}_{kd_{12}}\,\overline{i}_{kd_1} + \overline{r}_{kk_2}\,\overline{i}_{kd_2}$$ (IV.119)

$$0 = \frac{d}{dt}\overline{\psi}_{q_1} + \overline{r}_{kkq_1}\,\overline{i}_{kq_1} + \overline{r}_{kq_{12}}\,\overline{i}_{kq_2}$$

$$0 = \frac{d}{dt}\overline{\psi}_{q_2} + \overline{r}_{kq_{12}}\,\overline{i}_{kq_1} + \overline{r}_{kkq}\,\overline{i}_{kq_2}$$

Note in the above rotor equations the terms $\overline{r}_{kd12}$ and $\overline{r}_{kq12}$ are the per unit mutual resistances between amortisseur circuits.

Power and Torque

Equation (IV.66) expressed in per unit of 3ϕ power base (IV.77) becomes

$$\overline{P} = \overline{e}_d\overline{i}_d + \overline{e}_q\overline{i}_q + 2\overline{e}_o\overline{i}_o$$ (IV.120)

Similarly, the per unit torque expression is

$$\overline{T} = \overline{i}_q\overline{\psi}_d - \overline{i}_d\overline{\psi}_q$$ (IV.121)

4.4.7 Per Unit Base Quantities

In all the above per unit equations the following are the base quantities.

$e_{s_{base}}$ = peak value of rated line-to-neutral voltage (V)

$i_{s_{base}}$ = peak value of rated line current (A)

$E_{s_{base}}$ = RMS value of rated line-to-neutral voltage $(V) = \dfrac{e_{s_{base}}}{\sqrt{2}}$

$i_{s_{base}}$ = RMS value of rated line current $(A) = \dfrac{i_{s_{base}}}{\sqrt{2}}$

$$3\phi \quad VA_{base} = \frac{3}{2} e_{s_{base}} i_{s_{base}} = 3E_{s_{base}} I_{s_{base}}$$

$$Z_{s_{base}} = \frac{e_{s_{base}}}{i_{s_{base}}} = \frac{E_{s_{base}}}{I_{s_{base}}}$$

$$i_{fd_{base}} = \frac{L_{ad}}{L_{afd}} i_{s_{base}}$$

$$i_{kq1_{base}} = \frac{L_{aq}}{L_{akq1}} i_{s_{base}}$$

$$i_{kd1_{base}} = \frac{L_{ad}}{L_{akd1}} i_{s_{base}}$$

$$i_{kq2_{base}} = \frac{L_{aq}}{L_{akq2}} i_{s_{base}}$$

$$i_{kd2_{base}} = \frac{L_{ad}}{L_{akd2}} i_{s_{base}}$$

$$e_{fd_{base}} = \frac{3\phi \ VA_{base}}{i_{fd_{base}}} = \frac{\frac{3}{2} e_{s_{base}} i_{s_{base}}}{\frac{L_{ad}}{L_{afd}} i_{s_{base}}} = \frac{3}{2} \frac{L_{afd}}{L_{ad}} e_{s_{base}} = \frac{3}{\sqrt{2}} \frac{L_{afd}}{L_{ad}} e_{s_{base}}$$

$$Z_{fd_{base}} = \frac{e_{fd_{base}}}{i_{fd_{base}}} = \frac{3\phi \ VA_{base}}{\left(i_{fd_{base}}\right)^2} \qquad L_{fd_{base}} = \frac{Z_{fd_{base}}}{\omega_{base}}$$

$$Z_{kd_{base}} = \frac{3\phi \ VA_{base}}{\left(i_{kd_{base}}\right)^2} \qquad L_{kd_{base}} = \frac{Z_{kd_{base}}}{\omega_{base}}$$

$$t_{base} = \frac{1}{\omega_{base}}$$

The following inductances are shown in Figure 4.11:

$$L_{fd} = L_{ffd} - L_{ad} \qquad\qquad (IV.122)$$

$$L_{kd} = L_{kkd} - L_{ad} \qquad\qquad (IV.123)$$

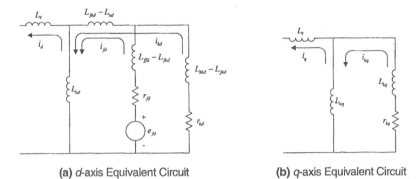

(a) d-axis Equivalent Circuit   **(b)** q-axis Equivalent Circuit

Figure 4.10 – Equivalent Circuits for the Synchronous Machine

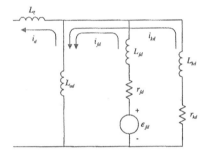

Figure 4.11 – d-axis Equivalent Circuit Neglecting L_{fkd} - L_{ad} term

Machine performance under a variety of transient and steady state situations can be derived from solution of the equations represented by these circuits along with the additional necessary equations representing the armature and connected system equations. We shall develop first the relations which describe machine steady state operation.

4.5 Synchronous Machine Performance – Steady State Operation

4.5.1 Saturation Neglected

The familiar steady state vector diagram of machine conditions for operation at a given steady state load will now be derived neglecting saturation.

Reference is made to the equivalent circuit of Figure 4.11 and the stator per unit voltage equations (IV.118).

Consider the case of a machine operating as a generator supplying power to an infinite bus at its terminals.

Let the machine phase voltages in per unit be:

$$e_a = e \cos(\omega t)$$

$$e_b = e \cos\left(\omega t - \frac{2\pi}{3}\right) \qquad \text{(IV.124)}$$

$$e_c = e \cos\left(\omega t + \frac{2\pi}{3}\right)$$

Also let the per unit phase current being supplied by the generator be

$$i_a = i \cos(\omega t - \phi)$$

$$i_b = i \cos\left(\omega t - \frac{2\pi}{3} - \phi\right) \qquad \text{(IV.125)}$$

$$i_c = i \cos\left(\omega t + \frac{2\pi}{3} - \phi\right)$$

Applying the d, q, 0 transformations (IV.33) to (IV.124)

$$e_d = +\frac{2}{3}\left[e_a \cos\theta + e_b \cos\left(\theta - \frac{2\pi}{3}\right) + e_c \cos\left(\theta + \frac{2\pi}{3}\right)\right]$$

$$e_q = -\frac{2}{3}\left[e_a \sin\theta + e_b \sin\left(\theta - \frac{2\pi}{3}\right) + e_c \sin\left(\theta + \frac{2\pi}{3}\right)\right] \qquad \text{(IV.126)}$$

$$e_0 = \frac{1}{3}\left[e_a + e_b + e_c\right]$$

where $\theta = \omega t + \theta_0$ is the angle between the d-axis and the center of phase "a". Since we are examining balanced steady state operation, the rotor per unit speed ω is the same as the frequency ω of the voltage and current waves and there are no zero sequence components.

Substituting (IV.124) in (IV.126)

$$
\begin{aligned}
e_d &= e \cos\theta_0 \\
e_q &= e \sin\theta_0
\end{aligned}
\tag{IV.127}
$$

Similarly for the currents (IV.125)

$$
\begin{aligned}
i_d &= i \cos(\theta_0 - \phi) \\
i_q &= i \sin(\theta_0 - \phi)
\end{aligned}
\tag{IV.128}
$$

Equations (IV.127) and (IV.128) show that for balanced steady state operation, e_d, e_q, i_d and i_q are constant (d.c.) quantities. With this in mind let us look at the voltage and flux linkage equations. The stator equations (IV.118) under steady state conditions become

$$
\begin{aligned}
e_d &= -\psi_q - r i_d \\
e_q &= +\psi_d - r i_q
\end{aligned}
\tag{IV.129}
$$

since for steady state balanced conditions $\dfrac{d\psi_d}{dt} = 0$, $\dfrac{d\psi_q}{dt} = 0$ and $\omega = 1.0$

Looking at the rotor voltage equations (IV.119) or visualizing them from the equivalent circuit of Figure 4.11 for steady state conditions we may set all rates of change of flux linkages equal to zero, whence

$$
e_{fd} = i_{fd} r_{fd}
$$

$$
i_{kd} = 0
\tag{IV.130}
$$

$$
i_{kq} = 0
$$

Also the flux linkage equations for these conditions become

$$
\begin{aligned}
\psi_d &= L_{ad} i_{fd} - L_d i_d \\
\psi_q &= -L_q i_q \\
\psi_{fd} &= L_{ffd} i_{fd} - L_{ad} i_d \\
\psi_{kd} &= L_{ad}(i_{fd} - i_d)
\end{aligned}
\tag{IV.131}
$$

From equations (IV.130) $i_{fd} = \dfrac{e_{fd}}{r_{fd}}$ which, when used in equation (IV.131), yields

$$y_d = e_{fd}\left(\frac{L_{ad}}{r_{fd}}\right) - L_d i_d \qquad\qquad \text{(IV.132)}$$

$$\psi_q = -L_q i_q \qquad\qquad \text{(IV.133)}$$

Remembering that equations (IV.132) and (IV.133) represent flux linkages in orthogonal axes, we may draw these relations as vectors as shown on Figure 4.12. Although all quantities in the above equations are scalar, they can be expressed symbolically as vectors where all q-axis quantities are 90° ahead of d-axis quantities. One choice of vector relations would be to have the d-axis as the axis of reals and the q-axis as the axis of imaginaries. It should be remembered that these axes rotate in space at the electrical speed of the rotor, and in this sense they are conceptually related to the phasor representing an a.c. quantity which rotates at synchronous speed. Figure 4.12 defines the voltages and currents in vector form.

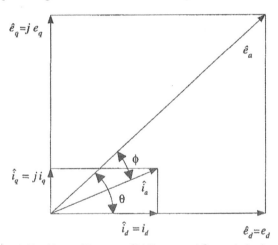

Figure 4.12 – Vector Diagram of Voltages and Currents in d-q Axes

Writing down a "^" to denote a vector quantity we may state:

$$\begin{array}{lll} \hat{i}_d = i_d & \hat{\psi}_d = \psi_d & \hat{e}_d = e_d \\[4pt] \hat{i}_q = ji_q & \hat{\psi}_q = j\psi_q & \hat{e}_q = je_q \end{array} \qquad\qquad \text{(IV.134)}$$

From equations (IV.124) and (IV.127)

$$\hat{e} = e_d + je_q = e\cos\theta_0 + je\sin\theta_0 \qquad\qquad \text{(IV.135)}$$

Note that equation (IV.135) was derived from a definition of $e_a = e \cos (\omega t)$ and $\theta = (\omega t - \theta_0)$ (angle by which the d-axis leads the center of phase "a") $= (\omega t - \theta_0)$. At $t = 0$, the d-axis lags phase "a" by θ_0.

Hence we can see that expressing "e_a" on the d-q axis plane is equivalent to lining up the "e_a" vector with $\hat{e}$ as given by equation (IV.135) from which it is noted that e_a leads the d axis by θ_0. In deriving the vector diagram, geometric relationships are required to locate the d and q axes, given the terminal voltage and current of the machine.

This will be done by the following vector relationships also described in the diagram of Figure 4.13. By definition the d-axis is the axis of reals and the q-axis is the axis of imaginaries.

Take equations (IV.132) and (IV.133) expressed in vector form

$$\hat{\psi}_d = e_{fd} \left(\frac{L_{ad}}{r_{fd}} \right) - L_d i_d \qquad (IV.136)$$

$$\hat{\psi}_q = -jL_q i_q \qquad (IV.137)$$

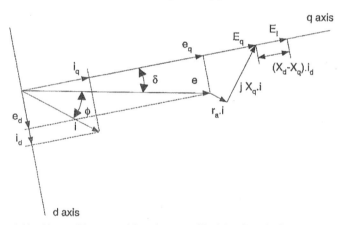

Figure 4.13 – Vector Diagram of Synchronous Machine Steady-State Relationships

Substituting equations (IV.136) and (IV.137) in (IV.129) and expressing in vector form (although in per unit $\omega = 1.0$, and thus inductances and reactances have the same per unit value, the dimensions of reactance are implied in the voltage equations):

$$\hat{e}_d = X_q i_q - r i_d \tag{IV.138}$$

$$\hat{e}_q = j e_{fd} \left(\frac{X_{ad}}{r_{fd}} \right) - j X_d i_d - j r i_q$$

$$= j e_{fd} \left(\frac{X_{ad}}{r_{fd}} \right) - j X_q i_d - j \left(X_d - X_q \right) i_d - j r i_q \tag{IV.139}$$

Combining (IV.138) and (IV.139)

$$\hat{e}_d + \hat{e}_q = e_d + j e_q =$$

$$= j e_{fd} \left(\frac{X_{ad}}{r_{fd}} \right) - j X_q \left(i_d + j i_q \right) - j \left(X_d - X_q \right) i_d - r \left(i_d + j i_q \right) \tag{IV.140}$$

Transposing equations (IV.140)

$$e_d + j e_q + \left(i_d + j i_q \right) \left(r + j X_q \right) = j e_{fd} \left(\frac{X_{ad}}{r_{fd}} \right) - j \left(X_d - X_q \right) i_d \tag{IV.141}$$

$$= j E_q$$

The left hand side of equation (IV.141) forms a vector along the q-axis, as is evident from the fact that all terms of the right hand side are imaginary, hence on the q-axis. The synthetic voltage E_q is obtained by adding to the terminal voltage e a voltage rise due to the armature current $\hat{i}$ across from the impedance $(r + j X_q)$. The phase angle of $\hat{E}_q$ relative to e locates the angle of the q-axis relative to the angle of the phase "a" terminal voltage. Note that the voltage E_q is only used to determine the angle of the q-axis, and has no other physical significance.

The term proportional to field voltage, e_{fd} is the steady state field current multiplied by X_{ad} also known as E_I

$$e_{fd} \left(\frac{X_{ad}}{r_{fd}} \right) = i_{fd} X_{ad} = E_I \tag{IV.142}$$

At this stage it is appropriate to introduce the variable E_{fd} which is proportional to e_{fd} by the ratio X_{ad}/r_{fd}:

$$E_{fd} = i_{fd} X_{ad} = E_I \tag{IV.143}$$

In the steady state, the procedure to establish the steady state relationships starting from terminal voltage and current conditions (Figure 4.13) are:

1) Take as reference the terminal voltage $\hat{e} = e$.

   From knowledge of load determine the current i in magnitude and phase relative to $\hat{e}$. $\hat{i} = |i| \underline{|-\phi}$.

2) Form the vector addition

   $$\hat{E}_q = \hat{e} + \hat{i}\left(r + jX_q\right) = \left|E_q\right| \underline{|\delta}$$

   Note: the angle δ is known as the machine internal power angle. This variable will have more significance when the subject of stability is discussed. The direction of the q-axis is established by the direction of $\hat{E}_q$.

3) The d and q components of voltage and current may now be determined by resolving $\hat{e}$ and $\hat{i}$ into the d and q axes

   $e_d = e \sin \delta$

   $e_q = e \cos \delta$

   $i_d = i \sin(\delta - \phi)$

   $i_q = i \cos(\delta - \phi)$

4) The internal field m.m.f $e_{fd} \dfrac{X_d}{r_{fd}}$ or $X_{ad}i_{fd}$ is determined from any of the following relations which can be seen to be equivalent from the vector diagram of Figure 4.13:

   $$\begin{aligned}
   E_I = X_{ad}i_{fd} &= E_q + (X_d - X_q)i_d \\
   &= e_q + ri_q + X_d i_d
   \end{aligned}$$
   (IV.144)

   It should be noted that saturation has not been accounted for in the above procedure. Also it should be realized that the relation $\dfrac{e_{fd}X_{ad}}{r_{fd}}$ is only equal to $X_{ad}i_{fd}$ in the steady state.

4.5.2 Open Circuit Operation

Steady-state open circuit operation is analyzed by having $i_d = 0$, and $i_q = 0$ in the above equations. When this is done we note that $e_d = 0$ and

$$e_q = E_q = X_{ad}I_{fd} = e \qquad \text{(IV.145)}$$

In all of the above derivations we note that the quantity of significance, in the field, is $X_{ad}i_{fd}$, which in per unit has a magnitude comparable to the magnitude of voltage. In the case of steady-state open circuit operation, $X_{ad}i_{fd} = \psi_d = e_q = e$.

Hence, rather than talking about per unit field current i_{fd}, it is customary and convenient to talk about $X_{ad}i_{fd}$ in per unit.

From the derivation of per unit quantities, we noted that to obtain an equivalent circuit with reciprocal mutuals, the volt-amp base in the field had to be equal to the 3ϕ stator volt-amp base. Since in actual operation the field volt-amps are in the order of 0.5% of the stator volt-amps, the value of per unit e_{fd} for typical operating conditions would turn out to be a number in the order of 0.005 p.u.

For this reason another set of per unit quantities are generally used in analyses of machine operation. Still preserving the relationships of the reciprocal per unit mutual system, we will define the additional variables as

$$E_I = X_{ad}i_{fd} \qquad \text{(IV.146)}$$

which is a variable proportional to field current i_{fd} such that when

$i_{fd} = \dfrac{1}{X_{ad}} \, p.u. \Leftrightarrow E_I = 1.0 \, p.u.$ Again on open circuit, neglecting saturation, when $E_I = 1.0$, the per unit terminal voltage e_a or $E_I = 1.0$ p.u..

The point to remember is that E_I is proportional to a field current or MMF, not to field voltage.

Field voltage is only proportional to field current in the steady state, i.e.

$$i_{fd} = \frac{e_{fd}}{r_{fd}} \text{ in the steady state} \qquad \text{(IV.147)}$$

When field voltage is intended, equation (IV.146) can be expressed using equation (IV.147) as

$$E_{fd} = \frac{X_{ad}}{r_{fd}} e_{fd} \qquad \text{(IV.148)}$$

We now have a new variable proportional to field voltage E_{fd}

Note that, in the steady state,

$$E_{fd} = E_I = X_{ad}i_{fd} = X_{ad}\frac{e_{fd}}{r_{fd}}$$

and all these quantities are equal to 1.0 per unit when e_a or $E_a = 1.0$. Also note that when $E_{fd} = 1.0$ p.u., e_{fd} is in the order of 0.005 p.u..

4.5.3   Effect of Saturation

The open circuit relationships just derived are shown on Figure 4.14.

The figure shows the "unsaturated" straight line relationship between per unit armature voltage E_a and per unit field excitation $E_I = X_{ad}i_{fd}$ or per unit field voltage (in the newly defined per unit E_{fd}).

The effects of saturation are indicated on Figure 4.14, showing that the actual excitation is greater than that shown by the straight line, also known as the air gap line. The amount of excitation "S" in excess of that determined by the air gap line, defined by the saturation curve, is a function of the flux level on the saturable parts of the machine.

The open circuit saturation curve is generally supplied as part of the data on machine parameters. In order to predict saturation effects under conditions of load one would need a great deal of information on the flux distribution in the various parts of the iron. However, approximations are made and the open circuit saturation curve is generally used in these approximations. These approximations involve establishing the right internal machine flux level which, when used with the open circuit saturation characteristics, gives the correct amount of saturation effect under load conditions.

A number of methods of accounting for saturation have been presented in the past. Some of these are well described in Reference 2 (p. 150) and Reference 3 (Chapter V).

We will describe here methods that are currently being used in computer representations of synchronous machines. For the case of round rotor machines the method used is similar to that described in Reference 4 (p. 368).

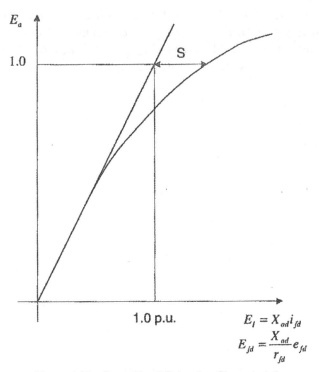

$E_t = X_{ad}i_{fd}$

$E_{fd} = \dfrac{X_{ad}}{r_{fd}} e_{fd}$

Figure 4.14 – Open Circuit Saturation Characteristic

4.5.4 Saturation In Round Rotor Machines

The assumption is made that the reluctance of the magnetic path is almost homogenous around the periphery of the rotor ($L_{ad} \approx L_{aq}$) and that the effect of saturation can therefore be represented by equal percent variations in the air gap inductance L_{ad} and L_{aq}. In one technique the only inductances that are made to saturate are these mutual stator-rotor inductances L_{ad} and L_{aq}.

Currently used saturation representation methods are covered in the discussion of computer representations of machines. A method which may be characterized as the "saturation factor" technique, and which has also been used in induction machines is presented below.

Referring to Figure 4.14 and the equivalent circuit of Figure 4.11 the linear relationship on the air gap line of the open circuit saturation curve is between $E_a = \psi_{ad}$ and $X_{ad}i_{fd}$ and, by choice of the per unit system, this linear relationship has a slope of 1.0. At any point where the saturation curve departs from the air gap line as shown on Figure 4.15, the slope $X_{ad}i_{fd} / E_a$ is greater than 1.0. Let this slope be labeled "k", the saturation factor. Figure 4.15 also shows this saturation factor plotted as function of the air gap flux linkage.

The procedure is to determine, from terminal voltage and current conditions, the per unit air gap voltage or flux ψ_a. Then determine the saturation factor "k" corresponding to this level of flux read off Figure 4.15. The values X_{ad} and X_{aq} are adjusted to saturated values by dividing them by the value k.

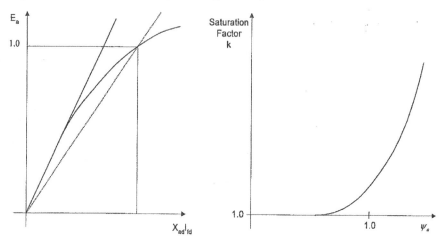

Figure 4.15 – Saturation Factor k as a Function of the Air-Gap Flux

Specifically the step would be:

1) Find air gap flux from terminal voltage and current

$$\hat{\psi}_a = \hat{\psi}_{ad} + \hat{\psi}_{aq} = \hat{e} + \left(r + j X_\ell \right) \hat{i}$$

2) Determine "k" in as a function of the air gap flux $k = f(|\psi_a|)$.

3) Adjust values of X_{ad} and X_{aq} as follows:

$$X_{ad_s} = \frac{X_{ad}}{k} = \frac{\left(X_d - X_\ell \right)}{k}$$

$$X_{aq_s} = \frac{X_{aq}}{k} = \frac{\left(X_q - X_\ell \right)}{k}$$

4) Proceed with the normal method of vector diagram construction as described in Figure 4.13 using the adjusted constants as

$$X_{d_s} = \left[X_\ell + \frac{X_d - X_\ell}{k} \right]$$

$$X_{q_s} = \left[X_\ell + \frac{X_q - X_\ell}{k} \right]$$

5) Obtain E_{I_s}, the value of excitation based on the vector diagram with saturated reactance values

6) The actual field current $L_{ad}i_{fd}$ is then equal to kE_{I_s}.

4.5.5 Saturation in Salient Pole Machines

In salient pole machines, because of the much greater air gap in the q- axis, the flux in this axis will seldom experience saturation. Hence in the case of salient pole machines saturation is made a function of some d-axis flux rather than the total flux as in the case of round rotor machines. Since saturation does not occur in the q-axis, it will be evident, from the construction of the vector diagram of Figure 4.13 that the machine power angle δ will not be affected by saturation in the case of the salient pole machine, whereas we noted that saturation, through its effect on X_d and X_q in the case of a round rotor machine, does affect the power angle δ. These effects will be discussed further under the subject of _stability_.

The procedure to determine field current under steady state load conditions for salient pole machines is:

1.) Construct the normal vector diagram as in Figure 4.13 locating the q-axis from the angle of E_q with respect to terminal voltage.

$$\hat{E}_q = \hat{e} + \left(r + jX_q \right)\hat{i} = \left| E_q \right| \underline{|\delta}$$

2.) As before obtain the d and q components of voltage and current.

$$e_d = e \sin \delta$$

$$e_q = e \cos \delta$$

$$i_d = i \sin (\delta - \phi)$$

$$i_q = i \cos (\delta - \phi)$$

where ϕ is the power factor angle of the load carried by the machine.

3.) Determine a flux level in the d-axis from which the amount of saturation will be derived. This flux level is generally obtained by adding a "transient reactance" drop to the d-axis flux representing some level of field leakage. "Transient" reactance will be discussed in a later section. Sometimes this value of reactance is taken as the leakage or Potier reactance.

$$\psi_d = e_q + ri_q$$

$$\psi_d' = e_q' = e_q + ri_q + X_d'i_d$$

4.) From the open circuit saturation curve determine the component of $X_{ad}i_{fd}$

= S which is due to saturation at a per unit voltage equal to e_q'.

5.) Determine the unsaturated $(X_{ad}\,i_{fd})$ in the normal manner, given in equation (IV.144)

$$\left(X_{ad}i_{fd} \right)_w = e_q + ri_q + X_d i_d \qquad (IV.144)$$

6.) Obtain the actual field current $\left(X_{ad}i_{fd} \right)_s$ by adding to (IV.144) the component "S" derived in Step 4.

$$\left(X_{ad}i_{fd} \right)_s = \left(X_{ad}i_{fd} \right)_u + S$$

4.6 Synchronous Machine Performance – Transient Analysis

The basic machine equations summarized in equations (IV.116) for stator flux linkages, in equations (IV.117) for rotor flux linkages, in equations (IV.118) for stator voltages and in equations (IV.119) for rotor voltages, define the performance of a machine given the necessary additional equations relating voltages to currents in the system to which the machine is connected.

Considerable additional insight can be derived by reduction of these equations with elimination of variables and simplification of transient effects by looking at them in terms of initial value and final value solutions. As a result of these reductions certain basic machine parameters have been derived and widely used, such as transient reactance, subtransient reactance, open circuit field and amortisseur time constants, etc.

In this section we will derive these simplified methods of machine transient analysis showing their relation to the basic equations derived thus far. Saturation will be neglected in this treatment which of necessity uses methods of linear systems analysis. The treatment of saturation effects will be included in the section dealing with machine models which are used in computer simulations of machine behavior.

4.6.1 Operational Methods of Machine Analysis

We shall restrict this treatment to a machine represented by one amortisseur and field circuit in the d-axis and one amortisseur in the q-axis. Similar methods can be extended to more complex representations which include multiple amortisseurs. Balanced conditions are assumed - hence the zero sequence components drop out.

The basic equations are written below in operational form. Recall that with the per unit system maintaining reciprocal stator-rotor mutual inductances,

$$L_{ad} = L_{afd} = L_{akd}$$

$$L_{aq} = L_{akq}$$

In line with the usual practice, we will also make the assumption that the per unit mutual inductances between rotor circuits in the d-axis are equal to L_{ad}, i.e.

$$L_{fkd} = L_{ad}$$

In order to help visualize the relations we will draw again the equivalent circuits in Figure 4.16.

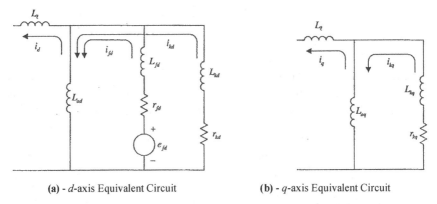

(a) - d-axis Equivalent Circuit (b) - q-axis Equivalent Circuit

Figure 4.16 – Equivalent Circuits for the Synchronous Machine

Stator Flux Linkages

$$\psi_d(s) - L_d\, i_d(s) + L_{ad}\, i_{fd}(s) + L_{ad}\, i_{kd}(s) \tag{IV.149}$$

$$\psi_q(s) - L_q\, i_q(s) + L_{aq}\, i_{kq}(s) \tag{IV.150}$$

Rotor Linkages

$$\psi_{fd}(s) = -L_{ad}\, i_d(s) + L_{ffd}\, i_{fd}(s) + L_{ad}\, i_{kd}(s) \tag{IV.151}$$

$$\psi_{kd}(s) = -L_{ad}\, i_d(s) + L_{ad}\, i_{fd}(s) + L_{kkd}\, i_{kd}(s) \tag{IV.152}$$

$$\psi_{kq}(s) = -L_{aq}\, i_q(s) + L_{kkq}\, i_{kq}(s) \tag{IV.153}$$

Stator Voltages

$$e_d(s) = s\psi_d(s) - \psi_d(0) - \psi_q(s)\,\omega - r i_d(s) \tag{IV.154}$$

$$e_q(s) = s\psi_q(s) - \psi_q(0) - \psi_d(s)\,\omega - r i_q(s) \tag{IV.155}$$

Rotor Voltages

$$e_{fd}(s) = s\psi_{fd}(s) - \psi_{fd}(0) + r_{fd}\, i_{fd}(s) \tag{IV.156}$$

$$0 = s\psi_{kd}(s) - \psi_{kd}(0) + r_{kd}\, i_{kd}(s) \tag{IV.157}$$

$$0 = s\psi_{kq}(s) - \psi_{kq}(0) + r_{kq}\, i_{kq}(s) \tag{IV.158}$$

The symbols (0) following a variable denote initial conditions at $t = 0$. All of the above equations can be expressed in terms of changes about the initial operating point, in which case the initial condition terms drop out and the variables in the equations represent changes from the initial values.

Expressing the rotor voltage equations (IV.156), (IV.157) and (IV.158) in incremental form and substituting the flux linkage terms by their expressions (IV.151), (IV.152), (IV.153) also in incremental form we obtain a set of 3 equations relating the incremental currents $\Delta i_d(s)$, $\Delta i_{fd}(s)$, $\Delta i_{kd}(s)$ and $\Delta i_{kq}(s)$ in terms of $\Delta e_{fd}(s)$.

From these equations, the currents $\Delta i_{fd}(s)$, $\Delta i_{kd}(s)$, and $\Delta i_{kq}(s)$ can be expressed in terms of $\Delta e_{fd}(s)$, $\Delta i_d(s)$ and $\Delta i_q(s)$.

These expressions are:

$$\Delta i_{fd}(s) = \frac{1}{A(s)}\left[\left(r_{kd} + L_{kkd}s\right)\Delta e_{fd}(s) + sL_{ad}\left(r_{kd} + sL_{kd}\right)\Delta i_d(s)\right] \tag{IV.159}$$

$$\Delta i_{kd}(s) = \frac{1}{A(s)}\left[-sL_{ad}\Delta e_{fd}(s) + sL_{ad}\left(r_{fd} + sL_{fd}\right)\Delta i_d(s)\right] \tag{IV.160}$$

$$\Delta i_{kq}(s) = \frac{sL_{aq}}{r_{kq} + sL_{kkq}}\Delta i_q(s) \tag{IV.161}$$

where

$$L_{kkd} = L_{ad} + L_{kd}$$

$$L_{kkq} = L_{aq} + L_{kq}$$

$$L_{ffd} = L_{ad} + L_{fd}$$

$$A(s) = \left(L_{kkd}L_{ffd} - L_{ad}^2\right)s^2 + \left(L_{kkd}r_{fd} + L_{ffd}r_{kd}\right)s + r_{kd}r_{fd}$$

When these expressions for rotor currents are substituted in the stator flux linkage equations (IV.149) and (IV.150) (incremental form) $\Delta\psi_d(s)$ and $\Delta\psi_q(s)$ are expressed as function of $\Delta e_{fd}(s)$, $\Delta i_d(s)$, and $\Delta i_q(s)$ as in the following

$$\Delta\psi_d(s) = G(s)\Delta e_{fd}(s) - L_d(s)\Delta I_d(s) \tag{IV.162}$$

$$\Delta\psi_q(s) = -L_q(s)\Delta i_q(s) \tag{IV.163}$$

where

$$G(s) = \frac{L_{ad}\left(r_{kd} + sL_{kd}\right)}{A(s)} \tag{IV.164}$$

$$L_d(s) = L_d - \frac{sL_{ad}^2\left[(L_{kd} + L_{fd})s + \left(r_{kd} + r_{fd}\right)\right]}{A(s)} \tag{IV.165}$$

$$L_q(s) = L_q - \frac{sL_{aq}^2}{sL_{kkq} + r_{kq}} \tag{IV.166}$$

Equations (IV.162), (IV.163) and (IV.159) give operational expressions between the significant dependent variables $\Delta\psi_d(s)$ $\Delta\psi_q(s)$ $\Delta i_{fd}(s)$ and the independent variables $\Delta e_{fd}(s)$, $\Delta i_d(s)$ and $\Delta i_q(s)$.

All of these expressions apply to the machine representation of the equivalent circuits of Figure 4.16. Whereas these equivalent circuits are quite adequate for a variety of purposes, in cases where better precision is required in the determination of rotor currents, the assumption of per unit mutual inductances between rotor circuits as being equal to the mutual between rotor and stator L_{ad}, may not be adequate. In these cases an equivalent circuit which allows L_{fkd} to be other than equal to L_{ad} is shown in Figure 4.17.

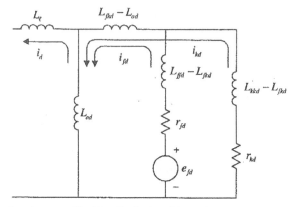

Figure 4.17 – Synchronous Machine Equivalent Circuit Considering the Term L_{fkd} - L_{ad}

For this circuit the operational expressions are:

$$\Delta i_{fd}\left(s\right) = \frac{1}{A^{*}\left(s\right)}\left\{\left(r_{kd} + sL_{kkd}\right)\Delta e_{fd}\left(s\right) + sL_{ad}\left[\left(L_{kkd} - L_{fkd}\right)s + r_{kd}\right]\Delta i_{d}\left(s\right)\right\} \quad \text{(IV.167)}$$

$$\Delta y_{d}\left(s\right) = G^{*}\left(s\right)\,\Delta e_{fd}\left(s\right) - L_{d}^{*}\left(s\right)\,\Delta i_{d}\left(s\right) \quad \text{(IV.168)}$$

where

$$G^{*}\left(s\right) = \frac{L_{ad}\left[r_{kd} + \left(L_{kkd} - L_{fkd}\right)\right]}{A^{*}\left(s\right)} \quad \text{(IV.169)}$$

$$L_{d}^{*}\left(s\right) = L_{d} - \frac{sL_{ad}^{2}\left[s\left(L_{kkd} + L_{ffd} - 2L_{fkd}\right) + \left(r_{kd} + r_{fd}\right)\right]}{A^{*}\left(s\right)} \quad \text{(IV.170)}$$

$$A^{*}\left(s\right) = \left(L_{kkd}L_{ffd} - L_{fkd}^{2}\right)s^{2} + \left(L_{kkd}r_{fd} + L_{ffd}r_{kd}\right)s + r_{kd}r_{fd} \quad \text{(IV.171)}$$

The q-axis circuit remains unchanged and, therefore, equation (IV.163) is still valid and is repeated here:

$$\Delta\psi_{q}(s) = -L_{q}(s)\Delta i_{q}(s) \quad \text{(IV.163)}$$

Another commonly used equivalent circuit which is adequate for many studies is the one which neglects amortisseurs as shown in Figure 4.18.

For this representation the relations are

$$\Delta i_{fd}(s) = \frac{1}{A^{**}(s)}\left\{\Delta e_{fd}(s) + sL_{ad}\Delta i_d(s)\right\} \qquad (IV.172)$$

$$\Delta \psi_d(s) = G^{**}(s)\,\Delta e_{fd}(s) - L_d^{**}(s)\,\Delta i_d(s) \qquad (IV.173)$$

$$\Delta \psi_q(s) = -L_q^{**}(s)\,\Delta i_d(s) \qquad (IV.174)$$

where

$$A^{**}(s) = r_{fd} + sL_{ffd} \qquad (IV.175)$$

$$G^{**}(s) = \frac{L_{ad}}{A^{**}(s)} \qquad (IV.176)$$

$$L_d^{**}(s) = L_d - \frac{sL_{ad}^2}{r_{fd} + sL_{ffd}} \qquad (IV.177)$$

$$L_q^{**}(s) = L_q \qquad (IV.178)$$

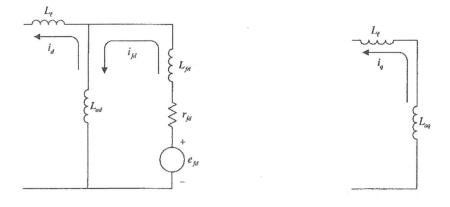

(a) - d-axis Equivalent Circuit   (b) - q-axis Equivalent Circuit

Figure 4.18 – Synchronous Machine Equivalent Circuits Neglecting Amortisseur Windings

4.6.2 Transient and Subtransient Reactances and Machine Time Constants

The reductions of the basic equations performed above with elimination of dependent variables, such as rotor currents, leads to operational expressions between stator flux linkages, field voltage and stator currents. Depending on the basic equivalent circuit chosen to represent rotor effects, these operational expressions take the form of the various expressions $G(s)$, $G^*(s)$, $G^{**}(s)$, $L_d(s)$, $L_d^*(s)$, $L_d^{**}(s)$, $L_q(s)$, $L_q^*(s)$ and $L_q^{**}(s)$ developed in the previous section.

Figure 4.19 is helpful in visualizing the basic machine representation.

We have developed the blocks $G(s)$, $L_d(s)$ and $L_q(s)$. However, for the complete solution, the stator currents $i_d(s)$ and $i_q(s)$ must be determined from additional relations which involve the stator and network voltage and current relations as well as rotor speed and angle dynamics responding to accelerating and decelerating torques. Note that although the d and q axis flux linkages and currents in the machine are basically uncoupled, the interaction between these occurs through the stator-network voltage/current equations represented within the dashed line block of Figure 4.19. Before developing these additional voltage/current relations which include the connected system, let us examine the reaction of machine flux to changes in field voltage while preserving current constant (equivalent to open circuit conditions) and the reaction to changes in armature currents.

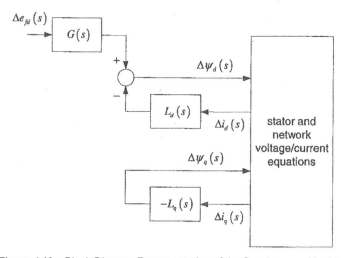

Figure 4.19 – Block Diagram Representation of the Synchronous Machine

Under open circuit conditions i_d and i_q are zero and the only active block in Figure 4.19 in $G(s)$ which is the transfer function between field voltage and direct axis flux. Let us examine $G(s)$. In the simplest representation (equivalent circuit in Figure 4.18) the expression for $G(s)$ given by equation (IV.176) is

$$G(s) = \frac{\Delta \psi_d(s)}{\Delta e_{fd}(s)} = \frac{L_{ad}}{r_{fd}\left(1 + s\dfrac{L_{ffd}}{r_{fd}}\right)} \qquad \text{(IV.179)}$$

From equation (IV.179)

$$\Delta \psi_d(s) = \frac{L_{ad}}{r_{fd}\left(1 + s\dfrac{L_{ffd}}{r_{fd}}\right)} \Delta e_{fd}(s) = \frac{1}{1 + sT'_{d0}} \Delta E_{fd}(s) \qquad (IV.180)$$

where $\Delta E_{fd} = \dfrac{L_{ad}}{r_{fd}} \Delta e_{fd}$ as defined previously in equation (IV.148) and $T'_{d0} = \dfrac{L_{ffd}}{r_{fd}}$ is the field open circuit time constant. Note that with the choice E_{fd} as a variable, there is a one to one relationship between ψ_d and E_{fd}, in the absence of saturation.

Relation (IV.180) indicates that for open circuit conditions the armature flux and therefore voltage responds to a change in field voltage exponentially with a time constant corresponding to the field L/R time constant, as shown in Figure 4.20.

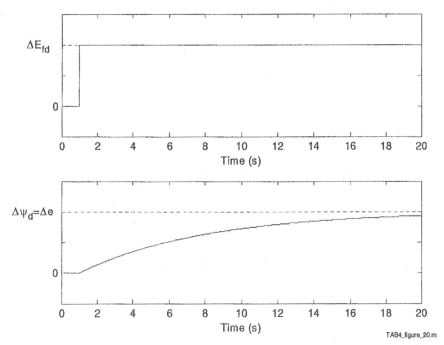

Figure 4.20 – Open Circuit Response to a Field Voltage Step – No Amortisseur Windings

Take now the same open circuit case except that a more detailed representation is used for the machine as in Figure 4.16. Using relations (IV.162) and (IV.164):

$$\Delta\psi_d(s) = \frac{L_{ad}}{r_{fd}} \frac{\left[\dfrac{L_{kd}}{r_{kd}}s+1\right]}{\left[\dfrac{L_{ad}\left(L_{kd}+L_{fd}\right)+L_{kd}L_{fd}}{r_{fd}r_{kd}}s^2 + \left(\dfrac{L_{kkd}}{r_{kd}}+\dfrac{L_{ffd}}{r_{fd}}\right)s+1\right]} \Delta e_{fd}(s)$$

(IV.181)

$$= \frac{\left(T_{kd}s+1\right)}{\left(T'_{d0}T''_{d0}s^2+\left(T_2+T'_{d0}\right)s+1\right)}\Delta E_{fd}(s)$$

where (note definitions of T'_{d0} and T''_{d0})

$$T_{kd}\triangleq\frac{L_{kd}}{r_{kd}} \quad T'_{d0}\triangleq\frac{L_{ffd}}{r_{fd}}$$

$$T_2\triangleq\frac{L_{kkd}}{r_{kd}} \quad T''_{d0}\triangleq\frac{1}{r_{kd}}\left(L_{kd}+\frac{L_{ad}L_{fd}}{L_{ffd}}\right)$$

Equation (IV.181) can be expressed in factored form as

$$\Delta\psi_d(s) = \frac{\left(1+sT_{kd}\right)}{\left(1+s\tau_{1d}\right)\left(1+s\tau_{2d}\right)}\Delta E_{fd}(s)$$

(IV.182)

where τ_{1d} and τ_{2d} are the principal time constants of the machine d-axis obtained by factoring the denominator of equation (IV.181). The values τ_{1d} and τ_{2d} can be calculated in terms of the parameters in (IV.181) as:

$$\tau_{1d} = \frac{\left(T'_{d0}+T_2\right)+\sqrt{\left(T'_{d0}+T_2\right)^2-4T'_{d0}T''_{d0}}}{2}$$

(IV.183)

$$\tau_{2d} = \frac{\left(T'_{d0}+T_2\right)-\sqrt{\left(T'_{d0}+T_2\right)^2-4T'_{d0}T''_{d0}}}{2}$$

Due to the relative values of field and amortisseur resistances, T'_{d0} is usually much larger than T''_{d0}. Hence, the approximation $(1+T'_{d0}s)(1+T''_{d0}s)$ as the factors of the denominator of equation (IV.182) is quite close. These time constants, known as the open circuit field and amortisseur time constants respectively were defined in (IV.181).

Note that in this per unit system the unit of time is $\dfrac{1}{\omega_0}=\dfrac{1}{377}$ seconds (for a 60 Hz system). Thus the values of time constants in equation (IV.182) should be divided by ω_0 to have them expressed in seconds. Also note that the effective inductance in the calculation of $T_{d0}^{''}$ is, so to speak, the driving point inductance as seen from the amortisseur, (with armature open circuited):

$$\left(L_{kd} + \frac{L_{ad} \, L_{fd}}{L_{ffd}} \right)$$

The response ψ_d to a step change in E_{fd} from the expression (IV.184)

$$\Delta\psi_d(s) = \frac{\left(1+sT_{kd}\right)}{\left(1+sT_{d0}^{'}\right)\left(1+sT_{d0}^{''}\right)} \Delta E_{fd}(s) \qquad \text{(IV.184)}$$

is shown in Figure 4.21, where the effect of the amortisseur is to slow down the

initial rise of flux due to the factor $\dfrac{\left(1+sT_{kd}\right)}{1+sT_{d0}^{''}}$ in which, as can be seen from the respective expressions, $T_{d0}^{''}$ is in the order of two times T_{kd}

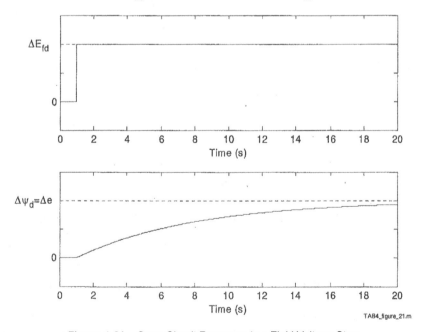

Figure 4.21 – Open Circuit Response to a Field Voltage Step

Referring to Figure 4.19, let us now look at the operational "inductance" terms $L_d(s)$ and $L_q(s)$. These terms describe the manner in which a change in stator currents i_d and i_q results into changes in armature flux linkages $\Delta\psi_d$ and $\Delta\psi_q$. Since the per unit rotational speed ω was chosen as 1.0 for rated speed, the per unit value of L and $\omega L = X$ is the same. Likewise the rotational voltage terms $e = \psi\omega$ have the same per unit value as ψ. For these reasons it is common practice to use the symbols X_d in lieu of L_d etc.

Take first the case of Figure 4.18 where amortisseur effects are neglected.

From expression (IV.177)

$$L_d^{**}(s) = L_d - \frac{sL_{ad}^2}{r_{fd} + sL_{ffd}} \tag{IV.177}$$

and remembering that $L_d = L_{ad} + L_\ell$ and $L_{ffd} = L_{fd} + L_{ad}$ expression (IV.177) can be reduced to

$$L_d^{**}(s) = \frac{L_d\left(1 + \dfrac{L_d'}{L_d}T_{d0}'s\right)}{\left(1 + sT_{d0}'\right)} \tag{IV.185}$$

where

$$L_d' = L_\ell + \frac{L_{ad}L_{fd}}{L_{ffd}} \tag{IV.186}$$

and $T_{d0}' = \dfrac{L_{ffd}}{r_{fd}}$ as previously defined.

The parameter L_d' defined in equation (IV.186) is called transient inductance, expressed more usually as transient reactance X_d'.

Using the initial value and final value theorems, expression (IV.185) shows that upon a step change in current Δi_d the initial change in flux linkages or in other words the initial drop or rise in voltage is $\Delta\psi_d = -L_d'\,\Delta i_d$. The final change is $\Delta\psi_d = -L_d\Delta i_d$. Expression (IV.185) shows that the inductance or reactance of the machine to fast changes is L_d' while for the steady state it is L_d. Figure 4.22

shows the change in direct axis flux linkages $\Delta\psi_d$ as function of time for an abrupt change in direct axis component of current Δi_d.

Note that the transition from the initial value $\Delta\psi_d = L_d' \Delta i_d$ to the final value $L_d \Delta i_d$ occurs with the time constant T_{d0}'.

The quadrature axis representation in Figure 4.18 does not have an amortisseur hence its effective inductance is not a function of time, $\Delta\psi_q = -L_q \Delta i_q$.

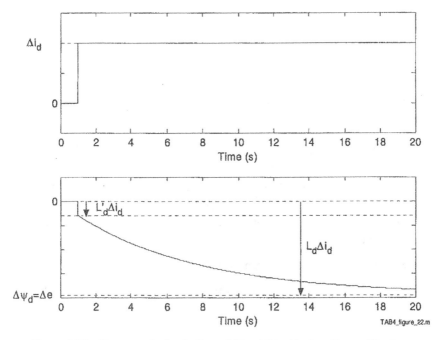

Figure 4.22 – Response to d-axis Current Step (Δi_d) – No Amortisseur Windings

Examine now the time response characteristics of the operational inductances corresponding to the equivalent circuit of Figure 4.16 where amortisseurs are represented.

Expression (IV.165) for $L_d(s)$ can be reduced to the form

$$L_d(s) = \frac{L_d\left(1+\left(T_d'+T_3\right)s+T_d'T_d''s^2\right)}{1+\left(T_{d0}'+T_2\right)s+T_{d0}'T_{d0}''s^2} \qquad \text{(IV.187)}$$

where T_{d0}', T_2 and T_{d0}'' were defined previously in connection with (IV.181). The other parameters in the numerator of (IV.187) are:

$$T_d' = \frac{1}{r_{fd}}\left(L_{fd} + \frac{L_{ad}L_\ell}{L_d}\right)$$

$$T_3 = \frac{1}{r_{kd}}\left(L_{kd} + \frac{L_{ad}L_\ell}{L_d}\right) \qquad \text{(IV.188)}$$

$$T_d'' = \frac{1}{r_{kd}}\left(L_{kd} + \frac{1}{\dfrac{1}{L_{ad}} + \dfrac{1}{L_\ell} + \dfrac{1}{L_{fd}}}\right)$$

T_d' and T_d'' are known as the short circuit field time constant and the short circuit subtransient time constant respectively.

As previously, in the discussion of the term $G(s)$ for the same equivalent circuit, the denominator of (IV.187) can be expressed approximately by the factors $\left(1+T_{do}'s\right)\left(1+T_{do}''s\right)$. Similarly the numerator of (IV.187) can be expressed approximately as $\left(1+T_d's\right)\left(1+T_d''s\right)$ where T_d' and T_d'' are the transient and subtransient short circuit time constants defined in equation (IV.188). The real roots of the numerator are the reciprocals of τ_{3d} and τ_{4d}.

Hence the exact factored expression for $L_d(s)$ is

$$L_d(s) = \frac{\left(1+\tau_{3d}s\right)\left(1+\tau_{4d}s\right)L_d}{\left(1+\tau_{1d}s\right)\left(1+\tau_{2d}s\right)} \qquad \text{(IV.189)}$$

and this expression for $L_d(s)$ can be approximated by (IV.190)

$$L_d(s) = \frac{\left(1+T_d's\right)\left(1+T_d''s\right)L_d}{\left(1+T_{d0}'s\right)\left(1+T_{d0}''s\right)} \qquad \text{(IV.190)}$$

The relationship between τ_{3d} and τ_{4d} and the numerator parameters in (IV.187) are:

$$\tau_{3d} = \frac{\left(T_d'+T_3\right)+\sqrt{\left(T_d'+T_3\right)^2 - 4T_d'T_d''}}{2}$$

$$\tau_{4d} = \frac{\left(T_d'+T_3\right)-\sqrt{\left(T_d'+T_3\right)^2 - 4T_d'T_d''}}{2} \qquad \text{(IV.191)}$$

Note that the equivalent inductances that figure in the expressions for T_d' and T_d'' in (IV.188) are

$$\text{for } T_d', \left(L_{fd} + \frac{L_{ad}L_\ell}{L_d} \right)$$

and

$$\text{for } T_d'', \left(L_{kd} + \cfrac{1}{\cfrac{1}{L_{ad}} + \cfrac{1}{L_\ell} + \cfrac{1}{L_{fd}}} \right)$$

Defining L_d' as previously in (IV.186), the per unit transient inductance or reactance

$$L_d' = L_\ell + \frac{L_{ad}L_{fd}}{L_{ffd}} = X_d' \qquad (IV.186)$$

and L_d'', the per unit subtransient inductance

$$L_d'' = L_\ell + \cfrac{1}{\cfrac{1}{L_{ad}} + \cfrac{1}{L_{fd}} + \cfrac{1}{L_{kd}}} = X_d'' \qquad (IV.192)$$

we note that

$$L_d' = L_d \frac{T_d'}{T_{do}'} \qquad (IV.193)$$

and that

$$L_d'' = L_d \frac{T_d' T_d''}{T_{do}' T_{do}''} \qquad (IV.194)$$

Notice the form of the inductances L_d' and L_d'' as defined by equations (IV.186) and (IV.192). By referring to the equivalent circuit of Figure 4.16, L_d' can be seen to be the driving point equivalent inductance viewed from the terminals with the amortisseur removed and with the field resistance set to zero. Similarly $L_d^{''}$ is the driving point inductance or Thevenin inductance as viewed from the terminals with field and amortisseur included and resistances set to zero.

The response of armature d-axis flux to an abrupt change in armature current is shown in Figure 4.23. It can also be visualized by applying the initial and final value theorems to the expression (IV.190) which, using (IV.193) and (IV.194) can also be expressed approximately as:

$$\Delta\psi_d(s) = L_d \frac{\left(1+s\dfrac{L_d^{'}}{L_d}T_{d0}^{'}\right)\left(1+s\dfrac{L_d^{''}}{L_d^{'}}T_{d0}^{''}\right)}{\left(1+sT_{d0}^{'}\right)\left(1+sT_{d0}^{''}\right)}\Delta i_d(s) \qquad\text{(IV.195)}$$

whereas the exact expression is:

$$\Delta\psi_d(s) = \frac{L_d\left(1+s\tau_{3d}\right)\left(1+s\tau_{4d}\right)}{\left(1+s\tau_{1d}\right)\left(1+s\tau_{2d}\right)}\Delta i_d(s) \qquad\text{(IV.196)}$$

Note that this behavior can be viewed in terms of the machine initially exhibiting an inductance $L_d^{''}$ called "subtransient", which gives way to an intermediate inductance $L_d^{'}$ called "transient" and finally, more gradually to the final steady state inductance L_d.

With a two-amortisseur representation in the q-axis analogous expressions to (IV.195) and (IV.196) apply with the appropriate change of subscripts from d to q.

It is important to note that, because of the relative difference between resistances of the two equivalent amortisseurs in the q-axis being much smaller than the difference between resistances in the field and amortisseur in the d-axis, the error in using $T_{q0}^{'}$ and $T_{q0}^{''}$ instead of the denominator time constancts τ_{1q} and τ_{2q} can be appreciable.

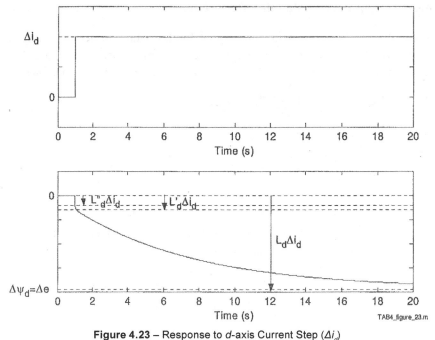

Figure 4.23 – Response to d-axis Current Step (Δi_d)

A similar derivation for the quadrature axis operational inductance in the case of only one amortisseur, gives:

$$L_q(s) = \frac{L_q\left(1 + s\dfrac{L_q'}{L_q}T_{q0}'\right)}{\left(1 + sT_{q0}'\right)} = \frac{L_q\left(1 + sT_q'\right)}{\left(1 + sT_{q0}'\right)} \qquad \text{(IV.197)}$$

where

$$L_q = L_{aq} + L_\ell$$

$$L_q' = L_\ell + \frac{L_{aq}L_{kq}}{L_{aq} + L_{kq}}$$

$$T_{q0}' = \frac{L_{kkq}}{r_{kq}}$$

$$T_q' = \frac{1}{r_{kq}}\left(L_{kq} + \frac{L_\ell L_{aq}}{L_{aq} + L_{kq}}\right)$$

4.6.3   Summary of Machine Constants

The following list contains a summary of fundamental and derived machine constants for the two equivalent circuit representations, that of Figure 4.16 including one amortisseur in each axis and of Figure 4.18, with no amortisseurs.

4.6.4   Equivalent Circuit Constants

r_a = stator resistance

r_{fd} = field winding resistance

r_{kd} = d-axis amortisseur winding resistance

r_{kq} = q-axis amortisseur winding resistance

L_{ad} = d-axis mutual inductance between rotor and stator windings

L_{aq} = q-axis mutual inductance between rotor and stator windings

L_ℓ = stator leakage inductance

$L_{ad} + L_\ell$ = L_d = d-axis synchronous inductance

$L_{aq} + L_\ell$ = L_q = q-axis synchronous inductance

L_{fd} = field winding leakage inductance

L_{kd} = d-axis amortisseur winding leakage inductance

L_{kq} = q-axis amortisseur winding leakage inductance

L_{ffd} = $L_{ad} + L_{fd}$ = field winding self inductance

L_{kkd} = $L_{ad} + L_{kd}$ = d-axis amortisseur winding self inductance

L_{kkq} = $L_{aq} + L_{kq}$ = q-axis amortisseur winding self inductance

In the case of round (solid rotor) machines, the q-axis is better represented by two equivalent amortisseurs giving the equivalent circuit a form analogous to that of the d-axis in Figure 4.16 (except for absence of excitation voltgage). In this case, in a fashion similar to that for the d-axis, the circuit parameters are:

r_{kq1} = "low resistance" q-axis amortisseur winding resistance

r_{kq2} = "high resistance" q-axis amortisseur winding resistance

L_{aq} = q-axis mutual inductance between rotor and stator windings

L_{kq1} = "low resistance" q-axis amortisseur winding leakage inductance

L_{kq2} = "high resistance" q-axis amortisseur winding leakage inductance

L_{kkq1} = $L_{aq} + L_{kq1}$ = "low resistance" q-axis amortisseur winding self inductance

L_{kkq2} = $L_{aq} + L_{kq2}$ = "high resistance" q-axis amortisseur winding self inductance

4.6.5　Time Constants

Refer to Figure 4.16 for the d and q axes circuits

$$T_{d0}' = \frac{L_{ffd}}{r_{fd}}$$

= d-axis field open circuit time constant

$$T_d' = \frac{1}{r_{fd}}\left(L_{fd} + \frac{L_\xi L_{ad}}{L_{ad} + L_\ell} \right)$$

= d-axis transient short circuit time constant

$$T_{d0}'' \approx \frac{1}{r_{kd}}\left(L_{kd} + \frac{L_f L_{ad}}{L_{ad} + L_{fd}} \right)$$

= d-axis subtransient open circuit time constant

$$T_d'' \approx \frac{1}{kd}\left(L_{kd} + \cfrac{1}{\cfrac{1}{L_{ad}} + \cfrac{1}{L} + \cfrac{1}{L_{fd}}} \right)$$

= d-axis subtransient open circuit time constant

$$T_{q0}'' = \frac{1}{r_{kq}}\left(L_{kq} + L_{aq} \right)$$

= q-axis subtransient open circuit time constant

$$T_q'' = \frac{1}{r_{kq}}\left(L_{kq} + \frac{L_{aq} L_\ell}{L_{aq} + L_\ell} \right)$$

= q-axis subtransient open circuit time constant

$$T_{kd} = \frac{L_{kd}}{r_{kq}}$$

= d-axis amortisseur leakage time constant

In the case of solid rotor machines, the q-axis is represented by a second order circuit analogous in form to that of the d-axis in Figure 4.16. For this representation the q-axis time constants are defined as:

$$T'_{q0} = \frac{L_{kkq1}}{r_{kq1}}$$

= q-axis transient open circuit time constant

$$T'_q = \frac{1}{r_{kq1}}\left[L_{kq1} + \frac{L_\ell L_{aq}}{L_{aq} + L_\ell}\right]$$

= q-axis transient short circuit time constant

$$T''_{q0} = \frac{1}{r_{kq2}}\left(L_{kq2} + \frac{L_{kq1}L_{aq}}{L_{aq} + L_{kq1}}\right)$$

= q-axis subtransient open circuit time constant

$$T''_q = \frac{1}{r_{kq2}}\left(L_{kq2} + \frac{1}{\dfrac{1}{L_{aq}} + \dfrac{1}{L_{kq1}} + \dfrac{1}{L_\ell}}\right)$$

= q-axis subtransient short circuit time constant

Note that all time constants are in per unit of the time base which is $1/\omega_0$ seconds

(1/377 seconds for 60 Hz systems). That is, T in seconds = $\dfrac{T\ p.u.}{\omega_0}$.

4.6.6   Derived Inductances

For the equivalent circuits in Figure 4.16, derived inductance parameters are defined as:

$$L_d = L_{ad} + L_\ell$$

= d-axis synchronous inductance

$$T'_d = L_d\frac{T'_d}{T'_{d0}} \approx L_\ell + \frac{L_{ad}L_{fd}}{L_{ad} + L_{fd}}$$

= d-axis transient inductance

$$L''_d = L_d\frac{T'_d T''_d}{T'_{d0} T''_{d0}} \approx L_\ell + \frac{1}{\dfrac{1}{L_{ad}} + \dfrac{1}{L_{kd}} + \dfrac{1}{L_{fd}}}$$

= d-axis subtransient inductance

$$L_q = L_{aq} + L_\ell$$

= q-axis synchronous inductance

$$L'_q = L_q\frac{T'_q}{T'_{q0}} = L_\ell + \frac{L_{aq}L_{kq}}{L_{aq} + L_{kq}}$$

= q-axis subtransient inductance

For the q-axis represented by two amortisseurs, similar to the d-axis, the three derived inductance parameters are:

$$L_q = L_{aq} + L_\ell \qquad\qquad\qquad = q\text{-axis synchronous inductance}$$

$$L'_q = L_q \frac{T'_q}{T'_{q0}} = L_\ell + \frac{L_{aq}L_{kq1}}{L_{aq} + L_{kq1}} \qquad = q\text{-axis transient inductance}$$

$$L''_q = L_q \frac{T'_q T''_q}{T'_{q0} T''_{q0}} = L_\ell + \frac{1}{\dfrac{1}{L_{aq}} + \dfrac{1}{L_{kq1}} + \dfrac{1}{L_{kq2}}} \qquad = q\text{-axis subtransient inductance}$$

4.6.7   Short Circuits

An analysis of the properties of the operational inductances $L_d(s)$ and $L_q(s)$ in Figures 4.19, as shown in Figures 4.21, 4.22 and 4.23 give a good basis to the understanding of machine behavior under abrupt changes such as are due to short circuits or switching of loads. The responses of ψ_d to step changes in i_d were illustrated in Figure 4.22 for a machine represented by field effects only and in Figure 4.23 by the joint effects of field and amortisseur.

Take the case of a suddenly applied short circuit starting from a specified initial loading condition. In order to solve for the new currents that will flow following the instant of application of the short circuits, the Laplace transformed equations must take into account initial conditions. One way of taking initial conditions into account is to define the variables in terms of their changes from initial values, i.e.:

$$\psi_d = \psi_{d0} + \Delta\psi_d$$

or

$$\psi_d(s) = \frac{\psi_{d0}}{s} + \Delta\psi_d(s) \qquad\qquad\qquad (IV.198)$$

$$i_d = i_{d0} + \Delta i_d$$

or

$$i_d(s) = \frac{i_{d0}}{s} \Delta i_d(s) \qquad\qquad\qquad (IV.199)$$

and likewise for all variables.

Equations (IV.162) and (IV.163) relate changes of flux linkages to changes in excitation and changes in currents.

$$\Delta\psi_d(s) = G(s)\,\Delta e_{fd}(s) - L_d(s)\,\Delta i_d(s) \tag{IV.162}$$

$$\Delta\psi_q(s) = -L_q(s)\,\Delta i_q(s) \tag{IV.163}$$

In addition to equations (IV.162) and (IV.163) we have stator voltage equations which must be put into total rather than incremental form. They are then equated to zero to specify the short circuit condition ($e_d = e_q = 0$).

$$s\psi_d(s) - \psi_d(0) - \psi_q(s)\,\omega - ri_d(s) = 0 \tag{IV.200}$$
$$s\psi_q(s) - \psi_q(0) - \psi_d(s)\,\omega - ri_q(s) = 0 \tag{IV.201}$$

In terms of the incremental variables such as in equations (IV.198) and (IV.199), (IV.200) and (IV.201) become:

$$s\Delta\psi_d(s) - \frac{\psi_{q0}}{s}\omega - \Delta\psi_q(s)\,\omega - r\frac{i_{d0}}{s} - r\Delta i_d(s) = 0$$

or

$$s\Delta\psi_d(s) - \Delta\psi_q(s)\,\omega - r\Delta i_d(s) = \frac{1}{s}\,(\psi_{q0}\omega + ri_{d0}) \tag{IV.202}$$

$$s\Delta\psi_q(s) + \Delta\psi_d(s)\,\omega - r\Delta i_q(s) = \frac{1}{s}\,(-\psi_{d0}\omega + ri_{q0}) \tag{IV.203}$$

Note that the right hand side of equations (IV.202) and (IV.203) can also be expressed $-\dfrac{e_{d0}}{s}$ and $-\dfrac{e_{q0}}{s}$ respectively.

Substituting equations (IV.162) and (IV.163) in (IV.202) and (IV.203) and solving for $\Delta i_d(s)$ and $\Delta i_d(s)$:

$$\Delta i_d(s) = \frac{\left[\dfrac{e_{d0}}{s} + sG(s)\Delta e_{fd}\right]\left[r + sL_q(s)\right] + \left[\dfrac{e_{q0}}{s} + G(s)\Delta e_{fd}\omega\right]L_q(s)\omega}{\left[r + sL_d(s)\right]\left[r + sL_q(s)\right] + L_q(s)L_d(s)\omega^2} \tag{IV.204}$$

$$\Delta i_q(s) = \frac{\left[\omega rG(s)\Delta e_{fd}(s) + \dfrac{e_{q0}}{s}r + sL_d(s) - \dfrac{e_{d0}}{s}L_d(s)\omega\right]}{\left[r + sL_d(s)\right]\left[r + sL_q(s)\right] + L_q(s)L_d(s)\omega^2}$$

$$\tag{IV.205}$$

where $G(s)$, $L_d(s)$ and $L_q(s)$ are operational expressions derived from the equivalent circuit representations.

In analyzing the meaning of expressions (IV.204) and (IV.205) we can expand these with the operational expressions for $L_d(s)$ and $L_q(s)$ and take the inverse Laplace transform of the resulting high order expression. (With $L_d(s)$ a second order expression and $L_q(s)$ a first order expression, the characteristic equation in (IV.204) and (IV.205) becomes a fifth order polynomial in s).

Rather than go through the immense amount of algebra, we will illustrate the fundamental effects with some simplifications and give the detailed expressions for the short circuit current as derived in Reference 1.

Let the three-phase short circuit be applied to the machine terminals at time $t = 0$. And let the phase of the d-axis relative to the center of phase "a" be θ_0 at $t = 0$.

The phase currents following the application of the short circuit are shown on Figure 4.24.

Inspection of Figure 4.24 reveals that the currents have a d.c. component superposed on an a.c. component. The d.c. component in each phase arises from the fact the armature flux linkages cannot change instantly hence the armature current in each phase must start from its initial value (which could be zero in the case of an open circuited machine).

The envelopes of the a.c. components can be seen to decay as function of time. This is due to the decay of flux in the rotor circuits according to the rotor time constants.

Let us first develop the initial value of the a.c. components and associated d.c. components of current. In order to simplify matters, we can forego for the moment the effects of flux decay in the rotor, by assuming zero resistances in the rotor (infinite time constants).

Under this assumption of rotor circuits resistances equal to zero, the expressions (IV.190) and (IV.197) for $L_d(s)$ and $L_q(s)$ become:

$$L_d(s) = L_d''$$ (IV.206)

$$L_q(s) = L_q''$$ (IV.207)

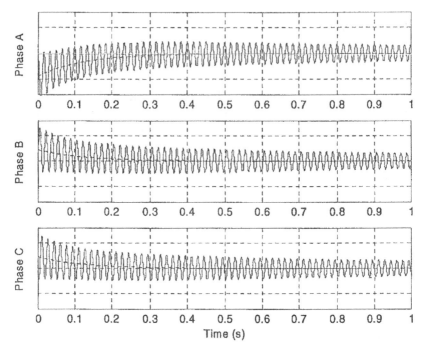

Figure 4.24 – Phase Currents following a Short-Circuit at Machine Terminals

Substituting equations (IV.206) and (IV.207) in (IV.204) and (IV.205), and holding the excitation constant ($\Delta e_{fd} = 0$),

$$\Delta i_d(s) = \frac{e_{qo} L_q'' \omega + e_{do}\left(r + sL_q''\right)}{s\left[\left(r^2 + L_q'' L_d'' \omega^2\right) + sr\left(L_d'' + L_q''\right) + s^2 L_d'' L_q''\right]} \qquad \text{(IV.208)}$$

$$\Delta i_q(s) = \frac{e_{qo}\left(r + sL_d''\right) - e_{do} L_d''}{s\left[\left(r^2 + L_q'' L_d''^{\,2}\right) + sr\left(L_d'' + L_q''\right) + s^2 L_d'' L_q''\right]} \qquad \text{(IV.209)}$$

Note that in all these expressions, with the choice of $\omega = 1.0$, it can be dropped from the expressions. We prefer to keep "ω" in the expressions for the sake of dimensional clarity and to help conversion to other time bases than $t_{base} = \dfrac{1}{\omega_0}$.

The denominator of equations (IV.208) and (IV.209) can be expressed as

$$s\, L_d'' L_q'' \left[s^2 + s \frac{r\left(L_d'' + L_q''\right)}{L_d'' L_q''} + \left(\omega^2 + \frac{r^2}{L_d'' L_q''} \right) \right] \qquad \text{(IV.210)}$$

and equation (IV.210) can be written using the classical form for a second order term

$$s L_d'' L_q'' \left[s^2 + 2\xi \omega_1 s + \omega_1^2 \right] \qquad \text{(IV.211)}$$

where

$$\xi = \frac{r\left(L_d'' + L_q''\right)}{2\left(L_d'' L_q''\right)\omega_1} \quad \text{and} \quad \omega_1^2 + \frac{r^2}{L_d'' L_q''}$$

The quadratic factor in equation (IV.211) is the characteristic equation of a damped sinusoid with frequency of "ω_1". Note that in the per unit system for

which these equations are written, the time base is often chosen as $\dfrac{1}{\omega_0}$ seconds, hence a frequency of $\omega_1 = 1.0$ p.u. is equal to ω_0 rd/s.

The inverse Laplace transform for equations (IV.208) and (IV.209) are:

$$\Delta i_d(t) = A + B e^{-\xi \omega_1 t} \sin\left(\sqrt{1-\xi^2}\, \omega_1 t + \gamma_d \right) \qquad \text{(IV.212)}$$

$$\Delta i_q(t) = C + D e^{-\xi \omega_1 t} \sin\left(\sqrt{1-\xi^2}\, \omega_1 t + \gamma_q \right) \qquad \text{(IV.213)}$$

where

$$A = \frac{e_{q0}\omega L_q'' + e_{d0}r}{r^2 + L_q'' L_d'' \omega^2} \tag{IV.214}$$

$$B = \left| \frac{e_{q0}\omega L_q'' + e_{d0}r + e_{d0}\left(-\xi + j\sqrt{1-\xi^2}\right)L_q''\omega}{\sqrt{1-\xi^2}\, L_d'' L_q'' \omega^2 \left(-\xi + j\sqrt{1-\xi^2}\right)} \right| \tag{IV.215}$$

$$\gamma_d = \tan^{-1}\frac{e_{d0}\left(\sqrt{1-\xi^2}\right)L_q''\omega}{e_{q0}\omega L_q'' + e_{d0}\left(r - \xi L_q''\omega\right)} \tan^{-1}\frac{\sqrt{1-\xi^2}}{-\xi} \tag{IV.216}$$

$$C = \frac{e_{q0}r - e_{d0}L_d'\omega}{r^2 + L_q'' L_d'' \omega^2} \tag{IV.217}$$

$$D = \left| \frac{e_{q0}r - e_{d0}L_d''\omega + e_{q0}L_d''\omega\left(-\xi + j\sqrt{1-\xi^2}\right)}{\sqrt{1-\xi^2}\, L_d'' L_q'' \omega^2 \left(-\xi + j\sqrt{1-\xi^2}\right)} \right| \tag{IV.218}$$

$$\gamma_q = \tan^{-1}\frac{e_{q0}L_d''\omega\sqrt{1-\xi^2}}{e_{q0}\left(r - \xi L_d''\omega\right) - e_{d0}L_d''\omega} \tan^{-1}\frac{\sqrt{1-\xi^2}}{-\xi} \tag{IV.219}$$

For $r = 0$

$$\begin{aligned}
\Delta i_d &= \frac{e_{q0}}{\omega L_d''} + \frac{\sqrt{e_{q0}^2 + e_{d0}^2}}{\omega L_d''}\sin\left(\omega t + \tan^{-1}\frac{e_{d0}}{e_{q0}} - 90°\right) \\
&= \frac{e_0}{\omega L_d''}\left[\cos\delta - \cos(\omega t + \delta)\right]
\end{aligned} \tag{IV.220}$$

$$\begin{aligned}
\Delta i_q &= -\frac{e_{d0}}{\omega L_q''} + \frac{\sqrt{e_{q0}^2 + e_{d0}^2}}{\omega L_q''}\sin\left(\omega t + \tan^{-1}\frac{e_{q0}}{-e_{d0}} - 90°\right) \\
&= -\frac{e_0}{\omega L_q''}\left[\sin\delta - \sin(\omega t + \delta)\right]
\end{aligned} \tag{IV.221}$$

where $\delta = \tan^{-1} \dfrac{e_{d0}}{e_{q0}}$ and $e_0 = \sqrt{e_{d0}^2 + e_{q0}^2}$

From equations (IV.220) and (IV.221) we see that Δi_d and Δi_q are each made up of a constant term and a sinusoidal term of fundamental frequency. The actual phase currents of Δi_a, Δi_b, Δi_c can be obtained by using the inverse transformation equations (IV.34).

$$\Delta i_a = \Delta i_d \cos(\omega t + \theta_0) - \Delta i_q \sin(\omega t + \theta_0) =$$

$$= \frac{e_0}{\omega L_d''}\left\{\left[\cos\delta - \cos(??? \right.\right. \tag{IV.222}$$

$$\frac{e_0}{\omega L_q''}\left\{\left[\sin\delta - \sin(\omega t + \delta)\right]\sin(\omega t + \theta_0)\right\}$$

By means of trigonometric identities, equation (IV.222) is reduced to

$$\Delta i_a = \frac{e_0}{2}\left[\frac{1}{X_d''} + \frac{1}{X_q''}\right]\cos(\theta_0 - \delta) + \frac{e_0}{X_d''}\cos\delta\cos(\omega t + \theta_0) +$$

$$= +\frac{e_0}{X_q''}\sin\delta\sin(\omega t + \theta_0) - \frac{e_0}{2}\left[\frac{1}{X_d''} + \frac{1}{X_q''}\right]\cos(2\omega t + \delta + \theta_0) \tag{IV.223}$$

Note that this is the change in current in phase "a". It was derived by assuming no resistance loss in armature or rotor. It is made up of a d.c. component (first term), a fundamental frequency component (2nd and 3rd terms) and a small double frequency component due to subtransient saliency (fourth term). Note that the d.c. component is of magnitude such that $\Delta i_a = 0$ at $t = 0$. This component arises

because of the terms $\dfrac{d\psi}{dt}$ in the stator voltage equations (IV.118).

The assumption of zero rotor resistance yields infinite rotor circuit time constants which means that the subtransient flux linkages are sustained indefinitely. When the effect of rotor resistances is included the a.c. components of phase current (d.c. components of d and q currents) will decay with the basic rotor short circuit time constants as shown in Figure 4.24.

The assumption of zero armature resistance yields a non-decaying d.c. offset component of phase current (undamped fundamental frequency component of d and q currents). When armature resistance r is included the fundamental frequency component of Δi_d and Δi_q, in equations (IV.220) and (IV.221), is damped by the term $e^{-\zeta t}$ where

$$\zeta \square \frac{r\left(L_d'' + L_q''\right)}{2 \quad L_d'' L_q''}$$

and $\dfrac{1}{\zeta}$ is known as the armature time constant.

Note that in expression (IV.223), θ_0 is the angle of the d-axis relative to the center of phase "a" at $t = 0$. The angle θ_0 merely determines the instant of time at which the short circuit is applied. The angle $\delta = \tan^{-1}\dfrac{e_{d0}}{e_{q0}}$ is a function of the initial load on the machine.

At no load $\delta = 0$ and equation (IV.223) reduces to

$$\Delta i_a = -\left(\frac{1}{X_d''} + \frac{1}{X_q''}\right)\frac{e_0}{2}\cos\theta_0 + \frac{e_0}{X_d''}\cos(\omega t + \theta_0) - \left(\frac{1}{X_d''} + \frac{1}{X_q''}\right)\frac{e_0}{2}\cos(2\omega t + \theta_0) \quad \text{(IV.224)}$$

Similar expressions apply to Δi_b and Δi_c by replacing θ_0 with $(\theta_0 - 2\pi/3)$ and $(\theta_0 + 2\pi/3)$ respectively.

Note that the fundamental frequency component of Δi_a, for this case of no initial load on the machine, is a function of X_d'' only. A study of the procedure of establishing the vector diagram on Figure 4.13 reveals that there will be no q-axis flux in the case of an unloaded machine, hence the results of equation (IV.224) are not surprising.

In the case of a heavily loaded machine, approaching the stability limit, δ will approach 90° in which case expression (IV.224) becomes

$$\Delta i_a = -\left(\frac{1}{X_d''} + \frac{1}{X_q''}\right)\frac{e_0}{2}\sin\theta_0 + \frac{e_0}{X_q''}\sin\left(\omega t + \theta_0\right) + \left(\frac{1}{X_d''} - \frac{1}{X_q''}\right)\frac{e_0}{2}\sin\left(2\omega t + \theta_0\right) \quad \text{(IV.225)}$$

In equation (IV.225), the fundamental frequency component of Δi_a is now a function of X_q'' for the basic reason that under these conditions the machine flux lies on the q-axis.

4.6.8 Initial Symmetrical Fault Currents-3ϕ Short Circuit

In expressions (IV.220) and (IV.221) we derived the expressions for the initial changes in currents Δi_d and Δi_q.

Likewise expression (IV.223) is for the initial changes in phase current Δi_a. Inspection of (IV.220), (IV.221) and (IV.223) shows clearly that the d.c. components in Δi_d and Δi_q, which are $e_0/X_d''\cos\delta$ and $e_0/X_q''\sin\delta$ respectively, translate directly into the fundamental frequency of components of Δi_a, which are $e_0 / X_d''\cos\delta$ $\cos(\psi t + \theta_0)$ and $e_0\ X_q''\sin\delta\sin(\omega t + \theta_0)$. The change in fundamental frequency component of phase current Δi_a can also be expressed in terms of phasors as

$$\Delta\hat{i}_a = \left[\frac{e_0}{X_d''}\cos\delta - j\frac{e_0\sin\delta}{X_q''}\right]e^{j(\omega t + \theta_0)} \quad \text{(IV.226)}$$

where $\theta_0 =$ the phase angle between the d-axis and the center of phase "a" winding.

If we should pick the reference axis as the d-axis, equation (IV.226) can also be expressed as

$$\Delta\hat{i}_a = \Delta\hat{i}_d + \Delta\hat{i}_q \quad \text{(IV.227)}$$

where

$$\Delta\hat{i}_d = \frac{je_{q0}}{jX_d''} \quad \text{(IV.228)}$$

$$\Delta\hat{i}_q = \frac{e_{d0}}{jX_q''} = -j\frac{e_{d0}}{X_q''} \quad \text{(IV.229)}$$

In order to obtain the total currents i_d and i_q, we must add the initial values of i_{d0} and i_{q0}.

Defining voltages behind subtransient reactance e_{d0}'' and e_{q0}'' as

$$\hat{e}_{d0}'' = e_{d0}'' = e_{d0} + \hat{i}_{q0} \; jX_q'' = e_{d0} + ji_{q0} \; jX_q'' = e_{d0} - i_{q0}X_q'' \qquad \text{(IV.230)}$$

$$\hat{e}_{q0}'' = je_{q0}'' = je_{q0} + i_{d0} \; jX_d'' = j\left(e_{q0} + i_{d0}X_d''\right) \qquad \text{(IV.231)}$$

From equations (IV.230) and (IV.231)

$$\hat{i}_{d0} = i_{d0} = \frac{j\left(e_{q0}'' - e_{q0}\right)}{jX_d''} \qquad \text{(IV.232)}$$

$$i_{q0} = \frac{e_{d0} - e_{d0}''}{X_q''} \qquad \text{(IV.233)}$$

Combining equations (IV.232) and (IV.228), and (IV.233) and (IV.229) to obtain the total currents,

$$\hat{i}_d = \hat{i}_{d0} + \Delta\hat{i}_d = \frac{j\left(e_{q0}''\right)}{jX_d''} = \frac{e_{q0}''}{X_d''} \qquad \text{(IV.234)}$$

$$\hat{i}_q = \hat{i}_{q0} + \Delta\hat{i}_q = -j\frac{e_{d0}''}{X_q''} \qquad \text{(IV.235)}$$

These expressions can be visualized in terms of the vector diagrams of Figure 4.25.

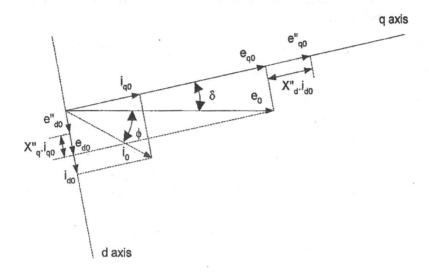

(a) Steady-State and Initial Conditions

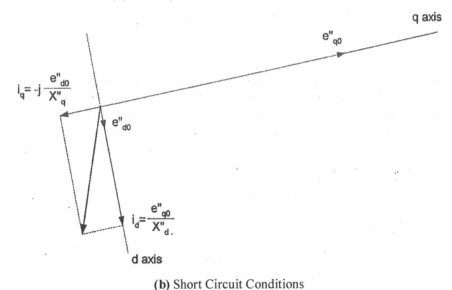

(b) Short Circuit Conditions

Figure 4.25 – Initial Symmetrical Fault Currents

Figure 4.25(a) is the steady state vector diagram to establish initial conditions. It is drawn following the procedures described in connection with the vector diagram of Figure 4.13. Included in this vector diagram is the formation of the "voltages behind subtransient reactance", e_{d0}'' and e_{q0}'' as defined in equations (IV.230) and (IV.231).

These voltages correspond to voltages generated by subtransient flux linkages.

The diagram on Figure 4.25(b) shows the derivation of the short circuit currents. Basically the machine is represented by sources in the d and q axes equal to e_{d0}'' and e_{q0}''. The machine reactance is represented by X_d'' and X_q'' in the d and q axes respectively.

Since X_d'' is nearly equal to X_q'', neglecting subtransient saliency is often justified and the procedure becomes one of establishing an equivalent voltage behind subtransient reactance.

$$\hat{e}_0'' = \hat{e}_0 + jX''\hat{i}_0$$

The short circuit current, neglecting the effect of stator resistance, is then simply

$$\hat{i} = \frac{\hat{e}_0''}{jX''}$$

The derivations of expressions for short circuit currents started from the basic machine stator voltage equations (IV.202) and (IV.203), from which the components of short circuit phase current were established: a d.c. component decaying with an armature time constant, a fundamental a.c. component and a small double frequency component due to subtransient saliency. (equations (IV.222) and (IV.223)).

It will now be shown that the a.c. components of phase currents can be derived from the basic equations by neglecting the $d\psi/dt$ terms in the stator voltage equations.

As mentioned before, these terms give rise to the d.c. components of phase current which, when superposed on the a.c. components, ensure that there is no instantaneous change in current from the initial value to the new value as dictated by the symmetrical a.c. components. Writing the stator voltage equations neglecting the $d\psi/dt$ terms, and expressing these in terms of incremental variables as in equations (IV.202) and (IV.203)

$$-\frac{\psi_{q0}}{s}\omega - \Delta\psi_q(s)\omega - r\frac{i_{d0}}{s} - r\Delta i_d(s) = 0 \qquad \text{(IV.236)}$$

$$+\frac{\psi_{d0}}{s}\omega + \Delta\psi_d(s)\omega - r\frac{i_{q0}}{s} - r\Delta i_q(s) = 0 \qquad \text{(IV.237)}$$

Equations (IV.236) and (IV.237) can be expressed as

$$-\Delta\psi_q(s)\omega - r\Delta i_d(s) = \frac{1}{s}(\psi_{q0}\omega + ri_{d0}) = -\frac{e_{d0}}{s} \qquad \text{(IV.238)}$$

$$+\Delta\psi_d(s)\omega - r\Delta i_q(s) = \frac{1}{s}(-\psi_{d0}\omega + ri_{q0}) = -\frac{e_{q0}}{s} \qquad \text{(IV.239)}$$

Substituting $\Delta\psi_d$ and $\Delta\psi_q$ in terms of Δi_d and Δi_q as in equations (IV.162), (IV.163) (with $\Delta e_{fd} = 0$), equations (IV.238) and (IV.239) become

$$\Delta i_q(s) = L_q(s)\omega - r\Delta i_d(s) = \frac{e_{d0}}{s} \qquad \text{(IV.240)}$$

$$-r\Delta i_q(s) - \omega L_d(s)\Delta i_d(s) = -\frac{e_{q0}}{s} \qquad \text{(IV.241)}$$

Solving for Δi_q and Δi_d from equations (IV.240) and (IV.241)

$$\Delta i_d(s) = \frac{\dfrac{e_{q0}}{s} - \omega L_q(s) + r\dfrac{e_{d0}}{s}}{\omega^2 L_q(s)L_d(s) + r^2} \qquad \text{(IV.242)}$$

$$\Delta i_q(s) = \frac{-\dfrac{e_{d0}}{s}\omega L_d(s) + r\dfrac{e_{q0}}{s}}{\omega^2 L_q(s)L_d(s) + r^2} \qquad \text{(IV.243)}$$

Again making the assumption of $r = 0$ and substituting for $L_q(s)$ and $L_d(s)$ by their subtransient values L_q'' and L_d'', equations (IV.242) and (IV.243) become

$$\Delta i_d(s) = \frac{e_{q0}}{sX_d''} \tag{IV.244}$$

$$\Delta i_q(s) = -\frac{e_{d0}}{sX_q''} \tag{IV.245}$$

which are the same results as obtained previously.

The changes in phase current Δi_a are obtained by applying the inverse d-q transformation to the d-q current change components $\Delta i_d = \dfrac{e_{q0}}{X_d''} = \dfrac{e_0 \cos\delta}{X_d''}$ and $\Delta i_q = \dfrac{e_{d0}}{X_q''} = \dfrac{e_0 \sin\delta}{X_q''}$, i.e.;

$$\Delta i_a = \frac{e_0 \cos\delta}{X_d''}\cos(t+\theta_0) + \frac{e_0 \sin\delta}{X_q''}\sin(t+\theta_0) \tag{IV.246}$$

which is equivalent to the expression (IV.224).

Note that the small double frequency component due to subtransient saliency in equation (IV.223) does not appear in equation (IV.246). Hence dropping out the $d\psi/dt$ terms in the basic equations eliminates both the d.c. offset component as well as the small second harmonic component (which is produced by the d.c. offset component reacting on saliency).

In calculating short circuit currents it is sufficient to derive the symmetrical fundamental frequency component. The d.c. components can be derived by merely noting the instantaneous change in each phase current at the instant of the short circuit. The amount of the d.c. offset in each phase will be equal to and negative in sign to this instantaneous change.

4.6.9   Rotor Short Circuit Time Constants

In the previous treatment the operational inductance terms $L_d(s)$ and $L_q(s)$ were taken as their initial values L_d'' and L_q'', in order to derive the initial value of short circuit current. We shall now explore the effects of rotor fluxes becoming demagnetized as a function of time. The effect can be viewed as being due to a transient change in the apparent machine inductances as originally described in Figure 4.23. We saw that the effect of neglecting the $d\psi/dt$ terms in the armature voltage equations was to lose the d.c. offset component of current in the solution, without affecting the fundamental frequency component. Continuing to use this simplification, and further, to make the algebra more straight forward, assuming that $r = 0$, expressions (IV.242) and (IV.243) become

$$\Delta i_d (s) = \frac{e_{q0}}{s\omega L_d (s)} = \frac{e_{q0}}{sX_d (s)} \tag{IV.247}$$

$$\Delta i_q (s) = \frac{-e_{d0}}{s\omega L_q (s)} \tag{IV.248}$$

For $L_d(s)$ and $L_q(s)$ we may substitute the operational expressions previously derived, which, when multiplied by ω can also be expressed as

$$X_d (s) = \frac{X_d \left(1 + T_d's\right)\left(1 + T_d''s\right)}{\left(1 + T_{d0}'s\right)\left(1 + T_{d0}''s\right)} \tag{IV.249}$$

$$X_q (s) = X_q \frac{\left(1 + sT_q'\right)}{\left(1 + sT_{q0}'\right)} \tag{IV.250}$$

Substituting equations (IV.249) in (IV.247) and (IV.250) in (IV.248)

$$\Delta i_d (s) = \frac{e_{q0} \left(1 + sT_{d0}'\right)\left(1 + T_{d0}''s\right)}{sX_d \left(1 + T_d's\right)\left(1 + T_d''s\right)} \tag{IV.251}$$

$$\Delta i_q (s) = \frac{-e_{d0} \left(1 + sT_{q0}'\right)}{sX_q \left(1 + T_q's\right)} \tag{IV.252}$$

Expanding equations (IV.251) and (IV.252) by partial fractions and taking the inverse Laplace transform

$$\Delta i_d (t) = \frac{e_{q0}}{X_d} + \frac{e_{q0}\left(\dfrac{T_{d0}'}{T_d'} - 1\right)\left(1 - \dfrac{T_{d0}''}{T_d'}\right)}{X_d\left(\dfrac{1}{T_d''} - \dfrac{1}{T_d'}\right)T_d''} e^{-\frac{1}{T_d'}} + \frac{e_{q0}\left(1 - \dfrac{T_{d0}'}{T_d'}\right)\left(1 - \dfrac{T_{d0}''}{T_d'}\right)}{X_d\left(\dfrac{1}{T_d''} - \dfrac{1}{T_d'}\right)T_d'} e^{-\frac{t}{T_d''}} \tag{IV.253}$$

$$\Delta i_q(t) = -\frac{e_{d0}}{X_q} - \frac{e_{d0}}{X_q} \frac{\left(T'_{q0} - T'_q\right)}{T'_q} e^{-\frac{t}{T'_q}}$$

(IV.254)

Expressions (IV.253) and (IV.254) can be viewed as the direct and quadrature components of the fundamental frequency phase currents as derived in equation (IV.226).

Looking at $\Delta i_d(t)$ first, we note that it is made up of a constant term e_{q0}/X_d known as the steady state component and two exponentially decaying terms, decaying with the transient short circuit and subtransient short circuit time constant T'_d and T''_d respectively. These time constants had been mentioned before in the derivation of $L_q(s)$ and $L_d(s)$ in (IV.190) and (IV.197).

An interesting point is that these short circuit time constants are related to the open circuit time constants by:

$$T'_d = \frac{X'_d}{X_d} T'_{d0}$$

(IV.255)

$$T''_d = \frac{X''_d}{X'_d} T''_{d0}$$

(IV.256)

$$T'_q = \frac{X'_q}{X_q} T'_{q0}$$

(IV.257)

Making approximations in equation (IV.253) based on the fact that T''_d and T''_{d0} are small compared with T'_d we may express

$$\Delta i_d = \frac{e_{q0}}{X_d} + e_{q0}\left(\frac{1}{X'_d} - \frac{1}{X_d}\right) e^{-\frac{t}{T'_d}} + e_{q0}\left(\frac{1}{X''_d} - \frac{1}{X'_d}\right) e^{-\frac{t}{T''_d}}$$

(IV.258)

Figure 4.26 shows these components of Δi_a.

The subtransient current is made up of all three terms of equation (IV.258), which at $t = 0$ is seen to be

$$\Delta i_d'' = \frac{e_{q0}}{X_d''} \qquad \text{(IV.259)}$$

The transient current is made up of the first and second terms of equation (IV.258). At $t = 0$ this is seen to be

$$\Delta i_d' = \frac{e_{q0}}{X_d'} \qquad \text{(IV.260)}$$

The steady state current is given by the first term

$$\Delta i_d = \frac{e_{q0}}{X_d} \qquad \text{(IV.261)}$$

All the above are <u>changes</u> in current from the steady state initial value i_{d0}.

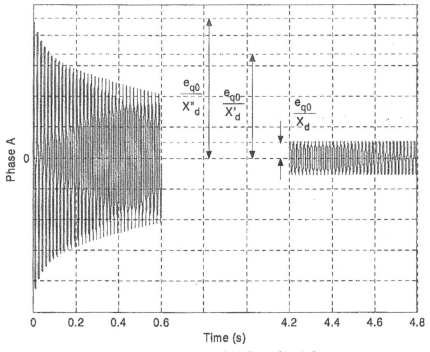

Figure 4.26 – Components of the Short-Circuit Current

By a procedure analogous to that developed in equations (IV.230) to (IV.235), where, to get the total subtransient current $\left(i_{d0}+\Delta i_d''\right)=i_d''$, we formed a voltage behind subtransient reactance $e_{q0}''=e_{q0}+i_{d0}X_d''$ and obtained $i_d''=e_{q0}''/X_d''$, we may likewise form voltages behind transient and synchronous reactances and obtain the total transient and steady state currents as:

$$i_d'=i_{d0}+\Delta i_d'=\frac{e_{q0}+i_{d0}X_d'}{X_d'}=\frac{e_{q0}'}{X_d'} \tag{IV.262}$$

$$i_d=i_{d0}+\Delta i_d=\frac{e_{q0}+e_{d0}X_d}{X_d}=\frac{E}{X_d} \tag{IV.263}$$

A similar procedure follows for the quadrature axis currents.

Figure 4.27 illustrates the construction of the vector diagram to establish the various internal voltages from initial loading conditions (Figure 4.27(a)), and to determine the subtransient, transient and steady state short circuit currents (Figure 4.27(b)).

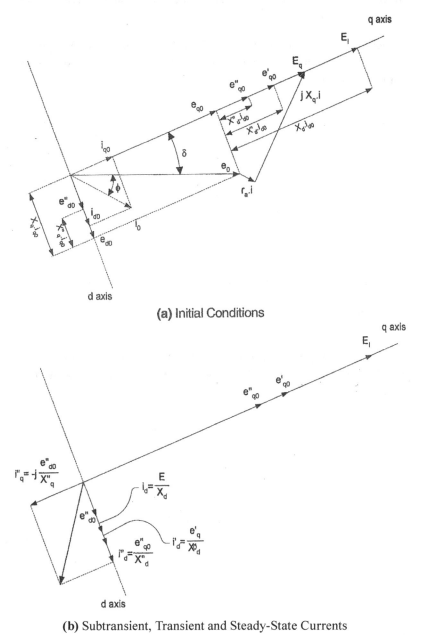

(a) Initial Conditions

(b) Subtransient, Transient and Steady-State Currents

Figure 4.27 – Vector Diagrams for Short-Circuit Calculation

4.6.10 Effect of External Impedance

The case of a 3ϕ short circuit on the terminals of the machine has been explored in the previous sections. The effect of a short circuit through external impedance will now be examined.

The inclusion of external impedance $R_E + L_E s$ can be viewed as equivalent to modifying the armature leakage inductance and armature resistance of the machine as shown in Figure 4.28.

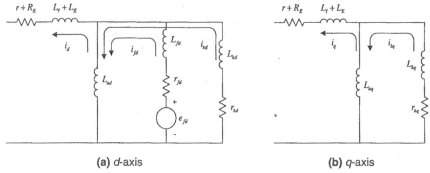

(a) d-axis   **(b) q-axis**

Figure 4.28 – Synchronous Machine Equivalent Circuit Including External Impedance

The analysis will be identical as for the case of a 3ϕ short circuit except that the operational impedances are now modified to include the external components.

Following the same procedure as in equation (IV.236) and following expressions, with the omission of armature $d\psi/dt$ terms, equations (IV.238) and (IV.239) becomes

$$-\Delta\psi_q(s)\,\omega - (r + R_E)\,\Delta i_d\,(s) = \frac{1}{s}\left[\psi_{q0}\omega + (r + R_E)i_{d0}\right]$$
$$= -\frac{1}{s}\left[e_{d0} - R_E i_{d0}\right] \tag{IV.264}$$

$$\Delta\psi_d(s)\,\omega - (r + R_E)\,\Delta i_q\,(s) = \frac{1}{s}\left[-\psi_{d0}\omega + R_E i_{d0}\right]$$
$$= -\frac{1}{s}\left[e_{q0} - R_E i_{q0}\right] \tag{IV.265}$$

Substituting $-[L_q(s) + L_E]\Delta i_q(s)$ and $-[L_d(s) + L_E]\Delta i_d(s)$ for $\Delta\psi_q(s)$ and $\Delta\psi_d(s)$, and solving for $\Delta i_d(s)$ and $\Delta i_q(s)$

$$\Delta i_d(s) = \frac{\left[e_{q0} - R_E i_{d0}\right]\omega\left[L_q(s) + L_E\right] + \left[r + R_E\right]\left[e_{d0} - R_E i_{d0}\right]}{s\left\{\omega^2\left[L_q(s) + L_E\right]\left[L_d(s) + L_E\right] + \left[r + R_E\right]^2\right\}} \qquad \text{(IV.266)}$$

$$\Delta i_q(s) = \frac{-\left[e_{d0} - R_E i_{q0}\right]\omega\left[L_d(s) + L_E\right] + \left[r + R_E\right]\left[e_{q0} - R_E i_{q0}\right]}{s\left\{\omega^2\left[L_q(s) + L_E\right]\left[L_d(s) + L_E\right] + \left[r + R_E\right]^2\right\}} \qquad \text{(IV.267)}$$

Expanding equations (IV.266) and (IV.267), finding the roots of the denominator and inverting by partial fractions leads to the time response of Δi_d and Δi_q. This is a rather tedious task and we shall illustrate the effects by analyzing some extreme cases.

First, the values of $\Delta i_d''$, $\Delta i_d'$ and Δi_d as well as the corresponding values of changes in quadrature axis current can be obtained from equations (IV.266) and (IV.267) by substituting X_d'', X_d' and X_d respectively instead of $\omega L_d(s)$ and X_q' and X_q instead of $\omega L_q(s)$.

The procedure is straight forward and the determination of the total currents follows the same technique of the previous section, viz.; of finding the initial internal machine voltages (behind subtransient, transient and synchronous reactances) and then determining the currents by having those voltages applied to a circuit composed of the appropriate machine reactances in series with the external impedance.

When this is done the total currents $i_d(s)$ and $i_q(s)$ are

$$i_d'' = \frac{e_{q0}''\left[X_q'' + X_E\right] + e_{d0}''\left[R_E + r\right]}{\left(R_E + r\right)^2 + \left[X_q'' + X_E\right]\left[X_d'' + X_E\right]} \qquad \text{(IV.268)}$$

$$i_q'' = \frac{e_{q0}''\left[R_E + r\right] - e_{d0}''\left[X_d'' + X_E\right]}{\left(R_E + r\right)^2 + \left[X_q'' + X_E\right]\left[X_d'' + X_E\right]} \qquad \text{(IV.269)}$$

And similar expressions apply with appropriate changes in internal voltages and reactances, to the transient and steady state values of currents.

Let us now look at the effect of external impedance on the rotor flux decay time constants, which, in the case of a full short circuit, were defined in equations (IV.255), (IV.256) and (IV.257).

Take first the case where the external impedance is only reactive, i.e.; $R_E = 0$ and let us also neglect r.

The denominator of equations (IV.266) and (IV.267) gives the roots from which the decay time constants are derived. Substituting the operational expressions for $L_d(s)$ and $L_q(s)$, this denominator characteristic equation becomes

$$\left[X_q\left(1+sT_q'\right)+X_E\left(1+sT_{q0}'\right)\right]\left[X_d\left(1+sT_d'\right)\left(1+sT_d''\right)+X_E\left(1+sT_{d0}'\right)\left(1+sT_{d0}''\right)\right]=$$

$$=\left[\left(X_q+X_E\right)\left(1+sT_{q0}'\frac{\left(X_E+X_q'\right)}{\left(X_E+X_q\right)}\right)\right]\left[\left(X_d+X_E\right)\left(1+sT_{d0}'\frac{\left(X_E+X_d'\right)}{\left(X_E+X_d\right)}\right)\left(1+sT_{d0}''\frac{\left(X_E+X_d''\right)}{\left(X_E+X_d'\right)}\right)\right] \quad \text{(IV.270)}$$

The time constants can be recognized as

$$T_{qz}' = T_{q0}'\frac{\left(X_E+X_q'\right)}{\left(X_E+X_q\right)} \quad \text{(IV.271)}$$

$$T_{dz}'' = T_{d0}'\frac{\left(X_E+X_d'\right)}{\left(X_E+X_d\right)} \quad \text{(IV.272)}$$

$$T_{dz}'' = T_{d0}''\frac{\left(X_E+X_d''\right)}{\left(X_E+X_d'\right)} \quad \text{(IV.273)}$$

Note that when $X_E = 0$, these time constants become equal to the short circuit time constants, and when $X_E \to \infty$ they approach the open circuit time constants. The effect of external resistance R_E on the time constants will be illustrated by taking the case where amortisseur effects are neglected, i.e.:

$$X_d(s) = X_d\frac{\left(1+sT_d'\right)}{\left(1+sT_{d0}'\right)}$$

and $X_q(s) = X_q$.

The characteristic equation of (IV.266) and (IV.267) becomes:

$$= X_q X_d \left(1 + sT_d'\right) + R_E^2 \left(1 + sT_{d0}'\right)$$

$$= \left(X_q X_d + R_E^2\right) \left[1 + s \frac{X_q X_d T_d' + T_{d0}' R_E^2}{X_q X_d + R_E^2}\right] \quad \text{(IV.274)}$$

The effective time constant is

$$T_{dz}' = \frac{T_{d0}' \left[X_q X_d' + R_E^2\right]}{X_q X_d + R_E^2} \quad \text{(IV.275)}$$

4.6.11 Field Current Transient

In the previous sections we were concerned with the effects of abrupt changes in network impedances on machine stator currents. Field voltage was considered constant. These same abrupt changes in network impedances (short circuits or impact loads) produce transient changes in field and amortisseur currents. Indeed, to maintain constant flux linkages the instant after the change, currents must be induced in the rotor circuits which cancel the demagnetizing effect of the increased armature currents.

We will examine these effects by taking first the case where the machine is represented without amortisseurs, as described in the equivalent circuit of Figure 4.18 repeated here for convenience in Figure 4.29.

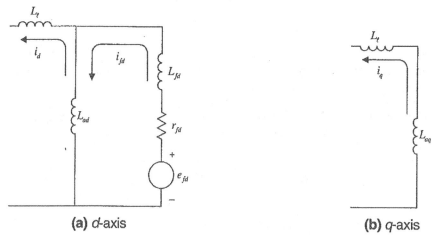

(a) d-axis   **(b)** q-axis

Figure 4.29 – Equivalent Circuit Neglecting Amortisseur Windings

The equations, as previously derived in equations (IV.172) to (IV.178), are

$$\Delta i_{fd}(s) = \frac{\Delta e_{fd}(s) + s L_{ad} \Delta i_d(s)}{r_{fd} + s L_{ffd}} \tag{IV.276}$$

or

$$\Delta i_{fd}(s) = \frac{\Delta e_{fd}(s)}{r_{fd}} \left(\frac{1}{1 + s T'_{d0}} \right) + \frac{s L_{ad}}{r_{fd} \left(1 + s T'_{d0} \right)} \Delta i_d(s) \tag{IV.277}$$

Recall that $L_{ad} i_{fd}$ was defined as E_I and $L_{ad} e_{fd}/r_{fd}$ as E_{fd}.

Equation (IV.277) can also be expressed as

$$\Delta L_{ad} i_{fd} = \Delta E_I = \Delta E_{fd} \left(\frac{1}{1 + s T'_{d0}} \right) + \frac{s L_{ad}^2}{r_{fd} \left(1 + s T'_{d0} \right)} \Delta i_d(s) \tag{IV.278}$$

Other flux linkage equations derived from equations (IV.172) to (IV.178), (IV.185) and (IV.186) are:

$$\Delta \psi_d(s) = \frac{\Delta E_{fd}}{1 + s T'_{d0}} - \frac{L_d \left(1 + \dfrac{L'_d}{L_d} T'_{d0} s \right)}{\left(1 + s T'_{d0} \right)} \Delta i_d(s) \tag{IV.279}$$

$$\Delta \psi_q(s) = -L_q \Delta i_q(s) \tag{IV.280}$$

Let us solve for the field current transient for the case of a 3ϕ short circuit at the machine terminals, starting from zero initial loading, i.e.; normal voltage, open circuit condition. ($e_{q0} = 1.0$, $e_{d0} = 0.0$).

As before, the armature voltage equations, in terms of changes, are as in equations (IV.202) and (IV.203), repeated here. Note that $d\psi/dt$ terms have been included.

$$s\Delta\psi_d(s) - \Delta\psi_q(s) \omega - r\Delta i_d = -\frac{e_{d0}}{s} = 0 \tag{IV.202}$$

$$s\Delta\psi_q(s) + \Delta\psi_d(s) \omega - r\Delta i_q = -\frac{e_{q0}}{s} \tag{IV.203}$$

Taking first the case of no change in field excitation, i.e.; $\Delta E_{fd} = 0$, substituting equations (IV.279) and (IV.280) in (IV.202) and (IV.203) and solving for Δi_d, we obtain:

$$\Delta i_d = \frac{e_{q0} L_q(s)}{s\left\{\left[r + sL_d(s)\right]\left[r + sL_q(s)\right] + \omega^2 L_d(s) L_q(s)\right\}} \tag{IV.281}$$

where $L_q(s) = L_q$ and

$$L_d(s) = \frac{L_d\left(1 + s\dfrac{L'_d}{L_d} T'_{d0}\right)}{\left(1 + sT'_{d0}\right)} \tag{IV.282}$$

Making the assumption $r = 0$ (recall that r controls the rate of decay of the armature d.c. offset component).

$$\Delta i_d(s) = \frac{e_{q0}}{sL_d(s)\left(s^2 + \omega^2\right)} = \frac{e_{q0}\left(1 + sT'_{d0}\right)}{sL_d\left(1 + s\dfrac{L'_d}{L_d} T'_{d0}\right)\left(s^2 + \omega^2\right)} \tag{IV.283}$$

Substituting equation (IV.283) in (IV.278) and assuming $\Delta E_{fd} = 0$

$$\Delta E_1(s) = \Delta L_{ad} i_{fd}(s) = \frac{L_{ad}^2}{r_{fd}} \frac{e_{q0}}{L_d T'_d\left(s + \dfrac{1}{T'_d}\right)\left(s^2 + \omega^2\right)} \tag{IV.284}$$

Using relations:

$$\frac{L_{ad}^2}{L_{ad} + L_f} = X_d - X'_d$$

$$T'_d = \frac{X'_d}{X_d} T'_{d0}$$

$$T'_{d0} = \frac{L_{ad} + L_f}{r_{fd}}$$

Equation (IV.284) can be expressed as

$$\Delta E_I(s) = \frac{e_{q0}\left(X_d - X'_d\right)}{X'_d\left(s + \dfrac{1}{T'_d}\right)\left(s^2 + \omega^2\right)} \tag{IV.285}$$

The inverse Laplace transform of equation (IV.285) is

$$\Delta E_I(t) = \frac{e_{q0}\left(X_d - X'_d\right)}{X'_d}\left[e_{q0}^{-\frac{t}{T'_d}} - \cos\omega t\right] \tag{IV.286}$$

Remembering that $E_{I0} = L_{ad}i_{fd0} = e_{q0}$, the total field current can be established as $E_{I0} + \Delta E_I$ and is illustrated in Figure 4.30 along with Δi_d.

Note that the change in field current is made up of two components. An abrupt d.c. component which decays exponentially with the field short circuit time constant T'_d, and a fundamental frequency component which is due to the fundamental frequency component of i_d or the d.c. offset component of phase currents. The assumption of armature resistance $r = 0$ leads to having no attenuation to the fundamental frequency component. Recall that the fundamental frequency component of i_d or d.c. offset component of phase currents, actually decays with the armature time constant which is finite for $r > 0$.

The above analysis could be extended to the case where amortisseur effects are included. Transient amortisseur currents would flow much like the transients in the field current. They would of course, decay to zero since amortisseur currents are zero in the steady state.

Ignoring the fundamental frequency component of field current, we note that the constant flux linkage theorem initially forces the field current to jump in order to offset the demagnetizing effect of armature current Δi_d. This is equivalent to making the machine appear to have a lower reactance, the transient reactance X'_d as we saw when dealing with the form of the short circuit currents. Since excitation was not changed, the jump in field current cannot be sustained and it decays to the original value with the characteristic short circuit time constant.

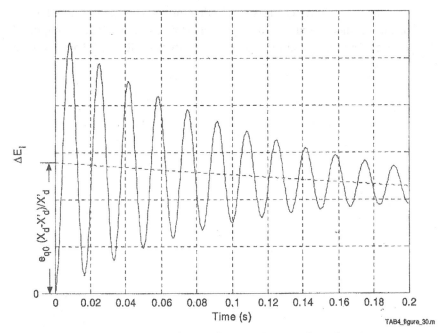

Figure 4.30 – Field Current Change after a 3ϕ Short Circuit

Likewise in the case of an abrupt loss of load wherein the initial load currents i_{d0} and i_{q0} are reduced to zero, we may use equation (IV.276), with $\Delta i_d(s) = -\dfrac{i_{d0}}{s}$ and see that for this case the field current

$$L_{ad}i_{fd}(s) = \frac{L_{ad}^2 i_{d0}}{r_{fd}\left(1 + sT_{d0}'\right)}$$

This means that the field current $L_{ad}i_{fd}$ abruptly drops by

$$\frac{L_{ad}^2 i_{d0}}{r_{fd}T_{d0}'} = \left(X_d - X_d'\right)i_{d0}$$

and gradually gets back to its original value with the time constant T_{d0}'. Since the circuit was opened, there are no d.c. offset armature currents to produce fundamental frequency currents in the rotor.

Figure 4.31 shows the field current transient for the case of load rejection.

The effect of field voltage changes can be determined by superposition. For the case of the 3ϕ short circuit, using equations (IV.204) and (IV.205) simplified for the case of $r = 0$, and taking into account only the effects of change in field voltage Δe_{fd}.

$$\Delta i_d(s)\Big|_{\text{due to } \Delta e_{fd}} = \frac{G(s)\Delta e_{fd}(s)}{L_d(s)} \qquad \text{(IV.287)}$$

$$\Delta i_q(s) = 0$$

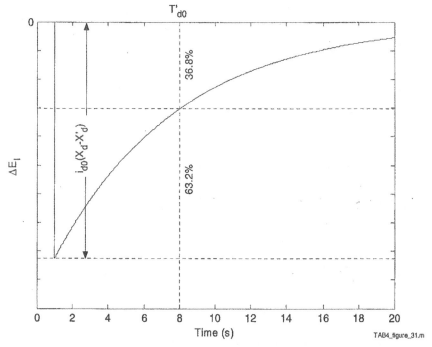

Figure 4.31 – Field Current Transient after Load Rejection

For the case of the machine without amortisseur effects, equation (IV.287) can be expressed as

$$\Delta i_d(s) = \frac{L_{ad}\Delta e_{fd}(s)}{r_{fd}\left(1+sT'_{d0}\right)L_d \dfrac{1+s\dfrac{L'_d}{L_d}T'_{d0}}{1+sT'_{d0}}} = \frac{L_{ad}\Delta e_{fd}(s)}{r_{fd}L_d\left(1+sT'_d\right)} \qquad \text{(IV.288)}$$

For a step change $\Delta e_{fd}(s) = \dfrac{\Delta e_{fd}}{s}$ and taking the inverse Laplace transform of equation (IV.288),

$$\Delta i_d(t)\Big|_{\text{due to }\Delta H_{fd}} = \frac{\Delta E_{fd}}{X_d}\left(1 - e^{-t/T_d'}\right) \qquad \text{(IV.289)}$$

where $\Delta E_{fd} = \dfrac{L_{ad}}{r_{fd}}\Delta e_{fd}$

For this case, the change in current due to the short circuit, neglecting the d.c. offset component and neglecting amortisseur effects, is derived from equation (IV.258) as

$$\Delta i_d(t)\Big|_{\text{due to short circuit}} = \frac{e_{q0}}{X_q} + e_{q0}\left(\frac{1}{X_d'} - \frac{1}{X_d}\right)e^{-\frac{t}{T_d'}} \qquad \text{(IV.290)}$$

where for the case of an initially open circuited machine with rated voltage, $e_{q0} = E_{fd0}'$.

From equations (IV.289) and (IV.290), if the effect of the change in excitation is to offset the transient demagnetization effect of the short circuit which changes the value of current from the initial e_{q0}/X_d' to e_{q0}/X_d, then

$$\frac{\Delta e_{fd}}{X_d}\left[1 - e^{-t/T_d'}\right] + \frac{e_{q0}}{X_d} + e_{q0}\left(\frac{1}{X_d'} - \frac{1}{X_d}\right)e^{-t/T_d'} = \frac{e_{q0}}{X_d'}$$

or

$$\Delta E_{fd} = E_{fd0}\left(\frac{X_d - X_d'}{X_d'}\right)$$

Figure 4.32 shows the effect of change in excitation voltage on the short circuit current. The value of ΔE_{fd} added to E_{fd0} gives the ceiling excitation. With conventional rotating exciters changes in excitation voltage ΔE_{fd} cannot occur instantaneously and this adds some lags to the response. However, with modern thyristor type excitation, nearly instantaneous changes in E_{fd} can be obtained and the effect of the voltage regulator is limited primarily by the ceiling voltage $E_{fd0} + \Delta E_{fd}$.

4.6.12 Short Circuit Torques

The expression for torque was derived in absolute units as

$$T = \frac{3}{2}\left[i_q \psi_d - i_d \psi_q\right]$$

In per unit the relation is:

$$T = \left[i_q \psi_d - i_d \psi_q\right] \tag{IV.291}$$

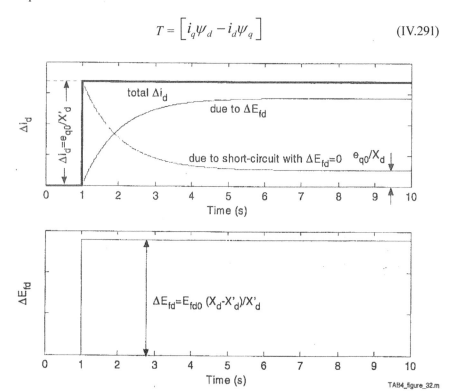

Figure 4.32 – Effect of Excitation Voltage on the Short Circuit Current

Examine the form of the torques for the condition of 3ϕ short circuit. All of the variables in equation (IV.291) have been defined previously (equations (IV.162), (IV.163), (IV.204) and (IV.205)) and the expression for torque could be derived by direct substitution of expressions for fluxes and currents. Using the complete form of the operational expressions for fluxes and currents will result in a rather unwieldy torque expression and as before, we shall make simplifications that permit better insight into basic effects.

For the case where changes in excitation are not considered, $(\Delta e_{fd} = 0)$, the rotational speed is a constant rated value, and initial values of currents and fluxes are sought, expressions for $\Delta i_d(s)$ and $\Delta i_q(s)$ were given in equations (IV.208) and (IV.209). With the further simplifying assumption that armature resistance $r = 0$, the expression for $\Delta i_d(t)$ and $\Delta iq(t)$ were given in equations (IV.220) and (IV.221).

These will be repeated here for convenience.

$$\Delta i_d = \frac{e_0}{X_d''}[\cos \delta - \cos(\omega t + \delta)] \tag{IV.220}$$

$$\Delta i_q = -\frac{e_0}{X_q''}[\sin \delta - \sin(\omega t + \delta)] \tag{IV.221}$$

Using the time domain equivalent of equations (IV.162) and (IV.163), with Δe_{fd} set to zero,

$$\Delta \psi_d = -L_d'' \Delta i_d \tag{IV.292}$$

$$\Delta \psi_q = -L_q'' \Delta i_d \tag{IV.293}$$

The total currents i_d and i_q are

$i_d = i_{d0} + \Delta i_d$

$i_q = i_{q0} + \Delta i_q$

Similar expressions apply to fluxes.

We may follow the development for inclusion of initial conditions in equations (IV.230) to (IV.235), and obtain a general expression for initial 3ϕ short circuit torques including the effect of initial load. On the other hand, since the purpose here is to develop an understanding of the phenomena, we can take the case of an initially open circuited machine at rated voltage and speed in which case

$$\left.\begin{aligned}
i_{d0} &= 0 \\
i_{d0} &= 0 \\
\psi_{d0} &= \frac{e_{q0}}{\omega} = \frac{e_0}{\omega} \\
\psi_{q0} &= -\frac{e_{d0}}{\omega} = 0 \\
\delta &= 0
\end{aligned}\right\} \tag{IV.294}$$

With these assumptions the currents and fluxes to be inserted in equation (IV.291) are (from (IV.220), (IV.221), (IV.279) and (IV.280)).

$$i_d = \frac{e_0}{X_d''}[1 - \cos\omega t]$$

$$i_q = -\frac{e_0}{X_q''}\sin\omega t$$

$$\psi_d = \psi_{do} + \Delta\psi_d = \frac{e_0}{\omega}\cos\omega t$$

$$\psi_q = \psi_{qo} + \Delta\psi_q = -\frac{e_0}{\omega}\sin\omega t$$

And the torque expression is

$$T = \frac{e_0^2}{X_q''}\sin\omega t\cos\omega t + \frac{e_0^2}{X_d''}(1-\cos\omega t)\sin\omega t =$$

$$= \frac{e_0^2}{X_d''}\sin\omega t - \frac{e_0^2}{2}\left(\frac{1}{X_d''} - \frac{1}{X_q''}\right)\sin 2\omega t \qquad\text{(IV.295)}$$

Note from equation (IV.295) that the short circuit torque is made up of a fundamental frequency term and a double frequency term due to subtransient saliency (when $X_d'' = X_q''$ this component vanishes). The average torque is zero as should be expected from the assumption of zero armature resistance. The peak torque can be quite high (for a value of $X_d'' = 0.15$ p.u. this value of peak torque could reach close to 7 p.u.).

Note that the assumption of $r = 0$, leads to the undamped sinusoidal expression (IV.295). When a finite value of r is used, the resultant expression will contain a d.c. torque term produced by the i^2r losses and attenuation of the sinusoidal components with the armature time constant T_a previously encountered in the discussion of short circuit currents.

Note that in this derivation of transient short circuit torques, the armature voltage equations must include the $d\psi/dt$ terms. These are the terms that give rise to the armature d.c. offset currents and to the alternating torque components. Reference

(1) derives a simplified expression for short circuit torque including the effect of armature resistance, making the assumption that $X_d'' = X_q''$ and that the rotor resistances are negligible (no decay of rotor flux linkages).

$$T(t) = \frac{e^2}{\left(X_d''\right)^2 + r^2}\left[e^{-\alpha t}\left(X_d'' \sin t - r \cos t\right) + r\right]$$
(IV.296)

where

$$\alpha = \frac{r}{X_d''}$$

Figure 4.33 shows the form of the short circuit torque.

The effect of rotor resistances will now be examined. Take again the case of a short circuit from an open circuit condition for which relations (IV.294) hold. Instead of taking the machine inductances as the subtransient values, express them in operational form. Then, using equation (IV.294) and $r = 0$ into previously derived expressions (IV.204) and (IV.205)

$$i_d(s) = \frac{e_0 \omega}{s L_d(s)\left(s^2 + \omega^2\right)}$$
(IV.297)

$$i_q(s) = \frac{e_0}{s L_q(s)\left(s^2 + \omega^2\right)}$$
(IV.298)

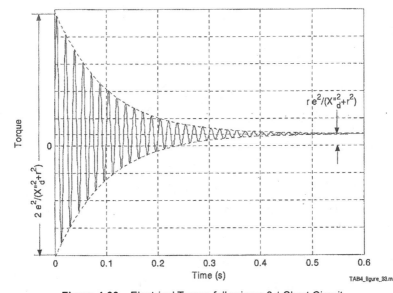

Figure 4.33 – Electrical Torque following a 3ϕ Short Circuit

In order to illustrate the effects of rotor circuit resistances, we will make the simplifying assumption that the operational inductances $L_d(s)$ and $L_q(s)$ are of first order, i.e.; single time constant expressions.

$$L_d(s) = \frac{L_d + sL'_d T_d}{1 + sT_d} = \frac{L_d\left(1 + sT'_d\right)}{1 + sT_d} \tag{IV.299}$$

$$L_q(s) = \frac{L_q + sL'_q T_q}{1 + sT_q} = \frac{L_q\left(1 + sT'_q\right)}{1 + sT_q} \tag{IV.300}$$

where $T_d = T'_{d0}$ and $T_q = T'_{q0}$

Substituting equations (IV.299) and (IV.300) in (IV.297) and (IV.298) and taking the inverse Laplace transform through partial fractions, the time expressions for the currents become:

$$i_d(t) = \frac{e_0}{\omega L_d} + \frac{e_0\omega\left[T_d - T'_d\right]T'_d}{L_d\left[\omega^2 T'^2_d + 1\right]} e^{-\frac{t}{T_d}} + \frac{e_0}{\omega L_d}\frac{\sqrt{1 + \omega^2 T^2_d}}{\sqrt{1 + \omega^2 T'^2_d}}\sin\left(\omega t + \gamma\right) \tag{IV.301}$$

where

$$\gamma = \left(\tan^{-1}\frac{\omega T_d}{1} - \tan^{-1}\frac{\omega T'_d}{1} - 90°\right)$$

and

$$i_q(t) = \frac{-e_0\left[T_q - T'_q\right]}{L_q\left[1 + T'^2_q \omega^2\right]} e^{-\frac{t}{T_q}} + \frac{e_0}{\omega L_q}\frac{\sqrt{1 + \omega^2 T^2_q}}{\sqrt{1 + \omega^2 T'^2_q}}\sin\left(\omega t + \beta\right) \tag{IV.302}$$

where $\beta = \tan^{-1}\omega T_q - \tan^{-1}\omega T'_q$

Reference (1) develops an interesting concept of the "stand-still" impedance of the machine viewed from the armature terminals.

This is the impedance of $sL_d(s)$ and $sL_q(s)$ with $s = j\omega$.

Substituting $s = j\omega$ in equations (IV.299) and (IV.300),

$$Z_d(j\omega) \qquad = j\omega L_d(j\omega) = \frac{j\omega L_d\left(1 + j\omega T_d'\right)}{\left(1 + j\omega T_d\right)}$$

$$= R_d(\omega) + jX_d(\omega)$$

where

$$R_d(\omega) = \frac{X_d\left(T_d - T_d'\right)}{1 + \omega^2 T_d^2} \tag{IV.303}$$

$$X_d(\omega) = \frac{X_d\left(1 + \omega^2 T_d T_d'\right)}{1 + \omega^2 T_d^2} \tag{IV.304}$$

and $X_d = \omega L_d$.

Similar relations hold for the q-axis with appropriate changes in subscripts.

Expressing (IV.301) and (IV.302) in terms of these newly defined "standstill" impedances.

$$i_d = e_0 \left\{ \frac{1}{X_d} + \frac{R_d(\omega)T_d'}{[Z_d(\omega)]^2} e^{-\frac{t}{T_d}} + \frac{1}{Z_d(\omega)} \sin\left[\omega t - \tan^{-1}\frac{X_d(\omega)}{R_d(\omega)}\right] \right\} \tag{IV.305}$$

where

$$Z_d(\omega) = \sqrt{R_d(\omega) + X_d(\omega)}$$

and

$$i_d = e_0 \left\{ -\frac{R_q(\omega)}{[Z_q(\omega)]^2} e^{-\frac{t}{T_q'}} + \frac{1}{Z_q(\omega)} \cos\left[\omega t - \tan^{-1}\frac{X_q(\omega)}{R_q(\omega)}\right] \right\} \tag{IV.306}$$

Expressions (IV.305) and (IV.306) suggest that the current responses i_d and i_q could also be derived from application of voltages $-\sin \omega t$ and $-\cos \omega t$ to the circuits with operational impedances $sL_d(s)$ and $sL_q(s)$ as shown in Figure 4.34.

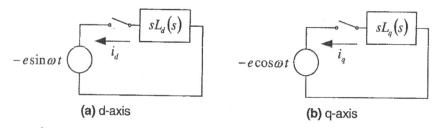

(a) d-axis   **(b)** q-axis

Figure 4.34 – Operational Impedances Circuits

This result can also be derived from inspection of equations (IV.297) and (IV.298) which can be written as:

$$i_d(s) = \left[\frac{e_0 \omega}{s^2 + \omega^2} \right] \frac{1}{sL_d(s)} \tag{IV.297}$$

$$i_q(s) = \left[\frac{e_0 s}{s^2 + \omega^2} \right] \frac{1}{sL_q(s)} \tag{IV.298}$$

Equations (IV.297) and (IV.298) are in the form of

$$i(s) = \left[\frac{1}{Z(s)} \right] e(s)$$

where

$$e_d(s) = \frac{e_0 \omega}{s^2 + \omega^2} = \mathcal{L}\{e_0 \sin \omega t\}$$

$$e_q(s) = \frac{e_0 \omega}{s^2 + \omega^2} = \mathcal{L}\{e_0 \cos \omega t\}$$

Note that the impressed voltages $e_d(s)$ and $e_q(s)$ are undamped sinusoids because r was set equal to zero.

Using equations (IV.154) and (IV.155) with proper initial conditions (IV.294):

$$\psi_d(s) = \frac{\psi_d(0)}{s} - L_d(s)i_d(s)$$

(IV.307)

$$= \frac{e_d}{\omega s} - L_d(s)i_d(s)$$

$$\psi_q(s) = -L_q(s)i_q(s)$$

(IV.308)

Substituting equations (IV.307) and (IV.308) in (IV.297) and (IV.298)

$$\psi_d(s) = \frac{e_0}{\omega s} - \frac{e_0 \omega}{s^2 + \omega^2}$$

(IV.309)

$$\psi_q(s) = -\frac{e_0}{s^2 + \omega^2}$$

(IV.310)

Taking the inverse Laplace transform

$$\psi d\ (t) = \frac{e_0}{\omega} \cos \omega t$$

(IV.311)

$$\psi q\ (t) = -\frac{e_0}{\omega} \sin \omega t$$

(IV.312)

Using the time expressions for i_d, i_q, ψ_d and ψ_q in equation (IV.291)

$$T = \frac{e_0^2}{2}\left[\frac{R_d(\omega)}{\left[Z_d(\omega)\right]^2} + \frac{R_q(\omega)}{\left[Z_q(\omega)\right]^2}\right] +$$

$$+ e_0^2\left(\frac{1}{X_d} + \frac{R_d(\omega)T_d'}{\left[Z_d(\omega)\right]^2}e^{-\frac{t}{T_d'}}\right)\sin \omega t - \frac{e_0^2 R_q(\omega)}{\left[Z_q(\omega)\right]^2}e^{-\frac{t}{T_q'}}\cos \omega t +$$

(IV.313)

$$+ \frac{e_0^2}{2}\left\{\frac{1}{Z_q(\omega)}\sin\left[2\omega t + \tan^{-1}\frac{R_q(\omega)}{X_q(\omega)}\right] - \frac{1}{Z_d(\omega)}\sin\left[2\omega t + \tan^{-1}\frac{R_d(\omega)}{X_d(\omega)}\right]\right\}$$

Summarizing this development on 3ϕ short circuit torques, the various expressions that have been derived are:

a) Equation (IV.295) for the case where all armature and rotor resistances are assumed equal to zero.

b) Equation (IV.296) for the case where armature resistance is included, but subtransient saliency is neglected $\left(X_d^{''} = X_q^{''}\right)$ and rotor $d\,q$ resistances are assumed equal to zero.

c) Equation (IV.313) in which armature resistance is neglected and the rotor circuits are approximated by an operational impedance with single time constant in each axis.

A discerning inspection of the form of these expressions reveals that the 3ϕ short circuit torque for an initial open circuit condition is made up of the following components.

1) A fundamental frequency component determined primarily by X_d''.

2) An unidirectional component due to armature i^2r losses where i is the fundamental frequency component of armature current.

3) A double frequency component of torque which is due to subtransient saliency.

4) A unidirectional component of torque produced by rotor i^2r losses where i is the a.c. component of rotor currents, i.e., the d.c. component of armature currents.

It should be appreciated that the components of torque in 1, 3 and 4 are produced by the d.c. offset component of armature current, which decays with the armature time constant. This time constant does not figure in equation (IV.313) due to the assumption of $r = 0$. When armature resistance is considered, the approximate torque expression becomes

$$T = e_0^2 \left[\frac{F}{X_d''} e^{-\frac{t}{T_a}} \sin \omega t + \frac{1}{2}\left(\frac{R_d(\omega)}{X_d''^2} + \frac{R_q(\omega)}{X_q''^2} \right) e^{-\frac{2t}{T_a}} + \frac{F^2 r}{X_d''^2} + \frac{1}{2}\left(\frac{1}{X_q''} - \frac{1}{X_d''} \right) e^{-\frac{2t}{T_a}} \sin \omega t \right] \quad \text{(IV.314)}$$

where

$$T_a = \frac{2X_d'' X_q''}{r\left[2X_d'' X_q'' \right]}$$

$$F = \left(1 - \frac{X_d''}{X_d'} \right) e^{-\frac{t}{T_d''}} + \left(\frac{X_d''}{X_d'} - \frac{X_d''}{X_d} \right) e^{-\frac{t}{T_d'}} + \frac{X_d''}{X_d}$$

$$T_d'' = T_{d0}'' \frac{X_d''}{X_d'}$$

$$T_d' = T_{d0}' \frac{X_d'}{X_d}$$

Evaluation of short circuit torques is important to the proper design of machine foundations and strength of shaft couplings etc.

Out of phase synchronizing produces torques that are even more severe than those under short circuit. The same methods can be used to solve for torques under out of phase synchronizing. References (2, 3, 4) contain useful information on this subject.

The importance of analytical closed form expressions for short circuit torques and other maching variables is to help understand the nature of; the phenomena. With the use of machine models the solution is readily achieved by digital computer.

4.7 Machine Models

In simulations of Power System dynamic performance, machines are represented in the form of models which can be executed in analog computers or through digital computation.

These models are expressed in terms of the derived parameters (L_d, L_d', T_{d0}', etc.) rather than the basic parameters in the equivalent circuit (L_{ad}, L_ℓ, r_{fd}, L_{kd}, etc.). The following sections outline the derivation of machine models.

4.7.1 Salient Pole Machine Without Amortisseurs

Figure 4.18 shows the basic equivalent circuits for the d and q axes for a salient pole machine without amortisseur effects. The figure is repeated here for convenience.

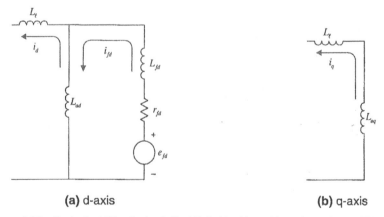

(a) d-axis **(b) q-axis**

Figure 4.35 – Equivalent Circuits for Salient Pole Machine without Amortisseur Windings

The open circuit saturation curve shown in Figure 4.14 discussed in section 4.5.3 is also displayed here as Figure 4.36.

S is the MMF component required by saturation. On open circuit S can be expressed as function of terminal voltage which is proportional to the internal flux of the machine. Under load conditions the value of voltage or flux that determines S from the curve is usually taken as the voltage behind transient reactance or voltage proportional to field flux linkages.

$$S = f\left(\frac{E_q'}{\omega}\right)$$

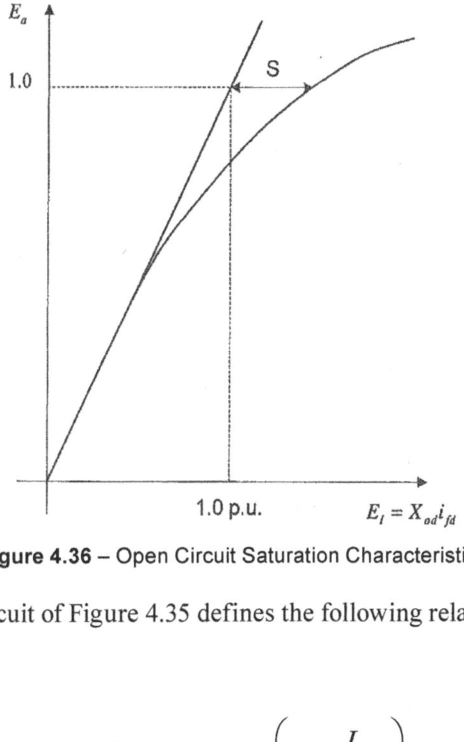

Figure 4.36 – Open Circuit Saturation Characteristic

The equivalent circuit of Figure 4.35 defines the following relationships:

_d_-axis

$$\psi_{ad} = L_{ad}\left(i_{fd} - i_d\right) - f\left(\psi_{fd}\frac{L_{ad}}{L_{ffd}}\right) \qquad \text{(IV.315)}$$

where $f\left(\psi_{fd}\dfrac{L_{ad}}{L_{ffd}}\right) = f\left(\dfrac{E_q'}{\omega}\right)$ = saturation component of MMF.

$$\psi_{fd} - \psi_{ad} = L_{fd}\, i_{fd} - \frac{L_{fd}}{L_{ad}} f\left(\frac{E_q'}{\omega}\right) \qquad \text{(IV.316)}$$

where the assumption is made that the saturation of field leakage flux is in proportion to the saturation of mutual air gap flux as the field leakage inductance L_{fd} is to mutual inductance L_{ad}.

$$\psi_d - \psi_{ad} = -L_\ell i_d \tag{IV.317}$$

From Equations (IV.315) and (IV.316) eliminating ψ_{ad}

$$\psi_{fd} = \left(L_{ad} + L_{fd}\right) i_{fd} - \left(1 + \frac{L_{fd}}{L_{ad}}\right) f\left(\frac{E_q'}{\omega}\right) - i_d L_{ad} \tag{IV.318}$$

Multiplying Equation (IV.318) by L_{ad}/L_{ffd} and transposing

$$L_{ad} i_{fd} = \frac{L_{ad}}{L_{ffd}} \psi_{fd} + \frac{L_{ad}^{\;2}}{L_{ffd}} i_d + f\left(\frac{E_q'}{\omega}\right) \tag{IV.319}$$

Noting the relationships between derived inductances and equivalent circuit inductances as follows

$$L_d' = L_\ell + \frac{L_{ad} L_{fd}}{L_{ffd}} \Rightarrow \left(L_d - L_d'\right) = \frac{L_{ad}^{\;2}}{L_{ffd}}$$

$$L_d = L_\ell + L_{ad}$$

and applying these to Equation (IV.319)

$$L_{ad} i_{fd} = \frac{E_q'}{\omega} + \left(L_d - L_d'\right) i_d + f\left(\frac{E_q'}{\omega}\right) \tag{IV.320}$$

The field circuit voltage equation is

$$e_{fd} = \frac{d}{dt}\psi_{fd} + r_{fd} i_{fd} \tag{IV.321}$$

Multiplying Equation (IV.321) by L_{ad}/r_{fd}

$$\frac{L_{ad}}{r_{fd}} e_{fd} = \frac{d}{dt}\frac{L_{ad}}{r_{fd}}\psi_{fd} + L_{ad} i_{fd} =$$

$$= \frac{L_{ffd}}{r_{fd}}\frac{d}{dt}\frac{L_{ad}}{L_{ffd}}\psi_{fd} + L_{ad} i_{fd} \tag{IV.322}$$

or

$$E_{fd} = T'_{do} \frac{d}{dt}\left[\frac{E'_q}{\omega}\right] + L_{ad}\, i_{fd} \qquad\qquad \text{(IV.323)}$$

where $E_{fd} = \dfrac{e_{fd}L_{ad}}{r_{fd}}$ and $T'_{do} = \dfrac{L_{ffd}}{r_{fd}}$.

Using Equations (IV.316), (IV.317) and (IV.318) to express ψ_d as a function of ψ_{fd} and i_d:

$$\psi_d = \psi_{ad} - L_\ell i_d$$

$$= \psi_{fd} - L_{fd}i_{fd} + \frac{L_{fd}}{L_{ad}} f\left[\frac{E'_q}{\omega}\right] - L_\ell i_d$$

$$= \psi_{fd} - \frac{L_{fd}}{L_{ffd}}\psi_{fd} - \frac{L_{ad}L_{fd}}{L_{ffd}}\cdot i_d - \frac{L_{fd}}{L_{ad}} f\left[\frac{E'_q}{\omega}\right] + \frac{L_{fd}}{L_{ad}} f\left[\frac{E'_q}{\omega}\right] - L_\ell i_d \quad \text{(IV.324)}$$

$$= \frac{L_{ad}}{L_{ffd}}\psi_{fd} - i_d\left[L_\ell + \frac{L_{ad}L_{fd}}{L_{ffd}}\right]$$

$$= \frac{E'_q}{\omega} - i_d X'_d \qquad .$$

q-axis

From Figure 4.37 the only relationship for the q-axis is

$$\psi_q = -i_q\,(L_{aq} + L_\ell) = -i_q L_q \quad \text{(IV.325)}$$

Relations (IV.323), (IV.320) and (IV.324) for the d-axis and (IV.325) for the q-axis, are described in the block diagram of Figure 4.37.

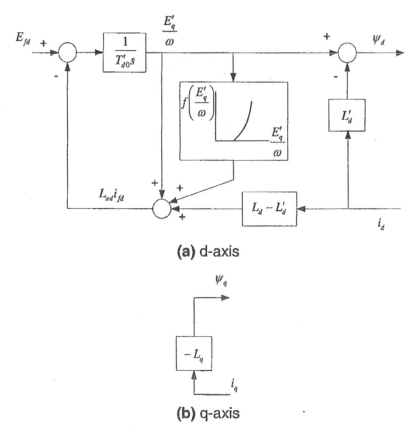

(a) d-axis

(b) q-axis

Figure 4.37 – Block Diagram Representing Salient Pole
Machine without Amortisseur Windings

4.7.2 Salient Pole Machine with Amortisseurs

Figure 4.38 shows the equivalent circuit for the d and q axes of a Salient Pole machine with amortisseurs.

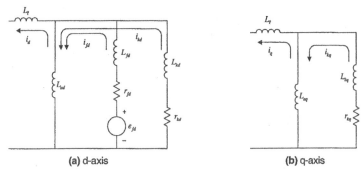

(a) d-axis　　　　　　　　　　　(b) q-axis

Figure 4.38 – Equivalent Circuits for Salient Pole Machine with Amortisseur Windings

d-axis

The flux linkage relations for the d-axis are

$$\psi_{ad} = L_{ad}\left(i_{fd} + i_{kd} - i_d\right) - \left(\frac{E_q'}{\omega}\right) \tag{IV.326}$$

$$\psi_{fd} - \psi_{ad} = L_{fd}i_{fd} - \frac{L_{fd}}{L_{ad}}f\left(\frac{E_q'}{\omega}\right) \tag{IV.327}$$

$$\psi_{kd} - \psi_{ad} = L_{kd}\,i_{kd} \tag{IV.328}$$

$$\psi_d - \psi_{ad} = -L_\ell\,i_d \tag{IV.329}$$

From (IV.326) and (IV.327) eliminating ψ_{ad}

$$\psi_{fd} = (L_{ad} + L_{fd})i_{fd} + L_{ad}\left(i_{kd} - i_d\right) - \left(1 + \frac{L_{fd}}{L_{ad}}\right)f\left(\frac{E_q'}{\omega}\right)$$

or multiplying by L_{ad}/L_{ffd} and transforming

$$L_{ad}\,i_{fd} = \frac{L_{ad}}{L_{ffd}}\psi_{fd} - \frac{L_{ad}^2}{L_{ffd}}\left(i_{kd} - i_d\right) + f\left(\frac{E_q'}{\omega}\right) \tag{IV.330}$$

543

Noting relationships between equivalent circuit and derived inductances

$$L'_d = L_\ell + \frac{L_{ad}L_{fd}}{L_{ffd}}$$

$$L''_d = L_\ell + \frac{1}{\dfrac{1}{L_{ad}} + \dfrac{1}{L_{fd}} + \dfrac{1}{L_{kd}}}$$

$$L_d = L_\ell + L_{ad}$$

$$L_d - L'_d = \frac{L^2_{ad}}{L_{ffd}}$$

Equation (IV.330) becomes

$$L_{ad} i_{fd} = \frac{E'_q}{\omega} + (L_d - L'_d)i_d - (L_d - L'_d)i_{kd} + f\left(\frac{E'_q}{\omega}\right) \qquad \text{(IV.331)}$$

Next solving for i_{kd} from (IV.326) and (IV.328)

$$\psi_{kd} = L_{ad}(i_{fd} - i_d) + (L_{ad} + L_{kd})i_{kd} - f\left(\frac{E'_q}{\omega}\right) \qquad \text{(IV.332)}$$

Substituting $L_{ad}i_{fd}$ from (IV.331), (IV.332) becomes

$$\left(L_{kd} + \frac{L_{ad}L_{fd}}{L_{ffd}}\right)i_{kd} = \psi_{kd} - \frac{E'_q}{\omega} + \left(\frac{L_{ad}L_{fd}}{L_{ffd}}\right)i_d \qquad \text{(IV.333)}$$

Also

$$\psi_d = \psi_{ad} - i_d L_\ell \qquad \text{(IV.334)}$$

Substituting for ψ_{ad} from Equation (IV.328)

$$\psi_d = \psi_{kd} - L_{kd} i_{kd} - i_d L_\ell$$

Substituting for i_{kd} from Equation (IV.333)

$$\psi_d = \psi_{kd} - \frac{L_{kd}}{\left(L_{kd} + \dfrac{L_{ad}L_{fd}}{L_{ad} + L_{fd}}\right)}\left(\psi_{kd} - \frac{E_q'}{\omega}\right) - \left[L_\ell + \frac{L_{ad}L_{fd}L_{kd}}{L_{kd}\left(L_{ad} + L_{fd}\right) + L_{ad}L_{fd}}\right]i_d \quad \text{(IV.335)}$$

Other relationships (identities) are

$$L_{kd} = \frac{\left(L_d' - L_\ell\right)\left(L_d'' - L_\ell\right)}{L_d' - L_d''}$$

$$\frac{L_{ad}L_{fd}}{L_{ffd}} = L_d' - L_\ell$$

$$L_{fd} = \frac{L_{ad}\left(L_d' - L_\ell\right)}{L_d - L_d'}$$

Hence (IV.335) becomes

$$\psi_d = \psi_{kd}\frac{L_d' - L_d''}{L_d' - L_\ell} + \frac{E_q'}{\omega}\frac{L_d'' - L_\ell}{L_d' - L_\ell} i_d L_d'' \quad \text{(IV.336)}$$

$$= \psi_d'' - i_d L_d''$$

In (IV.336) the state variables are ψ_{kd} and E_q'/ω which are obtained from integration of rotor voltage equations

$$e_{fd} = r_{fd}\, i_{fd} + \frac{d\psi_{fd}}{dt}$$

Multiplying by L_{ad}/L_{ffd} and transforming,

$$\frac{L_{ad}}{L_{ffd}}\psi_{fd} = \int\left(e_{fd}\frac{L_{ad}}{L_{ffd}} - \frac{r_{fd}}{L_{ffd}}L_{ad}\, i_{fd}\right)dt$$

i.e.

$$\frac{E_q'}{\omega} = \int \left[E_{fd} - L_{ad} i_{fd} \right] dt \qquad (IV.337)$$

Also

$$i_{kd} r_{kd} + \frac{d\psi_{kd}}{dt} = 0$$

or

$$\psi_{kd} = -\int i_{kd} r_{kd}\, dt \qquad (IV.338)$$

Using (IV.332) for i_{kd} in (IV.338)

$$\psi_{kd} = -\int \frac{r_{kd}}{L_{kd} + \frac{L_{ad} L_{fd}}{L_{ffd}}} \left[\psi_{kd} - \left(\frac{E_q'}{\omega} \right) + \frac{L_{ad} L_{fd}}{L_{ad} + L_{fd}} \right] dt = -\frac{1}{T_{do}''} \int \left[\psi_{kd} - \frac{E_q'}{\omega} + \left(L_q' - L_\ell \right) i_d \right] dt$$

Finally using (IV.331) and (IV.332)

$$L_{ad} i_{fd} = \frac{E_q'}{\omega} + \left(L_d - L_d' \right) i_d + \left(\frac{L_d' - L_d''}{\left(L_d' - L_\ell \right)^2} \right) \left[\frac{E_q'}{\omega} - \psi_{kd} - i_d \left(L_d' - L_\ell \right) \right]$$

A summary of the d-axis equations are:

$$\psi_d'' = \psi_{kd} \left(\frac{L_d' - L_d''}{L_d' - L_\ell} \right) + \frac{E_q'}{\omega} \left(\frac{L_d'' - L_\ell}{L_d' - L_\ell} \right)$$

$$\psi_d = \psi_d'' - i_d L_d''$$

$$\psi_{kd} = -\frac{1}{T_{do}''} \int \left[\psi_{kd} - \frac{E_q'}{\omega} + \left(L_d' - L_\ell \right) i_d \right] dt$$

$$E_q' = \frac{1}{T_{do}'} \int \left[E_{fd} - L_{ad} i_{fd} \right] dt$$

$$L_{ad} i_{fd} = \frac{E_q'}{\omega} + f \left(\frac{E_q'}{\omega} \right) + i_d \left(L_d - L_d' \right) \left[1 - \frac{L_d' - L_d''}{L_d' - L_\ell} \right] + \left(\frac{E_q'}{\omega} - \psi_{kd} \right) \left[\frac{\left(L_d - L_d' \right) \left(L_d' - L_d'' \right)}{\left(L_d' - L_\ell \right)^2} \right]$$

The q-axis equations for the single amortisseur can be similarly derived. Figure 4.39 is a block diagram for these equations. It should be noted that under the assumption of $\omega = 1.0$, inductances L and reactances $X = \omega L$ have the same per unit quantities, hence it is quite customary to see the parameters in the block diagrams expressed as $X's$ instead of $L's$ and voltages $e's$ instead of flux linkages $\psi's$.

Table 4.1 presents typical values for the parameters in this model.

Table 4.1 – Typical Parameters for Salient Pole Generator

TYPICAL VALUES	SAT. CURVE	
	E_Q'	$X_{ad}I_{fd}$
$X_d = 1.0$ p.u.		
$X_q = 0.75$ p.u.	0	0
$X_d' = 0.30$ p.u.	0.72	0.72
$X_d'' = 0.22$ p.u.	0.90	1.00
$X_q'' = 0.22$ p.u.	1.1	1.44
$T_{d0}'' = T_{q0}'' = 0.06$ s	1.35	2.50
$T_{d0}' = 5.5$ s		

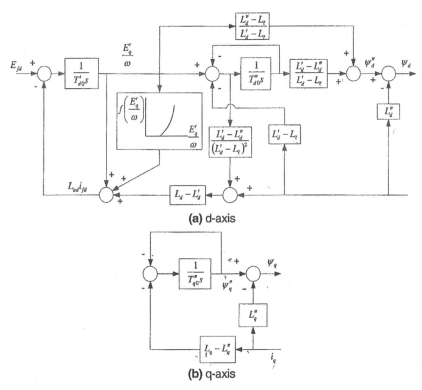

(a) d-axis

(b) q-axis

Figure 4.39 – Block Diagram Representing Salient
Pole Machine with Amortisseur Windings

4.7.3 Round Rotor Machine with Amortisseurs

The treatment of the round rotor machine is very similar to that derived for the salient pole machine except that due to solid rotor effects, it is more accurate to represent the q-axis with two equivalent amortisseurs as in Figure 4.40.

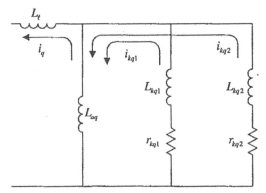

Figure 4.40 – q-Axis Equivalent Circuit for Round Rotor Machines

Also saturation is treated differently in as much as it occurs in both d and q axes.

The block diagram of Figure 4.41 shows the model for the round rotor machine. It should be noted that in these derivations the definition of time constants and reactances T_{d0}', T_{d0}'', X_d', X_d'', etc. were defined in section 4.6. As previously explained, T_{d0}' and T_{d0}'' are not exactly the reciprocals of the poles of $L_d(s)$ and $L_q(s)$. The block diagrams of Figures 4.39 and 4.41 show the interaction between the two states E_q'/ω and ψ_{kd}.

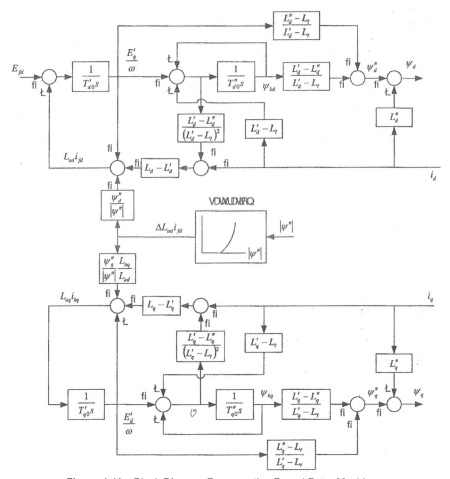

Figure 4.41 – Block Diagram Representing Round Rotor Machines

4.8   Unbalanced Faults

Currents flowing due to unbalanced fault conditions can be solved by imposing the constraint equations which define the fault. The resulting equations are complex and non-linear. Closed form solutions of the rigorous equations including rotor and armature resistance effects are extremely unwieldly and one must make simplifying assumptions to derive insight into the basic effects.

The general case of a machine under load suffering a sudden unbalanced short circuit can be solved rigorously by simulation of the pertinent machine equations and the equations which describe the relations between voltages and currents derived from the fault conditions. The general approach as well as simplified results that can be derived with appropriate assumptions will be illustrated with examples of typical unbalanced faults.

4.8.1   Line-to-Line Short Circuit

The equations defining the line-to-line short circuit condition shown in Figure 4.42 are:

$$e_b - e_c = 0 \qquad\qquad\text{(IV.339)}$$

$$i_a = 0 \qquad\qquad\text{(IV.340)}$$

$$i_b + i_c = 0 \qquad\qquad\text{(IV.341)}$$

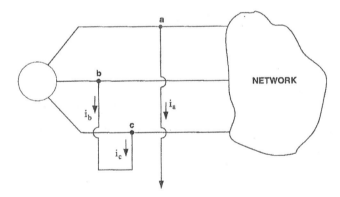

Figure 4.42 – Schematic Representation of Line-to-Line Short Circuit

These equations expressed in terms of d, q and 0 components become:

$$e_d \sin \theta + e_q \cos \theta = 0 \qquad\qquad\text{(IV.342)}$$

$$i_d \cos \theta = i_q \sin \theta \qquad\qquad\text{(IV.343)}$$

$$i_0 = 0 \qquad\qquad\text{(IV.344)}$$

where $\theta = \omega t + \theta_0$.

Equations (IV.342) to (IV.344) along with machine and network equations relating currents to fluxes and fluxes and rate of change of fluxes to voltages form a sufficient set for the solution of currents.

To gain insight consider the simpler case of an open circuit machine undergoing a sudden line-to-line short circuit.

Equations (IV.339) through (IV.344) still apply. For this case, fault currents are also the machine currents. To further simplify matters consider zero armature and rotor resistances. The voltage equations are:

$$e_d = \frac{d\psi_d}{dt} - \psi_q \tag{IV.345}$$

$$e_q = \frac{d\psi_q}{dt} + \psi_d \tag{IV.346}$$

The flux-current equations are:

$$\psi_d = \psi_{d0} - i_d L_d'' \tag{IV.347}$$

$$\psi_q = -i_q L_q'' \tag{IV.348}$$

Substituting equations (IV.347) and (IV.348) in (IV.345) and (IV.346)

$$e_d = -L_d'' \frac{di_d}{dt} - i_q L_q'' \tag{IV.349}$$

$$e_q = -L_q'' \frac{di_q}{dt} + \psi_{d0} - i_d L_d'' \tag{IV.350}$$

Use of equations (IV.349) and (IV.350) in (IV.342) yields

$$\left[-L_d'' \frac{di_d}{dt} + i_q L_q'' \right] \sin\theta + \left[-L_q'' \frac{di_q}{dt} + \psi_{d0} - i_d L_d'' \right] \cos\theta = 0 \tag{IV.351}$$

Combining terms and noting that

$$-L_d'' \frac{di_d}{dt} \sin\theta - L_d'' i_d \cos\theta = -L_d'' \frac{d}{dt} [i_d \sin\theta] \quad \left(\text{note that } \frac{d\theta}{dt} = \omega = 1.0 \right)$$

and $+L_q'' i_q \sin\theta - L_q'' \dfrac{di_q}{dt}\cos\theta = -L_q'' \dfrac{d}{dt}\left[i_q \cos\theta\right]$

equation (IV.351) can be written as:

$$\frac{d}{dt}\left[L_d'' i_d \sin\theta + L_q'' i_q \cos\theta\right] = \psi_{d0}\cos\theta \qquad (IV.352)$$

or, integrating,

$$L_d'' i_d \sin\theta + L_q'' i_q \cos\theta = \psi_{d0}\sin\theta\,\psi_{d0}\sin\theta_0 \qquad (IV.353)$$

Using equation (IV.343) in (IV.353)

$$i_d\left[L_d'' \sin\theta + L_q'' \frac{\cos^2\theta}{\sin\theta}\right] = \psi_{d0}\,[\sin\theta + \sin\theta_0]$$

or

$$i_d = \frac{\psi_{d0}\left[\sin^2\theta + \sin\theta_0\,\sin\theta\right]}{L_d'' \sin^2\theta + L_q'' \cos^2\theta} \qquad (IV.354)$$

$$i_q = \frac{\psi_{d0}\left[\sin\theta\cos\theta + \sin\theta_0\,\cos\theta\right]}{L_d'' \sin^2\theta + L_q'' \cos^2\theta} \qquad (IV.355)$$

Examine the nature of i_d and i_q in the above relations. Equations (IV.354) and (IV.355) can be put in the form

$$i_d = \frac{\psi_{d0}\left[\sin^2\theta + \sin\theta_0\,\cos\theta\right]}{L_d'' +\left(L_q'' - L_d''\right)\cos^2\theta} \qquad (IV.356)$$

$$i_q = \frac{\psi_{d0}\left[\sin\theta\cos\theta + \sin\theta_0\,\cos\theta\right]}{L_d'' +\left(L_q'' - L_d''\right)\cos^2\theta} \qquad (IV.357)$$

Take first the case where $L_q'' = L_d''$ (no subtransient saliency). i_d and i_q can be seen to exhibit a constant d.c. term (fundamental or positive sequence component of phase current), a second harmonic term (negative sequence) and a fundamental frequency term produced by the d.c. offset component. From equations (IV.356) and (IV.357), with $L_q'' = L_d''$.

$$i_d = \frac{\psi_{d0}}{2L_d''} - \frac{\psi_{d0} \cos 2\theta}{2L_d''} + \frac{\psi_{d0} \sin \theta_0}{L_d''} \sin \theta \qquad \text{(IV.358)}$$

$$\uparrow \qquad \uparrow \qquad \uparrow$$

d.c.   2nd harmonic   fundamental

$$i_q = \frac{\psi_{d0} \sin 2\theta}{2L_d''} + \frac{\psi_{d0} \sin \theta_0}{L_d''} \cos \theta \qquad \text{(IV.359)}$$

The no-load initial condition results in no initial quadrature axis flux hence no d.c. term in i_q.

The phase currents are derived with the appropriate transformation equation ($i_b = i_d \cos(\theta - 120°) - i_q \sin(\theta - 120°)$) yielding, after appropriate compaction with trigonometric identities,

$$i_b = \frac{\psi_{d0}}{L_d''} \frac{\sqrt{3}}{2} \cos(\theta - 90°) + \frac{\psi_{d0} \sin \theta_0}{L_d''} \frac{\sqrt{3}}{2} = -i_c \qquad \text{(IV.360)}$$

$$\downarrow \qquad \qquad \downarrow$$

fundamental frequency   d.c. offset

Use of symmetrical component transformations to the fundamental frequency component of i_b and i_c yields the positive sequence and negative sequence components of fundamental frequency as follows:

$$i_1 = \frac{1}{3}(i_a + ai_b + a^2i_c) =$$

$$= \frac{\psi_{d0}}{L_d''}\frac{\sqrt{3}}{2}\cos(\theta - 90°)(a - a^2) = \qquad (IV.361)$$

$$= \frac{\psi_{d0}}{2L_d''}\cos\theta$$

$$i_2 = \frac{1}{3}(i_a + a^2i_b + ai_c) =$$

$$= \frac{\psi_{d0}}{L_d''}\frac{\sqrt{3}}{2}\cos(\theta - 90°)(a^2 - a) = \qquad (IV.362)$$

$$= -\frac{\psi_{d0}}{2L_d''}\cos\theta$$

These results could have been derived directly from inspection of equations (IV.358) and (IV.359) for i_d and i_q. The magnitude of the d.c. component of $\sqrt{i_d^2 + i_q^2}$ yields the magnitude of positive phase sequence current.

Also it can be shown that if negative sequence currents flow in the stator,

$$i_a = I_{a2}\cos(\theta + \phi)$$

$$i_b = I_{a2}\cos(\theta + \phi + 120°) \qquad (IV.363)$$

$$i_c = I_{a2}\cos(\theta + \phi - 120°)$$

The corresponding d and q currents are second harmonic or double frequency currents

$$i_d = I_{a2}\cos(2\theta + \phi)$$
$$i_q = -I_{a2}\sin(2\theta + \phi) \qquad (IV.364)$$

Using this fact, the second harmonic terms in equations (IV.358) and (IV.359) could be translated directly into negative sequence components without having to go through the process in equation (IV.362).

Evidently the fundamental frequency phase currents could have been derived with the use of symmetrical components as in Figure 4.43, where X_1 is the machine reactance to positive sequence currents and X_2 is the reactance to negative sequence currents.

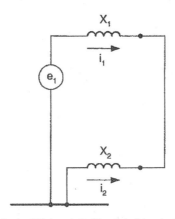

Figure 4.43 – Equivalent Network to Simulate Line-to-Line Short Circuits

The nature of X_1 is time dependent, varying from $X_d^{''}$ to X_d as seen in the discussion of 3ϕ short circuits and balanced machine performance. X_2 is the machine reactance to negative sequence currents which turn out to be second harmonic currents in the $d\text{-}q$ reference frame. At this high second harmonic frequency the machine impedance is the subtransient impedance. Negative sequence reactance is defined as the ratio of the fundamental-frequency reactive armature voltage due to the fundamental frequency negative sequence component of armature current, to this component of current, with the rotor rotating at synchronous speed and field winding short circuited through the exciter. As the MMF wave produced by the negative sequence currents rotates at synchronous speed in opposite direction to the rotation of the rotor, the reactance presented varies rapidly from that of the direct axis to that in the quadrature axis. It is approximately equal to

$$X_2 = \frac{1}{2}\left(X_d^{''} + X_q^{''}\right)$$
(IV.365)

4.8.2   Harmonics – Line-to-Line Short Circuit

When subtransient saliency effects are included the fault current will exhibit harmonics as may be seen from equations (IV.356) and (IV.357) which can be combined in the appropriate transformation equation to give

$$
i_b = \frac{\sqrt{3}\psi_{do}\left(\sin\theta - \sin\theta_0\right)}{L_d'' + L_q'' - \left(L_d'' - L_q''\right)\cos 2\theta}
\tag{IV.366}
$$

Reference I (Appendix A) has Fourier series expressions of the form

$$
\frac{\sin\theta}{A + B - (A - B)\cos 2\theta} = \frac{1}{A + \sqrt{AB}}\left[\sin\theta - b\sin 3\theta + b^2\sin 5\theta - \ldots\right]
$$

and

$$
\frac{1}{A + B - (A - B)\cos 2\theta} = \frac{1}{\sqrt{AB}}\left[\frac{1}{2} - b\cos 2\theta + b^2\cos 4\theta - \ldots\right]
$$

where $b = \dfrac{\sqrt{AB} - A}{\sqrt{AB} + A}$ from which equation (IV.366) can be written as

$$
\begin{aligned}
i_b = \ & \frac{\sqrt{3}\psi_{d0}}{L_d'' + \sqrt{L_d''L_q''}}\left(\sin\theta - b\sin 3\theta + b^2\sin 5\theta + \ldots\right) - \\
& - \frac{\sqrt{3}\psi_{d0}}{L_d'' + \sqrt{L_d''L_q''}}\left(\frac{1}{2} - b\cos 2\theta + b^2\cos 4\theta + \ldots\right)
\end{aligned}
\tag{IV.367}
$$

where $b = \dfrac{\sqrt{L_d''L_q''} - L_d''}{\sqrt{L_d''L_q''} + L_d''}$

In equation (IV.367) we see that if L_d'' and L_q'' are not equal b will be other than zero and the fault current will be composed of fundamental frequency ($\sin\theta$) and odd harmonics (3θ, 5θ etc.) as well as a d.c. component and even harmonics (2θ, 4θ etc.) which are produced by the trapped flux.

Limiting our attention to the fundamental components,

$$i_b = \frac{\sqrt{3}\psi_{d0}}{L_d'' + \sqrt{L_d'' L_q''}}$$

it is noted that the same result could be derived by symmetrical components if

$X_2 = \sqrt{X_d'' X_q''}$ i.e.; the negative sequence reactance is the geometric mean of X_d'' and X_q''.

Usually since X_d'' is nearly equal to X_q'', the difference between the geometric mean and the arithmetic average is small, i.e.;

$$X_2 \approx \frac{1}{2}\left(X_d'' + X_q''\right) \approx \sqrt{X_d'' X_q''}$$

Another relation for X_2 that arises from similar treatment for the line-to-neutral short circuit case is

$$X_2 = \sqrt{\left(X_d'' + \frac{X_0}{2}\right)\left(X_q'' + \frac{X_0}{2}\right)} - \frac{X_0}{2} \qquad \text{(IV.368)}$$

4.8.3   Practical Calculation Procedure – Line-to-Line Fault

The fault current was shown to contain a fundamental frequency component, a d.c. component and even and odd harmonics. Neglecting the harmonic components, the fundamental frequency component is calculated by means of symmetrical components with the use of the circuit of Figure 4.43 where the positive sequence reactance, as in the case of balanced faults, undergoes changes due to the rotor flux linkage decay.

The initial fault current is obtained by making $X_1 = X_d''$. The current expression, including flux decay effects, for the case of a machine initially under open circuit conditions is given by

$$i_b = -i_c = \sqrt{3}E_0\left[\left(\frac{1}{X_d'' + X_2} - \frac{1}{X_d' + X_2}\right)e^{-\frac{t}{T_{d\ell\ell}''}} + \left(\frac{1}{X_d' + X_2} - \frac{1}{X_d + X_2}\right)e^{-\frac{t}{T_{d\ell\ell}'}} + \frac{1}{X_d + X_2}\right] \qquad \text{(IV.369)}$$

$$\text{where} \quad \begin{cases} T''_{d_{\ell\ell}} = T''_{d0} \dfrac{X''_d + X_2}{X'_d + X_2} \\[4mm] T'_{d_{\ell\ell}} = T'_{d0} \dfrac{X'_d + X_2}{X_d + X_2} \end{cases}$$

Thus, as far as fundamental frequency positive sequence currents are concerned, the machine behaves much like it would for the case of a balanced fault through an external impedance X_2.

The d.c. offset current would be calculated from the fundamental and the knowledge of the instant of time at which the fault occurred. Its magnitude in each phase would be such that $\left(I_{dc} + i_{fund.\,freq.}\right)_{t=0} = 0$.

The time constant of decay of the d.c. offset current, as before is given by

$$T_a = \frac{X_2}{r} \tag{IV.370}$$

4.8.4 Line-to-Neutral Short Circuit

The terminal conditions for a line-to-neutral short circuit, with the machine initially on open circuit, are:

$$\begin{aligned} e_a &= 0 \\ i_b &= i_c = 0 \end{aligned} \tag{IV.371}$$

Expressing equation (IV.371) in terms of d and q components

$$e_d \cos\theta - e_q \sin\theta + e_0 = 0 \tag{IV.372}$$

$$i_d \sin\theta = -i_q \cos\theta \tag{IV.373}$$

Also

$$i_0 = +\frac{i_d}{2\cos\theta} \tag{IV.374}$$

As before, assuming zero armature and rotor resistances and substituting equations (IV.349) and (IV.350) in (IV.372).

$$\left[-L''_d \frac{di_d}{dt} + i_q L''_q\right]\cos\theta - \left[-L''_q \frac{di_q}{dt} + \psi_{d0} - i_d L''_d\right]\sin\theta - L_0 \frac{di_0}{dt} = 0 \tag{IV.375}$$

Combining terms and noting that

$$-L_d'' \frac{di_d}{dt} \cos\theta + i_d L_d'' \sin\theta = -L_d'' \frac{d}{dt}\left[i_d \cos\theta\right]$$

and

$$+L_q'' \frac{di_q}{dt} \sin\theta + i_q L_q'' \cos\theta = L_q'' \frac{d}{dt}\left[i_q \sin\theta\right]$$

Equation (IV.375) is rewritten as

$$\frac{d}{dt}\left[-L_d'' i_d \cos\theta + L_q'' i_q \sin\theta - X_0 i_0\right] = \psi_{d0} \sin\theta \qquad \text{(IV.376)}$$

Integrating and using equations (IV.373) and (IV.374)

$$\left[-L_d'' i_d \cos\theta - L_q'' \frac{i_d \sin^2\theta}{\cos\theta} - \frac{L_0 i_d}{2\cos\theta}\right] = -\psi_{d0} \cos\theta + \psi_{d0} \cos\theta_0 \quad \text{(IV.377)}$$

Solving for i_d and i_q,

$$i_d = \frac{2\psi_{d0}\left(\cos\theta - \cos\theta_0\right)\cos\theta}{2L_d'' \cos^2\theta + 2L_q'' \sin^2\theta + L_0} =$$
$$= \frac{2\psi_{d0}\left(\cos\theta - \cos\theta_0\right)\cos\theta}{L_d'' + L_q'' + L_0 + \left(L_d'' - L_q''\right)\cos 2\theta} \qquad \text{(IV.378)}$$

$$i_q = \frac{-2\psi_{d0}\left(\cos\theta - \cos\theta_0\right)\sin\theta}{L_d'' + L_q'' + L_0 + \left(L_d'' - L_q''\right)\cos 2\theta} = \qquad \text{(IV.379)}$$

For the case where subtransient saliency is neglected, expressions (IV.378) and (IV.379) yield

$$i_d = \frac{\psi_{d0}}{L_d'' + L_q'' + L_0}[1 + \cos 2\theta - 2\cos\theta_0 \cos\theta] \qquad \text{(IV.380)}$$

d.c.   2nd   fundamental
harmonic   frequency

$$i_q = \frac{\psi_{d0}}{L_d'' + L_q'' + L_0}[-\sin 2\theta + 2\cos\theta_0 \sin\theta] \qquad \text{(IV.381)}$$

$$i_0 = \frac{\psi_{d0}}{L_d'' + L_q'' + L_0}[\cos\theta - \cos\theta_0] \qquad \text{(IV.382)}$$

The positive sequence current can be derived directly from the d.c. component in equation (IV.380). The negative sequence component likewise is seen to correspond to the second harmonic.terms in equations (IV.380) and (IV.381). The d.c. offset in the phase currents correspond to the fundamental frequency component in i_d and i_q.

4.8.5   Harmonics – Line-to-Neutral Short Circuit

When subtransient saliency is taken into account, the phase current i_a obtained from appropriate d, q, 0-to-phase transformation and use of equations (IV.378), (IV.379) and (IV.374) is

$$i_a = \frac{3\psi_{d0}\left[\cos\theta - \cos\theta_0\right]}{L_d'' + L_q'' + L_0 + \left(L_d'' - L_q''\right)\cos 2\theta} \qquad \text{(IV.383)}$$

This can be expanded into infinite series using the Fourier series expressions in Reference 1, Appendix A.

The expression becomes:

$$i_a = \frac{3\psi_{d0}}{L_d'' + \left[\left(\sqrt{L_d'' + \dfrac{L_0}{2}}\right)\left(\sqrt{L_q'' + \dfrac{L_0}{2}}\right) - \dfrac{L_0}{2}\right] + L_0}\left[\cos\theta + b_0\cos 3\theta + b_0^2\cos 5\theta + ...\right]$$

$$- \frac{3\psi_{d0}\cos\theta_0}{\sqrt{\left(L_d'' + \dfrac{L_0}{2}\right)\left(L_q'' + \dfrac{L_0}{2}\right)}}\left[\frac{1}{2} + b_0\cos 2\theta + b_0^2\cos 4\theta + ...\right]\qquad\text{(IV.384)}$$

where

$$b_0 = \frac{\sqrt{L_q'' + \dfrac{L_0}{2}} - \sqrt{L_d'' + \dfrac{L_0}{2}}}{\left(\sqrt{L_q'' + \dfrac{L_0}{2}}\right)\left(\sqrt{L_d'' + \dfrac{L_0}{2}}\right)}\qquad\text{(IV.385)}$$

As in the case of the line-to-line fault, the phase current is seen to have a fundamental frequency component and odd harmonics whose magnitudes are related to this fundamental component and to the subtransient saliency factor b_0.

The constant (d.c.) term and even harmonics are related to the instant of time at which the short circuit occurred. Note that if $\theta_0 = 90°$ (cos $\theta_0 = 0$), no d.c. term or even harmonics would arise.

Inspection of the expression for the fundamental frequency term in equation (IV.384) shows that in order to obtain the same result by use of the method of symmetrical components, the value of negative sequence reactance is

$$X_2 = \sqrt{\left(X_d'' + \frac{X_0}{2}\right)\left(X_q'' + \frac{X_0}{2}\right)} - \frac{X_0}{2}$$

as previously mentioned in equation (IV.368).

It can be noted that this expression also yields $X_2 = X_d''$ when $X_d'' = X_q''$ and that although it is different from the expression $X_2 = \sqrt{X_d'' X_q''}$ obtained for the line-to-line fault, for most practical situations, the difference in numerical value is not significant.

The fundamental frequency component of line-to-ground fault current, with the effects of flux decay included becomes

$$
i_a = 3\psi_{d0}\left[\left(\frac{1}{X_d'' + X_2 + X_0} - \frac{1}{X_d' + X_2 + X_0}\right)e^{-\frac{t}{T_{d\ell-g}''}} + \right.
$$

$$
\left. + \left(\frac{1}{X_d' + X_2 + X_0} - \frac{1}{X_d + X_2 + X_0}\right)e^{-\frac{t}{T_{d\ell-g}'}} + \frac{1}{X_d + X_2 + X_0}\right] \tag{IV.386}
$$

where
$$
\begin{cases}
T_{d\ell-g}'' = T_{d0}'' \dfrac{X_d'' + X_2 + X_0}{X_d' + X_2 + X_0} \\[3mm]
T_{d\ell-g}' = T_{d0}' \dfrac{X_d' + X_2 + X_0}{X_d + X_2 + X_0}
\end{cases}
$$

4.8.6   Double-Line-to-Ground Fault

The case of the double-line-to-ground fault can be tackled in similar fashion. The relations are rather unwieldy. However, the basic symmetrical component approach can be used to determine the fundamental component of current. In this case the value of X_2 is given by

$$
X_2 = \frac{2X_0\left[X_d'' + \sqrt{X_d'' X_q'' \dfrac{X_d'' + 2X_0}{X_q'' + 2X_0}}\right]}{2X_0 + \sqrt{(X_d'' + 2X_0)(X_q'' + 2X_0)\dfrac{X_d''}{X_q''} - \sqrt{X_d'' X_q'' \dfrac{X_d'' + 2X_0}{X_q'' + 2X_0}}}} \tag{IV.387}
$$

Expression (IV.387) yields, for the limiting cases,

$$
X_2 = \frac{2X_d'' X_q''}{X_d'' + X_q''} \quad \text{for } X_0 = 0
$$

$$
X_2 = \sqrt{X_d'' X_q''} \quad \text{for } X_0 = \infty
$$

The expressions for fundamental frequency currents are:

$$i_{a_1} = \psi_{d0} \left[\left(\frac{1}{X_d'' + X_e} - \frac{1}{X_d' + X_e} \right) e^{-\frac{1}{T_{d\ell\ell g}''}} + \left(\frac{1}{X_d' + X_e} - \frac{1}{X_d + X_e} \right) e^{-\frac{1}{T_{d\ell\ell g}'}} + \frac{1}{X_d + X_e} \right] \quad \text{(IV.388)}$$

where

$$X_e = \frac{X_2 X_0}{X_2 + X_0}$$

$$T_{d_{\ell\ell-g}}'' = T_{d0}'' \frac{X_d'' + X_e}{X_d' + X_e} \quad \text{(IV.389)}$$

$$T_{d_{\ell\ell-g}}' = T_{d0}' \frac{X_d' + X_e}{X_d + X_e}$$

$$i_{a_2} = -i_{a_1} \frac{X_0}{X_2 + X_0}$$

$$i_{a_0} = -i_{a_1} \frac{X_2}{X_2 + X_0} \quad \text{(IV.390)}$$

From these developments it is apparent that the machine behaviour can be analyzed with symmetrical components. The positive sequence currents are readily determined by representing the machine as a positive sequence source in series with positive sequence reactance of the machine, and by loading it with the appropriate combination of negative and zero sequence impedances which represent the fault in question. Figure 4.44 shows the representations for the 3 types of fault discussed previously.

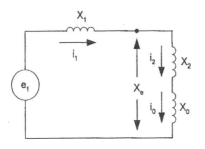

$$i_1 = \frac{e_1}{X_1 + X_2 + X_0}$$
$$i_1 = i_2 = i_0$$

(a) line to neutral fault

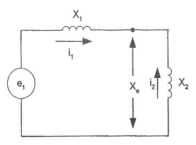

$$i_1 = \frac{e_1}{X_1 + X_2}$$
$$i_2 = -i_1$$

(b) line to line fault

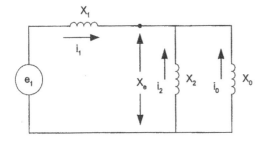

$$i_1 = \frac{e_1}{X_1 + \dfrac{X_2 X_0}{X_2 + X_0}}$$

$$i_2 = -i_1 \frac{X_0}{X_2 + X_0} \qquad i_0 = -i_1 \frac{X_2}{X_2 + X_0}$$

Figure 4.44 – Equivalent Circuits for Unbalanced Short Circuits Simulation

4.8.7 Negative Sequence Reactance

Three definitions of negative sequence reactance X_2 were derived from the point of view of matching calculated fault current by the method of symmetrical components with the value of the fault current calculated with the use of *d-q-0* components.

Another definition of negative sequence reactance can be derived by impressing fundamental frequency negative sequence currents into the machine and solving for resulting negative sequence fundamental frequency voltages. The ratio of voltages to currents then gives the negative sequence reactance.

In equation (IV.364) the currents i_d and i_q corresponding to negative sequence fundamental frequency phase currents i_{a2} were

$$i_d = I_{a2} \cos(2\theta + \phi)$$
$$i_q = -I_{a2} \sin(2\theta + \phi) \tag{IV.391}$$

The *d, q,* currents at this frequency (120 Hz) encounter subtransient reactances X_d'' and X_q'', i.e.;

$$\psi_d = -X_d'' i_d$$

$$\psi_q = -X_q'' i_q$$

Neglecting armature resistance the voltage equations are

$$e_d = \frac{d\psi_d}{dt} - \psi_q = \left(2X_d'' - X_q''\right) I_{a2} \sin(2\theta + \phi)$$

$$e_q = \frac{d\psi_q}{dt} + \psi_d = \left(2X_q'' - X_d''\right) I_{a2} \cos(2\theta + \phi) \tag{IV.392}$$

The phase voltages are

$$e_a = \frac{X_d'' + X_q''}{2} I_{a2} \sin(\theta + \phi) + \frac{3}{2}\left(X_d'' - X_q''\right) I_{a2} \sin(3\theta + \phi)$$

$$e_b = \frac{X_d'' + X_q''}{2} I_{a2} \sin(\theta + 120° + \phi) + \frac{3}{2}\left(X_d'' - X_q''\right) I_{a2} \sin(3\theta + \phi)$$

$$e_c = \frac{X_d'' + X_q''}{2} I_{a2} \sin(\theta - 120° + \phi) + \frac{3}{2}\left(X_d'' - X_q''\right) I_{a2} \sin(3\theta + \phi)$$

The first term corresponds to the negative sequence component of voltage hence the negative sequence reactance by this derivation becomes $X_2 = \dfrac{X_d'' + X_q''}{2}$. This is the most commonly accepted definition of X_2.

4.8.8   Negative Sequence Resistance

Negative sequence currents give rise to double frequency currents in the rotor and corresponding rotor i^2r losses which are in part supplied by power transferred from the shaft. The value of negative sequence resistance can be derived from the power transferred from the stator due to negative sequence currents.

One way of deriving this value is by means of a test whereby negative sequence voltages (reverse phase rotation) are impressed on a machine running at synchronous speed and measurement made of the power transferred from the stator.

The theory of the induction machine treated in the next section is helpful to the understanding of negative sequence power loss and hence to the derivation of negative sequence resistance.

Figure 4.45 shows the equivalent circuit of an induction machine with symmetry in both d and q axes. (For the case of asymmetrical d and q axes the circuit would be an average of the two axes.)

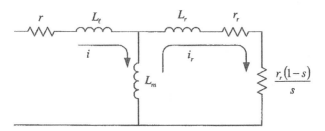

Figure 4.45 – Induction Motor Equivalent Circuit

This equivalent circuit can represent conditions for negative sequence components of voltages and currents by noting that, with the rotor at synchronous speed, the value of slip s is -2. The equivalent resistance $\dfrac{r(1-s)}{s}$ representing power transfer from rotor to shaft becomes $\dfrac{-r}{2}$ indicating that the shaft supplies power to the extent of $I_r^2 r/2$,.i.e.,; one half of the losses in the rotor.

The negative sequence resistance is therefore approximately equal to $r + r_r/2$ since L_m is relatively high so that its shunting effect may be neglected. This resistance corresponds to:

$$r_2 = \frac{\text{negative sequence power transfer from stator}}{\left| I_2 \right|^2}$$

4.8.9   Zero Sequence Impedance

In Section 4.3, in the derivation of d, q and 0 components, it was shown that due to the spacial distribution of the phases along the stator, fundamental frequency zero sequence components of currents (equal currents in each phase) produce no net MMF across the air gap. Impedance to zero sequence currents is therefore only due to the stator windings. The machine zero sequence equivalent circuit is therefore represented as in Figure 4.46.

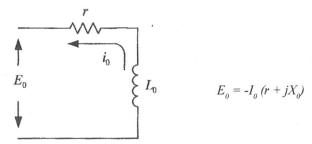

Figure 4.46 – Synchronous Machine Zero Sequence Equivalent Circuit

The above holds for the case where spacial distribution of the stator windings produces a pure sine wave of periodicity corresponding to the space between poles in the rotor. This spacial distribution is usually not purely sinusoidal and therefore is composed of higher harmonics.

Thus for given currents i_a, i_b and i_c in the stator phases, the spacial 3rd harmonic contribution due to these currents would be

$$MMF = K \left[i_a \cos 3\gamma + i_b \cos 3 \left(\gamma - 120° \right) + i_c \cos 3 \left(\gamma + 120° \right) \right] \qquad \text{(IV.393)}$$

For a balanced set of currents such as positive or negative sequence which add up to zero, expression (IV.393) shows that there is no net MMF produced due to spacial winding distribution harmonics.

However, for zero sequence currents such as $i_a = i_b = i_c = I \cos \omega t$, substitution of this value in equation (IV.393) yields

$$MMF \quad = \frac{3I}{2} \left[\cos \left(3\gamma + \omega t \right) + \cos \left(3\gamma - \omega t \right) \right]$$

$$= 3I \cos 3\gamma \cos \omega t$$

From the point of view of the rotor which travels at synchronous speed, $\gamma = \omega t$, this MMF wave due to zero sequence currents is

$$3I \cos 3 \, \omega t \cos \omega t = \frac{3}{2} I \, [\cos 4 \, \omega t \cos 2 \, \omega t]$$

It consists of fourth and second harmonic components which induce currents in the rotor and corresponding rotor heating.

4.8.10 Machine Airgap Power and Shaft Power for Unbalanced Faults

The actual net electrical power transferred from the shaft is of interest in determining machine behaviour during fault conditions.

From the theory of symmetrical components the average power at any given point in a circuit in per unit of the 3 phase power base is

$$P = |E_1| \, |I_1| \cos \theta_1 + |E_2| \, |I_2| \cos \theta_2 + |E_0| \, |I_0| \cos \theta_0 \qquad \text{(IV.394)}$$

The airgap power can be derived by adding the power loss in the stator to the power output at the terminals of the machine.

Take the case of a single line-to-ground fault through some resistance. The sequence network connection diagram is shown on Figure 4.47, giving relations of the sequence variables.

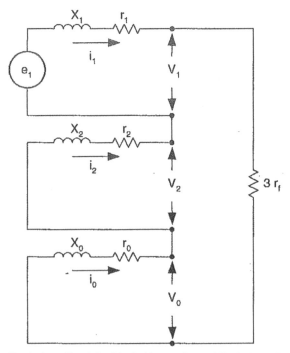

Figure 4.47 – Equivalent Circuit for Single Line-to-Ground Fault through a Resistance

Using equation (IV.394) the terminal power P_T is

$$P_T = |V_1| \, |I_1| \cos \theta_1 + |V_2| \, |I_2| \cos \theta_2 + |V_0| \, |I_0| \cos \theta_0 \qquad \text{(IV.395)}$$

From Figure 4.47 where the only active source is e_1

$$
\left.
\begin{aligned}
V_1 I_1 \cos \theta_1 &= 3 r_f I_1^2 + r_0 I_0^2 + r_2 I_2^2 = \left(3 r_f + r_0 + r_2\right) I_1^2 \\[2mm]
V_2 I_2 \cos \theta_2 &= -r_2 I_2^2 = -r_2 I_1^2 \\[2mm]
V_0 I_0 \cos \theta_0 &= -r_0 I_0^2 = -r_0 I_1^2
\end{aligned}
\right\}
\qquad \text{(IV.396)}
$$

Hence using equation (IV.396) in (IV.395)

$$P_T = 3 r_f I_1^2$$

Now the power loss in the stator is

$$I_1^2 r_1 + I_2^2 r_{stator} + I_0^2 r_0$$

where the negative sequence power loss is only that due to losses in the stator. Recall that the negative sequence resistance r_2 is made up of $r_{stator} + r_r/2$ where r_r is the equivalent rotor resistance.

The total shaft power is that transferred across the airgap plus that converted to supply rotor losses. Recall that half the negative sequence rotor losses are supplied from conversion of positive sequence energy, while the other half is supplied by conversion of mechanical power. Hence, the total shaft power is:

$$
P_s = \underbrace{\left(P_{ag} + \frac{r_r}{2} I_2^2 \right)}_{\substack{\text{from positive} \\ \text{sequence source}}} + \underbrace{\frac{r_r}{2} I_2^2}_{\substack{\text{from mechanical} \\ \text{power}}}
$$

$$= \left(3 r_f + r_1 + r_{stator} + r_0\right) I_1^2 + \frac{r_r}{2} I_2^2 + \frac{r_r}{2} I_2^2 = \qquad \text{(IV.397)}$$

$$= \left(3 r_f + r_1 + r_2 + r_0\right) I_1^2 + \left(r_2 + r_{stator}\right) I_2^2$$

since $I_1 = I_2 = I_0$ and $r_2 = r_{stator} + \dfrac{r_r}{2}$

Equation (IV.397) shows that the shaft power can be derived from the equivalent circuit of Figure 4.47 by calculating the positive sequence power from the source e_1 and adding the braking torque supplied mechanically given by the second term in (IV.397). The effect of unbalanced faults from a power loading standpoint is properly determined by connection of the negative and zero sequence networks in the appropriate manner as required to solve for the sequence currents corresponding to the particular fault.

The resulting positive sequence power in such a connection represents the actual power supplied electrically by the machine.

It should be noted that the shaft power calculated in this manner does not include components due to losses generated by harmonic currents and eddy currents.

The derivation above justifies the approach of representing the loading effects of faults by connection of the negative and zero sequence networks acting as a load on the positive sequence source. Where acceleration and deceleration effects on the shaft are sought, the power supplied mechanically through the induction motor effect should be added.

4.9   Induction Machines

The equivalent circuits of a synchronous machine and the theories of representing effects in synchronous machines can also be applied to represent the operation of induction machines. One simplification is immediately possible; i.e. due to the symmetrical construction of the rotor, the d and q axes equivalent circuits are identical in induction machines. Further there are no excitation sources in the rotor.

Figure 4.48 shows the d and q axes equivalent circuit for an induction machine. For the sake of simplicity the rotor effects are represented by only one circuit in each axis.

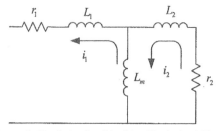

Figure 4.48 – Induction Machine Equivalent Circuit

The induction machine is characterized by asynchronous operation; i.e.; the speed of the rotor ω' is different from the speed of the MMF wave set up by the frequency of balanced positive sequence currents in the stator, ω.

The difference between rotor speed and synchronous speed is called slip $s = \omega-\omega'$. If ω and ω' are expressed in per unit with ω as base, s is the per unit slip. Using d, q transformations, yielding the armature quantities along fixed orthogonal axes on the rotor.

$$e_d = \frac{2}{3}[e_a \cos \omega't + e_b \cos(\omega't - 120°) + e_c \cos(\omega't + 120°)]$$

(IV.398)

$$e_q = -\frac{2}{3}[e_a \sin \omega't + e_b \sin(\omega't - 120°) + e_c \sin(\omega't + 120°)]$$

For balanced voltages with frequency ω,

$$e_a = e \sin \omega t$$

$$e_b = e \sin (\omega t - 120°)$$

(IV.399)

$$e_d = e \sin (\omega t + 120°)$$

Equation (IV.398) becomes

$$e_{d1} = e \sin st$$
$$e_{q1} = -e \cos st$$

(IV.400)

that is, the d and q components of armature voltage become sinusoidal quantities with slip frequency.

Writing the voltage equations for the stator (subscript 1) and for the rotor (subscript 2)

$$e_{d1} = \frac{d\psi_{d1}}{dt} - \psi_{q1}(1-s) - r_1 i_{d1} = e \sin st$$

(IV.401)

$$e_{q1} = \frac{d\psi_{q1}}{dt} + \psi_{d1}(1-s) - r_1 i_{q1} = -e \cos st$$

$$\frac{d\psi_{d2}}{dt} + r_2 i_{d2} = 0$$

(IV.402)

$$\frac{d\psi_{q2}}{dt} + r_2 i_{q2} = 0$$

where

$$\psi_{d1} = -(L_1 + L_m)i_{d1} + L_m i_{d2}$$
$$\psi_{d2} = -L_m i_{d1} + (L_2 + L_m)i_{d2}$$
$$\psi_{q1} = -(L_1 + L_m)i_{q1} + L_m i_{q2} \qquad \text{(IV.403)}$$
$$\psi_{q2} = -L_m i_{q1} + (L_2 + L_m)i_{q2}$$

Substituting equation (IV.403) in (IV.401) and (IV.402)

$$-(L_1 + L_m)\frac{di_{d1}}{dt} + L_m\frac{di_{d2}}{dt} + [(L_1 + L_m)i_{q1} + L_m i_{q2}](1-s) - r_1 i_{d1} = e \sin st$$

$$-(L_1 + L_m)\frac{di_{q1}}{dt} + L_m\frac{di_{q2}}{dt} - [(L_1 + L_m)i_{d1} + L_m i_{d2}](1-s) - r_1 i_{q1} = -e \cos st \tag{IV.404}$$

$$-L_m\frac{di_{d1}}{dt} + (L_2 + L_m)\frac{di_{d2}}{dt} + r_2 i_{d2} = 0$$

$$-L_m\frac{di_{q1}}{dt} + (L_2 + L_m)\frac{di_{q2}}{dt} + r_2 i_{q2} = 0$$

The set of equations (IV.404) are linear differential equations with sinusoidal applied voltages of slip frequency st. Hence there is a steady state solution for which the dependent variables i_{d1}, i_{q1}, ψ_{d1} and ψ_{q1} are also alternating quantities at slip frequency. The solution of the set can be obtained with the use of complex numbers.

Defining

$$e_{d1} = I_m\{E_m e^{jst}\} = I_m\{\sqrt{2}E_d e^{jst}\}$$

$$e_{q1} = I_m\{-jE_m e^{jst}\} = I_m\{-j\sqrt{2}E_d e^{jst}\} \tag{IV.405}$$

From equation (IV.405)

$$\hat{E}_d = \frac{E_m}{\sqrt{2}} \; \varDelta E$$

$$\hat{E}_q = -j\frac{E_m}{\sqrt{2}} \; \varDelta -jE$$

where E is the r.m.s. value.

If $\hat{I}_{d1}$, $\hat{I}_{q1}$, $\hat{I}_{d2}$, and $\hat{I}_{q2}$ are the phasors representing the r.m.s. values of the sinusoidal variables i_{d1}, i_{q1}, i_{d2}, and i_{q2} with frequency s, then equations (IV.404) can be written as

$$E = -js(L_1 + L_m) \hat{I}_{d1} + jsL_m\hat{I}_{d2} + [(L_1 + L_m)\hat{I}_{q1} + L_m\hat{I}_{q2}] (1 - s) - r_1\hat{I}_{d1} \quad \text{(IV.406)}$$

$$-jE = -js(L_1 + L_m) \hat{I}_{q1} + jsL_m\hat{I}_{q2} - [(L_1 + L_m)\hat{I}_{d1} + L_m\hat{I}_{d2}] (1 - s) - r_1\hat{I}_{q1} \quad \text{(IV.407)}$$

$$-jsL_m\hat{I}_{d1} + js(L_2 + L_m)\hat{I}_{d2} + r_2\hat{I}_{d2} = 0 \quad \text{(IV.408)}$$

$$-jsL_m\hat{I}_{q1} + js(L_2 + L_m)\hat{I}_{q2} + r_2\hat{I}_{q2} = 0 \quad \text{(IV.409)}$$

Solution of these equations or symmetry considerations will yield

$$\hat{I}_{q1} = -j\hat{I}_{d1}$$
$$\hat{I}_{q2} = -j\hat{I}_{d2} \quad \text{(IV.410)}$$

Using equation (IV.410) in (IV.406) and simplifying

$$E = -j(L_1 + L_m) \hat{I}_{d1} + jL_m\hat{I}_{d2} - r_1\hat{I}_{d1} \quad \text{(IV.411)}$$

Also dividing equation (IV.408) by s

$$-jL_m\hat{I}_{d1} + j(L_2 + L_m) \hat{I}_{d2} + \hat{I}_{d2} \frac{r_2}{s} = 0 \quad \text{(IV.412)}$$

Equations (IV.411) and (IV.412) can be represented by the equivalent circuits in Figure 4.49 where the time base is $1/\omega$ and where all quantities are at slip frequency. Converting to phase components (inverse d, q transformation)

$$e_a = \sqrt{2} \ E \sin st \cos(1 - s)t + \sqrt{2} \ E \cos st \sin(1 - s)t = \sqrt{2} \ E \sin(t) \quad \text{(IV.413)}$$

and similarly for currents

$$i_{a1} = \sqrt{2} \ I_{d1} \sin (t) \quad \text{(IV.414)}$$

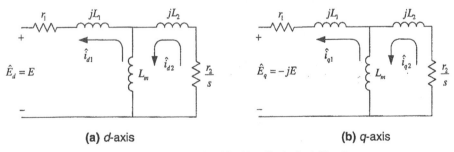

(a) d-axis   **(b)** q-axis

Figure 4.49 – Induction Machine Equivalent Circuit

Hence the equivalent circuit for the induction machine for phase quantities in steady state is also given in Figure 4.50 where the time base is seconds.

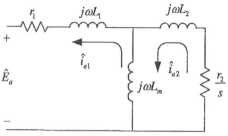

Figure 4.50 – Induction Machine Steady State Equivalent Circuit

Here all quantities are phasors at stator frequencies.

Since the actual resistance loss per phase in the rotor is $r_2 I_2^2$, the balance of the power transferred to the rotor is

$$P = \frac{r_2}{s} I_2^2 - r_2 I_2^2 = \frac{1-s}{s} r_2 I_2^2 \tag{IV.415}$$

This is the mechanical power transferred to the shaft. Another familiar form of the equivalent circuit is shown in Figure 4.51 where the power loss in the rotor is identified as resistance loss $r_2 I_2^2$ and shaft power is $\frac{1-s}{s} r_2 I_2^2$

The direction of currents is shown for the case of operation as an induction motor in which case "s" is positive; i.e., the rotor speed is less than synchronous speed and the power transfer to the shaft is positive as can be seen from equation (IV.415). Evidently, if the power transfer across the air gap of an induction motor is $P_{AG} = \frac{r_2}{s} I_2^2$ then the actual power loss in the rotor is $r_2 I_2^2$.

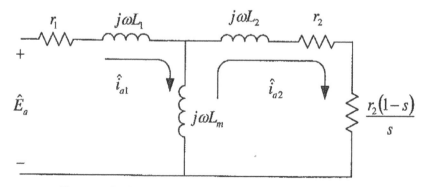

Figure 4.51 – Induction Machine Steady State Equivalent Circuit

Also since $P_m = \omega'T$, where P_m = shaft power, T = torque and ω' = $(1-s)$ is shaft speed, from relation (IV.415).

$$T = \frac{r_2}{s} I_2^2 \qquad \text{(IV.416)}$$

The equivalent circuit of the induction motor may also be derived from the following analysis of steady state a.c. fundamentals. The motor stator and rotor are analogous to the windings of a transformer. With the rotor stationary (blocked rotor) the case is analogous to that of a transformer with short circuited secondary.

Considering the coils of one phase of the stator, the terminal voltage of this phase may be expressed as

$$E_1 = E_{m1} + I_1 (r_1 + jX_1) \qquad \text{(IV.417)}$$

where E_{m1} is the induced voltage due to air gap flux, X_1 is the leakage reactance of the coils and r_1 the resistance of the stator coils. For balanced steady state conditions all variables in equation (IV.417) including the induced voltage E_{m1} must be sinusoidal of fundamental frequency. The air gap flux is the net result of MMF produced by stator and rotor currents. The MMF produced by balanced fundamental frequency stator currents results in a wave which rotates at synchronous speed around the periphery of the stator. This was derived in the discussion of the stator winding of a synchronous machine. The MMF produced by rotor currents must likewise result in a wave which rotates at synchronous speed with respect to the stator. If the rotor is stationary this is automatically produced by rotor currents of fundamental frequency which are induced much like in the case of the transformer. With the rotor at some speed ω' where $s = \omega - \omega'$ = slip, the synchronously rotating MMF with respect to the stator is contributed by rotor currents of slip frequency producing MMF rotation with respect to the rotor at slip frequency. This MMF wave added to the rotor speed, results in a synchronously rotating MMF with respect to the stationary stator frame.

If the voltage induced in the stator by the synchronously rotating flux wave is represented by the phasor E_{m1} then this same flux wave induces a voltage sE_{m1} of slip frequency in the rotor. It is this voltage which gives rise to currents of slip frequency in the rotor

$$sE_{m1} = (R_2 + jsX_2) I_2 \qquad \text{(IV.418)}$$

where X_2 is the rotor leakage reactance measured at fundamental supply frequency. Dividing equation (IV.418) by s

$$E_{m1} = \left[\frac{R_2}{s} + jX_2\right] I_2 \qquad \text{(IV.419)}$$

The air gap flux is the resultant from MMF's due to stator current I_1 and rotor current I_2. Expressing this relation in terms of the magnetizing reactance jX_m

$$E_{m1} = jX_m(I_1 - I_2) \qquad \text{(IV.420)}$$

The conditions of equations (IV.417), (IV.419) and (IV.420) are fulfilled by the equivalent circuit of Figure 4.51.

4.10   Motor Starting

Induction and synchronous motors are started from standstill by connection to the power source either at full voltage or at reduced voltage by means of an autotransformer.

Phenomena involved in starting induction or synchronous motors can be evaluated by the same computational methods. For the case of induction motors, the impedances are symmetrical in any axes and pulsations do not develop except in short periods following switching.

Starting of a synchronous motor introduces the pulsations due to the saliency effect. A complete solution of the starting transients is obtained by simulation methods solving the pertinent equations. Figure 4.52 shows a solution scheme which may be implemented on digital or analog computers.

The d-q transformation relates the source voltage onto the motor axes. The voltages e_d and e_q will be of slip frequency ($\omega - \omega_m$). The ψ_d and ψ_q loop can be recognized as giving oscillatory roots with a frequency ω_m.

At standstill $\omega m = 0$ and if there were no effect from source and stator resistance, the integration $1/s$ in the block diagram will yield a root $s = 0$. i.e., the familiar dc offset effect.

If we consider the quasi steady state where the initial switching transients have died down, and where the slip can be considered constant in relation to the variations in voltages and currents, then an analytical expression can be derived for currents and torque as follows:

Let the source voltage be $e_a = E \cos (\omega t)$, positive sequence, and let the position of the d-axis of the motor be $\theta = \omega_m t$. Using the d-q transformation

$$e_d = E \cos(\omega - \omega_m)t \qquad \text{(IV.421)}$$

$$e_q = E \sin(\omega - \omega_m)t \qquad \text{(IV.422)}$$

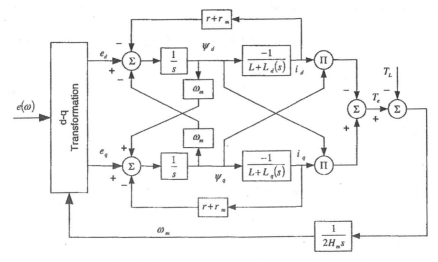

Figure 4.52 – Block Diagram Representing an Induction Machine

Park's voltage equations in Laplace form

$$e_d(s) = s\psi_d(s) - \omega_m \psi_q(s) - (r + r_m)i_d(s) \tag{IV.423}$$

$$e_q(s) = s\psi_q(s) - \omega_m \psi_d(s) - (r + r_m)i_q(s) \tag{IV.424}$$

Also, using the generator convention for current direction,

$$i_d(s) = \frac{-\psi_d(s)}{L + L_d(s)} \tag{IV.425}$$

$$i_q(s) = \frac{-\psi_q(s)}{L + L_q(s)} \tag{IV.426}$$

Equations (IV.421) and (IV.422) are linear differential equations with sinusoidal applied voltages e_d and e_q of slip frequency $(\omega - \omega_m)$. Hence a steady state solution of the equation may be obtained by substituting $s = j(\omega - \omega_m)$ and representing e_d and e_q as phasor quantities with this frequency.

$$\hat{e}_d = E$$
$$\hat{e}_q = -jE$$

Writing equations (IV.421) and (IV.422) in their steady state phasor form

$$E = j(\omega - \omega_m)\hat{\psi}_d - \omega_m\hat{\psi}_q - (r + r_m)\hat{i}_d \qquad \text{(IV.427)}$$

$$-jE = \omega_m\hat{\psi}_d + j(\omega - \omega_m)\hat{\psi}_q - (r + r_m)\hat{i}_q \qquad \text{(IV.428)}$$

Using (IV.425) and (IV.426) to express $\hat{i}_d$ and $\hat{i}_q$ in terms of $\hat{\psi}_d$ and $\hat{\psi}_q$, (IV.427) and (IV.428) becomes

$$E = \left[j(\omega - \omega_m) + \frac{r + r_m}{L + L_d\left(j(\omega - \omega_m)\right)} \right]\hat{\psi}_d - \omega_m\hat{\psi}_q \qquad \text{(IV.429)}$$

$$-jE = \omega_m\hat{\psi}_d + \left[j(\omega - \omega_m) + \frac{r + r_m}{L + L_q\left(j(\omega - \omega_m)\right)} \right]\hat{\psi}_q \qquad \text{(IV.430)}$$

Denoting

$$L + L_d\left(j(\omega - \omega_m)\right) = L_d^*$$
$$L + L_q\left(j(\omega - \omega_m)\right) = L_q^*$$
$$r + r_m = r^*$$

Solution of (IV.429) and (IV.430) yields

$$\hat{\psi}_d = \frac{jE\left(\omega - 2\omega_m - j\dfrac{r^*}{L_q^*}\right)}{\omega(2\omega_m - \omega) + j(\omega_m - \omega)r^*\left(\dfrac{1}{L_d^*} + \dfrac{1}{L_q^*}\right) + \dfrac{\left(r^*\right)^2}{L_d^*L_q^*}} \qquad \text{(IV.431)}$$

$$\hat{\psi}_q = \frac{E\left(\omega - 2\omega_m - j\dfrac{r^*}{L_d^*}\right)}{\omega(2\omega_m - \omega) + j(\omega_m - \omega)r^*\left(\dfrac{1}{L_d^*} + \dfrac{1}{L_q^*}\right) + \dfrac{\left(r^*\right)^2}{L_d^*L_q^*}} \qquad \text{(IV.432)}$$

Also

$$\bar{i_d} = \frac{-\hat{\psi}_d}{L_d^*} - \frac{\hat{\psi}_{dm}}{L_d} \tag{IV.433}$$

$$\bar{i_q} = \frac{-\hat{\psi}_q}{L_q^*} - \frac{\hat{\psi}_{qm}}{L_q} \tag{IV.434}$$

The motor fluxes are

$$\hat{\psi}_{dm} = \hat{\psi}_d \frac{L_d}{L_d^*}$$

$$\hat{\psi}_{qm} = \hat{\psi}_q \frac{L_q}{L_q^*}$$

i.e.,

$$\hat{\psi}_{dm} = \frac{jE\left(\omega - 2\omega_m - j\frac{r^*}{L_q^*}\right)\frac{L_d}{L_d^*}}{\omega\left(2\omega_m - \omega\right) + j\left(\omega_m - \omega\right)r^*\left(\frac{1}{L_d^*} + \frac{1}{L_q^*}\right) + \frac{\left(r^*\right)^2}{L_d^* L_q^*}} \tag{IV.435}$$

$$\hat{\psi}_{qm} = \frac{E\left(\omega - 2\omega_m - j\frac{r^*}{L_d^*}\right)\frac{L_q}{L_q^*}}{\omega\left(2\omega_m - \omega\right) + j\left(\omega_m - \omega\right)r^*\left(\frac{1}{L_d^*} + \frac{1}{L_q^*}\right) + \frac{\left(r^*\right)^2}{L_d^* L_q^*}} \tag{IV.436}$$

Torque = $(i_q \psi_{dm} - i_d \psi_{qm})$

Expressing (IV.433), (IV.434), (IV.435) and (IV.436) as

$$\psi_{dm} = \left|\hat{\psi}_{dm}\right| \cos\left[\left(\omega - \omega_m\right)t + \theta_{dm}\right] \tag{IV.437}$$

$$\psi_{qm} = \left|\hat{\psi}_{qm}\right| \cos\left[\left(\omega - \omega_m\right)t + \theta_{qm}\right] \tag{IV.438}$$

$$i_d = \frac{\left|\hat{\psi}_{dm}\right|}{\left|L_d\right|} \cos\left[\left(\omega - \omega_m\right)t + \theta_{dm} - \phi_d\right] \tag{IV.439}$$

$$i_q = \frac{\left|\hat{\psi}_{qm}\right|}{\left|L_q\right|} \cos\left[\left(\omega - \omega_m\right)t + \theta_{qm} - \phi_q\right] \tag{IV.440}$$

where $\left|\hat{\psi}_{dm}\right|$ and $\left|\hat{\psi}_{qm}\right|$ are the peak magnitudes and θ_{dm} and θ_{qm} are the angles of complex expressions (IV.435) and (IV.436); $\left|\hat{\psi}_d\right|$ and $\left|\hat{\psi}_q\right|$ are the peak magnitudes and θ_d and θ_q are the phase angles of same; ϕ_d and ϕ_q are the angles of complex expressions (IV.431) and (IV.432) and L_d and L_q.

The torque expression is:

$$T = -\frac{\left|\hat{\psi}_{qm}\right|}{\left|L_q\right|} \cos\left[\left(\omega - \omega_m\right)t + \theta_{qm} - \phi_q\right]\cos\left[\left(\omega - \omega_m\right)t + \theta_{dm}\right] +$$

$$+\frac{\left|\hat{\psi}_{dm}\right|}{\left|L_d\right|} \cos\left[\left(\omega - \omega_m\right)t + \theta_{dm} - \phi_q\right]\cos\left[\left(\omega - \omega_m\right)t + \theta_{qm}\right]$$

i.e.,

$$T = -\frac{\left|\hat{\psi}_{qm}\hat{\psi}_{dm}\right|}{\left|L_q\right|}\left\{\frac{1}{2}\cos\left(\theta_{qm} - \phi_q - \theta_{dm}\right) + \frac{1}{2}\cos\left[2\left(\omega - \omega_m\right)t + \theta_{qm} - \phi_q + \theta_{dm}\right]\right\} +$$

$$+\frac{\left|\hat{\psi}_{qm}\hat{\psi}_{dm}\right|}{\left|L_d\right|}\left\{\frac{1}{2}\cos\left(\theta_{dm} - \phi_d - \theta_{qm}\right) + \frac{1}{2}\cos\left[2\left(\omega - \omega_m\right)t + \theta_{dm} - \phi_d + \theta_{qm}\right]\right\} \tag{IV.441}$$

The torque is seen to consist of a steady component:

$$\frac{\left|\hat{\psi}_{qm}\hat{\psi}_{dm}\right|}{2}\left\{-\frac{1}{\left|L_q\right|}\cos\left(\theta_{qm} - \phi_q - \theta_{dm}\right) + \frac{1}{\left|L_d\right|}\cos\left(\theta_{dm} - \phi_d + \theta_{qm}\right)\right\}$$

and a pulsating component at twice slip frequency:

$$\frac{\left|\hat{\psi}_{qm}\hat{\psi}_{dm}\right|}{2}\left\{-\frac{1}{\left|L_q\right|}\cos\left[2\left(\omega - \omega_m\right)t + \theta_{qm} - \phi_q + \theta_{dm}\right] + \frac{1}{\left|L_d\right|}\cos\left[2\left(\omega - \omega_m\right)t + \theta_{dm} - \phi_d + \theta_{qm}\right]\right\}$$

With the source impedance as negligible and motor stator resistance as zero, the expression for torque becomes:

$$T = \frac{E^2}{\omega^2} \left\{ -\frac{1}{2|L_q|} \cos\left(0° - \tan^{-1}\left(\frac{\text{Im}\{L_q\}}{\text{Re}\{L_q\}} \right) - 90° \right) + \right.$$

$$+ \frac{1}{2|L_d|} \cos\left(90° - \tan^{-1}\left(\frac{\text{Im}\{L_d\}}{\text{Re}\{L_d\}} \right) - 0° \right) -$$

$$- \frac{1}{2|L_q|} \cos\left[2(\omega - \omega_m)t + 0° - \tan^{-1}\left(\frac{\text{Im}\{L_q\}}{\text{Re}\{L_q\}} \right) + 90° \right] +$$

$$\left. + \frac{1}{2|L_d|} \cos\left[2(\omega - \omega_m)t + 90° - \tan^{-1}\left(\frac{\text{Im}\{L_d\}}{\text{Re}\{L_d\}} \right) + 0° \right] \right\}$$

(IV.442)

i.e.,

$$T = \frac{E^2}{2\omega^2} \left\{ \frac{\text{Im}\{L_d\}}{|L_d|^2} + \frac{\text{Im}\{L_q\}}{|L_q|^2} + \right.$$

$$\left. + \left(\frac{\text{Re}\{L_q\}}{|L_q|^2} - \frac{\text{Re}\{L_d\}}{|L_d|^2} \right) \sin\left[2(\omega - \omega_m)t \right] + \left(\frac{\text{Im}\{L_d\}}{|L_d|^2} - \frac{\text{Im}\{L_q\}}{|L_q|^2} \right) \cos\left[2(\omega - \omega_m)t \right] \right\}$$

(IV.443)

Torque in per unit is given by this expression with E in per unit (1.0 p.u. for rated terminal voltage) and L_d and L_q in per unit.

With $r = 0$, the currents i_d and i_q will be:

$$\hat{i}_d = -j\frac{E}{\omega L_d} \quad \therefore \quad i_d = \frac{E \sin\left[(\omega - \omega_m)t - \phi_d \right]}{\omega |L_d|}$$

(IV.444)

$$\hat{i}_q = -j\frac{E}{\omega L_q} \quad \therefore \quad i_q = \frac{E \cos\left[(\omega - \omega_m)t - \phi_q \right]}{\omega |L_q|}$$

(IV.445)

Taking the inverse d-q transformation, the phase "a" current is

$$i_a = i_d \cos(\omega_m t)t - i_q \sin(\omega_m t)t$$

(IV.446)

With trigonometric substitutions using (IV.444) and (IV.445) in (IV.446)

$$i_a = \frac{E}{2\omega} \left\{ A \sin(\omega t - \alpha) + B \sin[(\omega - 2\omega_m)t - \beta] \right\}$$

where $A\underline{|\alpha} = \left[\frac{1}{j(\omega - \omega_m)L_d} + \frac{1}{j(\omega - \omega_m)L_q} \right]$ and $B\underline{|\beta} = \left[\frac{1}{j(\omega - \omega_m)L_q} - \frac{1}{j(\omega - \omega_m)L_d} \right]$

Nomenclature

E	=	amplitude of fundamental frequency source voltage $e_a = E \cos \omega t$
ω	=	source frequency
ω_m	=	motor speed
L_d^*	=	combined source and motor d-axis operational inductance at slip frequency $\omega - \omega_m$
L_q^*	=	combined source and motor q-axis operational inductance at slip frequency $\omega - \omega_m$
$\hat{\psi}_d, \hat{\psi}_q$	=	d and q axes total flux linkages phasors (motor+source) at slip frequency $\omega - \omega_m$
$\hat{\psi}_{dm}, \hat{\psi}_{qm}$	=	d and q axes motor flux linkages phasors at slip frequency $\omega - \omega_m$
θ_d	=	phase angle of $\hat{\psi}_d$
θ_q	=	phase angle of $\hat{\psi}_q$
θ_{dm}	=	phase angle of $\hat{\psi}_{dm}$
θ_{qm}	=	phase angle of $\hat{\psi}_{qm}$
ϕ_d	=	phase angle of $L_d (j(\omega - \omega_m))$
ϕ_q	=	phase angle of $L_q (j(\omega - \omega_m))$
ϕ_d^*	=	phase angle of $L_d^* (j(\omega - \omega_m))$
ϕ_q^*	=	phase angle of $L_q^* (j(\omega - \omega_m))$

Energy in Acceleration of Motors

Defining H = per unit inertia constant

ω_m = per unit motor speed

T = accelerating torque

ω = source voltage frequency (IV.447)

$$T = 2H\frac{d\omega_m}{dt}$$

or

$$Tdt = 2Hd\omega_m$$

582

With no load on, motor electrical torque accelerating torque

$$T = \frac{rI^2}{s} = \frac{rI^2\omega}{\omega - \omega_m} \qquad \text{(IV.448)}$$

where rotor losses $= rI^2$ and the rotor energy loss $= \int rI^2 dt$

$$\text{rotor energy loss} = \int T\frac{\omega - \omega_m}{\omega}dt \qquad \text{(IV.449)}$$

Substituting $2H\,d\omega_m$ for Tdt, expression (IV.449) becomes

$$\text{rotor energy loss} = \int 2H\frac{\omega - \omega_m}{\omega}d\omega_m$$

For complete acceleration from $\omega_m = 0$ to $\omega_m = 1.0$.

$$\text{rotor energy loss} = \int_0^1 2H\frac{\omega - \omega_m}{\omega}d\omega_m$$

$$= 2H\left[\omega_m - \frac{\omega_m^2}{2}\right]_0^1 = H$$

Rotor energy loss for full acceleration = H = Kinetic energy of motor at rated speed.

It is independent of time it takes to accelerate.

References

1) C. Concordia, "Synchronous Machines", John Wiley & Sons, Inc. New York, 1951.

2) Electrical Transmission and Distribution Reference Book, Westinghouse Electric Corporation, Fourth Edition.

3) S.B. Crary, "Power System Stability". Vol. I, John Wiley & Sons, Inc., New York 1945.

4) Fitzgerald and Kingsley, "Electric Machinery", McGraw Hill Book Co., 1952.

5) F.P. de Mello and L.N. Hannett, "Representation of Saturation in Synchronous Machines", IEEE Transactions on Power Apparatus & Systems. Paper 86WM0574, PES Winter Meeting 1986.

6) F.P. de Mello and L.N. Hannett, "Representation of Saturation in Synchronous Machine Stability Study Constants", EPRI EL-1424, Vol. 3, Research Project 997-3

Chapter 5

Electrical Machine Dynamics II

Contents

List of Figures

Electrical Machine Dynamics - II

5.1   Introduction

The successful operation of a-c power systems depends on the ability of various synchronous machines to maintain synchronism through transient conditions as might be created by credible disturbances. The study of the transient behavior of synchronous machines involves both the electrical phenomena relating fluxes, voltages, and currents as well as mechanical phenomena describing the variations in shaft speed and rotor angle as function of the imbalance between electrical and mechanical torques.

The transient behavior of synchronous machines has been characterized by useful concepts of "transient stability," "steady-state stability," and "dynamic stability." Much has been written on these subjects in textbooks and technical papers and it is not the intent here to replace this wealth of reference material but rather to present some fundamental concepts in convenient tutorial form. Pertinent technical papers are appended to these notes as reference material.

Whereas the entire subject of stability of synchronous operation can be described by one detailed set of dynamic equations, much useful insight has been developed by classification of certain basic phenomena into forms which allow particular simplifying assumptions.

We will explore the subject and most of the power system stability concepts by first considering the case of ideal machines represented by sources behind equivalent reactances; these sources having phase angles corresponding to the mechanical shaft positions of generator rotors. The additional effects due to the fact that a synchronous machine behaves differently than an ideal source behind a constant reactance will be considered separately following an exposition of basic stability concepts in their simplest form.

Although dynamic performance of power systems is generally associated with "stability phenomena," there are other dynamic aspects which may play an important role in the system design process. Overvoltage performance under load rejection conditions, and stability of subsynchronous oscillations in series capacitor applications are examples of these dynamic aspects which are also covered in these notes and reference material.

5.2   Stability Concepts - Idealized Machines

5.2.1   The Stability Phenomena

The mechanism whereby synchronous machines maintain synchronism, or remain in "step" with one another is through the development of restoring forces every time a given unit tends to accelerate or decelerate with respect to other units connected to the same network.

Constant shaft speed on a given machine is maintained when there is equilibrium between mechanical shaft torque and the braking electrical torque. Any imbalance between these torques produces acceleration or deceleration of the machine rotor following the laws of motion of a rotating body.

The derivations of the equation of motion and the inertia constants M and H were developed in the notes on Generation Dynamics and Control. For ready reference they are summarized here as:

$$p\delta(t) = \frac{1}{M} \int [T_m - T_e] dt \qquad (V.1)$$

where $p\delta(t)$ = deviation from normal frequency in per unit.
T_m = prime mover torque in per unit
T_e = electrical torque in per unit
M = $2H$ in seconds
t = time in seconds
H

= inertia constant in seconds; $= \dfrac{0.231 \times wR^2 \times (rpm)^2 \times 10^{-6}}{KVA\ base}$ $\qquad$ (V.2)

In the Generation Dynamics and Control notes (Section II), it was shown that, for small perturbations, (V.1) can also be expressed with little error as:

$$p\delta(t) = \frac{1}{M} \int [P_m - P_e] dt \qquad (V.3)$$

where P_m and P_e are per unit mechanical and electrical powers respectively.

A block diagram describing the momentum equation (also called the swing equation) in incremental form is shown in Figure 5.1, as applied to a single machine connected to a large network.

The accelerating power $(P_A = \Delta P_M = \Delta P_E)$ divided by the inertia constant M integrates into a change in speed $(p\delta)$ which in turn integrates into a change in angle $(\Delta\delta)$. The change in electrical power (ΔP_E) is seen to consist of two components, one a function of speed and the other a function of angle. In linearized form these functions may be represented by constants. $D = \partial P_E/\partial p\delta$ is called the damping coefficient. $T = \partial P_E/\partial\delta$ is called the synchronizing power coefficient.

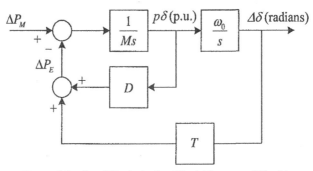

Figure 5.1 – Small Perturbation Block Diagram of Machine

The stability of this system may be analyzed by standard block diagram algebra to obtain the roots of the characteristic equation.

$$s = -\frac{D}{2M} \pm \sqrt{\left(\frac{D}{2M}\right)^2 - \frac{\omega_0 T}{M}} \qquad (V.4)$$

We have learned previously that a closed loop system is stable as long as the roots of the characteristic equation have no positive real parts. As applied to (V.4) this criterion requires that $D \geq 0$ and $T \geq \dfrac{D^2}{4 \times \omega_0 M}$ for stability. These results correspond well with physical reasoning since a negative value of D or T would constitute a positive feedback loop which would obviously be unstable.

The generalization of the phenomena to the multi-machine case of ideal constant voltage synchronous sources on a network is shown in Figure 5.2 where under small perturbations the relationship between power changes and angle changes is described by a linear power flow matrix.

The roots of the system characteristic equation would reveal the modes of oscillation and the stability of the system.

For larger perturbations the linearized treatment of Figures 5.1 and 5.2 is no longer valid. In particular the relationship between angle and electrical power must now be expressed as non-linear (sinusoidal) functions characteristic of power/angle expressions in networks.

Traditionally stability phenomena and associated methods of analysis have been characterized under the three categories "steady state," "transient" and "dynamic." The article "Introduction to Problems of Power System Stability" by Kimbark (Reference 3) presents in excellent tutorial form descriptions of these phenomena.

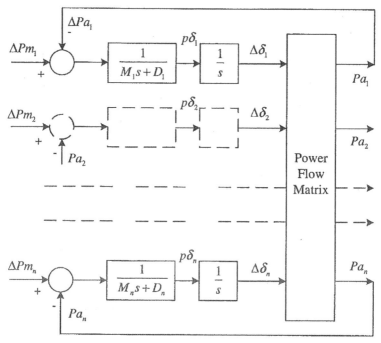

Figure 5.2 – Small Perturbation Diagram of Multi Machine System

Steady State Stability has been associated with the ability of machines to maintain synchronism under small disturbances. Steady state stability is a function of the system state or given operating condition and is not dependent on the magnitude of the disturbance which, by definition, is infinitesimally small. Under the regime of small perturbations relation (V.4) and the block diagram of Figure 5.1 shows that stability can be lost for lack of positive synchronizing power coefficient T or for lack of positive damping coefficient D.

In the early days of a.c. power systems, stable operation had to be assured without assistance from automatic excitation controls. Hence with excitation under close manual control the instability under small perturbations was usually associated with lack of steady state synchronizing torques ($\frac{\partial P}{\partial \delta} < 0$). Steady state stability has thus been associated with the existence or not of steady state synchronizing power and instability is manifested by an aperiodic drift in machine angle.

Transient Stability, as the name implies, is associated with the ability of a system to withstand transients or large disturbances. Angle excursions can be large and the loss of stability is due to the nonlinear relationship between angle and power. Stability is both a function of the operating state and the severity of the disturbance.

Dynamic or Oscillatory Stability has been associated with the linearized small-signal properties of the system which can be described by the roots of the characteristic equation of the overall system including controls. Instability is usually characterized by undamped oscillations and hence the condition cannot be detected by a simple test of a parameter such as the synchronizing power coefficient as was done for steady state stability. In studies of dynamic stability we shall see that the transient behavior of machine fluxes, in response to excitation control, can have a major role. As in the case of steady state stability, dynamic stability is not a function of the disturbance, but rather by the state of the system.

It is appropriate at this point to comment on the use of terminology which has historically suffered from past inability to analyze the complete phenomena and from the fact that certain modes of operation without the aid of automatic controls were possible in the days when stability phenomena were first talked about. The following observations may be helpful in placing the subject of stability into perspective:

Dynamic analysis in the dimensions involved with stability phenomena on multi-machine systems was practically impossible in the days before analog and digital computers, i.e., before the early fifties.

Automatic excitation controls were not sufficiently developed and trusted until the fifties. It was customary for system planners to design systems for stability under conditions of manual control of excitation. Steady state instability due to loss of steady state synchronizing power as characterized by an aperiodic drift in machine angle was, therefore, a germane problem and the analytical test of stability could be obtained from purely static versus dynamic considerations (steady state synchronizing power coefficients). . The earliest connotation to the term "steady state stability" was, therefore, associated with the aperiodic angle pull out due to loss of steady state synchronizing power.

Advances in the technology of automatic control (both in methods of analysis and hardware design), as well as in the design of generators yielding greater output per pound through improved cooling techniques, resulted in progressively higher reactance machines, the successful operation of which could only be assured in conjunction with use of automatic excitation control. Today's machines with $X_d \simeq 2\,p.u.$, could not maintain steady state stability at loadings considerably below rated without use of continuously acting (dynamic) voltage regulators.

The phenomena of *steady state stability*, i.e., stability under infinitesimally small disturbances, can no longer be treated analytically by a simple static test of steady state synchronizing power coefficient -- since the form of instability is not confined to an aperiodic drift in angle but, rather, usually involves undamped angle oscillations. The term *dynamic stability* and more recently *oscillatory stability*, was, thus, introduced to characterize this type of condition.

The phenomenon of *transient instability* was always associated with an energy shock which the system could not withstand without loss of synchronism on the part of some generation. The shock or imbalance in energy is due both to the change to the end condition (ultimate state of transmission) as well as during the transition (fault period).

From a purely operational (rather than computational) point of view there are two fundamental situations which lend themselves to the characterization of stability phenomena.

a) Performance under small disturbances involving no change in end state. Linearization and small perturbation analysis is applicable to determine stability. Instability can be of two forms: an aperiodic drift (unstable real root in the characteristic equation), or an undamped oscillation (unstable complex roots). The latter form of instability is much more common than the former since most units are on automatic voltage control.

  The end result of the oscillatory type of instability can be either a growth of oscillations to the point where the non-linear effects of the power angle curve cause pull out or loss of synchronism, or a growth of oscillations to a sustained amplitude level. In the latter case the limit cycle thus established is usually due to non-linear gain effects of control elements (amplifier limits or exciter ceilings). It should be noted that the oscillatory type of instability can develop in rare situations even without the action of excitation controls. (Reference 10)

b) Performance under large disturbances where the end state may or may not be the same as the initial state but where the electrical to mechanical energy imbalance due to the disturbance causes excursions in angles beyond the point where linear analysis is valid. The forms of instability that may result are:

First swing instability with the accelerating units pulling out on the initial angle excursion.

Second or subsequent swing instability when the superposition of several modes of oscillation cause larger angle excursions and pull out on the second or subsequent oscillations.

A stable first and subsequent swing in the sense that pull out does not occur, but a gradual growth of oscillations as the end state is approached. This occurs when the end state itself is "steady state" unstable. The transition to the end state can take several seconds as excitation systems adjust to the new condition. The result can then be either loss of stability as oscillations grow to excessive amplitudes, or growth of oscillations to a sustained level due to limit cycle effects as described in (a).

In the present state of the art all of the effects described above are analyzed with the same mathematical simulation tools capable of representing the full non-linear and linear, short-term and long-term effects.

5.2.2   Power-Angle Relations

Consider the system of Figure 5.3 showing two synchronous sources connected through impedance

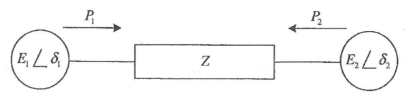

Figure 5.3 – Schematic of Two Machines Connected across Impedance

The vector diagram showing currents and voltages is shown on Figure 5.4.

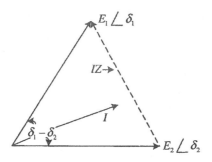

Figure 5.4 – Phasor Diagram for Voltages and Current in Machines Connected across Series Impedance

In vector notation:

$$\hat{I} = \frac{\hat{E}_1 - \hat{E}_2}{Z}$$

(V.5)

Also the expression for power is:

$$P = \mathrm{Re}\left[\hat{E}\hat{I}^*\right]$$

(V.6)

Hence:

$$
\begin{aligned}
P_1 &= \mathrm{Re}\left[\hat{E}_1\hat{I}^*\right] = \mathrm{Re}\left[\frac{\hat{E}_1\hat{E}_1^* - \hat{E}_1\hat{E}_2^*}{Z^*}\right] \\
&= \mathrm{Re}\left[\frac{|E_1|^2}{Z^*}\right] - \mathrm{Re}\left[\frac{\hat{E}_1\hat{E}_2^*}{Z^*}\right] \\
&= \frac{E_1^2}{|Z|}\sin\alpha + \frac{E_1 E_2}{|Z|}\sin\left(\delta_1 - \delta_2 - \alpha\right)
\end{aligned}
$$

(V.7)

where $Z = R + jX = |Z|\angle 90° - \alpha = |Z|(\sin\alpha + j\cos\alpha), \alpha = \tan^{-1}\left(\frac{R}{X}\right)\hat{E}_1 = E_1\angle\delta_1, \hat{E}_2 = E_2\angle\delta_2$

Similarly, $\qquad P_2 = \dfrac{E_2^2\sin\alpha}{|Z|} + \dfrac{E_1 E_2}{|Z|}\sin\left(\delta_2 - \delta_1 - \alpha\right)$

(V.8)

where the direction of power flow is by convention selected as being out of the source.

Expressions (V.7) and (V.8) show the familiar power angle expressions relating the power flow between two synchronous voltage sources as functions of the phase angle between them.

Figure 5.5 is a plot of P_1 and P_2 for the case of $E_1 = E_2 = 1$, $Z = 0.5$ and $\alpha = 5.7°$

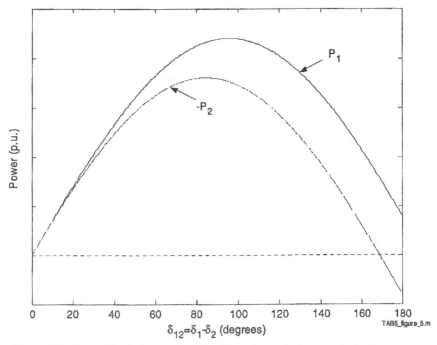

Figure 5.5 – Power Angle Curves for 2 Machines Connected across Series Impedance

Note the sinusoidal form of the power angle function. Also note that (P_1-P_2) represents losses and that for the case of a pure reactance, $Z = jX$, the lossless case, the power-angle expression is a sine wave

$$P = \frac{E_1 E_2}{X} \sin (\delta_1 - \delta_2) \qquad\qquad (V.9)$$

with no offset as shown in Figure 5.6.

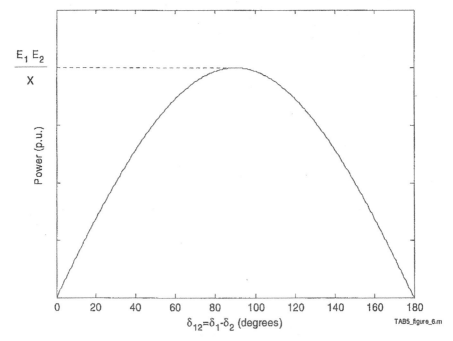

Figure 5.6 – Power Angle Curve for 2 Machines Connected across Series Reactance

The angle of source voltages E_1 and E_2 can be related to the shaft angle of the machine rotors. These rotors produce the MMF and flux wave whose rotation with respect to the stator generates the a-c voltage.

It is evident from the vector diagram of Figure 5.4 and expressions (V.7) and (V.8) that the transfer of power across impedances involves a change in angle between the voltages across the impedance.

In the general case of a network of impedances between several sources, as in Figure 5.7, the power angle expressions are:

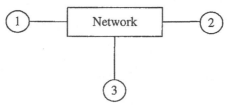

Figure 5.7 – Schematic of 3 Machine System

$$
\left.
\begin{aligned}
P_1 &= \frac{E_1^2}{|Z_{11}|}\sin\alpha_{11} + \frac{E_1 E_2}{|Z_{12}|}\sin\left(\delta_{12}-\alpha_{12}\right) + \frac{E_1 E_3}{|Z_{13}|}\sin\left(\delta_{13}-\alpha_{13}\right) \\
P_2 &= \frac{E_2^2}{|Z_{22}|}\sin\alpha_{22} + \frac{E_1 E_2}{|Z_{12}|}\sin\left(\delta_{21}-\alpha_{12}\right) + \frac{E_2 E_3}{|Z_{23}|}\sin\left(\delta_{23}-\alpha_{23}\right) \\
P_3 &= etc.
\end{aligned}
\right\} \quad \text{(V.10)}
$$

where: Z_{11} = driving point impedance $= |Z_{11}|\underline{\big|90°-\alpha_{11}}$

Z_{12} = transfer impedance $= |Z_{12}|\underline{\big|90°-\alpha_{12}}$

Z_{13} = transfer impedance $= |Z_{13}|\underline{\big|90°-\alpha_{13}}$

It should be noted that in the case of the straight series resistance and inductive reactance between two sources, $Z_{11} = Z_{12} = Z_{22}$, and the angle α_{12} curve is positive so that the peak of the power angle curve occurs at an angle between sources $(\delta_1 - \delta_2)$ of $(90° + \alpha_{12})$, as in Figure 5.5.

In the case where some shunt impedances are involved as in Figure 5.8:

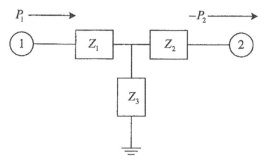

Figure 5.8 – Two Machine System with Shunt and Series Impedance

$Z_{11} \neq Z_{12}$ and for resistance and inductive reactance networks, α_{12} is negative so that the peak of the power angle curve occurs at $(\delta_1 - \delta_2)$ below 90° as shown in Figure 5.9.

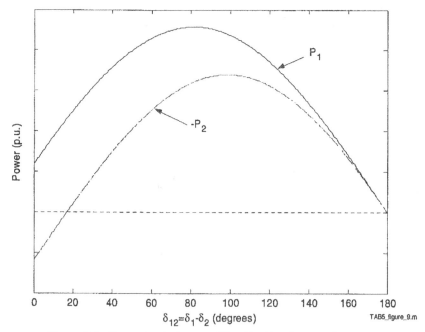

Figure 5.9 – Power Angle Curves of Two Machine System of Figure 8

5.2.3 Pull Out Power

Consider the system of a single synchronous machine connected to an infinite bus by a transmission line, as shown in Figure 5.10.

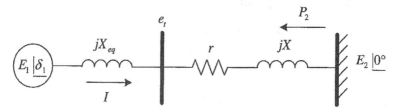

Figure 5.10 – Single Machine Connected to Infinite Bus

Note that the machine here is represented by a constant voltage source behind an equivalent reactance. Disconsidering saliency, that is assuming that the machine is represented by equal reactances in both axes, $X_{eq} = X_d = X_q$ and that the voltage source (E_t) is proportional to voltage behind this reactance.

Application of (V.7) allows us to derive the power-angle relations.

$$P_1 = \frac{E_1^2}{|Z|}\sin\alpha + \frac{E_1 E_2}{|Z|}\sin(\delta_1 - \alpha) \qquad (V.11)$$

$$Z = r + j(X + X_{eq}) = |Z|\underline{|90° - \alpha}$$

where $\alpha = \tan^{-1}\left(\dfrac{r}{X + X_{eq}}\right)$

$$|Z| = \sqrt{r^2 + (X + X_{eq})^2}$$

The synchronizing power coefficient for the machine is the slope of the power angle curve, or:

$$T = \frac{\partial P_1}{\partial \delta_1} = \frac{E_1 E_2}{Z}\cos(\delta_1 - \alpha) \qquad (V.12)$$

Which is non-negative whenever $-90° + \alpha \le \delta_1 \le 90° + \alpha$.

The maximum power which may be stably transferred, therefore, occurs when $\delta = 90° + \alpha$. This power is called the "pull out power at constant field current." Its magnitude is given by (V.13):

$$P_{MAX} = \frac{E_1^2}{|Z|}\sin\alpha + \frac{E_1 E_2}{Z}$$ (V.13)

5.2.4 Steady-State Stability

Although the concept of pull out power is an essential concept, the case of synchronous machines at constant excitation is not usually encountered in practice. Most modern generators are equipped with automatic voltage regulators which adjust field voltage to hold constant terminal voltage (e_t). It should be useful then to develop the equivalent of the pull out power for the case of constant e_t rather than constant E_{fd}. This limit is referred to as the "steady state power limit."

The vector diagram for the system of Figure 5.10 may be drawn as in Figure 5.11 using the infinite bus voltage as a reference.

If we start at no load, unity power factor, then $I = 0$ and $E_1 = e_t$. As we increase the load, we will require higher and higher values of E_1 to hold constant e_t. We may then say that the steady state excitation is a function of the steady state power, $E_1 = E_1(P)$. For each value of $E_1(P)$ we may define a pull out power at constant field excitation as a function of steady state power as in (V.14).

$$P_{MAX}(P) = \frac{[E_1(P)]^2 \sin\alpha + E_1(P)E_2}{\sqrt{r^2 + (X + X_{eq})^2}}$$ (V.14)

where $\sin\alpha = \dfrac{r}{\sqrt{r^2 + (X + X_{eq})^2}}$

The obvious definition for the steady state power limit is when:

$$P_{MAX}(P) = P$$ (V.15)

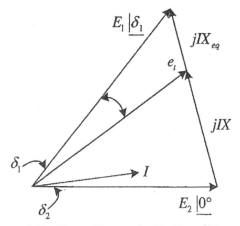

Figure 5.11 – Phasor Diagram for Machine of Figure 10

This concept can be more easily visualized by an example. Using the system of Figures 5.10 and 5.11 given the following per unit data:

$$r = 0 \qquad\qquad E_2 = 1.0$$
$$X = 1.0 \qquad\qquad e_t = 1.0$$
$$X_{eq} = 1.5$$

By means of trigonometric analysis of the vector diagram (not presented here) we can obtain the following data relating E_1 and P.

P	$E_1(P)$
0.00	1.0
0.25	1.11
0.50	1.42
0.75	1.88
1.00	2.92

At the value $P = .25$, we calculate $\delta_{12} = \sin^{-1}\left(.25 \times \dfrac{(1+1.5)}{1 \times 1.11}\right) = 34.2°$ and also that $P_{MAX} = \dfrac{1 \times 1.11}{(1+1.5)} = 0.445$. We may repeat this procedure for each value of power to compile the following table:

Point #	P	$E_1(P)$	δ_{12}	$P_{MAX} = \dfrac{E_1(P)E_2}{X + X_{eq}}$
1	0.00	1.0	0	0.400
2	0.25	1.11	34.17	0.445
3	0.50	1.42	61.98	0.566
4	0.75	1.88	85.32	0.752
5	1.00	2.92	120.96	1.166

Figure 5.12 shows these results graphically.

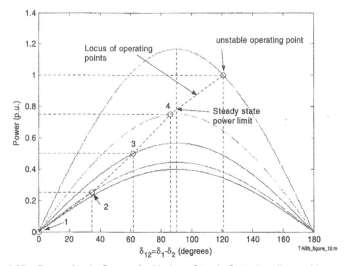

Figure 5.12 – Power Angle Curves for Various Steady State Loadings with $e_t = 1.0\,p.u.$

Although the concept of steady state stability has been discussed in terms of one or two machine cases, the principles involved are general. The general criterion for steady state stability in a multi-machine system is that $\partial P/\partial \delta$, known as steady state synchronizing power coefficient, be positive for each machine. The problem arises in the calculation of $\partial P/\partial \delta$ for large systems because this calculation is influenced by all the effects of machine interactions, governor settings, voltage regulators, etc. Chapter 3 of Reference 1 presents a very good discussion of this subject.

The need for evaluating steady state stability as described above has decreased markedly as the phenomenon rarely occurs in the present context where successful operation of machines must rely on action of continuously acting voltage regulators and the form of instability is usually due to lack of damping rather than synchronizing power. Nevertheless, steady state stability limits calculated with proper assumptions on equivalent machine reactance form useful benchmarks on power transfer limits.

5.2.5   Clarke Circle Diagram

One of the difficulties of steady state stability analysis of systems involves the complexity of the trigonometric relations of the vector diagram. A graphical method of finding steady state stability limits for a two machine system was developed by Edith Clarke and is presented in Chapter 6 of Reference 1.

Consider the two machine system of Figure 5.13.

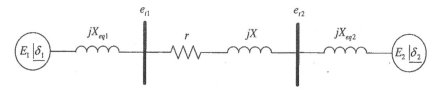

Figure 5.13 – System Structure for Clarke Circle Diagram

The information required to calculate the steady state power limit, consists of the impedance values, and the terminal voltages e_{t1} and e_{t2}. A vector diagram can be constructed by assuming a current reference vector and drawing the voltage drops throughout the system, as shown in Figure 5.14. The scale is arbitrary. The remainder of the problem is to obtain the origin "0" of the vector diagram (Figure 5.14e) in order to determine the magnitude and angular relationships.

We know that at the steady state power limit (sending end)

$$\delta_{12} = 90° + \alpha, \ \alpha = \tan^{-1}\left(\frac{r}{X_{eq1} + X_{eq2} + X}\right) \tag{V.16}$$

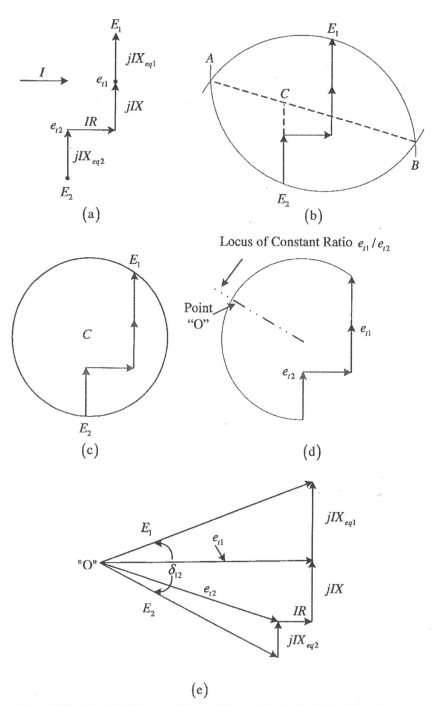

Figure 5.14 – Graphical Steps and Phasor Diagram Used with Clarke Circle Diagram

Using geometric relationships the locus of possible origins "0" which satisfy (V.16) is a circle whose circumference contains points E_1 and E_2 and whose center is on a straight line passing through points E_2 and e_{12}. The graphical location of this circle is shown in Figure 5.14b. The portion of the circle of interest is the largest arc as shown by the solid line in Figure 5.14c.

The other information given concerns the magnitudes of e_{t1} and e_{t2}. However, since we have not yet established a scale for the diagram, we cannot use these magnitudes directly. The ratio e_{t1}/e_{t2} is, however, independent of the scale and may be used. Figure 5.14d shows the graphical construction of the locus of possible origins "0" which satisfy the given ratio e_{t1}/e_{t2}. The intersection of this locus with the previously drawn circle satisfies both criteria and thus must be the point "0".

Figure 5.14e shows the final vector diagram with all the intermediate construction steps involving arcs, lines, etc. removed. We can now determine the scale of the diagram by comparison of the length of the vectors e_{t1} or e_{t2} with their known magnitude. The steady state power limit for this vector diagram is given by (V.13).

It is evident that the Clarke diagram can be very useful in visualizing the influence of variations in impedance, and system voltage levels on steady state stability.

Equation (V.17) is a convenient relation for estimation of steady state stability limits. It can be derived from the Clarke diagram by assuming that $e_{t1} = e_{t2} = 1$, and that $r = 0$.

$$P_{MAX} = \frac{\sqrt{\left(X_{eq1} + \dfrac{X}{2}\right)\left(X_{eq2} + \dfrac{X}{2}\right)}}{\left(\dfrac{X}{2}\right)^2 + \left(X_{eq1} + \dfrac{X}{2}\right)\left(X_{eq2} + \dfrac{X}{2}\right)} \qquad (\text{V.17})$$

Equation (V.17) can also be used to calculate stability limits for transmission lines with shunt impedances by application of Thevenin's theorem as shown in Figure 5.15.

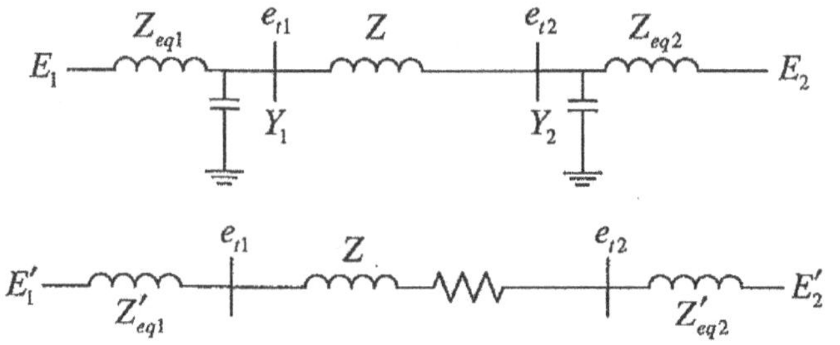

$$\text{where } Z'_{eq1} = \frac{Z_{eq1}}{1 - Z_{eq1}Y_1} \text{ and } Z'_{eq2} = \frac{Z_{eq2}}{1 - Z_{eq2}Y_2}$$

Figure 5.15 – Thevenin Equivalent for use of Clarke
Formula in Systems with Shunt Capacitance

For this method to be valid, Z_{eq} and Y must be lossless so that internal power equals terminal power.

5.2.6   Transient Stability

Up to this point we have studied those aspects of stability which can be analyzed by steady state relationships. These relationships are based on small perturbations about a given operating point and the linearized swing equations about that point. In discussing steady state stability, we have limited our attention to testing for positive synchronizing power coefficients for all machines in the system. In the study of transient stability, we are concerned with those cases where the magnitudes of the disturbances and corresponding angular excursions of machines are large, and the nonlinear power-angle relationships play a dominant role.

5.2.7   Equal Area Criterion

Much can be learned about transient stability from the study of the basic momentum equation.[*]

$$p\delta(t) = \frac{1}{M} \int (P_M - P_E)dt \qquad (\text{V.3})$$

---

[*] Note: Per unit power is used instead of torque based on the fact that speed remains very close to unity.

We know by definition that in the steady state, (if a steady state exists) $p\delta(t) = 0$ for a machine if it is to remain in synchronism with a system operating at rated frequency.

Thus:

$$0 = \frac{1}{M}\int_0^\infty \left(P_M(t) - P_E(t)\right)dt + p\delta(0) \tag{V.18}$$

Starting from an initial steady state, $p\delta(0) = 0$. Hence, (18) becomes:

$$0 = \int_0^\infty P_A(t)dt \tag{V.19}$$

A physical interpretation of (V.18) may be made by noting that the units of the integral are "power times time" or energy. If the electrical load on a generator is greater than (less than) the mechanical input, the mismatch must be supplied by the kinetic energy released (stored) by deceleration (acceleration). If we start at synchronous speed and return to the same speed following a disturbance, the net energy stored or released in the rotor inertia is zero.

Figure 5.16 shows time plots of P_A and $p\delta$. The graphical interpretation of (V.19) is that the net acceleration area ($P_A > 0$) must equal the decelerating area ($P_A < 0$) in order to return $p\delta$ to zero.

Without loss of generality, we would like to restate (V.19) in terms of angle (δ) rather than speed deviation ($p\delta$) since this form may be more useful. The equation relating angle to P_A is:

$$\frac{d^2\delta(t)}{dt^2} = \frac{\omega_0}{M}P_A(t) \tag{V.20}$$

Multiply both sides by $2\dfrac{d\delta}{dt}$:

$$2\frac{d\delta}{dt}\frac{\left(d^2\delta\right)}{dt^2} = 2\frac{d\delta}{dt}\left(\frac{\omega_0}{M}P_A\right)$$

or $\quad 2\left(\dfrac{d\delta}{dt}\right)^2 = \dfrac{2 \times \omega_0}{M} P_A\, d\delta$

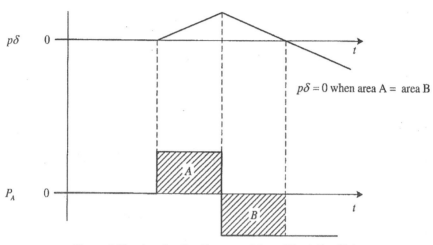

Figure 5.16 – Accelerating Power and Speed Deviation Plots

Integrating with respect to angle between the limits of δ_1 (initial angle) and δ_2 (final angle)

$$\left(\frac{d\delta}{dt}\right)^2_{\delta_1} = \frac{2 \times \omega_0}{M}\int_{\delta_1}^{\delta_2} P_A\, d\delta + \left(\frac{d\delta}{dt}\right)^2_{\delta_1} \tag{V.21}$$

Assuming an initial steady state at synchronous speed ω_0 at $\delta = \delta_1$

$$\left(\frac{d\delta}{dt}\right)^2_{\delta_1} = \omega_0^2$$

Hence, for a subsequent condition of $\dfrac{d\delta}{dt} = \omega_0$ at $\delta = \delta_2$ (21) becomes:

$$0 = \int_{\delta_1}^{\delta_2} P_A\, d\delta \tag{V.22}$$

EXAMPLE

Let us apply (V.22) to the system of Figure 5.17, showing a single machine connected to an infinite bus.

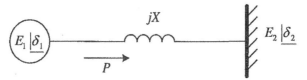

Figure 5.17 – Single Machine Connected to Infinite Bus

The power-angle equation for this system is:

$$P_E = \frac{E_1 E_2}{X} \sin (\delta_{12}) = P_{MAX} \sin (\delta_{12}) \qquad (V.23)$$

which is shown graphically on Figure 5.18. We shall assume mechanical power (P_M) constant. The initial steady state operating point is established as the angle for which $P_E = P_M$.

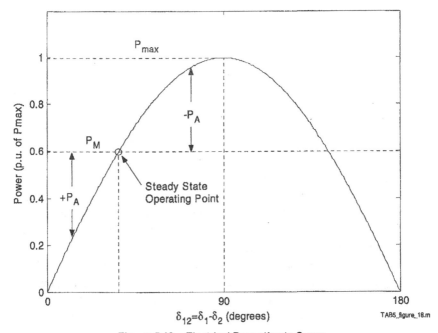

Figure 5.18 – Electrical Power/Angle Curve

Now assume that a transmission circuit was tripped such that the net reactance X was increased from X_B to X_A. With the higher reactance we will have to operate at a higher δ in order to transmit the same steady state power, such that:

$$P_M = \frac{E_1 E_2}{X_B} \sin \delta_B = \frac{E_1 E_2}{X_A} \sin \delta_A \qquad (V.24)$$

as shown in Figure 5.19.

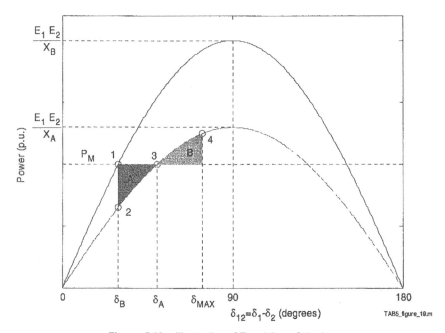

Figure 5.19 – Illustration of Equal Area Criterion

At the time of switching, we move from point (1) to point (2) on Figure 5.19 since the angle cannot change instantaneously. The lower power output causes an accelerating power P_A which causes an increase speed and thus an increase δ. When we have reached the point where $\delta = \delta_A$ (point (3)), the mechanical and electrical powers balance and the acceleration is zero. However, the speed at this point is still greater than normal so the angle continues to advance beyond $\delta = \delta_A$. In this region, however, the mechanical power is less than the electrical power (P_A < 0) and thus the machine will start to decelerate. At some point (point (4)) the machine will have been returned to normal speed and the angle will have reached a maximum ($\delta = \delta_{MAX}$). The angle δ_{MAX} satisfies Equation (V.25):

$$0 = \int_{\delta_B}^{\delta_{MAX}} \left(P_M - \frac{E_1 E_2}{X_A} \sin \delta \right) d\delta \qquad (V.25)$$

Graphically, δ_{MAX} is the angle which causes the decelerating area (Area B, Figure 5.19) to equal the accelerating area (Area A, Figure 5.19). Note that there is no restriction that δ_{MAX} be less than the angle for steady state stability (90° for this example).

Now that we have reached point (4) at which the speed deviation is back to zero, the speed will decrease if a net decelerating power exists at point (4) and consequently the angle will decrease. In a lossless system the angle will oscillate back and forth between δ_B and δ_{MAX}. In real situations due to losses and damping, these oscillations will die out with time and the angle reaches the post switching steady state δ_A.

5.2.8   Two Machine Systems

To further illustrate this concept, let us now consider a fault condition on the two-finite-machine system of Figure 5.20.

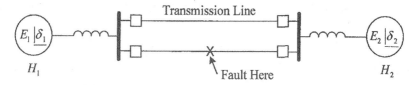

Figure 5.20 – Schematic of Two Machine System

Now that we have more than one machine, we also have more than one swing equation to consider. Hence, we cannot use Equation (V.22). However, we can derive a more general statement of the equal area criterion as follows:

$$\frac{d^2\delta_1}{dt^2} = \frac{\omega_1}{M_1} P_{A1} \qquad\qquad \frac{d^2\delta_2}{dt^2} = \frac{\omega_0}{M_2} P_{A2}$$

$$\frac{d^2\delta_{21}}{dt^2} = \frac{\omega_0}{M_1} P_{A1} - \frac{\omega_0}{M_2} P_{A2} \qquad \text{where } \delta_{12} = \delta_1 - \delta_2$$

Multiplying by $2\dfrac{d\delta_{12}}{dt}$

$$2\frac{d\delta_{12}}{dt}\left(\frac{d^2\delta_{12}}{dt^2}\right) = \frac{d}{dt}\left(\frac{d\delta_{12}}{dt}\right)^2 = 2\times\omega_0\left(\frac{P_{A1}}{M_1} - \frac{P_{A2}}{M_2}\right)\frac{d\delta_{12}}{dt}$$

Integrating with respect to δ_{12} between the limits of δ_{0_1} and δ_{0_2}.

$$\left(\frac{d\delta_{12}}{dt}\right)^2_{\delta_{0_1}} = 2 \times \omega_0 \int_{\delta_{0_1}}^{\delta_{0_2}}\left(\frac{P_{A1}}{M_1}-\frac{P_{A2}}{M_2}\right)d\delta_{12} + \left(\frac{d\delta_{12}}{dt}\right)_{\delta_{0_1}}$$

And when $\left(\frac{d\delta_{12}}{dt}\right)_{\delta_{0_1}} = 0 = \left(\frac{d\delta_{12}}{dt}\right)_{\delta_{0_2}}$

$$0 = \int_{\delta_{0_1}}^{\delta_{0_2}}\left(\frac{P_{A1}}{M_1}-\frac{P_{A2}}{M_2}\right)d\delta_{12} = \int_{\delta_{0_1}}^{\delta_{0_2}}\left(\frac{P_{A1}}{H_1}-\frac{P_{A2}}{H_2}\right)d\delta_{12} \qquad (V.26)$$

Equation (V.26) is the equivalent of (V.22) for a two-machine system. We can make graphical interpretations of (V.26) similar to those of Figure 5.18. The key to such an interpretation comes from the combined sending-receiving end power-angle equations. For the system of Figure 5.20 we shall neglect resistance such that:

$$\frac{P_1}{H_1} = \frac{1}{H_1}\left(\frac{E_1 E_2}{X_{12}}\sin\delta_{12}\right) \qquad \frac{P_2}{H_2} = \frac{1}{H_2}\left(\frac{E_1 E_2}{X_{12}}\sin\delta_{21}\right)$$

$$\frac{P_1}{H_1}-\frac{P_2}{H_2} = \frac{E_1 E_2}{X_{12}}\left(\frac{1}{H_1}\sin\delta_{12}-\frac{1}{H_2}(-\sin\delta_{12})\right) \qquad (V.27)$$

$$\frac{P_1}{H_1}-\frac{P_2}{H_2} = \frac{E_1 E_2}{X_{12}}\left(\frac{H_1+H_2}{H_1 H_2}\right)\sin\delta_{12}$$

Figure 5.21 shows the graphical interpretation of (V.27). In this form, the equal area criterion (V.26) may be applied directly.

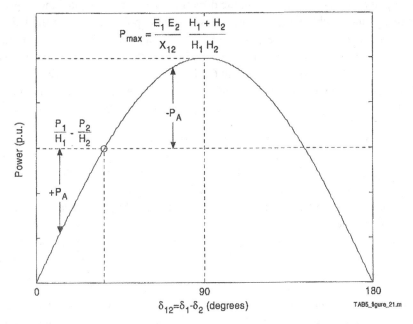

Figure 5.21 – Equal Area Criterion for Two Machine System

It is interesting to note that the machine inertias appear in Equations (V.26) and (V.27) but do not appear at all in Equations (V.22) and (V.23). It happens that the single machine against infinite bus case is one of two special cases of (V.26) and (V.27) in which the inertia term drops out. First, note that the inertias in Equation (V.27) combine like resistors in parallel. If H_1 is small compared to H_2, we may neglect H_2. If we allow H_2 to approach infinity, then Equation (V.26) reduces to Equation (V.22). The other case is when all resistances are neglected such that $-P_{E2} = P_{E1}$ and $-P_{M2} = P_{M1}$. If we make this substitution in (V.26) we obtain:

$$0 = \int_{\delta_{0_1}}^{\delta_{0_2}} \left[\left(\frac{P_{A1}}{H_1} \right) - \left(\frac{-P_{A1}}{H_2} \right) \right] d\delta_{12} = \int_{\delta_{0_1}}^{\delta_{0_2}} P_{A1} \left(\frac{1}{H_1} + \frac{1}{H_2} \right) d\delta_{12} = \left(\frac{1}{H_1} + \frac{1}{H_2} \right) \int_{\delta_{0_1}}^{\delta_{0_2}} P_{A1} d\delta_{12}$$

$$0 = \int_{\delta_{0_1}}^{\delta_{0_2}} P_{A1} d\delta_{12}$$

which is the same as Equation (V.22).

Returning to our example of Figure 5.20, we shall neglect all resistances. We shall assume also an initial transfer reactance (X_B), a faulted transfer reactance (X_f), and a post fault reactance (X_A) achieved by opening the breakers at A and A'. We would expect that $X_f > X_A > X_B$.

619

Figure 5.22 illustrates the relationships for this example. As before, by switching to a higher transfer reactance, we cause an instantaneous accelerating power (switch from point 1 to 2 - Figure 5.22) in the direction to increase δ_{12} (machine 1 speed increases and machine 2 speed decreases). At some point in time we shall clear the fault (at time t_{CLEAR} corresponding to the post-fault operating characteristic) (switch from point 3 to point 4, Figure 5.22). As before, once the angle is past the steady state operating point (point 6, Figure 5.22) P_A will be negative causing deceleration. Application of the equal area criterion establishes the maximum angle δ_{MAX} (point 5, Figure 5.22) where Area B equals Area A.

Consider now the same case but with slower operating breakers as shown in Figure 5.23. By comparison with Figure 5.22, we see that an increased clearing time (t_{CLEAR} causes an increased clearing angle (δ_{CLEAR}) moving line 3 - 4 - 5 to the right, thus increasing Area A and decreasing Area B. If the angle advances to point 5 of Figure 5.23, and Area B is still less than Area A, we are in trouble since any further increases in angle would be accompanied by acceleration rather than deceleration and the machines would fall out of step as the angle continued to advance. In such a case, we would say that the machines are transiently unstable on the first swing.

Given these examples, we can define the limiting case where the system is just stable. From Figure 5.22 we see that this case is the one where Area A just equals Area B. The switching time for this case is called the "critical switching time." It is applicable for the assumed voltage, power, and reactance values. Alternatively, we may define a maximum power transfer for first swing transient stability, applicable for the assumed voltage, reactances and clearing times.

Note that from the power-angle diagrams, using the equal area criterion, one can determine the critical clearing angle. To determine the critical clearing time the relationship between time and angle must be used involving acceleration power and equivalent inertia.

Figures 5.24 and 5.25 show the time response plots of angle, speed and accelerating power for the stable and unstable cases described above.

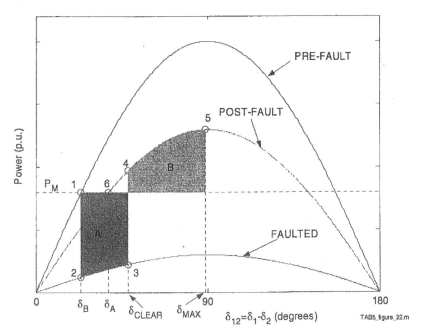

Figure 5.22 – Equal Area Criterion showing Stable Fault

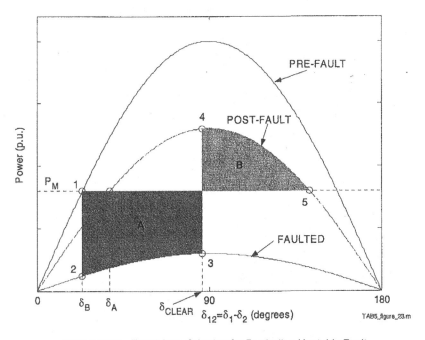

Figure 5.23 – Equal Area Criterion for Borderline Unstable Fault

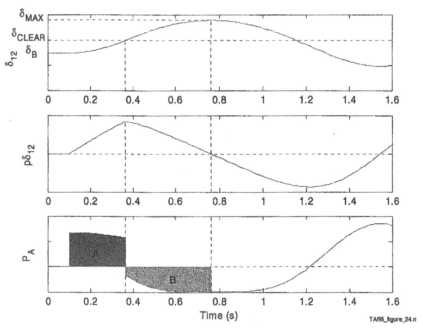

Figure 5.24 – Time Response for Stable Fault

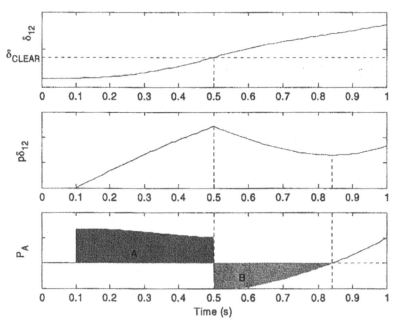

Figure 5.25 – Time Response for Unstable Fault

5.3 Multi-Machine Stability Analysis

The preceding development of the basic concepts of stability has been limited to very simple cases involving only one or two machines. Although the fundamental principles of stability are perfectly general, their application to systems of three or more machines by means of algebraic and/or graphical means involves solutions of the general Equations (V.10). In general, closed form solutions of these equations are extremely tedious and are considered impractical.

Before the advent of a-c network analyzers and computers, much effort was devoted to developing approximate closed form solutions for two or three machines, often utilizing some sort of lumped equivalent for the remainder of the system. More modern methods calculate swing curves by means of step by step integration procedures. Starting from an initial steady state, the swing transient begins with the application of the disturbance under study (fault, line trip, etc.). With the machine internal voltages held at angles corresponding to the initial rotor angles, the electrical power and hence accelerating power is obtained for each machine from a network load flow solution. Given these accelerating powers, the changes in speeds and angles are calculated over a small time step using the swing equations. (Integration of acceleration to yield speed and integration of speed to yield angle). The load flow solution is then repeated for the new interval $t_0 + \Delta t$ by having all machine rotors (internal voltages) at their new calculated angles and the process repeated.

Use of a-c network analyzers was made to yield rapid solutions of the load flow and the step by step integration procedure for angle change was performed manually. Today the whole process of integration of the swing equations as well as the solution of the load flow is performed by numerical methods in large-scale digital computers.

The representation of the system of equations involved is shown on Figure 5.26 for just one machine.

Shown in Figure 5.26 are the basic variables of machine internal voltages and angles. If the simplifying assumption of constant internal machine voltage and constant prime-mover power is made, then the set of equations reduce to a second order differential equation for each machine (swing equations) and the remainder of the computation task is the load flow solution, that is, the solution of algebraic equations.

Of course, once the computation is done digitally it is natural to extend the program to eliminate many of the simplifying assumptions inherent in the use of solid lines only of the diagram of Figure 5.26. These additional equations are differential equations that describe the variations in machine fluxes or internal voltages in response to excitation voltages and machine currents. Likewise, differential equations describe the behavior of excitation voltages and prime mover power where excitation system and governor systems are to be represented.

The solution of differential equations by numerical step by step techniques was described in Appendix D using a simple single pass integration algorithm. There are many methods of numerical integration ranging from the simple Euler's method to high order Runge-Kutta methods. In all cases, accuracy is increased by decreasing the time step. A compromise must be made between accuracy and amount of computation.

The procedures involved in step by step swing curve calculations will be illustrated with a simple example using Euler's method of numerical integration. In this example the machine will be represented by a voltage source behind some equivalent reactance assumed equal to the transient reactance X_d'. Subsequent material in these notes will be concerned with refinements of machine representations.

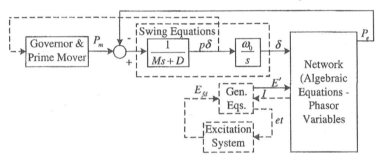

Figure 5.26 – Block Diagram for Dynamics of One Machine

EXAMPLE

An alternator shown in Figure 5.27 is generating 1 p.u. power at unity power factor and unity terminal voltage. Calculate the machine speed and angle transients caused by a 3ϕ fault at the high side of the generator step up transformer lasting 0.04 sec. and cleared by the trip-out of a transmission line.

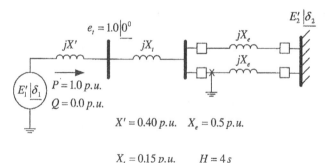

Figure 5.27 – Example System for Step-by-Step Calculation

1.   Calculation of Initial Conditions

The first step is the calculation of a base steady state load flow. Figure 5.28 shows the vector diagram from which the internal machine voltage, the infinite bus voltage and the angle between the two is derived.

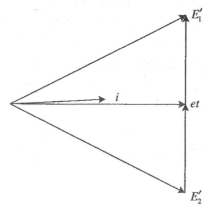

Figure 5.28 – Steady State Prefault Phasor Diagram

$$\hat{E}_1' = 1 + jX_d' \, \hat{I}$$

and

$$\hat{E}_2' = 1 - j\left(X_t + \frac{Xe}{2} \right)\hat{I}$$

where

$$\hat{I} = \frac{1}{e_t}(P - jQ) = (1 - j0)$$

$$\hat{E}_1' = 1.0 + j0.4 = 1.078 \,\underline{|21.8°}$$

$$\hat{E}_2' = 1.0 - j0.4 = 1.078 \,\underline{|-21.8°}$$

Hence, prior to the fault the initial conditions are:

$$\delta_1 \qquad = 21.8°$$
$$\delta_2 \qquad = -21.8°$$
$$\omega_{(0)} \qquad = 1.0 \; p.u.$$
$$P_{M(0)} \qquad = P_{E(0)} = 1.0 \; p.u.$$

2. Calculation of Load Flow at $t = 0+$

The occurrence of a 3ϕ fault at the high side of the transformer causes a new power flow. For this simple case, it turns out that, neglecting resistance, the power output and transfer to the infinite bus from machine 1 is zero. Hence, the accelerating power acting on machine 1 is $P_{M(o_+)_+} - P_{E(o_+)} = 1.0$. Since we have defined machine 2 as infinite, we are not concerned with solving for the swing conditions in machine 2.

3. Step by Step Integration of Swing Equations

Generator 1 speed and phase angle at $time = t_0 + \Delta t$ are obtained from the integral equations:

$$\Delta\omega(t_0 + \Delta t) = \omega(t_0 + \Delta t) - \omega_{(t_0)} = \frac{180f}{H} \int_{t_0}^{t_0 + \Delta t} (P_M - P_E) dt \qquad \text{(V.28)}$$

and

$$\delta(t_0 + \Delta t) = \int_t^{t_0 + \Delta t} (\omega - \omega_0) dt + \delta_{(t_0)} \qquad \text{(V.29)}$$

Using the approximation of a derivative as $\dfrac{d\omega}{dt} = \dfrac{\Delta\omega}{\Delta t}\bigg|_{\Delta t \to 0}$

and using a central difference formulation: $\Delta\omega\big|_{t_1 - \Delta t/2}^{t_1 + \Delta t/2} = \dfrac{180f}{H} \Delta t \times P_A(t_1)$

where $\Delta\omega$ is the speed change over the interval $t_1 - \Delta t/2$ to $t_1 + \Delta t/2$ and P_A is the value of accelerating power at t_1. Similarly, the change in angle from tl to $t_1 + \Delta t$ is obtained by integrating the average speed over the interval, which can be approximated as the speed at $t = t_1 + \Delta t/2$. At instants of switching, the accelerating power as shown in Figure 5.29 can suffer abrupt discontinuities. Hence, in keeping with the objective of using the average over the interval, the accelerating power during an interval centrally located with respect to a discontinuity is the average of the value before and after the discontinuity.

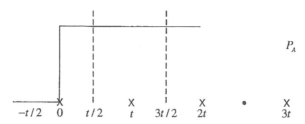

Figure 5.29 – Definition of Values at Discrete Time Steps

A step by step procedure used during the days of the network analyzer is illustrated with the table of Figure 5.30 applied to the above example.

$$K = \frac{180f}{H}(\Delta t)^2 = 1.08 \ for \ \Delta t = .02$$

Time	Power P_E	Accl. Power $P_M - P_E = P_A$	KP_A	$\Delta\delta_n = \Delta\delta_{n-1} + KP_A$	$\delta_n = \Delta\delta_{n-1} + \Delta\delta_n$
0	0	1 x ½	0.54	-----------	21.8°
Δt	0+	1	1.08	0.54	22.34°
2Δt-	0	1		1.62	23.96°
Fault Cleared	Average	0.604			
2Δt+	0.7915	0.2085	0.652		
3Δt	0.822	0.1915	0.207	2.27	26 23°
4Δt				2.48	28.71°

Figure 5.30 – Step-by-Step Calculation Procedure

In this example, the fault is cleared at $t = 0.04\ sec.$ and again the discontinuity is taken into account by averaging the accelerating power at the instant before and after the switching operation. Note that at $t = 0.04+$ the clearing of the fault has left a transmission system with one line only. The power output of the machine at $t = 0.04+$ is obtained from a load flow at the new system conditions and for the condition of machine rotor angle at

$$\delta_{12} = (23.96 + 21.8) \Rightarrow P_E = \frac{E_1' E_2 \sin(\delta_{12})}{(X' + X_t + X_e)} = \frac{1.078 \times 1.078 \sin(45.76)}{1.05} = 0.7915\ p.u.$$

Figure 5.31 shows the plot of power and angle as functions of time for this example.

In the general multi-machine case, the swing curve is plotted for every machine. An inspection of the plots will reveal whether the system is stable or unstable by noting the behavior of the angular difference between all machines. If these angular differences begin to decrease showing a tendency of machines to approach each other, the system is stable (Figure 5.32a). If the angular differences increase indefinitely, the system is unstable (Figure 5.32b).

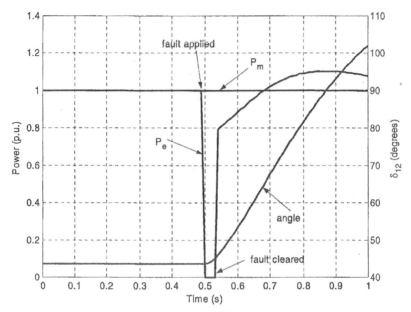

Figure 5.31 – Swing Curve for Single Machine Example

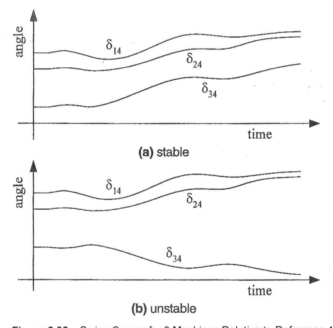

(a) stable

(b) unstable

Figure 5.32 – Swing Curves for 3 Machines Relative to Reference 4

As derived in the section on machine airgap and shaft power for unbalanced faults of Chapter IV – "Electrical Machine Dynamics - I," the effect of unbalanced faults on the loading of machines may be obtained by applying the negative and zero sequence network connections corresponding to the fault case across the positive sequence network. That is, between the point of fault and the zero potential bus, the fault impedance of $Z_0 \,/\!/\, Z_2$ applied for the case of a double line to ground fault. In addition to the electrical power supplied by each positive sequence source, there exist the components of negative sequence rotor losses which are supplied by mechanical shaft energy. These components of braking power should, strictly speaking, be accounted for in the computation of accelerating power for each source. This refinement is usually neglected considering other sources of inaccuracy in representation.

Hence, where negative sequence effects are significant, these components of braking power should be calculated as follows:

1) Determine for each source the negative sequence currents flowing (I2).

2) Determine $I_2^2\,(r_2 - r)$ of each generator, where r^2 is the negative phase sequence resistance and r is the stator resistance for that generator.

3) Include these terms as additional braking power in each machine in the solution of the swing equations.

5.4   Electrical Machine Effects

5.4.1   Power-Angle Relations

In the preceding treatment, the basic concepts of stability were introduced with the simplifying assumption that a machine could be represented by an ideal source behind an equivalent reactance, the phase angle of the source being related to the angular position of the machine rotor in relation to a synchronously rotating vector.

In Chapter IV we saw that the synchronous machine behavior is influenced by variations of rotor fluxes with time. These effects can also be viewed in terms of the machine exhibiting different values of effective reactance as a function of time. The variations in these fluxes are a time function of the armature currents and field excitation as described in Figure 5.33 where the operational machine inductances

$$L_d\,(s) \; = -\frac{\Delta\psi_d(s)}{\Delta i_d(s)} \text{ and } L_q\,(s) \; = -\frac{\Delta\psi_q(s)}{\Delta i_q(s)}$$

Recall that, neglecting transformer action terms, the equations for the d and q components of terminal voltage are:

$$e_d = -\psi_q \omega - r_{id}$$
$$e_q = -\psi_d \omega - r_{iq}$$

(V.30)

Also, $\quad \psi_d = G(s)\, E_{fd} - i_d(s)\, L_d(s) \text{ and } \psi_q = -i_q(s)\, L_q(s)$ (V.31)

Hence:

$$e_d \quad = i_q(s)\, Lq(s)\, \omega - ri_d$$
$$= i_q(s)\, Xq(s) - ri_d$$

(V.30)

and

$$e_q \quad = \omega G(s)\, E_{fd} - i_d(s)\, L_d(s)\, \omega - ri_d$$
$$= \omega G(s)\, E_{fd} - i_d(s)\, X_d(s) - ri_d$$

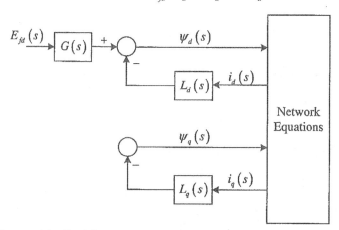

Figure 5.33 – Block Diagram Representation of the Synchronous Machine

In the derivation of machine behavior under short circuits or other abrupt load changes, we saw that it was possible to describe terminal conditions in terms of an initial internal voltage in each axis and a reactance in each axis. The internal voltage was established from initial conditions derived from the machine vector diagram.

Conceptually, one could visualize the machine as a source in each axis behind some equivalent reactance. Admittedly, these sources and reactances are changing as functions of time. Where the machine is represented by the differential equations as in Figure 33, these variations are automatically obtained as part of the solution.

The artifice of representing the machine as a fixed voltage behind a fixed reactance, and using different values of this voltage and reactance as an approximation to machine behavior for short term, intermediate term and long term effects, is a useful expedient to reduce the relations to algebraic equations.

Figure 5.34 is a review of the steady state vector diagram establishing the flux linkages or voltages behind subtransient, transient, and synchronous reactances.

From the vector diagram:

$$E_q^* - E \cos \delta = i_d (X_e + X_d^*) + i_q r_e$$

$$E \sin \delta - E_d^* = -i_d r_e + i_q (X_e + X_d^*)$$

(V.33)

where E_d^* and E_q^* are voltages in the d and q axes generated by flux linkages in the q and d axis derived from corresponding reactances X_d^* and X_q^* which may be subtransient, transient or synchronous depending on the case in question.

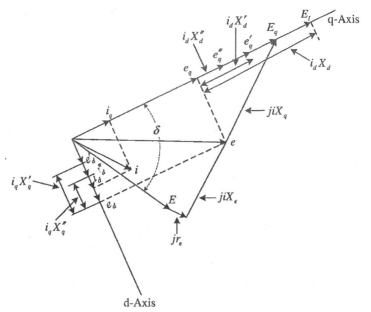

d-Axis

Figure 5.34 – Initial Condition Phasor Diagram

Solving for currents from (V.33):

$$i_d = \frac{\left(E_q^* - E \cos \delta\right)\left(X_e + X_q^*\right) - r_e \left(E \sin \delta - E_d^*\right)}{r_e^2 \left(X_q^* + X_e\right)\left(X_d^* X_e\right)}$$

(V.34)

$$i_q = \frac{\left(E \sin \delta - E_d^*\right)\left(X_e + X_d^*\right) + r_e \left(E_d^* - E \cos \delta\right)}{r_e^2 \left(X_q^* + X_e\right)\left(X_d^* X_e\right)}$$

The machine power output is:

$$P_E = e_d i_d + e_q i_q \tag{V.35}$$

$$= (E_d{}^* + i_q X_q{}^*) i_d + (E_q{}^* - i_d X_d{}^*) i_q$$
$$= E_d{}^* i_d + E_q{}^* i_q - i_d i_q (X_d{}^* - X_q{}^*) \tag{V.36}$$

Substituting (V.34) for i_d and i_q and using the simplifying assumption $r_e = 0$:

$$P_E = \frac{E_q{}^* E \sin \delta}{X_d{}^* + X_e} - \frac{E_d{}^* E \cos \delta}{X_q{}^* + X_e} + \frac{E^2 (X_d{}^* - X_q{}^*)}{2(X_d{}^* + X_e)(X_q{}^* + X_e)} \sin 2\delta \tag{V.37}$$

Note that the first two terms of (V.37) yield components of power which vary sinusoidally with angle while the third term produces the saliency component of power which varies with the 2nd harmonic of angle.

Note in particular that the coefficient of the third term of (V.37) is a function of:

$$\frac{(X_d{}^* - X_q{}^*)}{2(X_d{}^* + X_e)(X_q{}^* + X_e)}$$

This becomes insignificant as $X_d \to X_q$ or when $X_e \gg X_d$ or X_q,

Note also that the second term is proportional to $E_d{}^*$, the voltage behind the appropriate quadrature axis reactance.

If transient effects are neglected in the quadrature axis, $X_q{}^* = X_q$ and $E_d{}^* = 0$.

The effects of saliency are evidently a function of the speed of the phenomena of concern. If rapid transients are involved, we are concerned with <u>transient</u> saliency, that is the difference in transient reactances in the two axes. For this case, $X_d{}^* \ X_d'$ and $X_q{}^* = X_q'$ or sometimes $X_q{}^* = X_q$. If slow changing phenomena are involved, we are concerned with steady state saliency effects, that is the difference between X_d and X_q.

EXAMPLE

For the condition of Figure 5.35, plot the power angle curves assuming:

1) subtransient effects
   transient effects
   steady state conditions.

Note: Most transients involving rotor angle changes are too slow for subtransient conditions to be considered, however state of the art machine models permit inclusion of subtransient effects which, with the justified assumption of $X_d'' = X_q''$, actually make the step-by-step calculation process simpler, avoiding the need to iterate the machine model solution during the network load flow solution.

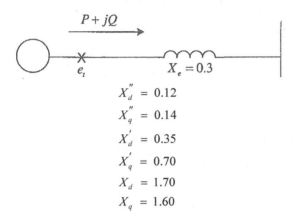

$$X_d'' = 0.12$$
$$X_q'' = 0.14$$
$$X_d' = 0.35$$
$$X_q' = 0.70$$
$$X_d = 1.70$$
$$X_q = 1.60$$

Figure 5.35 – Example Single Machine

Initial conditions from steady state vector diagram:

$$E_Q = 1.0 + (1.0 + j0)\,j1.6$$
$$= 1.888 \,\underline{|58°}$$
$$i_d = 1.0 \sin 58° = 0.848$$
$$i_q = 1.0 \cos 58° = 0.53$$
$$e_d = 1.0 \sin 58° = 0.848$$
$$e_q = 1.0 \cos 58° = 0.53$$
$$e_d'' = e_d - i_q X_q'' = 0.848 - 0.074 = 0.774$$
$$e_q'' = e_q + i_d X_d'' = 0.53 + 0.10 = 0.632$$
$$e_d' = e_d - i_q X_q' = 0.848 - 0.37 = 0.477$$
$$e_q' = e_q - i_d X_d' = 0.53 + 0.297 = 0.827$$
$$E_I = e_q - i_d X_d = 0.53 + 1.44 = 1.97$$

Receiving end infinite bus volts $= E = e_t - jX_e i$

$$E = 1.0 - j1.0 \times 0.3 = 1.044 \,\underline{|-16.7°}$$

Power Angle Curves

(a) Subtransient: using (V.37):

$$P_E = \frac{e_q'' E \sin \delta}{X_d'' + X_e} - \frac{e_d'' E \cos \delta}{X_q'' + X_e} + \frac{E^2 \left(X_d'' - X_q'' \right) \sin 2\delta}{2\left(X_d'' + X_e \right)\left(X_q'' + X_e \right)} = 2.42 \sin (\delta - 49.4°) - 0.059 \sin 2\delta$$

(b) Transient

$$P_E = \frac{e_q' E \sin \delta}{X_d' + X_e} - \frac{e_d' E \cos \delta}{X_q' + X_e} + \frac{E^2 \left(X_d' - X_q' \right) \sin 2\delta}{2\left(X_d' + X_e \right)\left(X_q' + X_e \right)} = 1.42 \sin (\delta - 20.57°) - 0.294 \sin 2\delta$$

(c) Steady State:

$$P_E = \frac{E_I E \sin \delta}{X_d + X_e} + \frac{E^2 \left(X_d - X_q \right) \sin 2\delta}{2\left(X_d + X_e \right)\left(X_q + X_e \right)} = 1.03 \sin \delta + 0.0144 \sin 2\delta$$

Obtain the transient and steady state power angle curves for a typical salient pole machine with the following constants, operating under the same conditions as the machine in Figure 5.35.

$$X_d' = 0.30$$

$$X_q' = X_q = 0.80$$

$$X_d = 1.2$$

Initial conditions from steady state vector diagram:

$$E_q = 1.0 + (1.0 + j.0) j0.8 = 1.28 \ \underline{|38.6°}$$

$$e_d = 1.0 \sin 38.6° = 0.625$$

$$e_q = 1.0 \cos 38.6° = 0.781$$

$$i_d = 1.0 \sin 38.6° = 0.625$$

$$i_q = 1.0 \cos 38.6° = 0.781$$

$$e_q' = 0.781 + 0.625 \times 0.30 = 0.9685$$

$$E_I = 0.781 + 0.625 \times 1.2 = 1.531$$

Transient Power-Angle

$$P_E = \frac{0.9685 \times 1.044}{0.6} \sin \delta \frac{1.044^2 \times 0.50}{2 \times 0.6 \times 1.1} \sin 2\delta$$

$P_E = 1.685 \sin \delta - 0.413 \sin 2\delta$

Note the plots of the power angle curves for these cases in Figure 5.36. Note in particular the effect of saliency which can add or subtract the 2nd harmonic term depending on whether $X_d{}^*$ is greater or smaller than $X_q{}^*$.

Steady-State Power-Angle

$$P_E = \frac{0.9685 \times 1.044}{0.6} \sin \delta \frac{1.044^2 \times 0.50}{2 \times 0.6 \times 1.1} \sin 2\delta$$

$P_E = 1.685 \sin \delta - 0.413 \sin 2\delta$

We will illustrate further the implications of machine transient effects with the following examples. Note that the machine power angle characteristic is a changing function of time. It is possible for a machine to be transiently (first swing) stable and steady state unstable.

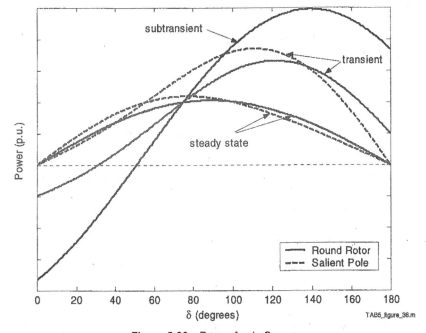

Figure 5.36 – Power-Angle Curves

635

The hydro machine shown on Figure 5.36 is subjected to a 3ϕ fault for 0.10 sec. followed by the loss of some transmission such that the post-fault transmission reactance is $Xe_a = 0.5$ versus a pre-fault reactance of $Xe_b = 0.3$.

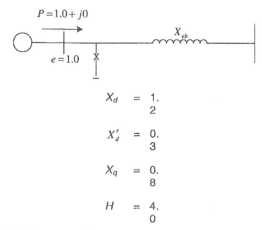

Figure 5.37 – Example of Stability Determination by Equal Area Criterion

Using the constant flux linkage assumption behind transient reactance in the d-axis, is this system first swing stable?

Initial conditions for this case are as in the previous example:

$$e'_q = 0.9685$$
$$\delta = 38.6° + 16.7° = 55.3°$$
$$E = 1.044$$

For the post-fault condition the power angle expression is:

$$P_E = \frac{e'_q E}{\left(X'_d + Xe_a\right)}\sin 2\delta + \frac{E^2\left(X'_d - X_q\right)}{2\left(X'_d + Xe_a\right)\left(X_q + Xe_a\right)}\sin \delta = 1.226 \sin \delta - 0.262 \sin 2\delta$$

For a 3ϕ fault lasting 6 cycles, assuming complete loss of power, the angle will move from 55.3° to:

$$55.3 + \frac{180 f}{H}\int_0^{0.1}\int_0^{0.1}[1.0]dt\ dt = 55.3° + \frac{180 f}{H}\left[\frac{t^2}{2}\right]_0^{0.1} = 55.3° + 13.5 = 68.8°$$

Figure 5.38 shows a plot of the power angle curve.

From the power angle expression, or curve, we may determine the angle at which $P_E = P_M = 1.0$ and $dP_E/d\delta$ is negative. This is $\delta = 144°$. Now the accelerating power-angle area during the fault is proportional to $P_A \times [13.5] = 13.5$.

The maximum decelerating area available is:

$$\frac{180}{\pi}\int_{68.8}^{144}[1.266\sin\delta - 0.262\sin 2\delta]d\delta - 1.0\times(1.44° - 68.8°)$$

$$= \frac{180}{\pi}\left[-1.266\cos\delta + \frac{0.262}{2}\cos 2\delta\right]_{68.8}^{144} - 75.2$$

$$= 92.5 - 75.2 = 17.3$$

This decelerating area *(17.3)* is greater than the accelerating area *(13.5)*. Hence, the system is first <u>swing stable</u> based upon the assumption of constant flux linkages.

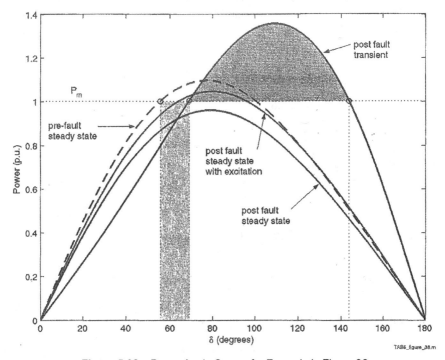

Figure 5.38 – Power Angle Curves for Example in Figure 36

Now, assuming no change in excitation, will the system be stable in the steady state?

The steady state power-angle curve for this system is derived from the initial conditions:

$$E_I \quad = 1.531$$

$$P_E \quad = \frac{E_I E \sin \delta}{(X_d + X_e)} + \frac{E^2 (X_d - X_q)}{2(X_d + X_e)(X_q + X_e)} \sin 2\delta$$

$$= \frac{1.531 \times 1.044}{1.7} \sin \delta + \frac{1.044^2 \times 0.4}{2 \times 1.7 \times 1.3} \sin 2\delta$$

$$= 0.941 \sin \delta + 0.0986 \sin 2\delta$$

The peak power of this expression is less than $P_M = 1.0$. Hence, the system will be unstable in the steady state for the assumption of constant excitation.

Now assume that excitation keeps the terminal voltage at 1.0 p.u. Will the system be steady state stable?

For a power transfer of 1.0 p.u. between machine terminal and receiving system, $E = 1.044$, the angle across the external system reactance, $X_{ea} = 0.5$, is given by:

$$\frac{e_t E}{X_{ea}} \sin \delta = 1.0 \sin \delta = 1.0$$

or $\delta = \sin^{-1} \dfrac{1.0 \times 0.5}{1.0 \times 1.044} = 28.6°$

Hence, machine current is:

$$i = \frac{e_t - E \lfloor -28.6° }{jX_{ea}}$$

$$= \frac{1}{j0.5} \{1.0 - 1.044 \left[\cos 28.6° - j \sin 28.6° \right] \}$$

$$= 1.0 - j0.164 = 1.013 \lfloor -9.3° $$

and the new steady state vector diagram gives:

$$E_Q = 1.0 + (1.0 - j0.164) j0.8 = 1.131 + j0.8 = 1.387 \lfloor 35.27° $$
$$e_d = 1.0 \sin 35.27° = 0.578$$
$$e_q = 1.0 \cos 35.27° = 0.816$$

$$i_d = 1.013 \sin (35.27° + 9.3°) = 0.711 \therefore E_I = 0.816 + 0.711 \times 1.2 = 1.67$$
$$i_q = 1.013 \cos (35.27° + 9.3°) = 0.722$$
$$P_E = \frac{1.67 \times 1.044}{1.7} \sin \delta + 0.0986 \sin 2\delta = 1.025 \sin \delta + 0.0986 \sin 2\delta$$

This expression shows that the peak will exceed $P_M = 1.0$. Hence, the system will be steady state stable.

From the above examples we have noted the difference between transient and steady state behavior of machines. In particular we should note that the so-called steady state criterion in the above examples is based on the assumption of no control of excitation. Evidently, this criterion is conservative or pessimistic since automatic voltage control will counteract the demagnetizing effect which is responsible for the transition from the transient to the steady state characteristic. As illustrated, two different tests can be made: one for steady state stability based on excitation conditions for the initial prefault conditions, the other test can be for steady state synchronizing power based on excitation conditions for a post-fault steady state if such a steady state can exist.

One can now appreciate that the complexity of the problem makes it necessary to resort to simplifying assumptions in order to establish benchmarks. Today, with the computing capability of digital machines, it is not necessary to compromise with various assumptions, as all transient effects can be accounted for. Nevertheless, the ability to establish benchmarks with simplifying assumptions will continue to be of prime importance.

In the days before the availability of digital computation a commonly used assumption was the constant field flux linkage assumption, i.e. the assumption that flux linkages behind transient reactance are constant during the critical time of the first swing. (1/2 to 1 sec). The classical solution approach was to use the same transient reactance in both axes. Studies have shown that with an excitation system response ratio of between 1 to 2 p.u., the assumption of constant field flux linkages in the d-axis gives reasonably accurate first swing effects. However, the classical approach of disregarding transient saliency can lead to substantial error.

In many situations, the stability performance can only be determined by simulations through subsequent swings where machine and excitation control effects must be considered (Reference 9).

5.4.2 Stability Capability Curves

A useful way of presenting stability information is in the form of plots of stability loci in the machine active and reactive load (P,Q) plane, for fixed terminal voltage. Figure 5.39 shows the case being considered.

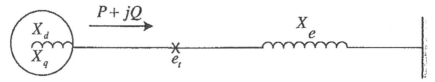

Figure 5.39 – System Diagram for Steady State Stability Calculations

Neglecting resistance and saturation, the steady state power-angle expression, from (V.37) is:

$$P_E = \frac{E_I E}{(X_d + X_e)} \sin \delta + \frac{E^2 (X_d - X_q) \sin 2\delta}{2(X_d + X_e)(X_q + X_e)} \qquad \text{(V.38)}$$

where E is the infinite bus voltage and E_I is the voltage behind X_d, i.e. proportional to field current.

Now, for the capability plots, where P, Q and e_t are given, the value of E_I and E are dependent variables varying with the loading conditions.

Take first the case of no saliency (i.e. $X_d = X_q$). Figure 5.40 shows the vector diagram where I_P and I_Q are the real power and reactive power components of current at the machine terminals.

From this diagram, the following relations can be derived:

$$P = \frac{E_I e_2}{X_d + X_e} \sin \delta \qquad \text{(V.39)}$$

$$Q = \frac{E_I^2 X_e}{(X_d + X_e)^2} - E_I e_2 \cos \delta \frac{X_e - X_d}{(X_d + X_e)^2} - \frac{e_2^2 X_d}{(X_e + X_d)^2} \qquad \text{(V.40)}$$

$$P = e_t I_p \qquad \text{(V.41)}$$

$$Q = e_t I_Q \qquad \text{(V.42)}$$

$$E_I^2 = (e_t + I_Q X_d)^2 + (I_p X_d)^2 \qquad \text{(V.43)}$$

$$e_2^2 = (e_t + I_Q X_e)^2 + (I_p X_e)^2 \qquad \text{(V.44)}$$

From (V.39):

$$\frac{dP}{d\delta} = \frac{E_I e_2}{(X_d + X_e)} \cos \delta \qquad \text{(V.45)}$$

Substituting the value of cos δ from (V.40):

$$\frac{dP}{d\delta} = \frac{E_I^2 X_e}{(X_d + X_e)(X_e - X_d)} - \frac{e_2^2 X_d}{(X_d + X_e)(X_e - X_d)} - \frac{Q(X_d + X_e)}{(X_e - X_d)} \qquad \text{(V.46)}$$

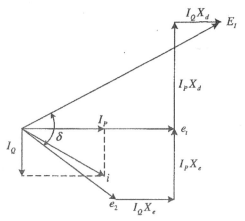

Figure 5.40 – Phasor Diagram for Symmetrical Machine ($X_d = X_q$)

The steady state stability limit occurs when $dP/d\delta = 0$ or from (V.46), when

$$Q = \frac{E_I^2 X_E}{\left(X_d + X_e\right)^2} - \frac{e_2^2 X_d}{\left(X_d + X_e\right)^2} \qquad (V.47)$$

Substituting (V.43) and (V.44) for E_I^2 and e_2^2 (V.47) can be reduced to equation:

$$\left(\frac{PX_d}{e_t^2}\right)^2 + \left[\frac{QX_d}{e_t^2} + \frac{1}{2}\left(1 - \frac{X_d}{X_e}\right)\right]^2 = \frac{1}{4}\left(1 + \frac{X_d}{X_e}\right)^2 \qquad (V.48)$$

Equation (V.48) is the equation of a circle in the P, Q plane where the center is located at:

$$P = 0$$

$$Q = \frac{e_t^2}{2X_d}\left(1 - \frac{X_d}{X_e}\right)$$

and the radius is $\dfrac{1}{2}\left(1 + \dfrac{X_d}{X_e}\right)\dfrac{e_t^2}{X_d}$

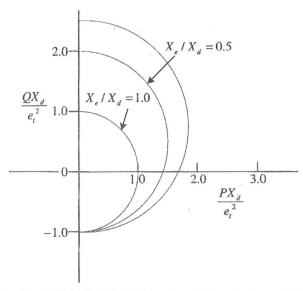

Figure 5.41 – Steady State Stability Limits on P vs Q Plane for Symmetrical Machine

Figure 5.41 shows a normalized plot of the stability limit in the $\dfrac{PX_d}{e_t^2}$ and $\dfrac{QX_d}{e_t^2}$ plane.

Note that the curves determine the points where there is zero steady state synchronizing power coefficient, $dP/d\delta = 0$. Points to the left of the curve denote stable operating points while points to the right of the curve are unstable operating points.

In the case of salient pole machines or round rotor machines with saliency considered, the vector diagram is as in Figure 5.42.

and as previously derived:

$$P_E = \frac{E_1 e_2}{\left(X_d + X_e\right)}\sin\delta + \frac{e_2^2\left(X_d - X_q\right)}{\left(X_d + X_e\right)\left(X_q + X_e\right)} \tag{V.49}$$

Differentiating (V.49):

$$\frac{dP}{d\delta} = \frac{E_1 e_2}{\left(X_d + X_e\right)}\cos\delta + \frac{e_2^2\left(X_d - X_q\right)}{\left(X_d + X_e\right)\left(X_q + X_e\right)}\cos\delta \tag{V.50}$$

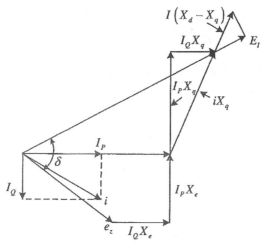

Figure 5.42 – Phasor Diagram Considering Saliency

Equation (V.50) can be expressed in terms of e_t, P and Q by substitution of E_I, e_2, and δ expressed in terms of these variables. The resulting expression is rather cumbersome and it is more practical to solve for the stability limits by trial and error.

The expressions for E_I and e_2 in terms of e_t, P and Q are:

$$E_I = \frac{\left(e_t + \dfrac{Q}{e_t}X_q\right)^2 + \left(\dfrac{P}{e_t}X_q\right)^2 + \left(X_d - X_q\right)\left[\left(\dfrac{P}{e_t}\right)^2 X_q + \dfrac{Q}{e_t}\left(e_t + \dfrac{Q}{e_t}X_q\right)\right]}{\sqrt{\left(e_t + \left(\dfrac{Q}{e_t}\right)^2 X_q\right)^2 + \left(\dfrac{P}{e_t}\right)^2 X_q^2}}$$

and

$$e_2 = \sqrt{\left(e_t - \frac{Q}{e_t}.X_e\right)^2 + \left(\frac{P}{e_t}.X_e\right)^2}$$

Two points on the P-Q plane can be obtained by solving (V.50) set equal to zero for the load condition of $P = 0$, for which case $\delta = 0$. In this situation:

$$E_I = e_t + \frac{Q}{e_t}X_d$$

and

$$e_2 = \left[e_t - \frac{Q}{e_t} . X_e \right]$$

Substitution of these values in (V.50) yields a quadratic expression in (Q/e_t^2) from which the roots are $\left(\dfrac{Q}{e_t^2} \right) = +\dfrac{1}{X_e}$ and $\left(\dfrac{Q}{e_t^2} \right) = -\dfrac{1}{X_q}$

The . reason for the stability limit at $P = 0$, $Q = +\dfrac{1}{X_e}$ (a theoretical operating condition) is that the receiving system voltage $e_2 = 0$ at this point. At the other extreme, the stability limit is reached at a point of negative excitation E_1 such that the negative contribution of the first term of (V.50) is equal to the second term of (V.50), which is the synchronizing torque coefficient due to saliency.

i.e. $\qquad \dfrac{E_1}{X_d + X_e} + \dfrac{e_2 \left(X_d - X_q \right)}{\left(X_d + X_e \right)\left(X_q + X_e \right)} = 0$

Figure 5.43 shows typical steady state stability curves for a salient pole machine.

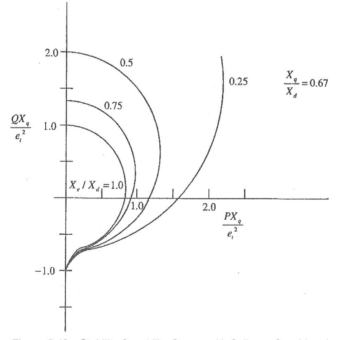

Figure 5.43 – Stability Capability Curves with Saliency Considered

5.4.3   Saturation Effects - Steady State Stability

The method of treating saturation in round rotor and salient pole machines was discussed in Electrical Machine Dynamics - I, pages 73-79.

In the case of the round rotor machine, the effect of saturation was accounted for with a reduction in synchronous reactances in both axes. This reduction was a function of the flux level behind leakage or Potier reactance. Evidently, the effect of saturation is to increase stability limits especially at operating conditions where the saturation level is high. Figure 5.44 shows typical effects of saturation on stability plots.

One method of treating saturation for a salient pole machine is to modify the field current calculated without considering saturation by a saturation component "S" corresponding to some flux level in the direct axis, such as the flux level proportional to voltage behind transient reactance.

The effect of saturation can be explored better by writing the machine dynamic equations, neglecting amortisseur effects. As a point of review of material presented in Electrical Machine Dynamics - I, Figure 5.45 gives the equivalent circuits of a salient pole machine without amortisseur effects.

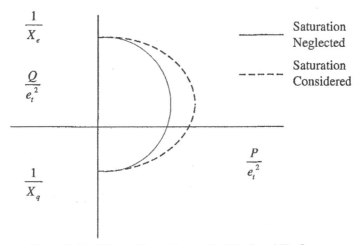

Figure 5.44 – Effect of Saturation on Stability Capability Curves

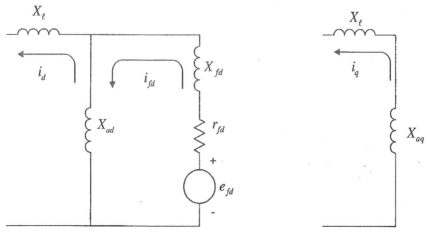

Figure 5.45 – *d* and *q* Axis Equivalent Circuits Neglecting Damper Winders

The open circuit saturation curve as well as the saturation function "S" of flux linkages describing the excess MMF required by saturation are shown on Figure 5.46.

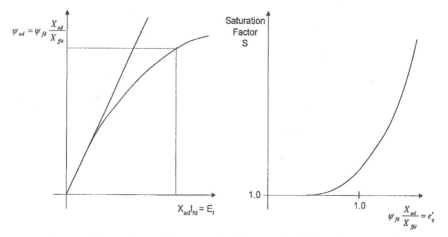

Figure 5.46 – Open Circuit Saturation Curve and Saturation Component

The field voltage equation is:

$$e_{fd} = \frac{d\psi_{fd}}{dt} + r_{fd}i_{fd} \qquad (V.51)$$

Integrating:

$$\psi_{fd} = \int(e_{fd} - r_{fd}\,i_{fd})\,dt + \psi_{fdo} \qquad (V.52)$$

Multiplying through by $\dfrac{X_{ad}}{X_{ffd}}$

$$\psi_{fd}\frac{X_{ad}}{X_{ffd}} = e_q' = \int\left(e_{fd}\frac{X_{ad}}{X_{ffd}} - \frac{r_{fd}}{X_{ffd}}X_{ad}\,i_{fd}\right)dt + \frac{X_{ad}}{X_{ffd}}\psi_{fdo}$$

i.e. $e_q' = \dfrac{1}{T_{d0}'}\displaystyle\int\left[E_{fd} - X_{ad}\,i_{fd}\right]dt + \dfrac{X_{ad}}{X_{ffd}}\psi_{fdo}$ \hfill (V.53)

where $E_{fd} = \dfrac{X_{ad}}{r_{fd}}e_{fd}$ and $T_{d0}' = \dfrac{X_{ffd}}{r_{fd}}$

If saturation is not considered, the field flux linkages are:

$$\psi_{fd} = X_{ffd}\,i_{fd} - X_{ad}\,i_d,$$

or

$$\frac{X_{ad}\psi_{fd}}{X_{ffd}} = X_{ad}\,i_{fd} - \frac{X_{ad}^2}{X_{ffd}}i_d \hfill (V.54)$$

Note that $X_d = X_{ad} + -X_\ell$ and $X_d'\ \Delta X_\ell + \dfrac{X_{ad}X_{fd}}{X_{ffd}}$

Hence:

$$\frac{X_{ad}^2}{X_{ffd}} = X_d - X_d'$$

Equation (V.54) can, therefore, be expressed as:

$$E_I = X_{ad}i_{fd} = e_q' + (X_d - X_d')i_d \hfill (V.55)$$

Note that these equations correspond to those in Appendix I of Reference 3, pages 22 and 23 referring to Model III.

Considering saturation, (V.54) gets modified by the term "s" which we will label:

$$s = f\left[\frac{X_{ad}\psi_{fd}}{X_{ffd}}\right] or\ f\left[e_q'\right]$$

$$i.e. X_{ad} i_{fd} = \frac{X_{ad} \Psi_{fd}}{X_{ffd}} + \frac{X_{ad}^2}{X_{ffd}} i_d + f\left[e_q'\right]$$

$$E_I = X_{ad} i_{fd} = e_q' + \left(X_d - X_d'\right) i_d + f\left[e_q'\right]$$

(V.56)

The above derivations are included to tie in with previous material and to make the following treatment of saturation in salient pole machines more easily understood.

Starting from Equations (V.53) and (V.56) which will be repeated here in equivalent form, with $\omega = 1.0$.

$$e_q' = \frac{E_{fd} - E_I}{sT_{d0}'} + \frac{e_{q0}'}{s}$$

(V.57)

$$E_I = X_{ad} i_{fd} = e_q' + f\left(e_q'\right) + \left(X_d - X_d'\right) i_d$$

(V.58)

$$\psi_d = e_q = e_q' - X_d' i_d$$

(V.59)

We may define the slope of the saturation function at a given operating point as a factor:

$$K = \frac{ds}{de_q'}\bigg|_{e_{q0}'} = \frac{\Delta\left(X_{ad} i_{fd} - e_q'\right)}{\Delta e_q'}\bigg|_{e_{q0}'}$$

The relations above can, therefore, be put into incremental form as follows:

$$\Delta e_q'(s) = \frac{\Delta E_{fd}(s) - \Delta E_I(s)}{sT_{d0}'}$$

(V.60)

$$\Delta E_I(s) = \Delta e_q'(s)(1 + K) + (X_d - X_d')\Delta i_d(s)$$

(V.61)

$$\Delta e_q(s) = \Delta e_q'(s) - X_d' \Delta i_d(s)$$

(V.62)

Recall that in Figure 5.33 the machine behavior was expressed as:

$$\Delta\psi_d(s) = G(s) \Delta E_{fd}(s) - L_d(s) i_d(s)$$

which with the assumption of $\omega = 1.0$ and neglecting $d\psi/dt$ terms also can be written as:

$$\Delta e_q(s) = G(s) \, \Delta E_{fd}(s) - X_d(s) \, \Delta i_d(s) \qquad (V.63)$$

Eliminating $\Delta e_q'$, and ΔE_I in (V.62) with the use of (V.60) and (V.61),we may express (V.62) in the same form as (V.63); where:

$$G(s) = \frac{1}{(1+K)+sT_{d0}'} \qquad (V.64)$$

and

$$X_d(s) = \frac{X_d + KX_d' + sT_{d0}' \, X_d'}{(1+K)+sT_{d0}'} \qquad (V.65)$$

Since in studying steady state stability we are only interested in the steady state or zero frequency values of machine reactance, from (V.65) we note that the effective saturated steady state reactance $X_{d_{sat}}$ of the machine is:

$$X_{d_{sat}} = \frac{X_d\left(1 + K\dfrac{X_d'}{X_d}\right)}{1+K} \qquad (V.66)$$

Note also that the effective steady state gain of the machine:

$$\left.\frac{\Delta e_q}{\Delta E_{fd}}\right|_{\Delta i_d=0} = \frac{1}{1+K} \qquad (V.67)$$

Checking for steady state stability, therefore, entails first the establishment of steady state operating conditions, the determination of linearized parameters about these operating conditions, and the calculation of the synchronizing power coefficient $\Delta P/\Delta \delta$ using these steady state operating conditions and linearized parameters.

Taking the vector diagram of Figure 5.47 for the case of zero resistance, and limiting our attention to the steady state case:

$$\begin{aligned} e_{bq} &= e_q - i_d x_e = \text{component of bus voltage along q-axis} \\ e_{bq} &= e_q + i_q x_e = \text{component of bus voltage along d-axis} \end{aligned} \qquad (V.68)$$

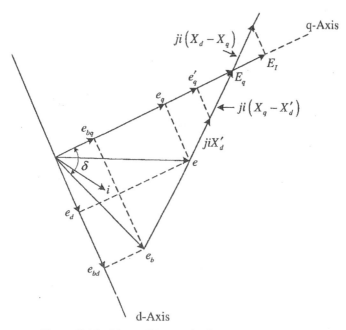

Figure 5.47 – Phasor Diagram for Salient Pole Machine

From the geometry of Figure 5.48, for small changes in angle $\Delta\delta$ we may write, for small $\Delta\delta$

$$\Delta e_{bq} = -e_{bq0}\,\Delta\delta$$
$$\Delta e_{bd} = +e_{bq0}\,\Delta\delta \tag{V.69}$$

Also, from (V.68):

$$\Delta e_{bq} = \Delta e_q - \Delta i_d X_e$$

And $\tag{V.70}$

$$\Delta e_{bd} = \Delta e_d + \Delta i_q X_e$$

Equating (V.69) and (V.70):

$$\Delta e_q = \Delta i_d X_e = e_{bq0}\,\Delta\delta$$
$$\Delta e_d = \Delta i_q X_e = e_{bd0}\,\Delta\delta \tag{V.71}$$

From (V.63) and (V.64), the steady state part of these relations yields:

$$\Delta e_q = \Delta E_{fd}\,\frac{1}{(1+K)} - \frac{X_d\!\left(1 + K\dfrac{X_d'}{X_d}\right)}{(1+K)}\,\Delta i_d \tag{V.72}$$

while for the quadrature axis, assuming no amortisseurs and no saturation:

$$\Delta e_d = + X_q \Delta i_q \qquad (V.73)$$

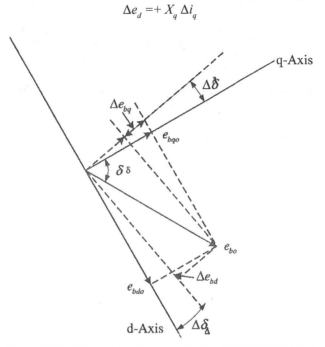

Figure 5.48 – Geometrical Relations for Small Perturbations in δ

Substituting (V.72) and (V.73) in (V.71):

$$\Delta i_d = \frac{e_{bd0}\Delta\delta}{\left(X_e + X_{d_s}\right)} + \Delta E_{fd}\left(\frac{1}{1+K}\right)\frac{1}{\left(X_e + X_{d_s}\right)}$$

$$\Delta i_q = \frac{e_{bq0}\Delta\delta}{\left(X_e + X_q\right)} \qquad (V.74)$$

where

$$X_{d_s} = X_{d_{sat}} = \frac{X_d\left(1 + K\dfrac{X_d'}{X_d}\right)}{\left(1+K\right)}$$

Now,

$$P = e_d i_d + e_q i_q \therefore \Delta P = e_{d0}\Delta i_d + i_{d0}\Delta e_d + e_{q0}\Delta i_q + i_{q0}\Delta e_q$$

Using (V.72), (V.73), and (V.74) ΔP can be expressed as a function of $\Delta\delta$ and ΔE_{fd}

For steady state stability we consider no excitation control hence, $\Delta E_{fd} = 0$ and hence ΔP is only a function of $\Delta\delta$.

$$\Delta P / \Delta\delta \;=\; \frac{\left(e_{q0} + i_{d0}X_q\right)}{X_q + X_e} - \frac{\left(e_{d0} + i_{q0}X_e\right)\left(-e_{d0} + i_{q0}X_{d\,sat}\right)}{X_e + X_{d\,sat}} \tag{V.75}$$

Equation (V.75) can be used to determine the steady state stability limit as will be demonstrated in the following example.

The salient pole generator with parameters and sat curve indicated in Figure 5.49 is connected to an infinite system through an external impedance which may be approximated by a simple reactance $X_e = 0.5\ p.u.$

Find the hand control steady state stability limit for the machine assuming unity terminal voltage and unity power factor. How does this limit compare with the stability limit calculated without considering saturation?

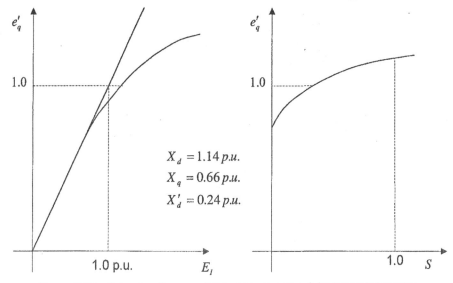

$$X_d = 1.14\,p.u.$$
$$X_q = 0.66\,p.u.$$
$$X'_d = 0.24\,p.u.$$

Figure 5.49 – Saturation Curve and Saturation Function S for Example Machine

SOLUTION

This problem requires a trial and error solution. Assume the operating condition of $P_0 = 1.2 + j0$ at $e_{t0} = 1.0$. From the vector diagram:

$$i_{q0} = \frac{P_0 / et_0 \left[\left(et_0 + \dfrac{Q_0}{et_0} X_q \right) - Q_0 / et_0 X_q \right]}{\sqrt{\left(et_0 + \dfrac{Q_0}{et_0} X_q \right)^2 + \left(\dfrac{P_0}{et_0} X_q \right)^2}}$$

$$i_{d0} = \frac{\left(\dfrac{P_0}{e_{t0}} \right)^2 X_q + \left(\dfrac{Q_0}{e_{t0}} \right) \left(e_{t0} + \dfrac{Q_0}{e_{t0}} X_q \right)}{\sqrt{\left(e_{t0} + \dfrac{Q_0}{e_{t0}} X_q \right)^2 + \left(\dfrac{P_0}{e_{t0}} X_q \right)^2}}$$

$$e_{q0} = \frac{\left(e_{t0} + \dfrac{Q_0}{e_{t0}} X_q \right) e_{t0}}{\sqrt{\left(e_{t0} + \dfrac{Q_0}{e_{t0}} X_q \right)^2 + \left(\dfrac{P_0}{e_{t0}} X_q \right)^2}}$$

$$e'_{q0} = e_{q0} + i_{d0} X'_d$$

$$e_{d0} = i_{q0} X_q$$

$$E_0 = e_{t0} - \left(\frac{P_0}{e_{t0}} - j \frac{Q_0}{e_{t0}} \right) j X_e$$

$$\sin \delta = \frac{e_{t0} \dfrac{P}{e_{t0}} \left(X_q + X_e \right)}{E_{q0} E_0}$$

From the saturation curve we may draw the saturation factor $K = \dfrac{\partial s}{\partial e'_q}$ as which is shown on Figure 5.50.

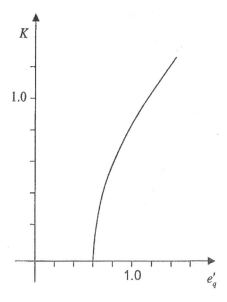

Figure 5.50 – Saturation Factor K as function of e'_q

From the 1st trial operating point:

$$i_{q0} = \frac{1.2(1)}{\sqrt{1^2 + 0.792^2}} = 0.936$$

$$i_{d0} = \frac{1.2^2 \times 0.66}{\sqrt{1.28}} = 0.742$$

$$e_{q0} = 0.783$$

$$e_{d0} = 0.620$$

$$e'_{q0} = 0.783 + 0.741 \times 0.24 = 0.961$$

$$K = 0.77$$

Hence: $X_{ds} = \dfrac{1.14\left(1 + 0.77 \times \dfrac{0.24}{1.14}\right)}{1.77} = 0.749$

Using the above values in (V.75): $\dfrac{\Delta P}{\Delta \delta} = 0.383$.

Note that with saturation not considered: $\dfrac{\Delta P}{\Delta \delta} = 0.153$.

For the next trial, take $P = 1.8$, $Q = 0$.

$$i_{q0} = 1.16$$
$$i_{d0} = 1.38$$
$$e_{q0} = 0.645$$
$$e_{d0} = 0.765$$
$$e'_{q0} = 0.975 \quad \therefore K = 0.80 \text{ and } X_{ds} = 0.74$$

Using these values in (V.75), $\dfrac{\Delta P}{\Delta \delta} = -0.163$.

Interpolating, the stability limit will be approximately at $P = 1.62\ p.u.$

With saturation not considered, $\dfrac{\Delta P}{\Delta \delta}$ for $P = 1.8$, $Q = 0$ is -0.441. Interpolating, the limit, not considering saturation, is approximately <u>1.355.</u>

5.4.4 Dynamic Stability

Aspects of linearized small perturbation stability considered thus far involved checks for existence of synchronizing power, i.e. checking that the coefficient $dP/d\delta$ is positive.

Use of continuously acting voltage regulators generally insure that $dP/d\delta$ is positive for most practical situations. Instability, therefore, does not usually result from lack of steady state synchronizing power but rather due to absence of positive damping in modes of oscillations resulting from the swing equations described by the block diagram of Figures 1 and 2, appropriately modified to include machine flux dynamics.

References 4 and 5 cover concepts of dynamic stability as affected by excitation control. The approach to the understanding of the phenomena is through development of linearized relations starting from the non-linear current, voltage and power relations describing synchronous machine behavior. An example of such linearized relations is shown in Appendix A of Reference 4.

The basic block diagram describing the phenomena is repeated in these notes for convenience (Figure 5.51 and Figure 5.52). Also for the simple case of a machine connected through external reactance to an infinite bus, with the machine represented without amortisseur effects, the parameters in the block diagram are:

$$K_1 = \left.\frac{\Delta T_e}{\Delta \delta}\right|_{E'_q} = $$ change in electrical torque for a change in rotor angle with constant flux linkages in the d-axis.

$$K_2 = \left.\frac{\Delta T_e}{\Delta \delta}\right|_{\delta} = $$ change in electrical torque for a change in d-axis flus linkages with constant rotor angle.

$$K_3 = $$ impedance factor $= \dfrac{X'_d + X_e}{X_d + X_e}$ for the case where the external impedance is a pure reactance X_e.

$$K_4 = \frac{1}{K_3}\frac{\Delta E'_q}{\Delta \delta} = $$ demagnetizing effect of a change in rotor angle.

$$K_5 = \left.\frac{\Delta e_t}{\Delta \delta}\right|_{E'_q} = $$ change in terminal voltage with change in rotor angle for constant E'_q.

$$K_6 = \left.\frac{\Delta e_t}{\Delta E'_q}\right|_{\delta} = $$ change in terminal voltage with change in E'_q for constant rotor angle.

$$T'_{d0} = $$ field open circuit time constant.

$$T'_{dz} = K_3 T'_{d0} = $$ effective field time constant under load.

It is important to recognize that, with the exception of K_3 which is only a function of the ratio of impedances, all other parameters change with loading, making the dynamic behavior of the machine quite different at different operating points.

$$K_1 = \frac{X_q - X_d'}{X_e + X_d'} i_{q0} E_0 \sin \delta_0 + \frac{E_{q0} E_0 \cos \delta_0}{X_e + X_q}$$

$$K_2 = \frac{E_0 \sin \delta_0}{X_e + X_d'}$$

$$K_3 = \frac{X_d' + X_e}{X_d + X_e}$$

$$K_4 = \frac{X_d - X_d'}{X_e + X_d'} E_0 \sin \delta_0$$

$$K_5 = \frac{X_q}{X_e + X_q} \frac{e_{d0}}{e_{t0}} E_0 \cos \delta - \frac{X_d'}{X_e + X_d'} \frac{e_{q0}}{e_{t0}} E_0 \sin \delta_0$$

$$K_6 = \frac{X_e}{X_e + X_d'} \frac{e_{q0}}{e_{t0}}$$

(V.76)

The analysis is based on frequency response techniques. The material in Appendix E of Generation Dynamics and Control will be helpful in the understanding of these techniques (Reference 7).

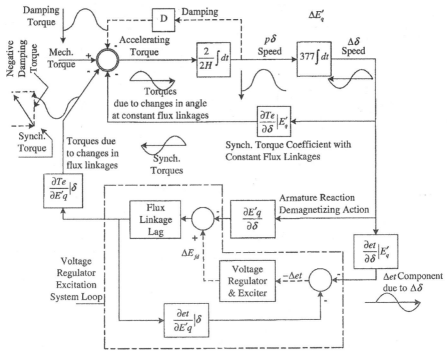

Figure 5.51 – Machine Torque Angle Relationship Including Effects of AVR and Exciter

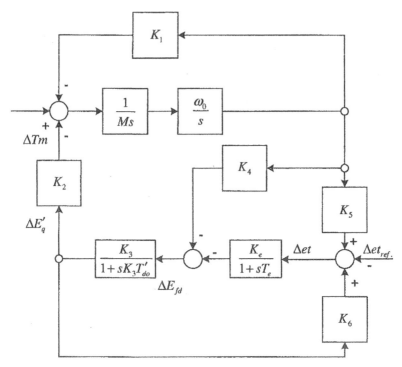

Figure 5.52 – Block Diagram of Single Machine Supplying an Infinite Bus through External Impedance Including Effects of Voltage Regulator-Excitation System

The use of these analysis methods will be illustrated with some examples. Take the case of the previous example of a machine whose data is given in Figure 5.49 and for the same loading condition considered previously of

$$P + jQ = 1.0 + j0 \text{ and } e_t = 1.0, \text{ and } X_e = 0.4, H = 5$$

Neglecting saturation and using (V.76) for the above operating conditions, with

$$
\begin{aligned}
i_{q0} &= 0.835, \ e_{q0} = 0.835 \\
i_{d0} &= 0.550, \ e_{d0} = 0.550 \\
E_{q0} &= 1.20, \ E_0 = 1.077 \\
\delta &= 55.22°
\end{aligned}
$$

The linearized parameters of the block diagram of Figure 5.52 are:

$$K_1 = 1.174$$
$$K_2 = 1.47$$
$$K_3 = 0.36$$
$$K_4 = 1.88$$
$$K_5 = -0.117$$
$$K_6 = 0.301$$

What is the synchronizing power coefficient with constant flux linkages?

$$K_1 = \left.\frac{\partial T_e}{\partial \delta}\right|_{E_q'} = 1.1745 \text{ p.u / radian}$$

What is the oscillation frequency of the machine swing equations assuming constant flux linkages?

$$\omega_n = \sqrt{\frac{\omega_0 K_1}{2H}} = 6.65 \text{ rd / s}$$

What is the steady state synchronizing power coefficient considering no regulator action (constant field voltage)?

$$\text{Steady State } \left.\frac{\partial T_e}{\partial \delta}\right|_{E_{fd}} = K_1 - K_2 K_3 K_4 = 0.180$$

What value of K_e would make the steady state synchronizing power coefficient equal to that with constant flux linkages?

From the block diagram of Figure 5.52, in the steady state,

$$\frac{\Delta E_q'}{\Delta \delta} = \frac{-K_4 K_3}{1 + K_e K_3 K_6} - \frac{K_5 K_e K_6}{1 + K_e K_3 K_6}$$

and steady state synchronizing coefficient:

$$= K_1 - K_2 \left[\frac{K_4 K_3 + K_5 K_e K_6}{1 + K_e K_3 K_6} \right]$$

From the above, with values of K_1 to K_6 previously calculated,

$$K_\varepsilon = 16.1 \frac{p.u. \, \Delta E_{fd}}{p.u. \, \Delta e_t}$$

This shows that it takes a fairly low gain voltage regulator to counteract the demagnetizing effect of armature reaction and make the machine exhibit a synchronizing power coefficient in the steady state equal to or better than that with constant flux linkages.

Assuming no regulator action (constant field voltage) at the natural frequency of oscillation, what is the magnitude of damping torque due to field effects?

With no voltage regulator action, the damping torques are contributed by the series of blocks whose combined transfer function is:

$$\frac{-K_4 K_3 K_2}{1 + s K_3 T'_{d0}}$$

For the frequency of oscillation, $\omega_n = 6.65$ rd/s and $T'_{d0} = 8s$.

This component of torque has the following magnitude and phase relative to angle:

$$\frac{-0.994}{1 + j19.1} = .0520 \underline{|93°}$$

Since speed leads angle by 90°, the component of torque in phase with speed is 0.052 cos 3° = 0.052. Note that the component of synchronizing torque coefficient at this frequency is negative, i.e. −0.052 sin 3° = −0.00272.

For an angle oscillation amplitude of 1 radian, at 6.65 rd/s, the p.u speed oscillation amplitude is 6.65/377 = 0.0177. Hence the equivalent damping constant $D = \Delta T p\delta$ at this frequency is $\frac{0.052}{0.0177} = 2.94$.

The damping ratio represented by this amount of damping torque can be derived approximately as follows.

The characteristic equation of a second order system represented by the block diagram of Figure 5.53

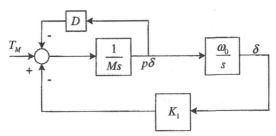

Figure 5.53 – Block Diagram of a Second Order System

is $\dfrac{\omega_0}{M}K + \dfrac{D}{M}s + s^2 = 0$. Comparing this expression with the form of the quadratic

$$\omega_0^2 + 2\xi\,\omega_0 s + s^2 = 0,$$

$$\omega_0 = \sqrt{\dfrac{K_1\omega_0}{M}} \text{ and } \xi = 1/2\dfrac{D}{\sqrt{K_1\,M\omega_0}}$$

At $s = j\omega_n$ the equivalent damping coefficient, $D = 2.94\ p.u.$ Hence the damping ratio produced by the flux demagnetizing effect is approximately:

$$\xi = \dfrac{1}{2} \times \dfrac{2.94}{\sqrt{1.174\times10\times\omega_0}} = \underline{0.22}$$

Assuming an infinite gain regulator - exciter, with zero lags, what are the damping torques?

With the idealized voltage regulator exciter in the picture, the function

$$\dfrac{\Delta E_q'}{\Delta\delta} \text{ becomes } \dfrac{-K_3\left[K_4 + K_e K_5\right]}{1 + sK_3 T_{do}' + K_e K_3 K_6}$$

with $K_e \rightarrow \infty$.

$$\dfrac{\Delta E_q'}{\Delta\delta} = \dfrac{K_5}{K_6} \text{ and } \dfrac{\Delta T_e}{\Delta\delta} = \left[K_1 - \dfrac{K_2 K_5}{K_6}\right]$$

Note that under this idealized situation of infinite gain and zero time constant the torque change contributed through the change in flux is in phase with angle hence, has no damping component.

Note also that because K_5 is negative, the net synchronizing power coefficient is greater than that with constant flux linkages.

663

$$i.e.\ K_1 - \frac{K_2 K_5}{K_6} = 1.745$$

compared with $K_1 = 1.174$ for constant flux linkages.

Note also that the synchronizing power coefficient for an ideal zero reactance machine (constant terminal voltage) under these loading conditions is:

$$\frac{e_0 E_0}{0.4}\ \cos 21.8° = 2.5$$

Take now the case where the excitation system has considerable lags as described by function

$$\frac{K_e}{(1+sT_e)(1+sT_v)}$$

Let $K_e = 20$
$T_e = 0.5$
$T_v = 0.2$

What are the damping torques produced by changes in flux at the natural frequency $\omega_n = 6.65$ rd/s? Is the operating point stable with this excitation system?

Referring to the block diagram of Figure 5.52 and labeling the voltage regulator-exciter function as $G(s)$, the torques resulting from changes in E_q' are:

$$-K_2 \frac{K_3}{1+sK_3 T_{d0}'} \left| \frac{K_4 + K_5 G(s)}{1 + \dfrac{K_3 K_6 G(s)}{1+sK_3 T_{d0}'}} \right| \Delta\delta(s)$$

Substituting $s = j6.65$ and $G(s) = \dfrac{20}{(1+s0.2)(1+s0.5)}$ – the above expression, with $T_{d0}' = 8s$, becomes:

$$= 0.0626\ \underline{|98.55°}$$

$$= -0.0093 + j0.0619$$

i.e. The damping torque developed by angle oscillations of 1 rad amplitude at a frequency 6.65 rd/s. is 0.0619 p.u., i.e. the amplitude of torques in phase with speed is $[.00619 \Delta\delta]$. It appears that this point is stable.

Note that stability can be determined by Nyquist's criterion with a check of the phase angle of the overall open loop function shown on Figure 5.54 at the frequency for which the amplitude ratio of this function is unity. We have assumed that this frequency is close to the natural frequency ω_n (assuming constant flux linkages).

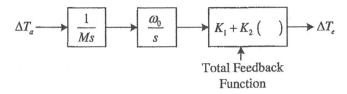

Figure 5.54 – Transfer Function $\dfrac{\Delta T_e}{\Delta T_a}$

This assumption is good when the magnitude of the feedback function $K_2(\Delta \dot{E}_q' / \Delta\delta)$ is small with respect to K_1.

Now take the same case with the regulator-exciter function as $\dfrac{100}{(1+s.05)}$

Is this excitation system stable in the open-circuit condition? The block diagram of the machine on open circuit is shown on Figure 5.55.

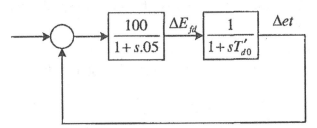

Figure 5.55 – AVR – Excitation System Flux Loop

A Bode plot of the open loop function (Figure 5.56) reveals that the control system is stable, with a crossover frequency of $\omega_c = 11$ rd/s. That is, the open loop function $\dfrac{100}{(1+ j0.05\omega_c)(1+ j8\omega_c)}$ has an amplitude of one at this frequency and a phase angle of -118.2°.

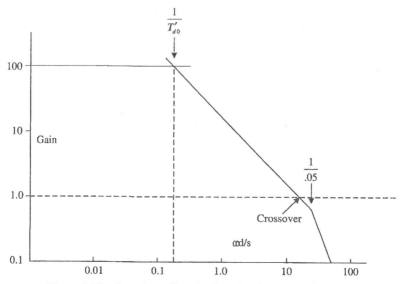

Figure 5.56 – Open Loop Transfer Function Frequency Response

Is the operating point, $P = 1.0 + j0$, stable with this excitation system? Repeating the procedure of determining the torques with use of the block diagram and

$$G(s) = \frac{100}{(1 + s0.05)}.$$

$\Delta T/\Delta\delta$ $(j\omega)$ through flux changes = 0.257 $\underline{/-78.03°}$ = .0533 – j0.252. The above value of $\Delta T/\Delta\delta$ at ω = 6.65 rd/s shows that the component of damping torque is negative –j0.252. Hence, in the absence of other sources of damping, this point will be unstable.

Note that if some external source of damping exists such that $D = 1.0$ in the diagram of Figure 53, then the net damping coefficient at this frequency would be:

$$\left(1 - \frac{0.252 \times \omega_0}{6.65} = (1 - 14.3) = -13.3\right)$$

which is still substantially negative. Hence, the operating point is unstable in spite of a nominal amount of external damping such as might be provided by the load/ frequency characteristic.

If one were to use a stabilizing signal derived from a measurement of rotor speed, determine the phase advance through which this signal would have to be processed for it to produce only damping torques. Determine also the magnitude of the signal required to make this operating point barely stable with the regulator-exciter function of $\dfrac{100}{1 + s0.05}$.

Figure 5.57 shows the pertinent part of the block diagram to solve for components of torque in response to a stabilizing signal working through the reference or set point of the voltage regulator.

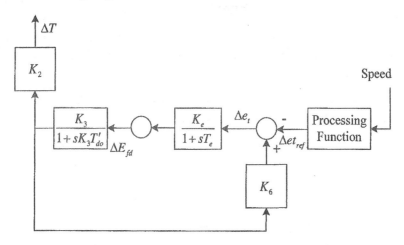

Figure 5.57 – Generator Excitation Open Loop Transfer Function $\Delta T\!\!\diagup\!\!\Delta\omega$

The phase lag of $\dfrac{\Delta T}{\Delta e_{t_{ref}}}$ is the phase lag of the function:

$$\frac{\Delta T}{\Delta e_{t\,ref}} = \frac{\dfrac{K_2 K_3 K_e}{\left(1 + s K_3 T'_{do}\right)\left(1 + s T_e\right)}}{\dfrac{K_3 K_e K_6}{\left(1 + s K_3 T'_{do}\right)\left(1 + s T_e\right)}}$$

Substituting numerical values and evaluating, at $s = j6.65$,

$$\frac{\Delta T}{\Delta e_{t_{ref}}} = 2.62 \underline{|-74.38°}$$

Hence the speed signal should be processed through a phase lead network such that the signal would be advanced by 74.38°. The resulting torque changes would then be in phase with speed.

The gain of the signal as measured at the reference of the voltage regulator should be such that a 1 p.u. change in speed should give $\frac{13.3}{2.62}$ change in Δe_t reference, i.e. a gain of 5.07 $\frac{p.u\ \Delta e_t}{p.u\ p\delta}$, so that the net effect will be the cancellation of the negative damping due to the regulator-exciter previously calculated as -13.3.

5.4.5   Induction Machine Effects

Although stability is usually associated with performance of synchronous machines operating in parallel, induction motors can also exhibit problems which may be categorized as stability problems.

Take the case of Figure 5.58 showing a synchronous source supplying a large induction motor load through some external reactance X.

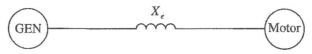

Figure 5.58 – Generator-Motor System

The equivalent circuit for this system can be described as in Figure 5.59.

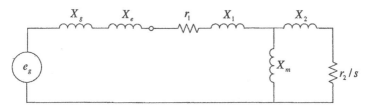

Figure 5.59 – Equivalent Circuit of System in Figure 5.58

Note that we have labeled the rotor resistance as r_2. We should avoid confusing this with the symbol for negative sequence resistance r_2 used in other sections.

As described in pages 212-222 and Class Problem X of Electrical Machine Dynamics - I, the performance of the motor can be obtained with the help of the following equivalent circuit.

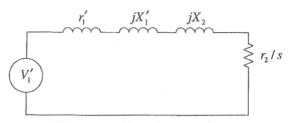

Figure 5.60 – Motor Equivalent Circuit

Where $V_1' = E_{Thev} = e_g \dfrac{jX_m}{r_1 + j\left(X_g + X_e + X_1 + X_M\right)}$

and $r_1' + jX_1' = \dfrac{jX_m\left[r_1 + j\left(X_g + X_e + X_1\right)\right]}{r_1 + j\left(X_g + X_e + X_1 + X_M\right)}$

For balanced conditions the per unit torque developed by the motor is:

$$T = I_2^2 \frac{r_2}{s} = e_g \frac{V_1'^2 r_2 s}{\left(r_1' s + r_2\right)^2 + \left(X_1' + X_2\right)^2 s^2} \tag{V.77}$$

The variable slip "s" should be solved from the motor momentum equations and motor mechanical load torque/speed characteristics as described in Figure 5.61.

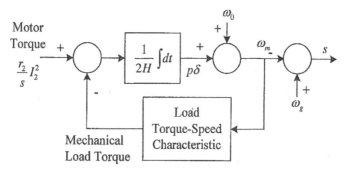

Figure 5.61 – Block Diagram of the Induction Motor Mechanical Equation

Recall the shape of torque slip motor characteristics as shown on Figure 5.62.

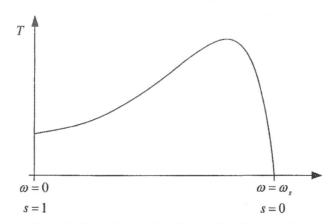

Figure 5.62 – Induction Motor Torque-Slip Characteristic

From the expression (V.77) for torque, it is apparent that torque varies directly with the square of system voltage and is decreased significantly with increases in system impedance. Hence, network disturbances resulting in voltage dips and changes in effective source impedances resulting in voltage dips and changes in effective source impedances can cause a reduction in motor torque sometimes to the point where motors stall. Once the motors stall, (s → 1.0) they present a high reactive load to the system causing excessive voltage drop and thereby impairing the ability of generators to maintain synchronism.

In the case of unbalanced faults, there are the additional effects of negative sequence currents and torques which can contribute considerably to the problem of stalling of motors.

When the system frequency cannot be assumed constant at rated value ω_0 evidently the value of slip will be $\left(1-\dfrac{\omega_m}{\omega_g}\right)$ where ω_g is the system frequency. The equivalent circuit constants of the motor, the reactances, that is, would have to be adjusted to the new system frequency, ω_g. Since, however, generated voltages which are a product of speed and flux are not generally made a function of speed (system speed variation being generally small), the errors introduced by this approximation are compensated by the errors of not adjusting the reactances.

It should be noted that the previous treatment is based on steady state relationships of motor currents, voltages and fluxes. A more rigorous analysis should take into account the electrical time constants of the rotor circuits. For small and not very efficient motors these time constants are small enough to justify the practice of neglecting them. A method of representation taking these time constants into account is nevertheless of value and may be required in certain cases that warrant detailed analyses. With reference to the equivalent circuit of Figure 5.63, the induction motor equations in terms of α, β components, also known as Stanley equations, modified to a synchronously rotating reference are:

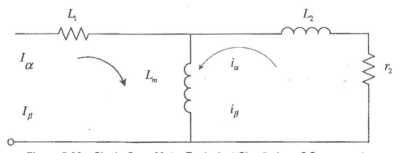

Figure 5.63 – Single Cage Motor Equivalent Circuits in α, β Components

Stator Voltages

$$E_\alpha = \frac{d\psi_\alpha}{dt} + r_1 I_\alpha - \psi_\beta \omega$$

$$E_\beta = \frac{d\psi_\beta}{dt} + r_1 I_\beta - \psi_\alpha \omega \qquad (V.78)$$

Note that these components are relative to axes rotating at synchronous speed, $\omega = 1$. For balanced operation E_α and E_β will be d.c quantities. ψ_α and ψ_β are the stator flux linkages.

Rotor Voltages

$$0 = \frac{d\lambda_\alpha}{dt} + r_2 i_\alpha + \lambda_\beta p\theta$$

$$0 = \frac{d\lambda_\beta}{dt} + r_2 i_\beta + \lambda_\alpha p\theta \qquad (V.79)$$

where λ_α and λ_β are rotor flux linkages expressed along the synchronously rotating axes. $p\Theta$ is

the negative of rotor slip. Under balanced conditions will be d.c. λ_α, λ_β, i_α and i_β will be d.c. quantities.

Stator Flux Linkages

$$\psi_\alpha = \left(L_1 + L_m\right)I_\alpha + L_m i_\alpha$$

$$\psi_\beta = \left(L_1 + L_m\right)I_\beta + L_m i_\beta \qquad (V.80)$$

Rotor Flux Linkages

$$\lambda_\alpha = \left(L_2 + L_m\right)i_\alpha + L_m I_\alpha$$

$$\lambda_\beta = \left(L_2 + L_m\right)i_\beta + L_m I_\beta \qquad (V.81)$$

Torque

$$T_e = \lambda_\beta i_\alpha - \lambda_\alpha i_\beta \qquad (V.82)$$

For balanced phase voltages of fundamental frequency,

$$e_a = E \cos \omega t$$

$$e_b = E \cos (\omega t - 120°) \qquad \text{(V.83)}$$

$$e_c = E \cos (\omega t + 120°)$$

The appropriate transformation of these to the α, β axes (which are same as d, q axes for a synchronously rotating rotor) gives:

$$\begin{aligned} E_\alpha &= E \\ E_\beta &= 0 \end{aligned} \qquad \text{(V.84)}$$

Under normal steady state conditions; the $\dfrac{d\psi_\alpha}{dt}$ and $\dfrac{d\psi_\beta}{dt}$ terms in the stator voltage equations (1) are zero. Omission of these $d\psi/dt$ terms will result in neglecting of the d.c offset currents in the stator which can arise during abrupt switching operations.

Rewriting (V.78) with the $d\psi/dt$ terms omitted and using (V.80) and (V.81) to eliminate rotor currents, we have:

$$E_\alpha = r_1 I_\alpha - \omega \left(L_1 + L_m - \frac{L_m^2}{L_2 + L_m} \right) I_\beta - \frac{\omega L_m}{L_2 + L_m} \lambda_\beta$$

$$E_\beta = r_1 I_\beta + \omega \left(L_1 + L_m - \frac{L_m^2}{L_2 + L_m} \right) I_\alpha + \frac{\omega L_m}{L_2 + L_m} \lambda_\alpha \qquad \text{(V.85)}$$

Also eliminating rotor currents in (V.79):

$$\frac{d\lambda_\alpha}{dt} = \frac{-r_2}{L_2 + L_m} \lambda_\alpha + \frac{r_2 L_m}{L_2 + L_m} I_\alpha - \lambda_\beta p\theta$$

$$\frac{d\lambda_\beta}{dt} = \frac{-r_2}{L_2 + L_m} \lambda_\beta + \frac{r_2 L_m}{L_2 + L_m} I_\beta + \lambda_\alpha p\theta \qquad \text{(V.86)}$$

From (V.85):

$$I_\alpha = \frac{\left(E_\beta - \dfrac{\omega L_m}{L_2 + L_m} \lambda_\alpha \right)}{\omega \left(L_1 + L_m - \dfrac{L_m^2}{L_2 + L_m} \right)} - \frac{r_1}{\omega \left(L_1 + L_m - \dfrac{L_m^2}{L_2 + L_m} \right)} I_\beta$$

$$I_\beta = \frac{\left(E_\alpha + \dfrac{\omega L_m}{L_2 + L_m} \lambda_\beta \right)}{\omega \left(L_1 + L_m - \dfrac{L_m^2}{L_2 + L_m} \right)} - \frac{r_1}{\omega \left(L_1 + L_m - \dfrac{L_m^2}{L_2 + L_m} \right)} I_\alpha \qquad \text{(V.87)}$$

Relations (V.86) and (V.87) can be simplified with redefinition of variables as follows:

$$\lambda'_\alpha = \frac{L_m}{L_2 + L_m} \lambda_\alpha$$

$$\lambda'_\beta = \frac{L_m}{L_2 + L_m} \lambda_\beta$$

$$L_1 + L_m - \frac{L_m^2}{L_2 + L_m} = L' \tag{V.88}$$

$$\frac{d\lambda'_\alpha}{dt} = \frac{-r_2}{L_2 + L_m} \lambda'_\alpha + \frac{r_2 L_m^2}{\left(L_2 + L_m\right)^2} I_\alpha - \lambda'_\beta p\theta$$

$$\frac{d\lambda'_\beta}{dt} = \frac{-r_2}{L_2 + L_m} \lambda'_\beta + \frac{r_2 L_m^2}{\left(L_2 + L_m\right)^2} I_\beta - \lambda'_\alpha p\theta$$

and

$$I_\alpha = \frac{E_\beta - \omega \lambda'_\alpha}{\omega L'} - \frac{r_1}{\omega L'} I_\beta$$

$$I_\beta = \frac{-\left(E_\alpha + \omega \lambda'_\beta\right)}{\omega L'} + \frac{r_1}{\omega L'} I_\alpha \tag{V.89}$$

The symmetry of equations (V.88) and (V.89) and the fact that components α and β are orthogonal, suggests use of a new set of complex variables as follows:

$$\lambda' = \lambda'_\alpha + j\lambda'_\beta$$

$$i_1 = I_\alpha + jI_\beta \tag{V.90}$$

$$e = E_\alpha + jE_\beta$$

Using these definitions in (V.88) and (V.89):

$$\frac{d\lambda'}{dt} = \frac{-r_2}{L_2 + L_m} \lambda' + \frac{r_2 L_m^2}{\left(L_2 + L_m\right)^2} i_1 - j\lambda'(p\theta)$$

$$i_1 = \frac{-1}{\omega L'}(\omega\lambda' + je) + j\frac{r_1}{\omega L'} i_1 \tag{V.91}$$

$$\alpha \rightarrow R$$

$$\beta \rightarrow I$$

673

Further, defining a complex voltage proportional to rotor flux linkages $e' = j\lambda'\omega$. (V.91) becomes:

$$\frac{de'}{dt} = \frac{-r_2}{L_2 + L_m}e' + j\frac{r_2 L_m^2}{(L_2 + L_m)^2}i_1 + je'(p\theta)$$

and   (V.92)

$$j\omega L'i = (e - e') - r_1 i_1$$

The parameters in (V.92) can be expressed as follows:

$$r_2/(L_2 + Lm) = \text{rotor open circuit time constant} = T'_{do}$$

$$\frac{L_m^2 r_2}{(L_2 + L_m)^2} = \frac{1}{T'_{do}}(L_1 + L_m - L')$$

Hence, (V.92) can be expressed as:

$$\frac{de'}{dt} = -\frac{1}{T'_{do}}\left[e' - j\omega(L_1 + L_m - L')i_1\right] + je'(p\theta)$$

$$i_1 = \frac{e - e'}{(r_1 + j\omega L')}$$

                                                                                          (V.93)

The motor per unit torque is equal to the per unit power transferred to the rotor, i.e.

$$T_e \approx P_e = \text{Re}[e'i^*]$$

where * denotes conjugate.

Relations (V.93) form a convenient set for the representation of induction motors in dynamic studies where rotor electrical transients are to be considered.

The motor can be represented by an internal voltage e' which is a complex state variable, in series with an impedance $r_1 + jX'$, where

$r_{1'} = $ stator resistance

$$X' = (X_1 + X_m) - \frac{X_m^2}{X_2 + X_m} = X_1 + \frac{X_m X_2}{X_m + X_2} \quad \text{(analogous to transient reactance)}$$

The derivative of e' is a function of e', $p\theta$ and i_1, as described by the block diagram of Figure 64.

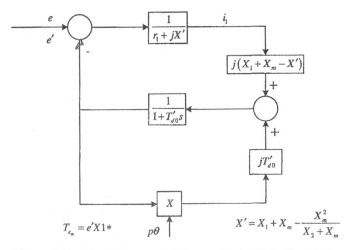

$$T_{e_m} = e'X1*$$ $$p\theta$$ $$X' = X_1 + X_m - \frac{X_m^2}{X_2 + X_m}$$

Figure 5.64 – Block Diagram of Motor considering Rotor Transients

5.4.6 Self Excitation

In addition to the oscillations caused by the rotor inertia interacting with synchronizing power, which have been the main phenomena of concern in dealing with stability, there are forms of instability which can occur in synchronous and induction machines and they concern *electrical self excitation*.

Electrical self excitation can only occur when the circuit to which the machine is connected contains capacitance. For instance, a synchronous generator may be connected to an open transmission line or an induction motor may be left connected to terminal capacitors.

Series capacitance can also give rise to pulsations of current, voltage and torque. Examine the case of a machine, as in Figure 5.65, left connected to a capacitance.

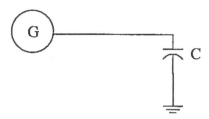

Figure 5.65 – Synchronous Machine Feeding a Capacitance

For a machine represented in terms of fluxes, currents, and voltages in the d & q axes, and limiting the representation to transient effects, i.e. one coupled circuit in each axis as described by the equivalent circuits of Figure 5.66, the circuit condition of Figure 5.65 may be described by the equations in the following development.

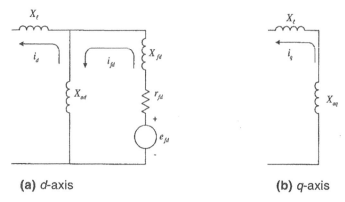

(a) *d*-axis   **(b)** *q*-axis

Figure 5.66 – Synchronous Machine Equivalent Circuits

Note that since self excitation phenomena are often associated with overfrequency conditions, the assumption of $\omega = 1.0$ and $\overline{X} = \overline{L}$ cannot always be made. Accordingly, flux linkages and voltages will be kept distinct.

The d-axis flux linkage and rotor voltage equations can be reduced to:

$$\frac{e_q'}{\omega} = \frac{L_{ad}}{L_{ffd}}\psi_{fd} = \frac{1}{T_{d0}'}\int\left[E_{fd} - L_{ad}i_{fd}\right]dt \tag{V.94}$$

where

$$E_{fd} = \frac{e_{fd}r_{fd}}{L_{ad}} \text{ and } T_{d0}' = \frac{L_{ffd}}{r_{fd}}$$

$$L_{ad}i_{fd} = \frac{e_q'}{\omega} + i_d\left(L_d - L_d'\right) + f\left[\frac{e_q'}{\omega}\right] \tag{V.95}$$

where $f\left[\dfrac{e_q'}{\omega}\right]$ is the excess field current due to saturation which is a function of

the flux level $\left|e_q'/\omega\right|$, and $L_d' = L_\ell + \dfrac{L_{fd}L_{ad}}{L_{ffd}}$

$$\psi_d = \frac{e_q'}{\omega} - i_d L_d' \tag{V.96}$$

Similarly, the *q*-axis flux linkage and rotor voltage equations are:

$$i_{kq}(L_{aq} + L_{kq}) - i_q L_{aq} = \psi_{kq} \tag{V.97}$$

or
$$i_{kq} = \frac{(\psi_{kq} + i_q L_{aq})}{L_{aq} + L_{kq}} \tag{V.98}$$

and
$$\psi_{kq} = -\int r_{kq} i_{kq} dt \tag{V.99}$$

Also

$$\psi_{kq} = L_{aq} i_{kq} - L_q' i_q \tag{V.100}$$

$$= \frac{L_{aq}}{L_{aq} + L_{kq}} \psi_{kq} - \left[L_q - \frac{L_{aq}^2}{L_{aq} + L_{kq}} \right] i_q$$

$$= -\frac{e_d'}{\omega} - \frac{L_\ell L_{kq} + L_\ell L_{aq} + L_{kq} L_{aq} i_q}{L_{aq} + L_{kq}} \tag{V.101}$$

$$= \frac{e_d'}{\omega} - L_q' i_q$$

where
$$\frac{e_d'}{\omega} = -\frac{L_{aq}}{L_{aq} + L_{kq}} \psi_{kq}$$

$$L_q' = L_\ell + \frac{L_{aq} L_{kq}}{L_{aq} + L_{kq}}$$

The stator voltage and current equations (neglecting $d\psi/dt$ terms and armature resistance) are:

$$e_q = \omega \psi_d = e_q' - i_d \omega L_d' \tag{V.102}$$

$$i_d = -\omega^2 \psi_d C = -\omega C e_q' + i_d \omega^2 L_d' C \tag{V.103}$$

$$e_d = -\omega \psi_q = +e_d' + i_q \omega L_q' \tag{V.104}$$

$$i_q = -\omega^2 \psi_q C = +\omega C e_d' + i_q \omega^2 L_d' C \tag{V.105}$$

From (V.103) and (V.105):

$$i_d = \frac{-e_q' \omega C}{1 - \omega^2 L_d' C} \tag{V.106}$$

$$i_q = \frac{e_d' \omega C}{1 - \omega^2 L_q' C} \tag{V.107}$$

Using (V.94) and (V.106) in Laplace Transform form and neglecting saturation:

$$\frac{e_q'(s)}{\omega} = \frac{1}{sT_{d0}'}\left[E_{fd}(s) - L_{ad}i_{fd}(s)\right]$$

$$= \frac{1}{sT_{d0}'}\left[E_{fd}(s) - \frac{e_q'(s)}{\omega} - i_d(s)\left(L_d - L_d'\right)\right]$$

$$= \frac{1}{sT_{d0}'}\left[E_{fd}(s) - \frac{e_q'(s)}{\omega} + e_q'(s)\frac{\omega C\left(L_d - L_d'\right)}{1 - \omega^2 L_d' C}\right]$$

$$e_q'(s)\left[\frac{1}{\omega} + \frac{1}{sT_{d0}'} - \frac{\omega C\left(L_d - L_d'\right)}{sT_{d0}'\left(1 - \omega^2 L_d' C\right)}\right] = \frac{E_{fd}(s)}{sT_{d0}'}$$

or

$$e_q'(s) = \left[\frac{\omega}{s + \dfrac{\left(1 - \omega^2 L_d C\right)}{T_{d0}'\left(1 - \omega^2 L_d' C\right)}}\right]\frac{E_{fd}(s)}{T_{d0}'}$$

i.e.

$$e_q'(s) = \left[\frac{E_{fd}(s)\omega}{T_{d0}'} + e_q'(0)\right]\left[\frac{1}{s + \dfrac{\left(1 - \omega^2 L_d C\right)}{T_{d0}'\left(1 - \omega^2 L_d' C\right)}}\right]$$

or   Initial condition   (V.108)

Similarly, for the q-axis, using (V.99), (V.100), (V.101), and (V.107):

$$\frac{e_d'}{\omega} = +\frac{r_{kq}}{L_{aq} + L_{kq}}\int L_{aq}\, i_{kq}\, dt$$

$$e_d'(s) = +\frac{1}{T_{q0}'s}L_{aq}\, i_{kq} \text{ where } T_{q0}' = \frac{L_{aq} + L_{kq}}{r_{kq}}$$

i.e. $\qquad = \dfrac{1}{T'_{q0}s}\left| \dfrac{e'_d(s)}{\omega} + i_q\left(L_q - L'_q\right)\right|$

$\qquad\qquad = \dfrac{1}{T'_{q0}s}\left| \dfrac{e'_d(s)}{\omega} + e'_d(s)\omega C\left(L_q - L'_q\right)\right|$

i.e. $\qquad e'_d(s) = -\dfrac{e'_d(s)}{T'_{q0}s}\left[\dfrac{1-\omega^2 L_q C}{1-\omega^2 L'_q C}\right]$

or $\qquad -e'_d(s)sT'_{q0} + e'_{d0}T'_{q0} = e'_d(s)\left[\dfrac{1-\omega^2 L_q C}{1-\omega^2 L'_q C}\right]$

$$\uparrow$$

Initial condition

i.e. $\qquad e'_d(s) = \dfrac{e'_{d0}}{s + \left[\dfrac{\left(1-\omega^2 L_q C\right)}{\left(1-\omega^2 L'_q C\right)T'_{q0}}\right]}$ $\qquad$ (V.109)

Examine Equations (V.108) and (V.109).

Flux linkages in the direct axis (e'_q) will exhibit self-excitation i.e. will increase exponentially with time as long as:

$$\dfrac{\left(1-\omega^2 L_d C\right)}{L'_{d0}\left(1-\omega^2 L'_d C\right)} < 0$$

Since $L_d > L'_d$, the largest value of capacitance that will barely avoid self-excitation in the direct axis will be:

$$C = \dfrac{1}{\omega^2 L_d} \text{ or } \omega L_d = \dfrac{1}{\omega C} \qquad\qquad (V.110)$$

Figure 5.67 shows the block diagrams of the d and q axes for this condition of machine connected to a capacitive reactance. It is evident that positive feedback (self-excitation) will occur in the q axis when $\omega^2 L_q C > 1.0$ and in the d axis when $\omega^2 L_d C > 1.0$.

In the absence of voltage regulators self-excitation will occur whenever the admittance $\frac{1}{\omega C}$ is greater than the direct axis synchronous reactance ωL_d. Note that the value of capacitance for self-excitation varies inversely with the square of frequency or speed.

It can be shown that the effect of voltage regulators which affect the direct axis flux is to alter this condition for self-excitation to the point where self-excitation does not occur in the direct axis but rather in the quadrature axis first as can be seen from relation (109).

Quadrature axis flux will decay as long as

$$\left[\frac{\left(1 - \omega^2 L_q C\right)\omega}{\left(1 - \omega^2 L_d' C\right)T_{q0}'} \right]$$

is positive.

Since $L_q > L_q'$ the point where quadrature axis self-excitation will first occur is where

$$\omega C = \frac{1}{\omega L_q} \text{ or } X_c = X_q$$

Self-excitation phenomena involve exponentially increasing fluxes and voltages as a function of time. The problem involves non-linearities due to saturation and, therefore, must be generally solved by direct simulation.

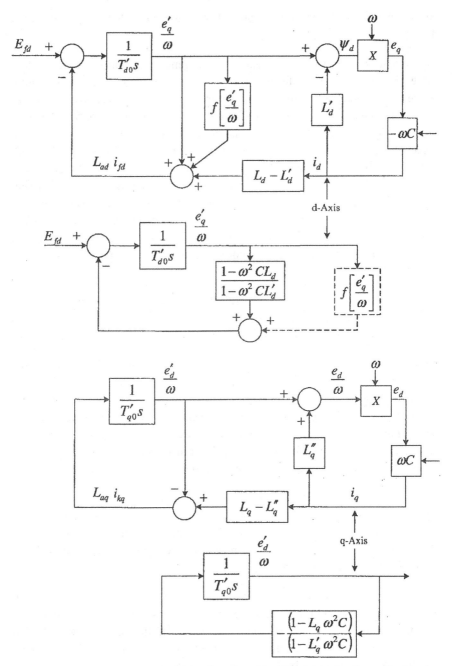

Figure 5.67 – Block Diagrams of d & q Axes for a Machine Supplying Capacitive Load

In order to illustrate with typical examples, Figures 5.68 through 5.72 are extracted from the paper "Analog Computer Studies of System Overvoltage Following Load

Rejections," IEEE Transactions, Power Apparatus and Systems, April 1963, pp. 42-49.

Figure 5.68 is a schematic of a remote steam-generating station connected to a large system through long-distance transmission lines. For conditions of opening of the transmission system receiving-end breakers, the system equivalent circuit, as seen by the machines, can be reduced to that shown in Figure 5.68(B). This approach provides voltage values at the generator and sending-end voltage bus. Receiving end voltage values may be calculated from knowledge of sending-end voltage and frequency. For steam systems where overspeeds following rejection are less than 10%, it was found sufficiently accurate to represent the transmission system as an equivalent capacitance, as shown in Figure 5.68(B). Where corona is appreciable, a non-linear equivalent shunt resistor can be included to simulate corona effects. The transformer magnetizing reactance exhibiting saturation characteristics is accounted for as a nonlinear inductive reactance.

Figure 5.69 shows a schematic of a hydro-generating system connected to a large power system through an extensive transmission network. A simplified system equivalent circuit used for computer simulation is shown in Figure 5.69(B). This equivalent is for conditions of the transmission system open at the receiving end.

The transmission system representation is more complex than the simple equivalent capacitance used in the steam turbine-generator example. The reason for the greater detail is that the range of overfrequency following load rejection for the hydro case is much greater, and the behavior of the network could not be approximated with one equivalent impedance element. Further, there were three saturable elements (transformers) along the transmission line, and the identity of sending and receiving end points of the 480 kV system had to be preserved.

The simulation of a transmission system is greatly simplified by assuming it to contain only reactive elements. This eliminates the need for retaining phase relationships between variables. To offset part of the error in this assumption, the transformer and part of the line resistance were lumped together with the generator armature resistance.

The assumption of a lossless line also made it easy to break down the line current into machine direct and quadrature-axes components. The transmission system constants were such as to permit the further simplification of lumping all the 250 kV line charging at the sending end of the 483 kV line. Even though the equivalent if reduction is valid only for rated frequency, the error in this equivalent for the range of frequency pertinent to this problem was not significant enough to warrant making the equivalent π capacitances and inductance functions of frequency or introducing a greater number of π sections to represent the lines.

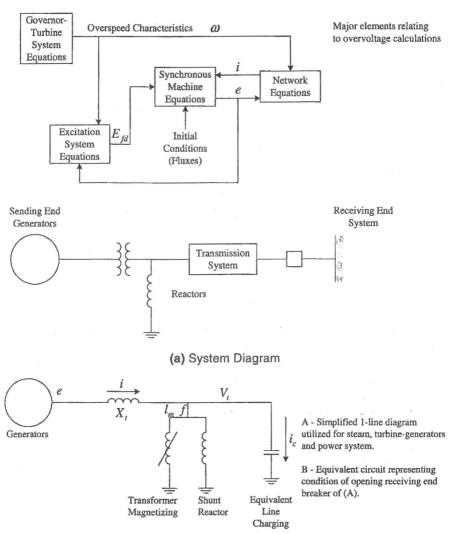

Figure 5.68 – System and Corresponding Dynamic Model
Considered in Load Rejection Studies

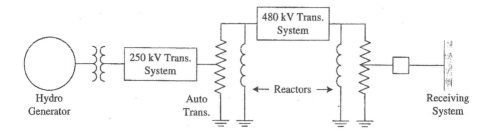

Figure 5.69(a) – System Diagram

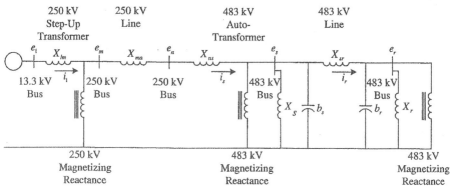

(b) – Equivalent Circuit for Opening Receiving End Breaker
Figure 5.69 – Load Rejection Example

Figures 5.70 shows the results of a typical computer run where rejection occurred by opening the receiving end of 186 miles of 345 kV line. There was no fault prior to opening of the line, and the transmission system did not have shunt reactor compensation. The generators had a 0.5 response excitation system. Figure 5.70 illustrates the fundamental phenomena that occur upon sudden rejection followed by self-excitation.

Basically, when a load is rejected, the generator terminal voltage almost instantaneously changes to a value derived by adding to the constant flux linkages in the rotor d and q axes equivalent circuits, the voltage rise components across the two axes transient reactances due to line-charging current. The transformer high-side voltage exhibit an additional rise due to line-charging across the transformer reactance. A gradual rise in flux linkages follows due to excess excitation voltage for the new loading conditions. The voltage regulator proceeds to decrease excitation and thereby check the increase of voltage. It should be noted that the voltage regulator controls d-axis flux only. Terminal voltage is made up of the flux components in the d and q axes. Normally, the q-axis component can exist only when load is other than purely reactive. During a transient from a load condition to a line-charging condition, the q-axis rotor-flux linkages will decay provided that the equivalent system capacitive reactance X_c is greater than the generator quadrature reactance X_q. When $X_c < X_q$, a condition of self-excitation exists and, instead of decaying, the quadrature axis flux builds up. On an unregulated machine, flux buildup in the d-axis would occur when $X_c < X_d$. With regulator action, however, self-excitation does not occur until $X_c < X_q$.

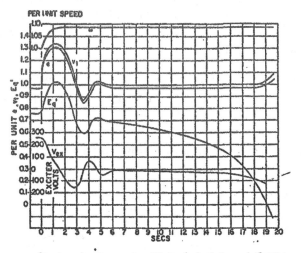

Generator and exciter parameters following load rejection and illustrating phenomenon of self-excitation. Transmission line—196 miles, 345-kv double-circuit, no-fault prior to opening of receiving-end breaker, no shunt reactor compensation. Excitation system response = 1/2 per unit American Standards Association

Figure 5.70 – Results of Load Rejection Study

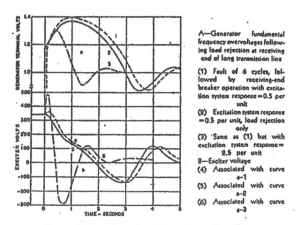

A—Generator fundamental frequency overvoltages following load rejection at receiving end of long transmission line

(1) Fault of 6 cycles, followed by receiving-end breaker operation with excitation system response = 0.5 per unit

(2) Excitation system response = 0.5 per unit, load rejection only

(3) Same as (1) but with excitation system response = 2.5 per unit

B—Exciter voltage

(4) Associated with curve a–1

(5) Associated with curve a–2

(6) Associated with curve a–3

Figure 5.71 – Results of Load Rejection Study

While the q-axis rotor flux ψ_{fq} is increasing due to self-excitation, the d-axis field flux ψ_{fd} under the impetus of a dynamic regulator is decreasing, with the net effect that the terminal voltage is maintained nearly constant for a time. A point is finally reached when decreasing ψ_{fd} can no longer maintain constant terminal voltage because of its small effect and because of the rapid rise of ψ_{fq}. When ψ_{fd} actually reverses sign under the action of a continued bucking exciter voltage the terminal voltage increases even faster as the voltage regulator system is now under conditions of positive feedback.

This phenomenon of self-excitation is illustrated in the run of Figure 5.70. At the borderline of self-excitation, the rate of flux buildup is very gradual. It can happen that a transient condition of self-excitation, will be restored to normal in time to avoid significant flux buildup.

For the hydro system of Figure 5.69, a typical case of self-excitation is illustrated in Figure 5.72(A). The curve of E_q' relating to generator field flux linkages becomes negative at approximately 4 seconds. The excitation system acting in the direct axis can no longer control generator terminal voltage which increases to a large value after having remained fairly constant near rated value under the control of the voltage regulator for several seconds.

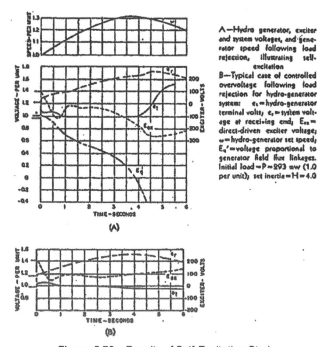

Figure 5.72 – Results of Self-Excitation Study

For the period prior to self-excitation, the generator terminal voltage increased approximately 10%, while the receiving end transmission voltage increased approximately 40%. The exciter operated with negative excitation in the period prior to self-excitation.

Figure 5.72(B) illustrates a typical case of controlled overvoltage with no generator self-excitation. Circuit and loading conditions for cases of Figure 5.72(A) and 5.72(B) were identical. The difference between the two cases was due to a change in transformer saturation which was sufficient to avoid self-excitation in the case of Figure 5.72(B). The generator overvoltage was less than 10%, while the receiving end transmission voltage increased about 30%. The transmission overvoltage is purely due to capacitive-inductive circuit constants which are brought close to resonant conditions by the overspeed. It should be noted that at the time the transmission voltage reached its peak value, the generator voltage was perfectly constant at the reference value.

The effects of static (thyristor) excitation systems can be very significant in the control of load rejection overvoltages, particularly the question of whether or not these systems are provided with negative field current capability (Reference 12).

In the foregoing analysis, only fundamental frequency effects have been considered. Since network nonlinearities due to saturating devices such as transformers and reactors introduce harmonics these effects would require modeling of the network in its full differential equation form.

To account for these effects, voltage and frequency transients that result from load rejection on generators left connected to portions of transmission systems have traditionally been analyzed in two parts (11,13).

The first part has dealt primarily with fundamental frequency effects. Simulations are performed using fundamental frequency dynamic programs using frequency dependent parameters and saturating elements. All plants are modeled in detail with rotor effects, excitation systems, governors and turbines. The network is solved as an algebraic problem relating fundamental frequency voltages and currents. Transformer saturation is accounted for in an approximate manner by using a magnetizing characteristic relating fundamental frequency components of current and voltage. Figure 5.73 is a schematic of the modeling detail involved in this first part of the analysis.

The second part has involved simulations on the Transient Network Analyzer (TNA) where the network is modeled in detail with physical scaled models of transmission lines, transformers and reactors. Voltage sources are set to represent voltage behind subtransient reactance covering range of magnitudes and frequencies as indicated by the simulation runs in Part 1. Voltages on an instantaneous cycle-by-cycle basis are recorded from an oscilloscope. In this way the solution includes harmonic distortions of wave shapes that arise due to saturating elements.

A new approach combining both parts is now possible for the study of load rejection over-voltages. With this approach both the machine and network are treated in full differential equation form as described schematically in Figure 5.74.

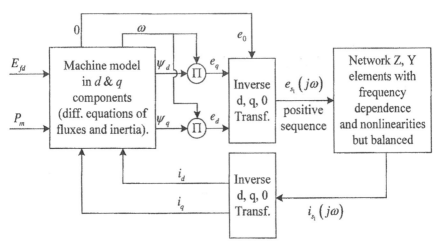

Figure 5.73 – Block Diagram for Solution of Fundamental Frequency Effects

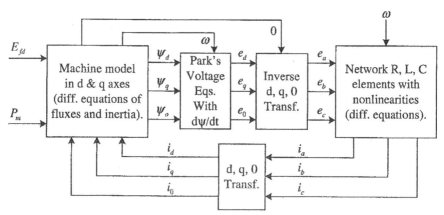

Figure 5.74 – Block Diagram for Solution of
Instantaneous Variables including Harmonic Effects

Figure 5.75 shows an example of a study system with rejection occurring at a switching station. Figure 5.76 shows the cycle-by-cycle voltage transients following load rejection.

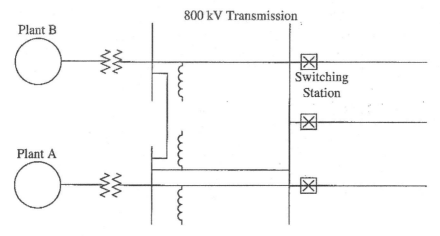

Figure 5.75 – Example of Study System with Rejection at Switching Station

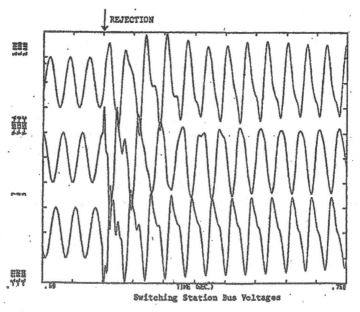

Switching Station Bus Voltages

Figure 5.76 – Switching Station Bus Voltages upon Rejection

Figure 5.77, on a larger time scale shows the behavior of machine parameters following rejection.

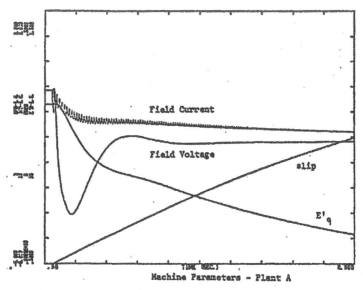

Figure 5.77 – Machine Parameters of Plant A following Rejection

5.4.7   Subsynchronous Oscillations

In most of the dynamic phenomena described thus far, the network has been adequately represented by algebraic relationships between fundamental frequency voltages and currents. The dynamic effects involving differential equations were thus confined to rotor fluxes, the inertial equations of torques, speed and angle, and control effects. An exception to this approach of using steady state fundamental frequency solutions for the network was described in Figure 5.75 in connection with solution of harmonic effects in the load rejection problem.

Reference (9) shows the modeling detail that is required depending on the phenomena under study. Usually the transient effects of the network elements are of a high enough frequency that when they must be studied, the machine dynamic effects can be ignored.

The study of network transients requires that the network differential equations be represented. While the machine can usually be represented as an ideal voltage source behind an inductance taken as the machine subtransient inductance.

There are situations however where the network natural modes of oscillation are of low enough frequency (subsynchronous, i.e. below fundamental frequency) to cause interactions with the machine rotor flux phenomena and sometimes with shaft mechanical torsional modes of oscillation. This usually occurs in applications involving series capacitors which give rise to synchronous network natural frequencies (frequencies for which the capacitive reactance equals the equivalent series inductive reactance). The subsynchronous oscillations that arise and particularly the possibility of their being unstable can only be analyzed by the complete treatment of network and machine as in Figure 5.74.

Subsynchronous oscillations are a potentially serious problem in transmission schemes with a high degree of capacitive compensation; and have on recent occasions caused serious damage to the rotors of large generators.

There are actually several different mechanisms by which troublesome subsynchronous oscillations can occur, but analyses of the problem have tended to obscure this fact. Further, analyses presented to date have dealt with only the simplest of transmission network configurations, while the actual problems may be observed in practice to be sensitive to condition changes over quite widespread areas of a complex transmission network.

5.4.8   Fundamentals

One aspect of the subsynchronous oscillation phenomenon, the purely electrical aspect, may be explained by reference to Figure 5.78 which shows a single generator connected to an infinite bus through a series compensated transmission line.

The generator should be regarded, for this basic discussion, as having infinite inertia so that its speed and angular position relative to the infinite bus are constant. We define per unit compensation, D, at rated frequency where X_L, X_C, L, and C are all per unit quantities.

$$D = \frac{X_C}{X_L} = \frac{1}{LC}$$

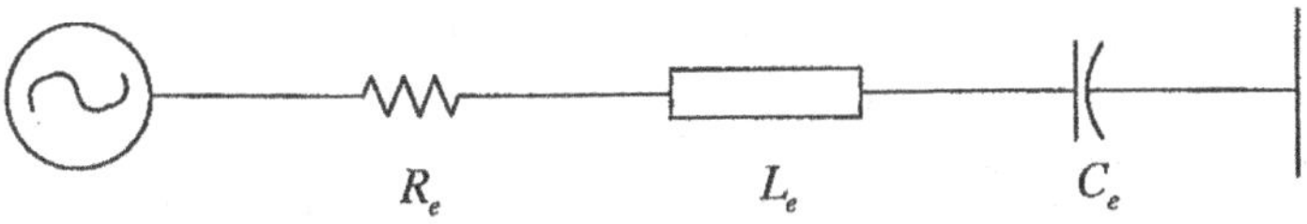

Figure 5.78 – System Circuit Giving Rise to Subsynchronous Oscillations

The generator is basically an inductive circuit element, and hence the system of Figure 5.78 has a natural resonant frequency. This natural frequency is given by

$$\omega^2 = \omega_0^2 D \qquad\qquad (\text{V.111})$$

and for practical degrees of compensation (D = 0.5 for example), its value is less than rated frequency; that is, subsynchronous.

Now visualize a synchronous machine whose rotor is turning at rated speed, ω_0, but whose armature has currents of frequency ω imposed upon it. Since the rotor of any round rotor generator or salient pole generator with connected amortisseurs; has low impedance short circuited current paths on the surface of its rotor, the generator will behave as an induction machine (of peculiar design, admittedly) under this condition. The slip of this induction machine must be

$$s = \frac{\omega - \omega_0}{\omega} \qquad (V.112)$$

which has a negative value for subsynchronous frequencies.

Next, assume that the capacitor in Figure 5.78 acquires a charge that is not identical to its steady state equilibrium value as the result of some small system disturbance. The RLC transmission circuit will "ring-down" at its subsynchronous resonant frequency, causing currents at this subsynchronous frequency to flow in the generator armature. But, at this subsynchronous frequency the synchronous machine behaves as an induction machine with a negative slip given by (V.112); that is, as an induction generator. It will, therefore, tend to feed energy into the RLC circuit at the subsynchronous frequency, and hence will tend to sustain or amplify the subsynchronous currents. Given unfavorable conditions, this action can cause subsynchronous currents to grow to magnitudes that disrupt transmission system protection elements and damage transformers and capacitors. It may also be shown that this subsynchronous current flowing in the armature of the synchronous machine will give rise to both an unidirectional component of shaft torque and an alternating shaft torque component at a frequency of (ω_0 - ω). This alternating component of torque may be large enough to damage the generator or turbine shaft.

The above line of analysis has been applied on a quantitative basis by Kilgore et al[14] to predict numerical values of system parameters for which subsynchronous frequency currents will be sustained or growing.

The important point to note from this fundamental analysis, as developed by Kilgore et al, is that subsynchronous oscillations can grow and be sustained by this simple induction generator effect without the effects of generator rotor speed variations. The phenomenon is, then, completely different from the phenomenon of unstable rotor angle oscillations which may be produced by the interaction of generator excitation controls and the air gap energy transfer process.

5.4.9   More Detailed Analysis

While the above analysis is simple and gives good insight into the basic phenomenon, it does not account for the fact that generator inertia is not infinite and that rotor speed is, therefore, are not constant. Further, it allows only a rudimentary treatment of saliency effects in deducing the equivalent induction motor parameters that should be used to represent the synchronous machine at the subsynchronous armature current frequency.

More detailed representation of the synchronous machine requires that the machine be modeled by its fundamental stator and rotor differential equations. These could in theory be expressed relative to either phase coordinates or to the direct and quadrature axis coordinates; but the latter choice is usually the more convenient.

Analyses based on the d and q axis differential equations have been presented in References 15 and 16. Reference 15 handled the solution of the differential equations of the system shown in Figure 78 and showed parametrically how variation of transmission resistance and capacitive reactance affect the onset of sustained subsynchronous oscillations in the armature current. Reference 16 extended the treatment of Reference 15 to include representation of turbine rotors joined to the generator by torsionally elastic shaft sections, and showed that the presence of shaft elasticity sharply modified the results predicted by References 14 and 15. Reference 16 showed the end effect of shaft elasticity in a parametric sense, but its analytical method was based strictly on digital computer processing, and did little to reveal the nature of shaft elasticity effects in a qualitative sense. Further, because Reference 16 used a matrix method in which each inductive and capacitive element in the generator and transmission network required one or two axes in a single large matrix, its treatment was limited to small numbers of generators and very simple transmission system representations.

There are therefore two aspects to the problem of subsynchronous oscillations:

1) Negative damping of subsynchronous electrical network natural frequencies -- a phenomenon that may be analyzed and predicted purely from a frequency response analysis of network and machine impedance. Here the indication of negative resistance in driving point impedance seen from a source, at frequencies exhibiting resonances, is in the direction to cause hunting or buildup of current and voltage oscillations at these frequencies. In practical situations this aspect does not cause, as the network including loads exhibits, sufficient positive resistance to overcome the negative rotor resistance effects.

2) Interaction between electrical resonant frequencies and mechanical shaft natural frequencies -- this phenomenon can give rise to negative damping of torques, currents, etc. at resonant frequencies of' the combined mechanical and electrical system. Even if the individual resonant frequencies of the electrical system and mechanical system

when considered by themselves may be damped, the coupling of the two systems may cause the overall system to be unstable. This phenomenon has also been called "modal interaction."

Negative damping of mechanical shaft natural frequencies caused by modal interaction effects is fostered by dissipation of power in the network and the greater the effective network resistance the more severe can be the problem of negative damping of shaft modes.

Figure 5.79 shows that the basic coupling between electrical and mechanical systems is through generator rotor speed. Knowledge of the transfer functions $H_1(s) = \frac{\Delta Te(s)}{\Delta n_G(s)}$ for the electrical system and $H_2(s) = \frac{\Delta n_G(s)}{\Delta Te(s)}$ for the mechanical system permits the evaluation of the stability of the feedback configuration in Figure 5.79. The important point remains that even though the individual functions $H_1(s)$ and $H_2(s)$ may be stable in themselves, the combination may produce an unstable interacting system.

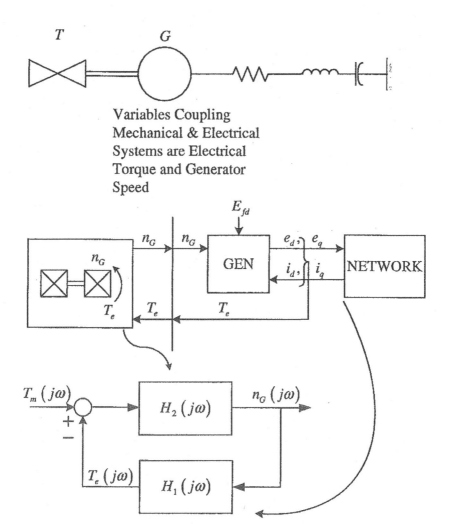

Figure 5.79 – System Representation Including Shaft Torsional Effects

The stability of the overall system is a function of the phase angle and gain of the open loop function H_1H_2. These in turn are dependent on the coincidence or near coincidence of natural modes of oscillation (torsional shaft frequencies with electrical system natural frequencies) as well as the degree of coupling between the mechanical and electrical systems. This degree of coupling is a function of the ratio of turbine to generator inertias.

Figure 5.80 shows the frequency response plots of the mechanical system transfer function $H_2(j\omega) = \frac{n_G(j\omega)}{Te(j\omega)}$ for two cases both with the same shaft torsional natural frequency: one where the turbine to generator inertia ratio is $J_t/J_G = 10$ and the other where $J_t/J_G = 1/10$.

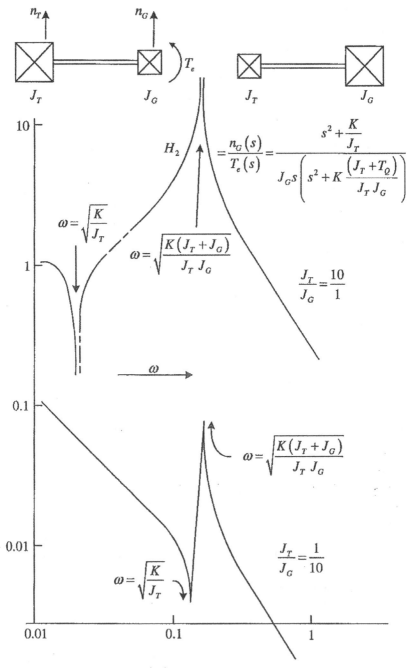

Figure 5.80 – Bode Plots of $\dfrac{dn_G(j\omega)}{dT_e(j\omega)}$ for Different Ratios of Turbine to Generator Inertias

It is evident that where the generator inertia is large the coupling is low. This is one reason why hydro generators generally do not exhibit shaft torque interactions with electrical natural frequencies in series compensated systems.

The stability of the combined mechanical and electrical systems can be analyzed by conventional methods of feed back control for the loop in Figure 5.78. However the derivation of the function $H_1 = \dfrac{Te(j\omega)}{n_G(j\omega)}$ in systems involving the effect of many connected units, including their mechanical shaft effects, requires very complex mathematical operations. The network impedance characteristics at $(\omega_0 + \omega)$ and at $(\omega_0 - \omega)$ where ω_0 is the fundamental frequency and ω is the perturbation frequency enter into these computations.

A much more powerful analysis technique is to examine the stability of the system by opening the loop at the machine terminals as shown in Figure 5.81.

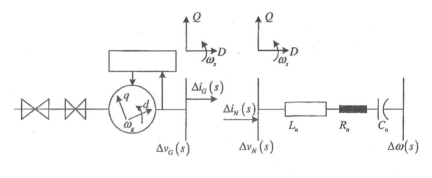

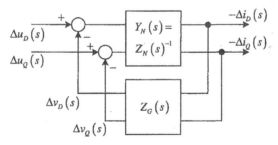

Nyquist Stability Criterion applied to

$$1 + Y_N(j\omega)\, Z_G(j\omega) \text{ or } Z_N(j\omega) + Z_G(j\omega) \text{ where } Z_N = Y_N$$

Figure 5.81

Reference 17 and 18 show the derivation and application of this method to evaluate the subsynchronous stability characteristics of units connected to a network including the electrical and mechanical effects of other units on the same network, as schematically shown in Figure 5.82. Reference 19 treats in greater detail the relationship between methods of subsynchronous oscillation stability analysis.

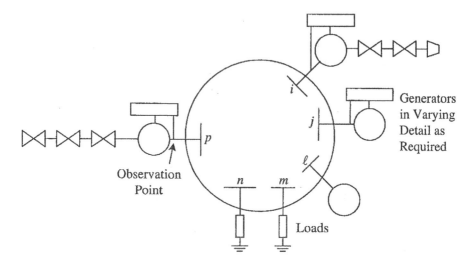

(a) System Configuration

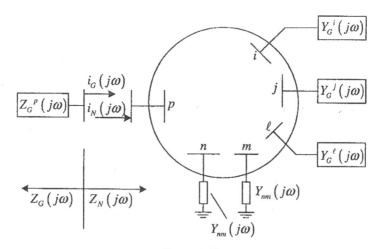

Figure 5.82

References

1. <u>Power System Stability,</u> Vol. I, S.B. Crary, John Wiley & Sons, Inc.

2. <u>Power System Stability,</u> Vol. II, S.B. Crary, John Wiley & Sons, Inc.

²3. "Modern Concepts of Power System Dynamics," IEEE Tutorial, Course Text 70 M-62-PWR.

*4. "Concepts of Synchronous Machine Stability as Affected by Excitation Control," F.P. deMello, C. Concordia, <u>IEEE Transactions</u>, Vol. PAS-88, No. 4, pp. 316-329.

*5. "A Digital Computer Program for the Automatic Determination of Dynamic Stability Limits," D.N. Ewart, F.P. deMello, <u>IEEE Transactions</u>, Vol. PAS-86, No. 7, pp. 867-875.

6. <u>Electrical Transmission & Distribution Reference Book,</u> Westinghouse Electric Corporation.

7. Appendices C, D, and E - Power Technologies, Inc. Course Notes - "Generation Dynamics & Control."

8. Power Technologies, Inc. Course Notes - "Electrical Machine Dynamics - I."

*9. "Power System Dynamics - Overview," F.P. deMello, 1975 Winter Power Meeting - Symposium on the Adequacy and Philosophy of Modeling Dynamic System Performance. IEEE Publication 75 CHO 970-4-PWR.

*10. "Concepts of Power System Dynamic Stability," F.P. deMello, T.F. Laskowski, <u>IEEE Transactions on Power Apparatus and Systems</u>, Vol. PAS-94, No. 3, pp. 827-833.

11. "Analog Computer Studies of System Overvoltages Following Load Rejections," <u>IEEE Transactions</u>, Vol. 82, No. 65, April, 1963. F.P. deMello, A.C. Dolbec, D.A. Swann and M. Temoshok.

*12. "Load Rejection Overvoltages as Affected by Excitation System Control," F.P. deMello, L.M. Leuzinger, R.J. Mills, <u>IEEE Transactions</u>, Paper T 74 337-2, 1974 Summer Meeting.

---

² References included in course notes. Vol. II

13. "Overvoltage Following Secondary Switching of Transformer Connected to High Voltage Lines," L.O. Barthold, I.B. Johnson, A.J. Schultz, <u>AIEE Transactions</u>, Vol. 77, 1958, pp. 1492-1500.

14. L.A. Kilgore, L.C. Elliott, E.R. Taylor, "The Prediction and Control of Self-Excited Oscillations due to Series Capacitors in Power Systems," <u>IEEE Transactions</u>, Vol. PAS-90, pp. 1305-1311, 1971.

15. C. Concordia, H. Rustebakke, "Self-Excited Oscillations in a Transmission System Using Series Capacitors," <u>IEEE Transactions</u>, Vol. PAS-89, pp. 1504-1512, 1970.

16. C.J. Bowler, D.N. Ewart, "Self-Excited Torsional Frequency Oscillations with Series Capacitors," IEEE Transactions, Vol. PAS-92. pp. 1689-1695, 1973.

*17. "Subsynchronous Oscillations: Part I, Comprehensive Stability Analysis," <u>IEEE Transactions</u>, Paper IEEE Winter Power Meeting 1975, J.M. Undrill and T.E. Kostyniak.

*18. Subsynchronous Oscillations: Part II, Shaft System Dynamic Interactions," <u>IEEE Transactions</u>, Paper IEEE Winter Power Meeting 1976, J.M. Undrill and F.P. de Mello.

*19. "Subsynchronous Oscillation Stability Analysis, by F.P. de Mello and J.M. Undrill to be submitted to the IEEE 1979 Summer Power Meeting.

*20. "Some Aspects of Transmission System Planning and Design in Large Developing Countries" by F.P. de Mello, Henniker Conference, Aug. 22-27, 1976.

*21. "Practical Approaches to Supplementary Stabilizing from Accelerating Power" by F.P. de Mello, L.N. Hannett, and J.M. Undrill, <u>IEEE Transactions</u>, Vol. PAS-97, pp. 1515, 1978.

*22. "Coordinated Application of Stabilizers in Multimachine Power Systems" by F.P. de Mello, P.J. Nolan, T.F. Laskowski and J.M. Undrill. Submitted to the IEEE 1979 Winter Power Meeting.

Appendix A

Dynamic Systems, Differential Equations – Transient and Steady State Solutions – Operational Impedance

Contents

List of Figures

F.P DE MELLO

Appendix A

Dynamic Systems, Differential Equations – Transient and Steady State Solutions – Operational Impedance

The study of "control and dynamics" requires the use of certain mathematical tools and techniques which have become an essential part of the technology of control. These tools are all related to methods of solution and analysis of systems described by differential equations. It is not the intent here to go through a detailed theoretical development of the pertinent mathematics that form the basis for the various analysis tools. There are numerous texts that may be referenced for this purpose, some of which are in the reference list.[25] The treatment in these appendices will be in the form of a brief review of some basic techniques to supplement and support the material in the main text on Chapter II – "Generation Dynamics and Control."

A.1   Dynamic Systems

The behavior of dynamic systems is expressed by differential equations relating the systems' variables. In many cases these equations turn out to be or can be approximated by linear differential equations. When this is the case, classical or closed form solutions can be obtained.

For the general case of non-linear differential equations, solutions must be sought through the use of simulation by analog computation methods or by numerical integration techniques carried out on digital computers.

Although any problem can be solved by these simulation methods, the insight that can be derived from linear system analysis is invaluable as a guide to control system design and performance evaluations.

A.2 System Differential Equations

Dynamic systems can be thermal, mechanical, electrical or a combination of all these. In order to stay on familiar ground we will illustrate with an electrical example and limit the discussion to linear differential equations.

Consider the circuit in Figure A-1.

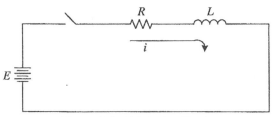

Figure A-1 – R-L Series Circuit

The differential equation is

$$E = iR + L\frac{di}{dt} \tag{A.1}$$

By separating variables, Equation (A.1) can be put in the form of (A.2)

$$L\int\frac{di}{E - Ri} = \int dt \tag{A.2}$$

Integration of Equation (A.2) yields

$$-\frac{L}{R}ln(E - Ri) = t + C_1 \tag{A.3}$$

where C_1 is the constant of integration.

Equation (A.3) may also be expressed in exponential form as

$$i = \frac{E}{R} + C_2 e^{-\frac{R}{L}t} \tag{A.4}$$

where C_2 is derived from constants of integration which in turn are determined from initial conditions in energy storage elements. The current in inductance L at time $t = 0$ before the switch is closed is $i_0 = 0$.

Substitution of $i = 0$ at $t = 0$ in equation A-4 yields

$$C_2 = -E / R \tag{A.5}$$

and Equation (A.4) can be written as

$$i = \frac{E}{R}\left[1 - e^{-\frac{R}{L}t}\right] i = \frac{E}{R}\left[1 - e^{-\frac{R}{L}t}\right] \tag{A.6}$$

plotted in Figure A-2 as function of time.

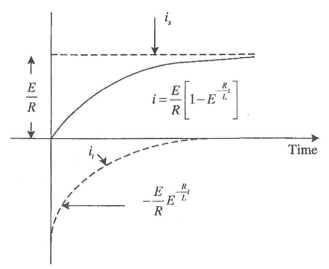

Figure A-2 – Steady State and Transient Response Components

This classical solution can be recognized as containing two components:

(1) The steady state component

$$i_s = \frac{E}{R} \tag{A.7}$$

which has the same form as the applied voltage.

(2) The transient component

$$i_t = -\frac{E}{R}e^{-\frac{R}{L}t} \tag{A.8}$$

which decays exponentially to zero.

An alternate method of solution for the current in the circuit of Figure A-1 is to solve separately for the steady state and transient components as follows:

Let $\qquad\qquad i = i_s + i_t \tag{A.9}$

Substituting Equation (A.9) in equation (A.1)

$$E = i_s R + L\frac{di_s}{dt} + Ri_t + L\frac{di_t}{dt} \tag{A.10}$$

Since E is constant $di_s/dt = 0$.

By definition also, i_t and $di_t/dt = 0$ in the steady state.

Hence

$$i_s = \frac{E}{R} \tag{A.11}$$

Substituting Equation (A.11) into Equation (A.10) yields the relation from which the transient component may be solved, i.e.:

$$Ri_t + L\frac{di_t}{dt} = 0 \tag{A.12}$$

By definition of the transient component it is exponential in nature, and one can express it as

$$i_t = I_T e^{pt} \tag{A.13}$$

Substituting Equation (A.13) in Equation (A.12)

$$(R + pL)\,I_T e^{pt} = 0 \tag{A.14}$$

From Equation (A.14) the value of p is determined as

$$p = -\frac{R}{L} \tag{A.15}$$

which can be noted, is independent of the applied voltage E but merely a function of the circuit parameters.

Substituting Equation (A.15) in Equation (A.13) we have

$$i_t = I_T e^{-\frac{R}{L}t} \tag{A.16}$$

The value for I_T is determined from initial conditions, i.e., the value of i at $t = 0$. The total current is $i = i_s + i_t$

$$i = \frac{E}{R} + I_T e^{-\frac{R}{L}t}$$

At $t = 0$

$$i = \frac{E}{R} + I_t = 0$$

whence $I_t = -\frac{E}{R}$

The resultant expression for current is naturally the same as obtained by the classical solution:

$$i = \frac{E}{R} - \frac{E}{R} e^{-\frac{R}{L}t}$$

This example was for a system described by a first order differential equation. For the general system of nth order the transient component must be chosen in the form $\sum_n I_n e^{P_n t}$. The values of p_n are evaluated by setting the coefficient of $I_n e^{P_n t}$ equal to zero. These principles are covered by other more commonly used methods of differential equation solution such as those which use the Laplace Transform method. We will not pursue the classical method of differential equation solution any further except to introduce the idea of the *characteristic equation* which is basic and which will also be derived with the Laplace Transform method.

A.3   Characteristic Equation

The choice of the exponential form for the transient component of the solution of a linear set of differential equations was guided by the results of the classical solution.

This form of solution has the following interesting properties.

If
$$i = I\, e^{pt} \tag{A.17}$$

Then
$$\frac{di}{dt} = Ipe^{pt} \tag{A.18}$$

And
$$\frac{d^2 i}{dt^2} = Ip^2 e^{pt} \tag{A.19}$$

Also
$$\int i\, dt = \frac{I}{p} e^{pt} \tag{A.20}$$

Hence in the equation for the transient solution, if i is substituted by Ie^{pt} the terms in the equation

$$\frac{d^n}{dt^n}$$

are replaced by p^n and the terms $\int^n ()\, dt^n$ are replaced by $1/p^n$. For instance the differential equation

$$a_0 \frac{d^n i}{dt^n} + a_1 \frac{d^{n-1}}{dt^{n-1}} i + \ldots + a_n i + a_{n+1} \int i\, dt + \ldots + a_{n+m} \int^m i\, dt^m = f(t) \qquad \text{(A.21)}$$

with $i = I e^{pt}$ becomes

$$a_0 p^n + a_1 p^{n-1} + \ldots + a_n + \frac{a_{n+1}}{p} + \ldots + \frac{a_{n+m}}{p^m} \qquad \text{(A.22)}$$

The polynomial form of the equation formed by substituting derivatives and integrals by the appropriate p and $1/p$ operators is called the operational form of the equation.

The basic equation which determines the transient modes is independent of the applied forcing function $f(t)$. It is known as the system characteristic equation and in the example above is

$$a_0 p^n + a_1 p^{n-1} + \ldots + a_n + \frac{a_{n+1}}{p} + \ldots + \frac{a_{n+m}}{p^m} = 0$$

or

$$a_0 p^{n+m} + a_1 p^{n+m-1} + \ldots + a_n p^m + a_{n+1} p^{m-1} + \ldots + a_{n+m} = 0 \qquad \text{(A.23)}$$

The values of p which satisfy Equation (A.23) are the roots of the characteristic equation and are the values that appear in the solution $i = I_n e^{P_n t}$ determining the transient modes of the system.

The characteristic equation of a system and its roots are fundamental to the evaluation of response and stability of dynamic systems.

EXAMPLE 1

Figure A-3 shows a series RLC network connected to a source $E(t)$ by switch S at $t = 0$.

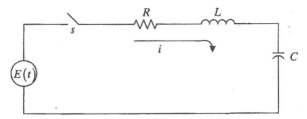

Figure A-3 – Series RLC Network

The circuit equation for the time after closure of S is

$$Ri + L\frac{di}{dt} + \frac{1}{C}\int i_s dt = E(t)$$

(A.24)

Breaking up the solution into two components (steady state, with same form as E (t) and transient) let us examine the case where E = constant.

The Steady State solution is found from Equation (A.24) by noting that i_s has the same form as E (t)

i.e.
$$\frac{di_s}{dt} = 0$$

(A.25)

Substituting Equation (A.25) in Equation (A.24)

$$Ri_s + \frac{1}{C}\int i_s dt = E$$

(A.26)

The only way that i_s can be a constant and satisfy Equation (A.26) is for $i_s = 0$ and $\frac{1}{C}\int i_s dt = E$.

The <u>Transient Solution</u> is found by writing the left hand side of Equation (A.24) in operational form and setting it to zero.

i.e.
$$\left(Lp + R + \frac{1}{Cp}\right)i = 0$$

(A.27)

where i is of the form $I_n e^{P_n t}$.

The characteristic equation of Equation (A.27) is

$$CLp^2 + RCp + 1 = 0$$

(A.28)

which yields the roots

$$p_1 = -\frac{R}{2L} + \frac{1}{2}\sqrt{\left(\frac{R}{L}\right)^2 - \frac{4}{LC}}$$

and $$p_2 = -\frac{R}{2L} - \frac{1}{2}\sqrt{\left(\frac{R}{L}\right)^2 - \frac{4}{LC}}$$

Depending on whether $(R/L)^2$ is greater or smaller than $(4/LC)$ the roots p_1 and p_2 will be real or complex.

The expression for the transient current is

$$i_t = I_1 e^{p_1 t} + I_2 e^{p_2 t} \tag{A.29}$$

To evaluate I_1 and I_2, we note that the system's initial conditions were $i = 0$ and the voltage across the condenser $= 0$.

i.e. $$i = 0 \tag{A.30}$$

and $$\frac{1}{C}\int i\,dt = 0 \tag{A.31}$$

Since the steady state component $i_s = 0$, condition Equation (A.30) applied to Equation (A.29) yields

$$I_1 = -I_2 \tag{A.32}$$

Also, applying Equations (A.30) and (A.31) to Equation (A.24) at $t = 0^+$

$$L\frac{d}{dt}\left(I_1 e^{p_1 t} + I_2 e^{p_2 t}\right)\Big|_{t=0} = E$$

i.e. $$I_1 p_1 + I_2 p_2 = \frac{E}{L} \tag{A.33}$$

Solving Equation (A.32) and Equation (A.33)

$$I_1 = \frac{E}{L(p_1 - p_2)}, \; I_2 = \frac{E}{L(p_2 - p_1)} \tag{A.34}$$

And the total solution for i is

$$i = \frac{E}{L}\left[\frac{e^{p_1 t} - e^{p_2 t}}{p_1 - p_2}\right] \tag{A.35}$$

For the case where p_1 and p_2 are complex conjugate roots $\left(\left(\dfrac{R}{L}\right)^2 < \dfrac{4}{LC}\right)$,

i.e.;   where $p_1 = -\alpha + j\beta$

           and $p_2 = -\alpha - j\beta$ (A.36)

Substituting these values in Equation (A.35)

$$i = \frac{E}{L} e^{-\alpha t} \left[\frac{e^{j\beta t} - e^{-j\beta t}}{2j\beta} \right] \tag{A.37}$$

which can be expressed as, from the definition of $\sin \beta t$

$$i = \frac{E}{L} \frac{e^{-\alpha t}}{\beta} \sin \beta t \tag{A.38}$$

Figure A-4 shows the nature of the current transient.

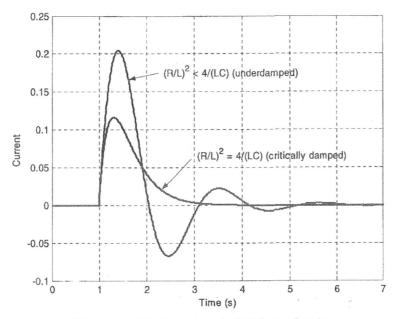

Figure A-4 – Step Response of a RLC Series Circuit

EXAMPLE 2

Take the same example except that let the applied voltage be a sinusoidal function $E = E \cos \omega t$ with the switch again closed at $t = 0$.

Again taking up the steady state solution, Equation (A.24) becomes

$$Ri_s + L\frac{di_s}{dt} + \frac{1}{C}\int i_s dt = \frac{E}{2}\left(e^{+j\omega t} + e^{-j\omega t}\right) \qquad (A.39)$$

where $\dfrac{\left(e^{+j\omega t} + e^{-j\omega t}\right)}{2}$ is the exponential form of cos ωt.

Since i_s by definition will be of the same form as the applied voltage, we may further divide i_s into components corresponding to the applied voltage components

$$i_{s_+} = I_+ e^{+j\omega t} \qquad (A.40)$$

$$i_{s_-} = I_- e^{-j\omega t} \qquad (A.41)$$

where I_+ is the complex magnitude of i_{s_+} and I_- is the complex magnitude of i_{s_-} components individually, from Equation (A.39)

$$R\left[I_+ e^{+j\omega t}\right] + L\frac{d}{dt}\left[I_+ e^{+j\omega t}\right] + \frac{1}{C}\int I_+ e^{+j\omega t} dt = \frac{E}{2}e^{+j\omega t}$$

or

$$RI_+ e^{+j\omega t} + LI_+ j\omega e^{+j\omega t} + \frac{I_+}{Cj\omega}e^{j\omega t} = \frac{E}{2}e^{+j\omega t} \qquad (A.42)$$

Dividing both sides by $e^{+j\omega t}$

$$üI_+ + {}_+j\omega + \frac{I_+}{Cj\omega} = \frac{E}{2}$$

Or

$$I_+ = \frac{E}{2\left(R + j\left(\omega L - \dfrac{1}{\omega C}\right)\right)} \qquad (A.43)$$

A similar derivation for I_- yields

$$I_- = \frac{E}{2\left(R - j\left(\omega L - \dfrac{1}{\omega C}\right)\right)} \qquad (A.44)$$

Equation (A.43) can be expressed as

$$I_+ = \frac{Ee^{-j\theta_z}}{2Z} \qquad (A.45)$$

where
$$Z = \sqrt{R^2 + \left(\omega L - \frac{1}{\omega C}\right)^2}$$
(A.46)

$$\theta_z = \tan^{-1} \frac{\left(\omega L - \frac{1}{\omega C}\right)}{R}$$
(A.47)

Likewise
$$I_- = \frac{E e^{+j\theta_z}}{2Z}$$
(A.48)

The total steady state current $i_s = i_{s_+} + i_{s_-}$. Using Equation (A.42) and Equation (A.43) and substituting Equation (A.47) and Equation (A.48),

$$i_s = \frac{E}{Z} \left(\frac{e^{j(\omega t - \theta)} + e^{-j(\omega t - \theta_z)}}{2} \right)$$
$$i_s = \frac{E}{Z} \cos(\omega t - \theta_z)$$
(A.49)

Z is the impedance of the network and indicates the ratio of voltage to current in the steady state for a sinusoidally varying applied voltage. Equation (A.49) is of the same form as the applied voltage $E \cos \omega t$. Its magnitude is E/Z and its phase angle with respect to the applied voltage sinusoid is θ_z.

The concept of operational impedance $Z(p) = R + Lp + \frac{1}{Cp}$ is self-evident from Equation (A.27). By substituting $p = j\omega$ one can derive the impedance to a fixed alternating voltage of frequency ω rd/s.

These concepts are important in the application of *frequency response* techniques which characterize the system in terms of its behavior as function of the frequency of the exciting function, ω.

Although the example was for an electric circuit, yielding the relationship between current and voltage the method is equally applicable to any variables of a system, be they mechanical, electrical or thermal, as long as they are related by linear differential equations.

F P de Mello

Power Technologies Inc

Appendix B

Laplace Transforms

Contents

List of Figures

Appendix

B

Laplace Transforms

The previous sections have reviewed the classical method of solving linear differential equations. We have seen how the transient solution and steady state solution are derived and have developed the concept of operational impedance and impedance to a constant frequency applied excitation function.

These same results can be derived in a greatly simplified fashion through the use of the direct and inverse Laplace transform which uses one approach for both the steady state and transient solution. Laplace transform operational calculus is the cornerstone of control system analysis.

B.1   Some Basic Theorems of the Laplace Transform

A function of time $f(t)$ has a Laplace transform $F(s)$ where

$$F(s) = \int_0^\infty f(t) e^{-st} dt \qquad (\text{B.1})$$

The value of the Laplace transform lies in the fact that a differential equation or expression of the variable "t" transforms into an algebraic equation or expression of the variable "s." This algebraic expression in turn may be operated upon and converted to a form easily recognized in terms of a time function. The process of obtaining the time function from the transform expression is called taking the inverse Laplace transformation. Mathematical operations which in the time domain involve convolution, convert to simple algebraic multiplications in the s domain. A summary of the important theorems governing the use of the Laplace transform are:

1. $$\mathscr{L}[f(t)] = \int_0^\infty f(t) e^{-st} dt \qquad (\text{B.2})$$

2. The inverse Laplace transformation $\mathscr{L}^{-1}$ is defined implicitly by the relation

$$\mathscr{L}^{-1}\{\mathscr{L}[f(t)]\} = f(t) \; 0 \leq t \qquad (\text{B.3})$$

3. If the functions $f(t)$, $f_1(t)$ and $f_2(t)$ have $\mathcal{L}$ transforms $F(s)$, $F_1(s)$ and $F_2(s)$ respectively and "a" is a constant of a variable which is independent of t and s, then

$$\mathcal{L}[a f(t)] = a F(s) \tag{B.4}$$

and

$$\mathcal{L}[f_1(t) \pm f_2(t)] = F_1(s) \pm F_2(s) \tag{B.5}$$

Also

$$\mathcal{L}^{-1}[a F(s)] = a f(t) \; 0 \le t \tag{B.6}$$

and

$$\mathcal{L}^{-1}[F_1(s) \pm F_2(s)] = f_1(t) \pm f_2(t) \; 0 \le t \tag{B.7}$$

4. If a function $f(t)$ has the $\mathcal{L}$ transform $F(s)$, then

$$\mathcal{L}\left\{\frac{df(t)}{dt}\right\} = s F(s) - f(0+) \tag{B.8}$$

where $f(0+)$ is the value of $f(t)$ at $t = 0+$. It is evident then that

$$\mathcal{L}\left\{\frac{d^2 f(t)}{dt^2}\right\} = s^2 F(s) - s f(0) - f'(0) \tag{B.9}$$

and

$$\mathcal{L}\left\{f^{(n)}(t)\right\} = s^n F(s) - \sum_{k=1}^{n} f^{(k-1)}(0) s^{n-k} \tag{B.10}$$

5. If the function $f(t)$ has the transform $F(s)$, its integral $f^{(-1)}(t) = \int f(t)dt = \int_0^t f(t)dt + f^{(-1)}(0^+)$ has the transform

$$\mathcal{L}\left[\int f(t)dt\right] = \frac{F(s)}{s} + \frac{f^{(-1)}(0+)}{s} \tag{B.11}$$

Similarly,

$$\mathcal{L}\left[\int f^{(-2)}(t)\right] = \frac{F(s)}{s^2} + \frac{f^{(-1)}(0)}{s^2} + \frac{f^{(-2)}(0)}{s} \tag{B.12}$$

and

$$\mathscr{L}\left[f^{(-n)}(t)\right]=\frac{F(s)}{s^n}+\sum_{k=1}^{n}\frac{f^{(-k)}(0)}{s^{n-k+1}} \qquad \text{(B.13)}$$

6. The Laplace transforms of some common functions are as follows:

Table B-1 - Table of Transforms

FUNCTION	$f(t)\ 0\leq t$	$F(s)$
Unit step	1 or $u(t)$	$\dfrac{1}{s}$
Exponential	$e^{-\alpha t}$	$\dfrac{1}{s+\alpha}$
Sine	$\sin \beta t$	$\dfrac{\beta}{s^2+\beta^2}$
Cosine	$\cos \beta t$	$\dfrac{s}{s^2+\beta^2}$
	$\dfrac{1}{\beta}e^{-\alpha t}\sin \beta t$	$\dfrac{1}{(s+\alpha)^2+\beta^2}$
Unit ramp	t	$\dfrac{1}{s^2}$
	$\dfrac{1}{n-1}t^{n-1}$	$\dfrac{1}{s^n}$
	$t\,e^{-\alpha t}$	$\dfrac{1}{(s+\alpha)^2}$
	$\dfrac{1}{n-1}t^{n-1}e^{-\alpha t}$	$\dfrac{1}{(s+\alpha)^n}$
	$u(t-a)$	$\dfrac{1}{s}e^{-as}$
	$u(t-a)-u(t-b)$	$\dfrac{1}{s}\left(e^{-as}-e^{-bs}\right)$
Unit Impulse	$u_1(t)=\lim\dfrac{u(t)-u(t-1)}{a}$ $a \to 0$	1

B.2   The $\mathscr{L}$ Transformation

We shall now apply Laplace transform methods to the solution of differential equations. Take for instance:

$$A\frac{d^2y}{dt^2} + B\frac{dy}{dt}Cy = f(t) \tag{B.14}$$

in which A, B, and C are known constants and $y \triangleq y(t)$.

The unknown $y(t)$ will be called the response function and the known $f(t)$ will be called the driving function. The initial values of the unknown and its first derivative are $y(0)$ and $y'(0)$.

Applying the $\mathscr{L}$ transformation to both members of Equation (B.14)

$$\mathscr{L}\left[A\frac{d^2y}{dt^2} + B\frac{dy}{dt} + Cy\right] = \mathscr{L}\left[f(t)\right] \tag{B.15}$$

Calling $F(s)$ the $\mathscr{L}$ transform of $f(t)$ and $Y(s) \triangleq \mathscr{L}[y(t)]$ the response transform. Then using equation (B.8) and Equation (B.9)

$$\mathscr{L}\quad[y'(t)] = sY(s) - y(0)$$

and

$$\mathscr{L}\quad[y''(t)] = s^2\,Y(s) - y(0)s - y'(0)$$

This discloses the way in which the initial conditions $y(0)$ and $y'(0)$ are incorporated in the solution during the process of transformation.

Equation (B.15) becomes

$$A\mathscr{L}\left[\frac{d^2y}{dt^2}\right] + B\mathscr{L}\left[\frac{dy}{dt}\right] + C\mathscr{L}[y] = \mathscr{L}\,f(t)$$

$$A\,[s^2Y(s) - y(0)\,s - y'\,(0)] + B\,[sY(s) - y(0)] + CY(s) = F(s)$$

or

$$(A\,s^2 + B\,s + C)Y(s) = F(s) + y(0)\,(A\,s + B) + y'\,(0)\,A \tag{B.16}$$

Equation (B.16) is called a transform equation. The polynomial coefficient of $Y(s)$ - in this case $(As^2 + Bs + C)$ - is called the characteristic function since it completely characterizes the physical system described by the differential equation. Note that this is identical with the system characteristic equation derived in Appendix A, except for the variable "s" instead of the operator "p". The equation formed by setting it to zero is called the characteristic equation of the system. Solving Equation (B.16) algebraically,

$$Y(s) = \frac{1}{As^2 + Bs + C}\left[F(s) + y(0)(As+B) + y'(0)A\right] \quad \text{(B.17)}$$

This algebraic equation has a form which will be found typical of all transform solutions, viz:

Response transform = System function x Excitation function

The system function in this example is the reciprocal of the characteristic function, but in general it will be a fraction of which the characteristic function is the denominator. It incorporates in one function all the essential knowledge regarding the physical system.

The excitation function includes the driving transform and the initial conditions. It contains all the essential specifications of the excitations applied to the system.

When the form of the driving function $f(t)$ is specified, the algebraic form of $Y(s)$ can be determined and

$$y(t) = \mathscr{L}^{-1}[Y(s)] = \mathscr{L}^{-1}\left[\frac{F(s) + y(0)(As+B) + y'(0)A}{As^2 + Bs + C}\right] \quad \text{(B.18)}$$

If $Y(s)$ were an algebraic function of the form of any one of the various transforms listed so far, the inverse could be written immediately by reference to the table. But since $Y(s)$ is a more complicated function than listed, such a direct method of determining the inverse transform fails.

This difficulty may be surmounted by resolving the function into a sum of simpler components whose inverse transforms are readily recognized.

B.2.1 $\mathscr{L}^{-1}$ Transformation

Consider the general rational algebraic fraction

$$F(s) = \frac{A(s)}{B(s)} \triangleq \frac{a_p s^p + a_{p-1}s^{p-1} + \ldots + a_1 + a_0}{s^q + b_{q-1}s^{q-1} + \ldots + b_1 s + b_0} \quad \text{(B.19)}$$

where $p \leq q$

By solving for the roots of the equation $B(s) = 0$, and calling these $s_1, s_2, \ldots, s_q$, the fraction may be expressed as

$$F(s) = \frac{A(s)}{B(s)} = \frac{A(s)}{(s-s_1)(s-s_2)(s-s_3)\ldots(s-s_q)} \tag{B.20}$$

and the above may in turn be written as a sum of partial fractions, each partial fraction having for its denominator one of the factors of $B(s)$. There will be "q" of these partial fractions, i.e.,

$$F(s) = \frac{A(s)}{B(s)} = \frac{K_1}{(s-s_1)} + \frac{K_2}{(s-s_2)} + \frac{K_3}{(s-s_3)} + \ldots \frac{K_q}{(s-s_q)} \tag{B.21}$$

To evaluate the typical coefficient K_k, multiply both members of Equation (B.21) by $(s - s_k)$ obtaining

$$\frac{(s-s_k)A(s)}{B(s)} = K_1\frac{(s-s_k)}{(s-s_1)} + K_2\frac{(s-s_k)}{(s-s_2)} + \ldots$$
$$+K_k + K_q\frac{(s-s_k)}{(s-s_q)} \tag{B.22}$$

In the fraction forming the left member of Equation (B.22), $(s - s_k)$ is a factor of both numerator and denominator and should be divided out. Then letting $s = s_k$, this left member becomes a number, and in the right member all terms except K_k become zero.

i.e.,
$$K_k = \lim_{s \to s_k} \frac{(s-s_k)A(s)}{B(s)} \tag{B.23}$$
$$= \frac{A(s_k)}{(s_k-s_1)(s_k-s_2)\ldots(s_k-s_{k-1})(s_k-s_{k+1})\ldots(s_k-s_q)}$$

But $(s_k-s_1)(s_k-s_2)\ldots(s_k-s_{k-1})(s_k-s_{k+1})\ldots(s_k-s_q) = \dfrac{d}{ds}B(s)\Big|_{s=sk} \triangleq B'(s_k)$ (B.24)

so Equation (B.23) can be written

$$\frac{A(s)}{B(s)} = \sum_{k=1}^{q} \frac{A(s_k)}{B'(s_k)}\frac{1}{(s-s_k)} \tag{B.25}$$

The actual problem of inverse transformation is now a simple one.

$$\mathcal{L}^{-1}\left[\frac{1}{s-s_k}\right] = e^{s_k t}$$

The above holds for $\dfrac{A(s)}{B(s)}$ having first order poles only; i.e., the roots of $B(s)$ being

$$(s+s_1)^n \, (s+s_2)^m \, (s+s_3)^\ell \dots$$

where $n, m, \ell = 1$

and $s_1 \neq s_2 \neq s_3 \dots$

EXAMPLE:

Find the $\mathcal{L}^{-1}\left[\dfrac{a_1 s + a_0}{(s+\alpha_1)(s+\alpha_2)(s+\alpha_3)}\right]$

in which α_1, α_2, and α_3 are real numbers, all different.

$$\mathcal{L}^{-1}\left[\frac{a_1 s + a_0}{(s+\alpha_1)(s+\alpha_2)(s+\alpha_3)}\right] = K_1 e^{-\alpha_1 t} + K_2 e^{-\alpha_2 t} + K_3 e^{-\alpha_3 t}$$

in which

$$K_1 = \left[\frac{a_1 s + a_0}{(s+\alpha_2)(s+\alpha_3)}\right]_{s=-\alpha_1} = \frac{-a_1\alpha_1 + a_0}{(-\alpha_1+\alpha_2)(-\alpha_1+\alpha_3)}$$

$$K_2 = \left[\frac{a_1 s + a_0}{(s+\alpha_1)(s+\alpha_3)}\right]_{s=-\alpha_2} = \frac{-a_1\alpha_2 + a_0}{(-\alpha_2+\alpha_1)(-\alpha_2+\alpha_3)}$$

$$K_3 = \left[\frac{a_1 s + a_0}{(s+\alpha_1)(s+\alpha_2)}\right]_{s=-\alpha_3} = \frac{-a_1\alpha_3 + a_0}{(-\alpha_3+\alpha_1)(-\alpha_3+\alpha_2)}$$

Special case: One pole lies at the Origin.

In $\dfrac{A(s)}{B(s)}$ of equation B-21 let $s_1 = 0$, then

$$\frac{A(s)}{B(s)} = \frac{A(s)}{s(s-s_2)(s-s_3)(s-s_4)\dots(s-s_q)} = \frac{A(s)}{s\,B_1(s)}$$

where $B_1(s) = \dfrac{B(s)}{s}$

The form above occurs frequently. It arises, for example, when the excitation function is a constant step and the system function does not have a pole or a zero at $s = 0$.

The final result can be shown to be

$$\mathcal{L}^{-}\left[\frac{A(s)}{s\,B_1(s)}\right] = \frac{A(0)}{B_1(0)} + \sum_{k=2}^{q} \frac{A(s_k)}{s_k\,B_1'(s_k)} e^{s_k t} \tag{B.26}$$

EXAMPLE:

Find $\quad \mathcal{L}^{-1}\left\{ \dfrac{a_1 s + a_0}{s\left[(s+\alpha)^2 + \beta^2\right]} \right\}$

here
$$A(s) = (a_1 s + a_0)$$
$$B_1(s) = [(s + \alpha)^2 + \beta^{\,2}]$$
$$B_1'(s) = 2(s + \alpha) \text{ and } s_2, s_3 = \alpha \pm j\beta \text{ and } s_1 = 0$$

Using Equation (B.26),

$$\mathcal{L}^{-1}\left\{ \frac{a_1 s + a_0}{s\left[(s+\alpha)^2 + \beta^2\right]} \right\}$$

$$= \frac{A(0)}{B_1(0)} + K_2 e^{(-\alpha + j\beta)t} + K_3 e^{(-\alpha - j\beta)t}$$

$$K_2 = \left[\frac{a_1 s + a_0}{2s(s+\alpha)}\right]_{s=-\alpha+j\beta}$$

where $\quad = \dfrac{a_0 - a_1\alpha + ja_1\beta}{2j\beta(-\alpha + j\beta)}$

$$\frac{\sqrt{(a_0 - a_1\alpha)^2 + a_1^{\,2}\beta^2}}{2\beta\beta_0} e^{j\left(\phi - \frac{\pi}{2}\right)}$$

where $\quad \beta_0^2 = \alpha^2 + \beta^2$

and $\quad \phi = \left[\tan^{-1}\dfrac{a_1\beta}{a_0 - a_1\alpha} - \tan^{-1}\dfrac{\beta}{-\alpha}\right]$

Similarly
$$K_3 = \left[\frac{a_1 s + a_0}{2s(s+\alpha)}\right]_{s=-\alpha-j\beta}$$

$$= \overline{K}_2 \text{ (conjugate } K_2)$$

Coefficients K_2 and K_3 are conjugate complex numbers.

The final result can be written

$$\mathcal{L}^{-1}\left\{\frac{a_1 s + a_0}{s\left[(s+\alpha)^2 + \beta^2\right]}\right\}$$

$$= \frac{a_0}{\beta_0^2} + \frac{\sqrt{(a_0 - a_1\alpha)^2 + a_1^2\beta^2}}{\beta\beta_0} e^{-\alpha t} \sin(\beta t + \phi) \tag{B.27}$$

A convenient rule to remember in obtaining the $\mathcal{L}^{-1}$ of a function where one pair of roots are $[(s + \alpha)^2 + \beta^2]$ is as follows:

The time function corresponding to the roots $[(s + \alpha)^2 + \beta^2]$ in

$$\frac{A(s)}{C(s)\left[(s+\alpha)^2 + \beta^2\right]} \text{ is } Ke^{-\alpha t} \sin(\beta t + \theta) \tag{B.28}$$

where
$$K = \frac{|A(-\alpha + j\beta)|}{B|C(-\alpha + j\beta)|} \tag{B.29}$$

and
$$\varphi = \text{angle of } A(-\alpha + j\beta) \text{ minus angle of } C(-\alpha + j\beta) \tag{B.30}$$

Similarly for a function where one pair of roots are $(s^2 + \omega^2)$ the time function component corresponding to these roots in the function

$$\frac{A(s)}{C(s)(s^2 + \omega^2)} \tag{B.31}$$

can be obtained as
$$K \sin(\omega t +) \tag{B.32}$$

where
$$K = \frac{|A(j\omega)|}{\omega|C(j\omega)|} \tag{B.33}$$

and
$$\varphi = \text{angle of } A(j) \text{ minus angle of } C(j\omega) + \tag{B.34}$$

B.3 Multiple Order Poles

Consider the function $F(s)$ which has poles of higher order. (s_1 occurs m_1 times, s_2 occurs m_2 times, etc.)

$$F\left(s\right) = \frac{A(s)}{B(s)} = \frac{A(s)}{\left(s - s_1\right)^{m_1}\left(s - s_2\right)^{m_2}..\left(s - s_n\right)^{m_n}} \tag{B.35}$$

The fraction $\dfrac{A(s)}{B(s)}$ may be resolved into a sum of partial fractions. For each pole s_k of multiplicity m_k there are m_k partial fractions

$$\frac{K_{k1}}{\left(s - s_k\right)^{m_k}}, \quad \frac{K_{k2}}{\left(s - s_k\right)^{m_k-1}}, \cdots \frac{K_{km_k}}{\left(s - s_k\right)}$$

in which the K's are constants yet to be determined. Thus the expansion of $A(s)/B(s)$ is

$$\frac{A(s)}{B(s)} = \frac{K_{11}}{\left(s - s_1\right)^{m_1}} + \frac{K_{12}}{\left(s - s_1\right)^{m_1-1}} + \cdots \frac{K_{1j}}{\left(s - s_1\right)^{m_1-j+1}} + \cdots + \frac{K_{1m1}}{\left(s - s_1\right)} +$$

$$+ \, ... \, +$$

$$+ \frac{K_{k1}}{\left(s - s_k\right)^{m_k}} + \frac{K_{k2}}{\left(s - s_k\right)^{m_k-1}} + \cdots \frac{K_{kj}}{\left(s - s_k\right)^{m_k-j+1}} + \cdots + \frac{K_{kmk}}{s - s_k} +$$

$$+ \, ...$$

To evaluate the K_k coefficients, first multiply both members of the equation above by $\left(s - s_k\right)^{m_k}$ obtaining

$$\frac{\left(s - s_k\right)^{m_k} A(s)}{B(s)} = K_{k1} + K_{k2}\left(s - s_k\right) + K_{k3}\left(s - s_k\right)^2 + ... + K_{kmk}\left(s - s_k\right)^{m_k-1}$$

$$+ \left(s - s_k\right)^{m_k}\left[\frac{K_{11}}{\left(s - s_1\right)^{m_1}} + ... + \frac{K_{nmn}}{s - s_n}\right]$$

In the left member $\left(s - s_k\right)^{m_k}$ cancels out with that factor which is also a part of $B(s)$. Letting $s = s_k$, this left member becomes a number which should correspond to K_{k1} of the right hand side since all other terms would be zero.

In order to obtain the other coefficients, we note that by differentiating both sides with respect to s, the following expression results:

$$\frac{d}{ds}(s-s_k)^{m_k}\frac{A(s)}{B(s)} = K_{k2} + 2K_{k3}(s-s_k) + \ldots + (M_k-1)K_{k_{mk}}(s-s_k)^{m_k-2}$$

$$+\frac{d}{ds}(s-s_k)\left[\frac{K_{11}}{(s-s_1)^{m_1}} + \ldots + \frac{K_{n_{mn}}}{s-s_n}\right]$$

Letting $s=s_k$ we note that K_{k2} is equal to the number resulting from the evaluation of

$$\left[\frac{d}{ds}(s-s_k)^{m_k}\frac{A(s)}{B(s)}\right]_{s=s_k}$$

(B.36)

Similarly for the other terms

$$K_{k3} = \frac{1}{2:}\frac{d^2}{ds^2}(s-s_k)^{m_k}\frac{A(s)}{B(s)}\bigg]_{s=s_k}$$

(B.37)

and

$$K_{kj} = \frac{1}{j-1!}(s-s_k)^{m_k}\frac{A(s)}{B(s)}\bigg]_{s=s_k}$$

(B.38)

EXAMPLE:

Find

$$\mathcal{L}^{-1}\left[\frac{a_2s^2+a_1s+a_0}{(s+\alpha)^3s^2}\right]$$

(B.39)

$$\mathcal{L}^{-1}\left[\frac{a_2s^2+a_1s+a_0}{(s+\alpha)^3s^2}\right] = \mathcal{L}^{-1}\left[\frac{K_{11}}{(s+\alpha)^3} + \frac{K_{12}}{(s+\alpha)^2} + \frac{K_{13}}{(s+\alpha)} + \frac{K_{21}}{s^2} + \frac{K_{22}}{s}\right]$$

(B.40)

$$=\left(\frac{K_{11}}{2:}t^2 + K_{12}t + K_{13}\right)e^{-\alpha t} + K_{21}t + K_{22}$$

(B.41)

where

$$K_{11} = \left[\frac{a_2s^2+a_1s+a_0}{s^2}\right]_{s=-\alpha} = \frac{a_2\alpha^2-a_1\alpha+a_0}{\alpha^2}$$

(B.42)

$$K_{12} = \left[\frac{d}{ds} \frac{a_2{}^2 + a_1 s + s_0}{s^2} \right]_{s=-\alpha} = \frac{-a_1\alpha + 2a_0}{\alpha^3} \qquad (B.43)$$

$$K_{13} = \left[\frac{d^2}{ds^2} \frac{a_2 s^2 + a_1 s + a_0}{s^2} \right]_{s=-\alpha} = \frac{-a_1\alpha + 2a_0}{\alpha^4} \qquad (B.44)$$

$$K_{21} = \left[\frac{a_2 s^2 + a_1 a + a_0}{(s+\alpha)^3} \right]_{s=0} = \frac{a_0}{\alpha^3} \qquad (B.45)$$

$$K_{22} = \left[\frac{d}{ds} \frac{a_2 s^2 + a_1 s + a_0}{(s+\alpha)^3} \right]_{s=0} = \frac{a_1\alpha + 3a_0}{\alpha^4} \qquad (B.46)$$

Let us complete this section by taking the same examples as in Appendix A.

Consider the circuit of Figure B-1.

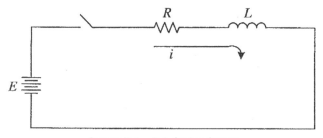

Figure B-1 – R-L Series Circuit

The differential equation for condition after closing of the switch at $t = 0$ is

$$E = iR + L\frac{di}{dt} \qquad (B.47)$$

Taking the $\mathscr{L}$ transform of both sides of Equation (B.47)

$$E(s) = Ri(s) + Lsi(s) - Li(0) \qquad (B.48)$$

where $E(s)$ denotes $\mathscr{L}\, E(t)$

and $i(s)$ denotes $\mathscr{L}\, i(t)$

and $i(o)$ = initial condition of i at $t = 0$

Since E is a constant; its $\mathscr{L}$ transform is E/S (see Table 1 - Table of Transforms). Also for this case $i(o) = 0$.

Hence Equation (B.48) becomes

$$\frac{E}{s} = i(s) \left[R + Ls \right] \tag{B.49}$$

Solving for

$$i(s) = \frac{E}{s[R + Ls]} \tag{B.50}$$

Equation (B.50) is the $\mathscr{L}$ transform solution of the current.

To obtain the time domain solution of current we must perform the inverse transform of Equation (B.50).

i.e.

$$i(t) = \mathscr{L}^{-1} \, i(s) = \mathscr{L}^{-1} \left\{ \frac{E}{Ls\left(s + \dfrac{R}{L} \right)} \right\} \tag{B.51}$$

Using the rules of partial fraction expansion (Equation (B.21) to Equation (B.23).

$$i(t) = \mathscr{L}^{-1} \left\{ \frac{K_1}{s} + \frac{K_2}{Ls\left(s + \dfrac{R}{L} \right)} \right\} \tag{B.52}$$

where

$$K_1 = \frac{E}{(R + Ls)} \bigg|_{s=0} = \frac{E}{R}$$

$$K_2 = \frac{E}{Ls} \bigg|_{s=\frac{R}{L}} = -\frac{E}{R}$$

Using the Laplace transform tables (Table B-1) to obtain the inverse of Equation (B.52).

$$i(t) = K_1 + K_2 e^{-\frac{R}{L}t}$$
$$= \frac{E}{R} - \frac{E}{R} e^{-\frac{R}{L}t} \tag{B.53}$$

which is the familiar form of the exponential rise in current in the inductive circuit of Figure B-1.

Of particular interest is the exponential term $e^{-R/Lt}$ which reveals the decay of the transient component.

The coefficient L/R has the dimensions of seconds, and is known as the "time constant" of the circuit. This time constant is defined as the time in seconds for the transient term to be reduced to $e^{-1} = 0.359$ of its initial value. Another useful interpretation of the time constant is the time that would be required for the transient to disappear completely if its rate continued at its initial value. (Figure B-2).

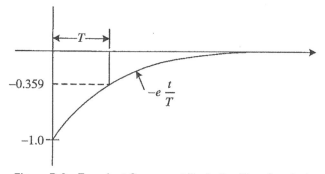

Figure B-2 – Transient Component Illustrating Time Constant

Take now the case treated in Appendix A of the RLC circuit with the sinusoidal excitation

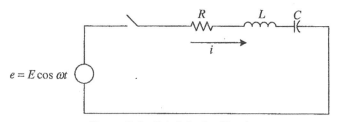

Figure B-3 – R-L-C Series Circuit

Again the circuit voltage drop equation is

$$Ri + L\frac{di}{dt} + \frac{1}{C}\int i\,dt = E\cos\omega t \tag{B.54}$$

Taking the $\mathscr{L}$ transform of both sides of Equation (B.54)

$$\left(R + Ls + \frac{1}{Cs}\right)i(s) - Li(0) + \frac{V_{c0}}{s} = \frac{Es}{s^2 + \beta^2} \tag{B.55}$$

where $i(o)$ = initial current at $t = 0$

and V_{c0} = initial voltage across the capacitor $\frac{1}{C}\int idt\Big|_{t=0}$

For the case where these initial conditions are zero, Equation (B.55) can be expressed as

$$i(s) = \frac{1}{\left(R + Ls + \dfrac{1}{Cs}\right)} \frac{Es}{s^2 + \beta^2} \tag{B.56}$$

Note that Equation (B.56) is in the form

Response transform $i(s)$ = $\left[\text{System function } i(s) = \dfrac{1}{\left(R + Ls + \dfrac{1}{Cs}\right)}\right]$

$$\times \left[\text{Excitation function } \frac{Es}{\left(s^2 + \omega^2\right)}\right]$$

Expressing Equation (B.56) in terms of poles and zeros

$$i(s) = \frac{EC\,s^2}{\left(1 + RCs + LCs^2\right)\left(s^2 + \omega^2\right)}$$

$$= \frac{EC\,s^2}{LC\left(s + \dfrac{R}{2L} - \dfrac{1}{2}\sqrt{\left(\dfrac{R}{L}\right)^2 - \dfrac{4}{LC}}\right)\left(s + \dfrac{R}{2L} + \dfrac{1}{2}\sqrt{\left(\dfrac{R}{L}\right)^2 - \dfrac{4}{LC}}\right)\left(s^2 + \omega^2\right)} \tag{B.57}$$

where the system poles are the roots of $(1 + RCs + LCs^2)$ which are the same as the roots of the characteristic Equation (A.26) $(1 + RCp + LCp^2)$ in Appendix A.

The time expression for $i(t)$ is obtained by taking the $\mathcal{L}^{-1}$ Equation (B.57) using the rules in Equations (B.28) to (B.34) and expressing Equation (B.57) as

$$i(s) = \frac{EC\,s^2}{LC\left[(s+\alpha)^2 + \beta^2\right]\left(s^2 + \omega^2\right)}$$

$$i(t) = K_1\varepsilon^{-\alpha t}\sin\left(\beta t + \phi_1\right) + K_2\sin\left(\omega t + \phi_2\right) \tag{B.58}$$

$$i(t) = K_1\varepsilon^{-\alpha t}\sin\left(\beta t + \varphi_1\right) + K_2\sin\left(\omega t + \varphi_2\right)$$

$$K_1 = \left. \frac{\left| EC\, s^2 \right|}{LC\, \beta \left| s^2 + \omega^2 \right|} \right|_{s=-a+j\beta}$$

where

$$= \frac{EC \left[\left[a^2 - 2ja\beta - \beta^2 \right] \right]}{LC\, \beta \left[\left[a^2 - 2ja\beta - \beta^2 + \omega^2 \right] \right]}$$

See Equations (B.28) to (B.30)

$$= \frac{EC \left[\left(a^2 - \beta^2 \right)^2 + 4a^2 \beta^2 \right]^{1/2}}{LC\, \beta \left[\left(a^2 - \beta^2 + \omega^2 \right)^2 + 4a^2 \beta^2 \right]^{1/2}}$$

$$\phi_1 = \tan^{-1} \frac{-2a\beta}{a^2 - \beta^2} \, \tan^{-1} \frac{-2a\beta}{a^2 - \beta^2 + \omega^2}$$

and

$$K_2 = \left. \frac{\left| EC\, s^2 \right|}{\omega LC \left| (s+a)^2 + \beta^2 \right|} \right|_{s=j\omega}$$

See Equations (B.31) to (B.34)

$$= \frac{EC\, \omega^2}{\omega LC \left[\left(a^2 + \beta^2 - \omega^2 \right)^2 + 4a^2\, \omega^2 \right]^{1/2}}$$

and

$$\phi_2 = \pi - \tan^{-1} \frac{2a\omega}{a^2 + \beta^2 - \omega^2}$$

Note that Equation (B.58) has the total solution, steady state (second term) and transient (first term) obtained by a straight forward routine use of the direct and inverse Laplace transform.

Appendix C

Transfer Functions, Block Diagrams

Contents

List of Figures

Transfer Functions, Block Diagrams

Recall that in the discussion of Equation (B.17), Appendix B, the form of the equation was stated as:

Response transform = System function x Excitation function

As will be shown below, another name for the system function is the *System transfer function.*

A transfer function is an operational expression describing the incremental functional relationship between two variables. An example will illustrate how a functional relationship or equation relating two variables is expressed in transfer function form. The term "incremental" implies that we are only concerned with changes from a quiescent point, hence initial conditions are assumed zero.

Take the equation

$$e(t) = Ri(t) + L\frac{di(t)}{dt} \tag{C.1}$$

describing the relations between current and applied voltage in an *R-L* circuit.

This equation may be expressed in Laplace transform form, assuming zero initial conditions, as:

$$e(s) = Ri(s) + Lsi(s) \Leftrightarrow e(s) = [R + Ls]i(s) \tag{C.2}$$

By algebraic manipulation we may express Equation (C.2) as a transfer function between $e(s)$ and $i(s)$

$$\frac{i(s)}{e(s)} = \frac{1}{R + Ls} \tag{C.3}$$

Figure C-1 shows the schematic representation of Equation (C.3) in transfer function block diagram form.

Figure C-1 – Transfer Function Representation

A block diagram is a schematic representation of mathematical relationships or equations between variables. Block diagrams are widely used in the area of control. There are basic block diagram relationships which are useful for reducing the number of branches of block diagrams. These relationships accomplish the same thing as the elimination of variables by substitution, in an array of simultaneous equations. These algorithms that can be used for block diagram reduction are analogous to the formulas that we use in combination of impedances or star-delta, series and parallel transformations so familiar in reduction of networks.

A frequent configuration is the feedback arrangement of Figure C-2.

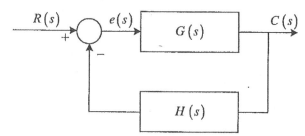

Figure C-2 – Block Diagram of a Closed Loop

which describes the following relationships

$$C(s) = G(s)\, e(s) \qquad\qquad (C.4)$$

$$e(s) = R(s) - H(s)C(s) \qquad\qquad (C.5)$$

where $G(s)$ and $H(s)$ are transfer functions.

Note the symbol

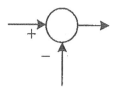

is a summing or difference junction forming the sum or difference of two or more variables.

Eliminating $e(s)$ by substitution of Equation (C.5) in Equation (C.4)

$$C(s) = [R(s) - C(s) \, H(s)] \, G(s)$$
$$C(s) = [1 + G(s) \, H(s)] = R(s) \, G(s)$$

i.e.,
$$\frac{C(s)}{R(s)} = \frac{G(s)}{1 + G(s)H(s)} \tag{C.6}$$

It is useful to remember relationship Equation (C.6) for purposes of block diagram reduction. This relationship defines the closed loop transfer function between the variables $C(s)$ and $R(s)$ expressible in a single block as shown in Figure C-3.

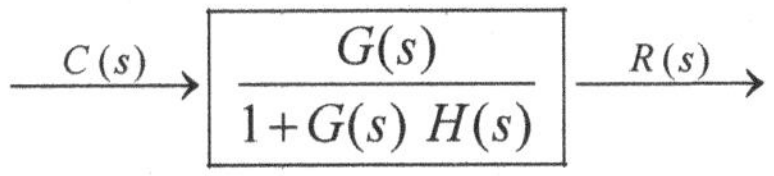

$$\xrightarrow{\quad C(s) \quad} \boxed{\dfrac{G(s)}{1 + G(s) \ H(s)}} \xrightarrow{\quad R(s) \quad}$$

Figure C-3 – Transfer Function of Clossed Loop $\dfrac{C(s)}{R(s)}$

Transfer functions in series can be combined by simple multiplication as shown in Figure C-4.

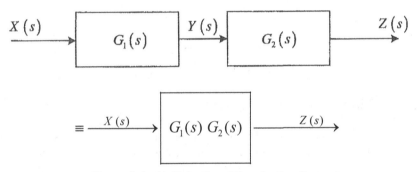

Figure C-4 – Multiplication of Transfer Functions

Transfer functions in parallel may likewise be combined by addition as indicated in Figure C-5.

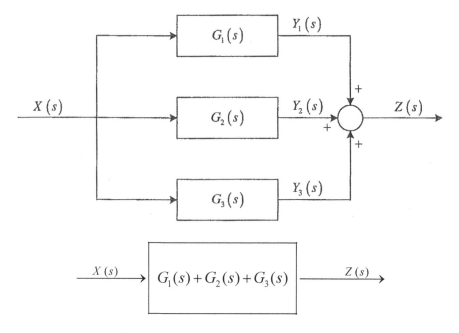

Figure C-5 – Summation of Transfer Functions

C.1   Final Value and Initial Value

Some special properties of the Laplace transform are of use in various design and analysis shortcuts. One of these is the "Final value theorem" which states that if $X(s)$ is the Laplace transform of $x(t)$ then the numerical value of x at time $t = \infty$ is given by the value of $sX(s)|_{s \to 0}$,

i.e., $x(t)|_{t \to \infty} = sX(s)|_{s \to 0}$

provided that $sX(s)$ does not have poles on the axis of imaginaries or on the right hand s plane (i.e., $x(t)$ is a stable function settling to a finite value at $t = \infty$).

This theorem is of particular use in evaluating the final value of the response of a transfer function to a unit step input.

Since the unit step input is $\dfrac{1}{s}$, the final value can be obtained by merely substituting $s = 0$ in the terms of the transfer function; e.g., the final value of $i(t)$, i.e., i at

$t = \infty$ following a unit step input in $e(t)$ to be evaluated from transfer function of

Equation (C.3) is $i(t = \infty) = \left.\dfrac{1}{r + Ls}\right|_{s=0} = \dfrac{1}{R}$.

A complementary theorem to the "Final value theorem" is the "Initial value theorem" which states that if $X(s)$ is the Laplace transform of $x(t)$, then the numerical value of x at $t = 0$ is given by the limiting value of $sX(s)$ as s goes to infinity.

i.e., $\quad x(t)\big|_{t=0} = sX(s)\big|_{s\to\infty}$

Again for the case of a transfer function $G(s)$, its output to a unit step function is $\dfrac{G(s)}{s}$ and the initial value of the output for the case of exciting it with a unit step function is

$$s\dfrac{G(s)}{s}\bigg|_{s=\infty} = G(s)\big|_{s=\infty}$$

e.g.: in the transfer function Equation (C.3), the initial response $i(t)$ to a unit step in $e(t)$ is

$$\dfrac{1}{R + Ls}\bigg|_{s=\infty} = 0$$

For instance, the function

$$\dfrac{1 + T_1 s}{1 + T_2 s}$$

has an initial value response to a unit step of T_1/T_2 and a final value of 1.

When $T_1/T_2 < 1$ the function is known as a lag/lead function (Figure C-6).

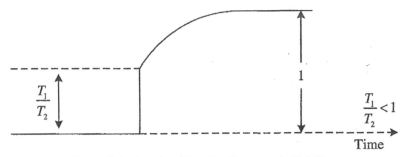

Figure C-6 – Lag-Lead Function Response to Unit Step

751

When $T_1/T_2 > 1$ the function is called a lead/lag function (see Figure C-7).

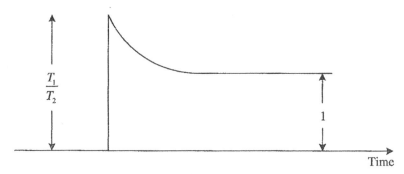

Figure C-7 – Lead-Lag Function Response to Unit Step

Similarly, the rate function $\dfrac{Ks}{1+Ts}$ has an initial response to a step of K/T and a final value of zero (Figure C-8).

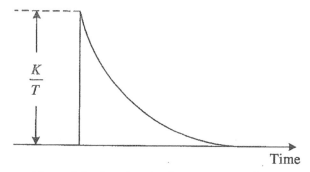

Figure C-8 – Rate Function Response to Unit Step

Appendix D

Analog Computers – State Space – Numerical Methods of Differential Equation Solution

Contents

List of Figures

Analog Computers – State Space – Numerical Methods of Differential Equation Solution

The advent of the analog computer or the electronic differential analyzer in the late 40's represented probably the greatest single breakthrough in the technology of dynamic analysis. This device permits the solution of the system equations by simulation and liberates the engineer from having to wrestle with the mathematics which, except for a limited number of fairly simple cases, become entirely unwieldy. Values of voltages correspond through appropriate scaling to values of the problem variables. That is the voltages in the analog computer are analogous to the problem variables, hence the name "Analog Computer."

The basic building block of the analog computer is the high gain operational amplifier, represented in Figure D-1.

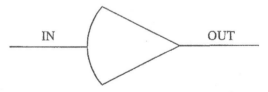

IN   OUT

Figure D-1 – Symbol for Operational Amplifier

This is a drift stabilized D.C. amplifier with a very high gain (between 50 and 300 $\times 10^6$ over the frequency range of interest), high input impedance and a phase shift of 180°, i.e., the output voltage is the negative of the input voltage.

The basic law which permits use of the operational amplifier as a device performing summing, integrating or other functions is Kirchoff's second law on the summation of currents into a node.

Consider the operational amplifier in the configuration of Figure D-2.

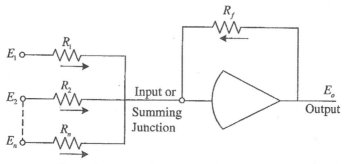

Figure D-2 – Amplifier Connections for Summer

Since the amplifier has a gain of almost infinity and the amplifier input impedance is very high, the summation of currents into the summing junction must equal zero from which fact we derive

$$E_0 = -R_f \left[\frac{E_1}{R_1} + \frac{E_2}{R_2} + \dots \frac{E_n}{R_n} \right] \qquad (D.1)$$

One notes that Equation (D.1) shows a summing relationship with scale factors of R_f/R_1, R_f/R_2 ... R_f/R_n on the various inputs E_1, E_2, ...E_n. Note that the amplifier inverts the sign of the inputs.

Examine now the configuration of Figure D-3.

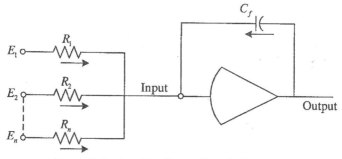

Figure D-3 – Amplifier Connections for Integrator

Again Kirchoff's law requires the summation of currents into the summing junction to be zero,

$$C_f \frac{dE_0}{dt} + \frac{E_1}{R_1} + \frac{E_2}{R_2} + \dots \frac{E_n}{R_n} = 0 \qquad (D.2)$$

i.e.

Integrating and rearranging terms

$$E_0 = -\int \left[\frac{E_1}{(R_1 C_f)} + \frac{E_2}{(R_2 C_f)} + \frac{E_3}{(R_3 C_f)} \cdots + \frac{E_n}{(R_n C_f)} \right] dt \qquad (D.3)$$

Equation (D.3) shows that the configuration of Figure D-3 is that of a summing integrator.

The same approach may be applied to an operational amplifier with arbitrary input and feedback impedances and the output voltage can be expressed as

$$E_0 = -\sum_{i=1}^{i=n} \left(\frac{Z_f}{Z_i} \right) E_i \qquad (D.4)$$

Although various combinations of operational amplifiers with especial arrangements of Z_f/Z_i are used on especial purpose analog process controls, for general purpose computation, the analog computer is composed mainly of the following linear elements

Summing amplifiers as in Figure D-2 with fixed ratio of R_f/R_i usually $R_f/R_i = 1$ or 10. In this configuration the symbol is shown on Figure D-4 where the feedback is implied and the gain R_f/R_i is indicated on the particular input by a "1" or a "10".

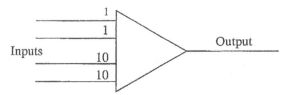

Figure D-4 – Symbol for Summing Amplifier

Inverters, Figure D-5, which are no more than summing amplifiers with a gain of "1".

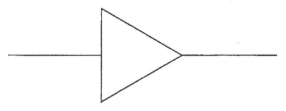

Figure D-5 – Symbol for Inverters

Integrators with the configuration of Figure D-3. By having $C_f = 1 \ \mu F$ and $R_i =$ 100kΩ or 1MΩ, input gains of "10" or "1" are obtained for the factors $\frac{1}{R_i C_f}$. The symbol for the integrator is shown on Figure D-6.

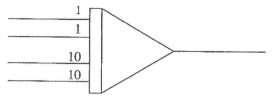

Figure D-6 – Symbol for Integrator Amplifier

Scaling or coefficient potentiometers with relatively low resistance compared with the input resistances R_i of the amplifiers. The symbol used is generally shown on Figure D-7.

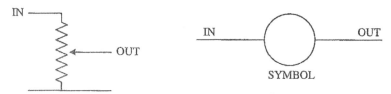

Figure D-7 – Scaling Potentiometer and Symbol

In addition to the above linear elements, there are a variety of non-linear elements such as function generators, multipliers (multiplying two variables) dividers, limiters, etc.

We will illustrate the use of the analog computer technique in the solution of the same RLC circuit problem as was discussed in Appendices A and B.

The basic differential equation for this circuit is

$$E(t) = Ri + L\frac{di}{dt} + \frac{1}{C}\int i \, dt \tag{D.5}$$

The basic rule in solution of differential equations by analog computer techniques is to convert the equation to integral form. The following rules are useful in setting up the equations for ready solution by analog computers.

1. Solve for the highest derivative. In the example of Equation (D.5), this becomes

$$\frac{di}{dt} = \frac{1}{L}E - \frac{R}{L}i - \frac{1}{CL}\int idt \qquad \text{(D.6)}$$

2. Integrate the highest derivative as many times as the order of the derivative. Equation (D.6) becomes

$$
\begin{aligned}
i &= \int\left(\frac{1}{L}E - \frac{R}{L}i\right)dt - \frac{1}{CL}\int\ \int idtdt \\
&= \int\left[\left(\frac{1}{L}E - \frac{R}{L}i\right) - \frac{1}{CL}\int idt\right]dt
\end{aligned} \qquad \text{(D.7)}
$$

3. Use the form of the resulting equation to connect the analog computer diagram as shown on Figure D-8. Note that summers and integrators invert the sign.

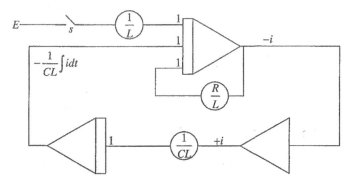

Figure D-8 – Analog Computer Solution of RL Circuit Equations

Upon closing the switch S, source E is applied and the solution of the current i will appear as a voltage as function of time out of integrator 1 (as $-i$) and out of inverter 2 (as $+i$). This voltage is recorded on a pen recorder yielding a plot of the solution.

D.1 Computer Scaling

Both amplitude and time scaling are generally required in the use of analog computers. In any physical system, many different dependent variables can exist, such as temperature, pressure, velocity, force, etc. In the analog simulation only one dependent variable - voltage - is possible. Thus a conversion from the physical variable to the computer variable is necessary. The amplitude scale factor specifies the number of computer volts which are analogous to one physical system unit (degree, psi, ft/sec or amps).

The choice of scale factors is an exercise in common sense from knowledge of the range of the physical variable and the fact that the computer voltage range is specified, usually - *100* to + *100* Volts.

Whereas amplitude scale factors represent a correspondence between computer and physical variable, the time scale indicates the relationship between the computer units of time which correspond to physical system units of time (e.g., 1 second on the computer represents 1 min, or 1 month of the physical system).

Time scaling is accomplished entirely in the gain of integrators. For instance if a 10 to 1 increase in speed is required this can be obtained by increasing the gain on all inputs to integrators by a factor of 10, or sometimes this can be accomplished by changing of integrator feedback capacitors from *1 μF* to *0 F*.

D.2   Initial Conditions

Every energy storage element of a physical system is represented by an integrator or combination of integrators. For instance, in the example of Figure D-8, the initial condition of current "i_o" is represented by an initial condition on the integrator *1*. Likewise an initial condition of voltage across the capacitor *C* is represented by an initial condition on integrator *3*.

Figure D-9 shows a method of setting initial conditions on integrators through establishment of the proper charge across the feedback capacitor.

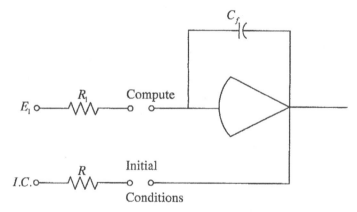

Figure D-9 – Connections for Integrator

D.3   State Space [29, 31]

A very popular formulation of differential equations is in the so called *State Space* form. Basically a differential equation of nth is expressed as a set of *n*, 1st order differential equations. Let us illustrate with examples.

Consider the circuit of Figure D-10.

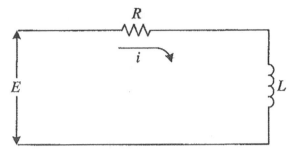

Figure D-10 – R-L Series Circuit

The differential equation for this circuit is

$$L\frac{di}{dt} + Ri = E \tag{D.8}$$

Now change the nomenclature as follows

Let i be replaced by x_1

and $\dfrac{di}{dt}$ be replaced by $\dot{x}_1$

Using these definitions, Equation (D.8) can be written

$$\dot{x}_1 = -\frac{R}{L}x_1 + \frac{E}{L} \tag{D.9}$$

Equation (D.9) is a state equation and x_1, is a state variable.

Consider now the case of the 2nd order differential equation describing the circuit of Figure. D-11.

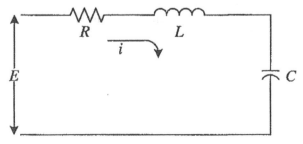

Figure D-11 – R-L-C Series Circuit

The equation is

$$Ri + L\frac{di}{dt} + \frac{1}{C}\int i\,dt = E \tag{D.10}$$

Defining $x_1 = i$ and $x_2 = \int i\,dt$ gives by definition

$$\dot{x}_1 = \frac{di}{dt} \text{ and } \dot{x}_2 = i$$

Equation (D.10) can now be written as two equations:

$$\dot{x}_1 = -\frac{R}{L}x_1 - \frac{1}{LC}x_2 + \frac{E}{L}$$

$$\dot{x}_2 = x_1 \tag{D.11}$$

As shown by Equation (D.11), the second order differential Equation (D.10) can be broken down into two first order equations. Similarly an Nth order system can be represented by N first order equations, which can be put into a very convenient matrix form.

For instance, Equation (D.11) can be expressed as

$$\begin{bmatrix} \dot{x}_1 \\ \dot{x}_2 \end{bmatrix} = \begin{bmatrix} -\dfrac{R}{L} & -\dfrac{1}{LC} \\ 1 & 0 \end{bmatrix} \begin{bmatrix} x_1 \\ x_2 \end{bmatrix} + \begin{bmatrix} \dfrac{E}{L} \\ 0 \end{bmatrix} \tag{D.12}$$

In this type of formulation one recognizes that the equations are ready for implementation on an analog computer, the $\dot{x}$ vector being the inputs to integrators and the x vector representing outputs to integrators.

Figure D-12 shows the corresponding analog computer diagram derived from matrix formulation Equation (D.12). Note that this is completely equivalent, as it should be, to the analog computer diagram in Figure D-8.

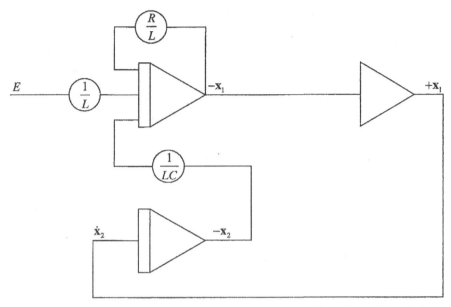

Figure D-12 – Analog Computer Diagram for RLC Circuit from State Space Formulation

D.4   Solution of the State Equation

The state space formulation yields a matrix equation of the form

$$\dot{x}(t) = Ax(t) + Bu(t) \tag{D.13}$$

where $\dot{x}(t)$, $x(t)$ and $u(t)$ are vectors and A is a square matrix and B is a matrix with appropriate dimensions ($n \times m$, where n is the number of state variables and m is the number of input variables).

The solution of (D.13) is

$$x(t) = e^{At}x(0) + \int_0^t e^{A(t-\tau)}Bu(\tau)d\tau \tag{D.14}$$

The term e^{At} in Equation (D.14) is called the *State Transition Matrix*. In conjunction with the forcing function $u(t)$, it determines the time trajectory of the system from its present state $x(0)$ to one in the future.

Matrices A and B in general may be functions of time (corresponding to time varying differential equations). For the case where they are constant, as well as the forcing function $u(t)$, we can integrate Equation (D.14) and obtain:

$$x(t) = e^{At}x(0) + A^{-1}[e^{At} - I]Bu \tag{D.15}$$

where $\mathbf{I}$ is the identity matrix of appropriate dimension.

As an example solve Equation (D.9) using Equation (D.15).

$$\mathbf{A} = -\frac{R}{L}$$

Here
$$\mathbf{Bu} = \frac{E}{L}$$

$$\therefore x(t) = e^{-\frac{R}{L}t} x(0) - \frac{L}{R}\left(e^{-\frac{R}{L}t} - 1\right)\frac{E}{L}$$

Which, for x(0) = 0, yields the familiar exponential rise in the inductive circuit

$$i(t) = x(t) = \frac{E}{R}\left(1 - e^{-\frac{R}{L}t}\right) \tag{D.16}$$

The first order example yields a very simple solution. For systems of higher order, the solution becomes complicated by the need to evaluate $e^{\mathbf{A}t}$ where $\mathbf{A}$ is a matrix. $e^{\mathbf{A}t}$ may be expanded into its series form

$$e^{\mathbf{A}t} = \mathbf{I} + \frac{\mathbf{A}t}{1!} + \frac{(\mathbf{A}t)^2}{2!} + \ldots \tag{D.17}$$

The larger the value of t, the more terms of the expansion Equation (D.17) must be included for the required accuracy.

Another approach is to use one or two terms of Equation (D.17) and limit the time step so that proper accuracy is obtained. The solution uses a recursive algorithm in that it repeats the process of transition from one state to another, where the initial state at the new time step is taken as the final state at the end of the last time step.

For instance if we use only the first two terms of Equation (D.17),

$$e^{\mathbf{A}t} \approx \mathbf{I} + \mathbf{A}t \tag{D.18}$$

Substituting Equation (D.18) into Equation (D.15) yields

$$x(t) = (\mathbf{I} + \mathbf{A}t)x(0) + \mathbf{Bu}t \tag{D.19}$$

Since Equation (D.19) is valid for a small time interval, we must use the recursive relationship

$$x(t + \Delta t) = (\mathbf{I} + \mathbf{A}\,\Delta)x(t) + \mathbf{Bu}\Delta \tag{D.20}$$

---

where Δ is the time increment. In general Equation (D.20) can be simplified to the form

$$\mathbf{x}(t + \Delta) = \mathbf{A}\mathbf{x}(t) + \mathbf{B'u} \qquad (D.21)$$

where $\mathbf{A'}$ is an $N \times N$ transition matrix and $\mathbf{B'u}$ is an N dimension column vector and $\mathbf{x}(t + \Delta)$ is likewise an N dimension column vector.

The recursive relationship Equation (D.21) brings to mind the general area of numerical methods of solving differential equations by using difference equation approximations or numerical integration algorithms.

This is a very vast subject and people have spent careers researching the merits of different algorithms such as Runge Kutta of various orders, Runge Kutta-Gill, Milne, Euler, and others. We will next explore a simple method of differential equation solution which gives good accuracy for most practical problems and will avoid being drawn into the many fine points which for the most part and from a practical point of view, are unnecessary frills.

D.5   A Digital Approach to Differential Equation Solution [25]

A logical step is to try to "digitise" the analog computer technique. This is done with a step by step procedure with the use of integration algorithms.

Before illustrating the method through an example, let us examine the operation of integration and one simple way of approximating this operation with a digital algorithm.

First look at the ideal continuous integrator whose transfer function is represented by $1/s$. When input with a unit impulse, the response of a continuous integrator is shown on the top trace of Figure D-13.

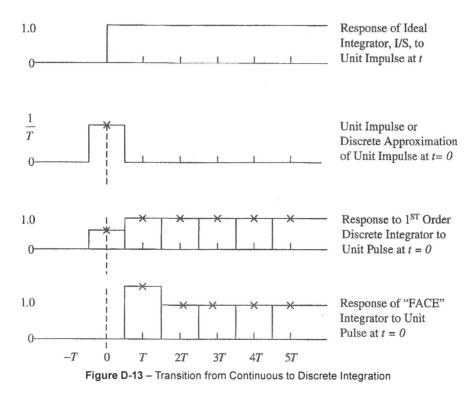

Figure D-13 – Transition from Continuous to Discrete Integration

D.6 Time-Domain Relationships Illustrating the Response of the FACE Integrator

In the discrete representation, values are defined at times $t = 0$, $t = T$, $t = 2T$... etc., and these values may be interpreted as the average value of the corresponding continuous function over the intervals about which the times $t = 0$, $t = T$, $t = 2T$ are centered.

On the basis of this interpretation of the digital sequence of numbers, the series that approximates the response of the continuous integrator is given by 3rd trace on Figure D-13, i.e., the sequence of numbers $1/2$, 1, 1, 1 ... at times $t = 0$, $t = T$, $t = 2T$, etc. This is basically Tustin's algorithm for integration.

The significant point here is that for this ideal first order integrator, there is an instantaneous undelayed output of $1/2$ at time zero when the input is a unit pulse centered around time zero.

Looking now at the analog computer diagram of Figure D-8 one notes that implementation of this type of algorithm in lieu of the integrators would require iterations since, because of the simultaneity of output and input, the input cannot be defined independent of the output. In order to avoid this interdependence of input on output at the same instant of time; the next best thing is to delay the output one time interval, breaking up the simultaneous dependence between input and output. When this is done, in order to preserve areas, the best thing that can be done is to tack on the missing *1/2* at *time = 0*, on to the output at the next time interval as shown on the last trace of Figure D-13. A block diagram of this simple one-pass digital integration algorithm is shown on Figure D-14.

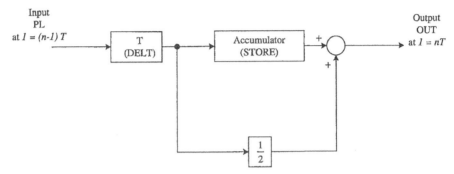

Figure D-14 – Computation Diagram for FACE Integrator

One can now visualize the process of differential equation solution by digital means as a straightforward recursive process of:

Defining inputs to integrators at times t_n from the outputs of these integrators (assumed fixed) and from other system inputs at time t_n.

Determining the outputs of the integrators at time $t_{(n+1)}$ from the inputs at time t_n in step (1) following the simple algorithm of Figure D-14.

Note that the output of the integrators can also be viewed as the "states" as explained in the previous section.

F. P de Mello

Power Technologies Inc

Appendix E

Feedback Control System Concepts

Contents

List of Figures

Feedback Control System Concepts

The term "Feedback Control System" is applied to a control system which compares a quantity to be controlled with a reference or desired value and operates on the error between these to bring the controlled quantity towards the desired value.

The closeness with which the controlled quantity is brought towards the desired value is a function of the type of control system. Regulators or type "0" servomechanisms require some finite error in the steady state. Type 1 servomechanism or controllers with "reset" (in process control terminology) have integration in the controller and wipe out the error to zero in the steady state.

One of the greatest aids in understanding control systems is the block diagram. This was introduced in Appendix C. A very common configuration of a feedback control is shown on Figure E-1.

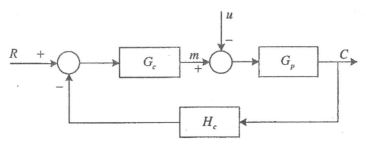

Figure E-1 – Generic Configuration of Closed Loop Control Systems

Here G_p is the process transfer function

        G_c is the controller forward function

        H_c is the feedback function

        R is the reference quantity or set point

        C is the controlled variable

        m is the input to the process manipulated by the controls

        u is the load or disturbance to the process.

This configuration may be understood better through an example. Take the case of a level control system.

$G(p)$ could be the transfer function K/s of a tank, c being the level of resident fluid

m the input controlled, flow rate

u being the uncontrolled (disturbance), drawdown from the tank

R is the reference level, or set point

H could be the sensor transfer function, such as a simple lag $\frac{1}{1+sT}$

G_c is the controller function which could be a simple proportional gain K_p or some more complex function.

Using the expressions on block diagram reduction of Appendix C, we can write down

$$C = \frac{G_c G_p}{1 + G_c G_p H} * R - \frac{G_p}{1 + G_c G_p H} * u \qquad \text{(E.1)}$$

The effect of closing the loop can be appreciated from Equation (E.1).

For instance the effect of a disturbance u on the system output C would have been $G_p u$ with the loop open. This has been reduced by a factor $\frac{1}{1+G_c G_p H}$ by closing the control loop. If for instance $G_c G_p H$ had a steady state value of 9, the effect of the disturbance will be reduced 10 to 1. If $G_c G_p H$ were to have an integration, (equivalent to having infinite gain in the steady state) the effect of the disturbance would have been zero in the steady state.

Another important point which may be drawn from equation (E.1) is the expression for C/R, i.e., the change of the controlled variable in response to a change in desired or reference value.

$$\frac{C}{R} = \frac{G_c G_p}{1 + G_c G_p H} \qquad \text{(E.2)}$$

For very large $G_c G_p$, $C/R = \frac{1}{H}$. This expression shows the importance of accuracy and linearity in the feedback element H, since for systems with large values of $G_c G_p H$ the controlled variable C depends mainly on the feedback element H, and the value of reference R.

Feedback control does not only reduce the effect of disturbances and drifts in the steady state. It also causes the output to respond more rapidly to the command of the references or to counteract dynamically the effects of load disturbances. Here we get involved with the important subject of response and stability of closed loop systems.

E.1 Closed Loop and Open Loop Time Response of Simple Systems

The concept of response and stability will be introduced with a couple of simple examples. Take the case of an open circuit generator whose terminal voltage response to a change in field volts is governed by a single time constant as described in Figure E-2.

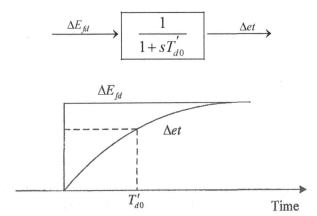

Figure E-2 – Process Open Loop Transfer Function and Its Step Response

Let us now regulate terminal voltage by means of an idealized regulator and exciter which may be represented by a simple gain as in Figure E-3.

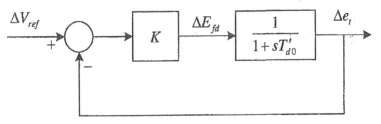

Figure E-3 – Closing the Loop with a Simple Proportional Control

The response of the closed loop

$$\frac{\Delta et}{\Delta V_{ref}} = \frac{G}{1+GH} = \frac{\dfrac{K}{1+sT_{d0}'}}{1+\dfrac{K}{1+sT_{d0}'}} = \frac{K}{1+K+sT_{d0}'} = \frac{K}{(1+K)\left(1+\dfrac{sT_{d0}'}{1+K}\right)} \tag{E.3}$$

For large K we note that equation E-3 has a steady state gain of almost unity but a response time constant of $T_{d0}'/(1+K)$ which is $(1+K)$ times faster than the open loop response of Figure E-2.

Figure E-4 shows the comparison of the open and closed loop performances

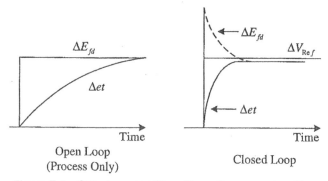

Figure E-4 – Open Loop and Closed Loop Responses to a Step

Note that the response of the closed loop is considerably faster than that of the open loop. This is due to the forcing action of the field in response to the high gain operating on the error.

On an idealized system containing only one time constant (first order system) such as in Figure E-3 there is theoretically no limit to the value of the gain K that can be applied. In practice most systems exhibit more than one time constant, i.e.; are of higher than first order, and a limit to the gain of the closed loop and hence a limit to closed loop's speed of response is reached due to stability considerations.

Let us illustrate by assuming the regulator exciter to be described by one time constant as in Figure E-5.

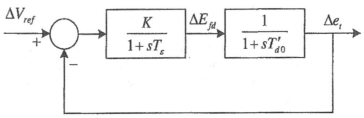

Figure E-5 – Second Order Closed Loop

Again solving for $\Delta et \Delta V_{ref}$ with the use of the $G/1+GH$ formula

$$\frac{\Delta et}{\Delta V_{ref}} = \frac{K}{(1+K)\left[1+s\dfrac{\left(T_\varepsilon + T'_{d0}\right)}{(1+K)} + s^2 \dfrac{\left(T_\varepsilon T'_{d0}\right)}{(1+K)}\right]} \qquad (E.4)$$

The nature of the closed loop response can be derived from the roots of the denominator of Equation (E.4), which are the roots of the closed loop characteristic equation

$1 + GH = 0$

Depending on the value of K, the roots of Equation (E.4) can be real or complex, the higher the value of K the more oscillatory (less damped) are the roots.

The quadratic form of the denominator can be expressed as

$$1 + \frac{2\zeta}{\omega_0}s + \frac{s^2}{\omega_0^2} \qquad (E.5)$$

where

$$\frac{2\zeta}{\omega_0} = \frac{T_\varepsilon + T'_{d0}}{(1+K)} \qquad (E.6)$$

and

$$\frac{1}{\omega_0^2} = \frac{T_\varepsilon \times T'_{d0}}{(1+K)} \qquad (E.7)$$

The roots of equation E-5 are

$$s_1, s_2 = \left[-\zeta \pm j\sqrt{1-\zeta^2} \right] \omega_0 \qquad (E.8)$$

where ω_0 is known as the natural frequency of oscillation and ζ is the damping ratio. A damping ratio; $\zeta = 1$, known as critical damping, yields two equal real roots $s_1, s_2 = -\omega_0$. Damping ratio less than 1 yield complex roots while those greater than one yield real (non oscillatory) roots. In terms of the parameters, K, T_e and T'_{d0}, Equation (E.6) and Equation (E.7) yield

$$\zeta = \frac{T_\varepsilon + T'_{d0}}{2\sqrt{\dfrac{1+K}{T_\varepsilon + T'_{d0}}}} \qquad (E.9)$$

$$\omega_0 = \sqrt{\frac{1+K}{T_e T'_{d0}}} \qquad (E.10)$$

From Equation (E.9) and Equation (E.10) we note that the higher K, the higher the natural frequency and the lower the damping ratio. The second order system of Figure E-5 cannot become unstable, i.e., cannot have roots with negative values of ζ. However, it can approach exhibiting sustained oscillations as $\zeta \to 0$ which is unacceptable performance. Systems with characteristic equations of higher orders can easily exhibit instability with increasing loop gains.

The inverse Lapace transform of expression (E.4) multiplied by $1/s$ (for the input step) yields the time function

$$\Delta e_t = \frac{K}{1+K}\left[1 + \frac{e^{-\zeta\omega_0 t}}{\sqrt{1-\zeta^2}} \sin\left(\sqrt{1-\zeta^2}\,\omega_0 t - \tan^{-1}\frac{\sqrt{1-\zeta^2}}{-\zeta} \right) \right] \qquad (E.11)$$

Figure E-6 shows the form of the response expression (E.11) as function of normalized time "$\omega_0 t$" for various values of ζ.

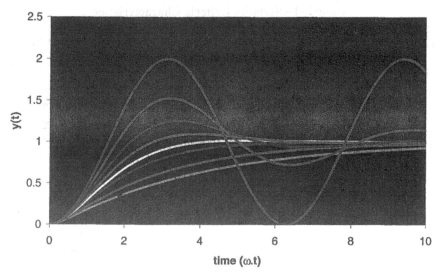

Figure E-6 – Normalized Step Response of a Second Order Differential Equation

E.2 Stability of Closed Loop Systems

From the above examples it becomes quite clear that the stability of closed loop systems can be investigated from knowledge of the roots of the characteristic equation

$$1 + GH = 0$$

Several methods are available to determine whether or not some of the roots of the characteristic equation lie in the right hand plane (a condition signifying instability). Such methods as Routh's criterion, root locus, etc. have their special application and it is not the intent here to expound further on these methods which may be readily found in the literature. We will merely explore briefly some of the very widely used Frequency Response techniques and Nyquist stability criteria. The table below summarizes briefly the features and names of some of the techniques used for determining stability.

Table E-1 - Stability Criteria Characteristics

METHOD	ANSWER OBTAINED	INFORMATION REQUIRED	APPLICATION	REMARKS
Routh	Yes-or-no stability	Closed-loop characteristic polynomial	Analysis	Difficult to assess effect of parameter variations
Hurwitz				Involved computation required
Meerov				Only computation needed is long division
Wall				Applicable to sampled data systems
Schur				
Root Locus	Complete system response	Open-loop transfer function, factored form	Analysis and synthesis	Can be extended to time delay systems
Nyquist Bode	Stability and approximate time response	Open-loop transfer function measured or computed for all frequencies		Application to time delay systems
Dzung	Yes-or-no stability	Closed-loop frequency response	Analysis	
Mickallov Leonhard	Absolute and relative stability			

E.2.1 Frequency Response

The concept of the operational impedance and the impedance to a sinusoidally varying excitation function was developed in example 2 of Appendix A.

A transfer function is an operational expression much like that of impedance. The complex number obtained by substitution of $s = j\omega$ in the transfer function gives information on the steady state sinusoidal response of the output of the function to a sinusoidal input excitation of frequency ω. The absolute value of this number corresponds to the magnitude ratio of the output sinusoid to the input sinusoid while the phase angle of the complex number expressed in polar coordinates indicates the angle by which the output sinusoid leads or lags the input sinusoid.

Frequency response techniques use the magnitude and phase characteristics of transfer functions or combinations of transfer functions to derive a great deal of information about the stability and response performance of control systems.

The frequency response characteristics of some common transfer functions encountered in control systems are described in Figure E-7.

Naturally the frequency response of a combination of transfer functions in series is easily obtained by taking the product of these functions, i.e.; the magnitude is the product of the magnitudes of the individual functions and the overall phase angle is equal to the summation of phase angles of the individual transfer functions.

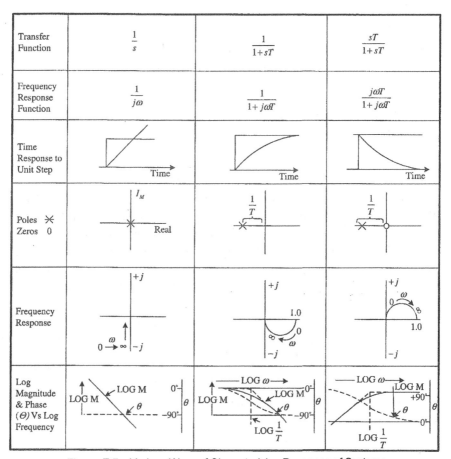

Transfer Function	$\dfrac{1}{s}$	$\dfrac{1}{1+sT}$	$\dfrac{sT}{1+sT}$
Frequency Response Function	$\dfrac{1}{j\omega}$	$\dfrac{1}{1+j\omega T}$	$\dfrac{j\omega T}{1+j\omega T}$
Time Response to Unit Step			
Poles ✕ Zeros 0			
Frequency Response			
Log Magnitude & Phase (Θ) Vs Log Frequency			

Figure E-7 – Various Ways of Characterizing Response of Systems

787

E.2.2 Nyquist Stability Criterion

Recall that the stability of a closed loop system was determined from properties of the characteristic equation $1 + GH = 0$.

The Nyquist criterion is a means used to determine whether or not $1 + GH$ has roots in the right hand half of the s plane. A rigorous derivation of the Nyquist criterion involves use of complex number theorems by Cauchey and examination of the number of cycles of phase rotation of the function $GH(j\omega)$ as $j\omega$ is taken around a closed path from $-j\infty$ to $+j\infty$.

Except for very unusual circumstances Nyquist's criterion applied to practical cases amounts to the following:

> For a closed loop whose characteristic equation is $1 + GH$, the stability of the system can be derived by examining the frequency response characteristic of the open loop function GH. This is done by finding the phase angle of GH at the frequency for which the magnitude of GH is 1.0. If the phase angle is 180° the system is borderline unstable. If the phase angle is more than 180° lagging, the system is unstable.

The phase angle of GH at the point where the magnitude of GH is 1 is known as the phase angle at crossover and the frequency ω_0 at this point is called the crossover frequency. Many guide rules have been established to relate the shape of the open loop frequency response function to the performance of the closed loop function. One point to remember is that the phase angle at crossover should in general not exceed 130 to $140°$. For such cases the closed loop system response will be oscillatory with good damping, the output exhibiting an overshoot of about 25%. The frequency of oscillation of the closed loop is related to and closely approximates the crossover frequency. For smaller phase angles at crossover, in the order of $100°$ the system in general looks critically damped.

Figure E 8 shows complex plots of typical $G(j\omega)H(j\omega)$ (open loop) functions as ω varies from zero to infinity. Such plots are called Nyquist diagrams. The third locus in Figure E-8 shows the case of a conditionally stable system - one where either an increase or a decrease in loop gain can cause instability. This is in contrast with the usual case where instability is only reached with increasing gain.

Figure E-9 shows typical time responses of the closed loop $\Delta C = \dfrac{G}{1+GH}$ to a step change in reference ΔR.

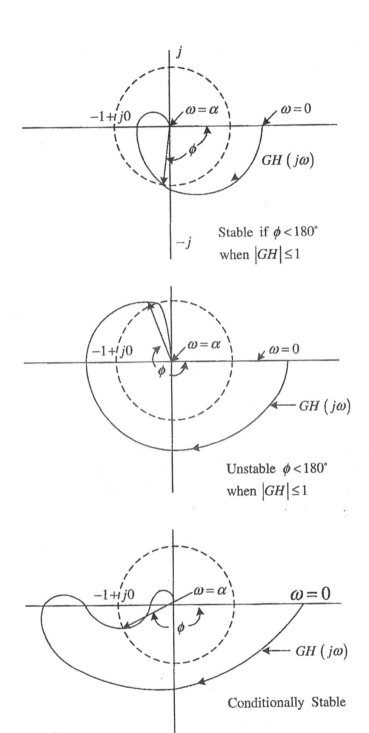

Figure E-8 – Nyquist Plots of Open Loop Function

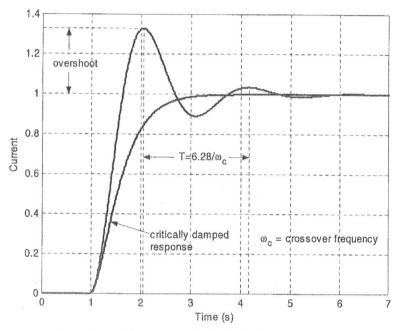

Figure E-9 – Underdamped and Critically Damped Responses

E.2.3 Bode Theorems

From the foregoing discussion, we note that the evaluation of the overall open loop frequency response characteristic $GH(j\omega)$ requires multiplication of transfer functions. The Bode method gives a simple technique for plotting transfer functions in terms of a log of magnitude plot and a phase angle plot.

If two transfer functions are written in polar form

$$A = A_1 e^{j\theta_1} \tag{E.12}$$

and

$$B = B_1 e^{j\theta_2}$$

Then

$$AB = A_1 B_1 e^{j(\theta_1 + \theta_2)} \tag{E.13}$$

That is, to obtain the frequency response of a product of transfer functions, the individual transfer function phases are added and their magnitudes are multiplied.

If the magnitudes are expressed as log A_I and log B_I then log $(A_I B_I)$ = log A_I + log B_I. The Bode diagram plots the logarithm of magnitude and phase angle of the open loop function $GH(j\omega)$ as separate functions of frequency.

The Bode plotting technique is based on asymptotic characteristics of transfer functions expressed in factored form. Let us illustrate with examples:

Take the transfer function of a single lag time constant

$$G(s) = \frac{K}{1 + sT} \qquad \text{(E.14)}$$

The frequency response of $G(s) = G(j\omega)$

$$= \frac{K}{1 + j\omega T} = \frac{K}{1 + j\left(\dfrac{\omega}{\omega_0}\right)} \qquad \text{(E.15)}$$

where $w_0 = \dfrac{1}{T}$

The asymptotes of Equation (E.15) as $\omega/\omega_0 \to 0$ and as $\omega/\omega_0 \gg 1$ are

$$K \text{ and } -j\frac{K}{\left(\dfrac{\omega}{\omega_0}\right)} \qquad \text{(E.16)}$$

The magnitude of $G(j\omega)$ plotted in log scale versus ω also on a log scale is shown on Figure E-10 as are also the two asymptotes for $\omega / \omega_0 \to 0$ and $\omega / \omega_0 \gg 1$.

Figure E-10 also shows the plot of phase angle of Equation (E.15) as function of ω_0. Note that plotted in this form all that is required is the location of the break frequency ω_0 and the shape of the frequency response function is then quickly determined.

A lead function is likewise described by asymptotic straight line approximations of log magnitude versus log ω as also shown on Figure E-10. The actual function can be quickly determined with the use of templates which give appropriate corrections to the asymptotic straight line approximations a function of the normalized value of ω/ω_0.

Likewise, templates give the phase angle contribution of each lag or lead factor, i.e.; the angle contributed by a pole or zero. Obviously the phase angle of Equation (E.15) as $\omega /\omega_0 \to 0$ as $0°$ and it is $90°$ as $\omega /\omega_0 \to \infty$. At $\omega /\omega_0 = 1$ it is $45°$.

Figure E-11 shows typical monograms for use with the Bode technique.

We will illustrate the use of Bode diagrams in the following example:

Consider the position control system described by the block diagram of Figure E-12. Find the maximum gain K for which this positioning system will be stable, and also the value of gain K 0 for which the phase angle at crossover is $-135°$, i.e.; the phase margin is $45°$.

Without ever knowing anything about Bode methods, this problem can be solved easily by plotting phase angle and magnitude of "G" with $K = 1.0$ as function frequency ω. From these plots we can determine the frequencies for which the phase angle is $180°$ and $135°$ respectively. Determine also the magnitude $|G|$ at these frequencies. Let these magnitudes be $M_{180°}$ and $M_{135°}$ respectively.

Then the values of gain K required to cause crossover at a phase angle of $180°$ and $135°$ respectively are

$$K_{180°} = \frac{1}{M_{180°}} = 12$$

and

$$K_{135°} = \frac{1}{M_{135°}} = 1.92$$

Figure E-13 contains a Bode plot $\frac{1}{s(1+T_1 s)(1+T_2 s)}$ of by use of the asymptotic approximation technique. Phase angle values are marked along the curve from which the value of $M_{180°}$ and $M_{135°}$ can be obtained by interpolation.

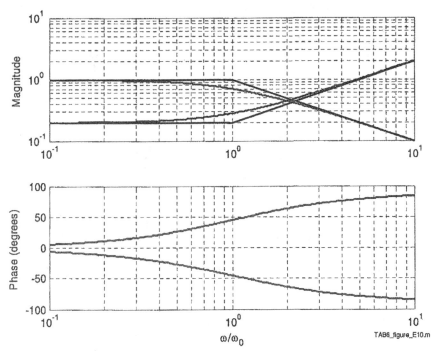

Figure E-10 – Bode Plots of Simple Pole and Zero

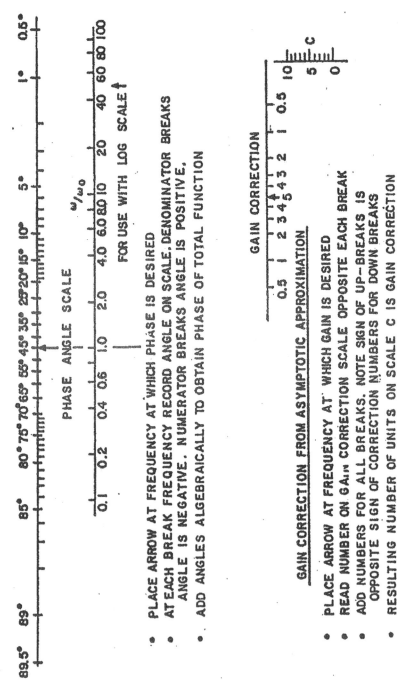

Figure E-11 – Templates in Bode Analysis

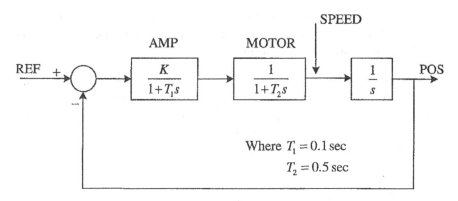

Figure E-12 – Block Diagram of Position Control System

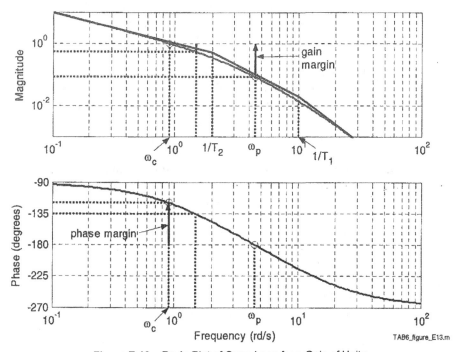

Figure E-13 – Bode Plot of Open Loop for a Gain of Unity

For the value of K which produces borderline stability, the phase angle is $180°$ and the crossover frequency is $\omega_c = 4.5$ rads/sec. The crossover frequency for the case where phase margin is $45°$ is $\omega_c = 1.5$ rads/sec.

Control design by frequency response techniques is concerned with the shaping of the frequency response of the controller function to provide the proper phase margin at crossover. Lead/lag functions of the form $(1 + T_1s)(1 + T_2s)$ with $T_1 >$ T_2 and lag lead functions with $T_1 < T_2$ are often used, with the location of T_1 and T_2 selected so as to produce the desired effect.

It is apparent that a high or infinite gain at zero frequency is necessary for good steady state and low frequency performance (low, or zero steady state error). The response of the control system is related to the crossover frequency, the higher this frequency the faster the control response, or bandwidth. However, a limiting constraint is the requirement of stability.

The rules of plotting Bode diagrams can be readily derived by elementary reasoning. These can be formulated as follows:

1. Determine the gain and slope at zero frequency.

   a) If all factors contain time constants $(1 + sT)$ both in the numerator as well as the denominator, then the initial gain, at $\omega = 0$, is equal to the steady state gain and the initial slope is zero.

   b) If $(s)^n$ appears in the denominator, the initial gain or magnitude of the function is infinite and the slope is such that the gain is decreased by a factor 10^n for every tenfold increase in frequency. The line can be located by making it pass through the point determined by $\omega = 1$ on the abscissa and overall gain on the ordinate.

   c) If $(s)^n$ appears in the numerator, the initial magnitude ratio is zero and the slope is such that the gain is increased by a factor of 10^n when the frequency is increased tenfold.

2. The initial line is carried to the first break frequency $\omega_0 = 1/T_1$, where T_1, is the longest time constant in the numerator or denominator.

3. At the first break, the change in slope is determined. Since the factor containing this longest time constant will be in the form $(1 + sT)^n$ the gain will change by a factor when the frequency changes 10 times.

   a) For instance, if the initial slope is zero and n = 2 (factor containing the longest time constant in the numerator of the transfer function), then the slope after the break will be such that the gain is increased a hundredfold (102) when the frequency changes by a decade. This is called a double break upward.

   b) As another example assume that the initial slope is S1; i.e.; the gain increases by ten times per decade increase in frequency and that the longest time constant occurs in the denominator at a break frequency 1/T1. Then the slope after the break will be horizontal since the downward slope contributed by the denominator time constant cancels the upward initial slope.

4. The slope thus determined after the first break is continued until the next break which is determined by the next longest time constant in numerator or denominator. The change in slope is determined as before and the process is repeated until all time constants have been accounted for.

Bode theorems relate the slope of the magnitude function to the phase angle. In general for minimum phase functions the phase angle can be approximately determined by the slope of the function.

A single slope, i.e.; magnitude decreasing 10 times for a tenfold increase in frequency carries about 90° phase lag. A slope of two (two decades, per decade), i.e.; 100 times decrease in magnitude for every tenfold increase in frequency represents about 180° phase lag and so on.

E.3   Frequency Response of the Closed Loop

The closed loop function can also be plotted in terms of its gain and phase as function of frequency.

$$\frac{1}{1+GH} \qquad (E.17)$$

Some easy guide rules can again be used to approximate the shape of the gain versus frequency curve.

Equation (E.17) can be approximated under two extreme conditions, i.e.; when $GH>>1$ and when $GH<<1$. Under the first condition Equation (E.17) becomes nearly $1/H$ and under the second condition Equation (E.17) is approximately G. This leads to the following set of rules to obtain the approximate shape of the closed loop response.

1. Plot gain curves for G, $\frac{1}{H}$ and GH.

2. Follow G when GH < 1, i.e.; follow G if $\frac{1}{H} > G$.

3. Change from the G curve to the $\frac{1}{H}$ curve when GH > 1, i.e.; follow $\frac{1}{H}$ if $\frac{1}{H} < G$.

4. The amount of resonant humping at near the transition from one curve to another is a function of the phase angle of GH at crossover, i.e.; at the point where $GH = 1.0$. Evidently if the phase angle at this point is $180°$, the resonant peak would reach infinity. The more oscillatory the system the greater the peak of the closed loop function. Figure E-14 illustrates the various points made above using the example of Figure E-12 for an arbitrary gain $K = 1.5$.

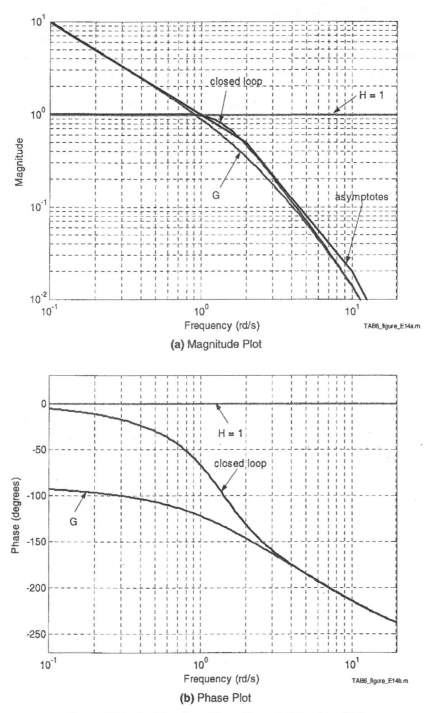

(a) Magnitude Plot

(b) Phase Plot

Figure E-14 – Deriving Closed Loop Characteristics from G&H

E.4　Tuning Criteria

There is a certain amount of subjectivity in deciding on what is an optimum tuning criterion, what is a desirable closed loop response shape and how much overshoot is considered to be acceptable. The answer is largely a function of the process.

Servomechanism theory using frequency response techniques was developed largely during World War II and the context was mainly radar tracking and gun turret positioning controls. In that context the need was for as great an accuracy as possible over as great a bandwidth as was needed. A tuning criterion with a 20% overshoot was often judged optimum because the bandwidth duty imposed by the targets did not reach to the cross over frequency where resonant amplification occurs. As an example, referring to Figure E-14, if this particular positioning system is being made to follow targets with frequencies in the range of 0.5 rads/sec or below, the control system will not be exercised in the region of cross over $(GH\ (j\omega) = 1)$.

Most power system processes have considerable noise in the bandwidths beyond crossover frequencies, hence the overshoot criterion of control tuning should be more conservative, i.e. little overshoot or no overshoot. This means that phase angle at crossover should be between -110° and -120°.

E.5　Dead Time or Transport Lag

There are many processes which exhibit significant "dead time" i.e., no perceptible response for the dead time period following a step change. Processes with multiple time constants close to each other also exhibit characteristics resembling a dead time.

Figure E-15 shows the transfer function of a pure dead time, its time response and frequency response. The pure dead time function $\xi^{-j\omega t}$ has no attenuation, i.e., its gain is unity, independent of frequency, but its phase lag increases linearly with frequency, but its phase lag increases linearly with frequency

$$\phi = \frac{-\omega T}{\pi} \times 180°$$

Take now a process with pure dead time to be controlled as in Figure E-16.

It is evident that if the control function G is a pure proportional gain K_p, instability would occur if K_p is greater than unity. Since the steady state closed loop response is $K_p/(1 + k_p)$, such a control with $K_p < 1$ would be as good as no control.

Remembering that the objectives of good control are:

1. High accuracy in the steady state which means high gain or infinite gain at $\omega = 0$.

2. Rapid response with acceptable stability (low overshoot).

It becomes obvious that the control function that is indicated for a pure dead time process is an integral control i.e. $G = K_I/s$.

Transfer Function

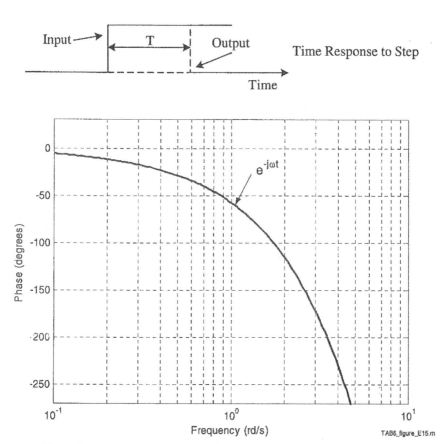

Time Response to Step

Figure E-15 – Frequency Response Characteristics of a Dead Time Process

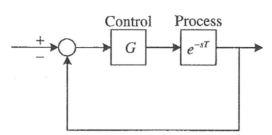

Figure E-16 – Control of a Process with Dead Time

Now the magnitude versus frequency characteristic of the open loop function is no longer flat as it was with proportional control but a straight line at 45° in the log $(G(j\omega))$ versus log (ω) plane, so that crossover $(G(j\omega) = 1)$ will occur at some frequency, while the steady state gain $(\omega = 0)$ is infinite, assuring perfect zero error control in the steady state.

The question now is what is an acceptable gain K_I which gives rapid response with low overshoot.

Using the criterion of an acceptable phase lag of between 110° and 120° at crossover for acceptable low overshoot, say 117°, the answer now involves determining the crossover frequency for which the phase lag of the open loop function (process and control) $\dfrac{K_I e^{-j\omega_c T}}{j\omega_c}$ is 117°. Since the denominator $j\omega_c$ accounts for 90° this means finding the frequency at which $e^{-j\omega T}$ exhibits a lag of $(117 - 90) = 27°$.

i.e.: $$\frac{\omega_c T}{\pi} \times 180 = 27$$

or $$\omega_c = \frac{27\pi}{180 T}$$

The gain K_I is then determined as the value required to make the magnitude of the open loop function $\dfrac{K_I}{\omega_c} = 1$

i.e.: $$K_I = \omega_c = \frac{27\pi}{180 T}$$

Appendix F

Notes on Process Control

Contents

List of Figures

Notes on Process Control

Historically automatic control technology developed along two parallel paths - one path being that taken by the instrumentation industry serving the process control field; such as control of chemical processes, steam plant controls, etc. The other path developed in the field of positioning, guidance controls, military gun turret controls, machine tool control, etc. This particular area saw developed the Bode, Nyquist, Root locus and other analytic techniques under the impetus of large outlays of Government research funds during and following World War II.

While the principles of control are universal, the usage of terms has been quite distinct among these groups. The latter talk about lead/lag functions, pole-zero locations, root locus, etc. While the former, rooted in process control terminology which precedes World War II, talks about two-mode and three-mode controls proportional bands, reset and rate times, etc. These brief notes are to familiarize the student with process control terminology and practices which form an important field in Power Plant and Power System control.

F.1   Control Modes

A controller is a device which shapes control action by operating on the error signal. Figure F-1 is helpful in defining terms.

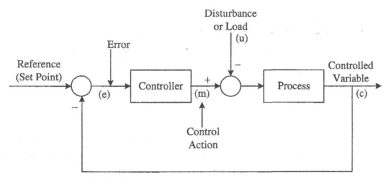

Figure F-1 – Block Diagram of Process and Controls

A <u>proportional controller</u> is one where the relationship between control action and error is a simple proportional gain, K_p.

$$m = K_p \qquad \text{(F.1)}$$

From previous discussions we note that a proportional controller cannot restore the error to zero unless there is an integration inherent in the process itself. The higher the gain the smaller the steady state error. Gain is expressed as "proportional band."

$$P.B = \frac{100}{K_p}\% \qquad \text{(F.2)}$$

A gain of 1 yields a proportional band of 100%. A gain of 20 is equivalent to a 5% proportional band, i.e.; it takes an error of 5% to drive the control action 100%.

A <u>proportional plus reset controller</u> (a two-mode controller) is one where integral action is added to proportional action.

The integral action resets the error to zero. The control equation is:

$$m = \left(K_p \varepsilon + K_I \int \varepsilon \, dt \right)$$

or
$$m(s) = \left[K_p + \frac{K_I}{s} \right] \varepsilon(s) \qquad \text{(F.3)}$$

Equation (F.3) can also be expressed as

$$\frac{m(s)}{\varepsilon(s)} = \frac{K_I \left(1 + \frac{K_p}{K_I} s \right)}{s} \qquad \text{(F.4)}$$

Reset action is generally expressed as the number of times that the integral action repeats the proportional action per unit of time. i.e.; Repeats per second $= K_I / K_p$

or Repeats per min (more commonly used) $= \dfrac{K_I \times 60}{K_p} \qquad \text{(F.5)}$

Another way of expressing integral action is by "reset time," i.e.; the time that it takes the integral action to repeat the proportional action for a given fixed error. Obviously "reset time" in mins. is the reciprocal of repeats per min.

A controller with <u>Proportional plus reset plus rate</u> action is called a 3-mode controller.

Its transfer function is generally expressed

$$K_p \left[1 + \frac{K_I}{K_p s} + T_R s \right]$$ (F.6)

where T_R can be expressed as rate time which can be interpreted as the gain to rate of change of the error relative to the proportional gain.

In Equation (F.6) the term $T_R s$ implies an ideal differentiator. In actual practice differentiation usually has a maximum cut-off frequency and of necessity must

be of the form $T_R s / \left(1 + T_R' s \right)$ where $T_R' \ll T_R$.

Practical 3 mode controllers, either pneumatic, hydraulic or electronic have the form

$$\frac{K_I \left(1 + \frac{K_p}{K_I} s \right) \left(1 + T_R s \right)}{s \left(1 + \frac{T_R}{K} s \right)}$$ (F.7)

where   Prop. Band in percent = $100/K_p$

Reset time $= \dfrac{K_p}{K_I} \times \dfrac{1}{60}$ mins

Rate time $= = T_R \times \dfrac{1}{60}$ mins

The additional time constant T_R/K in the denominator is usually about $T_R/10$. It sets the maximum instantaneous gain for a step input at 10 times the proportional gain.

Figure F-2 shows the time response characteristics of the various controller types discussed above for a unit step input of error.

Figure F-3 shows the frequency response characteristics of these controllers

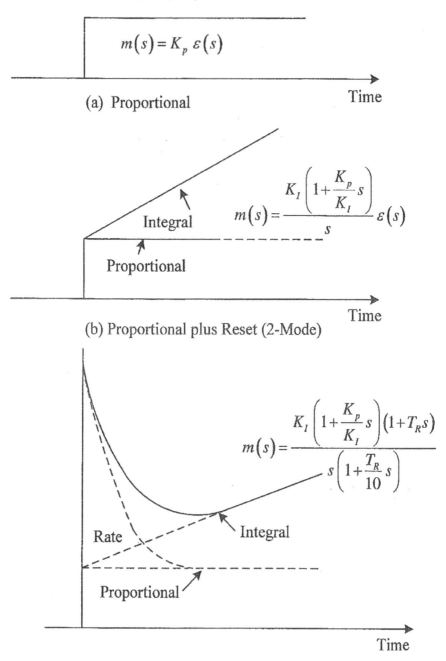

(a) Proportional

(b) Proportional plus Reset (2-Mode)

(c) Proportional Plus Reset plus Rate (3-Mode)

Figure F-2 – Responses of Controllers to Step in Error

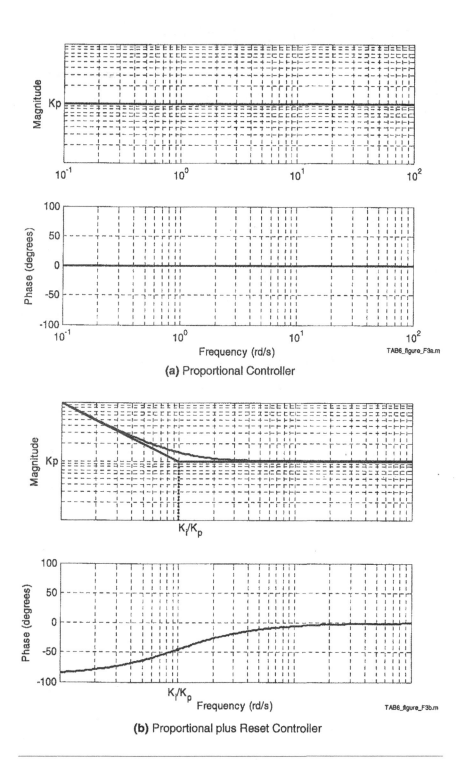

(a) Proportional Controller

(b) Proportional plus Reset Controller

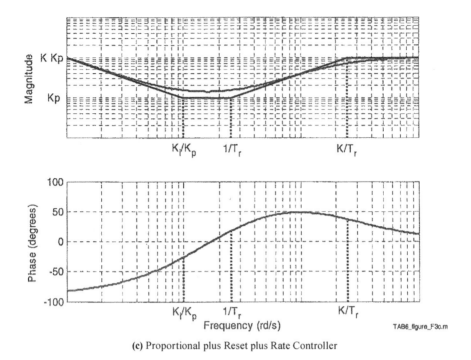

(c) Proportional plus Reset plus Rate Controller

Figure F-3 – Frequency Response Characteristics of Controllers

F.2   Tuning of Controllers and Process Response Curves

The important criteria in designing a process control system are:

1. Instability or cycling of the controlled variable must be avoided (except where on-off controls are used).

2. The steady state error should be minimized or even reduced to zero.

3. The control should return the process variable to set point as soon as possible.

The type of controller and its adjustments that should be used to meet these requirements should be a function of the process characteristics. The essential information on these characteristics can be derived from the step response curves of the process.

Figure F-4 shows typical response curves of systems with multiple lags. One simple way of characterizing the shape of these response curves is by noting the times T_1 and T_2 which, as indicated on Figure F-3, are the equivalent dead time and the time to maximize rate of rise of the response curve.

The relative case or difficulty of controlling a process is revealed by the shape of the response curve. In general the smaller the ratio L/D. i.e.; the sharper the "S" shape of the response curve the more difficult is the control task. In the limit, when $L/D = 0$ we have a process with almost pure "dead time" or "transport delay."

There are numerous articles giving guide rules on the choice of the type of controller and on the optimum values of controller parameters. Some references on this subject are included at the end of this Appendix.

In general these methods of controller tuning can be classified as "closed loop methods" or "open loop methods."

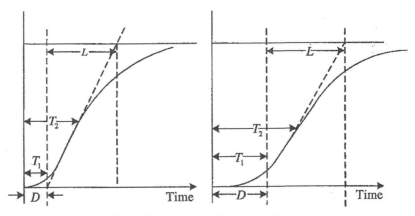

Figure F-4 – Process Response Curves

F.3 Closed Loop Methods

Some of the oldest guide rules on controller tuning were developed by Ziegler and Nichols [34] and involved tuning by means of on line experiments with the closed loop system. The experiment involves using proportional control only and determining the so-called "ultimate proportional gain," K_u which causes the control system to be barely unstable. The period of oscillation in seconds P_u is also noted. On the basis of these two values the controller parameters are found which give a control response characterized by the so-called 1/4 decay ratio. Figure F-5 summarizes the essentials of this method of tuning.

It should be noted that these guide rules are quite empirical and do not necessarily yield the optimum parameters in cases where the process has significant dead time. Also the 1/4 decay ratio criterion often may not be acceptable since there are many control situations where the criterion should be one with no overshoot.

F.4 Open Loop Methods

The derivation of control parameters from the process open loop characteristics is probably of much wider use since it permits tuning from knowledge of the process response.

The material included here is from the work of Chien, Hrones and Reswick[32]. Many others have developed useful and more sophisticated guide rules. Nevertheless the general rules listed here have fairly wide applicability, especially when it is recognized that the exact criterion of optimality of the closed loop response is rather subjective to begin with.

Referring to Figure F-4, the figure of merit R is defined as follows from the times L and D.

$$R = L/D$$

Also, let C be the plant gain. Based on these two figures of merit, R and C, the table below gives recommended controller parameters for two types of response, the quickest response without overshoot and quickest recovery with about 20% overshoot as shown in Figure F-6.

CLOSED LOOP METHODS – ZIEGLER & NICHOLS

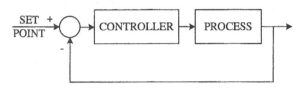

DETERMINE ULTIMATE GAIN K_u **AND PERIOD OF OSCILLATION** P_u **(IN PROPORTIONAL MODE ONLY)**	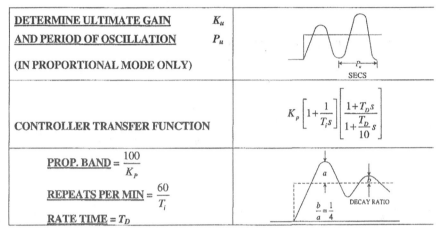
CONTROLLER TRANSFER FUNCTION	$K_p \left[1 + \dfrac{1}{T_i s} \right] \left[\dfrac{1 + T_D s}{1 + \dfrac{T_D}{10} s} \right]$
$\underline{\text{PROP. BAND}} = \dfrac{100}{K_P}$ $\underline{\text{REPEATS PER MIN}} = \dfrac{60}{T_i}$ $\underline{\text{RATE TIME}} = T_D$	$\dfrac{b}{a} = \dfrac{1}{4}$ DECAY RATIO

CONTROLLER ADJUSTMENT FORMULAE

MODES	GAIN	PROP. BAND	REPEATS/MIN	RATE TIME-MIN
PROPORTIONAL	$0.5\,K_u$	$\dfrac{200}{K_u}$	---	---
PROPORTIONAL & RESET	$0.45\,K_u$	$\dfrac{222}{K_u}$	$\dfrac{1.2 \times 60}{P_u}$	---
PROPORTIONAL RESET & RATE	$0.6\,K_u$	$\dfrac{167}{K_u}$	$\dfrac{2 \times 60}{P_u}$	$\dfrac{0.125\,P_u}{60}$

Figure F-5 – Ziegler and Nichols Tuning Methods

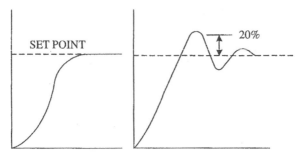

Figure F-6 – Tuning Parameters Based on Response Parameters of Figure F-4

TYPE OF CONTROL	QUICKEST RESPONSE WITHOUT OVERSHOOT		QUICKEST RESPONSE WITH 20% OVERSHOOT	
	Step Change in Set Point	Step Change in Load	Step Change in Set Point	Step Change in Load
STRAIGHT PROPORTIONAL Propostional band (percent) =	$\dfrac{333C}{R}$	$\dfrac{333C}{R}$	$\dfrac{143C}{R}$	$\dfrac{143C}{R}$
STRAIGHT PROPORTIONAL Propostional band (percent) =	$\dfrac{286C}{R}$	$\dfrac{167C}{R}$	$\dfrac{167C}{R}$	$\dfrac{143C}{R}$
Reset time (time units of D) =	3.33	$\dfrac{6.67DC}{R}$	1.67DC	$3.33\dfrac{D}{R}$
PROPORTIONAL AND RESET AND DERIVATIVE Propostional band (percent) =	$\dfrac{167C}{R}$	$\dfrac{105.2C}{R}$	$\dfrac{105.2C}{R}$	$\dfrac{83.3C}{R}$
Reset time (time units of D) =	1.67DC	$2.5\dfrac{DC}{R}$	1.43DC	$1.67\dfrac{DC}{R}$
Rate time (time units of D) =	$0.3\dfrac{RD}{C}$	$0.4\dfrac{RD}{C}$	$0.45\dfrac{RD}{C}$	$0.5\dfrac{RD}{C}$

Note that two types of disturbance for which the table above gives recommended control parameter values are:

1. Step change in set point or reference

2. Step load change

Refer to the block diagram of Figure F-1 for definition of these disturbances.

F.5 Controller Tuning Based on Open Loop Process Response Measurement

A wide range of processes exhibits responses to control action characterized by a combination of dead time and time lags. The response curve can be values of time to reach a certain fraction of the final value. An arbitrary characterization of the response curve is suggested in terms of the times to reach 10%, 63%, and 90% of the process final value as shown in Figure F-7.

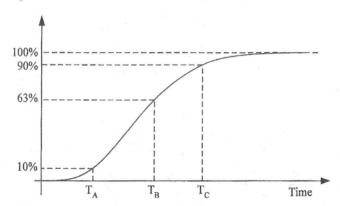

Figure F-7 – Process Response Characterized by T_A, T_B and T_C

Ratios of time T_C/T_B and T_A/T_B appear to characterize the type of response, i.e.; the relative amount of dead time to other lags.

A number of computer runs performed to optimize controller tuning, i.e.; to minimize a performance index of the form

$$I = \int_0^\infty \left(|\text{error}| \times \text{time} \right) \partial t + K \times (\text{Max. overshoot})$$

has yielded nomographs for arriving at two and three mode controller settings as function of the ratios T_A/T_B and T_C/T_B.

Figures F-8 to F-12 show these nomographs for three mode and two mode controllers.

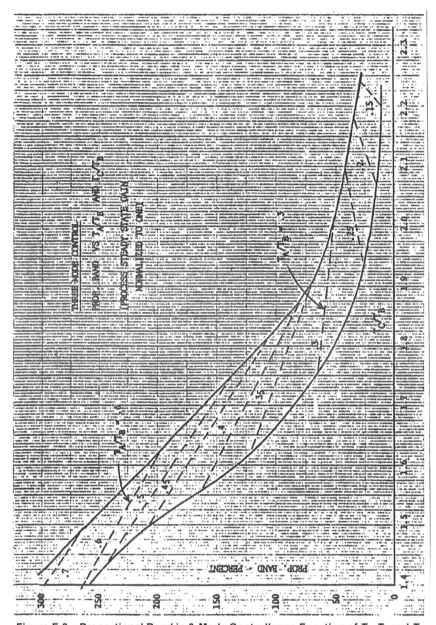

Figure F-8 – Proportional Band in 3-Mode Controller as Function of T_A, T_B and T_C

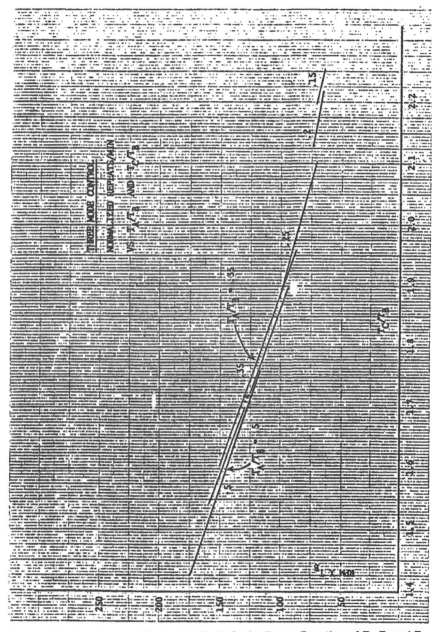

Figure F-9 – Repeats per Minute in 3-Mode Controller as Function of T_A, T_B and T_C

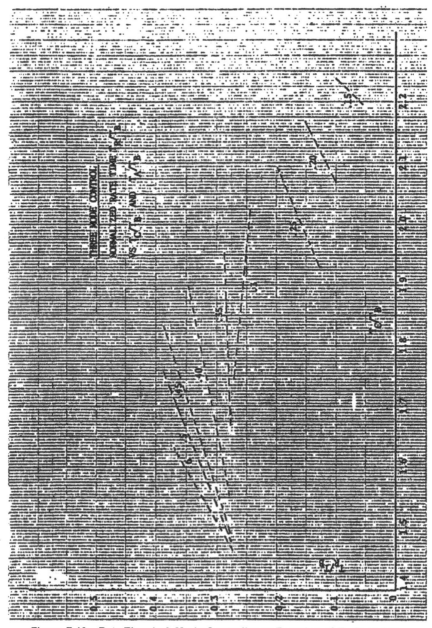

Figure F-10 – Rate Time in 3-Mode Controller as Function of T_A, T_B and T_C

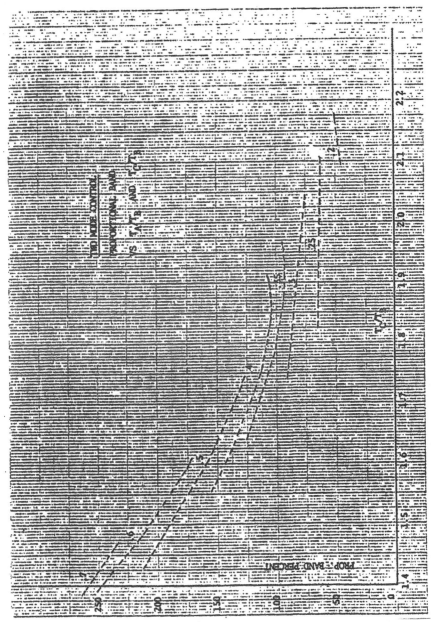

Figure F-11 – Proportional Band in 2-Mode Controller as Function of T_A, T_B and T_C

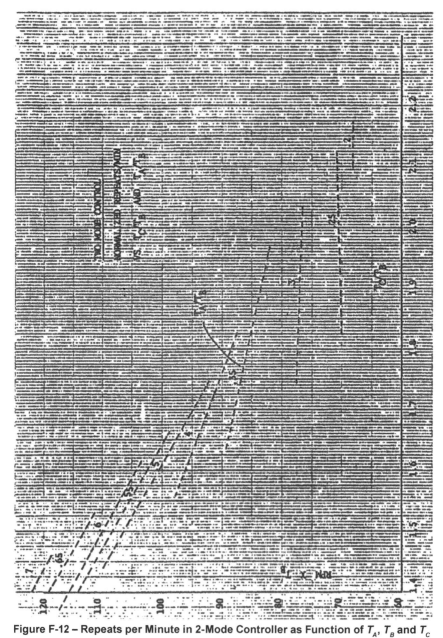

Figure F-12 – Repeats per Minute in 2-Mode Controller as Function of T_A, T_B and T_C

EXAMPLE

In order to illustrate the use of this method in determining controller settings, the following sample problem is presented.

A pressure controller modulates feeder speed as follows:

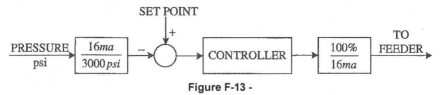

Figure F-13 -

With the controller in manual, a *2 ma* step in the manual signal to feeder produces the pressure response shown in Figure F-14. The steady state change in pressure is *1.6 ma.* Thus, we may measure the time to 10%, 63%, and 90% (*0.16 ma, 1.0 ma*, and *1.44 ma*, respectively) in order to obtain T_A, T_R and T_C.

$$
\begin{array}{llll}
T_A & = & 15.5 & \quad T_A/T_B & = & .3 \\
T_B & = & 52.5 & \quad T_C/T_B & = & 1.83 \\
T_C & = & 96.25 &
\end{array}
$$

Referring to Figure F-8 we may find controller settings as follows: Draw a vertical line through 1.83 on the $T_C/T_B = .3$ line by interpolation. Draw a horizontal line to the *PB* axis and read *PB = 180%*. This procedure may be repeated for each parameter using Figures F-8 through F-12.

For this example we obtain results:

	2 Mode			**3 Mode**	
PB	=	85%	PB	=	62%
$RPM \times T_B$	=	77	$RPM \times T_B$	=	105
			T_R/T_B	=	.265

We may now apply our gain correction factors due to time scaling (multiply *RPM/T_B*, and T_R/T_B by T_B) and due to loop gain correction.

(Multiply *P.B.* by *1.6 ma* pressure/*2 ma* feeder)

2 Mode		**3 Mode**
PB = 85% × 1.6/2 = 68%		PB = 62% × 1.6/2 = 49.6%
RPM = 77/52.5 = 1.467		RPM = 105/52.5 = 2.0
		T_R = .265 × 52.5 = 13.9

The controlled responses for these controller settings are shown in Figure F-15 for two and three mode controllers.

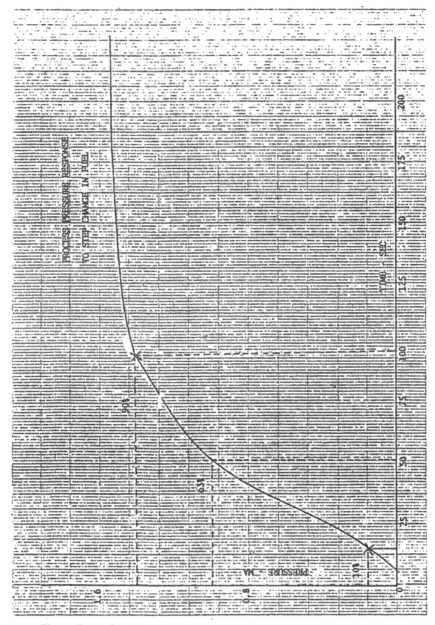

Figure F-14 – Step Response of Process (Pressure to Signal to Feeder

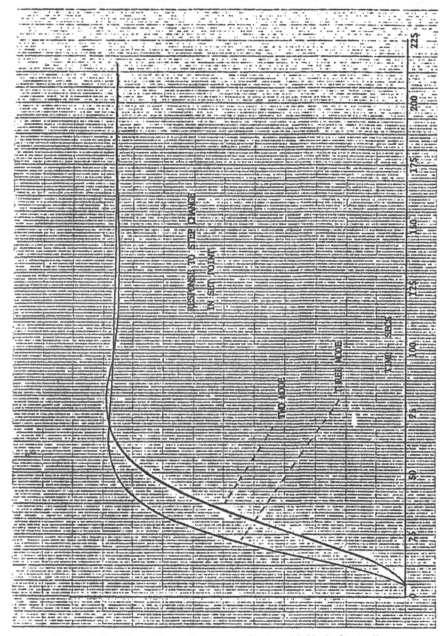

Figure F-15 – Closed Loop Responses for 2 and 3-Mode Controllers

F.6 Addendum

F.1.1 Digital Control Algorithms and Control Toning

Implementation of control laws with a digital computer can be done in an infinite number of ways. Many of these give essentially equivalent performance, and one should be careful not to spend a career analyzing trivial or marginal differences between algorithms. One of the great advantages of the digital computer is the flexibility with which all types of control and logic calculations can be incorporated to suit the particular need. Such different control modes as the use of limits and deadbands that may be fixed or functions of some variable, plus switching on or off of integral or other control action depending on input conditions are purely a function of the process requirements and the ingenuity of the control engineer.

Control know-how is nevertheless well rooted in analog practices, and it is logical to evolve from these practices developing digital equivalents to well known analog control modes, limiting enhancements to those easily implementable with the digital approach. Such enhancements, with particular reference to deadtime compensation, are proposed in this paper as are methods of parameter tuning from knowledge of the process open loop response.

As a preamble and for reference purposes, some terms frequently used in process control are described below.

F.1.2 Three Mode Control

Two most commonly used forms of three mode control are shown in Figures F-16 and F-17. The parallel configuration of Figure F-16 has non-interacting control modes in the time domain, i.e., proportional, integral or derivative gains can be individually set without interacting with each other.

When the overall control is expressed as one transfer function made up of zeros and poles, we note that the adjustment of individual terms of the time-domain function results in changes of the poles and zeros of the control function. For this reason, this form is known as interacting in the frequency domain. One should note that the parallel form of Figure F-16, when expressed into series form, can give rise to complex zeros which at times may be advantageous.

The form of Figure F-17, called the series form, is that normally encountered with analog three mode controllers using one operational amplifier. The form of the transfer function for this type of three mode controller is:

$$\frac{K_I\left(1+T_I s\right)\left(1+T_D s\right)}{s\left(1+\dfrac{T_D}{K}s\right)} \qquad \text{(F.8)}$$

and, the adjustments normally available are non-interacting in the frequency domain, i.e. proportional band $=\dfrac{100}{K_p}$ adjusts the gain of the overall function. Reset time T_i is generally expressed in reciprocal form as repeats per $\min = \dfrac{60}{T_i}$ and can be adjusted without affecting the other parameters of the transfer function, and likewise rate time T_D can be adjusted independent of the other parameters. Note that in this form there is no possibility of complex zeros. K is often fixed at some value such as 10.

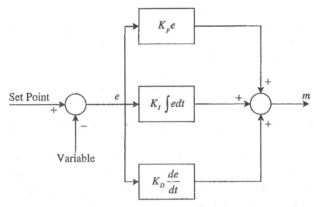

Figure F-16 – Parallel Configuration of 3-Mode Controller

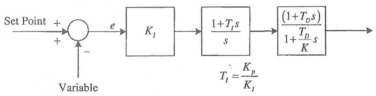

Figure F-17 – Series Configuration of 3-Mode Controller

The considerable amount of frequency response thinking, guide rules, etc., that have evolved over the years make it desirable to have control algorithms that are non-interacting in the frequency domain. In other words, the control engineer is more at home with locating such things as lead breaks (T_D and T_I) or corner frequencies $\left(\dfrac{1}{T_D}\right)$, $\dfrac{1}{T_I}$ and gain K_p as independent parameters than to work with the basic proportional reset and rate gains of the parallel system. As more control experience and guide rules are developed in the time domain, these preferences may change. Digital techniques permit, of course, a wide range of control laws which can be implemented with algorithms and algebraic Z form manipulations, as explained in many tests and technical papers.

Some of the variations that will find application are control modes written such that derivative and/or proportional action is bypassed on set point changes, provision for limiting the change in output per computation step and provision for automatic resetting of accumulators to prevent integral windup.

A major opportunity for digital control is the relative ease of accounting for process-deadtime and the implementation of linear, nonlinear, adaptive etc. algorithms not necessarily constrained by the linear differential equations of electrical circuits.

In addition to ensuring a control algorithm that is capable of coping with a wide range of process response characteristics, it would be very desirable to be able to derive parameter settings directly from the knowledge of process response and desired closed loop response characteristics. The derivation and examples below show a logical approach to achieve both objectives of having a flexible control algorithm whose parameters are directly relatable to the process response and desired control response characteristics.

F.1.3   Derivation of Desired Controller Transfer Function

The method outlined below is essentially similar to the ideas first introduced by Guillemin many years ago. The control design has been adapted for processes with deadtime and using the control logic capabilities of digital computers. Figure F-18 shows the traditional closed loop control structure with the controller function $g(s)$ and the process function $e^{-sT} G(s)$.

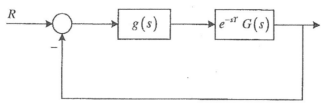

Figure F-18 – Closed Loop Control of Process with Dead Time

The process response characteristic is described by the transfer function $e^{-sT} G(s)$ where e^{-sT} represents a deadtime (transport lag) and $G(s)$ in a ratio of polynomials in s.

Let the desired controlled response (closed loop) be $e^{-sT} D(s)$. To be physically realizable the desired controlled response cannot avoid exhibiting a deadtime at least equal to the deadtime in the process response.

The control action to achieve the desired response would evidently be given by the impulse response function:

$$\frac{e^{-sT}D(s)}{e^{-sT}G(s)} = \frac{D(s)}{G(s)} \qquad (F.9)$$

This same control action expressed in terms of the elements of the closed loop in Figure F-18 is:

$$\frac{g(s)}{1+g(s)e^{-sT}G(s)} \qquad (F.10)$$

Equating (F.8) and (F.9) and solving for $g(s)$:

$$g(s) = \frac{D(s)}{G(s)\left[1 - e^{-sT}D(s)\right]} \qquad (F.11)$$

Expression (F.10) is the desired transfer function of the controller.

Application to Typical Processes

A wide range of process response characteristics can be described approximately by the function:

$$e^{-sT}g(s) = \frac{e^{-sT}\omega_p^2}{s^2 + 2\zeta_p\omega_p s + \omega_p^2} \qquad (F.12)$$

normalized to yield a steady state gain of one. This function exhibits a deadtime T and a second order response with a natural frequency ω_p and a damping ratio ζ_p.

Figures F-19 shows the step response of this function beyond the deadtime T for a range of values of ζ_p. Addition of deadtime results in a translation of the response by the amount of deadtime.

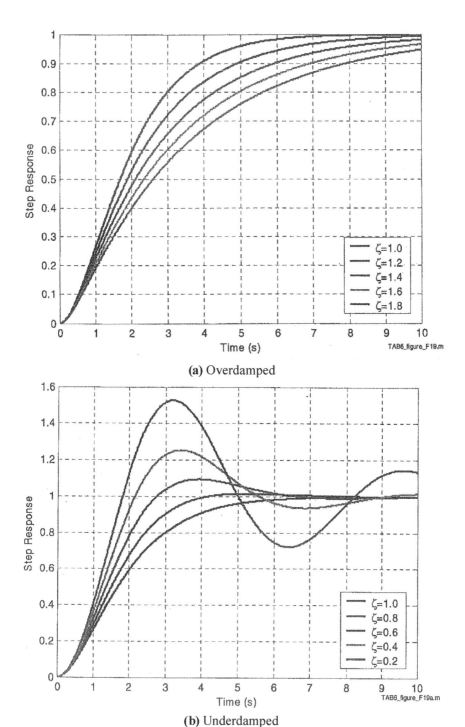

(a) Overdamped

(b) Underdamped

Figure F-19 – Normalized Step Response of a Second Order System

The desired closed loop response of the process can also be expressed by a similar function with symbols subscripted *"d"* for desired versus *"p"* for process in (F.12).

$$e^{-sT}D(s) = \frac{e^{-sT}\,\omega_d^2}{s^2 + 2\zeta_d\omega_d s + \omega_d^2} \tag{F.13}$$

The speed of response and overshoot of the desired function are controlled by the parameter ω_d and $_d$. Typically $\omega_d > \omega_p$ and $_d$ would be about 0.8.

Using (F.12) and (F.13) in (F.11), the controller function becomes

$$g(s) = \frac{\omega_d^2\left(s^2 + 2\zeta_p\omega_p s + \omega_p^2\right)}{\omega_p^2\left(s^2 + 2\zeta_d\omega_d s + \omega_d^2\left(1 - e^{-sT}\right)\right)} \tag{F.14}$$

A block diagram implementation of (F.14) in terms of integrations, time delays and other arithmetic operations is shown in Figure F-20.

The controller characteristics are thus completely specified if the process response can be expressed as a time delay followed by a second order response as in (F.12).

Figures F-21 to F-24 show examples of closed loop controlled performance for different process open loop response characteristics described by the parameters ω_p, ζ_p and T. As expected the control adjustments yield the same response shape whether or not the process has deadtimes, the difference being that the output response is delayed by the process deadtime. Figures F-21 and F-22 show the controlled response for the desired damping ratio $\zeta_d = 0.8$. Figures F-23 and F-24 are for a desired damping ratio $\zeta_d = 1.0$.

The sensitivity of the controlled performance to errors in estimates of the process deadtime is shown in Figures F-25 to F-28. Figures F-25 and F-27 show controlled performance for the case where the controller compensation is for a deadtime larger than the actual process deadtime. Figures F-26 and F-28 are for cases where the controller compensation is for less than the actual process deadtime.

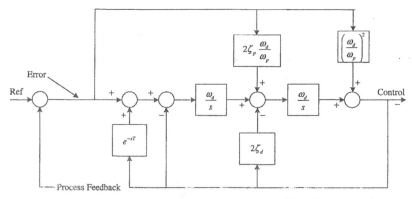

Figure F-20 – Second Order Controller with Dead Time Compensation

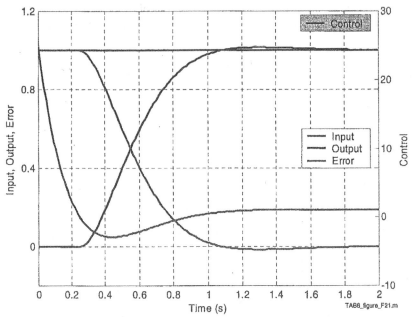

Figure F-21 – Closed Loop Response
(ω_p=1.0, ζ_p=0.3, ω_p=5.0, ζ_d=0.8, T=0.25, T1 = 0.25)

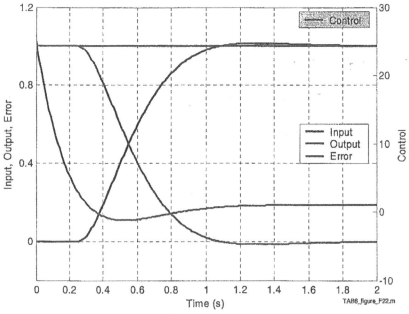

Figure F-22 – Closed Loop Response
(ω_p=1.0, ζ_p=1.0, ω_d=5.0, ζ_d=0.8, T=0.25, T1 = 0.25)

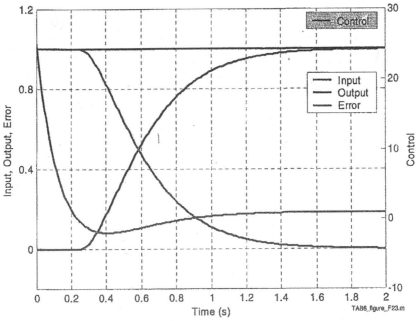

Figure F-23 – Closed Loop Response
$(\omega_p=1.0,\ \zeta_p=1.0,\ \omega_d=5.0,\ \zeta_d=1.0,\ T=0.25,\ T1=0.25)$

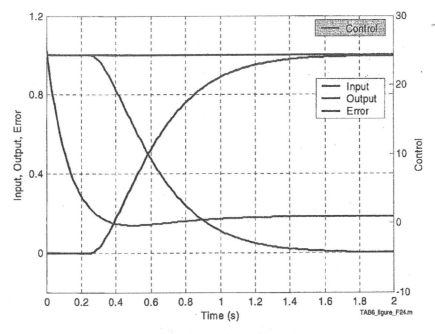

Figure F-24 – Closed Loop Response
$(\omega_p=1.0,\ \zeta_p=1.0,\ \omega_d=5.0,\ \zeta_d=1.0,\ T=0.25,\ T1=0.25)$

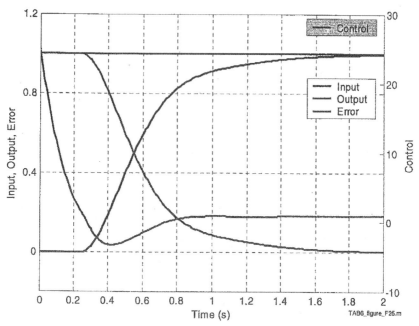

Figure F-25 – Closed Loop Response
(ω_p=1.0, ζ_p=0.6, ω_d=5.0, ζ_d=0.8, T=0.25, T1 = 0.30)

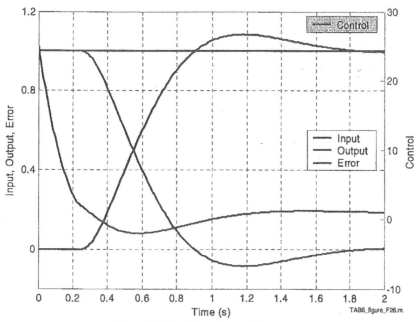

Figure F-26 – Closed Loop Response
(ω_p=1.0, ζ_p=0.6, ω_d=5.0, ζ_d=0.8, T=0.25, T1 = 0.20)

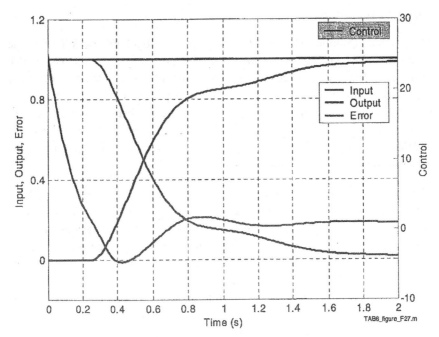

Figure F-27 – Closed Loop Response
(ω_p=1.0, ζ_p=0.6, ω_d=5.0, ζ_d=0.8, T=0.25, T1 = 0.35)

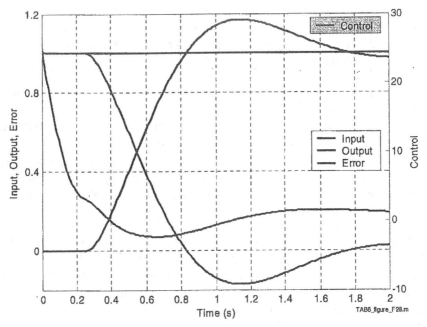

Figure F-28 – Closed Loop Response
(ω_p=1.0, ζ_p=0.6, ω_d=5.0, ζ_d=0.8, T=0.25, T1 = 0.15)

Turning Procedures

The previous examples show control performance obtainable by following the analytical rules starting from knowledge of the exact process response which turns out to fit the postulated second order function plus deadtime. In the more general problem, one does not know the process parameters or that the process necessarily fits exactly the second order plus deadtime form postulated. Rather, the process response function is likely to be known in terms of a response curve and thus the first step would be to approximate it by a second order plus deadtime function characterized by parameters T, ω and ζ.

The technique of picking the best fit of the approximation is simple on a CRT screen with an X-Y time response display of the process response. By having normalized response curves of the second order process for various damping ratios also displayed, the scale factor of the time axis of the process response curve can be adjusted until a fit is obtained with one of the normalized curves. Thus the damping ratio of the second order approximation to the process is established and the natural frequency can be obtained from the ratio of time scale factors of the process response curve and that of the normalized curve.

Another approach is to express the normalized response curves ($\omega = 1.0$) in terms of points characterized by specific ratios relative to the final steady state response and ratio of time to reach the particular point to the time to reach 50% of the final value. With the actual response curve also expressed by such ratios, it is easy to search for matches between the response curve to be fitted and a particular normalized second order curve.

Table F-1 gives the ratios of times to reach particular response values to the time to reach 50% of final value for normalized second order responses ($\omega = 1.0$) with various damping ratios ζ. Also listed in the row corresponding to response ratio of 0.5 is the actual time for the normalized response ($\omega = 1.0$) to reach 50% of the final value. For low values of damping ratio where the process has oscillatory responses, certain points are characterized by two time ratios, one corresponding to the response in the increasing direction and the other in the descending direction.

A third practical possibility is to have the normalized curves in transparencies with a variety of scale factors for the time axis. A fit is soon obtained by superposing the actual response curve onto one of the transparencies that produces the closest match. A set of second order system response curves platted for a range of time scales is contained in Figures F-45 to F-54.

TABLE F-1 – RATIO OF TIME TO REACH MAGNITUDE TO TIME TO REACH 0.5 (NORMALIZED: $\omega = 1.0$)

Magnitude	0.2	0.4	0.6	0.8	1.0	1.2	1.4	1.6	1.8
0.2	0.60	0.57	0.54	0.52	0.49	0.46	0.44	0.42	0.40
(time)*	(1.13)	(1.24)	(1.36)	(1.51)	(1.68)	(1.88)	(2.11)	(2.35)	(2.60)
0.5	1.00	1.00	1.00	1.00	1.00	1.00	1.00	1.00	1.00
0.8	1.36	1.41	1.51	1.63	1.79	1.93	2.04	2.11	2.17
1.0	1.60	1.75	2.04	2.76					
1.2	1.88 / 4.05	2.27 / 3.35							
1.4	2.25 / 3.45								

*Time to reach 0.5 of final value

Example of Tuning Technique

A process characterized by a deadtime and fourth order function (two second order functions in series) is to be used as an example of the tuning process. The actual process function is

$$\frac{e^{-sT}\omega_1^2\omega_2^2}{\left(\omega_1^2 + 2\zeta_1\omega_1 s + s^2\right)\left(\omega_2^2 + 2\zeta_2\omega_2 s + s^2\right)} \tag{F.15}$$

where
$$T = 0 \qquad \omega_2 = 0.3$$
$$\omega_1 = 1.0 \qquad \zeta_2 = 1.5$$
$$\zeta_1 = 0.8$$

Figures F-29, F-30 and F-31 show the actual process response to a step plotted to different time scales. One can clearly discern an equivalent deadtime of 1 sec: followed by a response which we wish to approximate with a second order function of natural frequency ω_p and damping ratio ζ_p.

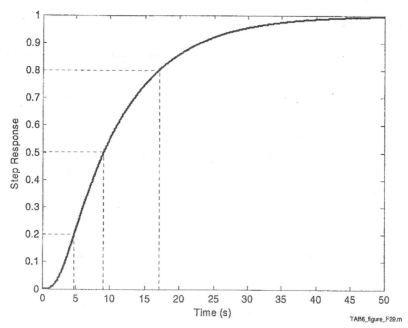

Figure F-29 – Fourth Order Process Step Response

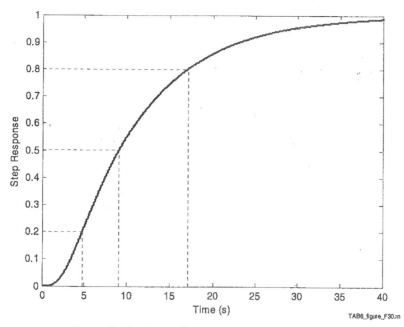

Figure F-30 – Fourth Order Process Step Response

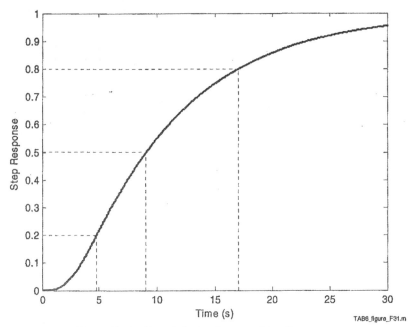

Figure F-31 – Fourth Order Process Step Response

Using any of the methods outlined above, we note that the actual process can be approximated by the function

$$\frac{e^{-sT}\omega_p^2}{\left(\omega_p^2 + 2\zeta_p\omega_p s + s^2\right)} \qquad (F.16)$$

Where $\omega_p =$ *0.22*

$\zeta_p =$ *1.1*

$T_p =$ *1.0*

Figure F-32 shows the response of the actual 4th order process and the 2nd order approximation.

If we now specify a desired ratio of closed loop to open loop response frequencies $\omega_d/\omega_p = 3.0$ and a desired closed loop damping ratio of 0.8, the resulting controlled response is shown on Figure F-33.

The closed loop response for a desired ω_d/ω_p ratio of 5 is shown on Figure F-34.

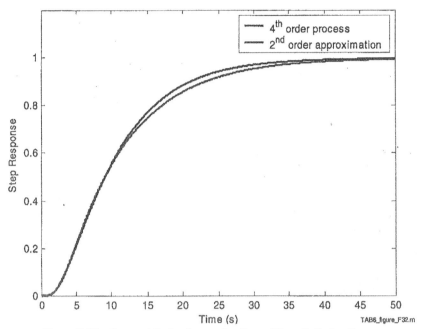

Figure F-32 – Second Order Approximation of Fourth Order Process

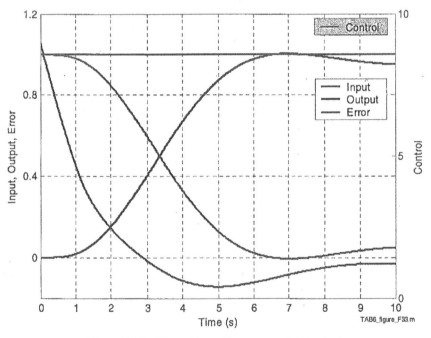

**Figure F-33 – Closed Loop Response with Control
Design Based on 2nd Order Approximation**

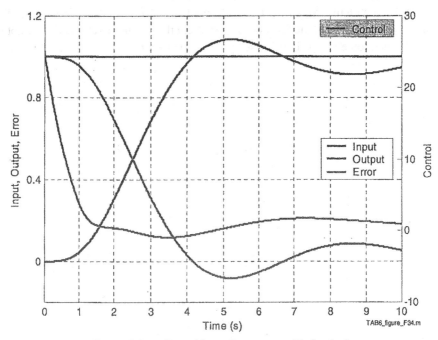

**Figure F-34 – Closed Loop Response with Control
Design Based on 2nd Order Approximation**

Relationship to Three Mode Control

The algorithm described in Figure F-20 has a similarity to that which describes a traditional three mode controller, except that it compensates for deadtime permitting faster controlled response for processes exhibiting deadtime.

If deadtime compensation is set equal to zero the diagram of Figure F-20 reduces to that in Figure F-35, and the corresponding transfer function can be expressed as

$$\frac{\omega_d^2}{\omega_p^2} \frac{\left(s^2 + 2\zeta_p \omega_p s + \omega_p^2\right)}{s\left(s + 2\zeta_d \omega_d\right)}$$

or   (F.17)

$$\frac{\omega_d}{2\zeta_d} \frac{\left(1 + \dfrac{2\zeta_p}{\omega_p}s + \dfrac{s^2}{\omega_p^2}\right)}{s\left(1 + \dfrac{s}{2\zeta_d \omega_d}\right)}$$

Comparing with the expression for one form of a three mode controller described in (F-8), one notes that the form is similar except that the numerator zeros are not constrained to be real as in the case in the three mode controller.

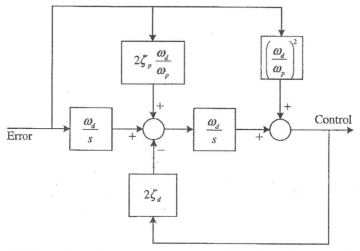

Figure F-35 – Second Order Controller without Dead Time Compensation

The correspondence between parameters of the three mode controller function

$$\frac{K_I\left(1+sT_I\right)\left(1+sT_R\right)}{s\left(1+sT_{R/K}\right)} \tag{F.18}$$

in Figure F-17 is

$$
\begin{aligned}
K_I &= \frac{\omega_d}{2\zeta_d} \\
\left(T_I + T_R\right) &= 2\zeta_p / \omega_p \\
T_I T_R &= \frac{1}{\omega_p^2} \\
\frac{K}{T_R} &= 2\zeta_d \omega_d
\end{aligned}
\tag{F.19}
$$

T_I and T_R would be real values for critically damped and overdamped processes i.e. those with $\zeta_p \geq 1$.

For such processes (second order, no deadtime and $\zeta_p > 1.0$). The adjustments in terms of ω_p, ω_d, ζ_d and ζ_p are

$$T_I = \frac{K_p}{K_I} = \frac{\zeta_p}{\omega_p}\left[1 + \sqrt{1 - \frac{1}{\zeta_p^2}}\right]$$

$$T_R = \frac{\zeta_p}{\omega_p}\left[1 - \sqrt{1 - \frac{1}{\zeta_p^2}}\right] \tag{F.20}$$

$$K_I = \frac{\omega_d}{2\zeta_d}$$

The controller zeros $1/T_I$ and $1/T_R$ are essentially positioned to cancel the process poles or roots. An overdamped second order process has two real roots s_1 and s_2. The ratio of the roots to the natural frequency as function of damping ratio is shown in Table F-2.

Table F-2

ζ	$S_{1/\omega}$	$S_{2/\omega}$
1.0	1.0	1.0
1.2	0.5367	1.863
1.5	0.382	2.618
2.0	0.268	3.732

When three mode controllers are used for processes with deadtime, the specification of a second order desired response cannot be made in the same way as was possible using the controller with deadtime compensation.

For second order processes with deadtime, i.e. where the process function is

$$\frac{\omega_p^2 e^{-sT}}{\left(\omega_p^2 + 2\zeta_p\omega_p s + s^2\right)} \tag{F.21}$$

and $\zeta_p = 1.0$ or greater, two of the three mode controller adjustments would logically be:

$$T_I = K_p / K_I = \frac{\zeta_p}{\omega_p}\left[1 + \sqrt{1 - \frac{1}{\zeta_p^2}}\right]$$

$$T_R = \frac{\zeta_p}{\omega_p}\left[1 - \sqrt{1 - \frac{1}{\zeta_p^2}}\right] \tag{F.22}$$

The denominator pole would normally be $T_R/10$ and thus the only remaining parameter to be established is K_I.

With the process poles cancelled by the controller zeros, the overall open loop function now becomes

$$\frac{K_I \, e^{-sT}}{s\left(1+\dfrac{T_R}{10}s\right)}$$

(F.23)

One method of determining K_I would be to establish the frequency $s = j\omega$ for which the function (F.19) has a phase lag of about 117.50, and then calculate the gain K_I which would make the magnitude of the function unity at this frequency. The choice of a higher phase lag than 117.5° would give more oscillatory performance.

ω is thus calculated from the relation

$$\tan^{-1}\left(\frac{T_R\omega}{10}\right) + \frac{\omega T \times 180}{\pi} = 27.5°$$

or   (F.24)

$$\frac{T_R\omega}{10} = \tan\left[27.5 - \frac{\omega T \times 180}{\pi}\right]°$$

making the approximation $\tan\theta = \theta$ for small θ,

$$\frac{T_R\omega}{10} = [.48 - \omega T]$$

or $$\omega\left[T + \frac{T_R}{10}\right] = 0.48$$

i.e. $$\omega = \frac{0.48}{\left[T + \dfrac{T_R}{10}\right]}$$

Hence $$K_I = \frac{0.48}{\left(T + \dfrac{T_R}{10}\right)}\left[1+\left(\frac{T_R}{10}\right)^2 \frac{(.48)^2}{\left(T + \dfrac{T_R}{10}\right)^2}\right]^{1/2}$$

(F.25)

$$= \frac{0.48}{\left(T + \dfrac{T_R}{10}\right)}\left[1+\frac{.0023\,T_R^{\,2}}{\left(T + \dfrac{T_R}{10}\right)^2}\right]^{1/2}$$

An example of three mode control tuning is illustrated for a process characterized by $\omega_p = 1.0$, $\zeta_p = 1.5$ and $T = 1.0$.

Using the above formulas

$$T_I = \frac{K_p}{K_I} = 1.5\left[1+\sqrt{1-\frac{1}{1.5^2}}\right] = 2.618$$

$$T_R = 1.5\left[1-\sqrt{1-\frac{1}{1.5^2}}\right] = 0.382 \tag{F.26}$$

$$K_I = \frac{0.48}{[1+.038]}\left[1+\frac{.0023\times 382^2}{(1.0382)^2}\right]^{1/2}$$

The corresponding adjustments would be: proportional band = $100/K_p = 100/2.618$ x $.46 = 83\%$. Repeats per minute = $60/2.618 = 22.9$ and rate time = 0.38.

The closed loop response of the process with the above three mode controller settings is shown in Figure F-36.

For comparison, using the controller of Figure F-22, with deadtime compensation, and $\omega_d = 5$, $\zeta_d = 0.8$, $T = 1.0$, one obtains the closed loop response also plotted on Figure F-37. The striking improvement in response is evident by noting that the process is essentially at set point within 1.8 s whereas it reaches set point and overshoots at 3.5 s in Figure F-36.

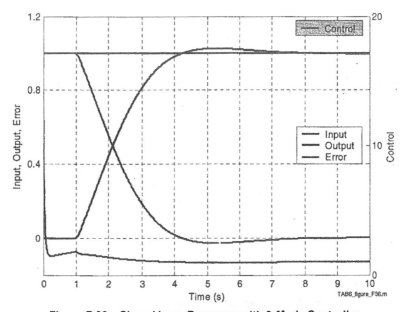

Figure F-36 – Closed Loop Response with 3-Mode Controller

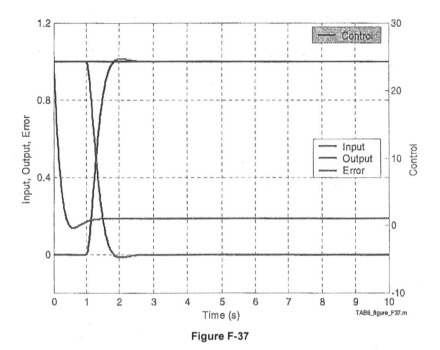

Figure F-37

Application to Process with Integration

For processes characterized by a deadtime, single time constant and an integration (typical of level control)

$$\frac{e^{-sT}}{s\left(1+sT_1\right)} \tag{F.27}$$

a similar derivation yields the control algorithm described in Figure F-38.

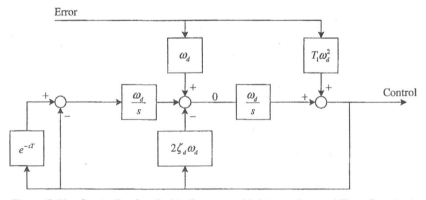

Figure F-38 – Controller Applied to Process with Integration and Time Constant

If one wishes to preserve integral action on the error, the same algorithm as was applied for a process with finite gain could be used by assuming the process with very large rather than infinite steady state gain, e.g. The process

$$\frac{e^{-sT}}{s(1+sT_1)}$$

(F.28)

could be approximated by

$$\frac{e^{-sT}\,T_2}{(1+sT_2)(1+sT_1)}\ \text{where } T_2 \text{ is very large.}$$

(F.29)

The equivalent natural frequency and damping ratio formulation is

$$\frac{T_2\,e^{-sT}\,\omega_p^2}{\left[\omega_p^2 + 2\zeta_p\omega_p s + s^2\right]}$$

(F.30)

Picking $T_2 \gg T$, or T say $T_2 = 100\,T_1$, or $100T$ whichever is larger.

$$T_1 + T_2 \approx T_2 = 2\zeta_p / \omega_p$$

and

$$1/T_1T_2 = \omega_p^2 \approx \frac{1}{100T_1^2}$$

i.e.

$$w_p = \frac{1}{10T_1}$$

(F.31)

$$\therefore \frac{2\zeta_p}{\omega_p} = 2\zeta \times 10T_1 = 100T_1$$

or

$$\zeta_p = 5$$

The process approximation is thus

$$\frac{100T_1\,e^{-sT}\,\omega_p^2}{\left[\omega_p^2 + 2\zeta\omega_p s + s^2\right]}$$

where

$$\omega_p = \frac{1}{100T_1}$$

(F.32)

$$\zeta = 5$$

$$\text{Gain} = 100T_1$$

The controller of Figure F-22 would be adjusted using the desired parameters ω_d and ζ_d and process parameters ω_p and ζ_p and the overall control attenuated (multiplied) by $1/100T_I$ or $\omega_p/10$.

Operation under Limits

When control output is limited, the output of the right band side integrator ω_d/s in Figure F-20 is continuously adjusted so that its output plus the error signal multiplied by $(\omega_d/\omega_p)^2$ is equal to the limit. This avoids reset windup and provides predictive characteristics to control action.

Figure F-39 shows performance for a step change in set point with limits on control action.

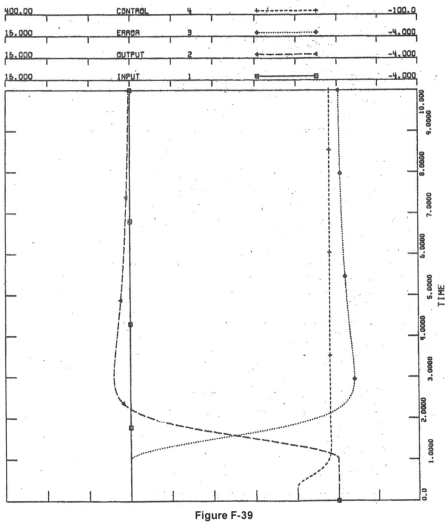

400.00	CONTROL	4	+--·-------+	-100.0
16.000	ERROR	3	•·············•	-4.000
16.000	OUTPUT	2	◄-------◄	-4.000
16.000	INPUT	1	▣━━━━▣	-4.000

TIME

Figure F-39

Digital Implementation

The power of modern computers and the bandwidth of a/d and d/a converters is so large that for most process applications the problem of sampling rate is no longer germane and suffice it to state that sampling will be executed at a rate compatible with the process response characteristics.

If ω_d is indicative of the desired response bandwidth it is natural to pick a sampling time smaller than $\frac{1}{4}\,\omega_d$.

Again if dead time is significant, an appropriate sub-multiple of the dead time could be the criterion for choice of sampling rate.

In any case there is no reason to have control response suffer because of' sampling rate.

The integration function in the controls denoted as $1/s$ in the continuous domain is accomplished with a simple accumulation algorithm.

EXAMPLES

The response of a process is characterized within the form of expression (F.12) by

$$\omega_p \quad = \quad 1\ rd/s$$

$$\zeta p \quad = \quad 0.3$$

$$T \quad = \quad 2\ s$$

The desired closed loop response is described by the parameters $T = 2$, $\omega_d = 2$ rd/s, $\zeta_d = 0.8$. Using a sampling time of 0.1 s and the control algorithm of Figure F-20, the closed loop response is shown in Figure F-40.

Another example for the same type of process except that the dead time is increased to *4 sec* is shown on Figure F-41.

The effect of faster sampling rate $T_{samp} = 0.05$ s for the process with the 0.2 s dead time is shown on Figure F-42. (Compare with Figure F-41.)

The performance with an ideal continuous controller which performs with dead time compensation as in Figure F-20 is shown for the process with a 2.0 s dead time in Figure F-44. (Compare with Figures F-39 and F-41.)

F.7   Conclusions

Digital control permits implementation of complex control logic with relative ease. Compensation for process deadtime, in particular, makes it possible to obtain practically the same controlled response (excluding the inevitable deadtime delay) independent of process deadtime.

The control structure and technique of arriving at control parameter adjustments have been developed using simple analytical operational methods that apply to continuous systems, it being recognized that translation into the discrete domain is not a problem provided adequate sampling rates are used.

The method is based on the observation that most process open loop response characteristics can be approximated by a deadtime in series with a second order transfer function whose parameters can be expressed in terms of a natural frequency ω_p and damping ratio ζ_p. Likewise the desired closed loop control response can be expressed in a similar form, where the achievable, hence desired, deadtime must be equal to the process deadtime, the natural frequency of the closed loop response ω_d selected as some reasonable multiple of the process natural frequency, and the damping ratio of the desired response ζ_d selected for acceptable overshoot (usually $\zeta_d \approx 0.8$).

The controller parameters are then directly related to these constants characterizing the process and closed loop control.

The relationship of the usual analog three mode controller (proportional with reset and rate) to the controller structure with deadtime compensation is demonstrated and rules established for parameter adjustment of three mode controllers from knowledge of the process as characterized by deadtime, natural frequency and damping ratio.

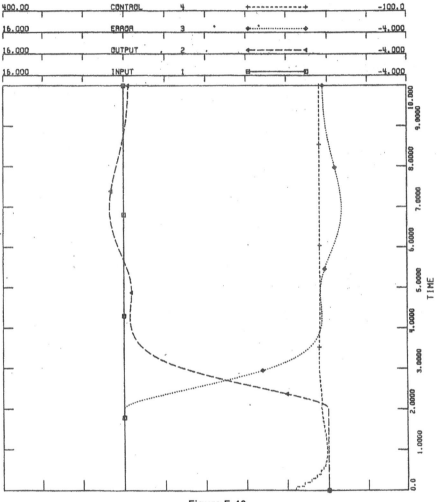

Figure F-40

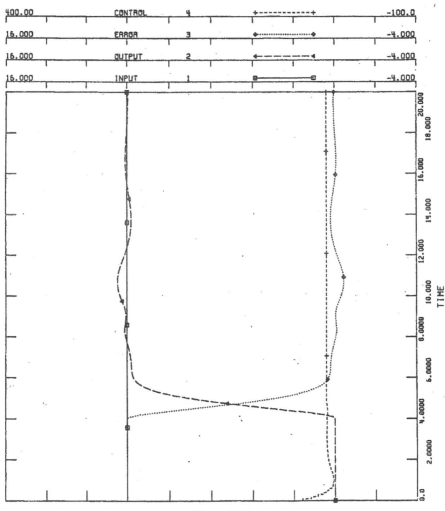

400.00	CONTROL	4	+-------+	-100.0
16.000	ERROR	3	◆········◆	-4.000
16.000	OUTPUT	2	◄-------◄	-4.000
16.000	INPUT	1	▣───────▣	-4.000

TIME

Figure F-41

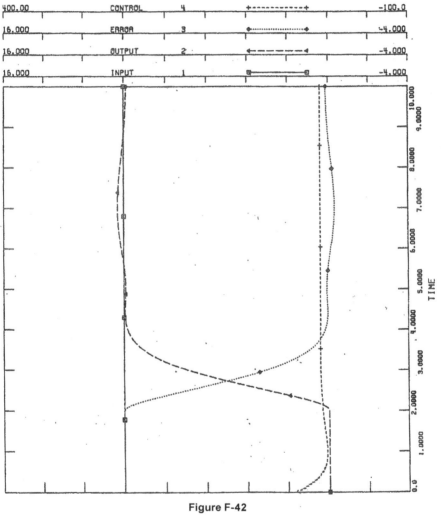

Figure F-42

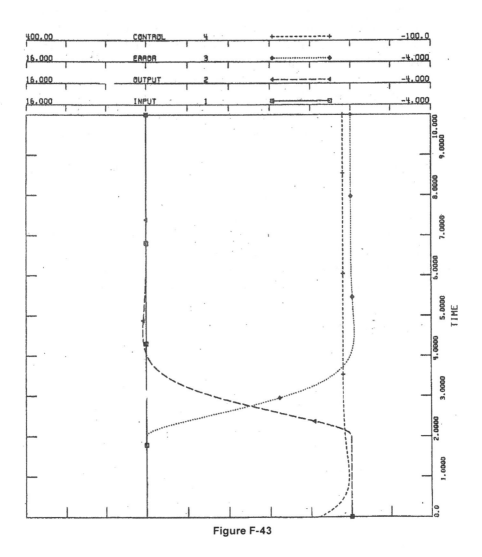

400.00	CONTROL	4	+----------+	-100.0
16.000	ERROR	3	●·················●	-4.000
16.000	OUTPUT	2	◄— — — — ◄	-4.000
16.000	INPUT	1	☐————————☐	-4.000

Figure F-43

REFERENCES

1. "Optimum Settings for Automatic Controllers", J.G. Ziegler and N.B. Nichols, Taylor Data Sheet No. TD5 10A 100, Taylor Instrument Companies. Rochester, NY.

2. "A Comparison of Controller Tuning Techniques", J.A. Miller, A.M. Lopez, C.L. Smith and P.W. Murrill, Control Engineering, Dec. 1967, pp. 72-76.

3. "Analytical Tuning of Underdamped Systems", C.L. Smith and P.W. Murrill, ISA Journal Sept. 1966, pp. 48-53.

4. "A More Precise Method for Tuning Controllers", C.L. Smith and P.W. Murrill, May 1966, pp. 50-58.

5. "Tuning Controllers with Error-Integral Criteria", A.M. Lopez, J.A. Miller, C.L. Smith and P.W. Murrill, Instrumentation Technology, Nov. 1967. pp. 57-62.

6. "A Controller to Overcome Deadtime", O.J. Smith, ISA Journal, Feb. 1959, Vol. 6, No. 2, pp. 28-33.

7. "How Modeling Accuracy Affects Control Response", W.M. Whicater, Control Engineering, Oct. 1966, pp. 85-87.

8. "Interactive Dynamic Simulation by Digital Computer", J.M. Undrill and T.F. Laskowski, ISA Transactions. Vol. 14, 1975, pp. 33-40.

9. Chien, Hrones & Reswick, "On The Automatic Control of Generalized Passive Systems," ASME Transactions, Vol. 74, No. 2, Feb. 1952, p. 175.

F. P. De Mello

Consulting Engineer

Mr. de Mello graduated with BS and MS degrees in Electrical Engineering from MIT where he was elected to Tau Beta Pi and Sigma Xi. His academic experience included several test engineering and laboratory assignments with the General Electric Company (GE) between 1945 and 1948.

In 1948, he joined the Rio Light and Power Company in Brazil and over several years held positions of increasing technical responsibility in system planning and design studies concerning expansion of the Rio, Sao Paulo, and City of Santos systems.

In 1955, Mr. de Mello joined the Analytical Engineering Section of GE's Apparatus Sales Division in Schenectady. Here he undertook design and analysis studies of controls of industrial, power apparatus and aircraft power systems, making extensive use of analog computers. In 1959, he was assigned to specialized studies of dynamics of electrical machines, excitation control, prime-mover systems, and overall power systems.

From 1961 to 1969, he conducted and guided extensive research efforts on modeling of dynamics of power systems and power plants for use in advanced boiler and plant control design studies. He made major pioneering contributions in the development of digital computer methods for dynamic analysis and process control design. Of particular note were the developments of computer techniques for the simulation of complex boiler dynamics and for the synthesis of multivariable boiler-turbine controls for which he was awarded GE's Managerial and Ralph Cordiner Awards. He also made significant contributions in the study of electrical machine dynamics, their voltage and governing controls and to the analysis and implementation of system load-frequency controls.

Mr. de Mello joined Power Technologies, Inc., at the time of its formation in August of 1969 as Principal Engineer, Dynamics and Control, and Secretary-Treasurer. He was appointed Vice President-Secretary in 1973. He was a Director of PTEL, PTI's affiliate in Brazil. From 1974 to 1976, he was project manager for PTI and PTEL in system and design studies for transmission from Itaipu, the world's largest 800 kV system and also served on the Advisory Board of the Study Group for Itaipu transmission. Prior to his appointment as Principal Consultant in 1987, he was Manager of PTI's Consulting Services Department.

Mr. de Mello has three patents and authored more than 100 technical papers in IEEE, ISA, American Power Conference, World Power Conference, and other utility industry publications, and also lectured to professional society groups. He has served on the IEEE System Controls Subcommittee and the joint IEEE Working Group on Plant Response and also served as US representative on CIGRE Study Committee 38. He teaches dynamic and operational subjects in PTI's Power Technology Course.

Mr. de Mello is a Fellow of IEEE, a Fellow of ISA, a member of the National Academy of Engineering, a registered Professional Engineer in New York State. He was a US representative on CIGRE Study Committees 38 and 39. He was awarded the IEEE Charles Concordia Award in 2003.

Printed in the United States
By Bookmasters